CHURCHILL'S NAVY

CHURCHILL'S
NAVY

THE SHIPS, MEN AND ORGANISATION
1939-1945   BRIAN LAVERY

CONWAY

ACKNOWLEDGEMENTS

This book is a new departure for a naval historian who has mainly worked on earlier periods, but I have had some experience of the later period in my *Hostilities Only*, about of wartime naval training, and in my forthcoming *Shield of Empire*, which tells the story of the Royal Navy and Scotland, as well as the forthcoming *River Class Frigates in the Battle of the Atlantic*. I am grateful to all the people who have worked with me on these projects, including Nigel Rigby, Rachel Giles and Abi Ratcliffe of the National Maritime Museum and John Tuckwell of Birlinn Books. I must also acknowledge the effects of numerous discussions with other historians and researchers over many years. These include Jock Gardiner, Malcolm Llewellyn-Jones, Jenny Wraight and Iain Mackenzie of the Naval Historical Branch; Campbell Macmurray, Matthew Sheldon and the late Chris Howard Bailey of the Royal Naval Museum; the staff of the Ships Plans section of the National Maritime Museum, especially Jeremy Michell, and to the library staff especially Jill Terrel and Liza Verity, and David Taylor and others in the Picture Library. I have also been helped by the staffs of the Imperial War Museum, National Archives and the London Library. As with all historians, my largest debt is to those of the period who kept records, wrote their memoirs, produced technical records and maintained some of the artefacts.

I would particularly like to mention the influence to two late friends, David Lyon and David Syrett, both of whom set an example in bridging the gap between eighteenth-century and twentieth-century history. At Conway Maritime Press, it was Robert Gardiner who supported me in my efforts over many years, and was partly responsible for the conception of my *Nelson's Navy*, which was a model for this volume. More recently, I must give thanks to John Lee, to Alison Moss for editing, for John Jordan for pointing out errors, and to Ross Watton for editing many of the drawings.

A Conway Maritime Book

© Brian Lavery 2006
© Volume, Conway 2006

First published in Great Britain in 2006 by Conway
An imprint of Anova Books Ltd
151 Freston Road
London W10 6TH
www.anovabooks.com

British Library Cataloguing in Publication Data:
A catalogue record for this book is available from the British Library

ISBN 10: 1 84486 035 3
ISBN 13: 9 781844 860357

Printed in China

Frontispiece: Landing craft under construction. Painted by Leslie Cole.
End page: Cleaning one of the pom-poms on Arctic patrol, 1942.

Contents

PART I

The Royal Navy in Peace and War

1 The Navy in 1939

The Royal Navy began the twentieth century on the crest of a wave. It was the main armament of the greatest empire in the world, and it was about to come even more into the public eye and have a vast expansion programme during an arms race with Germany. But the navy which went to war in 1914, though technologically advanced, was tactically cautious, socially backward and complacent. It failed to win a great victory against the German High Seas Fleet, as it had allowed the public to expect, and was very slow to adopt anti-submarine measures such as convoy when the country was under serious threat of starvation in 1917. Its highly developed air arm, the Royal Naval Air Service, was taken away and merged into the new Royal Air Force in 1918. The German fleet eventually surrendered at the armistice of November 1918, but regained its dignity by scuttling itself in the main British base at Scapa Flow seven months later.

Hard Times

The navy's troubles continued in peacetime. An arms race with the United States threatened, but the politicians and taxpayers were not prepared to pay for it and forced the navy to accept the Washington Treaty in 1922. Battleship strength, still regarded as the main determinant of naval power, was to be equal between Britain and the United States. France, Italy and Japan had their fleets regulated to a proportion of that size, while Germany was still allowed only a very small and limited fleet. The Americans were happy to be granted parity with Britain, and parity with France was welcomed by the Italians. However, the French were very unhappy with the demotion to a naval power of the third rank, and the Royal Navy was devastated at the blow to its prestige. Like the Americans and the French it took the treaty limits very seriously, with two long-term effects. The navy needed as many cruisers as possible to maintain patrols in an empire that was even more widespread than ever, but tended to build them as small as possible to keep up the numbers. And it spent a great deal of its limited budgets on ship construction, leaving little for updating the accommodation of its ships, for anti-submarine warfare, or for naval base facilities. Nevertheless the treaties were reaffirmed at London in 1930.

The navy had long been aware of its history and traditions, and began to turn increasingly towards them in a time of hardship. Sailors were aware that in 1805, in the culmination of a long series of wars and battles, the fleet under Horatio Nelson had defeated a larger French and Spanish force. From that time, the navy had maintained its position as the largest and best in the world for more than a century. In 1922 Nelson's flagship, the *Victory*, was put into a dry dock in the centre of the great dockyard at Portsmouth, equally visible by land and sea, and continued to serve as the flagship of the Commander-in-Chief.

Britain was close to financial ruin after the First World War, its people and politicians were traumatised by the death toll, and sceptical after the false hopes put in its generals and admirals. Money for the armed services was far harder to come by, and the army and navy now had to compete with a third service, the Royal Air Force, which presented an image of modernity compared with the traditional practices and ossified class structures of the others. For the first time in centuries the navy needed to justify its existence, as the more extreme advocates of bombing suggested that battleships would be easy prey to the aircraft, and that victory in any future war would only come by the destruction of cities. Naval officers were among the first to suffer from financial cuts. Under a programme of government cuts known as the 'Geddes axe' of 1922, up to a third of officers in certain ranks were made redundant. This was a hard blow to men who had placed all their hopes and expectations in the service, who had assumed a career for life and had not trained for any other job.

The next shock came from the lower deck of the navy. In September 1931 the crews of several ships of the Atlantic Fleet mutinied against pay cuts, which would bear hardest on long-service seamen. It was a small-scale affair compared with the mutinies that had overthrown governments in Russia and Germany at the end of the war and it was quickly settled with concessions, but it was publicised round the world and was a great blow to the prestige of a navy which still regarded itself as the greatest in the world. It also led to much soul-searching about relations between officers and men in an organisation that was not at the forefront of social change.

Meanwhile the air component of the navy, the Fleet Air Arm, continued to be shared between the navy and the RAF. By a compromise of 1922, the navy was to provide 70 per cent of pilots, who were to have dual rank in the two services. It provided all the observers, reflecting a justifiable lack of confidence in the RAF's navigation. The RAF would provide the aircraft to naval requirements. This system worked quite well on the decks of carriers, but it led to continued rivalry in Whitehall. It was a debilitating period, during which the British lead in naval aviation techniques was lost to the Americans and the Japanese. The navy was awarded control of naval aviation in 1937, but it was the eve of war in 1939 before it was implemented.

The navy sank to a low of 91,500 men in 1932–3 in the aftermath of the financial crisis, but began to expand slowly after that, to 127,500 men in 1937, and an authorised strength of 134,000 two years later. At the beginning of 1939 it had nearly 119,000 men in the Royal Navy proper plus more than 12,000 more in the Royal Marines.

Oposite: The Mediterranean Fleet in Grand Harbour, Malta, in 1937.

Reserves

In addition to the regular seamen, the Royal Navy had several classes of reserve to supplement it in wartime. It had retired officers, as well as naval pensioners who were liable to recall, and men of the Royal Fleet Reserve (RFR), who had all completed several years of naval service and

A poster advertising a navy week in the 1930s.

NAVY WEEK
PORTSMOUTH
AUG 2ND - 9TH

kept up with some form of training. This reserve was much favoured as all its members were known quantities and were familiar with naval ways. Of course most of them were too old for sea and were only fit for shore duties. Some had served many years ago and had established new lives on shore so were not keen to serve. Most were out of date and knew nothing of new fields such as aviation or radar. Moreover, the size of the reserve was determined by the number of men who had served a decade or two ago, which did not necessarily reflect current needs. Nevertheless the system produced nearly 55,000 officers and men in 1939, enough to increase the size of the fleet by about 45 per cent.

The next level was the Royal Naval Reserve (RNR), consisting of professional seamen from the Merchant Navy and fishing fleets. Members trained with the navy in peacetime, both in shore bases and in service with the fleet during breaks from their normal seafaring. The Admiralty placed a certain amount of faith in this, and it did produce a force of 1641 officers and 8397 ratings in 1939, who filled many important gaps in the early years of the war. But there were two main snags. The merchant seaman or fisherman was obviously familiar with the sea but not necessarily with naval ways and discipline. And more important, merchant seamen would be needed urgently in their own profession in the war that was to follow.

The third group consisted of the amateur seaman of the Royal Naval Volunteer Reserve (RNVR). The navy had long been suspicious of enthusiastic landsmen such as these, but it had reluctantly accepted their value during the anti-submarine campaign of the last war. In peacetime they trained in bases in the major ports such as London, Liverpool and Glasgow, with their own complement of officers as well as professional naval instructors. The public associated them with yachtsmen, but in practice few people had the time and leisure to combine yachting with weekend and evening training. However, the government also formed the Supplementary Reserve in 1937. This was simply a list of yachtsmen who were prepared to be called on in an emergency, but did no training for the present. The RNVR had 809 officers and 5371 ratings at the beginning of 1939, a relatively small addition to naval strength. In addition there were two specialist reserves, the Sick Berth Reserve with 1450 men and the Wireless Auxiliary Reserve with 20 officers and 579 men. None of the reserves would provide enough men to see the navy through the great expansion that was to follow.

The navy had a reserve fleet of about 140 ships, many of them veterans of the last war. They were maintained in the dockyards by nucleus crews and commanded by Admiral Sir Max Horton, who 'put a new spirit' into an area which had previously been regarded as a backwater.[1]

Mobilisation

The fleet was mobilised during the Munich Crisis of 1938 and many lessons were learned. The system was found to be inflexible and 'all and sundry arrived in barracks and there was no means of holding back or delaying call-up on any particular portion of the reserves to allow for delayed completion of ships or outward transport'.[2] The Reserve Fleet was mobilised and inspected by the King in Weymouth Bay in August 1939. As war threatened towards the end of the month, Class B and D of the RFR, who were to be ready for instant service, were called up by wireless and press announcements. Once war started on 3 September, the

RNVR were ordered to their depots to be sent on to the fleet in batches as required. The RNR took longer to mobilise as many men were still at sea, and others could not be called until replacements had been found in their regular jobs. Naval pensioners were called out as required, though some were no longer suitable for service – one man had become too fat to pass through engine-room hatches. A draft of 2000 was sent across France by rail and then by steamer to Malta, where some of the reserve ships were based. The older men were given shore jobs in the naval bases and protecting ammunition, which was often dispersed in railway tunnels and sidings. The younger men were put into destroyers, others in boom defence vessels which would not go far from the shore.[3]

Readiness for War

The fleet that went to war in September 1939 consisted of 129,000 officers and men, supplemented by 73,000 reservists. Including Australian and New Zealand forces it had 317 operational warships, consisting of 12 battleships and battlecruisers, 8 aircraft carriers, 58 cruisers, 100 fleet destroyers, 101 escort vessels and 38 submarines.

It is possible to find serious flaws in almost every aspect of the Royal Navy as it was in 1939. It had failed to predict the nature of the war it was about to fight, though that was a fault common to practically all the services, the politicians and public. Its officer corps was recruited from too narrow a base and had class attitudes which looked back to the Victorian age rather than forward to a 'people's war'. There were times when the peacetime officers seemed in danger of losing contact with the men they were supposed to lead. The lower deck was recruited on an antiquated long-service system, had too few opportunities for promotion, and was only just getting over its discontents of previous years. The navy's capital ships were too old, too slow, or too lightly armoured compared with rivals, and the newest ones were being built to compromise designs. Naval aviation was backward because of the conflict with the RAF. Ships lacked adequate anti-aircraft armament, and the means of directing its fire. Exaggerated faith in Asdic had led it to underestimate the submarine, which would prove to be the most serious threat. It had done almost nothing about coastal forces or amphibious warfare. The navy relied too much on ill-educated and poorly disciplined fishermen for one part of its reserves, and in general it had failed to tap into the enthusiasm and resources of the population.

Yet its record in the inter-war years was not one of failure. The enormous spirit of the Royal Navy had been maintained through many tribulations. It was a much more flexible organisation than in 1914, both tactically and in its ability to take new personnel and ideas. All this would be reflected in its wartime performance.

2 Society and Politics

When the Treaty of Versailles formally ended the First World War in 1919 and imposed severe penalties on a defeated Germany, the world entered a 20-year phase later known gloomily but not inaccurately as 'between the wars'. There were no 'normal' times in the period: Britain

was either recovering from one devastating war, enduring economic recession or preparing for another war that promised to be even more traumatic than the last. On the fringes, strong minorities supported doctrines such as communism or fascism, but the great mass of the population was increasingly disillusioned with politics. Religion was in decline after the horrors of the war and the sight of clerics claiming divine support on both sides. The 1920s had an image of hedonism, while the unemployment of the 1930s created despair more than anger.

Britain had a population of 46½ million in 1938, a small increase since 1919. The old landowning class, which had ruled for centuries, was in decline, having been forced to sell some of its land because of high taxes and death duties during the war. Great country houses were expensive to maintain and already their owners were beginning to make a living by opening them to the public. The idea of class, based on birth and social conditioning as much as wealth, was being increasingly challenged but it was still strong. An education in an expensive public school such as Eton or Harrow would bring a young man into contact with people who would help him in later life. The potential Nazi invaders of 1940 viewed this with an element of envy.

The entire system's purpose is to train those of strong willpower and boundless energy, who consider spiritual issues a waste of time, but know man's nature and understand how to rule. These are educated people who in conscienceless manner

Seamen at a service on board *Repulse* in the 1930s. Marines are in the foreground, the chaplain is in the centre with the officers and petty officers behind him, and most of the seamen on the deck below.

represent English ideals and see the meaning of their lives in the promotion of the interests of the English ruling class.[4]

The upper class maintained its 'society' centred round shooting parties, horse racing, and balls in London. Accent was still important, and a regional or 'lower class' one could debar a person from acceptance in society, or from a commission in the navy or certain regiments of the army. The middle class was growing, but felt insecure and lived in less opulent circumstances than in the past, with far fewer domestic servants and smaller numbers of children, who might need support to establish themselves in a career.

British Politics

Britain was a hereditary monarchy and King George V was held in great respect during his reign from 1910 to 1936. His eldest son, Edward VIII, was far more controversial. Apart from his plans to make an unsuitable marriage to an American divorcee, his views on politics and his tendency to interfere made him unacceptable to the political establishment and he was forced to abdicate. His brother and successor, George VI, was nervous and shy and unsuitable for public life in many ways, but these defects made him less likely to interfere in politics, and endeared him to his subjects.

British politics was controlled by the party which could command a majority in the elected House of Commons and thus provide a prime minister. The largely hereditary House of Lords was less powerful than in the past, although the Nazis viewed the whole system as a front.

Nowadays Britain appears as a parliamentary monarchy, but in spite of the democratisation of its constitution, parliamentary and governmental absolutism prevail. Today's state organisation is maintained by the monarchist and bureaucratic elements.

Naturally they saw the Jews as over-powerful, from the time of Benjamin Disraeli in the previous century. After 1922, '…no new cabinets were formed without including Jews. Baldwin's last cabinet contained two Jews from the financial world…'[5]

American servicemen were given a far rosier picture of the British political system.

…within this apparently old-fashioned framework the British enjoy a practical, working twentieth century democracy which is in some ways even more flexible and sensitive to the will of the people than our own.[6]

From 1918, for the first time in history, property tenure was no longer a factor in the right to vote and it was given to all men over the age of 21. Women were also allowed to vote for the first time, initially from the age of 30 and on the same terms as men from 1928. But these radical measures did not produce any radical solutions in British politics.

The old Liberal party, which had dominated British politics since 1906, collapsed quickly after the war, partly because of the conduct of its leader, the great wartime Prime Minister, David Lloyd George. Its place was largely taken by the Labour party, committed to a more working-class representation in Parliament and to moderate socialism. But the new party was still quite weak, and only formed two short-lived governments, in 1924 and 1929–31. It was almost fatally split after 1931, allowing the Conservative party, popularly known as the Tories, almost complete control of Parliament for a decade, partly in the guise of a 'National' government which included some former Labour and Liberal supporters.

Despite a good deal of hunger for change, the 1920s and 30s were a barren period for social reform. There was nothing to compare with the great Liberal reforms before the First World War, or Labour's setting up of the Welfare State after the second. The Conservative party had embraced social reform under Benjamin Disraeli in the 1870s, but now it reflected the mood of the middle classes, who feared socialism, communism, trade unions, high taxation, economic ruin, and change in general. Its main leader of the period was Stanley Baldwin, who was content to follow public opinion with his slogan 'Safety First' and had no ideas of his own. But governments of the 1930s did not deliver any kind of safety from economic recession, class conflict or war.

The British Economy

Britain had lost her position as the only real industrial power in the world more than half a century before, with the rise of the American and German economies in the 1870s. She was still a country which relied very much on manufacturing industry, which employed just under half the working population in 1931, compared with about a quarter in trade and transport, and less than 10 per cent in agriculture. There was a steady move towards new industries such as cars, chemicals and electricity. The largest single industry was coal mining, which employed more than a million men in 1930. It was

Theatre-goers pass through the market stalls in Covent Garden in London in 1939.

in private hands and was racked by strikes and poor industrial relations. The textile industries were also large, and iron and steel was next with more than a quarter of a million employees. The trade union movement was strong among skilled workers, while the Transport and General Workers Union was founded in 1921 under Ernest Bevin for the less skilled. But the unions were defeated in the 10-day General Strike of 1926 and had not fully recovered from that, while slumps and the threat of unemployment cowed what remained of the workforce. All this tended to breed resentment among the workers, and a certain amount of mistrust and cynicism about the management.

British industry had lost many overseas markets during the First World War, but even more important it had lost much of its old self-confidence. The Gold Standard, maintained enthusiastically by Winston Churchill as Chancellor of the Exchequer in the 1920s, meant that the pound was linked to the price of gold and was over-valued. This created stability but made exports far more difficult. British industry was not dead technologically and produced, for example, the first practical television sets (though to a design by EMI rather than the one by John Logie Baird which popular mythology favours). But the new leaders of industry, often the descendants of the buccaneers and entrepreneurs who had set up the great companies in the first place, were generally cautious and afraid of new ideas, not to mention the latent power of the trade unions.

Industry boomed for a time after the war, then entered a slump in the early 1920s. There was a recovery late in the decade, but the effects of the Wall Street Crash of 1929 soon spread to Britain, creating mass unemployment on an unprecedented scale. The position was worst in the areas reliant on heavy industry – in Scotland and the north of England – where unemployment reached 22 per cent of the workforce in 1932. Worst hit of all was the shipbuilding industry, where it reached more than 60 per cent in 1932. Industry offered few apprenticeships in these years, and became more timid than ever. There was much loss of industrial capacity, in shipyards as much as anywhere else, and the effects of this would be felt during the war of the next decade, when Britain came to rely on the United States for much of her war materials.

In the south, the position was much better and unemployment was less than 10 per cent in the London area. This reflected the rise of a new middle class, working as clerks and managers in banking and insurance. The period saw a great expansion of the London suburbs, with new-style housing designed for independent family units without live-in servants. It was yet another way in which Britain was divided in the years before 1939.

World Affairs

In the 1920s Germany was defeated and Russia, by then known as the Soviet Union, was cut off from world affairs because of the ideology of the regime. In the United States, politicians and people mostly favoured a policy of isolation, which kept her, too, out of full participation. As a result, Britain and France appeared to be the only real world powers. Both still had great empires, which had actually increased in the last few years. Under League of Nations mandate, Britain took over control of Palestine, Trans-Jordan and Iraq and had protectorates in Egypt, Sudan, Somaliland and Aden. Added to India,

large parts of Africa and many of the West Indian islands, the British Empire seemed stronger than ever. The only immediate setback was in Ireland, where the largest part of the country fought for independence and gained it in 1922. The colonies where large numbers of Europeans had settled – Canada, Australia, New Zealand and South Africa – were already largely self-governing and from 1931 they had full control of their own foreign policy. Since they tended to back Britain in world affairs, this was seen as a strength rather than a weakness for the empire, which now added the term 'Commonwealth' to include these self-governing parts. India was also given a measure of self-government in 1935, much against the wishes of Churchill. But in this case a strong opposition movement, and division between Hindus and Muslims, made the sub-continent very hard to govern. The newly acquired mandates were just as difficult to rule – Iraq was large and was partly controlled by the threat of bombing by the RAF, while in Palestine conflict between indigenous Arabs and immigrant Jews was already building up. Meanwhile the rising power of Japan in the Far East caused worries, especially after Britain was forced to give up her alliance with her in 1922 due to American pressure. A new and much-delayed naval base at Singapore was built in an attempt to cope with this threat.

The concept of empire was not particularly fashionable, except for a group led by the press barons Northcliffe and Beaverbrook, who campaigned for free trade within the empire and high tariffs on goods from outside. This cut across the more traditional policy of general free trade, and was defeated by the Conservative leader Baldwin. On the whole, the empire was a liability rather than an asset to Britain in the 1930s.

The famous Jarrow March of 1936. The marchers were protesting about high levels of unemployment, mainly caused by the permanent closure of Palmer's shipyard in Northumberland.

The British Empire coloured red in 1937, showing the distribution of British ships of 3000 tons and over. Note the large number of vessels in the North Atlantic, and also on passage to and from Latin America.

The Great War of 1914–18 had created more problems than it had solved. Britain had not suffered defeat, major bombardment or enemy occupation, but had lost three quarters of a million young men. The survivors talked about the horrors of the Western Front, and the new world seemed little better than the old. The sense of loss and futility created a strong pacifist movement in Britain, which was not reflected in other countries. German resentment at the savage terms of the Treaty of Versailles and the humiliating way in which they were applied finally exploded in the election of the Nazi party in 1933, committed to restore the country by any means necessary. Italy, part of the victorious alliance during the war, felt cheated by the peace terms and

this was an important factor in the rise to power of Mussolini and his Fascist party in 1922. They, too, were committed to aggression: Mussolini famously said 'War is to man as maternity is to woman'. Japan, another of Britain's allies in the war, had expanded by picking up German colonies in the Pacific and was developing far grander aims, while the military party rose to power in the state. The Soviet Union was not militaristic as such, and was largely turned inwards for industrial development and social repression on a grand scale; but the state's very existence posed a threat of revolution which was feared by the western powers, and was much exploited by the Nazis in Germany. British hopes of a more reasonable world were doomed.

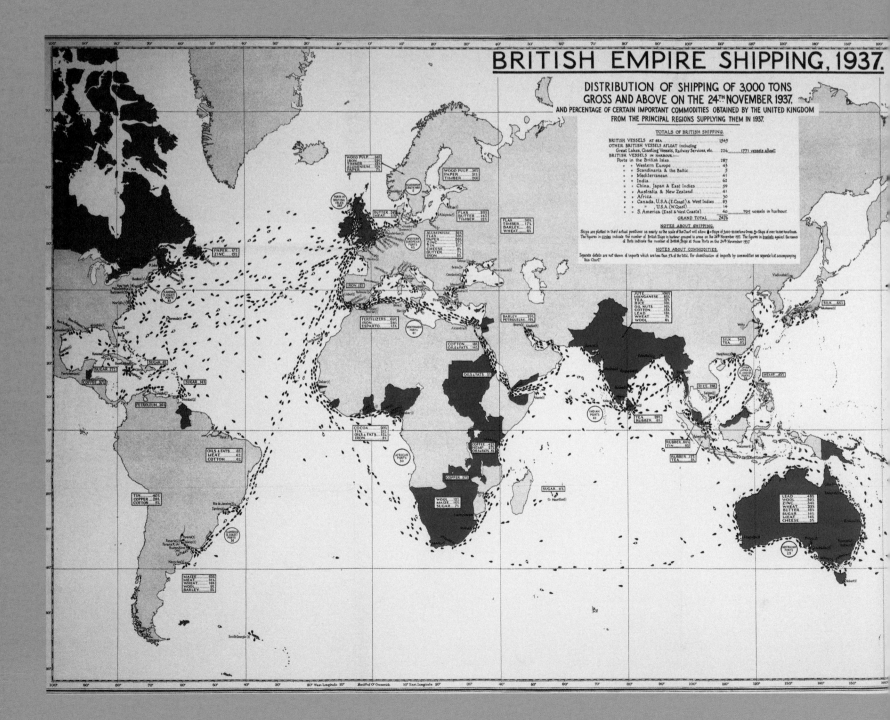

The Coming of War

The Nazis were relatively quiet in foreign policy for their first three years in power, but in 1936 they re-occupied the Rhineland, denied to them under the Treaty of Versailles. They began to build their army, navy and air force, the last of which was specifically banned under Versailles, as were submarines. In Britain there was a feeling that the Germans had been unfairly treated at Versailles and had a right to resume their place as a great nation, leading to the policy of appeasement that allowed the Nazis to take over Austria in 1938. But the Nazis' appetite was insatiable. When they demanded the border regions of Czechoslovakia, Britain and France combined in an attempt to stop them. Neville Chamberlain, the new Prime Minister, flew to Munich to meet Hitler and backed down, allowing the Germans to occupy the mountainous border areas which were the country's only means of defence. He proclaimed that it was 'peace for our time'. The Nazis took over the remaining part of Czechoslovakia the following year, then in August signed a non-aggression pact with the Soviet Communists, their ideological enemies. They demanded possession of the 'Polish Corridor' (another territory taken from them at Versailles). This time the western allies stood firm and declared war.

The Franco–British ultimatum to Germany to withdraw from Poland expired at 11.00 on Sunday, 3 September 1939 and Chamberlain made a mournful radio broadcast to the British nation. The people were pessimistic but resolute. Their political divisions largely disappeared, especially after the Fall of France in 1940 created a genuine threat to the country. The alliances with the Soviet Union and the United States from 1941 allowed people of almost all political persuasions, except a very small number of pre-war fascists, to unite in a common cause. They knew in general about the Nazi persecution of Jews and other minorities and saw this as another motive to fight. The Nazi policy of deliberate extermination was only adopted in the second half of the war, and there was some scepticism as the facts began to emerge, because of the scale of the horror and as a reaction against exaggerated atrocity stories from the last war. But there was no doubt that Hitler was a tyrant, the Nazi system was brutal and corrupt, and was a danger to the world. Despite the dangers and hardships there was no serious popular movement for peace or surrender. The young men and women who joined the navy and the Women's Royal Naval Service (WRNS), and the shipyard and dockyard workers who supported them, were sometimes lazy or corrupt as individuals, but as a group they were enthusiastic for the cause and proud of the role they played.

Over the next six years, the British people were more tightly organised and mobilised than at any time before or since. Men and, to a lesser extent, women up to their fifties could be conscripted into the armed forces, while the remainder often worked long hours on war production. Families were split as children and sometimes their mothers were evacuated from the major cities in the south and east. Food was rationed from the beginning and petrol rationing was so tight that private motoring almost became extinct. The threat of invasion was taken very seriously in the years after the Fall of France. There were restrictions on press and broadcasting and the government had the right to lock up any residents it suspected of disloyalty. By night the blackout of town and country was rigidly enforced. There were bombing raids on most of the major cities and civilian populations were often at risk, though not so much as in Germany when the British and Americans began to counter-attack. No group in the community endured more long-term danger and hardship than the sailors of the Royal Navy, but it must be seen against the backdrop of a country in which almost everyone faced danger, discomfort, lack of freedom, overwork, interrupted sleep, broken family life and shortage of material goods.

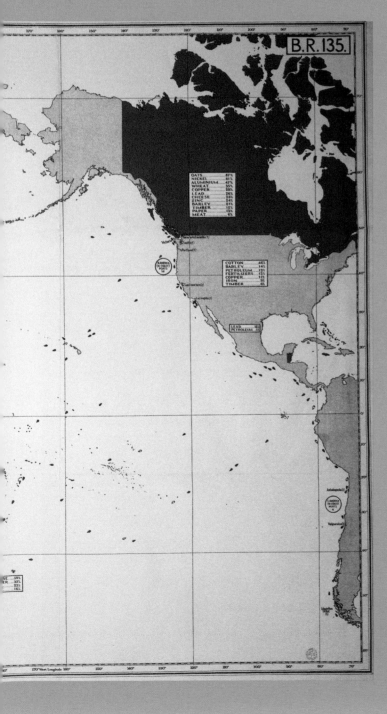

3 The Naval War

The 'Phoney War'

The war on land and in the air was almost dormant for the first autumn and winter and was dubbed the 'Phoney War' by the press. But this was never the case at sea. On the first day, against Hitler's wishes, *U-30* sank the liner *Athenia*, and after that the U-boats drifted inexorably towards unrestricted warfare, in which merchant ships could be sunk on sight without warning. Their most dramatic success came in mid October when *U-47* penetrated the British base at Scapa Flow and sank the battleship *Royal Oak*. But it was surface raiders which posed the greatest threat to the British position at that time, until the pocket battleship *Graf Spee* was cornered by British cruisers in Montevideo and scuttled herself. It gave the impression by the end of 1939 that the Royal Navy could reach out to some of the furthest seas in the world, but had failed to defend its own bases.

The Norwegian Campaign

In February 1940 the *Graf Spee's* supply ship, the *Altmark*, was carrying nearly 300 merchant navy prisoners to Germany when she was boarded in neutral Norwegian waters by the destroyer *Cossack* under Captain Phillip Vian. As well as showing British determination to carry on the war, the affair drew British and German attention to the north. Supplies of iron ore for Germany came from Sweden via the Norwegian port of Narvik and Churchill planned to stop it by mining the passages among the Norwegian islands, using troops to secure the position if necessary. The Germans planned a much greater breach of neutrality, by invading Denmark and Norway. It was a very daring operation and against the normal principles of strategy as Germany did not have command of the sea.

The British ships stood down just as the Germans launched a five-part invasion plan on 9 April. Apart from the troops which took Denmark without a struggle, forces sailed for Oslo, Kristiansand, Bergen, Trondheim and Narvik in the far north. The Norwegians sank the cruiser *Blücher*, and the British destroyer *Glowworm* rammed the cruiser *Hipper*, but the Norwegians were unprepared and the British failed to piece together the various intelligence sources and were wrong-footed. The Home Fleet failed to intercept the invasion forces.

There was some success at Narvik on the 10th and 13th, when two forces, the second led by the battleship *Warspite*, penetrated the fjord and sank 10 German destroyers. Counter attacks were launched and troops were landed in the Narvik and Trondheim areas, but the campaigns were poorly planned and led and lacked air support. The men had to be withdrawn early in June. During the retreat, the carrier *Glorious* was sunk because her captain had allowed her to sail within range of the guns of the German battlecruisers *Scharnhorst* and *Gneisenau*.

Dunkirk and the Fall of France

By this time the campaign in France was going very badly. German troops invaded the neutral Netherlands, Belgium and Luxemburg on 10 May 1940, just as Prime Minister Neville Chamberlain fell from office and was replaced by Winston Churchill. Blitzkrieg was even more successful than anticipated and the French were driven back while a large part of the British army retreated to Dunkirk. More than 300,000 Allied troops were evacuated, although two thirds were taken off by destroyers from the harbour, rather than by fishing boats and yachts from the beaches as is popularly thought. Hundreds of small craft did take part, mostly ferrying the troops from the beaches

Below left: German troops are welcomed as they enter the Rhineland in 1936, in breach of international treaties.

Below right: Neville Chamberlain arrives back from his meeting with Hitler in September 1938, holding aloft his 'piece of paper', which he believes guarantees 'peace for our time'.

to passenger ships offshore. The operation, directed by Admiral Bertram Ramsay in Dover, confirmed one of the lessons of Norway, that air attacks were very dangerous to shipping in confined waters. Another 200,000 troops were evacuated from other parts of France, despite the sinking of the liner *Lancastria* off St Nazaire with the loss of several thousand lives.

As France came close to surrender and Italy made an opportunistic declaration of war, Churchill became concerned about the fate of the French fleet. Force H, a powerful group of major warships, was formed under Admiral Sir James Somerville and sent to demand the surrender or demilitarisation of ships at Mers el-Kebir in Algeria. When they refused, Force H opened fire and disabled three battleships and many other ships, with heavy loss of French life. The British also moved against the French colony of Dakar in West Africa, but an attempted landing failed in September.

At home, all British energies were concentrated on the threat of a German invasion. The army was reorganised while the RAF fought the Battle of Britain to remove the immediate threat, and the Luftwaffe turned to the less productive night bombing of cities. The Home Fleet remained in the north but planned to send its destroyers south if the German invasion fleet ever sailed. Light craft of the Patrol Service and Coastal Forces would be the first to meet the invasion.

The Atlantic War

By the middle of 1940 a U-boat was allowed to sink on sight virtually any ship believed to be helping Britain. The German position was immeasurably boosted by the seizure of bases in Norway and France, and the battle moved out into the Atlantic, while southern and eastern British ports such as London and Southampton were largely closed due to bombing. During the winter of 1940–41 the U-boats developed the tactic of surfaced attack by night and had great success against weakly escorted convoys in an area north of Ireland and west of Scotland. In March 1941, as invasion seemed less likely and the German bomber offensive had clearly failed. Churchill declared that 'the Battle of the Atlantic has begun'. But there was some British success that month as three ace U-boat commanders – Gunther Prien, Otto Kretschmer and Joachim Schepke – were sunk or captured, convoy escorts became stronger and air patrols were intensified. Ultra intelligence began to give useful results and the U-boats were forced further out into the Atlantic. In September 1940 President Roosevelt allowed the transfer of 50 old American destroyers to Britain in exchange for the use of naval bases. In January 1941 Congress permitted the system of lend-lease, which allowed supplies to be sent to Britain in large quantities.

In May 1941 the great German battleship *Bismarck* and the cruiser *Prince Eugen* left Norway for a raid in the North Atlantic. They were spotted by British reconnaissance aircraft and shadowed by cruisers, while the battlecruiser *Hood* and the new battleship *Prince of Wales* left Scapa Flow to meet them west of Iceland. The *Hood* was sunk by the *Bismarck's* broadside and the *Prince of Wales* retreated. Meanwhile the Home Fleet and Force H were sent in pursuit, and the *Bismarck's* steering was fatally damaged by torpedo planes from the carrier *Ark Royal*. The British fleet caught up with her and destroyed her on the 27th. Surface raiders remained a threat, but in February 1942 the *Scharnhorst* and *Gneisenau* were withdrawn from Brest through the English Channel. The British were humiliated as their ships and aircraft failed to stop them, but in fact it marked a strategic retreat by the Germans.

Naval gunfire supports an army landing near Narvik in Norway.

Britain gained two powerful allies in the course of 1941, but that did not help the Atlantic war in the short term. The German invasion of Russia in June created the need for convoys to take supplies to Murmansk and Archangel in the north, past the U-boats, surface ships and aircraft based in Norway and through appalling sea conditions north of the Arctic Circle. One of the greatest disasters of the war came in July 1942 when the Admiralty, believing that the *Bismarck's* sister-ship *Tirpitz* was out, ordered convoy PQ17 to disperse. Two thirds of the ships were sunk. The United States entered the war after the attack on Pearl Harbor in December, but that opened the American East Coast to U-boat attack, and ships there remained unescorted for the first half of 1942, suffering great losses. Then in the second half of that year the U-boats moved back to mid-Atlantic, for the crisis of the U-boat war.

The Mediterranean War

The naval war in the Mediterranean began in June 1940, as France collapsed and Italy declared war. The elimination of the French fleet at Mers el-Kebir was traumatic and Britain's central base at Malta soon came under siege from the air, but the Royal Navy enjoyed some success against the Italians. In November Swordfish torpedo bombers from the carrier *Illustrious* sank or damaged three battleships in the

harbour at Taranto. Off Cape Matapan in March 1941 Admiral Andrew Cunningham led a fleet which sank three Italian cruisers. The navy co-operated with the army based in Egypt which was successful against the Italians in Libya, despite the lack of air support.

In April the navy took British troops to Greece to support the country against an Italian and German invasion, and withdrew them a few weeks later. In May the Germans invaded Crete by air against fierce resistance. The navy had little air support and during fighting round the island it lost nine major warships, mostly to German dive bombers. However, it succeeded in evacuating 18,600 troops from the island. Meanwhile the German *Afrika Corps* under Rommel advanced towards Egypt.

The second half of 1941 was a disastrous period for the Mediterranean Fleet, as German aircraft and U-boats entered the area and became increasingly effective. Malta had provided a base for air and submarine attack on the Axis supply routes to North Africa, but was heavily bombed from November. The famous carrier *Ark Royal* was sunk by U-boat on the 18th, followed by the battleship *Barham* on the 25th. Admiral Phillip Vian had some success against the Italians at Sirte on 17 December, but the following day a force of cruisers ran into a minefield and three were sunk or damaged. On the 19th Italian manned torpedoes penetrated the main British base at Alexandria and seriously damaged the battleships *Queen Elizabeth* and *Valiant*. The

The withdrawal from Dunkirk, painted by Richard Eurich. In the foreground, troops in small boats are carried out to a tug, a fishing boat, a paddle steamer and a Thames barge. In the background, troops on the mole are boarding destroyers.

Mediterranean Fleet had no serviceable capital ships by the beginning of 1942. There was an ambiguous success again at Sirte in March as two Italian destroyers were sunk in a storm but the British convoy was delayed and suffered heavy damage from the air. Cunningham left that month, with his fleet in much reduced circumstances.

The Retreat from the Pacific

The Royal Navy had long been aware how difficult it would be to defend the empire in the Pacific and Indian Ocean against Japan at the same time as fighting a war in Europe. Churchill optimistically believed that a moderate force of British capital ships could act as a deterrent so the *Prince of Wales* and *Repulse* were sent to Singapore, although no aircraft carrier was available to protect them. The Japanese attacked Pearl Harbor on 7 December 1941 to bring America into the war, and at the same time they launched attacks on the British colony at Hong Kong and threatened Malaya and Singapore. Admiral Tom Phillips took his two ships out despite the lack of air cover, and on the 10th they were sunk by Japanese torpedo bombers and bombers. Two months later the British Empire suffered perhaps its most humiliating defeat of all time when Singapore surrendered. The cruiser *Exeter* fought with the Americans at the Battle of the Java Sea, but was sunk a few days later. Admiral James Somerville, who took command of the fleet at Ceylon after Phillips' death, was forced to retreat to

the Indian Ocean, while the great Pacific war was left almost entirely to American forces, with help from the small Australian and New Zealand navies.

Victory in the Mediterranean

Convoys were forced through to Malta against heavy losses by air and U-boat attack during 1942. Operation Pedestal in August 1942 was escorted by 4 aircraft carriers (one of which was lost and two damaged), 2 battleships, 7 cruisers (two lost, two damaged) and 27 destroyers. Only 5 out of 14 cargo ships reached the island, including the tanker *Ohio*, which limped into harbour with vital supplies of oil.

But the tide began to turn, largely because of the land campaign in North Africa. In October General Montgomery began the Battle of El Alamein and eventually forced Rommel to retreat. In November, in Operation Torch, the Allies landed in French Morocco and Algeria, and Axis forces were trapped between them, being driven back to Tunisia and forced to withdraw to Italy in May 1943.

The Anglo-American forces were now on the offensive, as Cunningham returned. In July he led the naval side of the invasion of Sicily under the American General Eisenhower, the most heavily opposed invasion so far in the west. It used 580 warships and 2000 landing craft. Two months later Allied forces were put ashore at

The main campaigns fought by the Royal Navy in the Atlantic, North Sea, Arctic Ocean and Mediterranean.

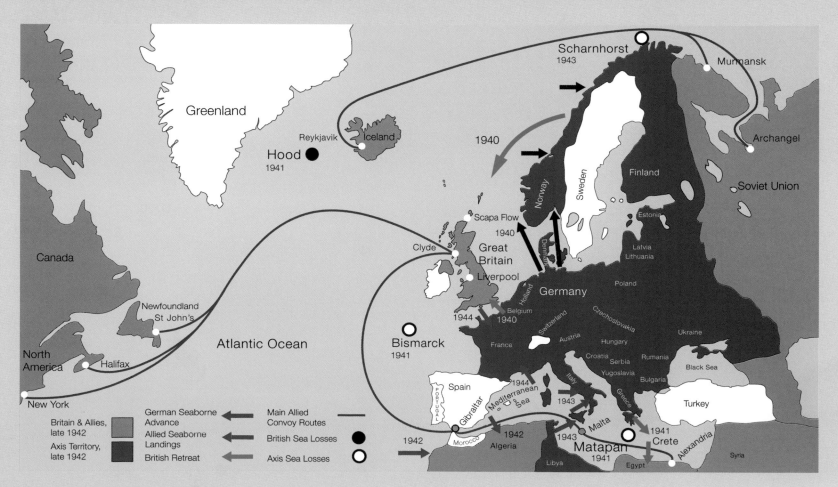

Salerno in Italy. Italy eventually surrendered but the Germans offered strong resistance. British naval forces on both sides of Italy aided the slow Allied advance and in January 1944 troops landed at Anzio near Rome but missed a chance to make spectacular advances.

By this time attention had shifted to events in northern Europe, but British forces helped a mainly American landing in the south of France in August 1944. British forces also operated in the Aegean, attacking the Germans in September and October as they withdrew from Greece.

The Crisis of the Battle of the Atlantic

During the second half of 1942 the 'wolf packs' of U-boats harassed Allied shipping in the North Atlantic. The Admiralty fought the high command of the RAF for more resources to be taken away from the hugely expensive bomber offensive against Germany, and for very long-range aircraft which could close the 'air gap' in the middle of the ocean. In the meantime 98 ships of 485,000 tons were sunk in September alone. There was a lull during the winter, but in March 1943 the U-boats returned to the attack against two eastbound convoys, HX229 and SC122, which lost 21 ships between them, against one U-boat sunk.

The crew of the *Prince of Wales* transfer to a destroyer as the ship is sunk by Japanese aircraft.

But the tide began to turn. Radar was increasingly used to detect U-boats on the surface, new models of Asdic and weapons such as Hedgehog were coming into use as were new escorts in the form of frigates. The air gap was gradually closed, while escort carriers went with many convoys to provide air support. As the supply of escorts increased, support groups were formed to go to the aid of beleaguered convoys. In May convoy ONS5 forced its way through a concentration of U-boats with the loss of 11 ships out of 42, but several U-boats were sunk. At the end of the month, worried about falling morale and losses by ship and aircraft, Admiral Dönitz withdrew the U-boats from the North Atlantic.

This secured the supply line for the Allied armies building up in Europe, but it was not the end. The U-boats eventually returned, some fitted with a powerful anti-aircraft armament. Towards the end of 1944 the Germans began to use the schnorkel, which allowed them to operate far more effectively underwater. They began a new campaign in British coastal waters, where they had not been since early 1940. They had even more effective boats such as the Walther type up their sleeve, but the war ended before they came into use.

In the north, the surface threat to the Russian convoys was gradually diminished. The *Scharnhorst* was trapped by the Home Fleet on Boxing Day 1943 and sunk. The *Tirpitz* was damaged by midget submarines in September 1943, and finally sunk by RAF bombers a year later.

Victory in the West

Although he set up a Combined Operations organisation immediately after the Fall of France, Churchill resisted American pressure to invade northern Europe until well into 1943. After that the whole of southern England became an armed camp as British, Canadian, Free French, Polish and American troops moved there in increasing numbers. A huge force of landing craft was built up. After several delays D-Day was set for 5 June 1944, but atrocious weather caused another delay to a weather window the next day. Seventy-nine per cent of combatant vessels would be British and Canadian, 16½ per cent American and 4½ per cent would be operated by the other Allies.

Allied forces landed on the Normandy beaches in the early hours of 6 June 1944. The three eastern beaches, code named Gold, Juno

Operation Harpoon, a Malta convoy of June 1942, escorted by the battleship *Malaya.*

and Sword, were attacked by British and Canadian troops in British landing craft. The Americans used mostly their own landing craft on Utah and Omaha beaches, but a large part of the covering forces were British. Apart from landing craft, warships patrolled the edges of the area for surface warships, E-boats and submarines and prevented any significant penetration. They provided anti-aircraft cover and bombarded enemy positions, both on the coast and several miles inland. Apart from heavy casualties on Omaha Beach, the landings were highly successful and naval casualties were unexpectedly light. But once ashore the armies were bogged down. Caen, a British objective for the first day, was not taken for a month. American armies now did the bulk of the fighting. After the final breakout from Normandy the lines of supply became increasingly long and the navies had to invade the island of Walcheren and clear the port of Antwerp to ease the situation. On 30 April 1945 Hitler committed suicide and power transferred to Admiral Dönitz until Germany surrendered a week later.

Back to the Pacific

The British Government was determined to return to the Pacific in some form. From late 1944, after victory in the Battle of the Atlantic, the success of the Normandy invasion, the surrender of the Italian fleet and the attrition of the German surface fleet, it had enough spare ships to do so.

The British Pacific Fleet was formed under Sir Bruce Fraser, but it was puny compared with the American forces in the area. Its equipment was largely outdated and it had much to learn about the latest techniques. Its crews were only too aware how far their pay and conditions had fallen behind those of the Americans. It carried out raids on oil refineries in Sumatra before the war ended with the first atom bombs.

British warships were present in Tokyo Bay and Fraser was one of the signatories of the Japanese surrender document, but the huge American force showed how far the British had slipped behind them in resources.

Right: Captain F J Walker's Second Escort Group returns to Liverpool after sinking six U-boats, to cheers from sailors and Wrens on the dockside.

Opposite: A heavily loaded soldier falls from the gangway of a Landing Craft Infantry during the Normandy landings.

PART II

The Structure of Naval Power

1 My Lords of the Admiralty

The Royal Navy was headed by the Admiralty. Technically this meant the Board of Admiralty, but colloquially it referred to the whole government department, its buildings and all its works. Like any government department the Admiralty was theoretically subject to the king. George VI had served as a naval officer in his youth and was much respected in the service, although he had no decisive influence over how it was run, except in matters of tradition, such as the naming of major warships.

The Admiralty was also subject to the control of Parliament, which voted the money to run the navy. In return Parliament expected an annual statement on naval affairs by the First Lord, and the right to question him or his ministers at regular intervals. But parliamentary control of the navy was rather light, especially in wartime. The Naval Estimates of the war produced only generalities about the amount of money to be spent, in the form of a vote for 'such numbers of Officers, Seamen, Boys and Royal Marines and of Royal Marine Police, as His Majesty may deem necessary to be borne on the books of His Majesty's Ships and at the Royal Marine Divisions…'. Even the number of men allowed for the navy, a figure which was almost sacred in peacetime, was dropped during the war. As Churchill explained in 1940:

…it is not expedient to lay precise facts and figures of the proposed strength and cost of the Navy in the coming year before the House as we should naturally desire to do. In the first place, it is physically impossible to make exact estimates for contingencies which are constantly changing; and in the second place, there is no need to tell the enemy more than is good for him about what we are doing.

In peacetime the Treasury also exerted a strong influence on the navy, by controlling budgets and keeping expenditure within estimates. This, too, was much less tight in wartime:

It has been agreed with the Treasury that forecasts of cash requirements for naval services in the financial year 1940, rendered by Departments and Branches, …may be treated as though they had been Navy Estimates approved in the ordinary way. … It will not be necessary to consult the Treasury merely because a proposed service may involve an excess on the Vote or Subhead concerned.[1]

Churchill's Role

Winston Churchill resumed his association with the Royal Navy on the first day of the war, when he took office again as First Lord of the Admiralty. A famous signal went out to the fleet: 'Winston is back'. Churchill had first taken charge of the Royal Navy in 1911 when it was the largest in the world and had unshaken prestige, during a period of rapid technological change and rising budgets. His fall from office after the Dardanelles campaign of 1915 was a bitter blow.

Churchill took a great deal of naval knowledge with him when he became Prime Minister in 1940, but that did not mean that he favoured the navy unduly. He had started his career as an army officer. After the Dardanelles he commanded a battalion on the Western Front. He was Secretary of State for War in the early 1920s, and while out of office in the 1930s his main project had been a four-volume biography of his forebear, an eighteenth-century general. General Sir Alan Brooke commented: 'Winston never had the slightest doubt that he had inherited all the military genius from his great ancestor Marlborough'.[2]

Churchill was equally at home with the air force. He had tried to learn to fly before and after the First World War, and had been instrumental in setting up the Royal Naval Air Service which became part of the RAF in 1918. He made a special study of the balance of power in the air in the 1930s. He became an honorary air commodore in the Royal Auxiliary Air Force and often wore the uniform. Churchill's knowledge of all three services was almost perfectly balanced, and it enabled him to supervise all of them.

As well as being Prime Minister, Churchill was Minister of Defence. The post had no real constitutional authority, and previous attempts to set up ministers 'for the Co-ordination of Defence' had been failures, but this did not stand in his way. His Chief of Staff General Ismay, wrote:

…the Prime Minister himself, with all the powers and authority which attach to that office, exercised a personal, direct, ubiquitous and continuous supervision, not only over the formulation of military policy at every stage, but over the general conduct of military operations.[3]

As his private secretary put it on the first weeks of his taking office as Prime Minister: 'Churchill scrutinises any document which has anything to do with the war and does not disdain to enquire into the most trivial point'.[4]

The Board of Admiralty

The Admiralty was a highly complex organisation. Unlike civilian ministries such as the Home Office or the Ministry of Education, it was directly responsible for every aspect of the lives of the servicemen under it. Like the other service ministries it had to be able to initiate and control every aspect of their organization rather than just regulate it. Commerce, for example, would continue in some form without the influence of the Board of Trade. Education was largely run by the local authorities and only lightly supervised by the ministry in London. But without a body such as the Admiralty, there would be no navy at all. Unlike the other service ministries the Admiralty was an operational as well as an administrative

Opposite: Churchill with Admiral Sir Dudley Pound (left) and Major General Loch (right).

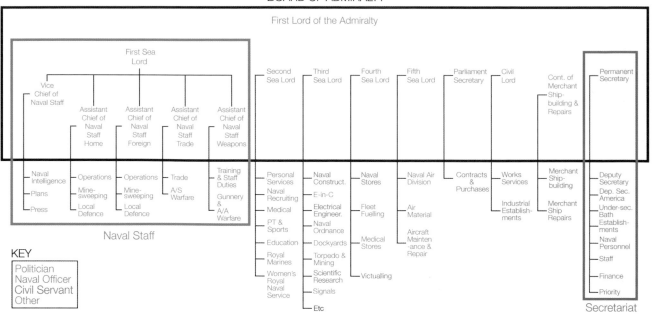

BOARD OF ADMIRALTY

First Lord of the Admiralty

First Sea Lord

| | | | | | Second Sea Lord | Third Sea Lord | Fourth Sea Lord | Fifth Sea Lord | Parliament Secretary | Civil Lord | Cont. of Merchant | Permanent Secretary |

Vice Chief of Naval Staff

Assistant Chief of Naval Staff Home / Assistant Chief of Naval Staff Foreign / Assistant Chief of Naval Staff Trade / Assistant Chief of Naval Staff Weapons

Ship-building & Repairs

- Naval Intelligence
- Plans
- Press

- Operations
- Mine-sweeping
- Local Defence

- Operations
- Mine-sweeping
- Local Defence

- Trade
- A/S Warfare

- Training & Staff Duties
- Gunnery & A/A Warfare

Second Sea Lord:
- Personal Services
- Naval Recruiting
- Medical
- PT & Sports
- Education
- Royal Marines
- Women's Royal Naval Service
- Etc

Third Sea Lord:
- Naval Construct.
- E-in-C
- Electrical Engineer.
- Naval Ordnance
- Dockyards
- Torpedo & Mining
- Scientific Research
- Signals

Fourth Sea Lord:
- Naval Stores
- Fleet Fuelling
- Medical Stores
- Victualling

Fifth Sea Lord:
- Naval Air Division
- Air Material
- Aircraft Mainten-ance & Repair

Parliament Secretary:
- Contracts & Purchases

Civil Lord:
- Works Services
- Industrial Establish-ments

Cont. of Merchant:
- Merchant Ship-building
- Merchant Ship Repairs

Permanent Secretary:
- Deputy Secretary
- Dep. Sec. America
- Under-sec. Bath Establish-ments
- Naval Personnel
- Staff
- Finance
- Priority

Naval Staff

Secretariat

KEY

Politician
Naval Officer
Civil Servant
Other

The organisation of the Admiralty during the Second World War.

---

headquarters, with power to direct ships and fleets at sea. In practice this was used sparingly and the two wartime First Sea Lords believed that the man on the spot was usually the better judge of what to do. The Admiralty was also responsible for procuring most of its own supplies, including ships, whereas the War Office worked through the Ministry of Supply and the Air Ministry through the Ministry of Aircraft Production. The Admiralty managed one of the world's largest civilian workforces in the royal dockyards, armament stores and other depots. There were 127,000 men and women in the home yards at the end of 1941, plus nearly 45,000 in overseas yards.

The Admiralty was well aware of its great powers. It was notoriously peremptory in the wording of its orders, and its pompous manner inspired mild satire among the recipients of its orders, who spoke of decisions by 'the Admiralty in its wisdom', or 'My Lords of the Admiralty'. According to Sir Oswyn Murray, who had retired as Secretary in 1936:

The Admiralty is the department of state which is charged with the administration of the naval business of the country. It is responsible for the maintenance and management of the Royal Navy, and for giving expert advice and taking executive action, when necessary, in matters relating to the defence of the interests and territory of the Empire by sea.[5]

Unlike some other government committees the Board of Admiralty was a fully working body with real control over the affairs of the navy. Early in the war Churchill decreed that the Board should meet at 4 p.m. every Friday and members wanting to raise a particular topic should inform the Secretary by Wednesday if at all possible. They were warned not to bring too much detail to the Board, but to use the meeting 'for the purpose of discussing…the large issues affecting the general policy of the Board, the strength of the Navy in material and personnel, changes of programme, changes in procedure or ceremonial, and matters of custom and tradition'.[6]

The expanded wartime Board of Admiralty consisted of 15 members including three politicians – the First Lord, the Parliamentary and Financial Secretary and the Civil Lord. There were ten naval officers, the five Sea Lords and their assistants, and two civilians – the Secretary, who was a civil servant, and the Controller of Merchant Shipbuilding and Repairs.

The Civilian Politicians

The First Lord of the Admiralty was the chairman of the Board of Admiralty, the main naval spokesman in Parliament and in charge of 'the general direction and supervision of all business relating to the Navy and merchant shipbuilding and repairs'.[7] Churchill's successor at the Admiralty in 1940 was a strong contrast. A V Alexander was a Labour MP, a man of no great personality. As Churchill said of him after a major gaffe, 'Such a nice fellow – but really…'.[8] Like the other service chiefs he was not a member of the War Cabinet, so he had no say in grand strategy. He was a good diplomat and administrator, respected by all those who worked with him. Alexander was a cog in the administrative machine, although quite an efficient one.

The First Lord was assisted by two junior ministers. The Parliamentary and Financial Secretary was always a member of the House of Commons, as only that house could deal with financial affairs. He deputised for the First Lord in Parliament and dealt with finance and contracts. The Civil Lord might be a member of either the Lords or Commons. He was mainly responsible for the buildings of the navy and the industrial staff. The Controller of Merchant Shipbuilding and Repairs was a wartime anomaly: neither politician, nor naval officer, nor civil servant. The post was held by Sir William Lithgow from a well-known Clyde shipbuilding family, and he was, as his title implies, responsible for merchant shipping which was largely under government control in wartime.

The Sea Lords

The key person in any naval administration was the First Sea Lord, the senior naval member of the Board and the chief naval adviser to the government. Admiral Sir Dudley Pound took office in 1939 after the untimely death or illness of several other candidates. He tended to head off Churchill's wilder ideas by quiet diplomacy rather than confrontation, which gave an impression of weakness. He was respected by Churchill, who usually followed his advice and wrote of 'our friendship and mutual confidence'. The Prime Minister had no hesitation in getting rid of senior officers he did not believe to be up to the job, and he removed two Chiefs of Imperial General Staff and one Chief of Air Staff during the war, but it was a fatal illness that removed Pound after four years of war. His habit of apparently nodding off during Chiefs of Staff meetings and waking when

A meeting of the
Board of Admiralty
in 1943. Those
present include
Alexander (1),
Pound (2),
Whitworth (3),
Markham (4) and
Lithgow (5).

the navy was mentioned was mocked by his colleagues, but Churchill saw it as a variation of his own practice of taking an afternoon nap. Pound had the traditional naval officer's reluctance to delegate, but he was a good administrator. According to his successor, he left the Admiralty 'running on oiled wheels', which were however 'rather inclined to run in a groove'.⁹

Andrew Brown Cunningham, who took over as First Sea Lord, was a very different officer. He served brilliantly as commander-in-chief in the Mediterranean during the most intense years of the naval war. He was widely regarded as the greatest British sailor since Nelson, although his impact on Whitehall was less than might have been expected. Apart from the invasion of Europe, the most intense part of the naval war was largely over by the time he took office in October 1943, and Cunningham was exhausted by his earlier command.

Cunningham began a typical day at 9 a.m., an hour before most of the civil servants arrived. He interviewed his staff officers on the previous day's operations, then attended the Chiefs of Staff meeting with the heads of the other services. After that he was back in the office 'seeing people, dealing with papers, or attending meetings'. He returned to the office after dinner and went to bed at 11 p.m., unless a meeting with Churchill kept him up late.¹⁰

The Second Sea Lord was a senior admiral in charge of all matters of naval personnel. The Third Sea Lord was also the Controller of the Navy, responsible for material matters. His department included the Director of Naval Construction and his staff, as well as the departments dealing with engines, electrical engineering, torpedoes, mines and naval ordnance. The Fourth Sea Lord was in charge of supplies and transport, while the Fifth Sea Lord, a position added to the Board in 1937, was responsible for the naval air arm.

The Chiefs of Staff

In the Second World War the navy had to operate far more closely with the other services than ever before, especially at the highest levels. Churchill emphasised that the First Lord of the Admiralty, the Chief of

Imperial General Staff who headed the army and the Chief of Air Staff each had an 'individual and collective responsibility for advising on defence policy as a whole'.¹¹ They met for two or three hours on six days a week, and spent at least 15 hours a week in one another's company in the Chiefs of Staff or COS meetings. Sir Alan Brooke describes meetings during the first weeks of April 1942. On Monday there was a 'useful' meeting on the defence of India against the Japanese advance. On Tuesday Brooke failed to convince 'old Dudley Pound' about the need for co-ordinated naval action with the Americans. On Wednesday the Chiefs of Staff discovered that Pound had agreed to Churchill sending out instructions to destroy the French battleship *Richelieu*. This had important ramifications and they had to meet again in the afternoon to find ways to talk Churchill out of it. Thursday's meeting was mercifully short but on Monday they heard more bad news about Japanese advances and by Wednesday they were discussing how to get more aid to Russia at a 'very difficult COS'.¹² All this meant that the First Lord had limited time to administer the navy, so he had a strong Vice Chief of Naval Staff to help him with much of the routine business.

The Naval Staff

The naval staff had been founded by Churchill in 1912 against the opposition of many admirals. It was formally headed by the First Sea Lord himself, with his deputy and Assistant Chiefs of Naval Staff for trade, foreign and home affairs and weapons. Its duties were 'the collection and dissemination of Naval Intelligence, the framing of long-term plans, the conduct of operations and in short the study of the whole field of naval strategy and tactics'. This involved taking a broad view of the whole field, although the staff had no executive authority in itself.

*It is not the business of the Naval Staff to design ships or guns or aircraft or to undertake the actual training of officers and men, but to indicate to the Departments responsible for those duties what their requirements are and to keep in touch with any changes which may affect the fighting efficiency of the fleet.*¹³

The staff was mainly made up of naval officers. The largest single group was in the Naval Intelligence Department. An important but much smaller division dealt with Plans, and others dealt with local defence, anti-submarine warfare, minesweeping, trade, economic warfare, operations, training, air warfare, naval air organisation and gunnery. The scientific departments also came under the First Sea Lord, though not formally part of the staff. These included the Hydrographic Department which produced charts and ran the Royal Observatory at Greenwich, the Signal Department, the Meteorological Branch and the Navigation Branch.

In January 1941 Churchill complained about the excessive numbers of naval officers employed at the Admiralty. More than a quarter of regular naval captains and commanders were employed there, a total of 545 officers. He recommended 'a through purge' and was not satisfied 10 weeks later when Alexander reported that very little could be done.[14] The staff continued to grow but in fact the number of officers based in the Admiralty remained quite small compared with the size of the navy or the civil service – around 2100 from the Royal Navy, Royal Marines and WRNS early in 1944. Their main job was to bring recent naval experience to bear, so they tended to rotate every two or three years, in contrast to the civil servants.

Naval officers had little training for the job. When Captain H K Oram was appointed Director of Training and Staff Duties in 1942, he admitted it was 'a job which I knew absolutely nothing about and therefore had to spend the first few weeks ferreting around to find out what it meant'.[15] As Director of Plans in the middle years of the war, Captain Charles Lambe complained about the amount of time he had to spend altering the wording of orders and memos, though he agreed that 'Careful and clear drafting is essential in all paper work. There must be only one meaning'.[16]

The Secretariat

The Secretary to the Admiralty was the senior civil servant in the department. He was the equivalent of a Permanent Secretary in another government department, but less powerful in that he had to share his influence with the naval officers on the Board of Admiralty. At the beginning of the war the Secretary was Sir Archibald Carter who had spent most of his career in the India Office and was never at home with the intricate and subtle structure of the Admiralty. In December 1940 he was replaced by Sir Henry Markham, who was relatively young at 43. He had served in the army on the Western Front during the First World War. He graduated from Oxford and joined the Admiralty in 1921, then worked as private secretary to successive First Lords from 1936–8. According to a colleague, his greatest gift was his 'flair for uniting correct constitutional procedure with efficiency of organisation'. He was a good leader with a sense of humour, and was almost totally devoted to his work, finishing not long before midnight most nights.[17] His duties included managing the office and its civil servants, supervising Admiralty procedure and acting as Accounting Officer, responsible to Parliament for the control of naval expenditure.

His subordinates also worked long hours, often interrupted by air raids. Celia L Jones and her colleagues 'did a ten-hour day, often much longer, seven days a week, with one Sunday off every three weeks.' They became deeply involved in the work, dealing with the accounts of individual ships. 'HM Ships assumed a very real identity and each one became very real to us. Through the accounts we became familiar with the pattern of life on board and in spirit we were very close to the officers and men forming the ship's company'.[18]

The civil service naturally expanded in wartime and the numbers in the Admiralty grew almost fourfold; it had just under 13,000 civil

Below left: The Admiralty Building in Whitehall.

Below right: The rear of the Admiralty from The Mall, showing the nineteenth-century extension and the Citadel.

servants at the start of the war and more than 48,000 by the beginning of 1944.[19] At the head of the civil service was the Administrative Class, recruited from young men in their early twenties with good degrees, mostly from Oxford and Cambridge. Like most civil servants they were selected by competitive examination. They tended to avoid specialisation but brought academic skills to a problem. The Class was quite small, less than 1 per cent of the service as a whole, but they filled the majority of the higher posts. Their main concern was with policy-making, and supervising the management.

Below them was the Executive Class, which carried out most of the management and had grades at the higher level which overlapped with those of the Administrative Class. It was a much larger group, recruited from men and women with a secondary school education. Early in 1944 the Admiralty Secretariat included more than 500 men in the Administrative and higher Executive grades. There were 58 women, mostly in temporary posts, at the lower end of the scale. Parallel to them were the scientific and technical staffs with their own systems of grading, and below them were the numerous clerical workers, women typists, and the messengers who carried paperwork from office to office.

In the 1930s one Treasury official suggested that the Admiralty was not a department in the usual sense but a congeries, or 'collection of things merely heaped together'. This was hotly denied by the Secretary who pointed out that it was a 'network' using a word that was far less of a cliché then. The departments of the Admiralty, he claimed, were far from watertight and had to work closely together at all levels to get things done. 'The whole of the work, indeed, is exceedingly closely interrelated, and has reference to a remarkably small number of common ends'.[20]

As a result, policy often had to be approved by several departments. For example, when it was decided to adopt standard nomenclature for aircraft carriers and their officers, the file circulated for 20 months and attracted more than 50 comments from various officers before it was eventually incorporated in an Admiralty Fleet Order.[21]

The Admiralty Buildings

The head office of the Admiralty was a well-known building on the west side of Whitehall, close to Parliament, Downing Street and other major government ministries. It was built in the early eighteenth century to an undistinguished design, partly redeemed by the screen in front intended to keep out rioting seamen. Admiralty House was put up in the 1780s as a residence for the First Lord. A large extension was built between 1888 and 1905, fronting on Horse Guards Parade. Admiralty Arch was added in 1911, at the entrance to The Mall and facing Trafalgar Square. In 1939 the concrete Citadel was added as an air raid shelter, and its unattractive bulk was eventually softened by the vegetation which grew on it.

The original boardroom was still used as in the days of Nelson, but the offices around it became crowded with more and more officers and civil servants. Originally it had been planned to evacuate most of the department from London and the Director of Naval Construction and his staff moved out hastily in 1939, but in the end most of the higher officials of the Admiralty stayed in Whitehall. New premises around London were used, often in temporary wartime buildings such as Northwick Park in north-west London where Celia L Jones worked in the Accounts Department in 1944.[22]

2 Admirals and Fleets

Flag Officers

The Admiralty was all-powerful in theory, but in reality much of its authority was delegated to the admirals on the spot, particularly the commanders-in-chief of the main fleets. 'Why have commanders-in-chief and do their work for them?' Pound wrote in 1939. 'The Admiralty should pass on all the intelligence it had and let the Admiral make the decisions, unless radio silence had to be maintained'.[23] But there were cases which cut across the boundaries of more than one command and Pound did intervene decisively during the chase of the *Bismarck* in 1941, and with disastrous effect in ordering the escort to abandon convoy PQ17 to Russia in 1942. Though the Admiralty was sparing in the use of its powers, Churchill was not always aware of the acceptable boundaries and as First Lord he perhaps intervened too much in the Norwegian campaign of 1940. This continued after he came to the premiership in May 1940 and Cunningham, Commander-in-Chief Mediterranean, wrote of his 'ungracious and hasty' messages urging more offensive action. But this was quite a short phase during which Churchill was under extreme stress and had not yet learned Cunningham's qualities. After that Churchill respected the authority of the admirals far more than of the generals, and interfered rather less with them.

By long tradition the senior officers of the fleet, the various grades of admiral, were known as flag officers, because each was entitled to hoist a flag indicating his status from the ship or shore base which formed his headquarters. Commodores were, in effect, temporary flag officers, promoted from the rank of captain to fill a specific appointment, such as the command of a cruiser squadron. The rank of Rear-Admiral, the most junior grade of flag officer proper, was more permanent. Normally seniority played a large part in the promotion but accelerated promotion was available in wartime – Phillip Vian benefited from this but found it was generally unpopular in the navy.[24] The next grade was Vice-Admiral, followed by full Admiral, who might well command one of the main fleets. The highest rank of all was Admiral of the Fleet, normally held by the First Sea Lord and others of great distinction. In 1939 there were four of them, including two who were retired, the Duke of Windsor and the Earl of Cork and Orrerey who was Commander-in-Chief at Portsmouth. Apart from a very small number of royal appointments, all admirals were regular officers – there was no provision for any officer of the RNR or RNVR to be promoted above commodore.

There was a large contingent of retired admirals at the beginning of the war, and roles were found for many of them. Some dropped their status and adopted RNR rank as commodores of convoys. Others were found subordinate roles in shore-based commands: for example, Vice-Admiral Sir Gilbert Stephenson became commodore of the famous training base at Tobermory. Vice-Admiral J A G Troup, author of a well-known seamanship manual, became flag officer at Glasgow and Admiral Sir Dudley Naismith was nominally in charge of sailors based in London. But the active seagoing commands were reserved for a relatively small number of people, professional naval officers who had been carefully selected for each step in rank and were not too old or unsuccessful.

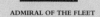

ADMIRAL OF THE FLEET

ADMIRAL

VICE-ADMIRAL

REAR-ADMIRAL

COMMODORE
FIRST CLASS

The stripes and badges worn by flag officers.

Admiral of the
Fleet Sir Andrew
Cunningham.

The Art of the Admiral

The Royal Navy was blessed with a number of very successful fleet commanders during the Second World War, with skill levels ranging from highly efficient to brilliant. At the highest level was Andrew Cunningham, who led the Mediterranean Fleet through its most difficult years and then became First Sea Lord. He was closely followed by Sir Max Horton, who commanded the submarine force until he took charge of the Battle of the Atlantic as Commander-in-Chief Western Approaches, in 1942; and by Bertram Ramsay who as Commander-in-Chief Dover organised the Dunkirk evacuation, and

with perfect symmetry led the naval side of the landings in Italy and Normandy. Other leading admirals included Sir James Somerville who commanded Force H and then the Eastern Fleet, Sir Bruce Fraser of the Home and the British Pacific Fleet, and Phillip Vian who commanded in the Mediterranean and the Pacific.

Not all the great wartime admirals had flourished in peacetime. Ramsay had retired in 1939 due to a dispute over his staff duties, Somerville had retired due to ill health and Horton had been in command of the Reserve Fleet. But the war soon brought these energetic and intelligent men into prominence.

Not all admirals were so successful. Some, such as Sir Dudley North at Gibraltar, were suspected of spending too much time before the war in social duties such as running the royal yachts. Sir Tom Phillips was regarded as highly capable as Deputy Chief of Naval Staff, but was put in command of the *Prince of Wales* and *Repulse* in 1941. Neither he nor his second-in-command had any experience of modern warfare afloat, and he totally underestimated the effect of air power, resulting in the loss of the ships.

An admiral could be expected to do many things besides leading a force of ships into battle. As a fleet commander he was largely responsible for the logistics and repair of his fleet. In a shore-based command he might be responsible for training, for local defence, or for directing a war far out in the ocean. There were different levels of skill partly reflected by rank. Sir Henry Harwood was highly successful leading a group of cruisers at the Battle of the River Plate in 1940. He was far less effective when he took over the much broader responsibilities of the Mediterranean Fleet from Cunningham in 1942.

Admirals still had to lead their fleets in battle from time to time, though only those in command of the Home and Mediterranean Fleets, or rear-admirals in charge of squadrons of cruisers. The trend

Admiral Sir
Bertram Ramsay
on the D-Day
beaches with Air
Chief Marshal
Tedder, who was
Eisenhower's
deputy.

The sinking of the *Scharnhorst* in December 1943, painted by Charles Pears. *The Duke of York*, the flagship of the Home Fleet, is coming up from the left, and star shells are being fired to illuminate the target.

was away from the over-centralised tactical control which had led to disappointment in the Grand Fleet in the last war, and in any case there was no large fleet of battleships to lead. A new generation of officers encouraged much more initiative and less detailed planning. When Cunningham's staff gave him a 60-page set of orders for a peacetime exercise, he ordered them to cut it. After it was reduced to a quarter he remarked that he agreed with one sentence – 'The fleet will be manoeuvred by the Commander-in-Chief'.[25] Furthermore, Cunningham had been brought up in destroyers rather than big ships and believed in leaving most of the initiative to the officers on the spot.

The Home Fleet

The Home Fleet was the main striking force in the navy, by far the most powerful group of ships except for the Mediterranean Fleet, which was only slightly smaller. Its name had been changed from the Atlantic Fleet in 1932, partly to wipe out the memory of the Invergordon Mutiny of the previous year. At the beginning of the war it had five battleships including the most modern ones, *Nelson* and *Rodney*, the battlecruisers *Hood* and *Repulse*, the *Ark Royal* which was the only modern aircraft carrier in service, three squadrons with a total of 14 cruisers and two destroyer flotillas of eight or nine ships. It did not greatly increase in strength during the war. It soon had to abandon its base at Scapa Flow until anti-submarine defences were fully prepared and operated from Loch Ewe, the Clyde and Rosyth at different times. The Home Fleet covered important convoys, such as those bringing Canadian troops to Europe in 1939–40. It was fully engaged under Admiral Sir Charles Forbes during the German invasion of Norway in 1940. It expected to send its destroyers south in the event of a German invasion of Britain, with the main force operating from Rosyth. It led the hunt for the *Bismarck* in 1941, but after that its operations were mainly in the north, covering convoys to

Russia. It formed a defence against any sortie by the *Tirpitz*, and under Sir Bruce Fraser it succeeded in sinking the *Scharnhorst* in 1943.

The Mediterranean Fleet

The Commander-in-Chief of the Home Fleet had relatively few administrative and diplomatic duties, because he was normally stationed near home and because the admirals commanding at Orkney and Shetland, and Rosyth took responsibility for his main bases. Commander-in-Chief Mediterranean, on the other hand, had a full range of responsibilities ashore and afloat. The Mediterranean Fleet was the largest and most popular peacetime command in the navy, but at the beginning of the war it had to take second place to the Home Fleet. This changed very rapidly in mid-1940 as France collapsed and Italy entered the war. Commanded very ably by Cunningham, the fleet operated against the odds in the Eastern Mediterranean, leaving the western sea to Force H. It suffered heavy losses from German air power in the Battle for Crete, from enemy submarines, and from daring Italian human torpedo attack which damaged two battleships in Alexandria Harbour.

In April 1941, as it approached one of its greatest crises in the Battle for Crete, the Mediterranean Fleet was run from Cunningham's flagship the famous battleship *Warspite*. The 1st Battle Squadron was commanded by a rear-admiral in the battleship *Barham*, and the lighter forces by a vice-admiral in the cruiser *Orion*. The 3rd Cruiser Squadron was also commanded by a rear-admiral, with a Rear-Admiral (Aircraft Carriers) in the *Formidable*. Force H was nominally under the command of the Commander-in-Chief Mediterranean, but generally operated separately. Ashore, there were bases in Alexandria (HMS *Nile*), Malta, Ismalia and Haifa.

In the second half of the war the Mediterranean Fleet was transformed as the Allies took North Africa and invaded Sicily, Italy and the South of France. In June 1944 it was commanded by Admiral Sir

The Fleet at Gibraltar in June 1939 during the naval manoeuvres. Mediterranean Fleet ships are in light grey; Home Fleet ships are in dark grey. Nearest to the camera are destroyers, a three-funnelled County class cruiser is to the left, and battleships lie outside the harbour.

John H Cunningham – no relation to his predecessor – who had his headquarters ashore at Algiers. It was now a series of area commands rather than a fighting fleet. Cunningham had flag officers for Gibraltar and the Mediterranean Approaches, Western Mediterranean, Malta and Central Mediterranean and Levant and the Eastern Mediterranean, with authority over the US naval commander in North West Africa, and French, Italian, Greek and Yugoslav forces in the area.[26]

The Anomaly of Force H

Normally a fleet or a command had a clear geographical base. It might be a small area like the Dover Command, or a huge one like the Pacific Fleet, but usually the fleet's limits were clearly defined. The major exception to this was Force H, a strong group of capital ships, aircraft carriers and supporting ships. It was formed late in June 1940 in response to the two new factors in the Mediterranean – the Italian entry to the war and the problem of keeping the French fleet out of German hands. It was based at Gibraltar, but not fully under the authority of the Flag Officer North Atlantic (FONA), who was also based there and was nominally responsible for ships in a large section of the east-central Atlantic. This caused much confusion in June 1940 when a French force of cruisers and destroyers escaped through the Strait. Force H had only been tasked with preventing Italian ships from exiting while FONA, Sir Dudley North, failed to intervene much to Churchill's fury.

Force H initially consisted of the battlecruiser *Hood* as flagship, the battleships *Valiant* and *Resolution*, the aircraft carrier *Ark Royal*, two cruisers and 11 destroyers. It was commanded by Vice-Admiral Sir James Somerville. In effect it became the main British force in the Western Mediterranean, while Cunningham's fleet was based in Alexandria and occupied in that region. Apart from its other orders, Force H could be switched to the Atlantic if needed, and it played a decisive part in the hunt for the *Bismarck* in 1941.

The British Pacific Fleet

In late 1944 with the Italian fleet surrendered and the German surface effort largely destroyed, the British attempted a return to the Pacific from which they had been driven in 1941–2. A new British Pacific Fleet was formed under Sir Bruce Fraser. Initially it was allocated five fleet aircraft carriers, two battleships, nine cruisers and 22 destroyers. This was a very powerful force by previous British standards, but it was small by recent

American ones in the Pacific. Furthermore, the Americans had no interest in supporting a return of British imperialism to the area and were sceptical about their ability to operate on such a scale. On arrival in the Pacific, the British Pacific Fleet was reduced to the status of 'Task Force 57' in the American scheme of things. It had to learn new techniques in replenishment at sea and was very much a poor relation to the Americans.

The Area Commands

At home, the coasts and seas around Britain were divided into area commands, each headed by an admiral and usually with several sub-commands. An area commander was responsible for the operation of naval harbour craft, local defence against raids and invasion, anti-E-boat warfare and convoy escort, dockyards and building slips in the area, the examination of shipping, training bases, and minesweeping.

The Portsmouth Command was one of the oldest in existence. Its area included most of the eastern English Channel, and it shared with the Dover Command the responsibility for sea links with France at the beginning of the war. Its first wartime commander-in-chief was Admiral Sir William James who in his childhood had been the model for the 'Bubbles' painting by his Sir John Millais, and had recently served as Deputy Chief of Naval Staff. Many of the troops evacuated in 1940, such as those from Le Havre, were taken off by ships of the command. After that it settled down to a routine. Portsmouth Dockyard was heavily bombed and even the *Victory* was damaged, but James spent much of his time welcoming VIPs such as the King and the Prime Minister, and in touring the many training bases in the area, publishing his story as *The Portsmouth Letters*.

The Nore Command was another ancient one, taking its name from an anchorage in the Thames Estuary where fleets of sailing ships used to assemble. It was somewhat reduced in area in wartime, having lost territory to both Rosyth and Dover. The Sheerness sub-command included the dockyard at the mouth of the Medway, and the larger dockyard at Chatham was another command. Its largest sub-command was at Harwich, which carried out a great deal of minesweeping and operated many of the ships which escorted convoys along the east coast of England. It had nearly 300 ships at its peak at the time of D-Day, including 27 destroyers, 33 coastal forces craft based at Felixstowe and 80 landing craft. Great Yarmouth was another sub-command, set up in July 1940. It operated coastal forces and minesweepers, protected convoys from air raids and carried out air-sea rescue operations to save

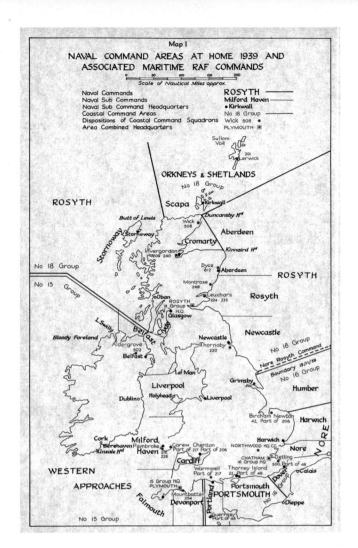

downed airmen. There were smaller sub-commands at Southend, Brightlingsea, Grimsby and on the River Humber. The command included several important training bases including *Royal Arthur* at Skegness and the Patrol Service depot at Lowestoft. All personnel based in London were nominally attached to HMS *Pembroke IV* under a rear-admiral, while thousands of men could be found in HMS *Pembroke*, the naval barracks at Chatham, at any given moment.[27]

In contrast the Dover Command was focused on more specific tasks, though these varied over the years. It was set up under Bertram Ramsay on the outbreak of war to protect the lines of communication with the army in France and to prevent enemy ships passing through the Strait of Dover. This changed radically in June 1940 and the command organised the evacuation of British and Allied troops from Dunkirk. After that it was in the forefront of the defence against invasion, in operating coastal forces and in attempting to block the channel to the enemy: it had a notable failure in that area in 1942 when the *Scharnhorst* and *Gneisenau* carried out their 'Channel dash'.

The Rosyth Command, formerly the Coast of Scotland Command, originally had responsibility for both sides of that country. It was divided in 1939 when an Orkney and Shetland Command was set up with responsibility for the north coast; the west coast of Scotland was transferred to Western Approaches in 1941. Rosyth Command was left with minesweeping on the east coast and with protection of the northern part of the east coast convoy route. Its southern boundary was at Flamborough Head in Yorkshire, where it met the Nore Command. Orkney and Shetland Command was responsible for the main fleet base at Scapa Flow, and in good weather it mounted coastal forces and other kinds of operations against the Germans occupying Norway.

Western Approaches

Western Approaches was perhaps the most diverse command in the navy. It was descended from the old Plymouth Command and at the

The home commands at the beginning of the war, and RAF Coastal Command group boundaries.

start of the war it included the coast from south-west England to the Firth of Clyde. At the beginning of 1941 the headquarters moved from Plymouth to Liverpool reflecting the increased importance of the Battle of the Atlantic. A new Plymouth Command was set up, including the area south of the Bristol Channel. The north-west coast of Scotland was taken over from the Rosyth Command.

The command included scores of ships for convoy escort, but it also had responsibility for all naval activity on the west coast of Britain north of the Bristol Channel. In 1944 it had no fewer than 25

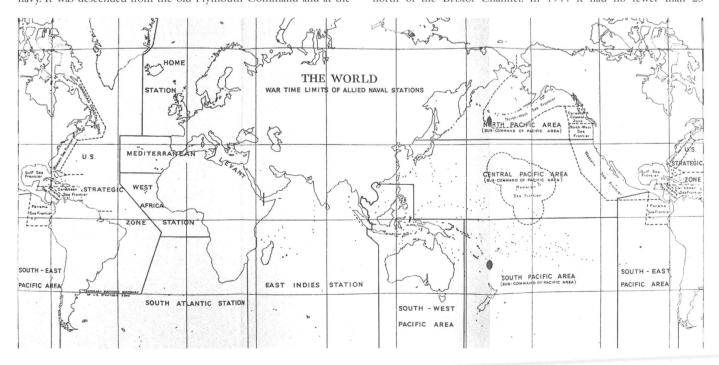

The overseas commands in 1943.

subordinate commanders, some of whom had little to do with the central task of the Battle of the Atlantic. It included the training bases on the Isle of Man and at Tobermory, Londonderry and Larne. The Flag-Officer-in-Charge at Glasgow was largely responsible for the crews of ships being built by contract on the Clyde, and for visiting VIPs. The area also included small ports such as Stranraer, Aultbea and Lamlash in Scotland.

The main task was to run the Battle of the Atlantic, and it was directly responsible for an area of sea reaching out to the middle of the ocean. Sir Max Horton developed his own style of directing it after he took over from Sir Percy Noble in 1942.

The scene in the great plotting room at Derby House, with every yard of the Atlantic marked and the walls covered with the symbols of convoys, U-boats, escorts and all sorts, changed with the arrival of Max Horton. The graciousness, the adept handling of overworked personnel by P.N. was missing. Nobody could say that Sir Max was a boor, but he certainly was direct, and without any frills whatsoever.

Battles were generally fought at night now. After dinner he would arrive in the Plotting Room to watch the battle develop, to order reinforcements, to build plans for the next time. His words were always direct. 'Where is…?' 'Why is …?' 'What is…?' and sometimes his decision would come in a flash.[28]

The Overseas Commands

Besides the Mediterranean and Pacific Fleets, there were many smaller overseas commands. The China Fleet operated in peacetime from Hong Kong, Shanghai and Singapore and had gunboats on the great Chinese rivers, but these stations were soon swept up by the Japanese advance. The South American Station hunted the *Graf Spee* at the beginning of the war but was not troubled much after that. The African Station provided support for troop and other convoys heading round the Cape for Egypt and the Far East. The East India Station held the line against the Japanese advance for a time, and escorted convoys in the area. The New Zealand and Australian Stations came into prominence as the war against Japan intensified. The America and West Indies station, based in Bermuda, ran training bases and organised liaison with the Americans.

Flagships

The amount of time an admiral spent afloat varied with the nature of his command. The area commanders naturally had little time at sea and were dependent on the facilities of their shore headquarters. There was no question of Commander-in-Chief Western Approaches going off to lead an individual escort group for example, while some area commanders had very few actual ships under their control. But the Home and Mediterranean Fleets did require the Commander-in-Chief to lead them into battle, as Admiral Tovey did against the *Bismarck* in 1941, Cunningham against the Italians at Matapan in the same year, and Fraser against the *Scharnhorst* in 1943. A seagoing admiral whether a commander-in-chief or the leader of a squadron of battleships or cruisers, would choose one ship, probably the largest, as his flagship which would become his floating headquarters. It retained its function as a fighting ship, and specialised headquarters ships were built only for Combined Operations.

The flagship was well equipped with cabins for the admiral and his staff in the stern, but in the case of the *King George V* class these proved uninhabitable in heavy seas. In a battleship there were separate bridges for the admiral and the flag captain, because the admiral was not expected to interfere in the running of the ship. In the *King George V* class, the admiral's bridge was one deck below the captain's. It had enclosed spaces along its centre line, including, from aft to forward, an admiral's chart house, a wireless telegraphy office, a 'remote control office' and a plotting office. Forward of that was the open space of the admiral's lookout platform, sheltered by an awning overhead. It had clear-view screens all around and was fitted quite simply, with a chart table and drawers and a compass in the centre. The area was well enough equipped to direct a battle in the early stages of the war, but soon radar would become essential and towards the end of the war the Action Information Organisation was set up to co-ordinate data from radar and other means. However, it was made clear that this was merely to inform the commander, not to make his decisions for him. A plotting room was set up close to the bridge, but admirals were not yet ready to abandon their position in the open. As late as December 1944:

In action the primary duty of the Command is to control and fight the ship or squadron. It is considered that this can, in general, best be done from the compass platform or Admiral's Bridge. Events in visual range will inevitably assume greater importance than those more remote, and it seems probable that the eye will always remain the final arbiter of human judgement.[29]

In a cruiser, the quarters could become rather cramped. As a flag captain, Angus Cunninghame-Graham found it inconvenient. 'Usually we captains like to have our ships to ourselves. From our personal standpoint we lose our spacious day and dining cabins and move into one of the two small cabin suites provided for captains on the admiral's staff'.[30]

Staffs

Traditionally British admirals had worked with very small staffs and many had not delegated enough to them; this was to become an increasing problem in the much more complex navy of the twentieth century. Sir Roger Backhouse centralised all staff work in himself as Commander-in-Chief of the Home Fleet in the late 1930s, with the result that Bertram Ramsay resigned as his chief of staff. Backhouse died just before the war, partly as a result of overwork. At the other extreme, Sir Roger Keyes was criticised for having a staff of 31 officers in the Mediterranean in the late 1920s, and this may have been a factor in stopping his promotion to First Sea Lord. The next generation of admirals had learned how to work with staffs, that a modern fleet was far too complex for the commander-in-chief to plan every detail. Cunningham recognised his own limitations as an administrator and used a very strong chief of staff, Sir Algernon Willis, to run that side of his command. Bertram Ramsay had learned much from his experience under Backhouse and ran a very efficient staff system.

It was usual for an admiral to use his flag captain, that is, the captain of the flagship, as his chief of staff, but this could cause difficulty when the admiral found it necessary to transfer his flag to another ship. This happened, for example, when Sir Phillip Vian moved from the cruiser *Naiad* to the *Phoebe*. He was heavily reliant on his flag captain Guy

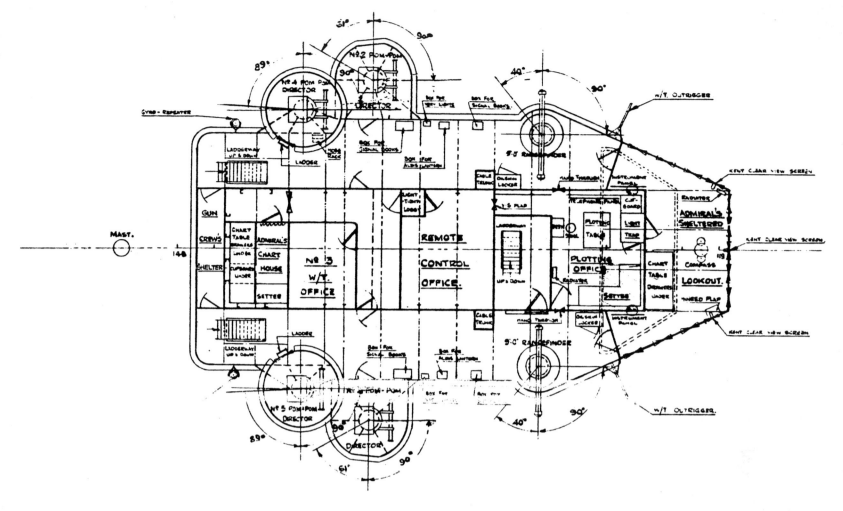

Grantham, whom Cunningham called 'that most brilliant and capable officer'. Grantham took command of the *Phoebe*, but such disruption could disorientate a crew if it took place too often.[31] Later in the war, it became more common to separate the flag captain from the chief of staff. It was never a problem in shore bases. Sir William James describes the qualities of his chief of staff at Portsmouth, Commodore Sir Atwell Lake, who 'had all the qualities for his post; a good seaman, an indefatigable worker, a tactful disciplinarian and a tidy mind'.[32]

Every admiral had a flag lieutenant, who might in fact be a sub-lieutenant or a lieutenant-commander. He had the dual role of organising the admiral's diary and social life, and composing signals in battle. Naturally the latter role became more important in seagoing

commands in wartime, and most were qualified signal officers. Unusually for the time, Sir Max Horton employed a woman flag lieutenant, Kay Hallaran, of Irish-American background.

She had immense poise and savoir-faire and never got rattled. A very good mixer, and equally charming to Admirals and ratings. She had so much tact and charm of manner that she was able to handle impatient senior officers much more effectively than any male junior officer could have done.[33]

All the admirals had a secretary, who was a senior officer of the administrative branch of the navy – a Paymaster Captain in the case of a commander-in-chief, and usually a Paymaster-Commander for a

The admiral's bridge of a *King George V* class battleship.

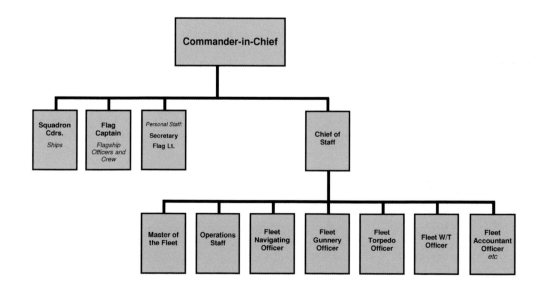

The organisation of the staff of the British Pacific Fleet in 1944–5.

The signal flags used by the navy for specialist purposes, in addition to the letters and numerals of the normal code.

junior flag officer. The Captain of the Fleet was largely responsible for maintenance, the Master of the Fleet for navigation. Other staff officers were taken on as the need expanded. The staff at Western Approaches numbered about a thousand by the time Horton took command. It was headed by a commodore and divided into Operations, Administration and Material. The British Pacific Fleet as founded in 1944 had one of the most developed staffs of the time, including four divisions with 11 officers dealing with Plans, three with Trade, seven with Personnel and nine with Material and Maintenance.[34]

In addition to his staff officers, an admiral needed large numbers of signallers, clerks and plotting room assistants. He was also entitled to a personal staff headed by his coxswain, usually a chief petty officer (CPO). Cunningham's CPO, Percy Watts, followed him from post to post during the war, as did his chief steward, Sackett.[35]

SPECIAL FLAGS USED IN NAVAL SIGNALLING.

AEROPLANE FLAG — BLUE FLAG — RED FLAG
AHEAD FLAG — CRUISER FLAG — SCREEN FLAG
AFFIRMATIVE — DESTROYER FLAG — SQUADRON OR FLOTILLA FLAG
AIRCRAFT CARRIER FLAG — DIVISION FLAG — STARBOARD FLAG
ASTERN FLAG — FISHERY FLAG — STATIONING FLAG
BATTLE CRUISER FLAG — NEGATIVE — SUB-DIVISION FLAG
BATTLE-SHIP FLAG — OPTIONAL — SUBMARINE FLAG
BLACK FLAG — PORT FLAG — UNION FLAG
BLUE AFFIRMATIVE — PREPARATIVE

3 Communications and Intelligence

Communication has always been vital in naval warfare, whether tactically in battle or in directing the strategic operations of fleets and convoys. It was more important than ever in 1939–45, because of the global nature of the war and because it was the first war to be dominated by electronics.

Visual Signals

In battle and on manoeuvres, the navy traditionally preferred to use visual signals for giving orders and inter-ship communication. Signal flags were the most common, using a set of 26 letter flags, 10 numerals, 26 special flags for naval purposes and 24 pennants, directly descended from the flag system used to transmit Nelson's famous signal at Trafalgar in 1805. They still had the great advantage that they were undetectable by an enemy. Using a pre-arranged code of operational orders it was relatively simple to manoeuvre a battle fleet or a destroyer flotilla in this way, but it was more difficult in other situations. A battle fleet was relatively compact, and manned by highly trained personnel in peacetime. A wartime convoy might be spread over many miles in bad visibility and it had very few fully trained signallers, so other means were necessary.

Another form of visual signalling was by lamp using Morse code. This was useful for transmitting longer signals which were not necessarily in the standard code book. It could be transmitted slowly to allow for partially trained signallers. The navy also had semaphore available. This could be sent by a man using flags, or by a semaphore machine fitted on larger ships; it was rarer in smaller ships.

The World Wide Communication System

The Admiralty needed a world-wide system to communicate both administrative and operational orders to naval bases round the world and to ships at sea. The Admiralty building was equipped with large radio masts on its roof to send and receive messages, and shore stations were accessible by landline and teleprinter. The world was divided into sea areas and the British Empire was extensive enough to provide a transmitting station in each – Colombo for most of the Indian Ocean, Bermuda for the Caribbean and west-central Atlantic, and the Falkland Islands for the South Atlantic, for example. Hundreds of thousands of radio messages were sent out from stations such as Simonstown in South

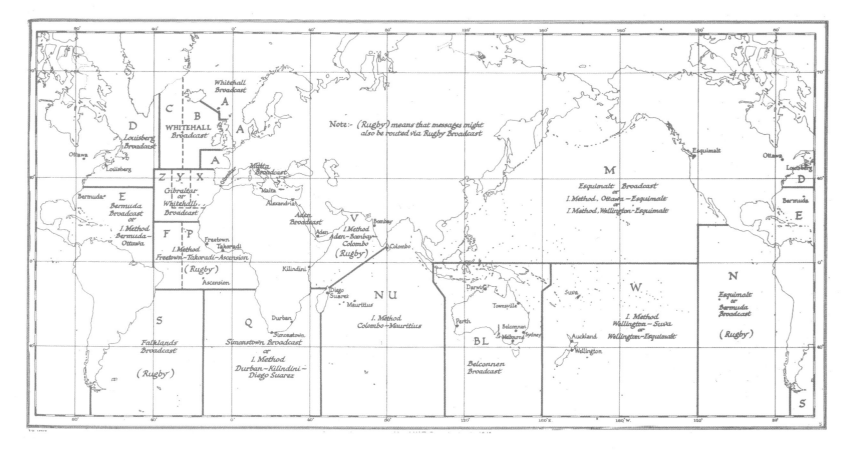

Africa every month, with the latest Admiralty orders and information to ships at sea – the Area Broadcast, which all ships in the region listened to.[36] Admiralty officials were warned not to save messages until the end of the working day and thus cause congestion as too many were sent at once, not to send messages that could be communicated equally well by letter or telegram, and to make them as concise as possible. The most secure messages of all were marked NOTWT (Not Wireless Telegraphy) and were not to go by radio even in the coded version.[37] Nevertheless the system became very crowded with routine messages and many stations had to transmit almost continuously on several wavelengths.

Wireless Telegraphy

When using radio, the navy still preferred wireless telegraphy (W/T), using Morse code, at the beginning of the war. The alternative, radio telephony (R/T) using voice, was difficult to keep records of and was viewed with suspicion.

Five different frequency bands were possible at this time. VLF or very low frequency was below 30 kilocycles. It was the only one that could be used to communicate with submarines underwater. LF or low frequency (30–300 kilocycles) was common at the beginning of the war. Its range was short but sufficient for the operations that were projected at the time, with closely organised fleets near the shore. MF or medium frequency (300–3000 kilocycles) was also used early in the war along with LF. HF or high frequency (3000–30,000 kilocycles) was vital for long-distance messages. Unlike other frequencies, these waves bounced off the Heavyside layer in the atmosphere and were not limited by the horizon. It was difficult for an enemy to use it for direction finding without highly sophisticated equipment, so it became the most common in the course of the war. VHF or very high frequency, on the other hand, could only be heard within the line of sight. It became common for contact with aircraft and within fleets where the ships were relatively close together. It might have been useful in convoy operations, except it was feared that some convoys would be too big and messages would be lost towards the fringes.

Radio Telephony

R/T or voice telephony became increasingly common within fleets, convoys and other formations. It was essential during operations, because of the need for fast communication and the shortage of highly skilled W/T operators. The navy was also short of suitable sets, and had to adapt them from civilian uses, or from the Americans. The most successful was the American TBS or talk between ships. According to Captain Donald Macintyre of the B2 Escort Group:

The transformation the TBS worked in the cohesion of the group dispersed around the sprawling convoy was wonderful. Instead of the tedious process of call-up by lamp and the laborious process of spelling out an order, or the shorter but insecure communication by HF radio, each ship was in immediate touch with the others simply by speaking into a telephone handset, the message coming through a loudspeaker on the bridge.

The main problem was when officers talked too much. Furthermore, 'The differing accents of two signalmen on TBS could produce moments of misunderstanding which would have brought the house down as a music-hall turn'. But as a whole, 'the efficiency of the group as a team rose tremendously'.[38]

Naturally the amount of radio equipment increased in ships of each class during the war. In 1939 Tribal class destroyers had four transmitters, all operating on low and medium frequency. Two were of medium power and two with low power, to make enemy interception more difficult. It had seven receivers for different frequencies, including four on high frequency for area broadcasts, plus direction-finding equipment on low frequency. The 1945 Battle class were fitted with eight transmitters, most of them on HF or VHF, with 10 receivers including one VHF, as well as sophisticated direction-finding equipment.[39]

Each type of operation evolved its own network of communication. In the Home Fleet in 1940, all ships listened to the area broadcast and the flagship monitored the adjacent area as well. The fleet wave was used for internal communication, on low or medium frequency and on low power to maintain security. There was an area low frequency channel

in the traditional sense of the term, in large numbers. It was intended to acquire military intelligence on behalf of the three services, but between the wars its budget was less than that needed to run a single destroyer in the Home Fleet, so it did not have a huge network of agents when war broke out. This was the only kind of work that the Foreign Office regarded as 'intelligence'. Its routine work involved diplomats acquiring information in the country they were in by reading newspapers, personal visits and talking to individuals in a normal way. The intelligence community also included the Government Code and Cypher Centre which was to prove crucial in the war, and the Industrial Intelligence Centre which collected information on the capacities of German industry. The Special Operations Executive or SOE was set up after the Fall of France to co-operate with resistance movements in occupied Europe and that, too, provided a source of intelligence, as well as friction with the other services.

The three services each had intelligence departments for their specialised purposes, and they tended to use a much broader definition of intelligence, including simple low-grade information, which was obtainable from newspapers, government statements and other public sources. According to an officer who served in the Naval Intelligence Department in the 1920s, 'The most valuable information is seldom secret. The difficulty is that people seldom realise its value'.[42]

The Joint Intelligence Committee was set up in 1936 and strengthened in 1939 to co-ordinate effort and dissemination. But this was still inadequate in the spring of 1940, when the Germans' planned their invasion of Norway and Denmark. There were reports from the British embassy in Stockholm, from a secret Foreign Office source inside Germany, from the American ambassador in Copenhagen and from photographic reconnaissance all pointing in the same direction.[43] The failure to put these reports together, plus a naval belief that an invasion on this scale was impossible without control of the sea, led directly to the first great Allied defeat of the war. After that the position was much improved; intelligence was assessed and shared much better, and other and more revealing sources came into play. From 1942 there was much sharing of intelligence at all levels with the American services.

A radio operator on board a submarine.

for communication with outlying ships, and a high frequency one for communication between senior officers. The auxiliary wave was 'an alternative action intercommunication and manoeuvring circuit for cruisers and above'. The flagship also kept watch on the RAF reconnaissance wave, and aircraft carriers on a striking force wave.

In convoys by the middle of the war, all warships listened to the area broadcast. They also listened to the convoy R/T wave, normally on a loudspeaker except when there was an alarm. Escort commanders had a convoy air HF wave for communication with patrolling surface-based aircraft, and a naval airwave for use with any carrier-based aircraft present. Merchant ships also manned channel M, for use in an emergency.[40]

The Intelligence Services

Intelligence was to play an essential part in the war, although for almost three decades following it the public had a misleading impression of the role of spies and agents. This was partly due to Churchill's own account, *The Second World War*, written at time when the extent of radio intelligence could not be revealed. The British premonition of the German invasion of Russia, for example, was attributed to 'one of our most trusted sources'. Many people took this to mean a spy, but in fact it was the decoding of enemy signals.[41]

In Britain, MI5 was responsible for internal security and counter-espionage. The Foreign Office ran the Secret (or Special) Intelligence Service, also known as MI6. This was the only department that used spies,

The Organisation of Naval Intelligence

The Naval Intelligence Department (NID) was formed late in the nineteenth century, mainly to collect basic data on foreign navies – under the 'two-power standard'. The Royal Navy was to be maintained at the level of the next two largest combined, and obviously it had to know what other navies had. Until Winston Churchill formed the naval staff in 1912, and it became truly effective in 1917, the NID provided the main body of naval officers at the Admiralty and was used for other tasks, but after that it was restricted to intelligence duties. The department was still one of the largest at the Admiralty. It employed 24 naval officers and 42 civilians in June 1939, and 291 naval officers in June 1944.[44] Its duties still included many matters that were quite routine and very far from any cloak-and-dagger associations. It was responsible for supervising naval attachés, advising on interpreters, postal censorship, and producing geographical handbooks for various countries. Lieutenant James Callaghan, a future prime minister, edited one on Japan, without any previous knowledge of the country.

The Director of Naval Intelligence for the first half of the war was

Rear-Admiral (later Admiral) John Godfrey, who had distinguished himself in staff work in the First World War and commanded the battlecruiser *Repulse* from 1936–9. His assistant was Commander Ian Fleming RNVR and he was a model for 'M' in the James Bond books, with his 'keen sailor's face', a house full of naval prints and relics, with stories of 'battles, tornadoes, bizarre happenings, courts-martial, eccentric officers, neatly worded signals'. Despite his great success in revitalising naval intelligence, Godfrey was too outspoken to win favour. After clashes with Churchill he was removed in 1942 and became the only admiral not to be honoured for war services. He was replaced by the more amenable Captain Edmund Rushbrooke.

Another distinguished officer was the barrister Ewen Montague, who masterminded the 'Man who Never Was' deception in which a body bearing papers was left in the sea off neutral Spain to mislead the Germans that the next invasion would be of the Greek islands, not Sicily.

RNVR officers were regarded as suitable for intelligence work; they generally had good, broad education and enquiring minds, which were not encouraged in regular naval officers of the day.

Sources of Intelligence

Espionage in the traditional sense played a small part in the Second World War compared with the Cold War that followed it. There were few highly placed agents close to the centre of the respective governments. It was less of an ideological war than the Cold War. It was much shorter, with less time to set up networks. All the governments concerned had full wartime powers, which could exclude suspected persons from the sensitive positions, and they used these powers with varying degrees of ruthlessness. Unlike the Cold War there was practically no regular communication between the opposing sides, so it was very difficult to get information out, and virtually impossible to defect if things went wrong. The spy still had his role, but he or she was not the main source of naval intelligence. In general, they were agents near the ports in enemy-held territory, such as Brest and Lorient in France and many Norwegian ports. Equipped with secret radios, they could transmit valuable information on shipping movements.

Another source was prisoners of war, and substantial numbers were captured from U-boats during the Battle of the Atlantic. At first the Admiralty was sceptical of their value. It used reports on their interrogation as indicators of morale in the U-boat service, but it discounted claims that boats could dive to 600 feet or could be refuelled at sea as mere boasting. From 1942 it began to take them more seriously and planted stool pigeons or used microphones to overhear conversations between prisoners. Captured or sunken vessels could also provide information of great value. British agents purchased the wreck of the *Graf Spee* off Montevideo to find out more about her early radar. Several U-boats were captured including *U-570*, which subsequently was operated as HMS *Graph*. Anti-submarine crews were carefully trained in mock-ups in case the opportunity of capture should ever arise.

Airborne photo reconnaissance developed rapidly during the war – it was a photograph of Bergen which told the Admiralty that the *Bismarck* had sailed on her famous mission in May 1941 – and it could be used to monitor progress in enemy shipyards as well as the movement of ships and the effects of bombing. It was generally carried out by the RAF using fast

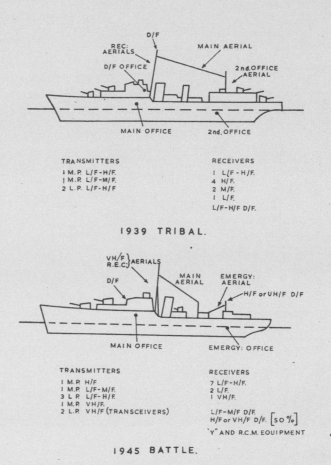

1939 TRIBAL.

1945 BATTLE.

Above: Rear-Admiral John Godfrey as Chief of Naval Intelligence.

Left: The increased radio equipment of destroyers, from 1939 to 1945.

Spitfire or Mosquito aircraft, but the Fleet Air Arm operated some aircraft including a flight from Gibraltar, because the government had assured the Spanish that the RAF would not operate from there. By 1942 the latest cameras could produce photos from 30,000 feet at a scale of 1:10,000, and had a magazine of 500 exposures. Nearly 3000 sorties were flown in 1943, although only a minority of these were for naval purposes. Several interpretation units were set up, some specialising in naval work.[45]

Radio Intelligence

Radio intelligence proved to be the most fruitful source by far. It came in several different forms. Traffic Analysis or TA consisted of noting the volume and origin of signals. A sudden increase, for example, might show that something was about to happen. Some basic codes might be understood, for example the U-boats' 'B-bar' (Morse .._..) meant the sighting of a convoy or target. An experienced listener could also identify the Morse operator, and hence his U-boat, by the characteristics of his touch on the key.

At another level was radio direction finding. The German tactical system demanded a great deal of signalling between the U-boats and their headquarters, using high frequency transmissions which could be picked up anywhere. At the start of the war the British had four Direction Finding (DF) stations; by 1942 there were 19 at home and more than 50 abroad, covering all the oceans.[46] U-boats transmitted on a constant frequency, within the high frequency range, and refused to believe that their signals were being used for direction finding, so their

system remained unchanged throughout the war. A single station could only find a direction for each transmission, at least two were needed to get a fix, at suitably varied angles, and preferably three or more. Information was transmitted very quickly across the oceans to a central point in Britain, and the positions of many U-boats were established. Closeness brought greater accuracy and High Frequency Direction Finding (HF/DF) installations were put in many ships from 1941, to find U-boats close to their convoy.

The third and most dramatic level was the actual decoding of German signals. Examples of the sophisticated German Enigma coding machine were obtained from allies or taken from captured U-boats. Thousands of people worked at Bletchley Park north of London to decode the messages it sent, and by early 1941 they were largely successful, though with some delays in the early period. There was a blackout from February 1942 when the Germans introduced a fourth rotor to the machine, but messages were again being decoded from December that year, and continuing until the end of the war. The decoding was more useful for the navy than other services. Aircraft tended to use un-coded voice messages, land troops kept in touch by other means as far as possible, but ships needed regular radio contact to find targets or avoid hazards. The decoding could give warning of ship movements and long-term plans, but it was most immediately useful in the Battle of the Atlantic. It allowed the Admiralty to follow the formation of patrol lines across the path of a convoy and takes steps to avoid it. It was only when the Atlantic became too crowded for this, for example in the renewed U-boat attack in March 1943, that this tactic failed. But it was balanced by the fact that the Germans, too, unknown to the Allies, were able to break codes. When convoy HX229

was re-routed to avoid the patrol line *Raubgraf* in March 1943, the Germans knew about it and the U-boats were shifted in order to counter it. According to Naval Intelligence it was difficult to understand this 'without assuming compromise', but the war had ended before the extent of German decoding was realised.[47]

The Submarine Tracking Room and the Battle of the Atlantic

As well as obtaining intelligence, it had to be assessed and interpreted. For general purposes, the Admiralty set up the Operational Intelligence Centre to do this in 1939. More specifically, the Submarine Tracking Room in the Admiralty dealt with the U-boat war. It was headed by a barrister, Captain Rodger Winn RNVR, and it was generally felt that lawyers, with their experience of assessing evidence, were ideal for this role. Naval officers found it too difficult to contradict their superiors and often had too many preconceived ideas, but accountants were found useful for the more detailed work. The small staff worked 24 hours a day in 'vile' physical conditions in Room 13 of the Admiralty, and then in the 'large and well equipped Room 41'. They assessed 'every scrap of information about U-boats, however obvious, insignificant or indirect'. They plotted known positions from Enigma decodes and were able to supply detailed information on the current position, long-term trends and technological advances.[48]

The latest background information was transmitted to the commanders of escort vessels in a magazine called the *Monthly Anti-Submarine Report*, edited by another lawyer. Each issue contained regular features on the latest British and German technology, reports of individual convoys and of coastal command activity. It started with a very perceptive assessment of the current position largely prepared by Winn and his staff. In May 1943 it assessed correctly that the turning point in the Battle of the Atlantic had been reached.

Comparison with Germany

The Germans were adept at the mathematical task of decoding Allied radio messages, allowing them to find convoys in the Atlantic. Otherwise, their sources of intelligence were far fewer. The nature of the U-boat war made it very unusual for them to take prisoners or capture ships. There were fewer occupied territories where they could deploy agents. In addition, the Nazi system did not foster the enquiring mind. As a result, the Germans had several spectacular and crucial failures of intelligence. They refused to consider the possibility that the British had centimetric radar, were using HF/DF at sea, or could decode their Enigma messages. These mistakes probably cost them the Battle of the Atlantic and, eventually, the war.

4 The Arts of the Seaman

Deck Seamanship

Every seaman had to learn the use of ropes, though it was far less central to his duty than it had been in the days of sail. He knew how to tie a bowline to put a loop in the end of the rope, a clove hitch to attach a rope to a fixed object, and many other ways of handling rope. He never used the term knot except to describe a specific operation such as a wall knot – he talked about bends and hitches, the former used to attach two ropes together, the latter to attach a rope to an object. He had learned something about more elaborate ways of treating rope by splicing or forming knots in the end and he was used to more difficult work with wire, which formed a great part of the standing rigging on modern ships. He knew how to throw a mooring line ashore and to tie the ship up to a shore mooring or a buoy.

The seaman learned how to raise and lower the ship's boats using cranes and davits, to row them and to handle them under sail and power. He could steer a boat or a ship according to order, using the compass or a fixed point on land. A fully experienced seaman knew a little about navigation in taking soundings by casting the lead, and to take readings from the ship's log. But the seaman of the lower deck, despite his desire for independence and his great skill at improvisation, was used to taking orders and did most of his seamanship under the direction of his officers. Only they knew the complex business of handling a big ship, and how to set a course (as distinct from steering one) through a narrow channel or over the open ocean.

The Bridge and the Chart Room

British officers generally favoured a bridge that was open to the wind and the weather. They argued that it allowed them to spot sudden changes in the wind, and to have a good view during an aircraft attack. The bridge was usually situated forward at the highest part of the superstructure to give a good view, both on deck and outboard. Too far forward, however, and it would suffer from breaking seas as happened with some American destroyers.[49] The main part, the compass platform, was usually quite small, for it did not have the wings which merchant ship officers used for docking on one side or the other. Some frigates had wings carrying light anti-aircraft guns. Capital ships had more than one bridge, with a lower one for the admiral. An older ship like the *Hood* had most of the bridge facilities in a spotting top in the mast, but the most recent trend was to simplify the bridge structure to avoid creating shot traps.

The central platform on the bridge was sealed off with a low partition, and only officers and men on duty would enter it. Its deck was wooden to prevent compass deviation. In the centre was the main compass, situated away from any iron. Forward of that was a Pelorus, high enough to look over the bulkheads and used for taking bearings on objects or ships. There were wooden chairs for the captain and the officer of the watch, and in a major warship there was a captain's sight on each side, used to indicate the bearing of a target to the guns. Some ships had a hooded table, covered with glass to allow the study of a chart in bad weather, but elaborate plotting or navigation was done in a separate chart room nearby. Round the sides of the bridge were voice pipes to communicate with the steering, engine room and the operators of the armament. There were boxes for various publications such as the signal books. From this position, the ship would be controlled in ordinary service, in exercises and in battle.

The chart room was as close to the bridge as the geography of the ship allowed but sometimes a deck lower in smaller ships. It was fitted with a table large enough to hold a full-size chart, which measured 41 x 27½ inches and drawers for many more charts below. It had bookshelves for navigational publications, and a couch for the navigator to snatch some rest during long spells when he had to be available.

Helm and Engine Orders

Steering the ship was a job for an experienced rating. All able seamen were assumed to be capable of doing it, but in action or in difficult manoeuvres a senior rating, the quartermaster or coxswain, would take over. On most ships the helmsman was stationed at least one deck below the bridge, where he was relatively safe from fire. If he had a view outside, it might be through a periscope or mirrors and it was intended to let him see if the ship was swinging slightly, not to let him make decisions, which were the prerogative of the officers on the bridge. The helmsman might be ordered to steer on a particular compass course. He would bring the 'lubber's line', a mark on the compass bowl that represented the heading of the ship, onto the appropriate number on the compass rose. If the course was to be used for some time, it was chalked on a blackboard ahead of him. He might be ordered to turn the helm to a particular angle, for example 'port 20' and he would watch an indicator to see that he got it right. He might be ordered to use the full angle of rudder of about 35 degrees, though 'hard a port' was obsolete, and full rudder was only used in emergency.

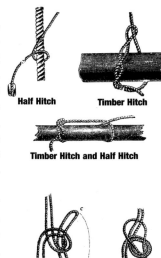

Half Hitch   **Timber Hitch**

Timber Hitch and Half Hitch

Fig. 1   **Fig. 2**
Bowline on the Bight

Figure of Eight Knot   **Overhand Knot**

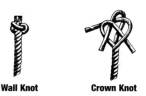

Wall Knot   **Crown Knot**

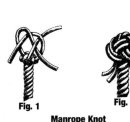

Fig. 1   **Fig. 2**
Manrope Knot

Examples of the ropework that every seaman had to learn.

The helmsman might be given the order 'steady' which meant to keep the ship on the course it was on at that moment, and to stop her swinging if necessary. This often involved applying the rudder in the opposite direction for a time. If given the order 'midships', he would put the wheel in its central position.

Orders from the bridge were transmitted to the engine room by a system of dials and levers, for the engine room was too noisy for voice orders to be used. The engine room telegraph was situated in the same compartment as the wheel. The captain or the officer of the watch gave orders down a voice pipe, and the telegraph operator pushed the lever round to one of the options available – 'full speed', 'half speed', 'slow' in both ahead and astern, and 'stop'. Another telegraph could be used to give an exact number of revolutions per minute to get across a more detailed control of speed. In some ships this was operated by a lever as with the engine room telegraph, in others the operator had to wind a handle to the appropriate speed.

Ship Handling

Often warships had to anchor where there was not a suitable wharf or mooring buoy. A ship usually anchored by steering directly into the current and stopping engines over the spot where the anchor was to be dropped. As a rule of thumb, a ship needed to let out chain equal to at least three times the depth of water she was in at high tide. The cable was paid out slowly as the ship moved astern, in order to prevent it piling up on the bottom, and was fixed on the capstan once the right amount was out. Dropping a single anchor was simple enough, but it might give the ship a huge turning circle as the tide changed. Two

anchors could be laid out to counteract this, but there was a danger that their cables might become twisted as the ship swung. A swivel could be attached to the cables to prevent this.

Giving instructions on bringing a ship into a mooring, whether a quay or a buoy, was recognised as the only task that the captain could not delegate, for he was expected to take personal charge of the manoeuvre. Some captains had commanded destroyers in mid-career and had kept in practice, but a gunnery officer such as Rory O'Conor had never done this kind of seamanship since he was in charge of a boat as a midshipman. He took advice from Admiral Jack Tovey, to:

(a) Never be in a hurry
(b) Never be proud
(c) When frightened, use full speed

But he still made mistakes and authorised the navigation officer to overrule him on the bridge if he looked like getting into trouble.[50]

O'Conor was not the only one to have difficulties. Lieutenant-Commander Wellings of the US Navy watched the *Hood* changing buoys in Scapa Flow in 1940 and remarked, 'Not a very good Job. Cut mooring buoy'.[51] In 1932 Commander Phillip Vian was appointed to command a destroyer without any previous experience in such ships and damaged her superstructure alongside the depot ship, and a few years later he failed to moor first time at Portsmouth, in the presence of the admiral. But he learned in the end, and in 1940 he carried out a series of intricate manoeuvres in the *Cossack* to board the German *Altmark* in a Norwegian fjord.[52]

Any manoeuvre had to be planned well in advance, because everything moved slowly. Engine orders were relayed by voice pipe to the telegraph operator in the wheelhouse below the bridge, who then sent them by engine telegraph to the engine room. There, throttles had to be opened or closed as quickly as possible. Steering orders went direct to the helmsman by voice pipe, but there was a time lag before the ship began to turn, especially at low speeds. Captains could use tugs in the major naval ports, but these were not always available in isolated anchorages. Most ships above the size of a corvette had two or more engines and propellers, and these could be operated in different directions to reduce the turning circle.

A captain always had to be aware that he was operating in a fluid medium – that the stern might swing uncontrollably during a turn, for example. In his book *On the Bridge*, Vice-Admiral J A G Troup offered much advice. On taking the ship out of harbour for the first time, the captain should use moderate speed and small turns of the wheel. He should then carry out exercises in open water, perhaps dropping a marker buoy as an aiming point. The essential thing in mooring or anchoring was to approach against the tide or current if at all possible, as that would allow the rudder to continue steering the ship while moving at very low speeds over the sea bottom. If there were a crosswind it would be all the more difficult, as different classes of ship behaved differently. 'Put, for example, the *Royal Sovereign* to approach an anchorage with a strong beam wind; as way is reduced, the vessel will try to turn to windward. A cruiser with a trawler bow will tend to do the opposite.'[53] When coming alongside a wall, the captain should be ready for a 'wall of water' created by interaction between the wash and the jetty.

Troup gave detailed instructions for mooring up at individual buoys in Grand Harbour, Malta. It was not just that the approach was difficult with sharp turns and variable winds; the harbour is like an amphitheatre and the whole of Maltese society might be watching as the fleet came in. More than one celebrated naval feud was started or fuelled by incidents in Grand Harbour. The approach to buoys 11 and 11A off the naval hospital at Bighi was difficult because of the sharp turn inside the harbour entrance. According to Troup, the task

…appears difficult, for it seems that if the ship goes fast enough to maintain steerage-way outside the breakwater, she will be going too fast when the buoys are reached , but this is not how it works out. All that is required is to reduce speed as soon as conditions allow. Slow ahead starboard, with perhaps 24 degrees of rudder for the turn around Ricasoli, brings down the way; the port engine, after clearing Imgherbeb Point, can sometimes be worked astern in preference to the starboard engine going ahead. The approach is a wide circle, the ship swinging all the time. With a north-west wind, a tug will be required to hold the stern to windward after the turn.[54]

For the actual mooring to a buoy, it was usually necessary to send men ahead in one of the ship's boats.

Course is shaped against the wind or tide for the buoy, keeping it on the same side as the sea-boat if possible. The sea-boat is lowered, ready manned, clear of the water line, and slipped when rather more than a ship's length from the buoy. The boat is hauled ahead by a grass line manned on the forecastle, and as she passes forward the picking-up rope is payed into her. The boat is then slipped and steers direct for the side of the buoy away from the ship, hooks on the picking-up rope, which is then brought to the capstan in the ship, and the ship is hauled up to the buoy and the cable shackled on.[55]

If mooring alongside a wall or jetty, light ropes known as heaving lines were thrown first. Each had a ball of rope called a monkey's fist at the end to make it travel better. Then the main mooring lines were hauled ashore and the loops at their ends were put over bollards, and the ship's crew hauled them tight. As well as the ropes at the bow and stern, a ship needed two springs – lines running from the bow to a position aft and from the stern to a position forward, to prevent her rubbing up and down the jetty with the change of tide. In home ports the rise and fall of the tide had to be taken into account and the ropes had to be slackened or tightened as required.

The Navigator

All officers of the executive branch would qualify to take charge of a watch on the bridge and were expected to know a certain amount of navigation. It was the defining skill which separated seamen officers from the lesser breeds of the engineering and paymaster branches, and from the seamen of the lower deck. Navigation had two main functions: to determine the position of the ship at a given moment, and to find the best route to a destination.

Radar was only just beginning to be useful in navigation, for identifying land features and avoiding collision in poor visibility. Radio navigation aids were coming into service and echo sounding could be used to determine depth, but mostly navigators had to rely on methods that had been in use since the nineteenth century and earlier. Accurate navigation was as important as it had ever been in avoiding the hazards of the sea, but new uses were found during the war. It was often necessary for an escort to find a convoy in mid-Atlantic, or to direct ships or aircraft onto a suspected U-boat. In amphibious warfare, it was vital to find the right spot on the right beach if the landing plan was not to be put in disarray. Every ship, down to a three-man landing craft, needed at least one navigator who was competent at the work in question.

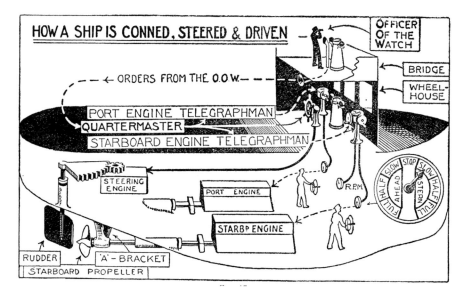

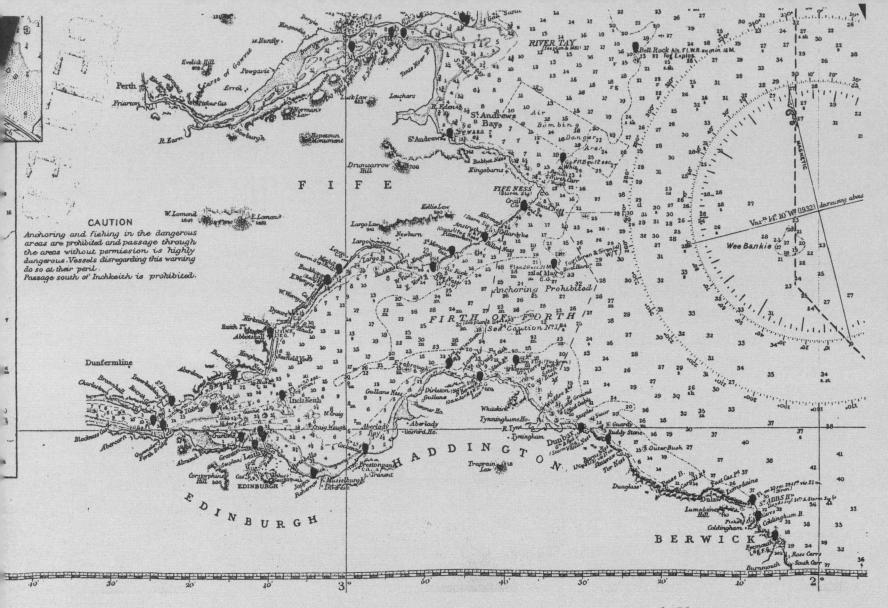

A chart of the Firth of Forth area as used in wartime, with the boundary of the east coast minefield marked by a dotted line to the right.

At the top of the navigational tree were the officers who had done specialist one-year courses in the School of Navigation at Portsmouth. They bore the letter (N) against their names in the Navy List, and tended to serve in large ships or in headquarters. At the other end were the yachtsmen of the Special Reserve who had made navigation their hobby. In John Fernald's *Destroyer from America*, the navigating officer was a 'mud squatting yachtsman…the art of Navigation had attracted his interest to the exclusion of almost every other aspect of naval knowledge…'.[56] In contrast, the great majority of naval officers had largely forgotten their highly technical education at Dartmouth and regarded navigation as a chore. Gorley Putt describes an RNVR navigator who 'more than any naval officer I have ever met, really did love the sea and everything about it'.[57]

A ship can be navigated by steering towards a fixed object such as a buoy or a prominent feature on shore; this is most common in narrow channels where the tide does not have much effect. It can be kept at a fixed bearing and distance from another ship, as when forming part of a fleet or a convoy. In other cases, especially when out of sight of land, a ship was navigated by ordering the helmsman to follow a particular course on the compass. This course was not so easy for the navigator to determine and he had to bear in mind that the ship would hardly ever go in exactly the same direction as the compass course. If he was using a magnetic compass he had to make allowances for variation caused by the earth's magnetic field and deviation resulting from metallic features in the ship itself. He had to allow for constantly changing tidal currents pushing the ship one way or the other, and for strong winds which might push her sideways.

Instruments and Charts

The basic navigational instrument was the compass. The magnetic version was used on the bridges of all ships and its needle pointed to magnetic north. This of course was subject to magnetic variation and deviation and in ocean-going ships it was supplemented by the gyro compass, which was based on the principle of the gyroscope. Depth under the hull was found by casting a lead attached to a line over the side, usually from a special platform off the side of the ship. It was also possible to do this by echo sounding – bouncing a noise off the bottom of the sea and measuring the time it took.

The log was used to measure the speed of the ship and the distance run through the water over a period. There were several types but the most common was trailed over the stern clear of the ship's wake. An impeller was turned by the movement of the water to give a reading of speed and distance on a dial on the ship's stern.

Over the previous century and a half, the Admiralty Hydrographic Department had produced charts of most of the seas and coasts of the world. They came in three main scales. Large-scale ones were used for crossing oceans and were on the gnomonic projection with lines of longitude converging towards the poles so that a straight line drawn on the chart would give a great circle course. Medium-scale charts were used for the bread-and-butter work. They used Mercator's projection in which the world was opened out to form a cylinder rather than a sphere, by stretching distances towards the poles and making the lines of longitude appear parallel. This meant that the same compass course would apply across the whole area of the chart, but the navigator had to remember that the scale varied from top to bottom. For example, Iceland would appear to be the same size as Borneo on such a chart, but the former was 260 miles long while the latter, closer to the equator, was 600 miles. Small-scale charts were drawn on the assumption that the world was flat, and were used for individual ports and harbours.

It was very important to keep charts up to date, especially in wartime when new minefields or wrecks might appear overnight. The navigating officer had a major task in adding corrections to his charts, based on information in the weekly Admiralty Notices to Mariners. Besides that, he kept numerous other Admiralty publications including the pilot books for the local area and lists of lights and radio signals.

For working on his chart, the navigator needed a soft pencil so that his lines could be rubbed out, parallel rulers to take bearings from the compass roses inset on the chart, a protractor for certain angles, and dividers for measuring distances based on the latitude marked on the side of the chart.

Coastal Navigation

Channel Navigation was defined as the navigation of a ship in 'narrow channels with dangers on both sides, and in rivers and harbours and their entrances'.[58] In normal circumstances a local pilot might be taken on to do this, but the ship's navigator had to be able to supervise the pilot and to do it himself if operational conditions made it necessary.

Established harbours were usually well marked with buoys to identify the channels and dangers. In the standard British system, a conical red or black buoy marked the starboard side of the channel as the ship was entering harbour, a flat-topped chequered red and white one marked the port. Others marked the division of a channel, the edges of a sandbank, wrecks and various dangers. Even within Britain there were variations from port to port and there was no universal world system, so the navigator needed his chart and pilot book. He also needed to be aware of local regulations, strong currents and other traffic and he was advised to prepare himself well before entering a strange port.

In sight of land the navigator fixed his position by taking compass bearings on two or preferably three or more fixed and easily identifiable objects on shore. His charts showed church steeples, chimneys and distinctive buildings to help him here, as well as more obvious navigational marks such as lighthouses. With no sights available he used dead reckoning. He knew the course steered from the compass and the distance run from the log. He could calculate the effect of the tide from his almanac and plot that, forming a triangle of 'course and distance steered', tide and 'course made good'. This, he hoped, would give his true position; but he was obliged to accept the possible inaccuracies of the data and hoped for a sight as soon as possible.

Ocean Navigation

For ocean navigation the main tools were the sextant which could take a very accurate measurement of the angle between a celestial body and the horizon, and the almanac which gave the position of the sun, moon, planets and the most useful stars over the course of a year. He needed an accurate measurement of time and for this he used a chronometer.

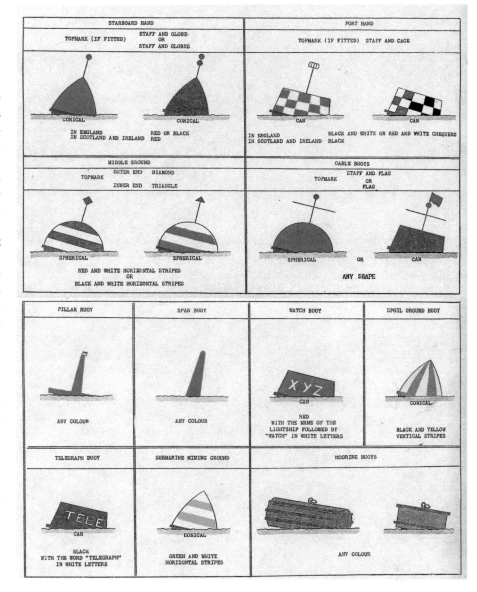

The standard system of buoyage in British waters.

When crossing an ocean, a good navigator would not simply work out the compass course which pointed the ship directly at the destination. He knew that the most efficient route was a great circle track, following a circle whose centre was in the centre of the earth. This meant plotting the route on a chart using the gnomonic projection in which the lines of latitude were show as curves, and changing course slightly every few hours. This was rarely practical in wartime and convoys, for example, were usually routed to avoid likely U-boats rather than on an ideal track from a navigational point of view.

Out of sight of land, there were two ways of determining position. One was by dead reckoning, but this had certain inaccuracies, especially over a long period, and the navigator would take sights of the sun, moon, planets and stars whenever the weather permitted. Finding the latitude was not very difficult. He used his sextant to take a very accurate measurement of the sun's angle above the horizon at noon. To that he would add the known angle of the sun angle from the equator to find his latitude.

Longitude was always more difficult. The navigator might also use an angle on the sun at a time other than noon, or the moon. This would give only a single position line, but he could calculate the distance run since the noon sight to give a reasonably accurate second line. The preferred method was to take the angles of three or more stars, preferably at twilight or dawn when the horizon was also visible. For each sight he could use the almanac to calculate the position of the star directly above the earth at that given moment, and his distance from that position, which would put him on a circle on the globe. With two sights he could make the circles intercept to give a definite position, and with three or four he could be more certain of it. The circles were usually too large to plot on his chart, so he would use the Marc St Hilaire intercept method to relate them to his estimated position and plot them from that. With good visibility and plenty of sights a good navigator would know the position within a mile or so in the middle of the ocean.

5 Logistics

A navy, more than other armed services, has to supply its men with all the necessities of life, even air in the case of submarines, though it did not have to be paid for. Sailors at sea cannot normally supplement their diets by foraging in wartime or by trips to local shops at other times. In addition a fleet needs vast quantities of fuel, ammunition and spare parts to stay operational. All this was the responsibility of the Admiralty, operating through various agencies mostly manned by civilians.

Gate of the Royal William Victualling Yard in Plymouth.

The Victualling Department

The Victualling Department was largely civilian manned, except for a very small number of naval officers who were attached to represent the interests of the users. It had six main tasks: the supply of provisions and clothing for the fleet; the examination, storage and accounting of the stores involved; running victualling yards at home and abroad; the victualling yard craft service which took stores out to ships in the dockyard areas; the cooking and bread-making arrangements of the fleet; and the administration of ships' canteens where sailors could buy additional food and small luxuries. It was headed by the Director of Victualling, and had divisions dealing with Administration, Finance and Accounts, Stocks and Supplies, War Organisation, and Transport and Personnel. During wartime it was responsible for a large number of local depots in 16 areas of the country. The Thatcham area, covering Portsmouth, had 21 depots alone. The central depot was at Deptford on the Thames near London. There were also overseas yards in all the places where the navy operated, divided into Mediterranean, USA, East Indies and Pacific areas.[59]

Normally ships' provisions were supplied by the local victualling depots, but if necessary the accountant officer of a ship could buy food from other sources, either through the Naafi or direct from local suppliers. Officers' stewards were trained in 'marketing', which in those days meant buying provisions in local markets. Officers were given some instruction on how to acquire provisions. Cattle, for example, were to be given 48 hours rest before slaughtering, then killed by humane methods.

The Messing System

Older ships, and those smaller than cruisers, mostly used the Standard Ration and Messing Allowance System. The Admiralty supplied a proportion of the food known as the Standard Ration, and paid a Messing Allowance to each mess, so that it was able to organise its own food to a certain extent. The mess prepared its food and took it to the galley to be cooked.

…each mess subtracts two of its members in rotation who, during the forenoon watch, clean the place and prepare the food, cutting up meat, cleaning vegetables, making puddings and pastries, with traction-engine heaviness of hand so that they look bad enough in the raw and taste, eventually, if they taste at all, like clay. The food thus prepared is sent along to our smoky galley in tins from which no amount of scraping and swilling could ever clear away the insidious taste of grease.[60]

The system was something of a shock to new seamen and trainees at HMS *Ganges* were warned that

*The mess caterer will decide what the mess will have to eat. **You**, when cook of the mess, will prepare the food – on the mess table – and take it to the galley to be cooked – after which you will hear what your messmates think about it as a **MEAL***

It was quite difficult to find recipes that could be prepared in one go without multiple trips to the galley, but seamen were recommended to learn how to make pastry and dumplings, and to prepare different kinds of vegetables – beetroot should not be skinned or its value would

The canteen in the cruiser *Bellona* during a Russian convoy in 1944.

be lost, beans and dried peas should be soaked overnight, parsnips should be washed well before eating. Simple recipes were suggested, such as cottage pie, 'poor man's goose', apple dumplings and a variety of suet puddings. The most exotic was beef curry with rice.[61]

The General Messing System was more modern and was applied on most ships of cruiser size and above, which had their own accountant officers. All meals – breakfast, dinner, tea and supper – were prepared centrally for the ship as a whole and the messes had much less initiative. Submarines tended to use the General Messing System, as did many auxiliaries and armed merchant cruisers. Other vessels, such as corvettes and minesweepers, used a third system, known as Victualling Allowance. They were usually too small to have their own accountant officer, so they bought provisions from the one at their shore base and were able to buy other goods from canteens or local sources to give more flexibility in their diet.

Cold storage was provided on most ships, with a cold room at a temperature of 15–18°F (minus 10–8°C) for keeping frozen beef and mutton, offal, poultry, butter and some kinds of fish. The cool room, with a temperature of 25–30°F, was used for smoked bacon and margarine.

Naval Diet

The Victualling Department issued instructions on sources and storage of certain kinds of food and drink. Coffee was usually from Kenya, with no chicory. Lime juice was much less in favour than it had been in the past: it was issued 'solely as a beverage since neither of the two commercial products has given satisfactory results when tested as anti-scorbutics'.[62] Instead, vitamin A was obtained from other sources. Potatoes were an important part of the British diet, and on board ship they were stowed in sacks in a well-ventilated compartment made up of wooden gratings. Rice was of the Patna variety, but some of the sources of it came under Japanese control during the war. Rum was the standard drink. It was 'purchased in the

The Royal Fleet Auxiliary ship *Cedardale*, one of a class of eight ships of 11,500 tons.

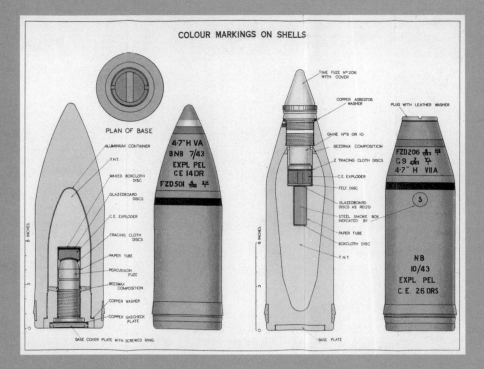

COLOUR MARKINGS ON SHELLS

open market upon sample. It consists of a blend of West Indian (mainly Demerera and Trinidad) with proportions of Natal and Mauritius rum'. Jamaica rum was rarely used, due to its strong aromatic flavour.[63] Tea was dear to the heart of the British, and came either blended or 'straight'. Corned beef was a convenient form of meat and was preserved and tinned; the tapered tin was preferred to the round one, but only because it gave the meat a better appearance when served up. Boneless beef was preferred by victualling officers, because it saved 20 per cent of weight and space when it was stored.

Naval surgeons often commented on the diet and its effects. Surgeon-Lieutenant Whitshed described a day's food in the destroyer *Worcester* in 1940.

Breakfast – Tea. White bread. Butter. Marmalade
Lunch – Meat. Potatoes. Cabbage or Peas. Tinned Fruit or polished rice or boiled pudding
Tea – Tea. White bread. Butter. Jam
Supper – Sausages and chips, or Bacon and Egg
Sunday supper – Salad and Tomatoes

It was typical of the British diet of the time, and sailors were as conservative as anyone else about their food. Whitshed pointed out some of its defects. The cabbages were tough and over-cooked, losing much of their vitamin content. The potatoes were often fried and there was too much reliance on tinned food.[64] The Admiralty kept the situation under constant review. Dehydrated foods, for example, became available from across the Atlantic in 1942, and the vegetables were found useful on long voyages, and the system saved on storage space. But trials of dried soups on submarines were not considered successful.[65] The authorities were well aware of the hardship, stress and heavy labour that were part of a seaman's life and he was fed quite well compared with the general population whose food was strictly rationed.

The typical working-class sailor was quite happy with his diet, although middle-class wartime entrants had different ideas: '…one goes pushing away excellent food for the quite inadequate reason that the roast potatoes are glassy with grease and the greens so sodden with water as to be, in the strict chemical sense of the term, saturated'.[66]

The Role of the NAAFI

The Navy, Army and Air Forces Institute, universally known as the Naafi, was founded in 1921 based on the experience of the First World War. It was a publicly-owned, non-profit-making company charged with supplying service personnel and their families with certain goods beyond the basic necessities provided by the state. As far as the navy was concerned, it operated canteens in the naval bases. Afloat, it ran a tiny canteen on board each ocean-going ship. By mid 1944 there were 760 canteens in shore establishments, and nearly 800 in ships. Many canteens, for example on destroyers, were converted from toilets and were so small that the canteen manager had to stand outside it and reach in for goods. Nevertheless, service as a naval canteen manager was very popular and 35,000 boys applied when the Naafi advertised for a thousand jobs. The canteen in the cruiser *Mauritius* played a vital part in the ship's life. 'Its shelves are always full of a varied array of little necessities and luxuries. Business is always good, and the staff kept constantly busy during the hours of opening. In the evenings there are for sale soft drinks'.[67]

The Naafi also developed its own supply sources, which might complement those of the navy. It bought foodstuffs in competition with other traders and had to endure the rationing imposed by the Ministry of Food, although it did get some priority in the purchase of fish and eggs. Overseas it set up breweries to supply service personnel, partly because local beer was often weak and unpopular, and supplies sent out from home would consume too much shipping space.[68]

The Royal Fleet Auxiliary

The Royal Fleet Auxiliary or RFA was a service manned by merchant seamen but owned and controlled by the government. Its main task was to keep British warships and naval bases supplied with fuel, as other goods (except ammunition) could travel in regular merchant ships or be acquired locally. It operated a fleet of 65 tankers at the beginning of the war. The largest was the Dale class of eight ships of 11,500 tons, and there were 13 other ships of 1000 tons each. Fifteen ships were lost during the war and a further 18 damaged, a high loss rate. New ships were added, beginning with the *Empire Salvage*, a German supply ship which was captured after the sinking of the *Bismarck*. By December 1944 there were 85 vessels, although about a third of these were of 500 tons or less, some of the smaller ones being water carriers. The Pacific war brought out the deficiencies of the fleet, not just in numbers. The Dale class, of which 13 were now in service, could do only 11–12 knots, whereas 15 knots was needed to keep station with warships while refuelling at sea.

The RFA was manned by about 4000 men. About 400 of these were deck and radio officers, the former recruited from nautical schools such as HMS *Conway*. There were about 600 engineering and electrical officers, usually trained by apprenticeship within the service. Officers had more permanent employment and slightly better conditions than most merchant navy officers in peacetime. There were about 3000 ratings, half from the United Kingdom or Malta, the remainder recruited in Asian ports such as Bombay, Singapore and Hong Kong, at reduced pay. Key ratings such as boatswains and carpenters had permanent employment and pension schemes.[69]

One method of refuelling at sea, by trailing a hose astern of the tanker. This was no use for passing goods such as ammunition and stores.

Ammunition Supply

In the past much of the navy's ammunition had been made in the Royal Ordnance Factory at Woolwich near London, but that was very vulnerable to bombing and the work was dispersed to numerous factories around the country. Cordite, the main propellant of shells, was mostly made at Holton Heath near Poole in Dorset. Torpedoes were manufactured in a large factory, formerly a car works, at Alexandria in Scotland. In peacetime ammunition was stored in secure conditions in huge depots near the main dockyards, for example Priddy's Hard for Portsmouth and Crombie for Rosyth. These, too, were vulnerable to bombing and many more were opened during the war, often in converted factories and warehouses. Disused railway tunnels, such as those at Colwall and Hawthorn, were used for safe storage. Some were used to disperse the ammunition inland, some served new or re-opened naval bases such as Lyness at Scapa Flow, and some supplied merchant ships with anti-aircraft ammunition. By late 1943 there were 33 depots in the United Kingdom, plus many sub-depots, with others at all the main bases abroad. There were also torpedo depots at all the main ports, and mine depots at Frater near Portsmouth and at Rosyth.

Normally ships came into port to take on ammunition supplies, which was done under conditions of great security. Explosives were towed alongside the ship in un-powered lighters to avoid contact with the fire of steam engines – a *Royal Sovereign* class battleship needed four lighters for its 15-inch ammunition and two for its 6-inch. Derricks were rigged to hoist it out of the lighter and lower it into the magazine. Cordite was hoisted in first because that was stored at a lower level in the magazine, followed by the shells themselves.[70] On a destroyer the work was less formal but just as hard.

Two deep drifters came alongside, their holds stocked with wooden boxes, and the ship's company set to work. Some got into the drifters and handed the heavy boxes to men above, who passed them along to others, who carried the boxes along the deck under the direction of the G.I. [Gunnery Instructor]. Other boxes and tins were unscrewed in the hold and their contents passed up singly – hundreds of shells and hundreds of charges. These were carried to the shell rooms and stored there in racks.[71]

Fuel

Before the war most of the navy's oil fuel was acquired by way of the Anglo-Persian Oil Company, in which the British Government had a 51 per cent stake. This became less certain after the Mediterranean was closed to shipping, so oil was obtained from Trinidad, Venezuela and the United States, though its quality was considered inferior. It was stored in great tank farms near the naval bases, buried underground as far as possible. Such tanks still dominate the landscape in twentieth-century bases such as Invergordon and Lyness. It soon became necessary to store quantities of diesel oil for landing craft engines, and petrol for aircraft and coastal forces.

Taking on oil fuel was a far less strenuous process than the older one of 'coaling ship', which still had to be done on a few antiquated vessels. In harbour, fuel could be taken on by going alongside a wharf or jetty, by coming alongside an oil tanker, by using pipes attached to buoys and connected to the oil plant on shore or by bringing an oil lighter alongside the ship. Naval officers were a little wary of tankers coming alongside, as they were 'unhandy' single-screw vessels which might do damage. Sometimes on destroyers the pipes had to be led through messdecks which required cleaning afterwards, but in general the process was painless, as pipes were connected and oil was pumped into the spaces in the double bottom and elsewhere.[72]

Refuelling at sea was a relatively unusual technique in 1939, as the navy relied on bases spread round the world. This proved inadequate first in the Atlantic, which has no natural refuelling stops in its centre; and later in the Pacific, where the distances were just too vast. The early technique was to refuel destroyers from larger ships. The destroyer was taken in tow at 12 knots, then speed was increased to 15 knots, while a hose was passed over. The next method, tried in the Atlantic in 1941, was to trail a floating hose. For the Pacific war the Royal Navy began to adopt the American technique of the two ships coming alongside, some distance apart due to the danger of rolling. Jackstays were passed between them, allowing refuelling at relatively high speeds, and also the transfer of ammunition and other stores, but it was not fully developed by the end of the war.

Enemies and Allies

1 Enemies

Britain faced three main enemies during the war, all of whom had ambitions to become great sea powers, although only the Japanese had the geographical situation and the determination to do this fully. Italy was largely confined inside the Mediterranean and lacked any kind of aggressive naval strategy, while Germany gave primacy to her army and air force and the navy concentrated on submarines, which could threaten routes over the sea but never control it. But the mere fact that all three navies were hostile and undefeated at the same time stretched British sea power to its limits, and led to disasters such as the loss of the *Prince of Wales* and *Repulse* in the Pacific in 1941.

All the enemy powers were totalitarian regimes, where service to the state was taken for granted. Unlike Britain, the United States and the Commonwealth countries, conscription was considered normal and the individual was expected to make sacrifices uncomplainingly.

The Strategy of the German Navy

The modern German navy was created by Admiral Von Tirpitz at the end of the nineteenth century, nearly three decades after the country had been united by Chancellor Bismarck. In 1906–14 it competed strongly with the Royal Navy in building Dreadnought battleships, though as a mainly land power Germany could never hope to outbuild the British. The naval officer corps believed it had won at Jutland in 1916, and was devastated when mutinies in 1918 led ultimately to the German defeat. It was further outraged when the armistice demanded the internment of the fleet, although it saved its honour by scuttling the ships at Scapa Flow in 1919.

Under the Treaty of Versailles which ended the war, Germany was forbidden to possess battleships over 10,000 tons, military aircraft or submarines. Hitler renounced the treaty when he came to power in 1933 and began to rebuild the U-boat arm. By an agreement of 1935, German was allowed to build up to 35 per cent of British naval

Opposite: A navy poster shows the two *Nelson* class battleships and an aircraft carrier and celebrates the defeat of Italy. It does not acknowledge the fact that the Germans in Italy continued to fight on. Painted by Forster.

Left: Karl Dönitz stands behind Hitler and Hermann Goering early in 1943.

tonnage. According to Plan Z of 1939, Germany was to have 13 battleships, 33 cruisers, 4 aircraft carriers and 267 U-boats by 1947. The naval high command was deeply disappointed when war with Britain broke out soon afterwards, as it was not nearly ready and the Führer had assured them that war would not happen for some years.

The German armed services co-operated well during the invasion of Norway in 1940, but rivalries and personal differences soon broke out. The army was always regarded as the primary service in Germany. The *Luftwaffe* was headed by Hitler's close associate Herman Goering and the navy took third place for much of the time. The *Luftwaffe* did little to support the U-boat offensive, with only minimal reconnaissance over the Atlantic and few raids on the key British ports. However, the naval air arm of the *Luftwaffe* employed 100,000 men in 1943.

Expecting a short war, the Germans abandoned Plan Z and concentrated on ships whose construction was already well advanced, and on U-boats. The only aircraft carrier, the *Graf Zeppelin*, was launched in 1938 but continually postponed and never completed. The surface fleet was used for raids on British supply routes and against the Russian convoys. It also served as a 'fleet in being', whose ships were a constant threat to the enemy even if they rarely left port. This was helped by the fact that most German warships were well designed, armed and constructed. But the surface fleet was reduced by attrition over the years and it was never large to begin with. The *Kriegsmarine* was obliged to rely increasingly on the U-boat as its means of attack.

The German navy, like most others, had no experience of amphibious warfare in 1940 when it was asked to plan the invasion of Britain – Operation Sea Lion. It did its best with improvised craft and converted barges, but it is doubtful how well they would have stood up to weather in the English Channel had the invasion ever been launched.

Hitler's interference had less effect on the navy than on the army, though his obsession that the Allies might invade Norway, for example, sometimes created difficulties. He took a strong interest in naval affairs, and on the surface at least, Admiral Karl Dönitz saw him as a strategic genius. After a meeting in 1943 he commented:

The enormous strength which the Fuehrer radiates, his unwavering confidence, and his far-sighted appraisal of the Italian situation have made it very clear in these days that we are all very insignificant in comparison with the Fuehrer, and that our knowledge and the picture we get from our limited vantage are fragmentary. Anyone who believes he can do better than the Fuehrer is silly.[1]

But in general German naval officers were apolitical. Apart from Admiral Canaris, the head of intelligence, very few were associated with the plot to kill Hitler in July 1944.

At the beginning of the war the *Kriegsmarine* was headed by Erich Raeder, who had served mainly in staff posts until he was appointed in 1928. Karl Dönitz was a former ace submariner of the last war. He began the war as the captain in charge of submarines, but he grew with the job and was a full admiral in 1943 when he was called on to succeed Raeder. Despite his background he persuaded Hitler not to scrap the big ships, and showed such determination in conducting the war that Hitler appointed him as his successor when he killed himself in 1945.

The German navy expanded rapidly in the first years of the war, from 78,000 men in August 1939 to 320,000 in March 1941. This number also included many of the men who operated coastal defences, an area which became important by 1943 as preparations were made to resist an Allied invasion. There were 37 heavy and 132 medium coastal artillery batteries in May 1941, and there were 371,000 men operating them in mid-1943.[2] But expansion of the navy proper had come to a stop. It was only about 7 per cent of the total *Wehrmacht* of nearly 10 million men, and resources were needed elsewhere. In June 1943 Dönitz wanted 438,000 men for new U-boats and other construction. He was offered only 103,000. Hitler told him:

I haven't got the personnel. The anti-aircraft and night fighter forces must be increased in order to protect the German cities. It is also necessary to strengthen the Eastern Front. The Army needs divisions for the protection of Europe.[3]

The Surface Fleet

Germany retained a few pre-Dreadnought battleships as training ships, but her first large modern ships were the three vessels of the *Deutschland* class begun in 1929–32 under the restrictions of Versailles. Armed with 11-inch guns, they were faster than battleships but better armed than cruisers: the Germans called them *Panzerschiffen* or armoured ships, the British, 'pocket battleships'. Originally intended for use against the Soviet Union, their long range made them effective as commerce raiders on the high seas, despite the loss of the *Graf Spee* in 1939. The agreement of 1935 allowed the *Kriegsmarine* to begin the *Scharnhorst* and *Gneisenau*, hybrid ships with high speed but relatively light armament. They caused the British many problems until the *Scharnhorst* was sunk

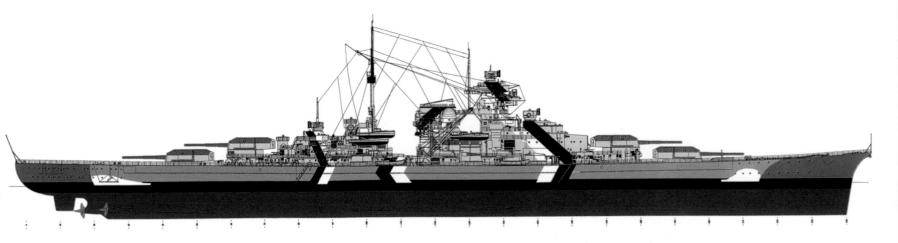

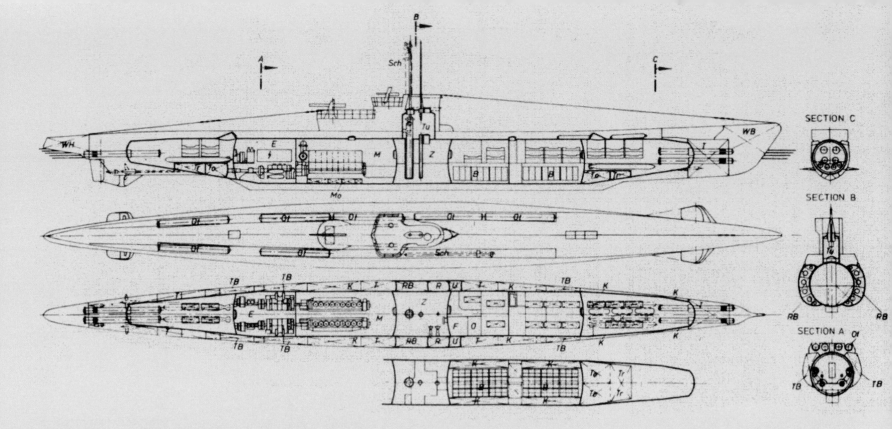

SECTION C

SECTION B

SECTION A

at the end of 1943. The *Bismarck* and *Tirpitz* were much larger and were even more of a threat with their 15-inch guns and a speed of 29 knots. Great effort was needed to sink the *Bismarck* in 1941, and to finally sink the *Tirpitz* by bombing in a Norwegian fjord in 1944.

The *Kriegsmarine* was not well provided with cruisers. The heavy cruisers *Blucher* and the light cruisers *Königsberg* and *Karlsruhe* were sunk during the invasion of Norway leaving only two heavy and four light cruisers to raid British commerce. They were supplemented by about 10 converted merchant ships which had some success on the high seas.

The decision to suspend work on larger ships at the beginning of the war was sensible enough and was parallel to similar decisions by Churchill, who nevertheless expected a long war. Less wise was the decision to build no more of those very useful ships, destroyers. The pre-war ships were fast and well armed, but 10 out of 21 were lost at Narvik in 1940 and only a limited number of replacements were built.

One area in which the *Kriegsmarine* excelled was in the small, fast motor torpedo boat, known as the *S-Boot* or *Schnell-Boot* to the Germans or the E-boat or enemy boat to the British. The Treaty of Versailles was vague about whether such boats were permitted, and the navy took advantage of this. The Germans were world leaders in the diesel engine and they developed a fast, lightweight version to power their boats. The typical E-boat was 114 feet long with three diesel engines giving a speed of almost 40 knots. It carried two torpedoes in tubes plus two reloads, and was big enough to have a heavy gun armament against aircraft and British MTBs. In all, 249 of them were built.

The U-Boats

Though it started in very weak condition, the German U-boat arm had as much influence on the war as most services of much greater numbers, and came closer than any other force to winning the war in the West. Germany had just 57 U-boats at the beginning of the war, of which 48 were operational. By the spring of 1941, with the failure of invasion plans and the bombing of cities, it was clear that the U-boat was the only realistic way to defeat Britain. In February Hitler decreed:

The object of our future war efforts must therefore be to concentrate every means of waging war by sea and air on enemy supplies for overseas as well as keeping down British aircraft production and inflicting still greater damage on the air armaments industry wherever possible.[4]

The standard U-boat was the Type VIIC, of which 665 were built. It was just large enough for Atlantic operation at 67.1 metres and 865 tons submerged, but it was highly manoeuvrable and suitable for mass production.

Officers

Officer selection used most of the same criteria as other nations, but with a National Socialist slant. Loyalty to the Führer was essential, and psychological tests were applied.

We had to grasp two ends of a bar, and once the apparatus was switched on and the current began to flow we couldn't let go of them. Many of us just screamed – quite the wrong thing – but others bit their cheeks and by drawing them in gave an impression off stern endurance. All this was filmed, but we never saw the film, though it must have been an interesting one.[5]

Successful candidates were enrolled as cadets and trained on the island of Danholm, where they wore a uniform similar to that of the army. In peacetime and early in the war they went on to a sail training ship to learn basic seamanship, and then had a long-distance trip on a cruiser. They went to the Naval Academy at Flensburg as midshipmen, to learn navigation, boat-handling, mathematics, physics and chemistry, and the general principles of guns and torpedoes.

As the navy expanded in the first years of the war, the proportion of officers to men declined noticeably – one officer to 16 men in 1939 and one to 28 men in March 1942. Training courses were shortened, men were brought in from the merchant navy and petty officers were promoted.

A large ship like the *Bismarck* had more than a hundred officers headed by a *Kapitan Zur See*. His second-in-command was a *Fregattenkapitan*, equivalent to a commander, and a *Korvettenkaptan* or lieutenant-commander as chief artillery officer and another as chief engineer. In contrast, a U-boat had a standard complement of four or five officers. The commander was usually a *kapitan-leutnant*, equivalent

U-552 returns to base after a successful mission.

to a lieutenant in the British or American service. There were two watch-keeping officers and an engineer officer, with perhaps another attached for training. The commander was usually appointed after one or two patrols as a watch-keeper and had great responsibilities. He had to run the boat, maintain morale in difficult circumstances, to find targets and conduct an attack. He was advised,

In all operations against the enemy, the commander of the submarine is entirely independent, and free to make his own decisions, unless special co-operation is called for.[6]

The Seamen

In peacetime, sailors volunteered for a period of 12 years' service. Men with engineering and other skills were particularly encouraged. They gained the single stripe of the *Gefreiter*, and other stripes with long service. Selected men were trained as petty officers or *Maats*, and at the beginning of the war there were schools at Kiel and Stralsund. *Maats* and *Obermaats* continued to wear the square ring of the seaman, but on promotion to *Feldwebel* they changed to fore-and-aft rig as worn by officers. There were four grades of *Feldwebel*, equivalent to chief petty officer or warrant officer in British or American service. The non-commissioned part of a U-boat's crew was led by four men with the rank of *Oberfeldwebel*. One was the *Oberbootsman*, who was the senior man, equivalent to coxswain. The *Obersteurman* was the navigator, a job that was always done by a commissioned officer in Britain and the United States. There was an *Obermaschinist* in charge of the diesel engines, and an *Elektro Obermaschinist*.

All navies had problems with the supply of petty officers and technicians, but this was particularly intense with the Germans. Because rearmament did not start until 1935, there was no large reserve of suitable men, except those who had served in the Imperial

Navy in the last war and were mostly fit only for shore duties. The nature of the war demanded smaller vessels such as U-boats, S-boats and patrol craft off the coast of France and Norway. These needed a higher proportion of petty officers.

Naval Bases

The traditional German naval bases were at Wilhelmshaven in the North Sea and at Kiel in the Baltic, which also served as headquarters of the fleet and the main training base. There were smaller bases at Cuxhaven and Wesermünde on the North Sea coast, and at Swinemünde in the Baltic. The great commercial ports of Hamburg and Bremerhaven were little used by the navy. The Fall of France meant that the U-boats moved to the Atlantic coast, where bombproof shelters were built by the Todt Organisation at Brest, St Nazaire, La Rochelle, La Pallice and Bordeaux.

The Japanese Navy

The Japanese navy was one of the most advanced in the world, at least equal to the United States in naval aviation when it attacked Pearl Harbor in December 1941. British planning had taken account of the Imperial Japanese navy in the 1930s, although in practice the war with Germany meant that Britain was never fully engaged with it. The *Prince of Wales* and *Repulse* were sunk by aircraft in December 1941. The cruiser *Exeter* was sunk after the Battle of the Java Sea in February 1942, and British ships chased Japanese submarines in the Indian Ocean, but the main campaign was almost entirely American. By the time the British returned to the Pacific in 1944, the Japanese had been comprehensively defeated and the remaining threat came from the *kamikaze* suicide pilots.

Japan was opened up to western ideas by the American Admiral Matthew Perry in 1852–4, but in naval matters she tended to follow British practice in the first instance. A naval college was set up at

The Japanese aircraft carrier *Ryuho*. She was converted from a submarine support ship and entered service as a carrier late in 1942.

Etajima, modelled on Dartmouth but with later entry and even stricter discipline. Early warships were built in Britain, and naval architects were sent to Greenwich to train. In the early 1920s a British mission introduced the Japanese to naval aviation, until the Americans insisted on the ending of the Anglo-Japanese alliance.

Japan had no independent air force, and rivalries between the navy and the army were more intense than in any other country. The army had five times as many officers as the navy, and they interfered decisively in the running of the state. Japan was already engaged in bloody and brutal war in China from 1931, and the army pushed for war with the United States after President Roosevelt imposed an oil embargo. The navy was far more reluctant, but launched the attack on Pearl Harbor in December 1941 despite its doubts.

The Japanese were the only Asian nation of the age to adopt modern western methods, combining them with a fanatical devotion to the Emperor and the code of *Bushido* or the Way of the Warrior. Japanese fighters almost never surrendered and were contemptuous of enemies who did, treating them very harshly. They became a uniquely effective fighting force. They beat the Chinese in 1894 and the Russians in 1905, but they had important gaps in their strategy. They followed the ideas of the American Captain Mahan too dogmatically, which led them to neglect commerce protection and the possibility of attack on American supply lines. Even more important, the Japanese had a large and powerful fleet at the beginning of the war, but lacked the resources to provide ships, aircraft and pilots for a long conflict against the industrial might of the United States. They failed to develop an efficient radar, and did not understand the extent to which American signals intelligence was being used against them.

Japanese Warships

Despite the effectiveness of her naval aviation, a strong faction in the Japanese navy still supported the battleship as the main weapon. They had a force of 10 capital ships at the beginning of the war, mostly quite old. The new *Yamato* class was originally intended to consist of four ships, but only two were launched in that form. They were far larger than anything used by any other power, the only ships with 18-inch guns. The Japanese hoped they would outclass anything the Americans could build for some years, and even then the latter ships would be too big for the Panama Canal. They were built to withstand tremendous punishment, but both were sunk by intensive air attack in 1944–5.

The eighteen Japanese heavy cruisers in service in December 1941 were large, fast and well armed, for Japan often built her ships behind high walls in a secretive society and exceeded treaty limits. Large destroyers of the *Fubuki* class were built in 1928–31 and forced other powers, including

Britain, to rethink their own destroyer programmes. The Japanese neglected the submarine as a means of attack on enemy supply lines, and instead concentrated on it as a tool of the battle fleet. They had a large force of boats and also developed midgets for inshore attack.

Naval Aviation

The Japanese first learned about naval aviation from a British mission of 1921–2 but soon developed it well beyond that. The first carrier, the purpose-built *Hosho*, was followed by two capital ship conversions, *Akagi* and *Kaga* in 1927–8. Rather than expand the officer corps, the Japanese trained large numbers of petty officer aircrew. Their carriers had small superstructures, or none at all. Admiral Yamamoto took charge of the aviation department in 1935 and had a vision of air power as the determinant of future naval wars. The carrier force grew from four to 10 ships in 1938–41. In the Mitsubishi Zero fighter, it had one of the most effective weapons of the naval war, though outclassed by the later American designs. The naval air arm also controlled the flying boats which patrolled the seas.

Japanese naval aviation initiated one of the most terrifying and effective weapons of the war, the suicide pilot, although at the time only Japanese culture would permit such tactics. Aircraft were fitted

A *kamikaze* attack on the USS *Columbia* early in 1945, using a Yosuka D4Y4 specially adapted for suicide missions.

Above: A two-man Italian manned torpedo.

Right: The Australian cruiser *Canberra*, built on Clydeside in 1925–8. Similar to a British County class ship, she was sunk by the Japanese in 1942.

with 550-pound bombs and steered directly onto warships, which proved devastating when first used and necessitated a much greater use of anti-aircraft guns. The British carrier *Indefatigable* was hit by one in April 1945, but her armoured deck saved her.

The Italian Fleet

The navy was very important to Mussolini's idea of Italian supremacy. He often talked of the Mediterranean and *Mare Nostrum* or 'our sea' but was also afraid that it might become a prison. This helped motivate the campaign in Ethopia in 1935, which offered bases outside the Mediterranean. The Italians, led by the inspirational Count Balbo, were enthusiasts for air power and formed a separate air force quite early. As in Britain and Germany, this hindered the development of naval air power, and was reinforced by Mussolini's belief that Italy was in effect an unsinkable aircraft carrier because of her central position in the Mediterranean. The navy was designed for a war against France, and ship design concentrated on speed rather than armour or gun power. Mussolini's declaration of war on Britain and France in June 1940 was purely opportunistic and the Italian people had no real motive or wish to fight, which was often reflected in their performance in battle.

In traditional surface ship actions, the British would have more contact with the Italian fleet than any other. When Italy entered the war she had four old but modernised battleships, with two modern ones of the *Littorio* class just completed, and another to enter service in 1942. Heavy 8-inch cruisers of the *Trento* and *Zara* classes were supplemented by various groups of the Condottieri class, intended originally to fight off French destroyers. From a peacetime strength of around 75,000

officers and men, the navy expanded to around 190,000 between 1940 and 1942. The *Regia Marina* also had 128 destroyers, and 115 submarines.

Besides the lack of naval air power, the *Regia Marina* was hampered by its leaders' belief in 'the fleet in being' – the idea that a naval force's very existence had an effect on strategy and sometimes it was better to protect it in harbour than risk it at sea. This was dealt a fatal blow by the Fleet Air Arm attack on Taranto in November 1940. The doctrine also resulted in the failure to take a historic opportunity earlier in the year. With the French navy out of action and the British fearing invasion at home, the Italians had a numerical superiority and might have won a decisive victory, had they not been so cautious. In fact the navy was used only to protect Italian supply lines in the Mediterranean, and avoided contact with the British fleet as much as possible. It was helped by German aircraft including Stuka dive bombers, and by U-boats which passed the Strait of Gibralter, but German surface ships were not risked on such a passage through the Strait, so the Italian surface fleet, with faulty doctrine and weak industrial resources, had to face the British alone. It suffered heavily. All four heavy cruisers of the *Zara* class, for example, were sunk during the war.

Torpedo Boats and Midget Submarines

If the Italians failed to deploy their surface fleet effectively, and had only moderate success with submarines, they had some spectacular victories with the smallest vessels. They developed the motor torpedo boat enthusiastically, for it was highly suitable for a weaker naval power in narrow seas, and it suited the dashing Italian temperament. Their motor torpedo boats had a good engine in the Isotta-Fraschini, and a continuous line of development in the inter-war years. The famous 10th flotilla or *Decimo MAS* operated both surface boats and manned torpedoes. It sank the cruiser *York* in Suda Bay in Crete in 1941, and disabled the battleships *Queen Elizabeth* and *Valiant* in Alexandria Harbour at the end of the year. Based secretly in Algeciras in neutral Spain, it penetrated Gibraltar harbour and sank merchant ships in convoys there.

It was to no avail and Italy surrendered to the allies in September 1943. This did not end the travail and the battleship *Roma* was sunk by a German glider bomb on the way to Malta.

2 Allies

The Commonwealth Navies

Within the huge British Empire, certain colonies had now become virtually independent under the Crown. These were the dominions of Canada, Australia, New Zealand and South Africa, where the descendants of white settlers either formed a majority, or had political control as in South Africa. Throughout the twentieth century there had been considerable debate about how these countries could contribute to the naval defence of the empire. Should they concentrate on local defence, or develop into regional naval powers, or should they send ships and men to form part of a Commonwealth naval force? These questions were never fully resolved, and each of the 'white dominions' resolved it in a slightly different way during the Second World War. All adopted the ships, rank and rating structures and most of the procedures of the Royal Navy, with small local modifications.

Canada

Canada was more determined than the other dominions to maintain a measure of naval independence from Britain, and this was reflected in its policy. Most of the major centres of population, apart from Vancouver, are far from the open sea, but the nation supported a remarkable expansion of naval forces during the war. There were only 2000 regular officers and ratings in the Royal Canadian Navy in 1939, supplemented by 3000 reservists, operating a force of destroyers. The Canadians used British instructors and methods but built ships in their own yards to produce a specialised naval force consisting of escort vessels for the Battle of the Atlantic. Two escort carriers were added late in the war, but a light fleet carrier was not ready until after it had ended. Two cruisers were commissioned in 1944–5 but apart from that the RCN was made up of ships of destroyer size and less.

The first Canadian training schools were at Halifax on the east coast and Esquimault in the west. Later, basic training was carried out in about 20 volunteer reserve divisions across the country. When the major convoy base at Halifax became overcrowded, a new training centre was opened at Deep Brook in the Bay of Fundy, Nova Scotia.[7] The Royal Canadian Navy increased nearly twenty-fold to a high point of 92,000 men and women in 1945. However, many ships proved rather inefficient when they first got to sea. Captain Donald Macintyre complained: 'The appearance of many of these travesties of warships was unbelievably dirty and unseamanlike'.[8] There were disasters to Canadian-escorted convoys late in 1942 and their ships were sent for extra training in the British bases at Tobermory and Londonderry, after which the situation was much improved.[9] The captain at Londonderry found that they were 'very bad at first but were very co-operative and learnt quickly'.[10]

British naval officers tended to assume that the fast expansion was the root of the problem, but it was also true that the Canadian escort groups were often the last to be issued with new equipment, and they were often treated as ill-disciplined 'colonials'. By the later stages the Royal Canadian Navy was much more efficient and provided nearly half the escorts in the Atlantic battle.

Australia and New Zealand

Naval affairs were considered important in Australia, a country which lives by the sea and had an obvious potential enemy in the shape of Japan. The cruiser seemed the natural ship, as they could be effective in the great distances across the Pacific. The Australians had six of them at the beginning of the war, and would lose three. They also had five destroyers and two sloops building. The naval force had 5440 men in 1939, which rose to nearly 37,000 in the course of the war, plus 2600 women. The Flinders naval depot carried out basic training and there were specialist schools in other parts of the country. There was a strong volunteer reserve force at the beginning of the war, and some officers were sent to serve with the Royal Navy in home waters. Yachtsmen were also trained in the supplementary reserve as in Britain. By the end of the war the Royal Australian Navy had four cruisers, 11 destroyers, three landing ships, eight sloops and frigates and nearly 300 escorts, motor launches and other vessels.[11] Sydney was being developed as a major base for Commonwealth forces in the Pacific.

New Zealand also favoured the cruiser before the war and provided half the crews of the light cruisers *Leander* and *Achilles*. The latter ship gained fame early in the war in the sinking of the *Graf Spee*. Twelve-year engagements in British style were used before the

The Engineer Officer carries out an inspection of the boiler room on the destroyer HMCS *Niagara*.

war but were not popular in a country where employment prospects were better. In wartime, men were taken on for hostilities only, and many yachtsmen were sent to Britain for training as officers, often serving with the Royal Navy after commissioning. A training school for ratings was opened at Auckland in 1941. New Zealand also produced more than 1000 aircrew for the Fleet Air Arm. The Royal New Zealand Navy reached a strength of 10,649 men and women in July 1945.[12]

South Africa

South Africa, with a substantial Afrikaner population, had a significant anti-British movement and was less committed to the naval war, so the dominion had less of an independent naval force. At the beginning of the war the South African Naval Service had no ships and just three officers and three ratings, with a volunteer reserve force of about 800, trained in Royal Navy ships on the South African Station. It was the newest and least prestigious of the country's armed services. A Seaward Defence Force of 29 vessels was set up early in 1940 to protect the base at Simonstown, and escort groups were formed to protect convoys in the region. Though the hard-line Nationalist party did not take power until after the war there was a considerable measure of segregation – black and white crew members messed separately, and commanders would have preferred to 'Europeanize' their crews if numbers had permitted. The SANF remained a small force on a world scale, peaking at 78 vessels and a total of just over 8000 officers and men, of whom nearly 3000 were seconded to the Royal Navy.[13]

The Royal Indian Navy

Of the remaining colonies under more or less direct British rule, India was by far the most populous and the only one to produce a substantial

The Free French crew on the fore decks of a destroyer.

naval force. It had a small fleet at the beginning of the war, operating a small force of sloops and supporting vessels. It consisted largely of Indian ratings under European officers. There were Indian officers, but the British Admiralty tried to restrict their right to command European personnel, or to sit on courts martial on them. The personnel of the Royal Indian Navy increased sixfold during the war, to man six escort vessels, 10 minesweepers and numerous coastal craft, but it was not easy to recruit suitable men. Indians were used to joining the army and many served in the merchant navy, but most of the recruits from coastal districts were considered too ill-educated for naval service.

The Free Navies

As successive countries were overrun by the Germans in the first half of the war, elements of their naval forces often escaped to support the Allied cause. In some cases ships and their crews were deployed to fight alongside the Royal Navy, although that could cause supply problems with unusual calibres of ammunition and so on. In other cases standard British warships were allocated to the exiled governments. The officers and ratings usually kept their old uniforms and ranks. The various free navies provided a useful supplement to the hard-pressed Allied forces. Just as important, they represented the peoples under occupation, and gave moral force to the Allied cause.

Poland had a moderate navy of four destroyers, five submarines and a few other ships when the country was invaded by Germany in 1939. Three of the destroyers were sent to Britain, and the rest of the fleet was quickly put out of action. British warships were added to the force, including two cruisers and six destroyers to be manned by exiles. The Polish navy helped escort nearly a thousand convoys and took part in operations far from home in the Mediterranean.

When the Germans invaded Denmark in 1940, the country was overwhelmed quickly and bloodlessly. In August 1943 the Germans attempted to take over the ships of the Danish navy, but most of them were scuttled by their crews. Resistance was much stronger in Norway and a large number of the antiquated and ill-prepared navy vessels were sunk. Some ships escaped, as did large numbers of seamen. A force of destroyers, escorts and coastal forces was built up and by 1945 the Norwegian navy was stronger than it had been in 1940. Belgium had very little of a naval force, but the Netherlands had a strong force both in Europe and in its colonies in the East Indies. Unlike the French colonies these supported the exiled government in London after the homeland was overrun, and fought alongside the Americans when the Japanese war began, suffering heavy losses. At the other end of Europe, the Greek navy was largely eliminated by German air attack in 1941. Two destroyers, 10 escort vessels and four submarines were provided by the Allies for Mediterranean operations.

The French Navies

The French navy had a more complex history than most of those of the occupied countries. It was one of the greatest in the world in 1939, with a fleet of seven old and new capital ships and two more on the way, 19 cruisers and 66 destroyers, some of which were virtually light cruisers. In 1940 it took part in the Norwegian campaign and when

France was invaded it suffered losses during the evacuation from Dunkirk. With the French surrender, a large part of the fleet was destroyed by the British at Mers el-Kebir. Ships in British waters and in Alexandria harbour were seized, though few of them were serviceable. Most of their crews were repatriated and only about 3000 remained to join the Free French under General de Gaulle. They manned escort vessels, some of which played a distinguished part in the Battle of the Atlantic. The remaining 'unfree' French fleet helped prevent a British invasion of Dakar in 1940, but was less successful when the Allies invaded North Africa two years later. When the Germans then marched into unoccupied France in November 1942, most of the remaining navy scuttled itself in Toulon.

The Soviet Navy

Despite several ambitious building programmes in the 1920s and 30s and its exclusion from the Washington and London treaties, the Soviet navy remained a minor force. There was excessive political control after a mutiny in the naval base at Kronstadt had nearly destroyed the regime in 1921. The country's industrial resources were stretched and technology was often backward compared with the West. Because of geography, the Soviet fleet was divided into four almost watertight areas – the Baltic, Arctic, Pacific and Black Sea. The Baltic Fleet gained a little operational experience during the war with Finland in 1939–40, but that was limited. When the Germans invaded in June 1941 the Baltic Fleet was the strongest in conventional terms, with two battleships and two cruisers, 19 destroyers and 65 submarines. But the war in the region was largely fought on land and the major units were kept in harbour, while small craft such as torpedo boats and improvised landing craft carried out the campaign on the coasts and rivers. The Pacific Fleet was numerically the largest, with 11 destroyers and 86 submarines, but it played no part in the war. The Black Sea Fleet was supreme in its area until the Germans used great efforts to bring in

ships and submarines over land. In the Arctic, the force began with eight destroyers and was built up to 16. Most of them were based on Italian designs, which were highly unsuitable in the area. They co-operated with the British and Americans in convoy escort, but they had little operational experience – they tended to operate too long at full speed and then run out of fuel. Because the campaign was mainly on land, nearly 400,000 sailors were transferred to the army in the course of the war and fought very well. The British battleship *Royal Sovereign* was loaned to the Russians in 1944, but saw no action.

The United States Navy

The British and United States navies had a certain amount in common in 1939. They shared a good deal of common heritage, as the United States Navy followed British lines when it was founded late in the eighteenth century. Officer ranks were very similar except at the top and the bottom: the highest American rank was Fleet Admiral and it was awarded very sparingly. Instead of sub-lieutenants the Americans had ensigns and lieutenants (junior grade). Both navies vied to be the greatest in the world in 1939, but there was no doubt about who had won the race in 1945. Both regarded themselves as the primary forces of their nation, especially after the attack on the fleet at Pearl Harbor brought the United States into the war. The Americans also suffered from competition from the air. There was no independent air force and naval aviation was firmly under naval control, but General 'Billy' Mitchell's extreme claims about the power of aircraft to sink ships caused some diversion of resources. Isolationism and financial stringency held back progress between the wars. But in many other respects the US Navy was more successful than the Royal Navy in dealing with the situation. On the whole its ships were better conceived than British ones, it made far more progress with naval aviation and slightly more in amphibious warfare. The pay and conditions of its crews were greatly improved.

Soviet torpedo boats in the Baltic late in 1942.

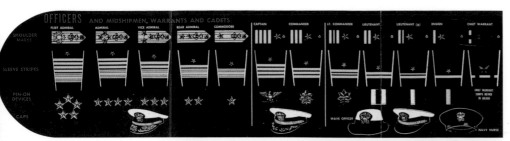

Officers' and enlisted men's rank distinctions of the US Navy.

The US Navy was under the authority of the President as Commander-in-Chief of the Armed Forces. Money was voted by Congress, which often imposed quite tight restrictions on how it should be spent. The political head was the Secretary of the Navy, a cabinet minister with direct access to the President: the post was held by Frank Knox during the war. The professional head was the Chief of Naval Operations, a post held by Ernest J King in 1942–5. Administration was through a series of bureaus dealing with Aeronautics, Yards and Docks, Medicine, Ordnance, Supplies, Ships and Personnel.

Personnel

The Navy Department had control of several other activities besides the navy proper. It ran the US Coastguard which prevented smuggling, surveyed the coast and carried out rescue operations. In wartime it was merged with the navy and provided many serviceable anti-submarine vessels and minesweepers. The United States Marines had far greater responsibilities than the British or any other marines, and often played a significant part in land activities. They held Iceland for the Allies and fought a hard campaign alongside the army in Guadalcanal, for example. They had far more publicity than their British counterparts and proudly used their slogan 'The first to land'. Naval aviation included shore-based aircraft, which in Britain would be operated by Coastal Command of the RAF. The navy used thousands of men in construction battalions (or 'seabees') to build impromptu naval bases and airfields. The navy proper doubled in size from 161,000 to 383,000 men in the 18 months before America entered the war. It multiplied nearly tenfold during the war itself, to nearly 4½ million men and women. The marines had a similar expansion, from 28,000 men in 1940 to 485,000 in 1945, while the coastguard also expanded approximately twentyfold, to 170,000 in 1945. This was achieved very efficiently, with a minimum of tension. The Bureau of Personnel (BuPers) used modern management methods to keep track of its men, plan their training and put them in specific jobs, unlike the old-fashioned and ad hoc system of the British.

In peacetime, naval officers were trained over four years in the Naval Academy at Annapolis, Maryland. Entry was on the recommendation of a congressman, and discipline was severe, especially in the first or 'plebe' year. But this source could only supply about a thousand men a year, about 1 per cent of those needed in wartime. The peacetime navy also developed its reserve officer programme with Naval Reserve Officer Training Corps in selected colleges. It commissioned more than 60,000 warrant and petty officers during the war, but its main source of officers was direct entry

by men with a college degree – far more common in the USA than Britain at that time. This source began to dry up as young men were conscripted before they had a chance to complete college. The navy developed the V-12 programme, by which suitable young men were enlisted in the navy and trained in colleges. The US Navy had no large body of engineer officers, and all 'line' officers were expected to take engineering in their stride.

The US Navy relied on volunteers during its first year of war, supported by the wave of enthusiasm after Pearl Harbor. Then it was forced to rely on conscription, partly because volunteers were drying up, partly to integrate it into the rest of the defence effort. With a vast inland population, the USN had long given up the idea that seamen could only be found in port towns and had an extensive recruiting and training organisation, well co-ordinated by the BuPers. A recruit started as an apprentice seaman then went on to become a seaman second and first class. If he had been trained in any specialised skill he would be rated as petty officer third class, for there were no 'non-substantive' ranks as in the British fleet. On being rated chief petty officer he gave up the square rig uniform and wore a collar and tie like the officers. Petty officers were usually known by their rate, such as torpedoman's mate third class, aviation radioman second class, yeoman first class or chief pharmacist's mate.

The women's naval force, the WAVES, was created in July 1942, and it expanded to nearly 9000 officers and 74,000 enlisted women – there were also equivalent forces for the marines and the coastguard. At first they were forbidden to serve overseas, until a law of 1944 permitted them to volunteer.

One fault line in the US armed forces was in the matter of race. At first African-Americans were not recruited to the navy except as domestics. By 1944 they were assigned to auxiliary vessels to make up to 10 per cent of the complement. A few all-black escort vessels were fitted out but the experiment was not pursued. In the meantime the African-American was often employed in menial duties ashore. Two hundred were killed when an ammunition ship blew up in California in 1944, leading to a mutiny.[14] On a more positive side, the first 26 black officers were commissioned in December 1943.

The Fleet

The US Navy was affected by the Washington and London treaties as much as any other, but on the whole the results were advantageous. In battleships, the Americans had several sunk or badly damaged at Pearl Harbor, but this was not to be a battleship war and it helped to release personnel and change perspectives towards aircraft carriers. The new battleships of the *North Carolina* and *South Dakota* classes were armed with 16-inch guns in triple turrets, outclassing anything in Britain or Germany. The four ships of the *Iowa* class, commissioned in 1943–4, had the same armament and a high speed of 32.5 knots.

Like other nations the Americans had built 8-inch cruisers until the early 1930s, then switched to ships with a large number of 6-inch guns. The *Brooklyn* class of the mid-1930s had 15 in triple turrets, the numerous *Cleveland* class, built from 1940 onwards, had 12. Modern American destroyers, such as the *Fletcher* class first launched in 1942,

were equipped with five or six of the highly effective dual-purpose 5-inch gun in single or twin mountings. On a hull of nearly 3000 tons light load displacement, the *Fletchers* also had 10 torpedo tubes and a speed of up to 38 knots. In escort vessels, the Americans sometimes followed British practice with the large number of escort destroyers based on the Hunt class, and frigates from the River class design.

The US Navy built a fleet of large, long range submarines for Pacific operation. The boats of the *Gato, Balao* and *Tench* classes were 311 feet 9 inches long with a submerged tonnage of up to 2415. With a crew of up to 80, they could operate over 11,000 nautical miles. US submarines had spectacular successes against the Japanese, who did not adopt convoy until late in 1943 and never developed effective measures to protect their supply lines. Deployed in small 'wolf-packs' of two or three boats, they sank more than a thousand merchant ships of over half a million tons: Japan was close to starvation even before the atom bomb was dropped in 1945.

Naval Aviation

With the battle fleet put out of action at Pearl Harbor, the US Navy quickly adopted the aircraft carrier as its main striking force, and it proved extremely effective from its great success in sinking four Japanese carriers at the Battle of Midway in 1942. The first American carrier was the *Langley,* converted from a collier in 1922. It was followed by the *Lexington* and *Saratoga,* adapted from battlecruisers under the Washington Treaty, and they gave the navy much valuable experience. The three ships of the *Yorktown* class of 25,000 tons carried nearly a hundred aircraft and were the most modern on the outbreak of war. They were quickly followed by the *Essex* class, enlarged *Yorktowns* which formed the basis of the fast carrier groups that came to dominate the Pacific. The smaller ships of the

Independence class were converted from cruiser hulls to fill gaps in production, and dozens of escort carriers carrying around 30 aircraft each were mass-produced under the entrepreneur Henry J Kaiser.

Naval aviation had relied heavily on enlisted pilots in the 1930s, but these were no longer recruited in wartime. By 1943 there were 773 enlisted pilots, compared with more than 20,000 officers. The centre of training was the air station at Pensacola, 'the Annapolis of the Air', but many other training bases were opened during the war. As well as single-seat fighters, two- or three-seat aircraft usually had officer pilots and enlisted men as gunners and radio operators.

US naval aircraft were outclassed by the Japanese at the beginning of the war, but soon began to overtake them. Classic designs included the Wildcat, Hellcat and Corsair fighters, the Avenger torpedo bomber and the dive bombers Dauntless and Helldiver.

US naval aviation was also responsible for shore-based naval aircraft, unlike the Fleet Air Arm, and it used PBY or Catalina amphibians and Liberator bombers, noted for their long range. It continued to develop lighter-than-air craft for sea patrol and had 146 'blimps' in 1944. US naval aviation peaked in 1945 with nearly 30,000 combat planes, nearly 3000 transport and utility aircraft and 8370 trainers. Looking to the future, it had 27 helicopters.

Amphibious Warfare

The US Marines had done more work in amphibious warfare than other forces in the 1930s, although that did not take them very far. The Pacific war was different from the European war in many respects, and invasions tended to be of tiny, isolated but heavily defended islands, so fire power was more important than accurate navigation. American landing craft also served in Europe in the invasions of Sicily and France. The full range of craft was needed,

Top: The US battleship *North Carolina*, completed in August 1941 with nine 16-inch guns. The two ships of this class could make 27 knots, slower than the later *Iowa* class.

Bottom: American escort carriers of the *Casablanca* class loaded with aircraft. Fifty of these ships were built by Henry J Kaiser in Vancouver.

sometimes developed with Anglo-American co-operation, though the Americans claim sole credit for the fast and adaptable Higgins craft, and most of the credit for the versatile Landing Ship Tank.

The Infrastructure

As well as the navy yards, the US Navy built ships in large private yards such as the one at Quincy in Massachussetts and the New York Shipbuilding Company's premises at Camden, New Jersey. Henry J Kaiser set up yards on many greenfield sites for the production of both warships and merchant ships. The one at Tacoma in Seattle built escort carriers. The Electric Boat Company of New England was one of the leading submarine builders, while the Higgins Boat Company of New Orleans produced innovative light landing craft.

Ashore, the US Navy was divided into 13 districts at home, including an inland one which included states such as Montana and Kansas, as well as much of the Great Lakes. There were well-established navy yards at New York, Philadelphia, Norfolk in Virginia and San Francisco, for the building and repair of warships and their supporting facilities. The navy also had the use of great fleet anchorages such as Hampton Roads in Virginia and San Francisco Bay. Overseas the greatest base was at Pearl Harbor with its natural anchorages and well-developed facilities. But once the war in the Pacific became mobile, the US Navy relied increasingly on a large fleet train which included depot ships for submarines and destroyers, and on island bases hastily constructed by the seabees. It also developed techniques of taking on fuel and other stores at sea, so that aircraft carriers could remain in operation for long periods.

3 The Merchant Navy

Protection of merchant shipping had always been one of the Royal Navy's key roles, and even more so in the Second World War when the country's survival depended on it. The navy also needed the Merchant Navy to provide a reserve of experienced officers and seamen, ships which could be converted to armed merchant cruisers, troop transports and landing ships and vessels to carry all kinds of naval supplies. The relationship between the two services was a complex one, and often there was misunderstanding on both sides.

The Size of the Fleet

Though the British Merchant Navy was by far the largest in the world and was almost exactly the same size as it had been a quarter of a century earlier, there were many who worried about its decline. Actual British tonnage had gone down slightly since 1914, though ships owned in the Empire and Commonwealth had risen in compensation, so Empire tonnage as a whole was up about 1 per cent since 1914. But it was relative rather than absolute decline that worried the strategists. Germany had not succeeded in rebuilding her fleet to pre-war standards, but smaller countries such as Greece and Norway had more than doubled theirs, as

had Italy, a potential enemy. Even worse, the Japanese merchant fleet had more than doubled. The USA was more of a commercial than military rival, and her seagoing tonnage had increased by 340 per cent with government support, giving her the second largest merchant fleet, nearly half the size of the British. The British Empire now controlled less than a third of the world's tonnage, compared with two fifths in 1914.

If that was not enough, the numbers of British seamen were falling faster, and there were 47,000 less in 1937 than in 1911. The number of masters had fallen by 52 per cent, deck officers by 33 per cent and engineers by 20 per cent. In fact this largely reflected a change to bigger ships and increased efficiency, but it was often taken as a sign of decline, and the nation had fewer reserves to draw on in wartime.[15] The Merchant Navy had endured hard times during the great depression, and things were little better on the eve of war. Freight rates were down in 1938, and in 1939 grain prices slumped, leaving 50 ships idle in Argentina for lack of a cargo.

The Merchant Navy was less structured and unified than the Royal Navy, but it was controlled in a different way by regulations, mostly by the Board of Trade. That department administered the Merchant Shipping Acts, especially the act of 1894 that controlled the qualifications of officers, regulated their relations with the crews, and provided for various safety measures for ships and passengers. Shipping was also controlled by the insurance market. Lloyds of London was the main institution in the world, and its inspectors laid down standards so that 'A1 at Lloyds', meaning that both the hull and rigging were up to scratch, became a universal expression.

The Shipping Companies

A shipping firm might be almost any size. The British India Steam Navigation Company had over a hundred ships in 1939. At the other end of the scale, a syndicate or an individual might own a single ship and charter it through an agent. For example, the Chine Shipping Company of Cardiff owned the *Canford Chine* of 5500 tons and used her for general tramping, until she was sunk by *U-52* in February 1941 with the loss of all 35 people on board.

Peacetime shipping was divided into liners and tramps. Liners were not necessarily passenger carriers, but were simply ships which operated on regular routes. Each of the major routes was controlled by conferences between the owners, who fixed prices and agreed on other matters. Tramps, which were not necessarily as decrepit as the name suggests, were those which sought cargoes around the world using the radio and the electric telegraph. They never carried passengers in great numbers, and usually transported bulk goods such as coal. Sometimes they were chartered by the liner companies to supplement the ships on their routes. Each of the major lines tried to foster its identity by its own distinctive house flag, and painted its funnels in a particular way. Cunard had its well-known red with black stripes, while Alfred Holt of Liverpool was universally known as the Blue Funnel Line.

Coastal shipping was mainly run by smaller companies, operating round the British coast and to the near continent, but largely carrying coal to London and other cities. Owners were often merchants who used the ships to carry their own goods, or captains who brought experience and commitment to the trade, or owners and brokers who had deep inside knowledge. They were spread around the coast but with concentrations in the major ports such as London, Glasgow, Liverpool and Newcastle.

As employers, the shipping companies were completely different to the Royal Navy. Rather than a single employer, they were a group of hundreds of very disparate companies. The Royal Navy offered permanent employment but very few people in the merchant service had any kind of job security and even captains were usually taken on for a single voyage only. The tanker companies, such as the Anglo-Saxon Petroleum Company or Shell Oil, were something of a contrast and offered more regular conditions.

In wartime the shipping companies continued to own and man their ships, but many were requisitioned by the Ministry of War Transport for naval use in the case of troopships and armed merchant cruisers, while other were subject to Admiralty control when they were directed into convoys. Ships under its direct control were given 'Empire' as a prefix to their names, except those provided by the United States where such a concept was not popular.

The Ships

At the pinnacle of the Merchant Navy were the great Atlantic liners – the largest, fastest and most prestigious ships by a long way. They were the pride, not just of the Merchant Navy, but of the nation as a whole. Their owners competed with other international companies in speed and design, with the Blue Ribband to be won by the ship which made the fastest trans-Atlantic crossing. Building had ceased during and after the First World War when the emigrant trade to America had collapsed. Since then firms such as Cunard had re-invented themselves for the luxury market. New building only resumed with the *Queen Mary*, which was launched in 1936 after several false starts during the depression. When the Second World War began the largest liners were quickly converted into troopships, initially carrying men from Australia and New Zealand to the war in Europe and North Africa. Other passenger ships were fitted with guns to become armed merchant cruisers, sometimes still with their civilian crews.

At the next level in social prestige were the passenger and cargo liners which operated the main services between Britain and the Empire. The *Athenia* was a cargo liner of 13,581 tons built by Fairfield in Glasgow in 1923. In peacetime she carried 310 cabin-class passengers and 928 third-class on a Glasgow to Canada service. She sailed from Liverpool on 3 September, the day that war was declared. At 19.30 that evening she was torpedoed by *U-30*, whose captain was exceeding his orders. She sank after 14½ hours.

The *Politician* was a cargo liner, built in 1923 as the *London Merchant*, and was later taken over by the Harrison Line. On 5 February 1941 her captain evidently mistook the Sound of Eriskay for the Sound of Barra in the Outer Hebrides and the ship went aground and was wrecked. Among her mixed cargo were 20,000 cases – more than a quarter of a million bottles – of whisky for export to the United States. Much of this was salvaged illicitly by the islanders and it became known as 'Polly' from the name of the ship.

The cross-channel steamer, operating between Britain and Europe or Ireland, was sometimes described as the 'Atlantic liner in

miniature'.[16] Those on the short sea crossings, for example from Dover to Calais, had no need for overnight accommodation as the journey only took a few hours. Those operating to the Netherlands or Germany needed more equipment. This was another market where speed was an advantage and Channel ferries, like Atlantic liners, had turbine engines and a speed of about 20 knots or more. Of course their market largely disappeared at the beginning of the war, to be replaced with carrying troops to France. That, too ended in 1940, and many of the ferries were converted to become the first Landing Ships Infantry.

Small passenger ships served the Thames Estuary and the Firth of Clyde. They were often paddle steamers and they, too, found a new role in wartime, as shallow-draught minesweepers. The *Talisman*, built by the London and North Eastern Railway Company for service on the Clyde, was converted into an anti-aircraft ship and served at D-Day.

Cargo ships were generally classed according to the arrangement of their decks. The most common was the 'three island' type with raised forecastle, centre island round the engine and under the bridge, and quarterdeck. Other types included the well-decker with the space between the forecastle and centre island filled in, and the shelter decked ship with the three islands joined together. They had no great need for speed and generally proceeded at 10 knots or less, with a crew of about 20 to 30 men.

Each estuary had its own type of local craft. The Clyde puffer was 88 feet long and designed to fit in the locks in the Crinan Canal between the Firth of the Clyde and the Hebrides. It operated from Glasgow to the remote towns in the Firth and on the islands. Sail survived much longer in the Thames Estuary and the well-known sailing barges still operated in some numbers, carrying bricks and agricultural goods.

Though British shipping had originally grown up with the transport of coal, it was now beginning to use the oil tanker in some numbers. In 1938 there were 470 in service in Britain and the Empire, totalling 3 million tons, about 30 per cent of world tonnage.[17] A typical example was the *San Demetrio* of 12,000 tons, built in 1938 for the Eagle Oil and Shipping Company. She was part of convoy HX84 from Halifax to the UK in November 1940, escorted by the armed merchant cruiser *Jervis Bay*. She was hit by shellfire from the German pocket battleship *Admiral Scheer* in mid-Atlantic and was severely damaged. Her crew abandoned her, but two days later the crew of one of her lifeboats encountered her still afloat and re-boarded her. She was taken to the Clyde with her cargo of gasoline.

The diesel engine had made some inroads in the coastal trades, but British shipping was still overwhelmingly powered by steam. Turbine engines were confined to the fastest merchant ships – the Atlantic liners and the Channel ferries. The rest used the slower but more economical triple-expansion engine, for it was generally believed that a ship operated most economically at a speed of 11 knots or less. Many of the older ships were still coal-fired, requiring a large crew of stokers.

Despite the huge merchant shipping losses, naval shipbuilding was given priority during the war, and the Ministry of War Transport looked elsewhere to replace losses. A few German ships were taken in the course of the war. Old laid-up ships were found in America and put into service, though their condition was often very poor. One hundred and eighty-two of the famous Liberty ships also operated under the British flag. Standard merchant ship designs were produced in British yards, including a tramp ship 425 feet long and around 10,000 tons deadweight, with a speed of 10–11 knots. Sixty-eight of them entered service. The standard fast cargo liner did not emerge until 1943. It was of 12,000 tons and had a speed of 15 knots, making it independent of convoy. The eight ships of the *Empire Malta* class of 1944 were much smaller, and designed for heavy lift. Three standard types of tanker were produced. The Ocean type, based on a design by Shell, was of 12,000 tons with a speed of 12 knots, the Norwegian type was slightly larger at 14,500 tons, and the Standard Fast type reverted to the smaller size but with a speed of 15 knots. One hundred and seventy coasters were built, including 63 Clyde puffers, mostly fitted with diesel engines to belie their name.[18]

The Officers

There were three main ways to become a deck officer in the Merchant Navy. The most certain and prestigious was to train in one of the schools and training ships, such as *Conway* in the Mersey, *Worcester* in the Thames or the Nautical College which was unexpectedly sited at Pangbourne in inland Berkshire. These institutions maintained good relations with the Royal Navy, which offered cadetships in the RNR and even the regular RN. They produced about a hundred graduates a year who tended towards the more prestigious shipping lines, such as P&O and Cunard. The second and most common route was by apprenticeship to a shipping line. About 650 entered in this way each year between 1928 and 1932. About a hundred also entered by promotion from the lower deck.

The deck officer began as a cadet then served time as a third, second and first officer to become a master after about 20 years or so – strictly speaking 'captain' was a courtesy title in the Merchant Navy. Since 1918 there had been a standard uniform, with four gold rings for a master and one for a third mate. The status of the Merchant Navy officer varied with the trade he was in. At the lower end of the scale was the mate of a barge or puffer; at the top was the master of a great liner.

Engineer officers trained by apprenticeship, either afloat or ashore. The junior engineers were the equivalent of skilled tradesmen, and the Royal Navy regarded them as the equal of ERA in their own service, rather than commissioned officers.

The Seamen

Culturally the Merchant Navy rating was very different from his Royal Navy counterpart. He rarely wore a uniform unless he was a steward, he changed jobs at will and he had little respect for formal discipline. Often he was not British: in 1938 there were more than 50,000 lascars, recruited in India, China and Africa at reduced rates of pay. There were also nearly 10,000 foreigners, compared with 132,000 British seamen. Stewards in the Merchant Navy were often of Goanese or Maltese origin, and there were comparatively few women.

Despite the obvious hazards, it was not difficult to recruit merchant seamen in wartime. They were exempt from conscription and had a certain amount of choice regarding which ship they served in. They were allowed to go to sea at 16 rather than 18 for the Royal Navy. Wages rose steadily in wartime, from an average of £9.12.6 (£9.62) a month in 1939 to £24 a month in February 1943, which compared well with both service and civilian wage rates.[19]

The Merchant Navy in War

Everything changed for the merchant seaman in wartime. Captains were used to sailing alone; now they had to work hard to keep a station in a convoy. The ships' funnels, hitherto painted brightly in house colours, were now grey or camouflage. Liners and tramps, passengers and cargo ships, sailed together in apparent equality. All were under the authority of the Ministry of War Transport, which arranged cargoes and routes instead of the ship owners. At sea the ships were controlled by the commodore of the convoy, who was often a retired admiral. There was constant danger, not from the sea but from enemy action, even if the seamen were civilians. The merchant seaman had been on the verge of unemployment in peacetime, but now he was in great demand.

The merchant service had suffered heavily in the First World War and no one had any illusions about how hard it would be in the Second. After the Fall of France coastal shipping was mostly deployed in keeping London supplied with coal. Convoys ran down the east coast through 'E-boat alley' off East Anglia where they might suffer heavy losses from light craft and bombers. Ocean-going ships were more likely to be attacked by U-boat. Perhaps they would be sunk instantly, perhaps the ship would catch fire, or the crew might escape to spend days or weeks in an open lifeboat. Nearly 56,000 crew were in ships sunk during the war and 25,864 of them – 46 per cent – died. The Merchant Navy had an overall death rate of 19 per cent, far higher than any of the armed services.

Armed Merchant Cruisers

The idea of converting merchant ships into warships, in the form of armed merchant cruisers (AMCs), had long been appealing. Fast ocean liners would be short of work in a major war, and had the speed and range to operate on the ocean. Most were designed to be fitted with guns in some form. They were not intended to face enemy warships, but they could help blockade Germany by patrolling the seas between Scotland and Iceland, and could assist with convoy escort. More than 50 merchant ships were taken over in 1939, complete with crews, and fitted with guns. The role of the armed merchant cruiser began to decline after 1941. The *Rawalpindi* and *Jervis Bay* were sunk by German warships, and the

Queen Mary wearing her wartime paint in Tasmanian waters in 1940, during her service ferrying Australian troops to the war in Europe and North Africa.

The life-line is firm
thanks to the
MERCHANT NAVY

A poster
celebrating th[e]
service of the
Merchant Nav[y]
showing an
idealised offic[er]
and crewman

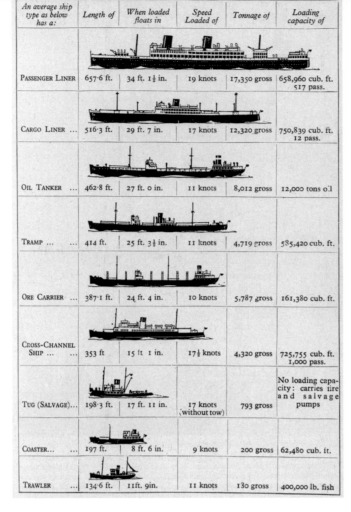

An average ship type as below has a:	Length of	When loaded floats in	Speed Loaded of	Tonnage of	Loading capacity of
PASSENGER LINER	657·6 ft.	34 ft. 1½ in.	19 knots	17,350 gross	658,960 cub. ft. 517 pass.
CARGO LINER ...	516·3 ft.	29 ft. 7 in.	17 knots	12,320 gross	750,839 cub. ft. 12 pass.
OIL TANKER ...	462·8 ft.	27 ft. 0 in.	11 knots	8,012 gross	12,000 tons oil
TRAMP	414 ft.	25 ft. 3½ in.	11 knots	4,719 gross	585,420 cub. ft.
ORE CARRIER ...	387·1 ft.	24 ft. 4 in.	10 knots	5,787 gross	161,380 cub. ft.
CROSS-CHANNEL SHIP	353 ft	15 ft 1 in.	17½ knots	4,320 gross	725,755 cub. ft. 1,000 pass.
TUG (SALVAGE)...	198·3 ft.	17 ft. 11 in.	17 knots (without tow)	793 gross	No loading capacity: carries fire and salvage pumps
COASTER... ...	197 ft.	8 ft. 6 in.	9 knots	200 gross	62,480 cub. ft.
TRAWLER ...	134·6 ft.	11ft. 9in.	11 knots	130 gross	400,000 lb. fish

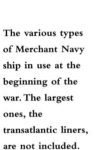

The various types of Merchant Navy ship in use at the beginning of the war. The largest ones, the transatlantic liners, are not included.

American entry to the war created a demand for them as fast troop carriers, while the supply of purpose-built warships was increasing. By the end of 1942 it was proposed to retain only 13 in service, mostly in the fringe areas of the South Atlantic, West Africa and the Indian Ocean.[20]

DEMS

Even before the war, the Admiralty planned to give merchant ships the means needed to defend themselves and chose the title 'Defensively Equipped Merchant Ships'. From 1941 the letters DEMS were borne as part of the non-substantive gunner's badge. Training began for Merchant Navy officers and men in eight major ports in July 1938, and a year later 1400 officers had been trained in fire control, with 180 a month passing through. Two seaman gunners were to be trained for each ship in a course lasting 10 working days,

Admiralty policy at the beginning of the war was centred on ships carrying 6-inch and 5.5-inch guns, but it soon became clear that aircraft were more of a threat than surface ships. In February 1940 the army provided 500 light machine guns and 1000 men, partly to give them some experience in anti-aircraft work. This grew steadily and in May 1941 they were formed into the Maritime Royal Artillery with an anchor shoulder patch. The numbers peaked at 14,200 men in September 1942.[21] In October 1943 the Admiralty outlined a new policy for manning guns on merchant ships on three scales: normal; double manning in areas particularly susceptible to air attack; and special rates for some ships such as 'monster' liners. Most ocean-going ships would now carry 20mm Oerlikon guns, although some only had machine guns.[22]

From January 1941 the basic training camp in Wales, HMS *Glendower*, was largely devoted to training Hostilities Only men for service in merchant ships. They did five weeks of basic disciplinary training, followed by two-and-a-half weeks each on advanced seamanship and gunnery, then three weeks on specialised DEMS training, to make a total of 13 weeks.

In service the DEMS gunners wore uniform, forming a striking contrast with the Merchant Navy crew in their 'miscellaneous garments', although dress code became much more relaxed at sea. DEMS gunners carried civilian clothes to avoid being interned as combatants in neutral ports. By February 1944 there were 33,000 Royal Navy men in the DEMS service, including 500 officers and 1000 in training schools.[23]

Convoy Commodores

In 1938 the Admiralty decided to employ its numerous retired captains and flag officers as commodores in charge of the merchant ships of a convoy. The first 53 were appointed in September, with the rank of Commodore Second Class, the highest available in the Royal Naval Reserve. The first course was held in the Admiralty a year late. Up to 14 officers could be trained at once, in a very intense course lasting two or three days. It included:

The organisation for forming convoys at various ports and the orders, manuals, and signal books issued for the conduct of convoys at sea, including their defence by ships and aircraft of the Royal Navy and of Coastal Command. The course also dealt with the installation of weapons, life-saving rafts, and bridge protection, the supply of signalling gear, smoke-making apparatus, the fitting of communications from bridges to engine rooms, the training of guns' crews in merchant ships, and other matters.[24]

The escort commander, in a commissioned warship, was put in overall charge of each convoy, rather than the commodore. 'The commodore of the convoy is to take charge of the convoy as a whole, subject to the Senior Officer of the Escort. He is responsible for the conduct of the convoy at sea and for its internal organisation'. At the same time the escort commander was to 'bear in mind the greater experience possessed by the Commodore as to the capabilities of the convoy, and he should refrain from interference with the latter's dispositions, unless the convoy is in danger'. The commander of the escort was usually only a commander and junior in both rank and experience to the commodore, cutting across centuries of naval tradition. It was justified on the grounds that the escort commander was in a commissioned warship flying the white ensign, and was at the centre of communications, with 'absolute power to enforce his orders'.

In all more than 150 officers were to serve as commodores of ocean convoys during the war, with 150 more as commodores of coastal and Mediterranean convoys (with a certain amount of overlap, as a few officers served as both at different times). The coastal convoy commodores were much less prestigious in their previous lives. Some had been lieutenant-commanders in the RNR; most were retired commanders or captains.

T124

Merchant seamen under Royal Navy command were normally signed on a T124 agreement, on a form provided by the Transport Board. Until 1940 this only covered an individual seaman in a particular ship, until the Admiralty introduced the T124X agreement, which meant that a man could be transferred from one ship to another, and that his services

Left: Captain Taylor of the *Cape Hawke* on the bridge with the helmsman.

could be retained 'for the period of the present emergency'. They would be 'Naval Auxiliary Members of the Armed Forces', and not required to register for conscription. All merchant seamen employed by the navy would be transferred to T124X in the course of time.[25]

T124 men were principally employed in armed merchant cruisers until about 1942, when many were used in merchant aircraft carriers or MACs. These ships were commanded and manned by Merchant Navy crews, with Fleet Air Arm aircrew and mechanics. It was said of the first one, *Empire Macalpine*:

The crew of the vessel was roughly fifty each merchant navy and fleet air arm, and these were under different codes of discipline and were paid at very considerably different rates. Also the accommodation provided was of the usual types for the two services – the merchant navy men having considerably the better part of the bargain. None of these problems provided any real difficulty in practice.[26]

John Kilbracken flew a Swordfish from *Empire Macalpine* and the informality of the Merchant Navy proved popular. The Fleet Air Arm officers adopted Merchant Navy language, calling the wardroom the saloon and lounge and the ship a boat, a great solecism in the Royal Navy. Some aircrews had the words 'Merchant Navy' painted on their aircraft, in place of 'Royal Navy'.[27] The same policy was applied to the first escort carriers, which were larger than MACs, but it was soon found to be more convenient to operate them with Royal Navy crews.

Allied and Neutral Merchant Shipping

Some of the countries with the largest merchant fleets – Norway, the Netherlands, Denmark and Greece – were occupied by the enemy during 1940–41. Many of the ships were already under charter to Britain when the countries were invaded, while others at sea were induced to come over to the Allied cause, though 40 per cent of the Danish dry-cargo fleet was captured by the Germans, and 28 per cent of the Norwegian fleet.[28] Nevertheless, there were 840 foreign dry-cargo ships under British control in 1940–41, including 156 from Greece, 147 from the Netherlands and 180 from Norway.

The United States Merchant Marine worked alongside the British in Atlantic and Russian convoys. American merchant shipping had

been in decline since the Civil War, despite government attempts to revive it. The Merchant Marine Act of 1920 gave US-registered ships preference on many trades but failed to inspire new vessels, and a subsidy of $250 million offered in 1928 produced only 42 ships, some of which were, however, of very good quality. The Maritime Commission of 1936 authorised loans of up to 75 per cent for new vessels, and some ingenious standard designs were produced, but little had been done before the start of the war in 1939. This was made up for after 1941, when Henry J Kaiser ran the famous Liberty ship programme, mass-producing more than 2751 standard ships of 7176 tons with a speed of 11 knots, a crew of 65 and a US Navy armed guard, the equivalent of the British DEMS gunners.

In 1940 the US Merchant Marine had only 65,000 officers and men and it was difficult to crew all the new ships. Huge training camps were

Below: Naval DEMS gunners with the 6-inch gun of a merchant ship at Liverpool.

set up on the East and West Coasts and on the Great Lakes. Boys of 16 were recruited to the service. Standards of training and licensing were reduced so that it was possible to become an officer after a year's sea service and a four-month course, and a captain after two years as an officer. By these means the Merchant Marine was increased to a quarter of a million men by the end of the war.

4 The Other Services

The Army

Below left: A convoy commodore and a captain on the bridge of a merchant ship.

Below right: The Commander-in-Chief of the British Expeditionary Force in France, Lord Gort, studies a map in a chateau in November 1939.

The army was by far the largest of the British services in wartime, rising to a maximum of more than 3 million men, compared with just over a million in the RAF and 855,000 in the navy. Its prestige was low for most of the war. Young men had heard of the horrors of the Western Front in the previous war from fathers, uncles and schoolmasters. In the current war, the army was tainted by defeat in Norway, France, Greece and Crete, while the navy appeared as the saviour who had rescued the troops at the last moment. After that, most of the army was based at home in apparent inactivity, but actually preparing to resist a German invasion or to launch one of its own. Its uniform, khaki battledress, was highly unattractive and one character in the film *The Way Ahead* of 1944 claims that it makes him feel like convict. The war in the North African desert ebbed and flowed and brought victory as well as defeat, but its lessons were not always transmitted home to the new armies under training. It was only with

victory at El Alamein late in 1942 and the invasions of Sicily, Italy and Normandy that the army's prestige began to rise, but there were still problems. The navy was more successful than the Americans in landing troops in Normandy, but the British army soon became bogged down and took a month to take Caen, one of their first-day objectives. After that, the bulk of the land fighting fell to the Americans.

More than any other service, the British army had an image of a class-based, snobbish society headed by upper-class officers but actually run by crafty, domineering sergeants. Regular privates, according to the legend, were brutish unemployables. This was never entirely true and for much of the time it was easier for a man to gain a commission from the ranks in the army than the navy. Moreover, just before the war, the War Office, which headed the army, made strenuous efforts to remedy any defects. Wartime recruits had to serve some time in the ranks before being considered for a commission, efforts were made to find suitable candidates whatever their class or educational background, and selection tests were more advanced and 'democratic' than those of the navy.

On being conscripted into the armed forces, a young man could volunteer for either the navy or the air force. If he did not tick either of these boxes on his application form, he was sent into the army, while many failed to get into the service of their choice and went into the army anyway. A character in *The Way Ahead* is asked by his officer if he thinks he will like the army. 'I wanted to join the navy', he replies. But this does not mean that all army recruits were so discontented. Some deliberately opted for the army because they did not like the idea of going to sea or flying, and RAF ground crews sounded too boring or menial. Others opted for particular regiments, because of family or local

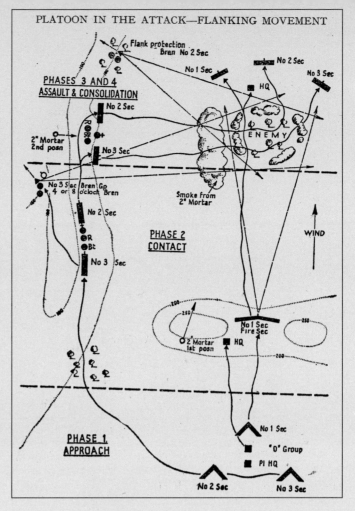

PLATOON IN THE ATTACK—FLANKING MOVEMENT

Left: The standard
method of attack
by an infantry
platoon of about 30
men, as developed
later in the war.

tradition. This was especially strong in country districts and in Scotland, where support for local regiments was, and remains, very intense. The army's regimental tradition was very useful in peacetime, but in war it was double-edged. Some regiments, such as those forming the Brigade of Guards, had a reputation for extreme snobbery. The regimental tradition made it more difficult for different units to co-operate in training, and for men to transfer from one unit or trade to another. Skilled engineers, for example, resented it when they were taken out of their infantry regiments to become far more useful in specialised units such as the Royal Electrical and Mechanical Engineers (REME). The army had a poor record in deploying men with useful civilian qualifications, but began to rectify it later in the war.

The navy had its own force of marines which took over much of the defence of isolated or advanced naval bases such as Scapa Flow, and Suda Bay in Crete. It came in contact with the army mainly as passengers in troopships or landing craft. Troopships carried soldiers and airmen on long voyages and the military class system was at its most intense on their decks, where the officers lived in first class, the sergeants in second class, and the other ranks in the hold. John Colville, Churchill's former private secretary, enlisted in the RAF as an aircraftman second class and was sent to South Africa for training. He complained to Mrs Churchill:

…while the overcrowding on the lower decks was so intense that it was only sometimes possible to lie flat on deck, or avoid bodily contact with others, the officers and nurses had two spacious to decks to themselves. In the evenings, as we stood or sat disconsolately below, we watched dancing on A-deck and listened to music from a string orchestra. The menus of the five-course dinners for the commissioned ranks were handed round the mess-decks while we fed on our unsavoury rations.

Colville admitted to being 'hoist with his own petard' when he returned later as a sergeant-pilot and the conditions were much more even.[29]

Troops were less likely to spend a long time on landing craft, but their use demanded ever-closer co-operation between the services if men were to be landed successfully on a well-defended beach. Soldiers, sailors and airmen trained together as part of the Combined Operations organisation. Naval officers had to be aware that the soldier was in an unfamiliar world on board ship.

He wears heavy 'ammunition boots' and his equipment is heavy and bulky. His equipment makes him liable to lose his balance if a ship lurches. His boots are not made for decks, many of them steel and many of them often wet. Nor do they make it easier for him to climb steep ladders or negotiate high coamings. The bulk of his equipment makes it extremely difficult to negotiate narrow gangways… Add to these difficulties pitch darkness and a desire to avoid all unnecessary noise, and one marvels that the troops manage so well, and appreciates the need of trained sailors to help and act as guides.[30]

The RAF

The very existence of an air force made some co-operation between the services essential, although that was not always fully recognised by the people concerned in the 1930s. The brash young Royal Air Force, founded in 1918, had an aura of modernity in contrast with the old-fashioned technology and class attitudes of the more established

services. The army had tended to see itself as an auxiliary to the navy, except during the European war in 1914–18, but air force officers believed that they could win the next war alone.

Aircraft, whether ship- or shore-based, could operate just as well over the sea as the land, and it was inevitable that they would play a part in sea warfare. By 1939 the main home operational commands of the RAF were Fighter, Bomber and Coastal, and all of these had some role in the naval war. Fighter Command was mainly charged with the aerial defence of the homeland. In 1940 it won its greatest glory in the Battle of Britain, which began with raids on convoys in June and July. The enemy attack then moved on to RAF airfields, later to London. Fighter Command also helped to defend east coast convoys from raiders, a campaign which peaked in the spring of 1941 before most of the German aircraft were sent to the Russian Front.

The navy's relations with Bomber Command were much more difficult. The strategic air offensive against Germany demanded huge resources in men and materials, and this caused diversion of effort from

Below: Cromwell
tanks line up for
an attack near
the River Orme
in Normandy,
July 1944.

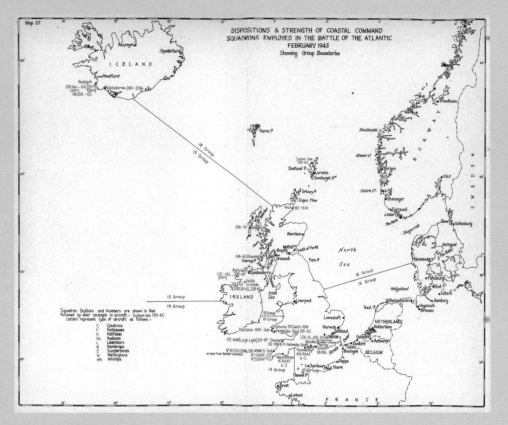

Map 37

DISPOSITIONS & STRENGTH OF COASTAL COMMAND
SQUADRONS EMPLOYED IN THE BATTLE OF THE ATLANTIC
FEBRUARY 1943
Showing Group Boundaries

The distribution of Coastal Command groups and squadrons, February 1943.

Coastal Command and the Battle of the Atlantic. Bomber Command failed to destroy the U-boat pens in the western French ports while they were being built in 1941, and they proved too strong to destroy afterwards. It did, however, carry out much of the offensive mining campaign against Germany, which sank or damaged more than 1300 ships. Its raids on U-boat building yards did irreparable damage towards the end of the war.

The RAF also competed with the navy for the best of the wartime recruits. In peacetime, young men joined one service or another because they loved the idea of the sea, or flying, or military life. In wartime, they had less choice but could opt for one or another in the hope of being accepted. In the aftermath of the Battle of Britain the RAF was far more successful in attracting conscripts than the navy, partly because naval expansion was much slower and there was not space for all the men who applied. At that stage, twice as many men applied for the RAF as the navy. Later in the war the proportions were reversed and far more men applied for the navy.

Coastal Command

Coastal Command of the RAF was set up before the war to operate flying boats, seaplanes and shore-based aircraft around the British coast, partly in co-operation with the navy. At the beginning of the war it patrolled the North Sea and the waters around Britain, but later its most important role was to operate in the former 'air gap' middle of the Atlantic, so its title rather understated its function. From the Fall of France, the story of Coastal Command was one of finding increasingly long-range aircraft to operate further out to sea, of improving navigation, of developing radar and other means of finding the enemy, and of acquiring weapons that could damage or destroy a U-boat or a surface ship.

Coastal Command began the war with less than 300 aircraft, mostly of low performance. It had four highly competent commanders-in-chief in succession during the war: Sir Frederick Bowhill, Sir John Slessor, Sir Phillip Joubert de la Ferte and Sir Sholto Douglas. The headquarters was at Northwood, just west of London. A key figure there was Captain D V Peyton-Ward, naval liaison officer and a submariner from the last war. Coastal Command remained part of the RAF but fell under the operational control of the Admiralty from April 1941. Sir Sholto Douglas

found that this made little difference provided there was goodwill on both sides, and needed very little written instruction from the Admiralty. Coastal Command was divided into groups, each covering a particular area of sea and partly reflecting the home commands of the navy. In 1939 No. 18 Group covered the area of Rosyth, Orkney and Shetland and part of the Nore Command and was based near Rosyth. No. 16 Group covered the rest of the Nore Command plus the Dover, Portsmouth and Portland naval commands. No. 15 Group covered the rest, meeting No. 18 Group in the North Channel between Northern Ireland and Scotland. This was clearly inconvenient in the kind of war that followed, and No. 15 Group took control of all the north-west approaches to Britain, with a northern boundary running from Cape Wrath in the north of Scotland to Iceland and its southern one in the middle of Ireland. It carried out most of the convoy escort patrols, while the new No. 19 Group took charge of south-western waters.

Coastal Command's war began with North Sea patrols mostly directed against German surface ships, but its aircraft proved inadequate. A great deal of time was taken up with anti-invasion patrols in the second half of 1940, but anti-submarine patrols were instituted in the north-western approaches and by the spring of 1941 they had succeeded in forcing the U-boats away from the British coast to the mid-Atlantic. Despite the occupation of Iceland and the use of bases in Newfoundland, there remained an 'air gap' in mid ocean, which the Germans exploited to the full in the first half of 1943. After that, Coastal Command began to benefit from new aircraft and technology. Long-range Liberator bombers helped to close the gap, along with escort carriers operated by the Fleet Air Arm. Radar became increasingly efficient at detecting U-boats in bad weather, and the Leigh Light was a kind of searchlight that was used in the final stages of an attack. The depth charge, usually set to explode at a depth of 50 feet, was the main anti-submarine weapon of Coastal Command and its aircraft became increasingly efficient at using it. Coastal Command sank 192½ U-boats in the course of the war, and shared in 21 more. With the use of Liberators, the medium-range aircraft had less to do and, in co-operation with the navy, they mounted an offensive against U-boats moving to and from their bases in the Bay of Biscay, with mixed results.

The other major role of the command was to mount an offensive against German coastal shipping using torpedo bombers. There was success when a Beaufort of 42 Squadron succeeded in disabling the *Lützow* in June 1941, but in general there were few results because of the poor performance of the aircraft. Re-equipment created much better results after 1942, and aircraft began to use rockets to attack German shipping with some success. In the Mediterranean, torpedo bombers had much impact in cutting Rommel's supply lines to North Africa.

Coastal Command also operated photo-reconnaissance flights, and ran the air-sea rescue service, which used aircraft and fast boats to pick Allied airmen up from the sea. The RAF had been interested in fast craft for some time, largely to service its flying boats. Lawrence of Arabia, using his pseudonym of Aircraftman Ross, played a leading part in the design. There was much transfer of technology with the naval motor torpedo boats and eventually the RAF air-sea rescue services used more than 700 vessels, in nearly 70 bases round the British coast and many more abroad. One common type was the British Power Boat Company's 63-foot launch with a speed of 39 knots powered by two Napier Sea Lion 500 horsepower engines, of which 69 were built.

Left: Coastal Command Beaufighters attack German minesweepers protecting a coastal convoy in the North Sea in August 1944.

Another type was the Thorneycroft 67-foot Whaleback, of which 105 were built. It had a speed of 25–26 knots and was defended against aircraft by two or three machine guns in aircraft-style turrets. Below decks, it had space for casualties in stretchers around midships, where the motion was least, with a cabin for an officer and crew accommodation forward. The RAF also used about 250 Supermarine Walrus amphibians to pick up survivors from the water, and developed airborne lifeboats to be dropped near them from converted bombers.

The Aircraft

At the beginning of the war Coastal Command's main aircraft was the Avro Anson, adapted from a civil airliner in 1934. It was only capable of carrying 360 pounds of bombs, had a speed of 173 miles per hour and its range of 790 miles did not allow it to patrol across the width of the North Sea, so the gap had to be filled by submarines. It was phased out and found a new life as the RAF's most popular utility transport. It was succeeded by the American Lockheed Hudson, which proved far more effective in the North Sea area. Obsolescent bombers, such as the Bristol Blenheim, Handley-Page Hampden and later the Vickers Wellington were often transferred to Coastal Command.

Coastal Command's main long-range aircraft at the beginning of the war was the Short Sunderland, a monoplane developed from a long line of mostly commercial flying boats. It entered service in 1938 but its intended successor, the Saro Lerwick, was a failure and production of the Sunderland had to be resumed. It had a speed of

Below: A cutaway view of a Sunderland flying boat. It gives much detail of the internal accommodation, but almost nothing is seen of the armament.

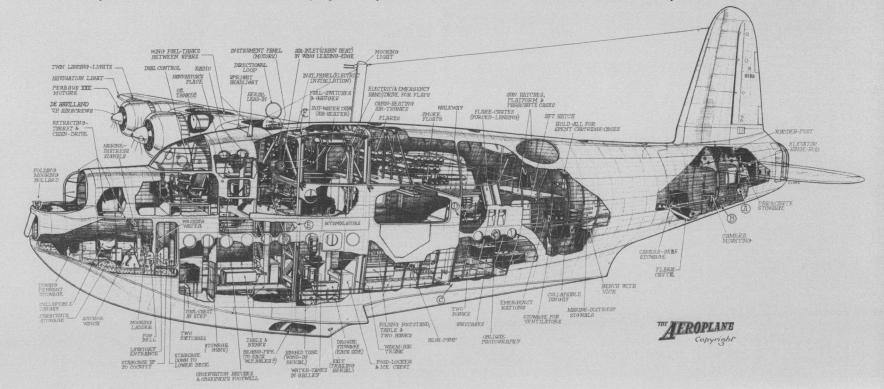

213 miles per hour and, more crucially, a range of nearly 3000 miles, which allowed it to stay in the air for 13.5 hours. It had a crew of 13 to allow watches to be kept on long flights. Its origin as an airliner gave it a deep hull with accommodation on two decks. Above was the flight deck with ample space for pilots, navigators, radio operators and engineers, and storage for some weapons. Below, the anchor compartment was in the bows with a winch and a collapsible dinghy. Aft of that were the sleeping quarters with canvas bunks and a separate galley. The Sunderland was so well armed that it was known to U-boat crews as the 'flying porcupine'. It carried two machine guns in the

The complicated procedure for mooring a Sunderland, often done in bad weather after a long mission.

nose turret and four in the tail turret, plus manually operated beam guns and a bomb or depth charge armament of up to 2000 pounds.

The American equivalent was the Consolidated PBY, known to the British as the Catalina. Developed by the US Navy since it first entered service in 1936, it was an amphibian which could alight on land or sea and was well adapted for naval operations. It had only a single deck compared with two of the Sunderland and a kind of pylon raised the wing and the engines clear of the water. This also housed the flight engineer. Accommodation was more compact than in the Sunderland, but still included rest bunks. Its two large gun cupolas, one on each side, provided excellent places for observation. Cooking facilities were very limited but a crew was able to eat a balanced diet on a long patrol, with four meals including cereal, bacon and sausage, soup, steak and poached or scrambled eggs.[31] Its range was greater than the Sunderland's so it could spend two hours patrolling 800 miles from base, compared with 600 miles for the Sunderland. Not everyone liked it. Alan W Deller found it '… an ugly duckling that was clumsy to handle in the air and on the water, compared with the Sunderland'.[32]

There was still not enough range to close the air gap, and eventually Coastal Command was able to take over some American Liberator bombers after Bomber Command rejected them as unsuitable. They were landplanes unlike the Sunderland and Catalina but had a huge range, which allowed them to patrol for three hours up to 1100 miles from its base. They first entered service with 120 Squadron in Northern Ireland in June 1941, but it was 1943 before enough were available to close the air gap.

RAF torpedo bombers had low performance at the start of the war. The Vickers Vildebeest was a biplane with a top speed of 150 miles per hour, which was in front-line service until 1942. It was replaced by the Bristol Beaufort, which first flew in 1938 and was more than 100 miles per hour faster. Its successor was the Beaufighter from the same company, which was first used as a night fighter in the London blitz, and then as a long-range fighter with Coastal Command. It first entered service as a torpedo bomber with 142 Squadron at North Coates in Lincolnshire in November 1942 and was used with some success.

Air Bases

Long-range aircraft were mostly flying boats in 1939. This was not because they expected to land in mid-ocean, for that was impracticable in any kind of rough weather, but because runways for large aircraft had not yet been built. The main bases before the war had been at such places as Felixstowe in eastern England, and Calshot near Southampton in the south. These were not much use in the Battle of the Atlantic and new bases were set up often in Scottish and northern Irish lakes and lochs to the north and west. The neutrality of Eire was a problem here, but by 1943 there were bases at Castle Archdale on Lough Erne in Northern Ireland, Sullom Voe in Shetland and Oban. Bowmore on Islay was situated in Loch Indaal and had 1½ clear miles of landing area with little tide and good anchoring ground in hard sand. It had no slipway to raise boats out of the water, but had squadron workshops, with a 5-ton crane and refuelling facilities. Six

SUNDERLAND Mooring procedure

Sunderlands of 246 Squadron were based there in April 1943.[33] Further south, Sunderlands continued to operate from Milford Haven in Wales and from a much better-established base at Mount Batten near Plymouth. A large contingent was based in Iceland, with 20 Hudsons, nine Catalinas and 15 Liberators. Maintenance of flying boats afloat had its own difficulties.

No-one who has watched the maintenance crew hanging precariously on small platforms attached to the leading edge of a Sunderland wing, exposed to a biting wind from the north-east, and fumbling with icy fingers in an endeavour to adjust some small mechanical part, can fail to understand why a land plane has a higher efficiency rate.[34]

The Men of Coastal Command

Long-range aircraft needed large crews. A Sunderland carried 13, while the smaller Catalina needed two pilots, an observer or navigator, one flight engineer and a rigger, and three wireless operators. All were trained as air gunners. Torpedo bombers had smaller crews, four in the Beaufort and two in the Beaufighter. They lived a far more intense life carrying out attacks on enemy shipping.

The greatest problem for Coastal Command crews, apart from navigation, was maintaining concentration and morale on long flights over a featureless ocean. The Command had little of the publicity associated with their colleagues in fighters and bombers. According to one wartime commander-in-chief: 'Though the work of the Coastal crews lacked glamour and any public recognition of their most important task, they seemed unaffected. Slogging along over thousands of miles of patrol, with an average chance of seeing one U-boat in 400 hours of flying, their morale remained high'.[35] The authorities did their best to remedy this. A booklet of 1942 described the work of the command in some detail, and the film *Coastal Command* inspired at least one youth.

To be on the flight deck as the captain of aircraft firmly moved forward the four long throttles, to hear the sound of the Pegasus engines and watch the four rpm indicators move up their vertical scales to 2600, and then pan back to the fast receding wake, was the kind of thing calculated to make a 15-year old impatient to do likewise.[36]

The RAF excelled at training both pilots and ground crew, but it had a long-standing problem with non-pilot aircrew. Before the war it planned daylight operations over land and did not recognise the need for specialist navigators. It only began to train 'observers' in 1934 – they had low status as corporals and were reluctantly spared from their ground duties. By the early stages of the war they were usually sergeants or junior officers and were fully responsible for navigation, but Captain Rotherham of the Royal Navy was unimpressed when he joined a raid on Wilhelmshaven in late 1939. He found it was a 'comedy of errors' in which navigation, among other things, was totally neglected. Before the war flying boat navigators were trained pilots who learned navigation as part of a long apprenticeship and had to work hard during a flight, for example, across the Mediterranean.

During the seven hours of the flight [the navigator] was never still. At one moment he would be in the forward gunner's position taking a drift with his bomb sight. At the next he was aft, throwing out a sea marker on which to take a tail drift with his hand compass, then to his chart table, where he would make his calculations.[37ix]

The crew of a Coastal Command Flying Fortress of 220 Squadron based on the Hebridean island of Benbecula in May 1943.

Such apprenticeship was not available in wartime and other means of training eventually had to be found. Heavy losses meant that Bomber Command had to switch to night operations, for which it was totally unprepared – a survey of 1941 showed that only a third of bombs dropped by night fell within 5 miles of their aiming point. The problem was at least as great with Coastal Command, for aircraft had to find convoys or U-boats in the middle of an ocean, or accurately report sightings. The status and training of the observer improved slowly, and in 1942 the category of 'navigator' was introduced, with the letter 'N' on his single-winged flying badge. Though he was often an officer, his status was well below that of a pilot and few were promoted beyond flight lieutenant, the equivalent of a naval lieutenant. Meanwhile other non-aircrew categories, such as air gunner, flight engineer and radio operator became more established. By 1940, all flying personnel had the rank of sergeant at least, equivalent to a naval petty officer, and were accommodated in separate messes from the rank and file on air stations.

PART IV
The Ships

1 Ship Design

Practically all the large ships of the navy were designed within the organisation, although in wartime some medium-sized classes, such as corvettes and frigates, were designed by private enterprise under naval control. Smaller vessels such as motor torpedo boats and landing craft often came from outside the navy. In wartime many ships, ranging from liners to fishing boats and yachts, were taken up from private owners. A few ships came from allies that dropped out of the conflict; many others, both old and new, came from America.

The navy's ship design was much criticised before and during the Second World War, and it is true that it never produced a classic design, except perhaps the light fleet aircraft carriers which only appeared at the end of the war. But there was no clear failure, except perhaps in the early stages of the Hunt class destroyer escorts. Any mediocrity was largely due to the constraints placed on the designers, for Britain took the naval treaties very seriously, and at the same time tried to keep up a world-class fleet on a limited budget. The poor gun power of the latest battleships, the confusion in frigate design, the weakness of anti-aircraft armament and the pre-war failure to develop anti-submarine warfare, landing craft and coastal forces, can all be attributed to policies imposed from outside the designers' control.

Every ship design is a series of compromises, between speed, sea-keeping, armament, accommodation, fighting power, range, cost in financial and real terms, and many other factors. The job of the ship designer was to reconcile these in the best way possible, according to standards set by his customer, the navy.

The Controller and the DNC

The navy's ship design fell under the responsibility of the Third Sea Lord and Controller of the Navy, who was in charge of 'material for the fleet, including ships and their machinery'.[1] Just before the war the post was held by Admiral Sir Reginald Henderson, a very experienced aircraft carrier officer who contributed much to design policy before his untimely retirement and death. His successor was Sir Bruce Fraser, later a great admiral in his own right, who had served as a gunnery officer and as director of naval ordnance. He was succeeded by Sir Frederick Wake-Walker in 1942.

Under the Controller was the Director of Naval Construction (DNC), '…the principal technical adviser to the Board of Admiralty, and the final authority on the design of warships and other vessels… Directly responsible to the Controller for all matters of design, stability, strength of construction, weight built into the hulls of ships, armour, boats, masting and all other nautical apparatus for all ships'.[2] Most of the ships in service at the beginning of the war had been designed under the authority of Sir Arthur Johns, who had begun his working life in

Devonport Dockyard. He had worked on Captain Scott's *Discovery* and designed submarines in the First World War. On becoming DNC in 1930 he did much to advance aircraft carrier design.

In 1936 he was succeeded by Stanley Goodall, who was unusual in that he had begun his career as a naval engineering officer. He kept long hours during the war, but avoided the overwork that damaged the health of many of his colleagues. He kept a diary and at the end of every year he summarised his feelings. The year 1937 was a 'thick year', 1938 was even worse, 1939 was 'most distressing' with the death of Henderson and Sir Roger Backhouse, 1940 was 'very trying'. The year 1941 started well with the success of many new ships such as the *Illustrious* class carriers and the L class destroyers. The loss of the *Hood* was 'not unexpected' but Goodall faced unfair criticism over the loss of the *Prince of Wales*, which continued into the following year. Although 1943 was far better, Goodall handed over the directorship to Sir Charles Lillicrap in 1944, continuing as assistant controller and elder statesman. One member of a succeeding generation of naval constructors regarded him as 'probably the most outstanding warship designer of all time'.[3] He designed ships to difficult specifications for a much wider range of functions than ever before, and coped with the demands of a prime minister who had little idea of the boundaries of his authority or competence.

Opposite: Men and women work side by side in the drawing office of a Tyneside shipyard in 1943. A photograph by Cecil Beaton.

Left: Sir Stanley Goodall in 1938.

The Empire Hotel in Bath, used as the administrative headquarters for the Naval Construction Staff during the war.

The Naval Constructors

Ship design was the task of the Royal Corps of Naval Constructors (RCNC), founded in 1883. It had 141 members on the eve of war. Constructors were recruited by examination from apprentices in the royal dockyards. They did a three-year course in naval architecture in the Royal Naval College at Greenwich, described as 'very severe and exacting' but 'not beyond the capacity of a man of sufficient intellectual calibre who is properly prepared for it and is prepared to work hard!'.[4] Those who passed the examination went through the ranks, starting with a year with the fleet as Constructor Lieutenant. They would reach the civil rank of Constructor at the age of about 30 and, if successful, they would be promoted to Chief Constructor about 10 years later. Only about a third of the corps was involved in ship design at any given moment; the others were in the dockyards, at sea or overseeing ships under construction. Critics felt that the system produced men who were too narrow in their outlook, and perhaps it is not a coincidence that Goodall reached the top by a different route.

The ship designers worked in the Admiralty in Whitehall in the 1930s. Each team designing a particular class was headed by a constructor in the centre of the room, called 'sir' in accordance with the custom of the time. Junior constructors carried out the numerous calculations of weight, resistance, stability and so on. They filled hundreds of pages of workbooks, which were kept permanently as a record, and they were not allowed to delete any mistakes. At the outbreak of war the department was evacuated to Bath, to find accommodation in the Pump Room Hotel and other grand establishments. Elderly residents were evicted from the hotels and even bathrooms were converted into drawing offices. But Bath was not safe from bombing; much sleep was lost in air raids and in April 1942 the Pump Room Hotel was damaged. The DNC moved back to London to be closer to the centre of affairs and his staff began to move to huts just outside Bath. By the end of the war the corps had 305 members, including 101 employed on ship design. Of the 305, 172 were permanent, while others included naval architects drafted in from private shipyards, and 11 Lloyds surveyors. Fifty-eight were in uniform with silver-grey cloth between the rank stripes of an officer.[5] There was a Constructor-Captain, equivalent to a Chief Constructor, with each of the main fleets.

The Design Process

The design of a new class of ship began with the naval staff in the Admiralty, who represented the users. Under the leadership of the Director of Training and Staff Duties, various divisions such as the gunnery, torpedo and engineering branches of the staff would be asked about the requirements for a new class of ship. These, the 'sketch requirements', went to the DNC who quickly commented on their practicability. After that the naval staff would draw the 'draft staff requirements', from which the DNC would prepare a more detailed study. These were circulated among up to a dozen divisions of the naval staff and then became the staff requirements after approval by the Board of Admiralty. They would describe the function of the class, its speed and endurance, armament and armour protection, manoeuvrability, radar and Asdic, signalling equipment, habitability and any other specialised needs. Using these parameters, the DNC's department set about designing a ship in the smallest detail.

Naval architects rarely start with a clean sheet of paper when designing a new class of ship, except perhaps in the case of landing craft in the Second World War. Normally the new design is solidly based on an old one. It might be a straightforward improvement, as when the aircraft carriers of the *Illustrious* class were followed by the *Indomitable* with better aircraft accommodation. It might combine several different trends of recent years. For example, wartime destroyers of the Emergency Programmes were intermediate in size between the I and J classes, with the armament of the former. It might be a reaction against the weakness of a previous type, for example with the River class frigates which were planned to be very different from the Flower class corvettes, but which also used many features of the sloops that had preceded them.

The dimensions of a class of ship were laid down in some detail in a four-page form known as the Legend of Particulars. They were often constrained by external factors. Large ships were sometimes planned with the width and length of the naval dry docks in mind. The River class frigates and the Castle class corvettes were designed to specific lengths, to fit the slipways of merchant shipbuilding yards.

By this stage the designer knew the number of decks of the ship, its general arrangement of guns, engines, accommodation and many other features. He was prepared to start on the detailed work. Naval architects knew that a long narrow hull was not necessarily the way to greater speed, as it had a greater wetted area for a given volume and this merely created skin friction and drag.

The midship section represented the widest part of the ship and was one of the first areas to be designed. A rounded or V-shaped bottom would not necessarily add to speed, and tended to produce greater draft for a given area. A completely square bottom would make streamlining difficult, but provided the corners, or bilges were rounded, it had little effect. Larger ships often had a completely flat bottom, smaller ones such as destroyers had a slight rounding or rise of the floor so that the bilges were slightly above the level of the keel. The area of the midship section compared with a rectangle was known as the midship coefficient. In a battleship it might be 90 per cent; in a destroyer it was rather less.

The shape of the bows was clearly important in how the ship moved through the water. The ram bow had been abandoned since the First World War, though frigates still had their bows strengthened for ramming submarines. The stem, the foremost part of the bow, was straight or almost so on most modern British warships. It was angled slightly from the vertical, ranging from 10 degrees on the *King George V* class to 20 degrees on Tribal class destroyers. Many aircraft carriers had a curved bow above the waterline, to bring the shape up to the forward part of the flight deck. A very fine entry at the bow would reduce wave-making and hence resistance, but it was useless as accommodation or storage space. The stern was a more complex shape as it had to accommodate both the propellers and rudder underwater, and the shape had to allow water to reach them without interference. Several different forms were available, including the cruiser stern, which sloped gently forward above the waterline, and the flat or transom stern, which became popular by the end of the war.

The designer drew the shape of the hull between the midship section and the bows or stern. The sides might be parallel for part of the hull, so that the midship section was simply continued forward or aft – this was quite common on destroyers. The fineness or otherwise of a design was measured by the prismatic coefficient. The shape of the midship section was projected forward and aft to the level of the bow and stern, and the volume occupied by the planned ship was compared with this shape, giving a good indication of the fineness or otherwise of the lines. The total area of each section was reduced using a formula based on the square root of the length and that was used to calculate the shape of the hull at various horizontal lines, or waterlines, at various levels. The designer's job was to make the lines of the hull as streamlined or 'fair' as possible. He also had to eliminate any irregularities round features such as rudders and propeller shafts, which might create eddies and hence resistance.

As soon as the lines plan was reasonably complete, a model was made in wax to test by towing through the tank in the Admiralty Experiment Works at Haslar near Portsmouth. The superintendent there, R W L Gawn, was one of the leading figures in naval architecture and commented on many designs. One feature to watch for was a sudden rise in resistance at a certain point as the speed increased. A clever design would minimise this and Gawn commented of the River class: 'We found this model so satisfactory with a negligible change of resistance constant over a wide speed range that we used it as a standard model for correcting results for a number of years'.[6]

During the age of the naval treaties between the wars, British naval constructors and their masters were obsessed with keeping within the weight limits, and all sorts of devices were used to keep weight down. This was less crucial in wartime, but the weight of each item in the structure and on board had to be calculated carefully. Too much weight and the ship would sink too deep in the water, although there was some room for manoeuvre here and most wartime ships ended up carrying far more gear than they had been designed for. Weight in the wrong place would make the ship unstable, or cause her to be in poor trim, which would reduce her speed or manoeuvrability. The weights of different

elements in a ship were also calculated. For a *Fiji* class cruiser of 10,354 tons (full load), for example, the biggest single item was the hull at 3819 tons or 37 per cent. Fuel was next at 1700 tons, machinery at 1413 tons, armour protection at 1289 tons and armament at 1188 tons. Aircraft and other equipment took up a relatively small amount of weight.[7]

Seaworthiness and Stability

A ship at sea is subject to six different motions, caused by the sea and, to a lesser extent, by the wind. Surging is variation in the forward motion, sway is displacement from side to side and heave is the up and down motion. The three other motions all involve rotation about the ship's axes: roll as the upper part of the hull moves from side to side, pitch as the bow is raised and lowered when heading into waves, and yawing as the steering is affected by outside forces. Pitching was felt most in the bows of the ship. Rolling was often what disturbed crews most, for example in the Flower class corvettes, which were too small for the North Atlantic where they did most of their service. It could cause extreme exhaustion, but what caused most seasickness was heave, the up and down motion, though that was not always appreciated at the time.

Using the weights he had calculated, the constructor was able to

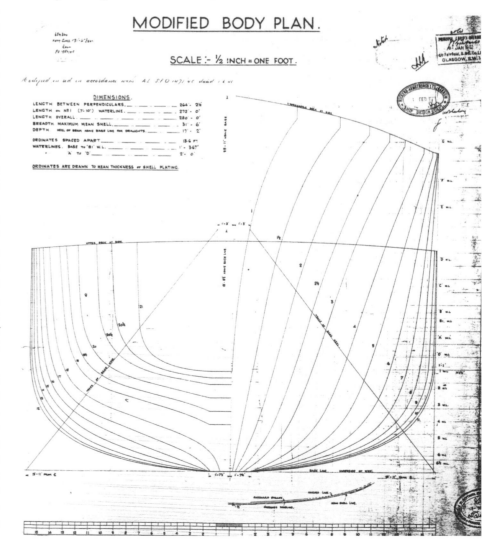

The lines of the Hunt class destroyer escorts, which had to be modified due to an error in the calculations. The drawing shows a series of cross sections of the hull, with those on the widest area at midships on the outside. Sections forward of that are shown on the right, those aft on the left, and the numbers correspond with the frames of the hull.

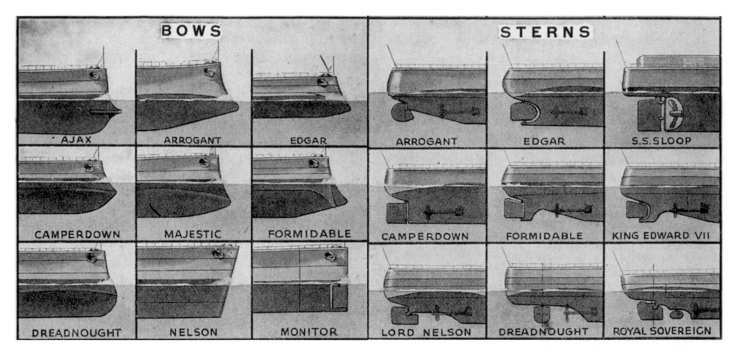

BOWS			STERNS		
AJAX	ARROGANT	EDGAR	ARROGANT	EDGAR	S.S.SLOOP
CAMPERDOWN	MAJESTIC	FORMIDABLE	CAMPERDOWN	FORMIDABLE	KING EDWARD VII
DREADNOUGHT	NELSON	MONITOR	LORD NELSON	DREADNOUGHT	ROYAL SOVEREIGN

Above: The bows and sterns of different types of ships. Ram bows were no longer being fitted by the 1920s, but some ships in service still had them. The sterns do not include the flat or 'transom' stern, which became popular by the end of the war.

Opposite: Fitting the wax model to a special rig inside the test tank in the National Physical Laboratory at Teddington in Middlesex.

find the centre of gravity of the ship. He was also able to find the centre of buoyancy from this lines plan. This would be directly above the centre of gravity if the ship was upright, but would move gradually away from it as the ship heeled over due to wind or waves. This created a motion that would tend to right the ship, unless it went too far and caused a capsize. The distance between the centres of gravity and buoyancy was the metacentric height. If it was too great, the ship would be in danger of capsizing. If it was too small, the ship would be too 'stiff' and would overreact, causing a fast and jerky motion. The Captain class frigates suffered from this problem and needed extra topweight to raise the centre of gravity.

No ship is ever perfectly stable in all conditions, and excessive motion causes low morale and exhaustion, seasickness, poor aiming and structural damage. Naval architects could take some steps to improve the position, though always at a price. The effects of pitching could be reduced by flaring out the bows as in the River class frigates, or just the lower part to create a 'knuckle' as in nearly all British cruisers. It was also less likely to happen with a longer hull, and the River class, 50 per cent longer than the Flowers, was quite successful in this respect. A broader hull could reduce rolling, but a much simpler solution was to fit bilge keels. These were fin-like structures which were fitted along the bilge for about half the length of the ship. They were belatedly fitted to the Flower class after they had been tested in the Atlantic, and did much to reduce their problems. Another solution was to fit Denny-Brown stabilisers, which used an arrangement of fins and gyroscopes. These were tried on Hunt class escort destroyers, but were not fully developed until after the war.

Stability was a rather different problem from seaworthiness. The Flower class corvettes were perfectly seaworthy in that they were not likely to be fatally damaged in rough seas. They endured the worst weather of the Battle of the Atlantic, and none was sunk from the action of the sea alone. But this was small comfort to their crews, especially in the early stages of the war, for they had to endure appalling rolling which caused seasickness and exhaustion.

Design to Building

As the design progressed, more and more passed to the draughtsmen who would settle many of the details according to standard rules, and draw plans that could be sent to the shipyards. Naval draughtsmen, like constructors, had trained in the royal dockyards but their status was rather lower. In wartime they were supplemented by draughtsmen in

the civilian shipyards. In the major programmes for corvettes and frigates, most of the design work was farmed out to private shipyards and then approved by Lloyds of London before being sent back to the Admiralty. Under the supervision of the constructors the draughtsmen would settle the details of construction. A shell-plating diagram would give the size and shape of each plate, while the individual members of the frame would be drawn out. The engine room was planned in some detail, including the supports for the engines and boilers and the complicated piping. Each compartment was drawn in detail with its fittings and furniture, while wiring and piping diagrams were needed for the whole ship. A set of several hundred plans was sent to each of the shipyards building the new class.

Even then the work of the naval constructor was not ended, for members of the corps were based in the yards as naval overseers to supervise the building. The completed ship was then tested on a measured mile, often the one off Arran in Scotland that offered deep water. Lessons might be learned about how the design worked out in practice.

Coastal Forces

Conventional naval architecture did not work so well on the smaller and newer types in the wartime navy. Most small landing craft abandoned any attempt at producing a streamlined hull, though stability was quite important in view of the heavy weights some of them had to carry. The fast craft used by Coastal Forces were different in another way. Larger warships had displacement hulls in which the amount of hull in the water was reasonably constant for a given load. Coastal forces largely used planing hulls, designed to lift much of the vessel out of the water at high speeds.

It would only work on small vessels of light displacement. It had angular bilges of 'hard chine' as it was called, which made it very inefficient at low speeds. It had to be short in proportion to its breadth, which also made it perform poorly at low speeds. The basic principle was that at high speed the shape of the hull would cause much of the vessel to be raised out of the water. It usually had a V-shaped bottom under the chines. This did not aid speed and a flat bottom would have done just as well. The V-bottom gave some directional stability, and it allowed the hull to settle back in the water as speed was reduced with less 'slamming'. Much of the early design of such craft was left to private contractors such as Fairmile, Vosper and the British Power Boat Company, but the whole process was supervised by W J Holt of the RCNC.

2 Shipbuilding

The Shipbuilders

British shipbuilding had suffered heavily in the great depression, perhaps more than any other industry. After a peak of more than 2 million tons of merchant shipping in 1920, it launched only 133,000 tons in 1933.[8] Unemployment in the industry reached 60 per cent in 1932, compared with a national average of 23 per cent. Industrial relations were notably bad, with the famous 'demarcation' strikes between unions and a multiplicity of trades doing various jobs – one authority wrote of 'the troubles that arise because of the rigid limits as to work which are laid down by a number of rival trade unions'.[9] The management, several generations on from the engineers and entrepreneurs who had founded the great companies, displayed a strange blend of complacency and fear – they were complacent that the skills of British shipbuilding could never be replicated anywhere else, but fearful that another depression would destroy them altogether. As a result, investment in capital equipment and in the training of labour was very sparse in these years. The largest shipyards were concentrated on the Clyde, the rivers of north-east England such as the Tyne and Tees, and the Mersey. Labour and land costs had driven the industry from the Thames, but yards could be found in small southern ports such as Cowes and Dartmouth. The Clyde did not have a monopoly of Scottish shipbuilding, which was carried out in Leith, Dundee and Aberdeen on the east coast.

The government had several main sources for its warships. The royal dockyards were the most obvious, but in fact their main function was repair rather than building. The three main yards, Chatham, Portsmouth and Devonport, did build some ships in peacetime, largely to keep the labour force together and stay in touch with the latest techniques, but in wartime they mostly went over to repair. The main

exception was Chatham, which built eight submarines during the war but only completed one cruiser. Devonport built the carrier *Terrible*, the only one built in a royal dockyard.

Most naval ships were built by private industry. During the peace the number of experienced warship builders had declined from about 20 to 14, with the loss of famous names such as Palmers of Jarrow and Beardmore of Dalmuir. Of the remaining yards, some, such as John Brown and Fairfield on the Clyde, Hawthorn Leslie and Vickers-Armstrong on the Tyne and Cammell Laird on the Mersey, built the largest vessels – battleships and fleet aircraft carriers. Intermediate yards, such as Scott of Greenock and Alexander Stephen of Glasgow, built cruisers, and a group of yards, Denny of Dumbarton, Yarrow of Glasgow, Samuel White of Cowes and Thornycroft of Southampton, specialised in destroyers and sloops. Three yards, Scotts, Cammell Laird and Vickers-Armstrong of Barrow-in-Furness, built submarines. The largest yards often built small warships as well as large ones and nearly every yard had a non-naval market. John Brown's built great liners such as the *Queen Mary*, Denny built cross-channel ferries, White of Cowes built motor and sailing yachts. Most of the warship yards carried on some merchant shipbuilding during the war, alongside their naval work, and Denny built 17 merchant ships.

Naval shipbuilding required different techniques and equipment from merchant shipbuilding. Work with armour plate was a problem for some, although it was not needed for those who specialised in destroyers. Warships were generally far more complex, with a good deal of internal subdivision. The navy used a large amount of D-grade steel for lightness, rather than the cheaper and more pliable mild steel used in merchant ships.

There was no time to set up new shipyards as happened in the United States in wartime, as Britain had far fewer suitable sites and they would have needed considerable land reclamation or movement of labour. A few old ones were re-opened, such as the Low Walker yard on Tyneside, but in general it was shortage of labour rather than land that constrained British shipbuilding. However, there were many other established and recently under-employed yards which built merchant ships. Rather than convert them to the skills of warship production, the Admiralty confined the building of capital ships, cruisers, destroyers, submarines and sloops to its usual yards. Other types of warship, such as the Flower class corvettes and the River class frigates, were designed to merchant ship standards, so that they could be built elsewhere. This opened up a large number of shipyards for warship production, led by Smith's Dock of Middlesborough, who initiated the Flower and River programmes.

Even the numbers of established merchant shipbuilders were not enough to meet wartime needs, and other companies outside the industry were deployed. Power-boat builders like Vosper and Fairmile dominated the coastal craft programme, and were helped by non-maritime companies such as furniture manufacturers who were skilled in woodworking. When pre-fabrication was introduced with the Loch class frigates in 1942, much of the work in constructing sections was handed out to inland steelworks such as bridge builders, although the highly skilled work of the final assembly was done in established shipyards.

Finally, the Royal Navy turned to the United States for many of its ships. Its early experience with the Town class of old destroyers was not

The Denny shipyard in Dumbarton in 1932. It built many destroyers for the navy, as well as sloops and merchant ships.

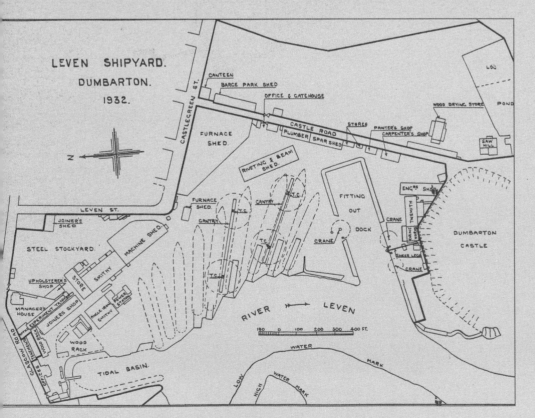

LEVEN SHIPYARD.
DUMBARTON.
1932.

entirely happy, but more recent designs such as the Captain class frigates and the *Attacker* and *Ameer* class escort carriers proved highly successful. American shipbuilders were far more advanced in prefabrication and welding and they could produce ships very quickly, though at a cost in both money and labour.

A Typical Shipyard

Most British shipyards had been laid out late in the nineteenth century when smaller ships were common. They usually had housing and other facilities built round them, so expansion was not easy. A report of 1942 stated that 'Most of the old yards on the North East Coast and Scotland

Shipyard workers, from the wartime publication *Build the Ship*.

FOREMAN

SHIPWRIGHTS

WELDER

CRANE-BOY

RIVETER

HEATER-BOY

LOFTSMAN

PAINTER

SHEET-METAL WORKER

are limited in size and cannot easily expand their boundaries. On the Tyne and Wear in particular the yards are generally limited by high ground a short distance from the river'.[10] One reasonably modern yard was Richard Dunston of Hull, which had been remodelled in the 1930s, but it was one of the smaller ones, specialising in tugs. Most yards were on narrow rivers, which also restricted the size of ships they could build. Clyde yards mostly launched diagonally into the river; a few, such as Pollocks of Faversham in Kent, launched sideways.

Alexander Stephen's yard at Linthouse, Glasgow, was on a 46-acre site first acquired in 1870. It was in two parts with river frontages of 1140 feet and 375 feet. The general offices represented the prestige of the firm and were 'designed to ensure ample light for all administrative and executive departments'. They also contained the drawing office and were decorated with models of ships the firm had built. There were separate workers entrances to the yard for the different trades, and plumbers', sheet-iron, tinsmiths and paint shops on the eastern side of the yard. The smithy was close by, along with a finishing shop for the making of furnishings. The steelworkers' shed ran parallel to the River Clyde, and contained a set of heavy rollers for bending plates up to 35 feet in length, an electric planing machine, a flanging machine and four punching machines. Behind this was an area for storing steel plates in the open, after they had been brought in by railway and tramlines along the Renfrew Road. The joiners' shop was at the western end of this range, with the mould loft on the second floor. There was a saw mill, and the yard used hydraulic pumps, air compressors and a boiler to power the machinery. In the centre of the yard was the series of six

building slips, laid out in 1927, fitted with electric cranes 120 feet high with an outreach of 70 feet and a working load of 6 tons. Most shipyards had rectangular basins where they fitted out their ships afloat, but Stephen's used the Clyde Trust Wharf at Shieldhall, and the famous 130-ton Princes Dock crane. However, the yard did have its own engine shed, with four bays over 400 feet long and served by electric cranes.[11]

The Labour Force

A shipyard was a noisy and dangerous environment, and workers on the ship itself were out in the open in all weathers. 'There are great and sudden clangs, an intoned mutter runs between the greater noises, and there are bell-like, gong-like crashes which astound the ear and mind'.[12] The usual discomforts of shipyard work were increased in wartime by air raids and precautions against them. At Smith's dock:

During the war we worked very long hours and it was hellish black down there. The sheds, even when the sun was shining, were dark and dingy. They had a coat of tar over them, there was no elaborate black-out curtains, it was just a rough tar over the glass sheets on the roof. All the doorways had great big sailcloth curtains across.[13]

In partial compensation, the workers had unusual pride in their trades and a unique satisfaction in seeing a ship take shape, and perhaps reading about a successful warship in the newspapers afterwards.

In the royal dockyards the shipwrights did most of the metalwork on the hull. In private yards the shipwrights were responsible for setting up the hull accurately while the actual fabrication was done by men of several different trades. These included blacksmiths who bent the frames, platers who shaped the plates and drilled them for rivets, and riveters who worked in 'black squads' each consisting of a riveter, a 'holder-up', a heater and a boy. The men of the finishing trades worked mainly in fitting out the ships, and unlike those who worked on the hull they could find jobs outside the industry. The war created little new demand for joiners and carpenters to equip cabins, but much work for electricians to fit out ever more sophisticated warships. This proved to be a serious bottleneck in the great frigate building programme of 1942–4. Fitting-out basins were taken over in the former Beardmore yard on the Clyde and at Hendon Dock in Sunderland. Ships were towed there so that the electricians could work to maximum efficiency.

The shipbuilding industry rebuilt its labour force as soon as the war started. Shipyard workers were made exempt from conscription, unemployed or retired workers were brought back, and skilled labour was 'diluted' as in the last war, by breaking jobs into smaller units or by using hastily-trained men who had not served a regular apprenticeship. American publicity made much of 'Rosie the Riveter' as the symbol of female participation in the war effort, but women made slow progress in British shipyards during the war. It was late 1941 before any serious attempt was made to recruit them on Tyneside, and employers conceded reluctantly that 'only as a last resort and in the event of it being found quite impossible to get male labour' would women be employed in large numbers.[14] From 140,000 employees just before the war, the industry expanded to a peak of 272,000 in September 1943. The number of women peaked slightly later, at 27,000, or about 10 per cent.[15]

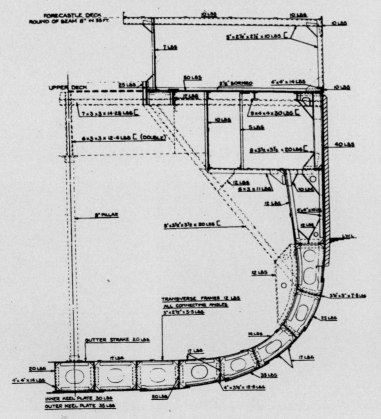

MIDSHIP SECTION – CRUISER

The cross section of a cruiser, showing the thickness of the different frames and plates, with armour on the outside.

Workers bending red-hot frames on the bending slab in a Tyneside shipyard in 1943. A photograph by Cecil Beaton.

Building Techniques

Warships used D-quality steel in key parts to save weight, a practice which had been encouraged while the limitation treaties were in force. Merchant ships, and those such as frigates and corvettes built to merchant ship standards, used mild steel which was much easier to work. Steel was brought into the shipyard mostly by rail and 'pickled' in a weak solution of hydrochloric acid to remove mill scale. Its grade was measured by the weight of a square foot. For example, a typical cruiser of the 1930s used 40-pound steel, which was an inch thick.

A ship was built on a building slip situated so that the finished product could be launched into the river. The ship was erected on blocks and was angled slightly to allow it to slide down the ways on completion. The keel was the backbone of the ship. Sometimes it was two vertical keels connected together, a box keel. In smaller ships it was a single series of vertical pieces of steel joined together. The bow of a warship was usually quite simple in this period, and the stempost which continued the keel upwards was normally straight or slightly curved. The stern was more difficult and often needed a complex casting to form the outline of its shape.

In the traditional transverse framing system, the frames that gave the hull its shape were attached along the length of the keel. They were made of U- or Z-section steel in warships, and bent to shape against pins placed in holes on the yard's bending slab. They might also require some bevelling, or angling of the bars. Frames were placed 6 feet apart in cruisers and 1 foot 9 inches to 2 feet 6 inches in destroyers. The engine bearers in the centre of the ship were thick plates and the shipwrights had to take particular care in lining up the propeller shafts, for a ship might never perform properly if it was done wrong. The *Nith*, a frigate launched at Leith in 1942, never did perform properly because of poor alignment.

In an alternative system, the main strength of the frames might be placed along the length of the hull rather than across it. When this was proposed for the J and K class destroyers just before the war, the conservative Clyde shipbuilders led a delegation to the Admiralty to warn against it. But it was highly effective in a long narrow vessel such as a destroyer and became standard.[16]

The plates which would form the skin of the hull were cut to shape and bent by special rollers. If riveting was used, they had to be punched very accurately so that the holes would line up with those on the frames. They would overlap on the finished ship, and various systems of 'joggling' were used to give a smooth outside hull. The hull was also plated internally in its lower part to create a double bottom for strength, safety and fuel storage.

Strong bulkheads were placed at regular intervals and were an important part of the structure. They gave strength to the structure and served to subdivide the hull in the event of damage. They had watertight doors and hatches to be closed when danger threatened. The decks were also part of this structure, helping keep water or oil out when necessary and bracing the sides against water pressure.

Riveting and Welding

Since the advent of iron and steel ships in the nineteenth century, riveting had been the standard method of fixing the parts together. Several types of rivet were used, including countersunk, pan head, straight neck and so on, according to how smooth the surface had to be, the strength needed and the appearance. Joints formed by riveting were not always completely watertight and had to be 'caulked' by splitting one edge of the pieces to be joined and driving it against the adjacent piece.

Welding was done by placing two adjacent parts of the structure alongside one another with a triangular groove in the join between them. A metal rod was melted by an electric arc and a join was formed as the metal solidified. Welding had many advantages. Plates could fixed at right angles to frames, reducing the need for the Z-section. They could be laid end to end without overlap, saving weight and creating a much smoother and more watertight surface than riveting. Once it had been learned, welding was much quicker and cheaper than riveting and needed less skill. It also allowed greater flexibility in construction, and made it possible to adopt prefabrication later in the war.

British shipbuilders had used welding on a small scale since the early 1920s either in less important parts of large ships, or in small ones. Denny of Dumbarton built the all-welded *Robert the Bruce* for the River Forth ferry service in 1934, for example. But shipbuilders believed that the weld, though strong in itself, might weaken the steel around it. They had experience of poorly-executed joints and were concerned about safety. They hesitated to invest in the equipment needed, and feared the

The frame of a ship erected on the building slip.

unions which might resist change. Also, D-quality steel, as used for British warships, was difficult to weld. American yards, starting with an almost clean sheet, were far more enthusiastic about welding and used it extensively, notably in the famous Liberty ship programme. British yards also began to adopt it during the war for thousands of landing craft and for a programme of 200 frigates, which began in 1942 and was to produce the Loch and Bay classes.

Prefabrication

The 1942 frigate programme was also the first British one to apply prefabrication on a large scale to ocean-going ships. Numerous sub-assemblies were made in different places, often by engineering and bridge-building firms with no experience of shipbuilding. The whole programme had to be very carefully planned, with a central drawing office in Glasgow. Contracts were placed for individual sections, none larger than 29 feet long, 8 feet 6 inches wide and 8 feet 6 inches high, to fit on road and rail transportation, or more than 2½ tons in weight to suit shipyard cranes. John Brown of Clydebank built the prototype *Loch Fada*, amidst their usual work in battleships and cruisers.

Other methods were used for some of the smaller craft, which were not built by conventional shipbuilders. Coastal forces craft were mostly constructed in plywood by yacht builders and landing craft by boat builders and others. More traditional wooden methods were used for motor minesweepers. Barges were built in concrete, and experiments were made with glass reinforced plastic, a material which could be moulded and was immune to the effects of the magnetic mine.

Launching

Since Queen Victoria's time it had been traditional for a ship to be launched by a woman breaking a bottle over its bows. Large ships were often launched by the highest in the land – in 1938 the cruiser *Belfast* was launched by Mrs Neville Chamberlain, and Clementine Churchill launched several. Queen Elizabeth launched the carrier *Implacable* in Glasgow in 1944. A launch is always a tense time for the shipbuilders, but the *Implacable* posed special problems for the naval overseer, Vic Hall. The ship had had her engines fitted before launch which made her unusually heavy, and the river was narrow, so she had to be turned through 75 degrees as soon as she entered the water.

I spent a sleepless night watching the ship and had the Shipyard Manager and Directors for company, all of us pretending we weren't nervous and anxious. Next day the Good Lord gave us an extra 1 ft 6 ins of tide – such a thing had never happened before on the Clyde – and the launch was a great success both technically and socially.[17]

The launch of a ship was less of an event in wartime when small warships were turned out by the hundred, and slightly humbler ladies were employed. The wives of local grandees, shipyard directors or naval officers might do the job. HMS *Trent* was launched at Bristol by Mrs Hodges, wife of a 'holder-upper' or riveter's assistant, chosen by a ballot of the workforce.[18] After that, the ship was towed to the local fitting out basin for completion.

Repair and Refits

Ship repair was obviously a very important concern in wartime, as both warships and merchantmen suffered from shells, bombs, mines and torpedoes as well as the usual hazards of the sea. It was made more difficult by the general shortage of dry docks, although many general shipyards did some repair. There were some well-publicised triumphs of reconstruction. Lord Mountbatten's destroyer *Javelin* was badly damaged after two torpedo hits and his *Kelly* almost capsized after another torpedo hit, but both were repaired and put back into service. The cruiser *Belfast* was almost rebuilt over more than two years, and emerged a very different ship from her sister *Edinburgh*. The resources of the royal dockyards were not adequate. Admiralty floating docks were moored in the Clyde, Oban and Fort William

and used naval ratings instead of dockyard workers. In addition, more than 52,000 repairs of warships were carried out in private shipyards. Denny of Dumbarton repaired over 50 ships and 35 landing craft, for example.[19]

Warships needed constant updating, or 'refits' as the navy called them. A certain amount of radar and other equipment could be fitted between voyages, but larger refits for big ships were mainly done in the royal dockyards. The *King George V* class, for example, had their aircraft catapults taken off from 1943, and the boats were moved down into the space, leaving the boat decks free for extra anti-aircraft guns, which soon proved essential in the Pacific. On a smaller scale, many of the V and W destroyers of First World War vintage were converted to long-range or anti-aircraft escorts, necessitating several months in dockyard hands.

Torpedo damage to the stern of the catapult ship *Ariguana*. She reached port to be put in dry dock.

3 Engines

The Royal Navy had almost completely abandoned sail by the early twentieth century. Many other navies used sailing ships as part of officer training, but Admiral Lord Chatfield had decisively rejected a revival of sail training in the 1930s. Sail was occasionally used as an auxiliary to power on very small craft on delivery trips, for example harbour defence motor launches on the way to foreign stations. It was also used in ships' boats and lifeboats, and all seamen had some training in handling small craft. Oars were also used in ships' boats and had some role in training and lifesaving. But all warships were powered craft, reliant on their engines for mobility and many other functions.

Naval engines were under the authority of the Engineer-in-Chief of the Navy, who was an Engineer Vice-Admiral in the Controller's Department. He was the 'Principal adviser to the Board on all questions affecting Naval Engineering', and was responsible to the Controller for,

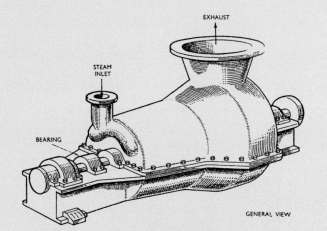

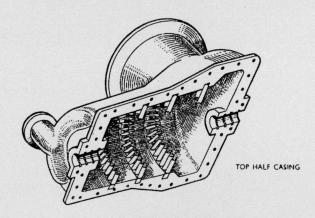

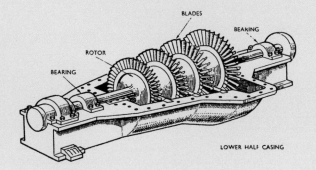

The basic arrangement of a turbine engine.

…all matters of design, inspection and production of propelling, auxiliary and other steam, hydraulic in internal combustion machinery (other than Gunnery or Torpedo equipment) fitted in warships, boats and auxiliary craft, and in Dockyards and Establishments.[20]

The Engineer-in-Chief's staff was largely made up of naval engineering officers – more than 80 of them in 1943, including seven rear-admirals. He also had civilian scientific officers and other civil servants on his staff plus those employed in the Admiralty Engineering Laboratory at West Drayton in Middlesex. Engineer overseers were naval officers, spread around the country to supervise work in the shipyards and to inspect coal bought for the Admiralty. But the Engineer-in-Chief's department rarely took the initiative in new developments, which usually came from private industry or the officers in the fleet.

Steam Turbines

Since the building of HMS *Dreadnought* in 1905–6, the steam turbine had been the main power plant of all new warships of destroyer or sloop size upwards. Its rotary motion needed fewer moving parts, hence less maintenance and a reduced engine room complement. It was more fuel efficient than the reciprocating engine at the high speeds which warships needed. It was lighter and its centre of gravity was lower, which aided stability.

The turbine engine needed high-pressure steam of about 200 pounds per square inch. There were several ways of converting this to a rotary motion but by far the most common British one, invented by Charles Parsons, was the reaction system. Inside a cylindrical casing, steam was passed through a series of rotors fitted with blades, alternating with fixed blades on the stationary casing. Many rows were used, so that the pressure of the steam did not drop too fast.

The turbine engine usually ran too fast for efficient ship use, so some kind of reduction was essential if both the engine and propeller were to run at maximum efficiency. This might be hydraulic, or electric as used in the Captain class frigates built for the Royal Navy in the USA in the 1940s. British ships used single reduction gearing, in which a pair of gears reduced speed by a factor of up to 20:1. The construction and design of the gearing was crucial, for only two teeth were in contact at any given moment and they had to bear a great weight. The most common system in 1939 used Parsons' 'all-addendum' or AA design of tooth, but the National Physical Laboratory continued to work on improvements.

British steam turbine design was still under the control of the Parsons company, which sent the basic design to one of the seven warship builders which also made turbine engines, or seven others which made them for cross-channel ferries and other fast merchant ships. The manufacture of turbine blades was something of a bottleneck, and a single engine needed many thousands. This caused the Admiralty to use other types of engine for ships which did not require great speed. Nevertheless, 880 sets of naval turbine machinery were made during the war, compared with 166 sets in the four years before it. They were capable of generating more than 12 million horsepower, far more than any other type of engine used by the navy.[21]

With falling warship orders there was little impetus from the naval side and British marine turbine design had not improved much since the First World War. Marine turbine makers did not keep in touch with the manufacturers of electricity generators, who were working in a greatly expanding market and made many advances between the wars. In contrast, there were better links between the two sides of the industry in the USA and real advances were made. American turbines had fewer blades, and there were improvements in the design of boilers, superheaters and gearing. As a result, the engines of the USS *Washington* were 39 per cent more fuel efficient than those of the *King George V* at low speeds, and 20 per cent at high speeds.[22] It was 1943 before the Engineer-in-Chief began to address the problem, but improvements only showed in the *Daring* class destroyers which appeared after the war.

Steam Reciprocating Engines

The steam reciprocating engine was far older, directly descended from those developed by James Watt and his predecessors in the eighteenth century. It was based on the principle that steam, when condensed, creates a partial vacuum and this can be used to make a piston move within a cylinder. It was a reciprocating engine in that the pistons moved up and down, rather than in a rotary motion. Watt added the separate condenser so that steam was drawn out of the cylinder to avoid wasting heat. From a maritime point of view, the biggest steps came in the late nineteenth century when high-pressure steam was used. A second cylinder was added to use up the lower pressure steam from the first cylinder, and a third was introduced in 1880 to create the triple expansion engine. This had three or four cylinders, a small one for high-pressure steam, a slightly larger intermediate one, and one or two larger ones for the remaining low-pressure steam. This gave much greater fuel efficiency and made the ocean-going steamship practicable, whether warship or merchant ship.

The navy had virtually abandoned the triple expansion engine after the *Dreadnought* was built, but its simplicity, efficiency at low speeds and low first cost made it attractive for the greater part of the merchant marine. It kept coming back to the navy as the power unit of requisitioned merchant ships and fishing boats, which were used in large numbers in wartime. It was also chosen as the engine for the new Flower class corvettes when they were designed just before the war, partly because it was believed they would be operated by Merchant Navy engineers who were familiar with the type, partly to avoid creating bottlenecks in turbine production. It proved remarkably reliable in service despite the severe conditions of the North Atlantic. It was retained for the Castle class corvettes which followed, and for the new frigates which employed two engines instead of one.

This engine was 22 feet 6 inches long and 8 feet 5 inches wide. It was 13 feet 8 inches high at the top of the casing, and the cylinder heads were a further 1 foot 8 inches higher than that. The high-pressure cylinder was near the centre of the engine and had an internal diameter of 18½ inches. Steam entered it at a maximum pressure of 225 pounds per square inch. At the end of its stroke it would exhaust to the intermediate pressure cylinder, with a diameter of 31 inches, then after another stroke the steam would be divided equally between the two low pressure cylinders, one at each end of the engine with an internal diameter of 38½ inches. Finally it would go to the condenser to be turned back into water. Each of the pistons travelled 30 inches up or down with each stroke. The piston rod was fixed to it, and was bolted in turn to the connection rod at the crosshead. This could pivot, and its lower end was attached to the crankshaft to translate the up and down movement into a rotary motion. The engine could be put into reverse by altering the direction of movement of the cylinders, so it needed no gearing.

Boilers

Both the turbine and the triple expansion engine required steam at high pressure. The Flower class corvettes were fitted with cylindrical Scotch boilers as used in the Merchant Navy, but these proved incapable of the sudden changes in speed needed in U-boat hunting and were the only real fault in the engines of the class. Other ships had water tube boilers.

According to the *Machinery Handbook* of 1941, the water tube boiler was 'lighter, more suitable for burning oil fuel, and steam can be raised quicker. Also a water-tube boiler can be arranged to withstand higher pressures and give a higher degree of superheat'.[23] It was designed to expose the maximum surface area to the heat of the furnace, and at the same time withstand the tremendous pressures that built up inside it. The Admiralty water tube boiler had been developed in the 1920s and tested against the commercial products of Babcock and Wilcox and Yarrow. It was tent-like in shape, with the steam tank forming its ridge along the top and two water tanks, of smaller diameter, as the eaves. Numerous water tubes formed the sides, and the furnace was inside that. It contained up to a dozen oil burners which provided the heat, each running the whole length of the boiler. The ends of the furnace were lined with firebricks.

The water in the lower tanks was heated and passed through the tubes into the steam tank above. This was suitable for triple expansion engines, which preferred the steam to be a little 'wet' as the moisture would help lubricate the cylinders. Turbine engines used 'dry' steam which was heated even more. From the steam tube it was passed through a series of smaller tubes running fore and aft among the main boiler tubes, so that it was raised to a higher temperature, and a pressure of 250 pounds per square inch.

The engines were situated as low as possible in the ship to improve the centre of gravity, simplify transmission to the propellers and to minimise the potential for action damage from shells. The bottom of the ship was especially strong in the engine room. Engine mountings were often of cast iron in the early stages but it tended to crack with action damage, so these were replaced by fabricated structures where possible. Much thought went into the layout of the boiler and engine rooms just before and during the war, largely to minimise action damage. Where possible on larger ships, each engine and boiler was in a separate compartment, with cross-over pipes so that a boiler could feed a different engine if needed. Access was needed on each side of every unit, so a greater amount of space was needed.

Internal Combustion Engines

The diesel engine had been fitted to ships since the *Selandia*, a Danish coaster of 1911, but it was only considered suitable for smaller merchant ships and the British shipping industry retained its confidence in steam. Diesel was very fuel-efficient and could be operated by a small crew compared with a steam engine. Plus it could be operated by a very small crew. Unlike petrol engines diesel fuel was

The motor room of the submarine *Tribune* in 1942.

not combustible unless compressed inside the cylinder, which was a great advantage for a ship that had to go into action.

Diesel engines were the main surface power plants of British submarines from 1907. This was one case where the Admiralty took a lead in engine development, largely because of the deficiencies of the British diesel industry. The Admiralty Experimental Laboratory at West Drayton tested single-cylinder examples of engines, and then multi-cylinder models were installed in submarines. Engines by Sulzer (Swiss) and MAN (German) were tested against British ones by the Admiralty and Vickers in the T-class submarines of the 1936–7 programme and were considered superior. The other way in which diesel and electric power was combined in the Royal Navy was in the Captain class frigates built in the USA. These used the electric motors as a means of gearing down the steam turbines.

Diesel engines were also used in many landing craft. The smaller types were imported from America, while many of those powering medium-sized vessels such as Tank Landing Craft were built by the British firm of Davy Paxman. According to one of its directors,

…the engines were non-reversible, but were connected to oil-operated reverse and reduction gears; the control of the machinery was arranged by two levers for

each unit, one to control the engine speed and the other to control the head or reverse clutches of the gear-box, and the control levers for all engines were grouped in a single station with gauge boards readily visible therefrom. Starting was effected by large electric starter motors, in the same way as a motor car; consequently, no skill whatever was necessary either to start or run the engine, or to control the operation of the propeller.[24]

The Germans used diesel engines in their E-boats, but British industry had failed to develop a lightweight, high-speed engine, so they had to use petrol engines, despite the obvious dangers of combustion. Even then the supply was doubtful, as units of over 1000 horsepower were needed. Engines such as the Rolls Royce Merlin were reserved for aircraft, and research and development also concentrated on aero engines. The engines of the first motor torpedo boats were built by the Italian firm of Isotta Fraschini. The Admiralty missed a chance to have them produced under licence in Britain and the supply was of course cut off when Italy entered the war. The Hall Scott Defender from America was used as a stop gap. It had been developed to combat bootleggers, but it had a horsepower of only 620, which meant that the speed of boats was less than 30 knots. The Packard engine of 1250 horsepower also came from America, and was far more satisfactory.

At the beginning of the war about half of low-speed ships' boats were equipped with petrol engines. These were unreliable in starting from cold and there was a policy to re-equip them with diesel. High-speed boats, with the hard chine hull form, were all fitted with petrol engines. Re-equipment was slow, but by the end of the war about 95 per cent of ships' boats used diesel. This created many supply problems, as there were more than 80 different types in use, with many different installations.[25]

Propellers

A few shallow-draft vessels such as minesweepers still used paddle wheels, and the navy had experimented with jet-drive in landing craft before the war. Apart from that, the navy relied on the screw propeller to drive all its ships. In general there was one propeller for each engine. A corvette had only one, whereas the much smaller motor torpedo boat might have three. Minor landing craft had one or two, destroyers and frigates had two, and cruisers, battleships and aircraft carriers had four. Unless it was mounted on the centre line, the shaft of the propeller had to be held out of the side by a V-shaped bracket.

Most naval propellers were three-bladed and made in manganese-bronze to protect them from decay. Diameter was constrained by the position under the hull. The blades had to be strong enough to bear the stress, but not too wide to create inefficiency. The edges of the blades were elliptical and a great deal of work and tank testing went into their design. As well as the outside diameter, propellers were also classed by their pitch. This was the distance it would travel through the water in a single revolution in ideal conditions, without any slippage. A smaller pitch was more useful at lower speeds, as with the low gear in a car, and the converse was true at high speeds. But variable-pitch propellers would have been too complex and vulnerable for the technology of the time. The correct pitch could be important. In 1943 Captain King of the frigate *Avon* found that his had been wrongly stamped with a pitch that was 2 feet less than what was intended, reducing the speed of the ship to 16 knots instead of 20.[26]

Electrical Systems

The Royal Navy had used electrical power in some form since the 1870s, for interior lighting, pumping and lifting, signalling and searchlights among other purposes. It was to become increasingly vital during the war as radar and sonar became more and more important, and degaussing systems were fitted to protect ships from the magnetic mine.

The navy had no electrical branch as such, for it was part of the torpedo officer's duties. As a result there was no corps of experienced naval electrical officers, and the Department of the Director of Electrical Engineering at the Admiralty was almost entirely civilian manned. The Director, Sir James Pringle, was the 'Principal Electrical Adviser to the Board' and 'Directly responsible to the Controller for all matters concerning the design, inspection, production and trials of all fittings, cables, apparatus, machinery and installations in warships and auxiliary vessels of all types, except W/T apparatus'.[27] His staff included many members and associate members of the Institute of Electrical Engineers, some with the degree of Bachelor of Science and one Ph.D. in 1943. It had only three naval officers, all retired, at the height of the war. Paper qualifications were far higher than in the engineering department, but practical experience afloat was far less.

Naval electrical equipment was divided into high power, which was effectively the muscles of the ship and operated gun turrets, winches, cranes and so on; and low power, which operated the 'nerves' such as radar, Asdic and other equipment. The navy retained direct current, whereas the US Navy began to go over to alternating current in 1932. However, AC generators had to be fitted when American equipment was adopted. Power was produced by generators operated mainly by the ship's engines, and was already fitted in ships supplied by the USA. Emergency power was also provided by smaller steam engines. In 1938 it was decided to stay with this, as they were considered more reliable than diesel engines. This was rethought after several wartime disasters, including the loss of the *Ark Royal* in 1941. If the main boilers were knocked out the electrical system would fail and there would be no power for the pumps. After that it was decided to fit emergency diesel generators in all ships, sited above the waterline where possible.

Power was transmitted round the ship by means of a ring main system, which was to 'extend fore and aft on each side of the vessel, behind armour and, where increased protection is secured thereby, below the waterline'. The policy on circuit breakers was that they should be 'constructed and adjusted so as to operate in the following sequence:- branch breakers shall open first, the speed of opening to clear heavy faults to be of the highest practicable without undue complication of design. Ring main and feeder breakers shall open next, and finally, supply breakers'.[28]

A propeller under test in a tank.

4 Armament

Guns were regarded as the primary naval weapon at the start of the war. They had dealt with the threat from the torpedo at the end of the nineteenth century and it was believed that the submarine could also be contained, while aircraft could be kept at bay by good gunnery. Naval guns were highly sophisticated weapons, often using the latest techniques of metallurgy and ballistics, and the largest could project a shell for more than 20 miles with a fair degree of accuracy. The gunnery branch was regarded as the elite of the navy. By the end of the war the position of gunnery was far more debatable, as aircraft showed their effectiveness and had much greater range, and the first guided missiles were coming into use.

Design and Production of Guns

Gun design and production was the responsibility of the Director of Naval Ordnance, a senior member of the gunnery branch. Rear-Admiral Oliver Bevir, who took office in August 1941, qualified as a gunnery officer in 1916 and had recently served as captain of the gunnery school HMS *Excellent*. He was responsible to the Controller of the Navy for 'all questions affecting naval ordnance material generally', including research, design, inspection and manufacture of guns, mountings, ammunition and bombs. He also co-operated with the DNC on such matters as ammunition hoists and periscopes. He

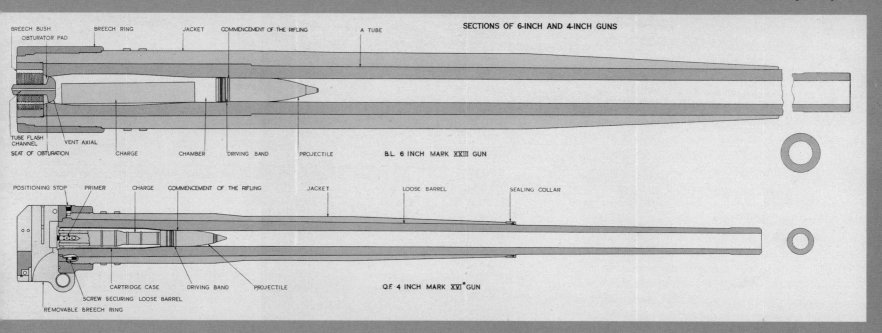

SECTIONS OF 6-INCH AND 4-INCH GUNS

B.L. 6 INCH MARK XXIII GUN

Q.F. 4 INCH MARK XVI* GUN

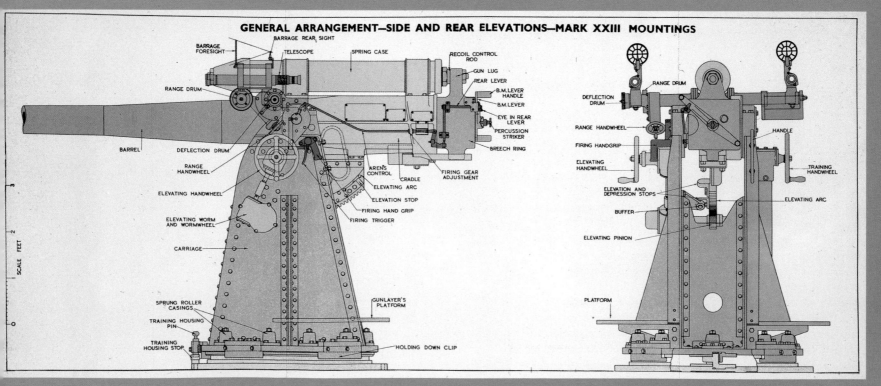

GENERAL ARRANGEMENT—SIDE AND REAR ELEVATIONS—MARK XXIII MOUNTINGS

had a large staff including the Inspectors of Naval Ordnance and many engineer officers.

These people did not undertake design themselves, but interpreted the needs of the customer, the navy. Gun design was largely carried out by Vickers-Armstrong, the armaments giant created by a merger of 1927. A new model took several years to perfect and most of the guns in use during the war had been designed some years earlier. The Naval Ordnance Department often modified guns in service, while the most effective anti-aircraft weapons, the 40mm Bofors and the 20mm Oerlikon, were designed in Sweden and Switzerland respectively.

Until about 1929, large guns were produced by winding wire round a central core then placing an outer shell round that. The wire was very effective in containing the blast, but did nothing to stop the barrel drooping. In the new method of built-up construction, tapered tubes were shrunk onto one another. All guns were rifled, which meant that there was a spiral groove inside the barrel to make the shell spin and give much greater accuracy. The inner tube containing the rifling could be replaced on many of the larger guns, as it wore out quickly. On the standard 15-inch gun, for example, it had to be replaced after 335 shots with full charge. The 6-inch gun used by most cruisers had a much longer life, of 1100 shots. Some guns, such as the Mark XIX 4-inch, used by many frigates, were moulded in a single piece apart from the breech ring which was shrunk on. This gave them inferior performance, with a range of 9700 yards compared with twice that for the Marks XVI and XXI fitted as the main anti-aircraft armament on many battleships and cruisers.

Until the First World War the Royal Ordnance Factory at Woolwich near London dominated naval gun and ammunition production, employing 70,000 workers at its peak. It seemed vulnerable to bombing but in fact it was little damaged during the London blitz of 1940–1. Attempts to move production to other sites came too late and Woolwich never had less than 20,000 workers during the war. Many ordnance factories of various types were opened for the making of guns, mountings and ammunition, run by the Board of Ordnance which supplied all three services. Guns were also made by Vickers-Armstrong at Elswick in Newcastle and by Beardmore in Glasgow. The Royal Ordnance Factory made 24 of the 14-inch guns for the *King George V* class, while Elswick made 30 and Beardmore 15, for example.

Gun Types

Naval guns came in three main categories. The largest, 6 inches and above, were known as breech loaders or BL – a misleading title, as all naval guns were loaded from the breech. Their main characteristic was that they were loaded with propellant inside a fabric bag. The next size down, from 4 to 6 inches, was known as quick firing or QF and had the charge in a metal cartridge case. Finally, there were automatic guns, mostly for anti-aircraft use, ranging from the 40mm Bofors to .3- and .303-inch machine guns, similar in calibre to an infantry rifle.

One important difference between the BL and the QF gun was in the breech. In the larger guns this was of the screw type. The block was roughly cylindrical with an interrupted screw thread round it. This was pushed into place at the after end of the gun and then turned to interlock with threads inside the breech, making a gas-tight seal. Most QF guns had a rectangular breech block which moved across the breech

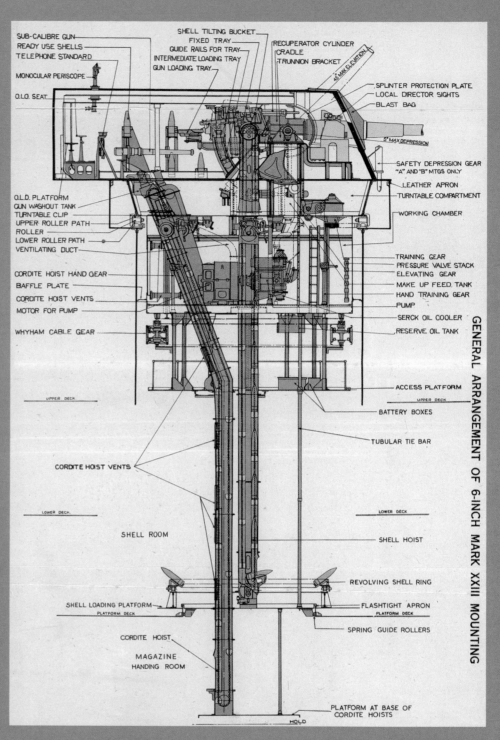

GENERAL ARRANGEMENT OF 6-INCH MARK XXIII MOUNTING

as it opened and closed. BL guns were usually fitted on hydraulically powered mountings, while QF mountings were operated by hand.

Heavy Guns

The 6-inch Mark XXIII gun was one of the most common 'breech loaders' in the navy, and was typical in design and construction. It was used by most modern cruisers, and 469 were manufactured. It consisted of an inner 'A' tube with the rifling, an outer tube known as the jacket, a breech ring set round the last 22 inches of the after part, and the breech bush inside the aftermost part of the jacket. It was mounted inside a cradle, which had trunnions that let the gun be rotated up and down for aiming. It also allowed it to recoil and this was restrained and its effect spread by the recuperator cylinder above and the recoil cylinder below. The recuperator cylinder was fixed to the cradle and filled with air which was compressed by a ram fixed to the gun when it was fired. The recoil cylinder moved with the gun. The whole assembly was on a pedestal mounting inside a gun turret.

A 6-inch gun mounting as used on many light cruisers, showing the method of ammunition supply from the magazines.

The Mark XXIII gun weighed nearly 7 tons and fired a shell of 112 pounds over a range of up to 25,480 yards or more than 14 miles. Other versions of the 6-inch gun included the Mark XXII, which was similar but rather heavier and formed the secondary armament on the *Nelson* and *Rodney*, and the elderly Mark VII, which had been introduced in 1901 and was still used on a few ships and many liners and armed merchant cruisers. There were still 629 of these in service when the war began.

The 8-inch gun was developed for the heavy cruisers built between the wars. Some were wire-wound, some were built-up, reflecting the change in construction. One hundred and sixty-eight were made, with a range of more than 30,000 yards and a 256-pound projectile.

The 12- and 13.5-inch guns of the First World War were obsolete so there was a substantial gap to the next size, the 14-inch gun of the *King George V* class. The design incorporated the latest technology and the range of more than 38,000 yards was greater than that of the much older 15-inch, while the projectile was slightly lighter at 1590 pounds.

The 15-inch gun was a classic design which equipped all the later capital ships of the First World War – The *Queen Elizabeths,* the R class and the battlecruisers *Hood, Repulse* and *Renown*. It was a great advance in its day and could still more than hold its own in 1939–45. There were 179 of them available to the navy in 1939, though some were lost with the *Royal Oak, Barham, Hood* and *Repulse*. It had a maximum range of 33,550 yards or 19 miles and fired a projectile weighing 1938 pounds.

The 16-inch gun, exclusive to the *Nelson* and *Rodney,* was the largest type in the navy, and the last heavy wire-wound gun. It had the longest range at 39,780 yards and the largest projectile weight at 2048 pounds, although that was less than the more modern 16-inch guns used in the American *Iowa* class.

Quick-Firing Guns

The Royal Navy produced a variety of guns in the medium range, unlike the US Navy which concentrated on the 5-inch as the main gun of destroyers and the secondary armament of battleships and cruisers.

The 4.7-inch Mark IX gun was used on most destroyers, apart from the older V and W classes of the First World War, and some of the L and M classes which had a more modern version. The Mark IX was built up in three pieces – the gun of 'A' tube, the jacket and the breech ring. The breech could be set to quick firing or semi-automatic. In the later case the breech opened automatically after firing ready to load the next round, which weighed up to 50 pounds and had a maximum range of nearly 17,000 yards. Another type of 4.7-inch gun formed the anti-aircraft armament of the *Nelson* and *Rodney* and older aircraft carriers. It used fixed ammunition in which the cartridge and shell were secured together for easier loading.

The only larger quick-firing gun was the 5.25-inch, used for the secondary armament of the *King George V* class and the main armament

Fitting shells into cartridge in a Ministry of Supply filling factory, 1941.

of most of the *Dido* class cruisers. It was designed to function equally well as an anti-aircraft gun and to fight surface craft. It could fire 80-pound shells at a rate of 10 to 12 per minute.

The twin 4.5-inch gun was developed for 1930s aircraft carriers and came in several versions It was fitted in modernised battleships in the late 1930s. Another version was used in the *Ark Royal* and in submarine depot ships. The Between Decks or BD version was used in *Illustrious* class carriers – this was a countersunk mounting designed to keep it clear of the aircraft on deck. It was used in single mountings in the later wartime destroyers of the S, Z and C classes and in twin mountings in Battle class destroyers, but most of these were not ready until after the war.

The 4-inch gun also came in several versions. The Mark V was the oldest, still carried on some of the oldest cruisers and aircraft carriers. The Marks XVI and XXI were very common as the anti-aircraft armament of many older battleships, modern cruisers, armed merchant cruisers and most Tribal class destroyers. It had a 35-pound projectile with range of 19,850 yards against surface targets and a ceiling of 39,000 feet against aircraft when the gun was elevated to 80 degrees. More than 2500 of them were made. The Mark XIX was a cheap, low velocity gun moulded in a single block, arming corvettes and frigates against surfaced submarines.

Gun Mountings

The navy was almost totally dependent on a single company for the design and manufacture of its heavy and medium gun mountings. As a matter of policy they were produced by Vickers-Armstrong, for the work required very expensive equipment, which would be difficult to maintain during the naval slump between the wars. As a private company, Vickers-Armstrong could support it by taking on foreign orders. Nevertheless, development time was very slow and it took several years to produce a new gun, which was an important factor in choosing the 14-inch for the *King George V* class battleships at an early stage of their design in 1936. Capacity at Vickers was expanded with rearmament and £500,000 was spent on plant for new guns at Barrow-in-Furness, with more money spent at Elswick in Newcastle. Vickers-Armstrong was headed by Sir Charles Craven, a former naval commander. He was a very effective leader and worked very closely with the DNO's department, but there is a suspicion that he was overawed by the gold braid at the Admiralty. He took on the ambitious specifications produced by the navy, but many mountings had excessive teething troubles. The early twin 8-inch turret of the 1920s was intended to have high elevating and training speeds for anti-aircraft use, but these were never realised. The *Prince of Wales* was forced to abandon action with the *Bismarck* in 1941 after her turret mechanism broke down.

The pedestal mounting was the older type. It consisted of a central casting, which kept the gun low but tended to restrict elevation and depression. The newer type was the central pivot mounting in which the trunnions were supported by a steel plate on each side with a third plate forward to connect them. On a lighter gun on a single mounting, the whole assembly was secured to a flat circular plate mounted on rollers to allow training. A larger gun was trained by the movement of the turret.

A heavy gun mounting was a huge construction. The quadruple 14-inch turrets of the *King George V* class were 60 feet deep over four decks and weighed about 1550 tons. On a smaller scale the Mark XXIII triple 6-inch turret was used on *Edinburgh* and *Fiji* class cruisers and a similar mounting was used on the *Southampton* class. The upper part was the gunhouse, protected by 2-inch armour on the sides, rear and roof, and 4-inch on its front face. The middle gun was mounted 2 feet 6 inches back from the others, partly so that adjacent crews would not interfere with one another. At the rear of the turret was a platform and periscope for the officer in charge, and a seat for a telephone operator. Cordite and ammunition hoists came up through holes in the floor, close to the loading trays of the guns, which could only be used if the elevation was 12½ degrees or less. Each gun had a seat for the layer who controlled the elevation. There was only one trainer, for the turret was moved as a whole, and he sat between the first and second gun. The hole where each gun penetrated the shield was covered by a canvas blast bag. The turret used hydraulic power in two engines to train at a maximum rate of 5 degrees per second. Local sights were fitted for use if the director failed and a small gun, known as 'sub-calibre' was stowed on one side of the turret for use in practice.

Three feet below the floor of the turret was the turntable compartment which contained the elevating and training gear, and the rollers on which the turret rotated. Below that was the working chamber with the main power unit, an oil cooler, and hand training gear for use in an emergency. At the next level down was an access platform for inspecting the gear leading into the turret to be inspected. The shell hoists ran down from the turret to the armoured shell rooms well below decks. The cordite hoist ran a deck further down, into the magazine. Both types of hoist were protected by doors to prevent a flashing passing down to the magazine. Nine men worked in the shell room of each turret, three in the cordite handling room and eight in the magazine proper. The whole turret assembly weighed more than 630 tons.[29]

The 4.7-inch single mounting of a destroyer was much simpler. It was elevated by hand, turning a wheel on the left side of the gun which operated gears to raise or lower it. Training was also by hand, and the gun and its mounting turned by means of a two-speed gearbox, bevel wheels, a worm gear and pinion. In fast gear for anti-aircraft use it could move through 4 degrees per second, and 2 degrees in slow gear. There was a semi-circular loading tray on the left side, where the ammunition was placed before it was rammed into the breech by a handle operated by steel wire ropes. There were platforms on each side for the crew of seven. The gun was protected by a lightly-armoured shield rather than a full turret. The rear was open and the breech protruded some way behind the shield.[30]

Ammunition

Cordite was the main propellant of all naval guns from the 16-inch to the .303 machine gun, although it came in different grades according to the size of gun. It consisted of the explosives nitro-glycerine and nitro-cellulose with petroleum jelly as a lubricant. It could be made in blocks (originally cords, hence the name). It did not explode in the true sense of the term, but burned very rapidly pushing the shell along the length of the gun barrel. The Royal Navy had its cordite factory at Holton Heath on the south coast of

England near Poole. For BL guns, sticks of cordite were tied together with silk thread and put in a silk cloth bag, because that cloth would disappear completely on ignition. In the case of QF guns, they were placed in a brass cartridge case. Smaller guns within this class tended to use fixed ammunition in which the cartridge and shell were secured together. Others had separate ammunition with the shell loaded first, then the cartridge.

Shells were made in more than 20 different factories, mostly in the north of England. The basic shape was forged, then it was turned very accurately to a streamlined shape in a lathe. The explosives were made at Woolwich and in other factories, and unlike cordite they were high explosives, 'instantly converted to gas with great violence'.[31] Types used included TNT, RDX, Lyddite and Shellite. Filling the shells was in many ways the most dangerous part of the process and was done in government factories under the control of the Board of Ordnance.

Shells came in several types. Armour-piercing shells had a thick head and walls and a hard steel penetrative cap. They were not intended to explode immediately on impact, so the fuse was set in the base rather than the cap. High-explosive shells had thinner walls and higher charges to create the maximum effect against un-armoured targets including aircraft. They had their fuses in the nose. Shrapnel was thin-walled and contained balls of lead which would be spread on impact, for use against troops or aircraft. Star shell contained an illuminating charge which was lowered slowly by parachute during a night action. Smoke shell could be used as a target for anti-aircraft practice, or for creating a smoke screen. Low-angle or LA practice shells were often

old shells with their explosive replaced by an inert substance. HA or high-angle shells were filled with a small powder burster and a few smoke pellets. All were clearly marked with their size and function, and with colour-coded bodies, caps and rings.[32]

Ammunition was stowed in boxes on racks in the magazine in the bowels of the ship, as far as possible from damage and protected by armour in the case of capital ships and cruisers. This was an important point for the Royal Navy, which had lost several major ships in both world wars due to ammunition explosions.

Directors

Though all guns could be fired using 'local control' if necessary, those on capital ships, cruisers, aircraft carriers, destroyers and the more sophisticated escort vessels used a central method of control, the director system. The director itself was mounted high up, usually at the after end of the bridge of a modern ship, with a subsidiary one on the after superstructure. It was pointed towards the target in action or practice, and the guns were aimed by following its movements, and fired by an electrical circuit operated by the gunnery officer in the director. The director offered several advantages. It was high enough to be clear of most of the spray and smoke, and to spot the fall of the shot. It was easier to indicate a target to the director than to individual guns, and central aiming and firing meant that the effect of each salvo could be assessed accurately. The typical director was a vertical cylinder large enough to house a team of five or six officers and men. The after part was raised slightly to allow windows for the control officers to look out, and equipped with instruments including gyro-stabilised sights.

Range was obtained by means of coincidence range finders. The target was viewed through two points as far apart as possible, and a system of mirrors brought the halves of the view together, one above the other. When these were lined up, the range could be measured on a scale. Range finders were made by the firm of Barr and Stroud in Glasgow. In the last war their critics had considered them inferior to the German range finders using the stereoscopic principle, but this was probably unfair, and the German system needed much more training to be effective. The real problem was that the ends of the range finders were not far enough apart. On modern ships like the *King George V* class they were fitted on the outside of the gun turrets, projecting like ears. By 1945 they were being replaced by radar which gave a more accurate reading in all weather.

The data on the movement and range of the target and many other factors were fed down to the transmitting station in the bowels of the ship. This contained the Admiralty Fire Control Clock, a manual computer operated by the ship's Royal Marine bandsmen in a capital ship or cruiser. Again British methods had proved inadequate in the last war, but the faults had been rectified by 1939 to produce a generally efficient system.

Anti-aircraft Guns

Many quick-firing guns were suitable for anti-aircraft use, and even the heavier BL guns could be deployed on occasion, though to little effect.

Below left: The single 20mm Oerlikon gun.

Below right: The interior of a director control tower showing the instruments used by the crew.

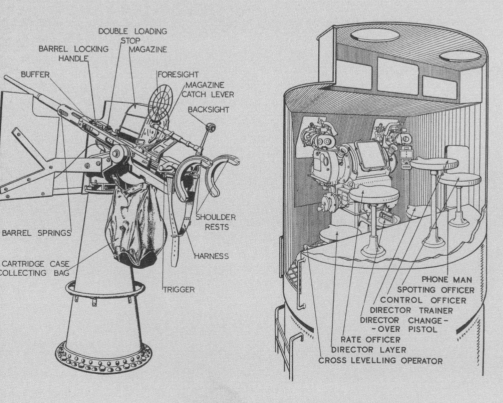

With poor aiming systems, close-range anti-aircraft weapons needed a very fast rate of fire to stand a chance of a hit, and a target was only in range for a very short time. Three main types were used during the war, two of which were designed abroad in neutral countries.

The home-grown weapon was the 2-pounder 'pom-pom' gun which was ubiquitous in the early days of the war. It was water-cooled and used the recoil to reload itself on the same principle as a machine gun. It was used in single mountings on some escort vessels and older destroyers, on a quadruple mounting on small carriers, light cruisers and modern destroyers, and on an eight-barrelled mount on larger ships. The *King George V* class had six or eight of these mountings. The multiple pom-pom was quite successful in producing the volume of fire that helped to reassure crews, but apart from the deficiencies of the aiming system, it was handicapped by a low muzzle velocity of 2040 feet per second, compared with 2750 feet per second for a typical naval gun. More than 7000 guns served with the Royal and Commonwealth navies in 1939–45.

The first of the imported designs was the 20mm Oerlikon, made in Switzerland and introduced in 1939. It was to a simple design in which the breech block was simply blown back by each shot to allow the entry of the next round. It was usually on a single manual pedestal mounting, operated by a gunner by means of shoulder rests. Aiming was usually by means of ring sights. The 'loading number' changed the 60-round drum magazine when required. Spent cartridges were evicted into a bag. It had a light armoured shield. Oerlikons were also used in twin mountings, sometimes powered. The gun was a great success, far better than the .5-inch machine guns it superseded, but it was not powerful enough to stop a kamikaze in the Pacific war. Fifty-five thousand of them were issued to the British and Commonwealth navies during the war and they were to be found on almost every type of ship. Some capital ships carried as many as 70 in the Pacific.

The 40mm Bofors gun came from Sweden and was first brought to Britain by the army just before the war. The navy began to use it in small numbers from 1941. Its projectile of nearly 2 pounds was more than seven times heavier that that of the Oerlikon and it had a range of more than 10,000 yards. Mostly used in single and twin mountings of increasing sophistication, it was perhaps the best naval anti-aircraft gun of the war but was rather slow to enter service, and only became common near the end.

Anti-aircraft Systems

The aiming of anti-aircraft guns posed much greater problems than against ships. The target moved much faster, and aircraft speeds were increasing rapidly before and during the war. An aircraft was highly manoeuvrable and could change course instantly in three dimensions. The ship itself was an unstable platform, and the director had to be stabilised against it, or the crew had more difficulty in following the target.

Light anti-aircraft guns used simple methods such as hosepipe and eyeshooting, but heavier guns, such as pom-poms and Bofors, used directors which paralleled those used for low-angle firing. The British had rejected a highly sophisticated tachymetric system, which Lord Chatfield claimed was the worst decision the navy made between the wars. Modern research suggests that it would not have made much difference: what was needed was a proximity fuse which

An eight-barrelled, 2-pounder pom-pom gun with its crew. The circular sights are near the top of the picture, the ammunition boxes are on each side of the gun barrels.

would be activated by sound or radar to explode in the vicinity of the target.[33] The early pom-pom directors relied on eyeshooting to a great extent and merely removed the direction of the guns to a more remote station, without adding greatly to the accuracy of the firing. The Mark IV director, introduced in 1940, used an instrument known as the Gyro Rate Unit or GRU to measure this more accurately. It was not stabilised against the movements of the ship, and needed a crew of eight. A time fuse could be set to explode the shell close to the target. But of course the target position had to be predicted a few seconds in advance, so it was less effective against aircraft approaching fast, such as dive bombers.

Range was found by means of a high-angle range finder, which was installed in the director. This was conventionally known as the height finder, though in fact it measured the vertical angle to the target. By 1942, it became increasingly common to fit radar to assist in range-taking. The Mark VI director, introduced late in the war, was a complete redesign with radar incorporated. Fully stabilised directors were not in general use until after the war.

The Torpedo

The torpedo was the primary weapon of the submarine and the motor torpedo boat, and started roughly equal with the gun in destroyers, though it had probably been overtaken by the end of the war. It was carried by most cruisers and some of the older capital ships. It was self-propelled, which meant that its handling equipment was less expensive than that of a gun, but the projectile itself cost much more. It could be set to keep the same depth underwater, which meant that it was easier to aim than a gun, but of course it was far slower, with a speed of 40 to 45 knots. It exploded underwater so that a single hit was likely to sink a merchant ship or do serious damage to a warship with good armour and subdivision. Its nineteenth-century inventors had dreamed of launching it from a small, cheap boat and sinking a great battleship. This was not entirely unrealistic and the *Royal Oak*, *Ark Royal* and *Barham* were

Torpedoes being fired from the tubes of a destroyer.

all sunk by torpedoes from U-boats. British seaborne torpedoes had less dramatic success, but surface ships carried out 383 successful attacks during the war, and submarines carried out 776.[34]

Torpedoes were developed in the Royal Naval Torpedo Factory at Greenock, though one disgruntled officer complained that:

It had magnificent workshops, all kinds of laboratories staffed by enthusiasts, with superb test-firing facilities of all kinds on its doorstep. I was told that during its lifetime it had never actually produced a new torpedo that functioned as intended, although doubtless it laid the groundwork for several that were later produced by private enterprise.[35]

Torpedoes were manufactured in another factory at Alexandria on the other side of the River Clyde, and tested on a range at Loch Long nearby.

Sea-launched British torpedoes were 21 inches in diameter, whereas airborne ones, and some of those on MTBs, were 18 inches. The most common type was the Mark VIII★★, used by modern submarines. The Mark VIII was the first British torpedo to use the burner cycle engine, in which compressed air was heated to about 1000°C and then mixed with oil and ignited in a chamber. It had developed somewhat by 1939, hence the asterisks in its designation. It was 21 feet 7 inches long and had a range of up to 7000 yards. At its head was the warhead, filled with TNT early in the war and more powerful Torpex after about 1943. Behind that was the compressed air cylinder and the last section included the engine, a depth gauge

The interior of a 21-inch torpedo.

to keep it at the right level, and gyroscopes to keep on a straight course. Externally it had horizontal and vertical rudders and two propellers rotating in opposite directions on the same axis. The latest torpedo in service, the Mark IX, was similar in principle but slightly longer, with a range of up to 15,000 yards. First used in 1930, it, too, had developed by 1939 and gained two asterisks. It was issued to some of the latest destroyers and cruisers and its longer range would have been an advantage in the Pacific. Attempts to develop homing torpedoes were unsuccessful.

Torpedoes were carried below the waterline on a few old battleships. Motor torpedo boats had two or four single fixed tubes, submarines had up to 12, but other torpedoes were fired from tubes on deck, which could be rotated to aim over the side of the ship at a target. Some of the old First World War destroyers had triple mountings with one tube superimposed on the other two, but inter-war development had concentrated on the quadruple tube, with all of them on the same level. A standard destroyer carried a pair of these, though the I class of 1935 introduced quintuple tubes. After that the importance of the torpedo seemed to diminish. The Tribal class destroyers were designed with gun power in mind and had only one set of quadruple tubes. Later classes had two sets, but many had one set removed to make way for extra anti-aircraft guns. One major development during the war was the fitting of gyro-angling. Destroyers could only fire torpedoes about 30 degrees forward of the beam and had to turn broadside on to launch an attack. Gyroscopes were used to turn the torpedo through the remaining 60 degrees so that they could fire directly ahead or astern of the destroyer's course.[36]

5 Sensors

The Human Eye

Despite all the developments in technology, the navy still relied on the eye as its main means of observing the world outside the ship and finding the enemy. Medical officers knew that: 'The eyes of man are the most highly developed sense organs found in the animal kingdom'.[37] Entrants to the seaman branch had thorough eye tests before they were accepted.

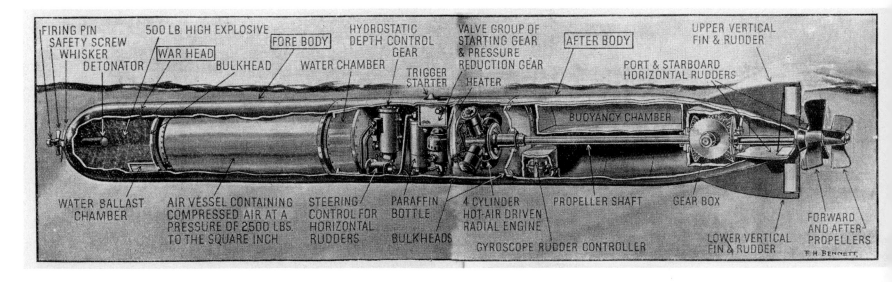

FIRING PIN / SAFETY SCREW / WHISKER / DETONATOR — WAR HEAD — 500 LB. HIGH EXPLOSIVE — FORE BODY — BULKHEAD — WATER CHAMBER — HYDROSTATIC DEPTH CONTROL GEAR — TRIGGER STARTER / HEATER — VALVE GROUP OF STARTING GEAR & PRESSURE REDUCTION GEAR — AFTER BODY — BUOYANCY CHAMBER — PORT & STARBOARD HORIZONTAL RUDDERS — UPPER VERTICAL FIN & RUDDER

WATER BALLAST CHAMBER — AIR VESSEL CONTAINING COMPRESSED AIR AT A PRESSURE OF 2500 LBS. TO THE SQUARE INCH — STEERING CONTROL FOR HORIZONTAL RUDDERS — PARAFFIN BOTTLE / BULKHEADS — 4 CYLINDER HOT-AIR DRIVEN RADIAL ENGINE — GYROSCOPE RUDDER CONTROLLER — PROPELLER SHAFT — GEAR BOX — LOWER VERTICAL FIN & RUDDER — FORWARD AND AFTER PROPELLERS — F. H. BENNETT.

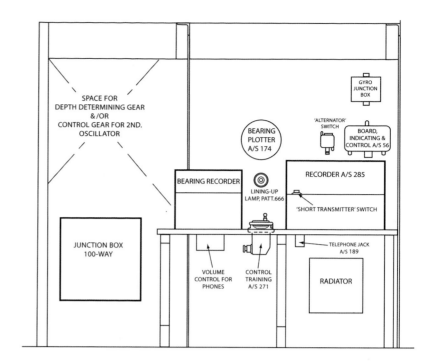

Far and near lookouts were stationed for surface work, and fog lookouts if necessary. Special anti-aircraft lookouts were also posted. They used binoculars and were carefully instructed in their care and use.

Surface Look-outs should sweep their arcs systematically, going over the whole extent of the arc each time, and taking from half a minute to a minute according to weather conditions, and then resting for half a minute.

At night the eye is much slower in seeing than the normal eye working in daylight, and sweeping should therefore be done more slowly at night.[38]

Lookouts were trained not to look directly at an object at night, but to aim a little way off. 'The very centre of the eye, which is the most sensitive part of all in day time, is almost useless at night. ... Train yourself to look just to one side of a suspected object and a little above them. Never stare directly at the suspected object; you will only lose it'.[39] When going on night duty they were made aware that it would take 10 minutes for their eyes to adapt to the dark, though if they were exposed to red rather than white light beforehand, it would be much quicker.

Early Asdics

The eye was no use against a submarine, except perhaps in the clearer waters of the Mediterranean. In the Atlantic and North Sea, the navy relied on the echo-sounding device known as Asdic, developed late in the First World War. It was based on an oscillator or transducer, a disc of about 2 feet in diameter mounted in a 'dome' under the hull. Fast vessels such as destroyers used a retractable dome so that it did not impair them at high speed. A current of 14–24 kilocycles was passed through the transducer, producing a sound wave with a range of about 2500 yards in good conditions. It would bounce off any object it hit, and the echo would be heard and the time measured, giving both a bearing and range for the target. It could also be used passively to listen for the engines and movement of submarines, known as the 'hydrophone effect'. The Asdic 'office' was situated on or near the bridge to allow the captain or officer of the watch to interpret echoes.

There was steady development of Asdic between the wars. The latest set in 1939 was Type 128, originally fitted in destroyers but later in escort vessels. Asdic was not confined to escort vessels. Type 132 of 1938 was designed as a purely defensive set for cruisers – they would use it to avoid submarines, but most had no direct means of attacking them. It was also fitted to some battleships. At the other end of the scale, much smaller sets were developed for coastal forces, boom defence vessels and merchant ships. There were special sets for submarines and even midget submarines. Landing craft sometimes used them to detect underwater obstacles.

Bearing Recorders

The main development during the war was not in Asdic itself, but in the means of recording and interpreting its results. Type 144 was the first to incorporate the bearing recorder in its design. During trials in 1942:

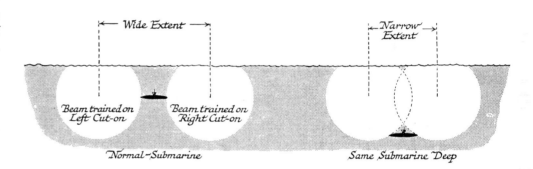

The bearing recorder was found to be of the greatest assistance in keeping contact with a target. The plot will show at once if the target has a high rate of change of bearing and in such a case the oscillator is trained so that the Bearing Recorder stylus is moved 10–20 degrees off the target and in the direction in which the target is moving. The oscillator is then allowed to step back to meet the target and, if the plot again shows that the target is still changing bearing rapidly, the process is repeated.[40]

At the beginning of the approach stage of an attack, after the bearing-recorder had been lined up, the First Operator trains across the target, stopping at the 'cut-on'. If an echo is heard the echo-push is pressed to mark the record and simultaneously to step the oscillator 2½ degrees off the target. On the next transmission, if no echo is heard, the oscillator automatically steps back 2½ degrees on to the 'cut-on'. A second echo on this bearing confirms the 'cut-on' and permits the operator to train across immediately to the other side. The time taken to cross the target is, in the early stages of the attack, inappreciable, and the first echo on the other boundary may be obtained with the next transmission.[41]

Type 144 was also designed to operate with the new ahead-throwing weapons coming into use, such as Hedgehog and Squid. It could be linked to the steering so that the helmsman would follow directions directly from the Asdic, allowing the captain to concentrate on the strategic situation. It could operate at a maximum speed of 25 knots and proved highly successful, becoming the main Asdic set of the later stages of the Battle of the Atlantic.

Top: The layout of an Asdic office fitted with a Type 144 set.

Bottom: Asdic operation. The white circles show the area of an Asdic beam at some distance from the target, and show how it can be difficult to assess the extent of a target if the depth is not known.

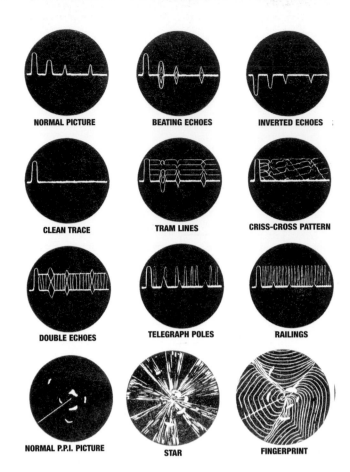

NORMAL PICTURE   BEATING ECHOES   INVERTED ECHOES

CLEAN TRACE   TRAM LINES   CRISS-CROSS PATTERN

DOUBLE ECHOES   TELEGRAPH POLES   RAILINGS

NORMAL P.P.I. PICTURE   STAR   FINGERPRINT

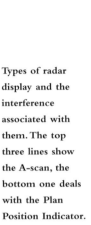

Types of radar display and the interference associated with them. The top three lines show the A-scan, the bottom one deals with the Plan Position Indicator.

Depth Finding

Early Asdic development had assumed that naval warfare would take place in relatively sheltered waters such as the North Sea. In the much deeper waters of the Atlantic, U-boats could dive to a depth of 780 feet.[42] Early escort vessels had to guess the depth of a target, or use a large pattern of depth charges to cover many possibilities. The beam of an Asdic covered about 15 degrees in the vertical plane, so it gave little indication of depth. From 1943, Type 144 sets were fitted with the Q attachment, an additional oscillator that deflected the beam lower and allowed detection at a closer angle to the target. Type 147 Asdic, introduced late in 1943, used a much narrower beam in the vertical plane and could find depth accurately. Fitted initially to the Loch class frigates, it was only used during the later stages of an attack, but with good effect. Combined with new weapons such as Squid, it had a very high success rate against submarines.

The Development of Radar

Radar was one of the classic developments of the Second World War. Almost unknown at the beginning, it was indispensable by the end. The Royal Naval Signal School at Portsmouth was in close touch with Sir Robert Watson-Watt's early experiments in the late 1930s, and radar sets were fitted to the battleship *Rodney* and the cruiser *Sheffield* in 1938. But in the early stages of the war priority had to be given to the RAF's needs for ground-based radar to defend Britain from the air. Initially it was known as RDF for Radio Direction Finding. The American term 'radar' for Radio Direction and Ranging was in use by 1943.

The invention of radar took place almost simultaneously in several countries including Britain, Germany and the USA. It depended on recent developments in radio, such as research into the propagation of short waves, and the development of television. The general principles of radar were outlined in a naval manual of 1942.

The action of the set depends on the fact that, when wireless waves in the course of their travel encounter any object, a certain amount of energy is reflected back along the original path, somewhat as sound is reflected in an 'echo'.

Energy is sent out from the transmitter in the form of a narrow beam, the receiver is also most sensitive in the same direction.

The bearing of an object is found by rotating the transmitter and receiver around until the receiver signal is a maximum.

The range of an object is determined by measuring the time interval which elapses between the departure of a very short signal or 'pulse' from the transmitter, and the arrival of the reflected energy or 'echo' onto the receiver. This time is measured on a cathode ray tube.[43]

The first naval set, Type 79, proved effective in its main role of detecting aircraft at ranges of up to 60 miles, and it was adapted for other purposes. Re-designated the Type 279, range finding for gunnery and searching for surface ships were added to its functions. After that, different sets were developed for more specialised uses, much aided by Sir James Somerville, a signal officer, as Controller of the Navy. A distinction was made between search sets which used a relatively broad beam to find an enemy and types intended to attack aircraft or surface ships. Metric sets used wavelengths of 7, 3 or 1.5 metres and had a very wide beam which gave 'rough and ready warning where a floodlight effect is required'.[44] Decimetric sets used 50 centimetres and were found to be most useful for gunnery ranging. Centimetric radar used a wavelength of 10 centimetres or less to give a much narrower beam and was able to detect surface ships and low-flying aircraft, as well as superseding the decimetric sets in gunnery ranging.

Warning Radar

In 1940, with the threat of invasion, an air and surface warning set for destroyers was a priority. Type 286M was an adaptation of the ASV (Air to Surface Vessel) Mark I used by the RAF, which was quickly pressed into service. It used a fixed aerial covering the forward half of the ship, so it could give warning of range but very little indication of direction. Thirty-two sets had been fitted by the end of the year, and it had some success in finding the enemy at Matapan in March 1941. In the same month the destroyer *Vanoc* sank U-100, the first success against the U-boat attributed to radar. More than 200 ships had been fitted by the middle of June, when a new version, with a lightweight rotating aerial was produced. But in general its wavelength was not suitable for the anti-submarine war.

Early radar could detect large ships in good conditions, but a smaller object such as a surfaced U-boat presented far more difficulty, especially among the waves of the North Atlantic. This was of vital importance, as surfaced night attack was the U-boat's most devastating tactic in 1941. As early as 1938 the Admiralty was interested in the narrower beam of a centimetric system, but three scientific breakthroughs – the cavity magnetron valve, the reflex kryston valve and the crystal mixer – were needed for it to succeed. The first set was ready by February 1941 and the type was tested on the corvette *Orchis*. Twenty-five were in service by the middle of the year and they proved a great success. The aerials and set were enclosed inside a cylindrical Perspex 'lantern', which was fitted to the rear of the bridge on corvettes and frigates. This made it difficult to fit it high up and a new version, Type 272, was developed with the radar office up to 40 feet from the aerial. A version for big ships, known as Type 273, had larger aerials for longer range.

Type 281 was originally planned in 1940 as an all-purpose set which could be fitted in ships as small as the *Dido* class cruisers. In fact it found its main use as a long-range anti-aircraft warning for cruisers, battleships and aircraft carriers. It proved successful in the *Prince of Wales* and was fitted to all fleet aircraft carriers from 1941. The original version needed two aerials on separate mastheads; the B version of 1943 was designed for a single mast.

Radar in Gun Control

The idea of mounting radar on gun directors rather than masts first surfaced late in 1939, and this led to the development of three different types of 50 centimetre radar – 282 for short-range anti-aircraft guns, 284 for the main armament and 285 for long-range anti-aircraft.

Type 284 was first tested on *King George V* at the end of 1940, and could pick up a cruiser at a range of 10 miles. It was used for range finding, for its beam was too wide to give accurate direction. It was fitted on many battleships and cruisers, but its defects soon became apparent. The range was still too short, it took too long to start from cold and different sets on the same ship could interfere with one another. Transmitter power was increased in Type 244P and range was doubled, while accuracy was within 25 yards. It was used against the *Bismarck* in 1941 and at the sinking of the *Scharnhorst* in 1943. In 1944 Type 274 entered service, with a range of 24 miles and the ability to be used in 'blind' firing. Radar could also be used to spot the splashes of shell and hence correct the aim. Types 274 and 284 could do this, but only if the shots were within the beam. Special splash-spotting radar was developed in Canada, but was not ready until after the war.

In anti-aircraft gunnery, Type 282 was introduced in 1941 for fitting on the top of pom-pom directors. The 282M introduced greater electrical power and later models had beam-switching. This used two beams giving separate echoes: when the two matched, the range was correct. Fitting of Type 282 was complete by the end of 1943. One way of dealing with fast-approaching aircraft was to use barrage fire, setting shells of the main or secondary armament to explode at a range of between 2000 and 5000 yards. Radar could give an indication of when the aircraft was likely to pass through this point, and Type 283 was introduced in 1943 for this purpose. It was found to be most effective at 2000 yards, but this proved unpopular at sea as it meant that aircraft were allowed to come very close before fire was opened.

For the 40mm Bofors gun, a new type of mounting known as Stabilised Tachymetric Anti-Aircraft Gun or STAAG was developed from 1942. It was a self-contained unit with its own radar, Type 262. The system would have rectified most of the faults of British anti-aircraft gunnery, but it was not ready until 1945.

Smaller Ships

Radar soon proved its effectiveness in big ships, destroyers, and during the Battle of the Atlantic. It was extended to smaller craft in the course of the

war, as equipment, and particularly aerials, became more compact. Type 286P was fitted to the submarine *Proteus* in mid-1941, and by August 1941 more than 60 boats had been fitted with a special version, 286W. There were special difficulties in operating from a surfaced submarine, including finding space, and the fear that it might give the position away.

Coastal forces often used shore-based radar to direct them in the narrow seas. In 1941 some MTBs, MLs and MGBs were fitted with Type 286U, with its fixed aerial. From mid-1942, boats were fitted with 286PU with a rotating aerial, and from 1943 the more powerful 291U was fitted.

Other Developments

Early radar used the A-scan display. A cathode ray tube showed a line above a range scale. A blip in the line meant that a contact had been obtained and the range could be read off the scale, but the direction could only be read from the current bearing of the aerial, and the position had to be plotted manually. In the case of the Type 271, for example:

The relative bearing of the aerials is read on a scale at the bottom of the shaft. The true bearing of the aerials can be estimated by means of the direction indicator (when fitted). The direction indicator is a simple form of gyro compass which, however, drifts slowly and must be re-set frequently. … The principal object of the Indicator is to indicate (roughly) the bearing of the aerials, relative to a fixed direction in space so that the operator, when observing a particular 'echo', is assisted in keeping his aerials continuously trained on the target despite the ship's yawing or altering course.[45]

It was an awkward arrangement, and from 1942 it was gradually replaced by the Plan Position Indicator or PPI. This used a cathode ray tube to give an overall view of the area within range, with one's own ship as the centre.

As the aerial sweeps round, echoes are traced out (or 'painted') not only at the correct range (from the centre of the tube) but also on the correct bearing, leaving a bright arc to mark their position. An after-glow tube is used, so that echoes do not immediately die away, and provided the aerial is kept rotating at reasonable speed the result is a complete picture of plan display of the relative position of all objects within radar range.[46]

This had many advantages, but the A-scan was retained for gunnery radar, as it gave a more accurate measurement of range.

Early radar gave no indication of whether a contact was friendly or not, so the system of Identification, Friend or Foe or IFF was introduced. This was a low-powered radio inside the friendly aircraft, which would be activated by a friendly radar signal and would create a pulsating echo on the cathode ray tube. Various types of interrogators were fitted to different radar sets to pick up the pulse.

It was necessary to know the height of approaching enemy aircraft in order to direct fighters against them, but this was difficult to do accurately in conventional warning sets which used a broad beam in both the horizontal and vertical plane. The range at which the targets were first detected might give some indication, but that did not allow for any changes. Radar officers used much ingenuity in interpreting the echoes, but a separate narrow-beam set was needed, which was not available until after the war.

Radar Aerials

Ideally the size of an aerial should correspond with the wavelength used, so that a metric set would require a much bigger one than a centimetric set. This conflicted with the need to keep topweight low and generally the navy used 'dipole' aerials which were half the length of the wave. There was a natural desire to place an aerial as high as possible, to give the longest range. This had an adverse effect on stability and created a need for much stronger masts. Another problem with early centimetric radar was that the cable had to be kept as short as possible, but the display had to be within reach of the officer of the watch on the bridge.

Second World War radar aerials came in many shapes and sizes. Most systems needed two aerials, one for transmitting and one for receiving. Type 271 had two 'cheeses' or hollow segments of a circle inside its lantern. Type 282, the pom-pom director, had two Yagi or fishbone-shaped aerials pointing towards the target. Type 277, the replacement for 271 on small ships late in the war, had a skeletal dish shape. Type 286M used an early 'bedstead' aerial, intended to create the greatest width for the minimum weight.

Some aerials were fixed pointing forward, such as the Type 286. Other early ones had to be turned by hand using a wheel in the radar office. They could not rotate through more than about 400 degrees without the cable becoming twisted, so it had to reverse direction after each sweep. From 1944, new air warning sets had powered continuous rotation, which was far more suitable for a PPI and for plotting in an action information room.

Operating Radar

Radar sets were not normally kept in constant use, and switching an early one on was a considerable operation – it took 21 separate stages in the case of a Type 271. A set needed between 5 and 20 minutes to warm up, according to the model. After that the operator would begin to sweep, unless he had other orders. Again the rate of sweep depended on whether or not a PPI or continuous rotation were in use. Sets fitted with both rotated at about 6 rpm for surface warning. The operator might also carry out a sector sweep if trouble was expected from a certain area, or the rest of the spectrum was covered by other ships. One of his main tasks was to eliminate interference from the set, by good maintenance and good adjustment. He learned how to eliminate faulty displays such as 'tram lines', 'criss-cross pattern' and 'railings'. He reported the echoes of ships or aircraft to the bridge, unless they were identified as ships in company. On finding a hostile echo, he might be ordered to hold on it, or to resume his sweep.[47]

In the early days of radar, bearing and ranges were communicated verbally to the captain on the bridge and he interpreted them, perhaps using a plotting table. This became far more difficult as more types of set were fitted, and the Action Information Organisation (AIO) evolved to cope with it. On a large ship this operated in several compartments, each with a different function. The Operations Room dealt with the surface situation and used both local and general plots of the area. It often used an instrument called a Skiatron, which projected the picture from a PPI to the underside of a translucent circular table so that more than one person could

Right: The array of radar aerials on a cruiser, *c.* 1945.
1. Type 279, long-range air warning.
2. Type 243, interrogator.
3. Type 272P, warning of surface craft, in a circular Perspex lantern.
4. Type 242 receiver.
5. Type 284, used to direct the main armament against surface targets.
6. Type 285, for anti-aircraft fire control.

Far right: A-scan operators in a Type 279 receiving office. One operator turns the handle and the other logs the reports.

view it. The Aircraft Direction Room dealt with the situation in the air and was ready to direct fighters onto an enemy attack if required. It, too, had a Skiatron. Sometimes there was a separate Target Indication Room nearby. The Radar Display Room was used by the radar officer to carry out technical supervision as well as undertake centralised control, height finding and IFF. There was a Bridge Plotting Room close to the command position where the captain could view the data as it filtered through the AIO. In smaller ships there was no Aircraft Direction Room, the Operations Room was combined with the chart house and the whole affair was sited on or near the bridge, making a separate Bridge Plotting Room unnecessary. About a quarter of the fleet had effective Action Information Organisation by 1945.[48]

One of the fastest moving tasks was the control of fighters in defence of the fleet. Destroyers in the British Pacific Fleet were not equipped with radar to act as pickets, so the carriers of a task force had to defend themselves. With attacks from several directions, the PPI then looked like 'a bursting bag of small peas'.[49]

From two ships at the beginning of the war, radar equipped thousands at the end. The *Prince of Wales* was the first ship to carry multiple sets in 1941: Type 281 for air warning, Type 284 for the main armament director, four Type 285s for anti-aircraft directors and four 282s for the close-range weapons.[50] Such fittings became common by the end of the war. Later ships in the War Emergency Destroyer Programme had Type 286 or 291 for combined surface and air warning, 276, 285 for air gunnery and 282 for combined air and surface gunnery, while some ships also had 271 or 272 for surface warning. The use of radar was already beginning to alter the whole nature of naval warfare, as the main centre of command began to move from the bridge to a position below decks. Many captains resisted this and nearly all remained on the bridge in battle, with the result that in action the real decisions were often made by the operations officers rather than the captain.

6 Fittings

After launch, a ship went for fitting out, usually afloat in a basin in or close to the yard which had built her. The process included the installation of engines and armament, and also the fitting of other essential features. Most of these – rigging, boats, anchors, and pumps, for example – were based on equipment that had been used for centuries, but were adapted for modern purposes.

Masts and Rigging

A warship usually had two masts, the foremast situated just aft of the bridge, which was the larger, and the mainmast. At the beginning of the war they were used for signal flags, lamps and wireless telegraphy aerials and navigation lights. Small ships, especially escort vessels, had crow's-nests for look-outs. Most capital ships and cruisers had tripod masts, especially the foremast. Each mast came in one, two or three portions

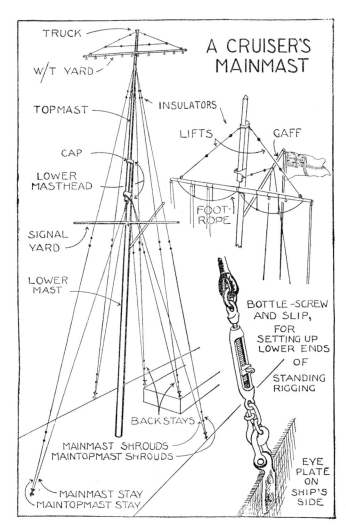

The rigging of a cruiser's mast.

known from the bottom as the lower mast, topmast and topgallant. The *King George V* class were fitted with an 85-foot long, steel foremast with its heel resting on the main deck, and it was 2 feet in diameter at its widest. It had a 55-foot wooden topmast that overlapped with the lower mast by 10 feet, and a 22-foot 'Admiral's pole' above that. Both the upper masts could be lowered or 'struck' for passing under bridges, so that the maximum height above the waterline was 145 feet. The masts were fitted with an upper 24-foot yard across the ship, for signal halyards and W/T aerials; and a 36-foot lower yard for more signal halyards. The mainmast was only 70 feet long and there was a 20-foot jackstaff in the bows and a 27-foot ensign staff at the stern.

Destroyers and smaller ships had simple pole masts at the beginning of the war. The O and P classes of the War Emergency programme were originally to have 'a steel tubular signal mast, with two steel tubular struts, one signal yard, and one W/T aerial ...complete with all stays, signal halyards, dressing lines, deck plates, lightning conductors, vane masthead flashing lights, yard arm flashing lanterns, steaming, fighting and "not under control" lights etc'. But some masts were to prove inadequate in practice – the destroyer *Sardonyx* lost its wooden mast during an Atlantic gale in June 1941, because of the weight of its 286M aerial.[51] By the end of the war the latest ships were being built with lattice masts like pylons, to support the increasing amount of radar equipment.

Steering

Most warships had a single rudder in the centreline of the ship as far aft as possible to give greater leverage. It was able to turn up to 35 degrees on either side, for more than that would tend to cause undue resistance through the water. In the case of twin-screw ships it might have increased manoeuvrability by having one rudder behind each

The anchor gear of the battlecruiser *Repulse*.

propeller, but this was not done even on frigates where it might have given some advantage. Nearly all ships used a balanced rudder which pivoted about its centre so that it took a minimum of effort to turn it.

The traditional wooden steering wheel was still in use in some ships, although many now used a metal version without the handles outside the rim. Major warships needed powerful steering arrangements to move their rudders, especially at high speed. Older and smaller ships used a mechanical system in which power was transmitted by means of screws. Others used electro-hydraulic steering gear, in which the rudder crosshead was turned by two hydraulic rams. In the *King George V* class this consisted of 'two separate motors in the steering compartment aft, and a steam driven pump in the starboard engine room'. A 'telemotor' system of transmission allowed this to be controlled from either the steering wheel on the bridge or the action position lower down in the hull. In an emergency it could be controlled directly from the rudder head.

The specification for the O and P class destroyers demanded:

The steering gear is to be tested to show that the vessel can be thoroughly controlled with the rudder hard over on either side, with the machinery developing the same power as on the full power trials and driving the vessel full speed ahead.[52]

Habitability

The Royal Navy of 1939–45 had to cope with a greater range of weather conditions than ever before, because it had rarely operated in Arctic waters in peacetime. It fought for a longer period than any modern war and often with improvised and overcrowded ships. Living conditions on the decks could be uncomfortable, particularly in the extremes of the Arctic and the tropics. Air conditioning was only used in selected magazine spaces before the war. It was added to some control compartments, to aid the operators' concentration, and a few other areas, but its weight was considered prohibitive and it was not used in living spaces. Trunking was used to bring fresh air, whether hot or cold, to the messdecks and living spaces. Trunks had to be kept small to avoid interfering with the structural integrity of the ship. Air was spread around the compartment in question by means of directional centrifugal fans known as 'punkah louvres', which came in various sizes from 5 inches to 17½ inches and could be operated at two speeds. At full blast the fans of a major warship could in theory change the air in a galley every half-minute, and that on a traditional messdeck every five minutes. The messdecks created many problems. The air might be directed towards particular hammocks, whose occupants had more than they needed. The hammocks added to the problem as they tended to restrict the circulation. Officers (apart from medical officers) generally took little interest in ventilation and it was left to the occupants of the mess. The surgeon-lieutenant of the frigate *Aire* in the North Atlantic reported that there was a great deal of condensation or 'sweating', caused by inadequate lining of the bulkheads with cork. More was added, but this did not change the culture of the lower deck. He described an

…unhealthy disrespect, that seems to be traditional among seamen, for fresh air on the mess decks. Punkah louvres were often closed, flaps closed down over exhaust trunks although the latter was justified to some extent as some cases are on record where considerable quantities of ocean found their way to the mess decks via these passages.

Furthermore, the seamen were prone to an 'indiscreet use of electrical heaters', which made the situation even worse.[53]

The navy was rather less prepared for conditions in the Indian Ocean than might have been expected, for its ships had usually spent short periods at sea there in peacetime. Canvas awnings were used to keep the sun off the deck in harbour, and at sea the men were often allowed to sleep on deck, but they still had to spend a good deal of time below.

It is one thing to spend a week or two under such conditions, but quite another to spend months on end with little prospect of relief. As far as possible, it was arranged that ships should refit in South African ports, to give ship's companies a tonic, but the next relief seems a long way off when the last is a thing of the past.[54]

With a temperature of over 90°F (32°C) in his cabin, the constructor captain of the Eastern Fleet wondered if 'conditions would be less uncomfortable if taking part in a convoy to Murmansk'. He concluded that they would not, though one of his colleagues did think so. 'Arctic conditions present appreciable problems. These, however, are not as severe as those in tropical theatres of operation'.[55] Those on the Arctic convoys might not have agreed. Punkah louvres were generally operated at low speed in colder conditions, and messdecks were fitted with steam radiators in any case. There was a problem with condensation on many ships. Lagging was found useful in both Arctic and tropical conditions, as it helped to keep the heat in or out as required. Modern centralised messing created new problems, as there was greater pressure on the system at mealtimes. Galleys ideally needed a height between deck of 8 feet to allow enough air, but this was rarely possible.

Anchors and Mooring Gear

An anchor is a device for holding a ship or boat to the sea bottom, used when there is no other means of keeping the ship in position. Naval ships needed a good supply of them, because in wartime replacements were not always to hand, and they would often be at anchor in bases such as Scapa Flow or Halifax, rather than alongside jetties in the traditional naval bases. The older type of anchor had two arms fitted with flukes, with a shank and a stock set in a plane at right angles to the arms. It was known as the Admiralty pattern and it featured prominently in the flag and on cap and arm badges. But it was obsolete except for boats and for smaller anchors known as kedges. The standard modern pattern was the stockless anchor. It had a shank and two arms, which pivoted at one end of the shank. Both of these would sink into the sea bottom when the anchor was in use, holding the ship in place against the wind and current. It was much easier to stow than the Admiralty pattern, and could simply be hauled up into the hawse pipe in the bows of the ship. The Admiralty continued to experiment with new anchors during the war and in 1943 it began trials with various different patterns resulting eventually in one of the first High Holding Power anchors; but this had little effect during the war.[56]

A large warship usually had two large bower anchors, which as their name implies were kept in the bows, in constant readiness for use. Those of *Hood* were of 190 cwt or 9½ tons. The sheet anchor was of similar size and was used as a spare. It was in a hawse hole on the starboard side of the ship, just abaft one of the bowers. (Later in the war, sheet anchors were

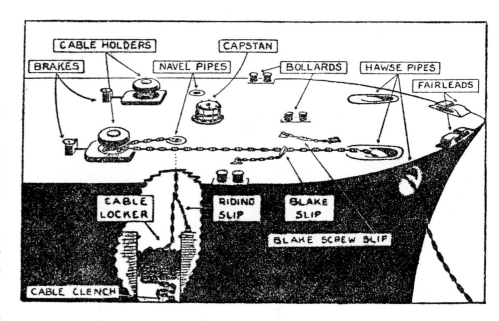

The layout of the anchor gear in the bows of a ship.

removed from many ships to save weight and the hawse pipe blocked off.) The stream anchor was used at the stern and was much smaller – 60 cwt in the case of the *Hood*. Kedge anchors were 'smaller anchors, used for light work such as kedging, warping or hauling the launch out when laying out a bower or sheet anchor &C. They are stowed in any convenient positions under suitable derricks or davits usually one on each side of the ship'. The kedge anchors of the *Hood* were of 16 and 12 cwt.[57] Smaller ships had fewer and smaller anchors. A Flower class corvette had three bowers of 21¼ cwt and a stream anchor of 5¾ cwt.

Chain cable was used with all ship's anchors. Apart from its greater strength compared with rope, it did not get tangled and its weight tended to make it lie horizontally on the sea bed, providing a more efficient pull on the anchor. It was usually studded cable, with a bar across the centre of each link to make it stronger and less likely to kink. The size of cable for an individual ship was based on the tonnage, using a formula worked out by W J Holt of the Royal Corps of Naval Constructors. It was measured by the diameter of the iron which made up each link and varied from 7/16 inch to 3⅜ inch. Length also varied with the size of the ship. It was measured in shackles, each of which was 12½ fathoms or 75 feet long. The *Hood* had 35 shackles, a V-W class destroyer had 14. When raising anchor, the chain was hauled up through the hawse hole in the bows. It was then led to a steam or electric winch or capstan, which did the work of hauling it up, and let it down through the navel pipes to the cable locker well below decks. When hauled up, a device known as a Blake's slip was fitted to the cable between the capstan and the hawse pipe to secure it, but the main work of holding the anchor was done by the brake on the capstan itself.

For mooring alongside a pier or jetty, the ship was equipped with bollards along both sides to which ropes could be attached. These were usually led through fairleads on the edges of the deck to take the mooring rope clear of obstructions and take some of the strain.

Boats

Every naval ship carried a complement of boats, which were used for communication with the shore and other ships when at anchor, for taking on supplies and allowing men to go ashore on leave, for racing and recreation and for many other purposes. A boat could also be used to lay out a small anchor, for example in water that was too shallow for the ship herself. Larger boats could be fitted with guns, but these were rarely used

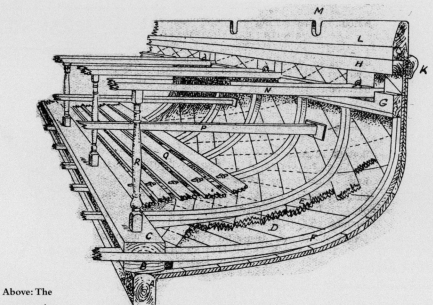

Above: The construction of a typical pulling boat.

Below: A typical, fast motorboat of 1939.

boats were a common feature of harbour life, especially in places like Malta and Scapa Flow. Officers considered that boat-pulling was superior to the lower deck's first love, football, because it involved a far great proportion of the crew. 'Eleven men only can represent their ship at football…but in a big-ship regatta a team of nearly three hundred officers and men go forth in the boats to do battle for their ship'. Each branch produced its own crew, perhaps for several different kinds of boat. Such contests were rarer in wartime, but the cruiser *Mauritius* was able to organise a contest at Taranto in 1943, involving 27 crews from several ships.[61] Mostly, boats had far more serious uses in wartime. They helped evacuate troops from the beaches of Dunkirk, until the flotilla of small craft arrived. They rescued crews of torpedoed merchant ships and boarded sinking U-boats, as with HMS *Spey* in February 1944.

want to wear a uniform like yours, I want to command a boat like yours, to belong to a ship like yours, like you to be part and parcel of the Navy.[59]

Boats were vital in training midshipmen. According to O'Conor: 'The finest training as a seaman and for command that he can possibly have is in a boat if he is given complete charge'.[60] Rowing races between

The whaler had some difficulty in getting alongside the U-boat because of the slight sea that was running, but eventually my First Lieutenant and one Rating managed to scramble on board. There was one dead rating on the gun platform and the Commanding Officer was lying severely wounded in the stomach alongside the conning tower hatch. The First Lieutenant actually got down to the lower control room, finding the inside in complete darkness but free from fumes. At the bottom of

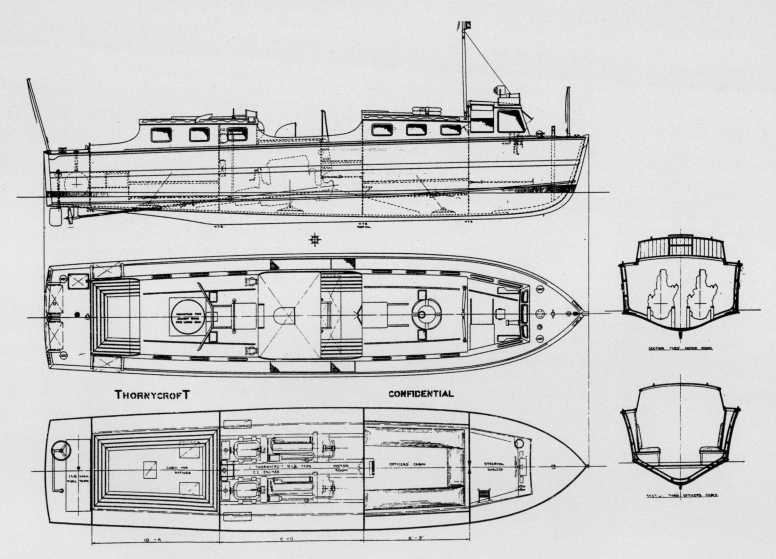

THORNYCROFT CONFIDENTIAL

officers and men go forth in the boats to do battle for their ship'. Each branch produced its own crew, perhaps for several different kinds of boat. Such contests were rarer in wartime, but the cruiser *Mauritius* was able to organise a contest at Taranto in 1943, involving 27 crews from several ships.[61] Mostly, boats had far more serious uses in wartime. They helped evacuate troops from the beaches of Dunkirk, until the flotilla of small craft arrived. They rescued crews of torpedoed merchant ships and boarded sinking U-boats, as with HMS *Spey* in February 1944.

The whaler had some difficulty in getting alongside the U-boat because of the slight sea that was running, but eventually my First Lieutenant and one Rating managed to scramble on board. There was one dead rating on the gun platform and the Commanding Officer was lying severely wounded in the stomach alongside the conning tower hatch. The First Lieutenant actually got down to the lower control room, finding the inside in complete darkness but free from fumes. At the bottom of the hatch was a large bag, possibly containing books, but it was too heavy for him to get up the conning tower; he therefore climbed up again to get a line, the Rating on board being fully occupied securing the whaler and keeping an eye on the wounded captain. The First Lieutenant had barely gained the open air once more when the boat began to sink and water to lap over the conning tower hatch. He and the Rating both jumped over the side and swam to the whaler which then backed clear of the disturbance caused by the U-boat sinking.[62]

Pulling, that is, rowing boats came in two main types, both clinker built with overlapping planks. The 32-foot cutter was a development of a type used by the navy for nearly 200 years. It had a wide beam of 8 feet 6½ inches for good sailing, and a square or transom stern. It was double-banked, that is, it had two oarsmen on each thwart, one on each side, to a total of 12. They were carried by cruisers and capital ships. The 27-foot whaler was derived from the boat used to harpoon whales and was used on most types of ship. It too was clinker built, but was double ended with a sharp bow and stern and a narrow beam of 6 feet, which made it better at rowing than sailing. It was single-banked, with its five oarsmen sitting on alternate thwarts. Smaller types of sailing boat, such as the 14-foot dinghy, were mainly used for recreation and training.

The navy had virtually abandoned steam-powered boats in recent years, reducing the weight by two-thirds and eliminating the need for stokers to go with every boat. By 1939 it was also moving towards high-speed motorboats with planing hulls, opening 'a new chapter of seamanship' according to Commander O'Conor.[63] Meanwhile, the 'slow type' of motorboat survived in the service, ranging from the 50-foot motor pinnace carried by battleships and fitted with two cots for overnight stays, to the 13½-foot motor dinghy used by submarines.

Fast motorboats had hard chine for planing. They were carvel built with two layers of diagonal planking running in opposite directions. They had cabins and some accommodation. At the top end of the scale was the 45-foot motorboat used by capital ships. It could be fitted out as an admiral's barge, or for general purposes. It had three engines for a total horsepower of 100. The 35-foot boat was similar, used by cruisers and as a crash tender by aircraft carriers. The 30-foot boat was used by light cruisers, while the 25-foot boat was used by most ships – the largest power boat on destroyers and escorts and a utility boat on larger ships.

A medium-sized power boat was crewed by four men. The coxswain was in charge unless an officer or midshipman was present. The bowman was responsible for the bow lines when coming alongside, the stern sheetman did the same job aft. A stoker was carried for engine maintenance and general duties, but he no longer had to operate the engine during manoeuvres as with a steam boat, because it was under the full control of the coxswain, who operated the throttle from his position at the wheel.

A destroyer or frigate usually carried three boats, slung from davits on both sides of the ship. A River class frigate, for example, had a 27-foot whaler, a 25-foot motorboat and a 15-foot dinghy of a type used by trawlers. In 1939 *Belfast* was issued with two 35-foot motorboats, one as an admiral's barge; a 36-foot motor and pulling pinnace of a type that was becoming obsolete; a 25-foot fast motorboat, a standard 32-foot cutter and 27-foot whaler, a 16-foot motor dinghy and a 14-foot dinghy designed by the Royal Naval Sailing Association for racing against the boats of other ships. Such a large complement could not be carried on davits without restricting the secondary armament, so the larger ones were stowed in the centre of the ship between the funnels. The *Prince of Wales* carried 10 of her boats on a special deck abaft of the funnels and above the wardroom, varying from 45 feet to 16 feet. The larger ones were stowed fore and aft, some were set athwartships to fill in vacant spaces, while the smaller ones might be nested inside slightly larger ones. Aircraft carriers had their boats in recesses on either side of the hull and obviously there was no place for central stowage.

The larger boats of battleships and cruisers were lifted out using a derrick or the aircraft crane. Davits were more convenient for launching boats. Normally the boat was stowed inboard of the davit and 'turned out' or manoeuvred into place above the water when required. On the Welin type of davit, used on destroyers and smaller ships, the davit was hinged backwards with the boat stowed outboard and on top of it. A whaler could be launched quickly by simply turning a handle and extending the davit over the water. Some davits were hinged to be lowered flat when in action. Sea-boats were kept ready on each side of a ship to launch in any emergency, such as man overboard. If launched while the ship was making way a boat used a device called Robinson's disengaging gear to release the falls which had lowered it into the water.

Pumps and Damage Control

Ships needed pumps and drainage for routine tasks such as removing water from the bilges. They also needed them for fire fighting, for flooding magazines to prevent explosion, or to correct heeling caused by damage. They also needed them to remove large quantities of water that might enter after underwater damage by mine or torpedo.

Typically, the O and P class destroyers were designed to have the means to remove water from every compartment. A main galvanised-steel suction pipe 2½ inches in diameter ran the length of the ship, with another under the upper deck and branch pipes leading off to the sides. It was served by fire and bilge pumps in the engine room and an electric pump in one of the boiler rooms. The main machinery spaces had circulating pumps and ejectors, set as low down as possible. For fire fighting, a pipe led forward and aft from the engine room under the upper deck, served by the same pumps. It had various branches and screw-down valves and hose

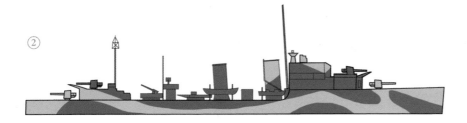

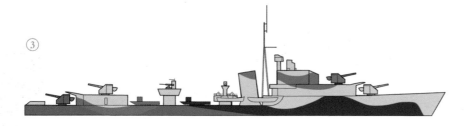

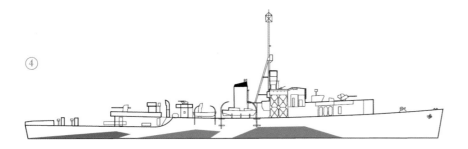

Examples of camouflage schemes.

1. The battleship *Rodney*.

2. An A to I class destroyer in the Admiralty Intermediate Scheme.

3. An Emergency War Programme destroyer in the Admiralty Light Scheme.

4. A River class frigate in the Western Approaches scheme.

connections. The magazines could be flooded direct from the sea by opening 6-inch sea-cocks and flood valves. They could be opened from positions on the upper and lower deck.

Despite these provisions, damage control proved inadequate in the early stages of the war. Men were not fully trained to carry it out, and often the equipment showed fatal flaws. The *Ark Royal* sank slowly because her steam plant was out of action and she had no diesel generators to supply power to the pumps. These defects were only partly remedied during the war, but new ships were fitted with at least one diesel generator placed above the waterline.

Painting

In peacetime ships were painted dark grey in British waters and light grey on foreign stations. Many continued in this state for some months after the start of the war, but the Admiralty issued various orders outlining camouflage schemes to be adopted. These relied on the use of light and dark shades of grey, green and blue to form a disruptive pattern. They were painted in bands, loops and patches across the hull and superstructure to break up the outline of the ship

and hopefully confuse the enemy about her type or intentions. Meanwhile, Western Approaches Command used the services of Peter Scott, son of a naval gunnery officer, and a yachtsman, painter and naturalist himself. He attempted to see the ships through the eye of a U-boat commander, and used lighter shades of grey and green. This was successful and was adopted by many ships in other commands. 'Mountbatten pink' proved far less effective.

There was no set scheme for landing craft at first and Alec Guinness 'devised a pattern of pale blue and white rectangles, rather like a Braque. My fellow officers complained that I had made mine look like a hospital-ship and far too conspicuous; but when we were out on the ocean they equally complained that they couldn't see me'.[64] Standard patterns were allocated by Admiralty Fleet Orders in May and November 1943. But by this time the whole concept of camouflage was coming into question and radar was beginning to make it redundant. Ships were now to be painted in light grey again, with a dark blue or grey patch in the central part of the hull.

Underwater, the hulls were covered with anti-fouling paint. This contained either mercury or copper, though scientists were divided about whether it poisoned marine life or merely deterred it from growing on the hull. It generally had a reddish colour. It would deteriorate if the hull was out of the water for any length of time, so the upper level near the load waterline had a composition with less anti-fouling known as 'boot topping', which separated the lower from the upper part of the hull. Wooden decks usually became very white after cleaning and sun-bleaching, and sometimes they were painted to prevent recognition from the air. Iron ones had non-slip paint of various types. Non-slip deck painting such as Cemtex was used on steel decks and gave a natural dark grey tone.[65]

Life-Saving Gear

The Royal Navy did not like to think about the possibilities of defeat, and perhaps that is why it tended to neglect life-saving gear until well into the war. In September 1939 there were still no plans to issue men with personal equipment. After urging by the Commander-in-Chief Home Fleet, the Admiralty began to issue inflatable life belts to crews. Each consisted of 'a rubber belt contained in a blue stockingette cover'. It was 'comfortable to wear, easy to swim in, and to give fair support to the wearer. It has been found that it is possible to carry out all normal duties in ordinary temperatures when wearing it'. It was fitted round a man's waist and supported by shoulder straps. It was inflated by mouth and this had to be done before leaving the ship if the man was to stand any chance of survival. It did nothing to keep an exhausted or unconscious man's head out of the water. 'His head invariably fell forward, causing death by drowning'.[66]

Ships' boats had some role in life-saving, but it is unlikely that many of them could be launched quickly enough from a sinking ship. The navy relied heavily on the Carley float, first introduced in 1915. This was an 0-shaped raft with its flotation round its edges and a grating in the middle. It came in three sizes, varying from the largest which was 10 feet long, 5 feet broad and 17 inches deep and designed for 20 men, to the small-ship version, which was 6 feet long, 4 feet wide and 12 inches deep and could take ten men. Each was equipped with water containers,

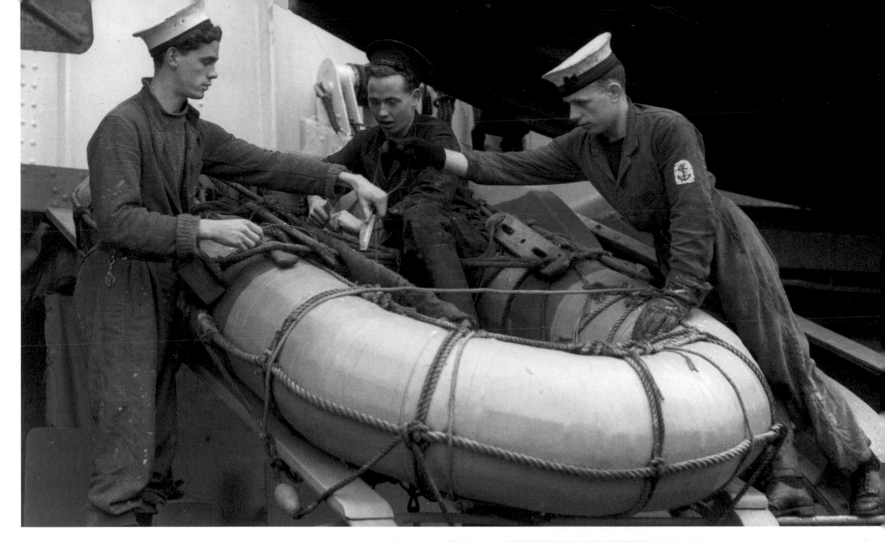

distress flares, tins of energy tablets, a torch and a signalling mirror, first-aid outfit, de-salting kit and Jacob's ladder. It offered no protection against cold and rain, and was designed so that half the men would be outside the raft clinging to ropes, and the rest, sitting round the rim, were never completely dry. It was barely adequate for war in the North Sea or Mediterranean, and completely unsuitable for the Atlantic or Arctic, where rescue might be delayed and the men were vulnerable to exposure. An inquiry of 1946 reported, 'Time and again large numbers who have reached their refuge have collapsed from cramp and cold, and died before rescue arrived'.[67] When the *Wild Swan* was sunk in 1942, all the men got into the water but they had to wait there for 13 hours for rescue. Thirty-one of them were affected by cold, three more became exhausted and drowned. Men in motorboats and whalers were safe, but those in the Carley floats suffered. As the ship's medical officer commented, 'No lives would have been lost if the life-saving equipment had been adequate to keep the men out of the water.'[68] The Carley float was supplemented by a device called a flotanet, which, as its name implies, is a net supported by floats. It was useful as 'a first refuge until the more solid support of a raft could be reached'.

Despite their faults, increasing numbers of Carleys and flotanets were issued during the war. The battleship *Howe* had 54 Carleys and 101 flotanets for a complement of more than 1800 men, while the carrier *Indomitable* had 74 Carleys and 28 flotanets for just under 2000 men. Carley floats might be stacked on odd corners of the deck, as on many battleships. Cruisers and aircraft carriers usually had rows of them stowed vertically along the sides of the ship, ready for use. Even so, many could not be launched, either because bad maintenance allowed the slips to seize up, or no knife was available to cut the ropes. It was claimed that only about 10 per cent of Carley floats became waterborne on a sinking. There is good reason to believe that many of the 50,000 sailors who died in the war could have been rescued by better lifesaving methods.[69]

Above: Seamen secure a Carley float before putting to sea.

Left: Officers wearing life vests in the wardroom.

PART V

Naval Society and Culture

1 The Administration of Naval Personnel

During the war the Royal Navy and Royal Marines would expand from 131,000 regulars and 73,000 reservists at the beginning of 1939, to a maximum of 783,000 men and 72,000 women in June 1945. The great majority of the new recruits were conscripts or short-term volunteers who had no plans to make the navy their career. This rapid expansion was less than the army, which had 3 million men at its peak, or the RAF, which had over a million. But a navy's personnel needs are far more complex than those of armies or air forces. Most of its men will spend a large part of their time at sea, which is not man's natural environment. They will live there in very difficult and dangerous conditions, and have to be supplied with needs of every kind. In addition a navy requires almost every type of skill. As well as seamanship and engineering, the wartime navy needed many of the techniques of the army for the Royal Marines, and most of the air force's skills for the Fleet Air Arm. The expansion put great strain on the navy's personnel system but brought into play one of the navy's greatest strengths – the ability to improvise and modernise within a traditional framework.

Naval manning was dominated by two rather archaic principles. In the first place, in theory it was not possible for a rating to be a member of the navy as such: a rating had to be borne on the books of a particular ship. Of course many thousands of men were in shore bases, but these usually had ship names, such as HMS *Ganges*, the training base on the River Orwell. The fiction was taken even further and every base actually had a ship or a boat. For example, HMS *Valkyrie*, the radar training base on the Isle of Man, had a converted lifeboat which was supposed to bear its complement of many hundreds of men.[1] Even senior officers were part of the fiction: staff officers at the Admiralty were technically attached to HMS *President,* a depot ship moored in the Thames. It was a custom that had perhaps had some meaning in the early days of the sailing navy when ships were manned for single campaigns or voyages only. It survived the transition to continuous service in the 1850s, and the building of shore bases from the 1890s onwards and did not end until the Naval Discipline Act of 1959.

The names of shore bases were often a matter of chance, based on some ancient warship which had been reduced to harbour service in that port many years earlier. The original *Ganges*, for example, was an 80-gun ship of the line built in 1821 and broken up more than a century later. Some bases had rather frivolous names. HMS *Varbel,* the base for midget submarines on the Island of Bute, was a combination of the names of Varley and Bell, the officers who founded it.

Secondly, all peacetime and most wartime ratings and warrant officers were attached to one of three 'home ports' or 'manning divisions' – Chatham, Portsmouth and Devonport (Plymouth). The new dockyard at Rosyth was never developed as a manning port despite ambitious plans, so peacetime naval recruitment tended to be concentrated in the south of England. In wartime this was somewhat modified and several specialised manning divisions were set up, for example for coastal forces, but more than half the navy remained with the three traditional divisions in 1944. Each 'general service' ship of the navy – including capital ships, cruisers, carriers and escort vessels – was attached to one of the three divisions and its crew would come from there. It was a system that had worked well in peacetime, allowing each man to settle his family in the area of the port in the knowledge his ship would return there sooner or later and he would be sent on leave or courses in the area. In wartime it came under considerable strain.

The Second Sea Lord and his Staff

Naval personnel policy was the responsibility of the Second Sea Lord, a senior admiral and member of the Board of Admiralty. In 1939 the post was held by Sir Charles Little. In 1941 he was succeeded by W J Whitworth, who had led the *Warspite* into action at the Second Battle of Narvik, one of the few successes of the Norwegian campaign. In 1944 the post went to Sir Algernon Willis, a great administrator and Cunningham's former Chief of Staff, but one of the 'Never complain, never explain' school, according to his future son in law.[2] The Second Sea Lord was responsible to the Board for recruiting and training the

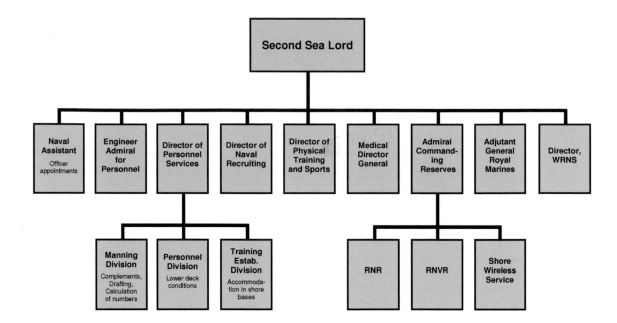

The organisation of the Second Sea Lord's department.

fleet, setting the levels of complements for ships, the appointment of officers, and for the administration of the Royal Marines, WRNS, reserve forces and naval hospitals. His Naval Assistant was responsible for officer appointments, and the Engineer Admiral for Personnel dealt with postings within his own branch. The Director of Personal Services was responsible for most of the manning issues. Under him, the Manning Division calculated the number of men needed for each period, the Personnel Division advised on the welfare of the lower deck and the Training Division co-ordinated the accommodation in training bases. But, in fact, the power of the Second Sea Lord's department was rather weak and vague. The actual training was done in schools under the authority of the area commands, and the content of the training, where it was laid down officially, was much more influenced by the branches such as engineering and gunnery.

Naval manning was determined by the numbers of men of particular skills needed for the ships that were likely to be in commission in the coming year, with a proportion for shore bases, training and so on. Again this came under strain in wartime as ships, such as the 50 American

destroyers, were acquired unexpectedly, others were lost in action, or individuals became casualties at unpredictable rates. New types, such as landing craft, were developed and the Fleet Air Arm expanded rapidly, so it was almost impossible to predict numbers accurately.

The crew of an individual class of warship was decided within the Second Sea Lord's office, after consultation with the various departments involved. This could become highly complex because of the different trades, and the situation became worse as new equipment was fitted to ships, including radar and anti-aircraft guns.

Volunteers and Conscripts

In peacetime, and even in wartime in 1914–18, the navy relied on voluntary entry. The terms of the seaman's normal 12-year service were harsh, and life at sea was often uncomfortable and restrictive, but the navy had unrivalled prestige, while a long period of guaranteed employment seemed attractive in the harsh economic climate of the 1930s. There was no shortage of good-quality volunteers.

The navy was slightly reluctant to rely on conscription even in 1939, but it soon became part of the fabric of wartime life. By the spring of 1942, men between the ages of 18 and 46 were liable, and women between the ages of 18 and 31. Even within that there was an element of volunteering. Every man was allowed to volunteer for either the navy or the RAF. If he did not, or failed to get into the service of his choice, he went into the army. No one joined the navy entirely against his will and, in fact, a large number of men were attracted by the prestige and the travel opportunities, and were not put off by the dangers and discomforts. For most of the war the numbers selecting the navy were about three times those needed and the service was able to pick and choose its men to a certain extent. The only exception was in the great expansion period of 1943–4, when almost everyone who came up to the minimum medical and psychological standards was accepted.

The numbers each service was allowed to recruit was set by the War Cabinet, balancing their needs against those of civilian industry and other services. Churchill, with his inside knowledge of all services, played a key role here and wrote in 1941: '…there is practically no Treasury control on War Service demands, and that it is my responsibility to see

The expansion of the navy, army and air force in 1939–45.

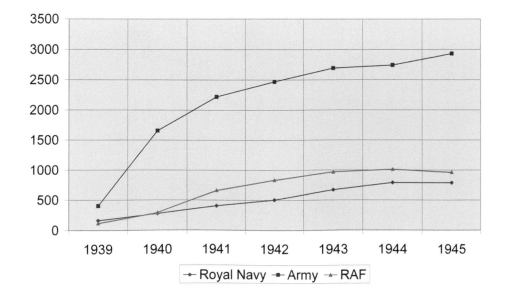

that our limited man-power is used to the best advantage'.[3] The issue of the 'manpower budget' became more intense by 1943 as the population became fully mobilised and there was no slack left in the system.

The navy expanded more slowly than the other services in the early stages of the war. Big ships took several years to produce and smaller vessels, such as coastal forces and landing craft, did not come into full use until the second half of the war. The fastest expansion came in 1943–4 as the navy grew from 671,000 to 790,000 men. The fleet was building up for D-Day, escort carriers from the United States were becoming available, and the great building programme for escort vessels was bearing fruit. In general the navy's demands for personnel were satisfied in the early stages. By 1942 the army and air force demands were being cut back, but the navy was allowed 85 per cent of its requests and took in more than 20,000 men and women in the month of August alone. In the following year it was allowed 190,000 new entrants, but in October the manpower crisis began to bite and its demand for 247,000 men was cut to 67,000 and many older ships had to be taken out of service to man the new ones.[4]

A man who was not in a reserved occupation and was of a suitable age was called to a strict medical examination. He needed good eyesight without glasses unless he had trade qualifications or was entering the administrative, domestic or medical branches. He had to have good teeth or wear dentures, for naval food was often tough and few ships carried dentists. If he passed he went on to an interview. In the first years of the war these were conducted by retired chief petty officers, who knew the service backwards but had little or no experience of newer branches such as aviation or radar. They were replaced by well-educated Wren petty officers trained by psychologists, and they proved a great success.

Ranks and Ratings

In many ways the navy was a more homogenous body than the army, whose regiments retained a very distinct identity even in wartime. Sailors, on the other hand, were often transferred from ship to ship without any regard for tradition. But in one respect the navy was more clearly divided. The army and air force had adopted the utilitarian battledress as the garb of a nation in arms, and it was worn proudly by General Montgomery himself. On shore and in big ships at least, most ratings wore a completely different uniform from the officers. In battle the ranks were slightly less obvious, as everyone wore steel helmets and many had anti-flash gear with less obvious rank distinctions. Afloat in

New entrants are greeted by a warrant officer on arrival at HMS *Royal Arthur* in the holiday camp at Skegness in February 1940. They are rather more mature than the usual peacetime recruits.

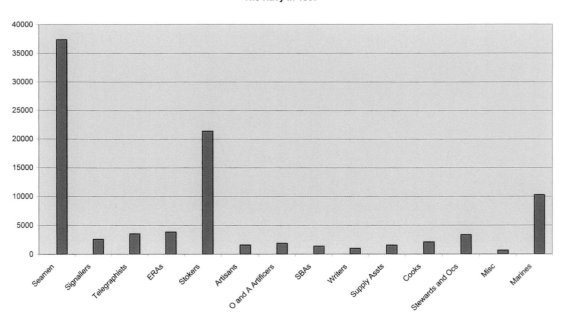

The numbers of
ratings in the
different branches
of the navy in 1937.

the smaller ships, dress tended to be informal but the men's caps said much about their rank even if they were in overalls or working dress. A senior officer had gold braid round the edge of the peak of his cap. A junior or warrant officer had the same distinctive badge, with oak leaves spreading out from an anchor under a crown. A chief petty officer had an anchor within a ring of laurel leaves, while a petty officer had the anchor in a simple gold ring. Junior ratings, if they wore peaked caps, had the same design in red. Junior petty officers and the great majority of those in lower ranks wore the famous round sailor's cap.

Like all modern armed services, except revolutionary ones, the navy had officers who were kept apart from the men when off duty. The non-commissioned ranks were known as 'ratings', reflecting the fact that each man was rated to do a particular job at a certain level of experience and authority. In this respect the terminology was different from the US Navy, in which a 'rated man' was a petty officer.

The Manning Divisions

After his basic training, a man would probably find himself attached to one of the three naval barracks to await posting to a ship. They were overcrowded, unsanitary slums. Even the legendary optimism of the journalist Godfrey Winn, who joined as an ordinary seaman, could not hide the defects of the tunnel at Chatham where many men had to sleep for fear of air raids.

...I suspect that if Charlie hadn't been with me that night, I wouldn't have had the guts to push my way right to the end of the tunnel, now dipping my head, now squeezing past – there was just room for us both to walk abreast – other early comers who had already slung their hammocks from hooks in the low roof, and were busy tying the laces of their boots together and hanging them next to their bed ... Even when we reached the farthest end it looked as though I should have to sleep standing up all night. Every hook was already doubly employed. ... Eventually Charlie spread my hammock on a shelf...I hid my watch, put my boots between myself and the outer wall of the tunnel, made a pillow of the rest of my clothes and crawled into my blankets...I was too tired to care.[5]

There were 48,500 men in the three naval barracks in February 1944. Some were permanent staff, some were undergoing courses, but 12,000 of these were ratings awaiting posting. As well as the barracks

they lived in temporary and requisitioned camps around the ports. New entrants hated the barracks and were only too keen to get a sea draft. Older long-service men, on the other hand, looked for comfortable billets ashore in order to become 'barrack stanchions'. But a man would remain attached to his division wherever he went. His service number was prefixed with the letter P for Portsmouth, D for Devonport and C for Chatham.

The commander of each barracks was responsible for the drafting of seaman ratings to each ship, as requested. In peacetime he would try to give each man a fair deal, with appropriate periods of foreign and home service, sea and shore jobs; this was impossible in wartime. Men would be called out by Tannoy or given 'draft chits', then marched to the nearest railway station to take a train to the yard where the ship was completing. Often they did not know the name or type of ship at this stage, but could only guess by the size of the draft.

The Branches

The navy was divided into many branches representing different trades. Naturally the seaman branch was the largest, and it included gunners, torpedomen, Asdic and later radar operators. It formed about a third of the navy. Signallers, both visual and radio, were close to the seaman branch and were about 3 per cent. Stokers came next behind the seamen. They provided the semi-skilled and heavy labour force in the engine rooms and formed about 20 per cent of the navy, whereas their more skilled counterparts, the engine room artificers and mechanicians, formed only 3 or 4 per cent. Other highly skilled men such as artisans and ordnance and electrical artificers were about 3 per cent. Marines, who were recruited and trained separately from the sailors, were about 10 per cent of the total fleet. The remainder formed the medical, domestic and administrative side of the navy and included sick berth attendants, cooks, stewards and writers or clerks. They formed about 6 per cent and were distinguished from the others, in that even junior ratings wore 'fore and aft rig', a version of the uniform worn by officers and petty officers, with peaked cap and collar and tie.

Each branch had evolved separately over the years, with its own badges, system of promotion and informal rules. The seaman was a very different animal from the stoker, and equally separate from the marine. The smaller branches relied more on technical skill for

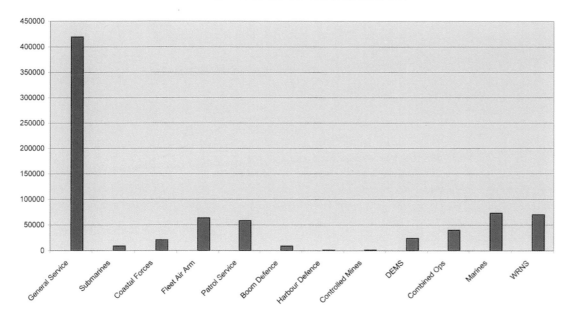

Naval Ratings and Marine Other Ranks, September 1944

advancement, and some were traditionally more genteel in their manners than the seamen or stokers. The different groups were often fierce rivals, but at heart they knew that every branch had its part to play in an efficient ship and navy.

Navies Within the Navy

The members of the three port divisions made up about 60 per cent the navy. The Submarine Service was largely separate since its foundation early in the century. In addition, a new division was set up for the Fleet Air Arm in 1939, and remained a permanent part of the navy, though aircraft carriers and the non-aeronautical parts of their crews remained attached to the three traditional divisions. The Patrol Service was manned by fishermen at the beginning of the war and continued on a separate basis, with its depot at Lowestoft. Coastal Forces was also set up early in the war, to man small, fast craft around British shores and later in the Mediterranean. Combined Operations manned landing craft, and was only loosely under naval control at the best of times. Some of the other groups were incongruously small. There were fewer than 9000 men in the boom defence section in September 1944, and precisely 1368 in the controlled minefields division, presumably kept separate because they were not expected to go far out to sea.

Rear-Admiral Ford discussed the defects of this rather haphazard system in 1943. Conditions of service varied in different manning pools, there was little exchange of information between them and it could be an inefficient use of manpower if there was a miscalculation of future resources or needs suddenly changed. On the other hand:

The great advantage of the present system is that these forces have an esprit de corps of their own and their ratings know that their welfare and advancement depend on their own officers who have a somewhat freer hand in this matter than would be the case if the forces were manned from some centralised pool.[6]

Even within the traditional manning ports, escort vessels such as corvettes and frigates were, in practice, kept separate from the larger warships. As Nicholas Monsarrat wrote on taking command of a frigate: 'Together with ocean convoy escort, it was in point of fact the only sort of navy I knew anything about; the ship I was going to command would be the biggest I had ever boarded, and her job, convoy escort, had been my life for as long as I could remember'.[7] Destroyers might move easily between

fleet and escort duties, but the crews of more specialised escort vessels tended to remain in the same line of business of the whole war.

In effect, there were six or seven different navies within the Royal Navy in 1939–45, each with the same uniform and ranks and often the same trades and qualifications, but manning different ships and fighting different kinds of war. Each of these navies needs to be considered separately.

2 Naval Medicine

Medical officers were involved at every stage in a seaman's career. They helped to select him for entry to the navy and for special tasks such as aircrew and submarines. They looked after his health on board a ship on active service and treated his wounds from accident or battle. Most of these duties were done by men who were almost as raw as the majority of seamen in the navy. There was very little in the life of a peacetime general practitioner to prepare him for the crowded, stuffy conditions of ships' messdecks, for sudden changes in climate between the tropics and the Arctic, or the horrific injuries that men might suffer in battle.

The medical department of the navy came under the Second Sea Lord and was headed by a Surgeon-Vice Admiral. This was Sir Percival Nicholls until he was succeeded by Sir S F Dudley in July 1941. His staff at the Admiralty was divided into four sections, dealing with personnel, material and finance, sickness and surveys, and statistics. His pre-war staff consisted of four naval medical officers and 25 civilian administrators and clerks; by 1943 this had risen to 18 medical officers including three dentists and one from the WRNS.

Naval Surgeons

For historical reasons naval doctors were known as surgeons, though most had no specific training in surgery and were in fact physicians in the usual sense of the term. There were about 400 of them in the pre-war navy – three to a large ship such as a battleship, one to a destroyer flotilla of eight or nine ships. In peacetime a naval surgeon was given a six-month course in subjects of special interest, such as treatment of casualties and preventive medicine, which were rarely taught adequately in normal medical schools. Early in the war it was decided

Naval ratings and marine other ranks in the different parts of the navy in September 1944.

that, as destroyers no longer operated with their flotillas all the time, a medical officer was needed on each one. In 1942 new escorts such as frigates were given a doctor each, greatly increasing the demand. The service peaked with more than 2500 medical officers in 1945.

Wartime naval surgeons were mostly recruited from general practice, from situations where there was another partner to carry on the practice.[8] They joined the Royal Naval Volunteer Reserve as temporary surgeon-lieutenants. In wartime, an induction course of about two weeks was all that was possible before the new naval surgeon was sent to sea, perhaps as the only medical officer in a destroyer or frigate. Surgeon-Lieutenant Whitwell joined the destroyer *Woolwich* in 1940, after two weeks in the navy, with little knowledge of procedures. In May he found himself as part of the Dunkirk evacuation, carrying up to 800 troops at a time and suffering 238 casualties in one trip alone. He was not able to keep up with the paperwork and was rebuked by the Medical Director General for 'the untidy and careless way' in which his journal had been compiled and for failing to 'appreciate the importance of the record'.[9]

From 1943 each new surgeon-lieutenant was issued with an eight-page booklet, *Notes for Medical Officers on Entry into the Royal Navy*,[10] but that dealt mainly with protocol and administration, apart from a few instructions such as 'It is very much better that a malingerer should get away with it for a day or two than that a serious illness should be missed', and that the crew should be trained in first aid in 'not so much what would be ideal as what is going to be possible in "Action" conditions'. It ended with the rousing injunction:

You are at the beginning of a fine adventure and of new experiences. No one is 'behind the lines' in a ship nowadays, and you will share all the risks and dangers equally with your brother officers and men. This is great privilege. Strive to be worthy of it.[11]

At sea, the surgeon found his practice very different from what he was used to ashore. It included only fit young men, who were nevertheless under great stress and discomfort. He could forget his skills in dealing with pregnancy or with the diseases of children or old age. He might have a very small practice compared with what he was used to, perhaps 140 men in a frigate, with distant responsibility for seamen in other warships and in a convoy being escorted. In normal times he had little to do and he might be asked to take on extra responsibilities, from censoring letters to supervising the catering, or acting as a sports officer. He might take a strong interest in preventive medicine, which could lead him into enquiries into the living conditions on the messdecks. He was expected to lecture regularly on first aid, which might save many lives in action conditions. The Admiralty advised him to study the construction of his ship.

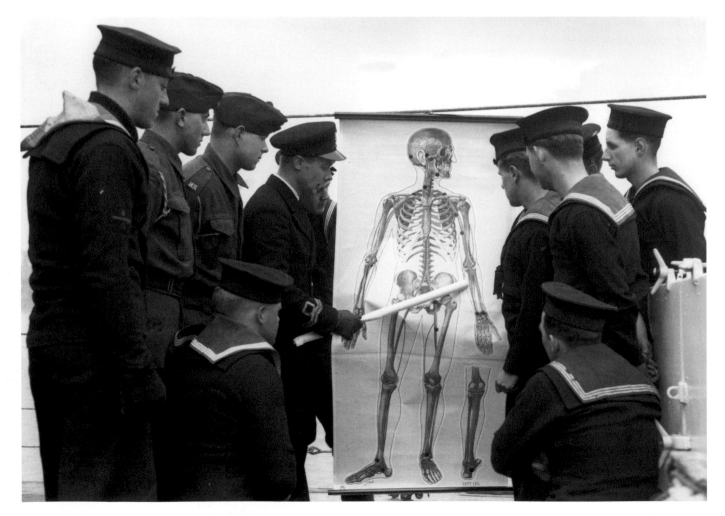

A surgeon-lieutenant RNVR instructs seamen in first aid in the destroyer escort *Atherstone* in 1942.

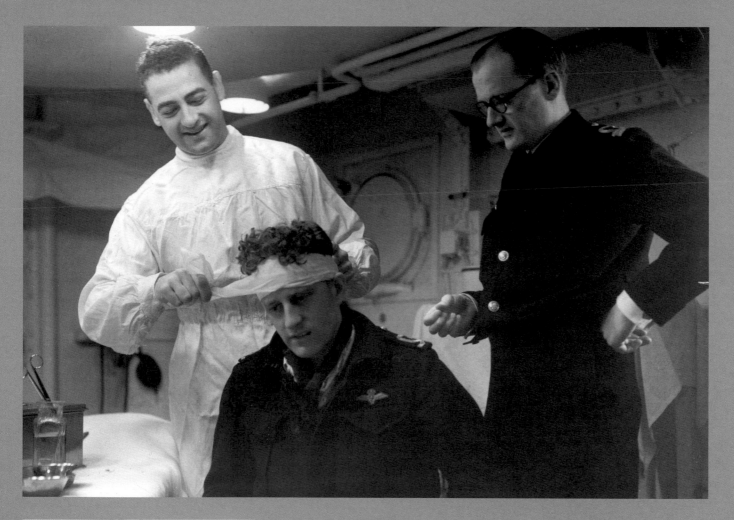

Above: A sick berth attendant dresses the wound of a Corsair pilot injured by anti-aircraft fire in June 1944, as the surgeon-lieutenant looks on.

Left: The sick berth of HMS *Hood*.

He should be well acquainted with the numbers and positions of the main bulkheads, the hatches and the water-tight doors which are open or closed during action, the precise situation of the fresh-water tanks and main ventilating trunks. … the havoc wrought by an explosive shell between decks will often render the task of reaching the wounded in the darkness extremely difficult.[12]

In action, everything changed and a surgeon who lived a comfortable life ashore might suddenly find himself in great

personal danger and dealing with the most traumatic casualties in great haste and with little experience.

Sick Berth Attendants

The Sick Berth Attendant or SBA was a male rating, usually recruited without any previous medical experience. He could be asked to carry out a wide variety of duties, from ward orderly to what would be called a paramedic today; he would be the only fully-trained medical personnel on board a corvette, for example. In between, he might be used as a male nurse or specialise in a subject such as X-ray or as a dental assistant. He was not the equivalent of a commissioned officer like the fully trained female nurses. His 'fore and aft uniform' gave him a certain amount of status, though no more than a cook, steward or clerk. To the lower deck he was sometimes known as 'Doc', implying commissioned status even if loaded with irony. He was also known as the 'sick berth tiffy', equivalent to an artificer or chief petty officer. In a similar vein, Joseph Wellings of the US Navy referred to the 'Chief Pharmacist's Mate' of the destroyer *Eskimo*, but the person he was talking about was almost certainly an ordinary SBA. In fact an SBA was the equivalent of an able seaman or a stoker, with the usual prospects of promotion to leading rate, petty officer and chief. Numbers in the branch peaked at 12,000 at the end of the war.

In the early days of the war, some were very hastily trained indeed. The medical officer of the destroyer *Foresight* complained of his SBA, William Stanmore in 1940. He was aged 23 and had worked as a butcher's boy before being conscripted in 1939. At Haslar Naval Hospital he had had a few lectures on first aid, but had spent most of his time filling sandbags. He did his best, but his intelligence was limited and he was very seasick, but he distinguished himself during the Norwegian campaign that spring, helping the survivors of the torpedoed *Eskimo*.[13]

Sick berth attendants wore a red cross inside a white circle on the right arm as their distinguishing badge. More specialist ones, mainly recruited with previous civilian experience, wore a further distinguishing letter under the badge. These included dental technicians, chiropodists and X-ray operators, who worked in the very largest ships or in shore bases.

The Sick Bay

The main medical compartment of a warship was known as the sick bay. It served as a small hospital, as a doctor's consulting room and sometimes as accommodation, for example in the *Worcester* in 1940 when the coxswain slept in it when it was vacant. The general policy was to have 'a Sick Bay in the upper part of the ship, convenient to the main living and working spaces and sited where the amenities of natural light and ventilation are available'.[14] Ship designers had to make the impossible compromise between a small area for normal use and a much larger one for battle casualties or the treatment of survivors from other ships. A new battleship like the *Prince of Wales* had a large area for its crew of 1400.

Accommodation in the Sick Bay consists of 22 swinging cots, 4 of which are in an isolation ward. There is also provision for the slinging of 8 hammocks. In an emergency there would be sufficient floor space for 12 or more stretcher cases.[15]

The surgeon-commander of the new aircraft carrier *Indomitable* was not happy with the sick bay when the ship was completed in 1941, comparing it unfavourably with the County class cruisers of the 1920s.

The seating accommodation is very poor indeed and the mess table inadequate. It has not been borne in mind that in the present war ships are operating on the oceans for considerable periods and it is therefore imperative that adequate provision is made for the sick or injured who may have to remain on board for many days.[16]

In contrast, the accommodation in the war-built River class frigates was much approved of. The surgeon-lieutenant of HMS *Barle* reported:

This is satisfactory in every way. … The furniture consists of two very comfortable swinging cots, folding operating table, folding armchair, two ordinary chairs, desk, wooden cabinet for drugs and dressings, metal cabinet used for instruments, dressings etc, and larger metal wall rack for stretchers and splints. In addition there are two wooden wall racks used for books and papers. The lighting is good, including shadowless lighting for the operating table, but the emergency floodlight and head light which should be available have not yet been fitted.[17]

Hospital Ships

Naval policy was to get sick and wounded men off the ships as soon as possible, to more specialised facilities ashore or afloat. This was not easy in the middle of the Atlantic, but slightly simpler in narrower seas such as the Mediterranean. The naval hospital ship had three main functions.

It could follow a main fleet around at a discreet distance, though this was comparatively rare in wartime. It could serve as a more or less static ship at an improvised naval base, such as Scapa Flow or Alexandria, where facilities ashore were inadequate. Or it could be used to transport casualties between the fleet and shore hospitals, which was the most common role.

The navy used 11 hospital ships during the war, and only five up to 1942. At the beginning of the war only the *Maine* of 8599 tons was in service. Built in 1902 for P&O, she had originally been designed for the cattle trade with South America and had a speed of 8 to 10 knots. No purpose-built hospital ship was completed, and the others were a mixed bag of converted merchantmen. Only one had been built more recently than 1922. Their size varied from 2000 to 10,000 tons and speed from 11 to 18 knots. Some were powered by diesel engines, some by oil-fired steam and some by coal – an arrangement that produced a great amount of dust and was very unsatisfactory. Some carried 500 patients, the smallest carried 170.

One of the most active hospital ships was the *Oxfordshire* of 8646 tons, built in 1912 for the Bibby Line. She was fitted for 505 patients and had a medical staff of 10 doctors and nine nursing sisters, plus sick berth attendants. She spent the first part of the war as base hospital ship at Freetown, Sierra Leone. Then she served in the North African landings and spent 1943 carrying patients between various Mediterranean ports. After that she was sent east to join the British Pacific Fleet. She treated more than 22,000 patients during the war, and returned prisoners of war and internees after it.[18]

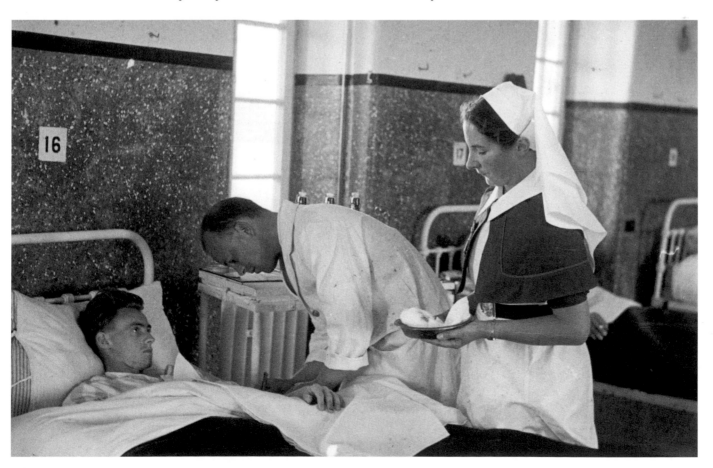

Opposite above: The Hospital Ship *Tjitjalengka* at Liverpool. Built in the Netherlands, she was taken over by the Admiralty in 1942 and served mainly in African ports before going to Australia in 1945.

Opposite below: Haslar Hospital near Portsmouth in the 1920s.

Left: A naval nursing sister in the hospital at Malta.

Shore Hospitals and Sick Quarters

The Royal Navy had used shore hospitals for nearly two centuries. The oldest was at Haslar on a peninsula near Portsmouth. It had been located to prevent press-ganged seamen from escaping and access was better by sea than by land. In 1939 there were also hospitals in the established naval bases at Plymouth, Portland, Chatham, the Firth of Forth and great Yarmouth. All these gained temporary extensions during the war, and auxiliary hospitals were added at places such as Londonderry, which the navy had not used much in peacetime. Civilian hospitals were converted, or large houses were taken over. One of the biggest was Barrow Gurney, a large mental hospital near Bristol, planned as an evacuation centre if bombing became too intense. It had about 25 medical officers under a surgeon rear-admiral, 45 nursing sisters, and about 270 sick berth attendants. It treated more than 26,000 patients, although the projected number of casualties from bombing never materialised.

Overseas, the navy had hospitals in all its main bases. One of the most important was at Bighi close to the entrance to Grand Harbour in Malta, but it had to be evacuated and its facilities moved further inland. Meanwhile more hospital facilities were set up at Alexandria, the headquarters of the Mediterranean Fleet during this time, to supplement the hospital ship. Smaller naval medical centres were known as sick quarters. Some were attached to shore bases, some dealt with minor illnesses among men from visiting ships. There were about a hundred of them in the United Kingdom, ranging from HMS *Pembroke IV* at Southend in the Thames Estuary which treated more than 75,000 patients, to the facilities at HMS *Gordon* further up the river, which treated 330.

The Nursing Services

Queen Alexandra's Royal Naval Nursing Service was founded in 1902. At the outbreak of war it was quite a small organisation, with 85 women, plus 168 in reserve. They wore a dignified but rather old-fashioned nurse's uniform, modified in conditions of active service. They were treated as the equivalent of officers. They were fully qualified nurses, with a hierarchy of sisters, senior sisters, matrons and principal matrons who might take charge of a hospital of 600 beds or more. A sister was largely engaged in training and supervisory duties; she might have a number of partially trained sick berth staff and women Voluntary Aid Detachments or VADs under her. The typical ward had 40 beds, with two sisters in charge. Naval nurses served in shore hospitals, sick quarters and hospital ships; they were not employed in seagoing warships. A total of 1341 sisters served during the war.[19]

VADs were less highly trained women nurses. They were members of charitable societies that provided first-aid training – the Order of St John of Jerusalem and the British Red Cross Society – and worked as nurses, clerks, cooks and dispensers in naval hospitals. More than 5000 of them served during the war, mostly under the instructions of QARNC nurses. Nurses were treated as equivalent to WRNS petty officers for accommodation.

Preventive Medicine

Naval surgeons reported on the life of the men in their messes, and were deeply concerned about overcrowding, the lack of ventilation and the problems of condensation. The surgeon of the old cruiser *Emerald* reported in 1943: 'The accommodation of this ship is inadequate for the present complement (702). Passageways are obstructed by lockers and men asleep for whom there is not sufficient room in the messdecks'.[20] They also commented on the seamen's diet, finding that there was often still a lack of fresh vegetables and excessive use of tinned foods.

Surgeons also had to deal with the ill effects of the seamen's 'run ashore'. Drunkenness was, of course, common, as were venereal diseases, and sometimes the ill effects of fights between rival ships' companies. Officers were generally tolerant of all of these: '…at 2100 hours our sick bay was full of "casualties", mostly with black eyes. … I gather there are similar casualties in the sick bay of the other ship involved!'.[21] Some medical officers were less understanding. In 1944 the surgeon of the frigate *Helford* gave a very detailed report on the hazards of the local brothels in Aden.[22]

The naval dental service included 686 officers at its peak in 1945. There was no question of distributing them among smaller ships as with doctors, and only battleships and fleet aircraft carriers had their own. Instead, dentists kept a good watch on the seamen's dental health on their visits to shore bases. It was an important matter, as dental treatment could not be arranged at sea, and naval food tended to require good teeth. Hostilities Only seamen were, however, allowed to wear dentures to replace missing teeth.

Organisation for Battle

In the early stages of the war, much of the peacetime order of battle was adhered to.

In larger ships this consisted of evacuating the Sick Bay to Distributing Stations situated in protected positions, which acted merely as places of refuge for medical stores and personnel. Pending a lull in the action casualties could receive only minimal first aid locally … When the action was over, the Sick Bay, if still serviceable, reverted to its ordinary function; otherwise, some upper deck space had to be chosen where the casualties would be given more methodical treatment.

More flexible arrangements soon became necessary, particularly in the case of air attacks which might continue for many hours. By 1943 the defects of the old sick bay were generally recognised. 'In war this exposed position is extremely vulnerable, and it becomes necessary to provide a more protected place to which existing sick can be quickly transferred and where casualties can be received.'[23] It was also necessary to set up distributing stations close to the men's action stations, to treat the wounded as quickly as possible, and with the minimum of movement. The 1942 pamphlet *The Treatment of Battle Casualties Afloat* cited the bad example of Nelson's death at Trafalgar, when he was carried down several decks despite a spinal injury. 'The man-handling entailed must have greatly exaggerated the shock from his injuries!' It was now emphasised that 'the most imperative necessity in the immediate care of wounded is treatment of surgical shock. Shock is invariably present in severe injuries, but its presence must be expected in the case of burns'.

First-aid posts were to be set up round the ship – a cruiser, for example, would have four, port and starboard, fore and aft. Each had either a medical officer, a sick berth rating or an especially well-trained first aider, plus one less skilled man An operating theatre would be set up below decks, though the principal medical officer was advised 'not to be immobilised permanently at any one post', but 'able to move about as necessary'. The surgeon should wear overalls with large pockets to carry equipment and tools from place to place. But in battle he should not expect to achieve too much.

During action, conditions in the operating theatre are such that no serious surgical work can be attempted; the traditional silence is replaced by a confusing medley of sound – the roar of salvoes and shattering detonations as the ship gives and receives punishment, the din of Fire Parties clearing burning debris and Repair Parties shoring up bulkheads and fixing temporary lighting between decks. There are the added discomfort of fumes, smoke and water, and the ship's evolutions will increase the extent and frequency of her roll and pitch.

In a small ship the single medical officer was expected to stay at his post unless summoned elsewhere, for example to liberate a casualty who was pinned down or to give first aid to an officer who could not leave his post. Otherwise he was required to do two things; 'To administer skilled First Aid to the injured' and 'By the manner of his so doing, to reinforce the courage of the seriously wounded and re-establish the morale of those who may be more frightened than hurt'.

The first-aid manual of 1943 suggested that it was not to be left to the first-aid parties, and that 'Everyone must accept this as part of his duty, realising that the treatment of casualties cannot always be left to the Medical Department alone'.[24] It was not clear how this was to be reconciled with the instruction from the gunnery branch, that '…whatever happens in action, the gun must be kept in action to the last man'.[25]

Most people who study first aid are dealing with remote possibilities, but when a seaman looked at the manual in 1943, he must have reflected how close it was to reality. He might well have to deal with a penetrating wound of the chest ('Remember that as well as the danger of sucking air into the chest there are also the dangers of fractured ribs and internal bleeding with this kind of wound'), or a man in flames ('When a man's clothing is on fire, the flames ascend and burn his neck. By laying him down, his head and neck are protected').[26] There was a real chance that he might suffer these wounds himself, though perhaps he preferred not to reflect on that.

Navies and air forces used a greater variety of weapons than ever before, producing many new types of injury. The problems of shellfire and bullet wounds were familiar to experienced naval surgeons, though not necessarily the hastily trained newcomers. It was known, for example, that the blast of a bomb or shell between decks would kill everyone within about 20 feet, often disintegrating the body. Beyond that distance there might be slight injuries, or perhaps concussion. Ships had long been sunk by torpedoes, but now it often happened in the middle of the Atlantic or in Arctic waters where the problems of exposure were greatly magnified. In addition, there was intensive bombing, which might last for many hours and severely damage morale. The explosion of a magnetic mine under a ship would cause numerous fractures in the lower part of the body, and far worse injuries in its immediate vicinity. In 1940 one medical officer of a destroyer reported: 'a scene of indescribable horror met me. Men were cut in two, internal viscera strewn about and intestines wrapped around the mast which was visible when I looked up through a large hole in the upper deck'.[27]

The Problem of Fatigue and Stress

By the time of the Second World War, most armed services had some system for resting personnel. The army tended to rotate units in the front line unless a major operation was in progress. Air forces rested men after a specific number of operations or a few months in combat. But the Royal Navy was very slow to accept the necessity for this. The needs of the ship came before the men, who were usually given leave only during a dry-docking or a boiler clean. The navy had always believed that its sailors were tough enough to endure almost anything – 'the men can stand it, the machines can't', Admiral Beatty wrote to Churchill early in the First World War.[28] But the Second World War would put far more strain on personnel than ever before, in terms of length, intensity and range of operations. As a result, many officers and men would become burnt out through stress.

A British seaman covered in oil after his tanker was sunk by U-boats in January 1943.

There were few cases of outright cowardice, because on the whole men were well selected and trained. The incident in the film *In Which We Serve*, in which a young stoker played by Richard Attenborough deserted his post in action, was apparently true but untypical. More common was the reaction observed by a medical officer under severe air attack during a Russian convoy in 1942.

During one attack today, I carefully observed a sailor at the back of the bridge, whose job was to telephone the orders for the gunnery officer. I must say the attack was very heavy, and the general noise and confusion were unbelievable. … I have never seen anybody quite so terrified as this sailor. His head, body and limbs were trembling, and he transmitted his orders in a high-pitched squeak. Nevertheless, he continued to do his job, and managed somehow to keep himself from breaking down completely.[29]

But even the bravest could not endure this forever. Marine Pearson of the cruiser *Kent* had already seen action in the *Exeter* and *Berwick* before he went to see his sergeant-major in 1942. He was becoming very agitated at the possibility of combat, was easily depressed and drank heavily on shore. He asked for a station on board where he could not see the action, and hoped for a shore job eventually.[30] Captain 'Johnny' Walker, the famous commander of the Second Escort Group, died of cerebral thrombosis caused by overwork in 1945. The medical service began to develop ways of recognising problems before they became too serious. By 1943 the category of 'fatigue' was recognised (though not always dealt with adequately). A ship's commission normally lasted 12 to 18 months, with some shore time after it, if the situation permitted.

3 Naval Law and Discipline

Like any armed force, a navy needs its own laws to prevent desertion, to punish cowardice in the face of the enemy, and to enforce the authority of officers and petty officers. It has to operate well beyond normal civil law, extend the authority of the state to foreign waters and lands, and to deal with the high spirits of young men during temporary relief from discipline. It employed severe punishments, because in wartime men are already operating in extremely unpleasant conditions and under threat of injury and death. British armed forces were traditionally recruited from the lowest levels of society (though far less so by the Second World War) and military and naval law tended to reflect that by its strictness. Navies are different from armies and air forces, in that their ships often operate well away from higher authority for months at a time, and the ship is a very enclosed world. Nevertheless, there were many who thought that naval law was too harsh. The pacifist playwright George Bernard Shaw wrote:

I do not believe for a moment that the British Fleet is manned by a horde of intimidated blackguards who cannot be trusted with the liberties of a tramp in a casual ward. … It is held that, if the man or boy were free to go when he liked on reasonable notice, as in civil employment, and their commander equally free to sack a man who was not worth his salt, the officers would lose all their

authority, and the men would instantly give a month's notice and leave England at the mercy of her enemies.[31]

The Naval Discipline Act and King's Regulations

The Naval Discipline Act was the legal authority by which the navy operated. Descended from the Articles of War first issued by Oliver Cromwell's regime in the 1650s it was passed in its modern form in 1860 when the death penalty was still common. It was amended slightly over the years, but still had a very old-fashioned ring to it. For several crimes it was decreed that the offender 'shall suffer death or such other punishment as is hereinafter mentioned'. It laid down severe penalties for mutiny, though it did not define it. It had a long section on prize money paid for captured enemy ships, though that was no longer relevant to the modern navy. Its out-dated language gave it an almost biblical ring, which tended to increase its authority.

Every officer subject to this Act who shall forbear to pursue the chase of any enemy, pirate or rebel, beaten and flying, or shall not relieve and assist a known friend in view to the utmost of his power, or who shall traitorously forsake his station, shall if he has therein acted traitorously, suffer death.

The act could also be used to punish ordinary offences such as murder, manslaughter, indecent assault, sodomy and theft. In case anything was left out, it allowed punishment of acts 'to the prejudice of good order and naval discipline' and others which could be dealt with 'according to the laws and customs in such cases used at sea'.

At the next level of authority were the *King's Regulations and Admiralty Instructions*, issued by the Board of Admiralty. The 1943 edition was nearly 900 pages long. It covered matters such as ceremony, the authority of commanders, the qualifications, appointment and duties of officers, the powers of various courts, the fighting efficiency and navigation of the ship and various accounting procedures.

Courts Martial

The court martial was the pinnacle of the naval disciplinary process. It was attended with 'considerable ceremonial' and enjoyed 'a high degree of prestige amongst officers and ratings'. It was quite rare in the navy – there were only 40 in 1939, rising dramatically to a peak of 1134 in 1945. This was not entirely due to the increasing size of the navy. In 1939 there was one court martial for every 2833 officers and men, by 1945 it had risen to one in 644, more than four times as many. However, it was far more common in the RAF, which had 3868 in 1945, and the army, which had the huge number of 49,113 in that year. This was not entirely because the navy was more law-abiding, as the threshold for the court martial was set much higher in the navy. It was a clumsy procedure that required the presence of many senior officers and witnesses and was difficult to hold at sea, impossible in small ships. As a result, most offences by ratings were dealt with by summary punishment by the captain or his subordinates. About 40 per cent of courts martial were on officers, for they were not subject to summary punishment. In wartime, officers

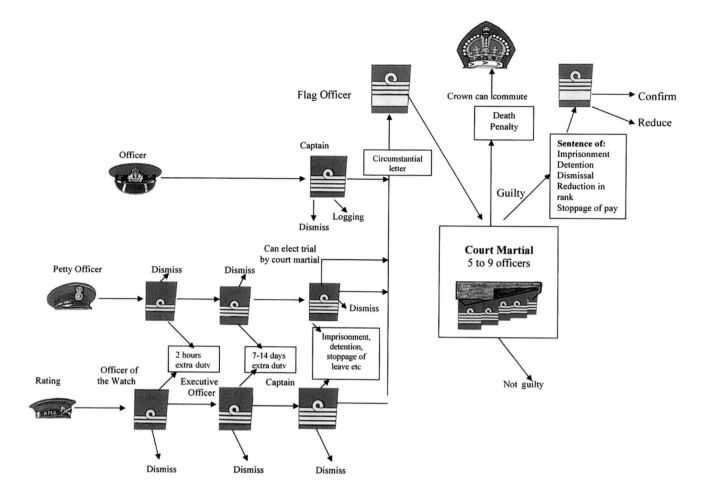

The system of naval
discipline.

could also be tried by disciplinary court, which was less formal and time-consuming than a court martial. In 1942, 2744 ratings and marines were tried by court martial, 205 officers by disciplinary court and 92 by court martial. Chiefs and petty officers also had the right to elect trial by court martial, if the offence might involve dis-rating.

If he decided that a court martial was necessary, a captain sent a 'circumstantial letter' to the admiral. If the admiral decided to convene one, he nominated a president and the rest of the officers were appointed by seniority, to a total of five to nine. Legal advice came from the office of the Judge Advocate, who might send one of his deputies, a barrister, to an important trial. In other cases an officer of the supply and secretariat branch with some legal training might be deployed. The captain or executive officer of the accused's ship normally acted as prosecutor while the defence was conducted by the 'prisoner's friend', who might be his divisional officer or a civilian lawyer. The procedure followed the adversarial system used in civilian courts and witnesses were called on both sides, followed by summing up. The members of the court then voted on the verdict, with the junior officer deciding first. A simple majority was sufficient, except in cases involving the death penalty, when two fifths were needed. The verdict was announced, and if it was 'guilty' the prisoner's friend produced evidence of mitigation or good conduct, after which the court retired to consider the sentence. A single sentence covered all the crimes that the accused was found guilty of, and any imprisonment began the moment it was passed by the court. The Admiralty had the power to modify the sentence, except the death penalty which could only be remitted by the Crown.[32]

Officers and crew were no longer court-martialled for the loss of their ship, as it was recognised that in the days of torpedoes and bombing it was not likely to be preventable. One exception was the loss of the cruiser *Manchester* to Italian torpedo boats in 1942. It was felt that the captain had scuttled his ship prematurely and the First Sea

Lord commented: 'So long as a ship remains afloat and has even one gun in action she may cause damage to the enemy'. The captain was dismissed and was considered unfit to command a ship again.[33]

Although the death penalty was far less common than in the past, it remained the supreme penalty for several offences. It was carried out by a firing squad consisting of 10 marines under a senior NCO, with the whole operation under the direction of the Naval Provost Marshal. Two of the rifles were loaded with blanks so that no one would ever be sure that he had killed the man. Members of the squad were told that the best service they could do to the victim was to kill him instantly, but there were cases, such as one at Naples in 1945, when he had to be finished off by the Provost Marshal's pistol.[34]

Cells and Detention Quarters

Naval offenders could be sentenced to detention in the ship's own cells, if she was large enough to have them. The *King George V* class had six, well forward on the lower deck. They might be used to contain offenders awaiting trial or too drunk to go to their messdecks, or they could contain men sentenced to up to 14 days by the captain. A man was denied bedding for the first four days of his sentence, then only on alternate nights after that. He was fed on the 'low diet' of biscuits and water and only allowed religious or instructional books. When these conditions were mitigated towards the end of the war, some officers considered that the punishment was now a 'welcome relaxation' to many offenders.

Men sentenced to longer periods of confinement were put in prisons ashore. The navy distinguished between 'detention' and 'imprisonment' – the former was less rigorous and did not carry the same stigma which might follow a man after he left the navy. In peacetime, offenders went to the Detention Quarters at Portsmouth where they were subjected to a regime that was 'sufficiently unpopular to act as a deterrent to further

'It says nothing about your being married here!'

Discipline on Board Ship

A large ship had its own police force, headed by the master-at-arms, a chief petty officer under the authority of the commander. According to the *King's Regulations,* the master-at-arms's regulating duties were 'mainly those connected with the prevention of irregularities and offences, and the custody of offenders, and not with the detailing of individual ratings for work to be performed on board or on shore'. He had a small number of regulating petty officers under him, and together they were to 'visit the various parts of the ship to see that due order prevails' and 'to report to the Officer of the Watch all offences and irregularities in the ship which may come to their knowledge'.[36] Naturally they were not popular with the rest of the crew.

Officers and petty officers were encouraged to develop 'power to command' to get their orders across firmly and clearly. Naval orders came on three different levels. The imperative meant that it should be done instantly, the volitive in which it should be carried out at the first opportunity, or 'unless there appears reason not to', and the admonitive, a suggestion, 'disregard of which may be a little tactless'.[37] This system broke down rarely, but disobedience of orders by officers or ratings was regarded as a serious matter and was dealt with by the disciplinary procedure. In examining a case of alleged disobedience, officers were enjoined to assess whether it was a direct order of merely a message; whether it was properly heard and understood, and if it was deliberately disobeyed. If the answer to all of these was yes, then the man would be placed under arrest.[38]

Offences relating to drink were far more common and happened at all levels. Wardroom drinks for officers, and the rum issue for ratings, encouraged heavy drinking even at sea. Ashore, the drunken sailor, suddenly released from shipboard discipline and with money in his pocket, was a legendary figure. Captains were advised that

…the great majority of offences committed by officers are caused directly or indirectly by drink, by which is not meant drunkenness, but a lapse of duty or conduct through drink. Any of those, which appear ordinary offences in neglect of duty, are brought about by the weakening of willpower and sense of duty by drinking too much.[39]

The drunken sailor returning from a 'run ashore' was another problem. Officers were told that 'There is no such thing in Naval Law as "Having drink taken." A man is either Drunk or Sober'. A difficult man should be placed in the charge of a sentry for his own protection, not as an arrest. The officer would assess whether he was fit to perform his duty, '…and that means any duty which a man of his rate could legitimately be called on to perform'.[40]

The great majority of naval punishments were awarded and carried out within the confines of the ship or shore base. Discipline on board an individual ship depended on many factors, including its size and the character of its captain and officers. Good officers tried to prevent matters reaching formal disciplinary level and new captains were advised: 'Punishments under the King's Regulations and Admiralty Instructions and the Naval Discipline Act should be used as a last resort. Bear this in mind and do your best to prevent serious cases arising'.[41] Officers also took care not to let an offence

**Above left:
Requestmen and
defaulters on board
a destroyer.**

**Above right:
A naval patrol
armband.**

serious offences'. The naval quarters were far too small for the expanded wartime navy with its greater disciplinary problems and many more were needed in Scotland for example, where many ships were based. Military prisons were used – the army detention barracks at Cartsdyke near Glasgow had more than a hundred sailors and marines in mid 1942. Barlinnie Prison in Glasgow had 19, including some sentenced by the civil power for ordinary offences and some undergoing imprisonment in lieu of detention. The Captain (D) of the Third Destroyer Flotilla based at Greenock complained that the food was excellent in civil prisons and a man sent there had 'a positively good time' compared with naval life. One man put on 8 pounds during 17 days. Moves were made to set up naval camps, for example at Kyleakin on the Isle of Skye. It had 28 wooden huts for 300 inmates, but there was no containing wall, no local work for the men, and no electricity or drainage. In Britain as a whole there were 751 members of the navy in prison in July 1942, including 428 undergoing detention, 236 having imprisonment in lieu of detention and 87 in proper imprisonment.[35]

become more serious. A drunken man would be restrained by those of equal rank so that he would not become guilty of assaulting a superior officer. If an offence was alleged to have taken place, it was brought before the officer of the watch who had the power to sentence the man to two hours of extra work or drill. If that was not enough, he was sent to the executive officer, who would normally investigate the offence the day after it was committed. If he had the rank of commander, for example in a battleship or cruiser, he could sentence the man to up to 14 days' extra work and drill on his own initiative. If he was the first lieutenant of a smaller ship and of lesser rank, he could award 7 days.

If this was considered inadequate, the case went before the captain, who heard 'requestmen and defaulters' at a fixed time. Requestmen might ask for promotion, for special leave or some other privilege. In an ex-American destroyer, '"Captain's Requestmen and Defaulters" took place periodically, rain or shine, at sea or in harbour. A rickety card-table was placed in the centre of the deck amidships, the captain and his officers stood on one side of it, and the requestmen and defaulters were lined up on the other'. Ordinary Seaman Brennan was denied permission to apply for a transfer and the captain asked, 'Can you imagine what would happen if everybody were allowed to be transferred wherever they liked?' After that, 'The rest of the requestmen followed, with requests about pay, about allowances, about being considered for promotion to a higher rate, about all sorts of things to which the Captain was always able to bring a penetrating insight and a ready judgement'.[42]

The defaulters were dealt with on the same occasion. In Nicholas Monsarrat's corvette early in her commission, the first defaulter was brought forward.

'Halt! Left turn! Off caps! Ordinary Seaman Jones, sir: one, was absent over leave two and a half hours, two did return on board drunk, three, did create vandalism in the mess-decks.' …

'What have you got to say, Jones?'

'Had a few drinks, sir' …

'Serious offences, all these. And you made a nuisance of yourself, too, keeping a lot of people awake. First Lieutenant's report.'[43]

If the captain found the case proved he could use a variety of punishments – stoppage of grog, or leave for up to 60 days, deductions from pay, reduction to the second class for leave which meant losing some pay and short leaves, and caning for ships' boys. With the approval of his admiral he could hand out much more severe sentences, of up to three months imprisonment or detention.

Discipline Ashore

When ships were in port, the officers and the master-at-arms organised patrols to deal with drunken and disorderly seamen. These were under the general control of the Naval Provost Marshal for the area. Each patrol included men below the rank of petty officer, 'in order to remove from drunken men the opportunity to strike their superior officer'.[44] They were often selected from those in shore bases or training camps in the area. At the Plymouth gunnery school, for example, men had to do a shift after they had already done a day's

work. Such men were found to be inexperienced and unmotivated, and oscillated between officiousness and negligence. They compared unfavourably with the regular military police of the army and in 1944 it was proposed to train leading patrolmen who would police naval ports under the control of more senior ratings.[45]

The three royal naval barracks were particularly difficult to govern. They mainly housed men in transit and did not have the sense of purpose of most shore bases. They tended to attract more than their share of bad characters among men evading sea drafts and there was easy access to alcohol in the nearby towns. As commodore of the Royal Naval Barracks at Chatham, Angus Cunninghame-Graham found it was difficult to maintain order among a shifting population.

I do not know what proportion professional criminals take up in our community, but a community of over 20,000 provided us with some in most branches. No murderers, I am glad to say, while I was there, but burglars, pickpockets, thieves, forgers, street gangsters, swindlers and no doubt others that I cannot remember all found a place with us. The unavoidable lack of close supervision of our continually transient troops gave them every opportunity to practice their unpleasant skills.

On average, 10 defaulters a day were brought before the commodore for serious offences, seven or eight times the normal figure in the navy. One man was punished for hiding himself in the barracks for two months and the admiral rebuked the commodore. Cunninghame-Graham 'patiently explained to him that the place was not the same as when he was commodore just before the war. With a daily turnover of a thousand we didn't know how many men we had, far less who anyone was'.[46]

The Threat of Mutiny

Mutiny, or collective disobedience by a group of men, was the most serious breakdown of naval discipline. British officers had strong memories of Invergordon, and they knew that earlier in the century naval mutinies had sparked off revolutions in Russia and Germany. There was no general mutiny of that kind during the Second World War, but there were many small ones on individual ships, only a few of which came to court martial. These included one in the headquarters ship *Lothian* in 1944 and the destroyer *Relentless* in 1945. There is no doubt that there were many more cases which never reached a trial, because one side or the other backed down or the matter blew over. The cruiser *Mauritius*, for example, was in a delicate state early in 1944 when leave was refused before sailing from Plymouth and some men refused duty. The anchor had to be raised by loyal petty officers.[47] Roderick Macdonald describes a case in the destroyer *Fortune*. When the hands refused to go on deck for work, the first lieutenant went round the messdecks reading the relevant articles from the Naval Discipline Act and 'dwelt specially on the Draconian punishments meted out by Their Lordships to silly, as he put it, sailors, guilty of such a heinous crime as mutiny in time of war'. Eventually the men gave in.

Like badgers emerging cautiously from the cosy gloom of their winter sett, sailor after sailor stumbled onto the iron deck in the burning sunlight.

Rubbing their eyes, they stood in an embarrassed line to be detailed off for a variety of mundane cleaning jobs by the Chief Boatswain's Mate. Nobody looked at anyone else.[48]

By 1944 the Admiralty was concerned about such incidents becoming more general, especially as sailors were being sent to a different war in the Far East while their army and air force brothers prepared for demobilisation. *Notes on Dealing with Mutiny or Massed Disobedience* advised captains to avoid the development of grievances if possible. If mutiny did occur, they were to try to separate the loyal men from the rest, to address any meeting from an unexpected angle and to set up a citadel defended by officers and loyal sailors and marines. Sir Max Horton objected to the tone of the document and pointed out that it was likely to scare inexperienced captains and undermine its purpose. The document was limited in its distribution and no general mutiny took place, perhaps because the war with Japan ended unexpectedly with the atom bomb.

4 Naval Custom and Traditions

Traditions weighed very heavily in the Royal Navy, though many of them were not as old as people assumed – the sailor's collar, for example, did not date from the time of Nelson but from the mid-nineteenth century. There was an ambiguous attitude to tradition. It often had to be neglected in wartime, especially in small ships such as corvettes, MTBs and landing craft which could not be operated like battleships even if the will was there. Moreover, continuous operation put great stress on the system, but most officers were aware of naval tradition and tried to implement it where they could. While training as an officer at *King Alfred* Geoffrey Willans was told:

It is possible…that some of you may find yourselves in command of a dirty little ship dropping anchor for the night in a lonely little bay. I would suggest to you that it is worthwhile postponing your bath and your shave and seeing personally that colours are saluted at the proper time. St Vincent outside Toulon, at a period when men really did sea time, set a personal example by appearing in full dress with sword and decorations. Meridians are passed, weeks and years go by, but this custom has survived. You, too, would do well to insist on this discipline of the colours, even if your White Ensign is only the size of a pocket-handkerchief.

You felt then that you were in contact with something that had roots. It gave you a sense of responsibility.[49]

Respect for Higher Authority

The Royal Navy always felt it had a special relationship with the monarch and the royal family. Since the funeral of Queen Victoria in 1901, the men of *Excellent* had hauled the royal coffin on a gun carriage. Both King George VI and his father had served in the navy, and every ship bore the title HMS or His Majesty's Ship. Out of respect for Queen Victoria's husband, Prince Albert, sailors never wore moustaches without beards. They also had to ask permission from the captain to grow a beard or 'full set'.

In theory a head of state was entitled to 21 guns at five-second intervals, a full admiral had 15, down to a commodore with 11. Gun salutes were uncommon in wartime, as there was no need to give one's position and strength away to the enemy. Even the historic meeting between Churchill and Roosevelt in Placentia Bay in August 1941 was relatively low key.

…Mr. Churchill was standing to attention on the quarter-deck, his hand raised to the peak of his cap. The bosun's pipes shrilled. The crew stood to attention, and the band of the Royal Marines crashed into the Star Spangled Banner. *Like an echo, across the strip of water came the notes of* God Save the King.[50]

Flag etiquette, however, was largely maintained. The Royal Standard was only flown when royalty was on board, the Admiralty flag of a 'fouled anchor' when several members of that Board were present. The main naval flag was the white ensign, with the Union Jack in the upper corner nearest the flagstaff, and the St George's cross on a white background. The Merchant Navy used the red ensign with a red background, and the blue ensign was for civilian-manned ships in government service and for ships with a proportion of reserve officers on board. The white ensign was normally lowered at sunset and raised again on the jackstaff at the stern next morning. In action, three ensigns might be worn in case one was shot away. In harbour, the Union flag was hoisted on the jackstaff in the bows, hence the popular name 'Union Jack'.

Otherwise, the Union flag was only flown, from the mainmast, when an admiral of the fleet was on board, which happened rarely. A full admiral flew the St George's cross from the mainmast, a vice admiral had a red ball in the upper canton nearest the jackstaff, and a rear-admiral had a ball in the lower canton as well. A commodore had a triangular flag known as a pennant.

The Ship

Sailors and officers both gave great loyalty to their ships, though their attachment was not permanent and most were likely to be transferred after about two years. Rivalries between seamen and stokers might well be buried when ashore and replaced with conflict between the crews of different ships. This might lead to violence on the streets and, like modern football hooligans, sailors believed that they were defending their collective honour by such fighting.

Ships' names were decided by a committee in the Admiralty. For the largest vessels they used names that had been established by long tradition, although some like *Warspite* were obscure, while others like *Arrogant* had taken on a less complimentary meaning – the ship that was to bear that name was cancelled in 1945. Cruisers had themed names such as counties, colonies or towns, or figures from classical mythology such as the *Leander* class. Each class of destroyer and later submarine had names beginning with a particular letter of the alphabet, with exceptions such as the Tribal class. The flower names of corvettes provided a large number of possibilities, though not martial in tone. Frigates were named for rivers, bays, lochs and naval captains. Smaller vessels, such as landing craft and torpedo boats, were given numbers rather than names, but even so some rather peculiar names were used in wartime. Submarine names such as *Tally Ho, Tiptoe* and *Truncheon* must have seemed strange to foreign ears.

The commissioning of a warship was a matter of some ceremony, rather truncated in wartime. Before the event the commander and his assistants prepared a detailed list of duties for each man of the ship's company, based on his substantive and non-substantive rating rather than on personal knowledge. On the day he was issued with a commissioning card, 'made out from the watch bill, giving an extract for each man showing his name number on the watch bill, watch, part and subdivision of the watch, quarters, arms, boat, division, special duty (if any), mess, kit locker, and hammock stowage'.[51]

Organisation had to be precise on the day of commissioning as the new crew arrived.

The officers and regulating petty officers should be ready with commissioning cards at various tables, according to the men's ratings. Fall in the ship's company, march the various ratings to the tables, turning over the stokers and marines to their own officers. A lieutenant, with a regulating petty officer, should be on the mess deck with a plan showing the positions of the different messes. Another officer, with assistants, should be detailed to show where the kit lockers are and where the hammocks should be stowed. Much time is saved by posting up notices showing the number of each mess, and labelling each group of lockers and hammock bins.[52]

The cruiser *Mauritius* was a typical example of a wartime commissioning, late in 1940.

The previous day had been spent in a series of conferences and inspections, a necessary prelude to the handing over of the ship by the builders, Messrs. Swan, Hunter & Wigham Richardson of Wallsend-on-Tyne, to whom she was more familiarly known by her 'job' number.

By noon the ship's company arrived, with an all-night train journey from Chatham, and with great interest took up their allotted places in the ship. Getting on board was no easy task, as the ship was lying alongside the future Anson and not the jetty.

Lunchtime saw the officers entertaining some of the employees of the firm who had give such grand co-operation during the building.

To the sound of cheering from the men on the dockside, the Mauritius, *aided by tugs, left the yard and proceeded down the Tyne, to the Tyne Improvement Commission's Quay, and work began in earnest.[53]*

Since 1919 each ship had been entitled to its own badge, which could be carried on the bows of its boats for example, although for security reasons this was in abeyance during wartime. When still in use, capital ships had a round badge, cruisers had a pentagonal shape, destroyers a shield and other types a diamond, all approved by the College of Heralds.

Battle honours, on the other hand, were likely to be enhanced in wartime. The honours were awarded for presence at a notable victory or campaign, and transferred from one ship to another bearing the same name, so some had very long histories. There had been five *Orions* in the Royal Navy since 1787 and the ship had 20 honours, ending with Normandy in 1944. They were borne on a board mounted in a prominent place on the ship. In all, nearly 50 honours were awarded during the war, from the River Plate in 1939 to Japan in 1945, with some awarded for participation in long-term campaigns such as the Atlantic, Mediterranean and Arctic Convoys.

Ceremonies

Crossing the line, or equator, was an ancient practice, which allowed the crew a kind of Saturnalia during which the authority of the officers was temporarily dispensed with. Lists were made beforehand of men who had not crossed the line before, and on the day the officers and crew assembled in front of an improvised swimming pool on deck, led by one of their number dressed as King Neptune. New men had their faces covered with paste or soap suds and were shaved by the 'barber' using a large wooden razor, then ducked in the pool amid great ribaldry.

Burial at sea was naturally a much more somber occasion, of Christian rather than pagan origin. It was much less used than in past times, as most voyages were quite short and it was better to get the

King George VI is received on board the battleship *Duke of York*.

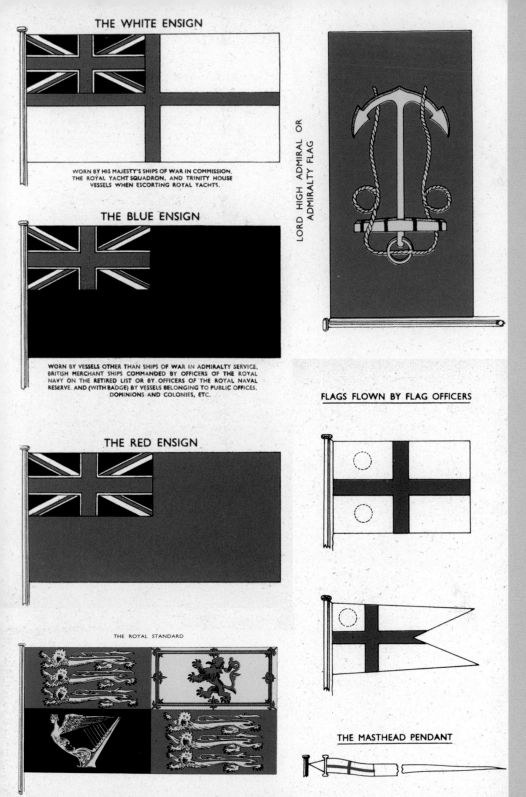

THE WHITE ENSIGN

WORN BY HIS MAJESTY'S SHIPS OF WAR IN COMMISSION,
THE ROYAL YACHT SQUADRON, AND TRINITY HOUSE
VESSELS WHEN ESCORTING ROYAL YACHTS.

THE BLUE ENSIGN

WORN BY VESSELS OTHER THAN SHIPS OF WAR IN ADMIRALTY SERVICE,
BRITISH MERCHANT SHIPS COMMANDED BY OFFICERS OF THE ROYAL
NAVY ON THE RETIRED LIST OR BY OFFICERS OF THE ROYAL NAVAL
RESERVE, AND (WITH BADGE) BY VESSELS BELONGING TO PUBLIC OFFICES,
DOMINIONS AND COLONIES, ETC.

THE RED ENSIGN

THE ROYAL STANDARD

LORD HIGH ADMIRAL OR ADMIRALTY FLAG

FLAGS FLOWN BY FLAG OFFICERS

THE MASTHEAD PENDANT

The main flags flown by British warships and merchant ships. The Royal Standard indicates the presence of the King, the Admiralty flag is for members of the Board of Admiralty.

body ashore to bury the man, with some ceremony, in a cemetery. But there were many deaths in the Battle of the Atlantic which took place far from shore, especially of rescued merchant ship survivors, and no room to store bodies on a terribly overcrowded ship. The corpse was prepared for burial by being sewn up in a canvas shroud and the last stitch was put through the nose to prevent the body falling out. It was placed under a Union flag on a plank against the ship's side and tipped overboard. Normally the captain supervised if there was no chaplain on board, but Nicholas Monsarrat did the job in *Campanula*.

I came to know that burial service by heart. I could easily have closed the book on 'Man that is born of woman hath but a short time to live, and is full of misery,' and run right on through the 'Stop engines' signal to the bridge, and 'We therefore commit his body to the deep' *and finished strongly on* 'Blessed are the dead which die in the Lord; even so, saith the Spirit, for they rest from their labours,' *without a written text to help me.*[54]

Officers Customs

All officers (including warrant officers) were entitled to a salute from those junior to them, and were expected to return it if in uniform and wearing a cap. The naval salute was different from the army one, in that the hand was held with the palm facing downwards.

The naval salute is made by bringing up the right hand to the cap, naturally and smartly, but not hurriedly, with the thumb and fingers closed together, elbow in line with the shoulder, hand and forearm in line, with the palm of the hand turned to the left, but inclined slightly inwards.[55]

At the beginning of the war, salutes were still considered important and Nicholas Monsarrat spent his time at *King Alfred* 'learning how to salute and how to respond in a seamanlike manner to the Loyal Toast'. By the later years even the Royal Marines were becoming careless in this respect, and it was complained, '…there is something wrong with the saluting training in the Corps – the technique of drill or the salute itself. … only a proportion of the Corps now salutes with head properly poised and with the tip of the forefinger one inch above the right eye'.[56] Salutes were almost abandoned in many of the smaller ships of the navy, where few of the officers and crew wore proper uniforms in any case.

There was much ceremony in connection with ships' boats. A junior officer always got into a boat first and out of it last. One approaching a ship was challenged by a sentry and would reply with the word 'Standard' if a member of the royal family was on board, 'Flag' and the name of the flagship if carrying an admiral, the name of the ship for a captain, and 'Aye, aye' for any other officer. When the captain arrived on board the side party by the gangway stood to attention and he was 'piped aboard' by the boatswain's whistle.

The wardroom, where the majority of the officers lived, tried to maintain the atmosphere of a gentleman's club, with many naval features added on and, of course, greatly modified by overcrowding and the necessity to live together for months at a time. Officers paid into funds to supplement the naval rations, and tried to keep up a high standard of tradition where ever possible. Naval officers had the unique privilege of drinking the loyal toast to the King sitting down, because of the danger, in old wooden ships, of banging heads on beams. There was a separate toast for each day, for example Thursday's was 'A bloody war and quick promotion', Friday's was 'a willing foe and plenty of sea room' and Saturday's was 'Sweethearts and wives (may they never meet)'.

Music

Sea shanties were the work songs of the Merchant Navy but were not encouraged on warships, where they might be considered subversive of discipline. Ships organized concert parties, and messes had their occasional singsongs using a combination of naval and popular songs.

On larger ships the Royal Marine band provided entertainment. For more formal occasions 'Heart of Oak' was used as the official naval anthem, with 'A Life on the Ocean Wave' for the Royal Marines, while 'Rule Britannia' always had strong naval connections by its very words 'Britannia rule the waves'. But the band had a much wider range than that, and in the case of the cruiser *Mauritius,* from 'Beethoven to Scott Wood via Sousa, all tastes have been satisfied'. The bandmaster had to deal with 'revolutionaries like Smith who think that Beethoven only wrote his stuff that way because swing hadn't been discovered'. The same Musician Smith gave a half-hour show on South African radio, while the band as a whole felt its best concert was done at Kilindini in East Africa, in co-operation with the band of the *Warspite,* and included the *Finlandia* symphony. A more popular favourite was 'Colonel Bogey', played ironically 'with appropriate words' to the crew of the *Frobisher* when *Mauritius*'s men had to break the leave to take over her convoy.[57]

Though some might question its musical status, and loudspeakers had replaced it for most purposes, the boatswain's call was used to summon the men on occasion, such as calling the hands to dinner. According to one officer that particular call was 'almost sacred' but 'difficult to describe'.

The boatswain or one of the petty officers starts off with a few short chirps to call up the others. When all are together each draws a long breath and then all pipe a long-drawn ascending note, starting at the bottom of the scale and gradually rising to the top, then slowly falling to the bottom again. Next comes a long-drawn note again but with modulations in the middle; then come the trills as well as the modulations. Lastly comes the 'pipe down' call, a long-sustained trill on the top note dropping suddenly to a trill on the bottom note, and the call is ended with a short, sharp upward note.[58]

The Rum Issue

The navy had always supplied its seamen with alcoholic drink to keep them happy amidst many hardships. Rum had long competed with beer, wine and brandy as the standard issue, and at first it was only used in the West Indies. However, by the twentieth century it was well established as the sailor's favourite.

Boys under 18 were not allowed rum, and others could become teetotalers for this purpose and have a cash payment instead. The *Mauritius* was regarded as 'a big rum-drinking ship' in that 500 out of 700 crew drew their 'tot'. Rum was issued at 11 a.m. with a good deal of ceremony. The duty gunner, regulating petty officer, sergeant of marines, supply petty officer and ship's butcher got the barrel up from the spirit room. The cooper opened it under the eye of the duty officer and the hands were called by bosun's pipe. The petty officers were given half a pint of neat rum each, the allowance of the other ratings was diluted by one part rum to three parts water. Officially each man was supposed to drink it himself, but lower deck custom allowed a man to be offered 'sippers' by his mates on an occasion like his birthday, or 'gulpers' as a reward for a special favour. The rum issue was an essential part of lower deck life, even if it encouraged a hard-drinking culture that was often reflected ashore when the men were on leave.

Lower Deck Culture

The seaman's lifestyle was very restricted on board ship, but he found ways to express his collective or individual identity. One was by modifications to his uniform.

The 'little round hat' as far from the central position as authority will permit, with the bow of its ribbon teased into a flat, symmetrical rosette. The spotless 'blue jean' collar, with its white borders gleaming. The black silk ironed to impeccable smoothness. The ribbons attaching it to the jumper are as long as possible, with swallow tail ends: by the length of these ribbons a man's taste is judged, and the longer the more dashing. And your mess-deck masher will affect a white silk scarf (not regulation, this, but allowed) tucked coyly beneath the black. The 'bell-bottoms' as wide as canny selection from 'Pusser's stores' or instructions to the ship's tailor can achieve, and for the first few moments at least bearing some trace of latitudinal folding (for trousers are stowed very carefully: first turned inside out and then folded concertina-wise lest a vertical crease appear).[59]

Another was by the use of slang, for many naval terms were of purely lower deck origin. 'Oppo' or 'opposite number' implied a more equal kind of friendship. According to George Melly, 'Winger' or 'wings', meaning a younger or less experienced friend, 'can, though far from inevitably, imply a homosexual relationship'.[60] A girlfriend was known as a 'party'. Collectively the navy was known as 'the Andrew'. Traditional nicknames were often attached to particular surnames.

For instance we have 'Shiner' Wright, 'Dusty' Miller, 'Pincher' Martin, 'Nellie' Wallace, 'Topsy' Turner, 'Pusser' Combe, 'Hookey' Walker, 'Smouge' Smith,

King Neptune and his cohorts during a Crossing the Line ceremony in a cruiser in 1942.

'Paddy' Walsh, 'Nobby' Clark, 'Bungy' Williams, 'Jack' Hilton. All Thomases are 'Tommo', and all members of the Day clan are 'Happy'. Tall men are alluded to as 'Lofty', short men as 'Stumps', 'Sawn-Off' or 'Shorty'.[61]

The rum issue on board HMS *Rodney* **in 1940.**

Swearing, which was almost universal on the lower deck, was another means of keeping the seaman separate from his officers. In his semi-fictional account of basic training and destroyer life *Very Ordinary Seaman*, J P W Mallalieu evaded the censor by having the men say 'flicking' in almost every sentence and had to explain it away. 'Though I have tried to give an accurate account of life on the lower deck of a destroyer, I have not been allowed to carry realism to the point of printing some of the words which were constantly used there. I have had to substitute words which no seaman would deign to use, but which seem preferable to blanks'.[62] Alec Guinness says of his first days in *Raleigh*, 'There's a sailor telling a story as I write this. "Fuckin" has occurred 3 times every word of the story'.[63]

RIBBONS OF MEDALS AWARDED TO MEMBERS OF THE ROYAL NAVY AND ROYAL MARINES, 1939-45

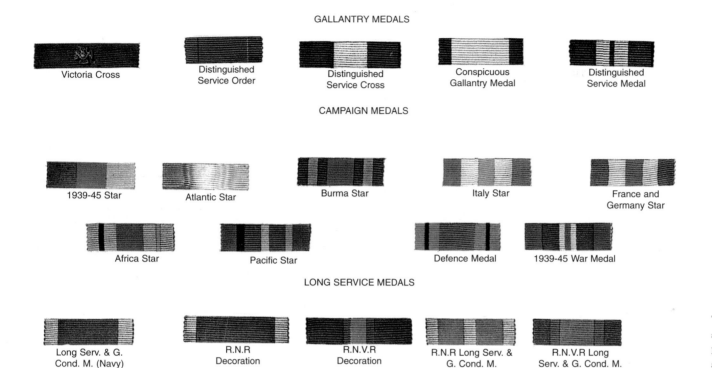

GALLANTRY MEDALS

Victoria Cross   Distinguished Service Order   Distinguished Service Cross   Conspicuous Gallantry Medal   Distinguished Service Medal

CAMPAIGN MEDALS

1939-45 Star   Atlantic Star   Burma Star   Italy Star   France and Germany Star

Africa Star   Pacific Star   Defence Medal   1939-45 War Medal

LONG SERVICE MEDALS

Long Serv. & G. Cond. M. (Navy)   R.N.R Decoration   R.N.V.R Decoration   R.N.R Long Serv. & G. Cond. M.   R.N.V.R Long Serv. & G. Cond. M.

The medals awarded to Royal Navy personnel in 1939–45.

Medals and Decorations

One aspect of naval tradition which was greatly augmented in wartime was decorations and medals. Again it was rather less old than most people thought. In Nelson's time medals had been issued by government and private enterprise to senior officers after great victories, but the first campaign medal issued to all was the Naval General Service Medal, which covered service in the great wars of 1793–1815, but was not issued until 1848. A clasp was awarded for each action. The custom survived and seven medals were issued for specific campaigns during the Second World War, including one for the Battle of the Atlantic. In addition, all who had served in the navy, marines or WRNS were entitled to the Defence and War Medals.

The gallantry medal originated not long after the campaign medal. The first Victoria Cross was awarded to Mate J D Lucas RN in 1854, during the Crimean War. It was soon supplemented by other medals, though it remained the only one (apart from the George Cross of

1940) which could be given to all ranks, and awarded posthumously. The Victoria Cross was held in even greater respect in 1939–45, as it had become rarer than before. Only 182 were awarded compared with 634 for 1914–18. Naval personnel were awarded 23 Victoria Crosses in 1939–45. Other medals for bravery included the Distinguished Service Order or DSO, awarded to senior officers of all services. Naval officers were eligible for the Distinguished Service Cross, and ratings for the Conspicuous Gallantry Medal and the Distinguished Service Medal. There were long service medals for the Royal Navy, the RNR and the RNVR.

In addition to medals, very senior officers were usually bestowed orders of chivalry. Vice-admirals and above could usually expect a knighthood – Admiral John Godfrey, formerly of naval intelligence, was the only officer of his rank in the twentieth century not to be honoured in this way. A very small number might become lords, and Cunningham and the other Chiefs of Staff became viscounts at the end of the war.

PART VI
Officers and Ratings

1 Officers

Most naval officers were members of the executive or seaman branch, trained in seamanship, navigation, leadership and fighting skills, and eligible to command ships and fleets when the time came. They were supported by the more specialised officers of the engineering and accountant branches, with more restricted career prospects.

Every naval officer requires a suitable blend of leadership qualities and technical skill, and it has never been easy to get this quite right. Conventional wisdom suggested that good officers could only be created from suitable material, by means of rigorous training and long experience. It would clearly be very difficult to expand the navy beyond a certain point in wartime without modifying or breaking these rules. The Royal Navy did not consider reducing the proportion of officers to men, as the Germans did. In fact, new fields such as aviation and landing craft required more officers than ever, and the rapidly expanding wartime navy was insatiable in its demands.

The Training of Regular Officers

It was normal for a potential naval officer to begin his training at the age of 13. A young man would put himself forward for competitive examination, perhaps after a time at a naval 'crammer'. Great store was placed on the interview by an admiral and senior officers, and a family naval background was an advantage. If successful, the young man would go to the Royal Naval College at Dartmouth in Devon, where he would take on the rank and uniform of cadet. He would undergo a general education in the style of an English public school, with a technical bias and with a certain amount of naval training added on. After some years he would be promoted to the rank of midshipman, with a white patch on each collar of his jacket. His shore education would continue, but he also spent time at sea in a battleship or cruiser, perhaps taking charge of a ship's boat and supervising parties of seamen.

There were many criticisms of the peacetime officers' training. Few other navies insisted on such an early entry and the Americans, Germans and Japanese produced very efficient forces while recruiting officers in their late teens. Selection depended very much on a suitable preparatory school education and a good class background – at the beginning of the war Churchill had to intervene after a candidate with a 'slightly cockney accent' was rejected.[1] The training was often too technical, and did not always prepare the candidate for the varied problems an officer might encounter.

For the most part what emerged was a definite breed of fit, tough, highly trained but sketchily educated professionals, ready for instant duty, for parades or tea parties, for catastrophes, for peace or war; confident leaders, alert seamen, fair administrators, poor delegators; officers of wide interests and narrow vision, strong on tactics, weak on strategy; an able, active, cheerful, monosyllabic elite.[2]

The only other way to enter as a regular officer was by 'special entry' at the age of 18. Regular officers were nearly all public school boys who underwent a strict examination and then spent 18 months doing what the Dartmouth candidates had done over five years. Many thought that the Special Entry scheme was the more efficient of the two, and it produced, for example, Terence Lewin, a future Admiral of the Fleet and Chief of Defence Staff during the Falklands War of 1982.

After promotion to midshipman, Dartmouth and Special Entry boys joined the training ship *Vindictive*. According to her captain the boys

…carried out all the duties that a seaman performs in a ship, viz:- quartermaster, boatswain's mate, sideboy, L.T.O. and S.T. of the watch, helmsman, leadsman, crew of all types of boats, sailmaker's mate, boatswain's party, gunner's party, signalman of the watch, seaboat's crew, lookouts etc. For a short period they have lived on the messdeck under the same conditions as a seaman.

They learned 'the general principles of Gunnery, Torpedo and Electrics', they 'acquired a certain amount of "Power of Command"'

Opposite: Petty Officer Jenman, aged 48, tells yarns to 16-year-old seamen on *King George V* in 1940.

Below: Cadets in the Royal Naval College after it moved from Dartmouth to Eaton Hall in 1943.

and 'a measure of self-confidence and enough knowledge, practical and theoretical, on which to build real officer-like qualities'.[3]

The navy was often ambivalent about the status of a midshipman. Commander Rory O'Conor claimed that on board ship they could be treated as a messenger by the thoughtless, as 'schoolboys and their natural prey' by 'Training and Educational experts (whose name is legion, for they are many)', or as an officer. O'Conor was strongly in favour of the last.

A midshipman is an officer, and must be treated as such and given a task which he feels he can make his own, whether in charge of a boat or as Midshipman of the Watch, and only his Action Station must take precedence. Once he realizes that he will be treated with the full consideration due to his status as an officer, no-one gives a readier response than a Midshipman, in keenness in his job and on the ship, both in her work and in her play.[4]

In wartime, both groups of cadets were eventually moved from Dartmouth to Eaton Hall in Cheshire, away from the threat of bombing. At the age of about 20, midshipmen were promoted to sub-lieutenant, the lowest rank of commissioned officer.

An Officer's Career

After commissioning a young man would spend a relatively sort time as a sub-lieutenant, mostly on courses at Greenwich and in the gunroom of a big ship, supervising midshipmen. His promotion to lieutenant would partly depend on his exam results as a midshipman. After that, he

would be considered a fully fledged naval officer. He might be a junior officer in a battleship or cruiser, rising perhaps to first lieutenant of a destroyer. He might well do a year's training and enter one of the sub-specialisations open to junior officers – gunnery, torpedo, navigation, submarines, signals or aviation. In peacetime the last of these involved subordination to the RAF and was a backwater. Navigation involved much work on one's own and did not necessarily train an officer in leadership. The torpedo branch had an 'octopus tendency' and took on too many technical roles such as electricity, so it was not necessarily the path to high rank. Submarines were far too specialised for the majority of officers. The signal branch was very technical, though it offered some influence as flag lieutenant to an admiral. This left gunnery, which was regarded as the most important specialisation between the wars. Critics of the branch claimed that the gunnery school taught officers everything except how to hit the target. According to Vice-Admiral K G B Dewar:

If Whale Island's methods were followed in other walks of life, applicants for motor driving licences would be examined in thermodynamics, and the manufacture of motor-car steel, whilst medical students would undergo a course of cutlery before being allowed to handle surgical instruments.[5]

After eight years as a lieutenant an officer was promoted to lieutenant-commander and had a thin or 'half' stripe sewn between his lieutenant's stripes. This did not necessarily affect his position greatly, and in a battleship or cruiser his role might not change, though he might become the senior navigation or gunnery officer. In aviation he

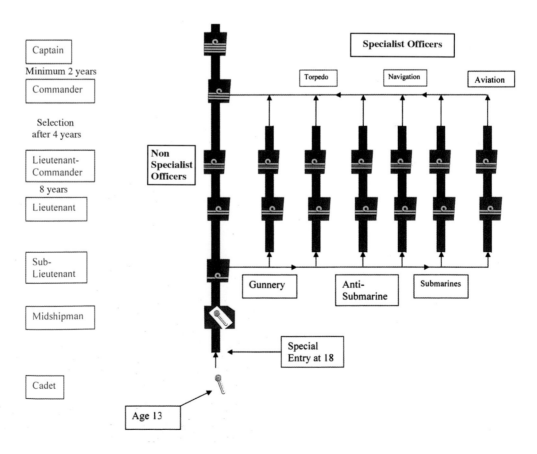

The career structure for regular naval officers.

Captain

Minimum 2 years

Commander

Selection after 4 years

Lieutenant-Commander

8 years

Lieutenant

Sub-Lieutenant

Midshipman

Cadet

Non Specialist Officers

Specialist Officers

Torpedo   Navigation   Aviation

Gunnery   Anti-Submarine   Submarines

Special Entry at 18

Age 13

was eligible to command a squadron, if he had served in destroyers or smaller ships he might be given his first command.

After that, promotion was by selection to the rank of commander, with three full-width stripes in his sleeve. For a seaman officer, the most important posting was as the second-in-command of a large ship, where he had to prove himself as an administrator and leader of the crew. A commander might serve on the staff of an admiral or at the Admiralty in London. If successful, the officer would be promoted to the rank of captain, one of the high points in any naval career. Apart from staff duties, he might command a battleship, cruiser or aircraft carrier or a flotilla of destroyers.

The Reserves

On the outbreak of war, the navy was able to supplement its officer corps by calling on several different groups of reserves. Retired officers could be used in many tasks, such as the commodores of convoys. They often had to drop their former rank and take on lower ones in the Royal Naval Reserve – the most famous example was Sir Gilbert Stephenson, who was a Vice-Admiral before the war, but served as a commodore in charge of the training base at Tobermory.

The next group was the seaman officers of the Royal Naval Reserve. They had spent a great deal of time at sea in the Merchant Navy, and done long and short periods of naval training in peacetime. They had ranks equivalent to those of regular officers, but with intertwined gold braid instead of the straight stripes of the regular officer. More than 1500 of these were brought into the navy at the beginning of the war, but after that the supply was soon exhausted, and Merchant Navy officers were in great demand in their own service. RNR officers played a vital role in commanding escort vessels as the Battle of the Atlantic began in earnest, and this is symbolised by Nicholas Monsarrat's Lieutenant-Commander Ericson in *The Cruel Sea*. The character was modelled on Charles Cuthbertson, who survived the sinking of the corvette *Zinnia* in a Gibraltar convoy in 1941.

The peacetime officers of the Royal Naval Volunteer Reserve were amateurs compared with the others. According to a traditional saying, the RNR were seamen trying to become gentlemen, the RNVR were gentlemen trying to become seamen. It was traditionally believed that they were yachtsmen, but in fact the part-time training 'meant giving up so much leisure, that it was almost impossible to combine the two', according to one officer.[6] Peacetime RNVR officers were quite a small group and there were only 809 of them in 1939. They wore wavy stripes to distinguish them from regular and RNR officers and were known as the 'wavy navy'. Naval opinion was sceptical about their value and one was told before the war, 'You'll never get a command, Rayner – the Navy won't give R.N.V.R.s command of a ship, no matter how long the war lasts'.[7] But this was soon disproved in practice and many rose to take charge of escort vessels and submarines.

One reserve that did rely on yachtsmen was the Royal Naval Supplementary Reserve, founded in 1936. This was simply a list of men with suitable experience who agreed to be called up for officer training in the event of war. It proved very useful in the early stages of the conflict. Those eventually trained included Ludovic Kennedy, the broadcaster, Ewen Montagu of *The Man Who Never Was* fame, and

Monsarrat, the novelist. Training at HMS *King Alfred* in Hove was often brief. According to Kennedy, 'At 7.30 each morning we walked the few hundred yards to the car park, dressed (for uniforms took time to be made) in an odd assortment of sports jackets, casual trousers, Trilby hats and caps'.[8] Ewen Montagu describes the course.

From the very first day of operations in the King Alfred *the staff of that 'ship' began, not only to train us in the skills which we would need, navigation, seamanship, gunnery and so on, but also to instil into us what was almost more important – the spirit of the Navy and its discipline.*[9]

These officers also filled a vital gap. Some of the trainees were diverted to take charge of the 'little ships' at Dunkirk in 1940, and later many of them became junior officers in the Battle of the Atlantic. But like the other reserves the scheme was naturally limited in numbers, and it was virtually defunct by the end of 1941.

Temporary Officers

The only way the navy could expand beyond these limits was to open up officer entry to the general, non-seafaring population. Following the example of the army, the navy decided just before the war that all candidates for temporary commissions should enter through the ranks and be selected after some service on the lower deck. Some young men entered through the Y Scheme, set up in 1941. This had the reputation of being an officer-producing scheme, open to young men with a good education who applied before being called up into the navy. In fact it was designed to recruit potential technicians as much as officers, and the scheme perhaps raised expectations too high. The navy also set up university units to give pre-entry training to undergraduates, though with limited success.

A group of officers of a minesweeper flotilla, showing the different stripes worn by RN, RNR and RNVR.

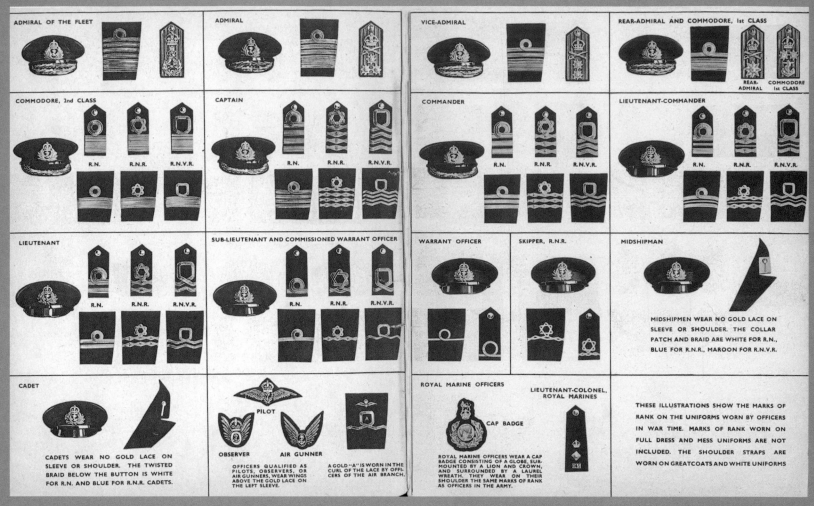

The rank stripes and other badges worn by officers.

Otherwise, potential officers were identified at the initial training schools, largely from the quality of their education, which excluded many suitable candidates.

Every trainee fills in a questionnaire which is examined. Men with suitable qualifications are noted and watched. The snag is that no one who has not at least had a secondary school education is even considered, no matter what brilliance he may show while at the training establishment, thus many who might make very brilliant officers are overlooked. The official excuse for this is that without a secondary school education men cannot master the officers' training course. This, speaking from personal experience, is not true. Any intelligent man can easily master the course, while no matter how high his educational qualifications, unless they are linked with intelligence a good officer does not result.[10]

Having been selected, the man was put in a special group at the training school and became a CW or Commission and Warrant candidate. He went to sea as an ordinary seaman for at least three months, where he was supposed to be under the observation of his captain. There is perhaps no better test of character than on the decks of a wartime destroyer, but busy captains rarely had time to assess the men properly, and most seem to have passed this stage. After 1943, candidates were sent to a special squadron based in the Firth of Forth for training and assessment.

Trainees were now cadet ratings, still wearing the square rig of the lower deck but with a white 'purity band' round the cap. They went to *King Alfred* at Hove and its satellites for a three-month intensive course. They learned navigation, gunnery, torpedo work, ship organization, naval law and other skills. It was commanded with great skill by Captain John Pelly, but Chief Petty Officer Vass, a gunner's mate and fierce disciplinarian, was far more prominent among the cadets.

In 1940 Geoffrey Willans felt that:

Time was too short for anything but a smattering of naval background. We did squad drill, physical training, and trotted round in gas masks. …but one also encountered the tradition of the Navy in a manner that was quite accidental. At times it shone like a beacon through all the other brouhaha of calling one end of the building 'the bow'. There was an unwilling poetry about it that was immensely stimulating.

Certainly it was intense and F S Holt commented: 'The whole course called for maximum concentration while at the same time being immensely practical'.[11] Furthermore, 'the great majority of Cadet-ratings suffer from over anxiety that they may fail. This is not unnatural when one considers the stakes involved:– Commissioned rank or return to the Lower deck'.[12]

A candidate went before a selection board, like Alec Guinness.

Each of the Admirals had a paper and pencil before him. They looked as if they were about to take part in a quiz and I had hardly completed my hat-off salute before their pencils started to scribble. One or two of them just stared at me with wind-watered eyes. The Admiral in charge of the proceedings appeared to be a shrewd, friendly-disposed frog.

Thus the great actor began 'the best performance I have given…that of a very inefficient, undistinguished junior officer in the Royal Naval Volunteer Reserve'.[13]

King Alfred was one of the great success stories of the war. It produced 22,500 officers, and about 88 per cent of the whole officer corps was temporary RNVR by 1945. They wore the wavy stripes of the RNVR but had no badge which distinguished them from the more permanent members, causing some resentment, as they were not volunteers in any real sense. They, too, had to overcome the doubts of regular officers about their abilities, and take on yet more responsibility as the war went on. Nicholas Monsarrat took command of a corvette in 1943 after two and a half years as junior officer and first lieutenant. Others, such as Edward Young, took command of submarines, while Coastal Forces were dominated by RNVR officers in all grades up to lieutenant-commander. But many others were in dead-end jobs as junior lieutenants, 'chained to their oars' as Monsarrat put it.

Engineer Officers

The problems of integrating technical skill and officer-like qualities were most intense in the engineering branch of the navy. Early in the century Admiral Fisher had tried to make engineering a sub-specialisation of the seaman branch, rather like gunnery or navigation. That failed, and regular engineer officers were trained at Keyham in Plymouth Dockyard and the half-completed Manadon College just outside the city. It was recognised that an engineer officer needed a greater depth of knowledge than a seaman officer, and he was not likely to serve at sea until he was a lieutenant. He had far less authority over his men than an executive officer, and he was distinguished by purple cloth between the stripes. He was never going to command a fleet or a ship, and his promotion path ended with the Engineer-in-Chief of the Fleet, a vice-admiral. The engineer officer of a frigate or cruiser was a commander, but those of destroyers and smaller ships were often warrant officers, well below the captain in rank and status.

The supply of engineer officers was particularly difficult in wartime. There were very few outside resources to draw on, as the Merchant Navy and civilian industry needed all they could find. Many artificers were promoted to warrant officer to take over the engine rooms of destroyers and frigates. Courses were set up in civilian colleges to give hasty training to well-educated young men, although the supply never quite met the demand. The engine rooms of corvettes were manned by artificers, the equivalent of chief petty officers, while the motors of coastal forces demanded a new breed of engineer altogether.

Accountant Officers

The navy's accountant officers were responsible for all financial matters of a ship, flotilla or shore base, as well as general administration and supervising the cooks and stewards. In peacetime, most were recruited through the Special Entry scheme, and they wore white between their stripes. The navy did not plan for a large-scale expansion of the branch, and most of the administrative work of small ships devolved on the executive officers, or on shore and flotilla staffs. More were recruited through the CW scheme, though only men who had accountancy qualifications, or defective eyesight which would have prevented them becoming executive officers.

Normally all naval officers were expected to go to sea if called upon, but there were some specialists, such as intelligence officers, meteorologists and administrators to whom this did not necessarily apply. These formed the special branch of the RNVR, wearing a green stripe between the gold ones. The branch also provided a home for many radar and radio specialists.

A poster advertising the Y-Scheme for young men to get pre-entry training to the navy.

Promotion from the Lower Deck

The emphasis on formal education tended to preclude many experienced candidates from the lower deck in the *King Alfred* system, as one MP told the House in 1942.

People have been selected as candidates for commissions and put through their course of sea training, and have never been able to conduct themselves in a sailor-like way, yet they have been passed as fit to take charge of ships and men. There have been extreme cases where chief petty officers, with 20 or 30 years experience, have not been thought worth considering for commissions, yet people

It was far more difficult for regular, experienced seamen to be commissioned than well-educated Hostilities Only men. There was an accepted wisdom that a man who had left school at 15, undergone the rigorous training at *Ganges* or a similar school and then spent years absorbing the culture of the lower deck would never be suitable for a commission. There was, however, a scheme known as 'upper yardsmen', by which promising young seamen would be specially trained and eventually commissioned. Its predecessor had been set up by Churchill just before the First World War, but it had experienced many difficulties in the inter-war years. Regular officers tended to close ranks against incomers, and there was little time for study on the lower deck, so the numbers of entrants were small.

Warrant Officers

The other route to a commission from the lower deck was a slower one, through warrant rank. The naval warrant officer was a very different animal from his army or air force namesake, although both had risen from the ranks. He was a junior officer with restricted promotion prospects, while in the army or air force he was in effect a senior NCO. Naval warrant officers were descended from the boatswains, gunners and carpenters who had kept Nelson's ships running. They were still specialists of considerable experience and their ranks now included warrant torpedo gunners, signal boatswains, telegraphists, engineers and air engineers. Schoolmasters were the only ones who were recruited direct into the navy. Others might be promoted from petty officer in their twenties, like Edward George Mason who was a gunner in the destroyer *Eskimo* at the age of 28. They might remain in warrant rank for many years, like John Webster who was boatswain of the Royal Naval Barracks at Devonport at the age of 73. A warrant officer wore the fore-and-aft uniform of an officer, with the same cap badge and a single thin stripe. After 10 years he was eligible to promotion to commissioned warrant officer, the equivalent of sub-lieutenant, and then to lieutenant and even lieutenant-commander after another eight years of service.

Apart from the engineers of destroyers and frigates, warrant officers were mainly found in larger ships, depot ships and shore bases. In 1939 large cruisers such as *Norfolk* had two commissioned gunners and a commissioned torpedo gunner, a commissioned ordnance officer, a schoolmaster, a gunner, a warrant telegraphist, warrant shipwright, warrant engineer, warrant mechanician and a warrant electrician. A destroyer flotilla leader, such as HMS *Duncan*, carried a torpedo gunner and a warrant engineer for flotilla duties, with another gunner in a different ship of the flotilla.[15]

From the lower deck, George Melly thought that warrant officers were:

Martinets, sticklers for the letter of the law, hard resentful men who realised they had risen from the ranks on merit but been blocked for a commission on class grounds. Caught uneasily between the relaxed bonhomie of the PO's mess and the easy formality of the wardroom they were punctilious in their insistence on outer form, correctitude, the marks of respect as laid down by King's Regulations.[16]

The Admiralty was aware of the warrant officer's faults. 'The type of officer obtained from this source may be very much "set in his ways" and unsuitable for staff appointments, but with his limits he is an extremely valuable officer'.[17]

2 The Higher Rates

The holders of the higher substantive ratings, the chief petty officers, petty officers and leading seamen, were the essential link between the officers and the lower deck, the true backbone of the navy in the eyes of many. In the seaman branches and many others they were invariably promoted from the junior rates. There was always controversy about how far they were technicians, how far they were disciplinarians. The senior rates, from petty officer upwards, needed mastery of their particular skill in torpedo or gunnery for example, they needed 'power to command', and they needed considerable experience. In many ways they were harder to find than officers, and a definite skills gap was emerging by the latter half of the war.

Leading Seamen

The rating of leading seaman had emerged as a skilled man above an able seaman rather than as having authority to command. This soon began to change, especially after the rating of petty officer second class was abolished in 1907, and by 1939 it was well established that a leading seaman should be able to take charge of men. He, and his equivalent in other branches, was distinguished by an anchor badge on his left arm above his good-conduct stripes. This gave rise to the nickname of 'killick', meaning a small anchor, and a man's promotion was referred to as 'getting his hook'. A large ship before the war was allowed nine leading seamen for every 100 of the crew. Each mess had a leading hand in charge, but often he found it difficult to maintain his authority. 'Due to their messing with the men the Leading Hands of a ship have a difficult job to maintain the extra dignity of their rate'. Captains were urged to 'Render them all the help you can with advice and privileges in giving real meaning to the word "Leading"'.[18]

The Admiralty did nothing to make life easier for the leading seaman. His pay rise on promotion to the rate was small. He did not have a change of uniform and his badge of a single anchor did little to mark him out in the public eye. Unlike the petty officer he continued to live with the men in the mess and he had to establish his authority there. This could be difficult for younger men, as older hands gave more respect to long-service stripes than to substantive rate. When John W Davies was promoted just before he qualified for his first good-conduct stripe, he was told it would 'provoke senior ratings, and must not be allowed to happen'.[19] Moreover, the leading hand had much less formal authority than a petty officer. He was not a superior officer within the meaning of the Naval Discipline Act, so insubordination, for example, was only considered 'an act to the prejudice of good order and naval discipline'. Yet leading seamen were an essential part of the chain of command, and the only source for potential petty officers. An ambitious regular seaman would see the rate as a step on the ladder towards the privileges and status of a petty officer or chief. An Hostilities Only man was not likely to look so far ahead, and many considered that the promotion was more trouble than it was worth; especially since some them had their pay made up to civilian standards by their former employers.

An able seaman had to spend a certain time at sea and pass an examination to be eligible for promotion. Even then, in peacetime he might have to wait up to seven years for a suitable vacancy. There was no formal shore training for leading seamen, but Commander O'Conor suggested that able seamen who were eligible and showed promise should be given a chance to develop 'power to command' by taking charge as the leading hand of the watch or second-in-command of large parties. 'The objective is to ensure that every Able Seaman passed for Leading Seamen has chances, both in his daily work and at his action station, to take charge of one or more men'. In wartime,

Opposite above: Cadet ratings, wearing 'purity bands' round their caps, learn steering and pilotage at HMS *King Alfred* in 1943.

Opposite below: Engineer sub-lieutenants in a lecture in the Royal Naval Engineering College at Manadon, near Plymouth.

POs and Leading Seamen: gold on blue dress uniform, red on blue service uniform, blue on white uniform. Able Seamen and below wear no rating insignia.

CHIEF PETTY OFFICER
Both sleeves, blue or white uniform.

PETTY OFFICER
Upper left sleeve.

LEADING SEAMAN
Upper left sleeve.

GOOD CONDUCT CHEVRONS
Colours same as Rating Insignia. Not worn by CPO.

FOR 13 OR MORE YEARS
Upper left sleeve.

FOR 8 YEARS
Upper left sleeve.

FOR 3 YEARS
Upper left sleeve.

CAP INSIGNIA

CHIEF PETTY OFFICER

PETTY OFFICER
SUN-HELMET INSIGNIA

MISCELLANEOUS
JUNIOR RATING

CHIEF PETTY OFFICER

PETTY OFFICER

MISCELLANEOUS
JUNIOR RATING

The sleeve and cap badges worn by chiefs, petty officers and leading seamen.

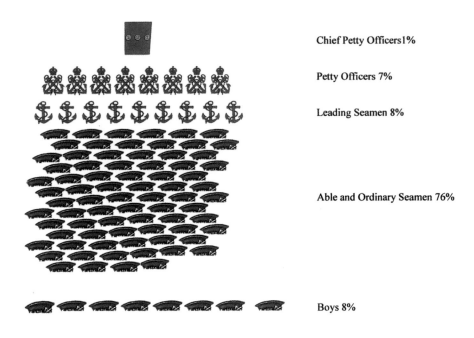

Chief Petty Officers 1%

Petty Officers 7%

Leading Seamen 8%

Able and Ordinary Seamen 76%

Boys 8%

The proportions
of seamen and
petty officers on
a battleship or
cruiser, c. 1935.

Officers were urged to give petty officers 'every reasonable indulgence' and to 'make them feel that confidence is reposed in them'. It was hoped that they would be addressed by all ranks by their formal titles of 'chief petty officer' and 'petty officer', but these did not trip off the tongue as easily as the army's 'sergeant' and 'corporal', and discipline was often less formal on board ship, so first names and nicknames were used more often by the lower deck. The petty officer had the right to trial by court martial instead of summary punishment in certain circumstances, and he was freed from some of the more irksome restrictions on leave and such matters. He was able to avoid the menial work of the lower deck, and his mess usually had a mature three-badge able seaman to clean, cook and set up hammocks.

Officers were advised that:

Petty Officers are not advanced to that rating solely as a result of seniority and on passing examinations. They must possess personality and tact, and be ready to accept the responsibility of their position. They should work at all times for the well-being and efficiency of the service as a whole. They should set an example of loyalty and discipline.[21]

Petty officers' posts had various archaic titles, often as 'mates' to warrant officers who were not necessarily present in smaller ships. Boatswain's mates were members of the seaman branch, detailed to run the daily routine, including rousing the men from their hammocks and keeping watch in the wheelhouse. The chief quartermaster was usually a petty officer or chief, according to the size of the ship. He supervised the steering and assisted the navigating officer. Gunner's mates were experienced members of that branch who had risen above the more specialised structure of quarters ratings, and so on. They, too, were disciplinarians, in the tradition of the branch. The yeoman of signals was the head of the visual signallers, while a wireless operator had the more mundane title of petty officer telegraphist. Petty officers were distinctly short in the newer branches of radar and Asdic, because of rapid advancement and a policy of slow promotion. In escort vessels the senior Asdic operator was rarely more than a leading seaman, though he had great responsibility and would have to guide the ship into action against a submarine. In the radar branch, an Admiralty Fleet Order pointed out early in 1942 that, 'Advancement to P.O. (R.D.F.) has not yet taken effect in sufficient numbers to allow these ratings in complements'. All this was designed to maintain the status of the petty officers by avoiding too fast promotion; but it may well have had the opposite effect, in giving high status to junior ratings.

There were seven chiefs and petty officers of the seaman branch for every 100 of the crew. They were given routine duties on board ships. Some served as captains of tops, in charge of the seamen of the forecastle, quarterdeck, fore top or maintop. In a large ship, each division had a senior petty officer in general charge as captain of the top, with assistants to take charge of the men's bags and hammocks, to instruct the young seamen and to supervise the messdecks. At sea, the petty officer of the watch was to muster the watch five minutes before it was due to go on, to do the rounds of the ship every hour, to take charge of the keys, the navigation lights and the lowering of the sea-boat in the absence of an officer. He was to supervise the leading hand of the watch.[22] Petty officers could also serve as instructors for the ships' boys, though officers were

promotion was faster and there was little if any gap between passing and promotion, so such grooming was unnecessary. After at least six months of good conduct, a man could pass for leading seaman at any time after his AB rating, though it would be acting for the first year.

Petty Officers

The petty officer was far more ancient than the leading seaman, and originally the title referred to the holder of a particular minor office, such as the yeoman of the sheets who controlled certain ropes on a sailing ship. In those days rate was often lost on transferring from ship to ship, but the Victorian navy turned 'petty officer' into a permanent rank. When faced with indiscipline or mutiny, the Admiralty's first reaction was to question the role of petty officers in suppressing it, and then to try to increase their status. Following various incidents after the First World War, it grudgingly gave petty officers of four years' seniority the right to wear the 'fore and aft' uniform with peaked cap and collar and tie. After Invergordon this was extended to those of one year's seniority, but junior petty officers continued to wear 'square rig'. Petty officers had always lived in separate messes, with slightly more space and better amenities than junior ratings. Their badge was a pair of crossed anchors on the left arm, and unlike the leading seamen they had a crown above to symbolise their greater formal authority.

Promotion was relatively slow even in wartime, and John Whelan observed: 'It was not until 1944 that the first H.O. Petty officers qualified as S.D.I.s [Submarine Detector Instructors]. It was possible to become a junior R.N.V.R. Officer within six months of joining, but it took far longer to make an asdic instructor'.[20] His own elevation came after a Luftwaffe bomb had killed many petty officers and chiefs in Devonport Barracks, creating many vacancies.

'Recommended for advancement,' said the Divisional Officer, an R.N.V.R sub-lieutenant hardly qualified to know or judge my ability.

'Recommended for advancement.' Said the First Lieutenant, who was eminently qualified.

'Request granted,' said the Captain.

'Request granted,' repeated the Cox'sn.

advised that 'Instructional petty officers, although generally well up in their particular subject, are frequently unable to distinguish between the essential and the unimportant', and were to be supervised carefully.[23]

On arriving on board his first ship, the armed merchant cruiser *Cameroon*, Tristan Jones was amazed to find that the petty officers were very different from the martinets he had known as a boy in *Ganges*.

It was a shock to me to be addressed in the least bit so civilly by anyone over the rank of Leading Seaman. The PO's voice was almost gentle, and there was a welcoming gleam in his eye. He was dressed in his Number Three blue serge uniform, but unlike the barrack bullies', his was worn and greasy in patches, and his shoes looked as though they had hardly ever been polished. The badge on his cap – the crown and anchor – was tatty beyond belief. His face – he was no more, I would guess, than in his middle twenties – was, like his cap and uniform, worn and tatty. He looked as if he had not had a good night's sleep in weeks.[24]

George Melly also found that petty officers were an amenable race.

Long association with the sea and its ports had given them a certain tolerant sophistication, part cynical but certainly affectionately so. They had learnt to mistrust the moral imperatives of any one place because they had seen them replaced by others, often equally rigid and ridiculous, elsewhere. The [sic] made allowances too for us temporary sailors. We were there because we had to be. One day the war would be over and the Navy its old self; a machine for sailing in.[25]

Even in a destroyer with a high complement of regulars in the early stages of the war, Joseph Wellings of the US Navy noticed how much the officers depended on the petty officers.

For example the signalmen not only read but interpret the signals. They always tell the OOD [Officer of the deck] the meaning of the signal but not the signal itself. They also know the tactical publications very thoroughly. The officers were not concerned with such matters, except the captain who knew the meaning of all the signals. Other petty officers perform their duties in the same manner as the signalmen. [Most of] the officers…did not have even a working knowledge of the equipment with which they worked. They did not seem interested in such matters. This is no doubt due to the great reliance placed on their petty officers.[26]

The dependence was even greater with temporary officers, arriving bewildered for their training schools.

…when we sailed in Clematis *leaving the dock in Bristol and down the Avon, I was in theory in charge aft. An order came down to get out a spring. Extraordinarily, I had absolutely no idea what the order meant and simply turned to one of the Petty Officers. I told him to get out a spring and was intrigued to watch what happened.[27]*

Despite the greater privileges, many newly promoted men felt that the duties of a petty officer were not very different.

On a watch, it didn't really alter when you became a PO. You still had a watch to keep. If there were any panics during the night you would make certain that people had closed up properly. I would check. I went to the 4-inch gun whenI was a PO. When I was a leading hand I went on to the Oerlikon, *but if, for instance, a boat was called away for a rescue, when I was buffer I would be responsible for getting that boat into the water and lowering it or hoisting it.[28]*

Chief Petty Officers

The chief petty officer had no badge as such on his normal uniform but instead he was distinguished by three brass buttons on his sleeve and a cap badge with a wreath round the anchor and a crown above. The navy tended to protect him more than any other rating. In the seaman branch, even in wartime, he had to have served at least three years after passing for petty officer, and at least five years as leading seaman and petty officer, so the rank was not open to many Hostilities Only sailors. The navy did not compromise on this, so some chief petty officers' messes were rather empty later in the war, despite the recall of large numbers of pensioners. The chief petty officers were entitled to their own mess, with slightly more space than the petty officers. The highly skilled artificers were equivalent in rank to them, but often much younger and were kept apart in separate messes. In a large ship before the war there was one chief of the seaman branch for every seven petty officers, although not all these billets were filled in wartime.[29] Chiefs tended to predominate in shore bases, where their experience was invaluable in training and administration.

In destroyers and smaller ships the coxswain, the senior chief petty officer, was a key figure. To D A Rayner, 'In a small ship the coxswain is the third most important man, as far as the happiness of the ship is concerned'.[30] According to Nicholas Monsarrat:

A good coxswain is a jewel; … The coxswain can make all the difference on board. As the senior rating in the ship, responsible for much of its discipline and

The master-at-arms inspects the crew of *Rodney* in 1943 in advance of captain's rounds.

administration, he has a profound effect on producing a happy and efficient ship's company. Usually he is a 'character', to use an overworked but explicit word: that is, a strong personality who would make himself felt in any surroundings, and who is, in his present world, a man of exceptional weight and influence. He keeps his eye on everything, from the rum issue to the cleanliness of hammocks, from the chocolate ration to the length of the side-whiskers of the second-class stokers. It is his duty to find things out, however obscure of camouflaged they may be – a case of bullying, a case of smuggled beer, a case of 'mechanised dandruff' in the seaman's mess – and either set them right or else report them forthwith to a higher authority. In the majority of cases, as might be expected, he is fully competent to set them right himself, and can be trusted to do so.

He is the friend of everyone on board, and a good friend too – if they want him to be, and if they deserve it: failing that, he makes a very bad enemy.[31]

The Admiralty urged new captains to recognise his importance.

The Coxswain in particular has an especial position in the ship's company. There is no reason why he should not be a Second Officer of the Watch at sea. He should be a constant link between the Captain and the messdeck. He should know of any bad feeling in any mess; of any leading hand who is running his mess badly. If he can have an office of his own, his position is greatly enhanced. He must have the respect, but also the confidence of the ratings. He must be capable of reprimanding the other Petty Officers. He must have the welfare of the ship's company consistently at heart. If the junior ratings call him 'Sir', so much the better, and he should see that the other Petty Officers when on duty are addressed in a manner befitting their state.[32]

Rayner felt that there should be 'a special bond between Captain and coxswain. It is he who takes the wheel in action, or when entering or leaving harbour. One of the most comforting sounds I know is the voice of your trusted coxswain coming up the voice-pipe, "Coxswain at the wheel, Sir"'.[33]

Shortages

By early 1943, as the navy expanded faster than ever before, the Director of Personal Services [sic] was increasingly concerned about the shortage of leading seamen and petty officers. The navy was 18 per cent short of leading seamen and 8 per cent short of petty officers. More petty officers would be promoted soon, but this would only reduce the numbers of leading seamen, and there was no immediate sign of relief there. The First Lord of the Admiralty was equally concerned.

There is increasing evidence that the number of higher and trained technical ratings is not keeping up with the rate at which the navy has expanded and that a large proportion of men entered for 'Hostilities Only' lack the normal incentive for advancement. This may be partly due to the fact that the wages of many are being 'made up' by their civilian employers, and in any case they do not contemplate a career in the navy with its attendant responsibilities.

The shortages in the ratings concerned are chiefly in Seamen Petty Officers and Leading Seamen, Petty Officer and Leading Telegraphists, Yeomen and Leading Signalmen, Senior Artificers (Electrical and Engine Room, the latter with certificates qualifying them to take charge of watches) and in Supply and Writer Petty Officers.[34]

The Royal Navy was always reluctant to use temporary rank, to give men status that would have to be taken away after the war. It was used more in new branches such as Combined Operations, and in the Submarine Service, but if a man became entitled to a 'fore and aft' uniform after a year's temporary service, he had to buy it himself.

To some extent the problem was insoluble, in that the rating of petty officer demanded experience that could not be produced in a hurry. But the British system compared unfavourably with the US Navy, where men were given far more encouragement to advance themselves. The Royal Navy tended to prevent unsuitable men for rising, rather than to train more to become suitable. There was no equivalent of the wavy RNVR stripes to distinguish wartime petty officers from regulars, and that would probably not have been acceptable on the lower deck, which was very conscious of status. But more leadership training and greater use of temporary rank could have done something to solve the petty officer problem.

3 Jack Afloat and Ashore

Long Service Men

Since the middle of the nineteenth century naval seamen had joined as boys at the age of 15 or 16 and remained in the service for at least 12 years from the age of 18, with the option to sign on for another 10 years to get a pension at the age of 40. In periods of rapid growth men were sometimes allowed to sign on for seven years followed by five in the reserve, but long service was the central feature of the naval seaman's life. That, and the natural separation from society caused by his lifestyle, led to the development of a strong and unique naval culture.

The Admiralty was strongly attached to it, but the system of early entry and long service had its critics. In 1941, one man told John Davies, 'Joined as a boy when I was fifteen. ... Me old man shoved me in. I ain't forgiven the old bastard to this day'.[35] Fifteen years of steady employment might have seemed attractive during the great depression, but was less so by the end of the war. In 1946 a petty officer wrote:

Is our public aware that its young sailors are kidnapped into its senior service at the tender age of 15, and, to ensure that the sentence is binding, they have to sign or have signed for them a document stating that for 12 years, from the age of 18, their souls belong to the Admiralty. Imagine: 15 years signed away by children unaware of life's meaning. Having procured the body, the service proceeds to divorce the mind from its natural environment, from every aspect of life save that of the naval service (early nineteenth century)[36]

New entrants were sent to the Boys' Training Establishments, where life was harsh, especially HMS *Ganges*. Tristan Jones joined one of the last boys' courses there in spring 1940 and saw much of the pre-war system.

Since I left Ganges I have been in many hellish places, including a couple of French Foreign Legion barracks and fifteen prisons in twelve countries. None of them were nearly as menacing as HMS Ganges as a brain-twisting, body-racking ground of mental bullying and physical strain.[37]

The long-service seaman was marked out by his early entry to the navy and the effects of naval discipline at an early age, but he still retained the free and easy attitude of a sailor. He was different from a stoker, who had entered later and worked at a dirtier and more technical trade; and the marine who had also entered later but was more dependent on the disciplinary structure.

In a navy which valued long service very highly, it is not surprising that it was regarded as the most important factor by some. Long service in ratings was marked by chevrons on the left arm, under the badge of a leading seaman or petty officer, if worn. A man was awarded one stripe for three years' service, a second for eight years and a third for 13 years. Each stripe brought 3d per day extra pay and increased prestige on the messdecks. The stripes were more prominent than the rank badges, and the public, and sometimes new entrants to the navy, often mistook them for army NCO's stripes. The 'three-badge AB' who had done his 13 years without any promotion was a substantial figure in the pre-war navy where advancement was slow, and he had something of a revival in wartime as pensioners were recalled and posted to the training camps. Nicholas Monsarrat describes him as a 'legendary character'.

…either he hasn't the brain and energy to pass for Leading Seaman, or he doesn't welcome responsibility, or he 'likes it where he is', or for any other reason… He may sound dull and stupid but he is rarely that; more often than not he knows it all… Give him a job and he will work his way through it; not with any flash display of energy, like one of those jumped-up young Petty Officers, but at a careful and steady pace, which escapes both commendation and criticism. … and (assuming that time doesn't matter) you will be able to rely on the job when it is finished.[38]

The Hostilities Only

Drafted into this, the Hostilities Only (HO) man generally found himself overwhelmed and took on the culture of the regulars. The wartime navy was a melting pot, recruiting men from a greater social and geographical range than ever before. Despite his experience as an actor, Alec Guinness was bewildered at HMS *Raleigh* in 1941. 'I can't understand what anyone says – they have the thickest Scots, Irish, Yorks, Lancs, Stepney accents. … There are 30 of us in class 54 – mostly factory hands, lorry drivers, navvies, half wits, nondescripts (the majority) and a Glasgow University man, and a young school master'.[39]

Training camps for HO ratings were set up round the coast, in converted holiday camps such as Butlin's at Skegness or Ayr, in converted boys' training camps such as *Ganges* at Shotley, or purpose-built such as *Raleigh* near Plymouth. A medical officer describes the situation at a camp in Cornwall in 1941.

HMS Impregnable is a training establishment for the Communications branch. There is a permanent Ships Company of about 170 men, which includes Instructors, Regulating Staff, Supply Branch, Cooks etc. The trainees, most of whom come here straight from civilian life, number on average about 480. Of these 120 are telegraphists and the other 380 are signalmen. …

The usual routine is for the men, who come in batches of 58 at a time, to arrive on a Wednesday. They are first inspected medically, then kitted up. … After this the new entries sit for an intelligence test, and those getting less than

50% marks are sent over to HMS Raleigh. *This is to avoid wasting time trying to teach hopelessly stupid men the difficult art of Signalling. The remainder then have 2 weeks instruction in Squad Drill, Seamanship, etc, before starting their actual course.*

The accommodation is very satisfactory. The Trainees are accommodated mostly in wooden buildings, though the Mess Decks are of brick. There are 9 Sleeping Huts, each holding 52 beds. These beds are in pairs one over the other, thus allowing ample space between the beds, which accounts for the good health of the men.

Most of the camps were used to train ordinary seamen over 10 or 12 weeks. They did a good deal of foot drill, which was familiar to the retired chiefs and petty officers who made up the bulk of the instructors. They learned knots, how to steer a ship and row a boat, were taught about naval discipline and organisation, but rarely saw an actual ship unless they happened to be stationed near a naval base. The men left the bases as ordinary seamen, or the equivalent in other branches, recognised as 'Men not fully trained, but generally employed at sea'.[40] As one officer of a training base wrote of a class:

F[robisher] 88, fashioned and welded together in five weeks, was returning to its individual components, but each man was taking away with him more than he brought in. Each could look after himself and his kit; whatever his category, each could swim, and pull and sail a lifeboat; each knew enough about fighting a ship not to be a nuisance at sea. And, above all, they had a sense of belonging, a rock-bottom foundation for living together, in preparation for the time when they would be locked together for months on end in a steel box far from land.[41]

The HOs, including Commision and Warrant candidates who were just passing through the lower deck, were amazed by what they saw

A training class at HMS *Royal Arthur* at Skegness, with the leading seaman instructor in the centre. The variety in ages is clearly seen.

and some of them published accounts, such as J P W Mallalieu's *Very Ordinary Seaman* and S Gorley Putt's *Men Dressed as Seamen*, which revealed messdeck culture for the first time. New men were quickly swept up by the attitudes of the lower deck and aped the regulars. Captain Oram of *Hawkins* wrote of 'the wartime sailor, faithfully modeling himself upon his glamorous predecessor…conscious of the ready-made aura which attached to his own interpretation of the part'.[42] The future Prime Minister James Callaghan wrote:

We were taught how to tie knots and we discovered how to launder our new, dark-blue collars so that they appeared as faded and washed out as those of any veteran seaman. We risked the wrath of the chief gunner's mate by cutting the tapes of our collars so that they showed a U-front instead of the regulation V-front, and we made sure we had seven horizontal creases (no more, no less) in our bell-bottomed trousers. All these matters were important to us.[43]

Uniform

Unlike soldiers and marines, seamen took no oath of allegiance, so the issue of uniforms was a defining moment and the first introduction to the strange naval culture. John Davies wrote that the seaman's shirt was an 'amazing garment'. It had a square-cut neck and short sleeves and many men had difficulty at first in finding which way to put it on. The seaman's trousers were 'outlandish'. Then came the jumper.

Getting into the jumper was an all-in struggle, no holds barred, a wild waving of arms followed finally by a condition of complete helplessness. Breathless and outwitted I at last stood still, my shoulders and upper arms relentlessly caught in blue serge, the extremities dangling helplessly before me. Then as though in

response to an intuitive feeling that all was not well, one of the white-shirted ones suddenly appeared, ducking under the screen. Without ceremony he heaved out the collar of my jumper, which had been the major cause of the stoppage, and then he tugged industriously at my waist until jumper and trousers met, and finally, with a superhuman effort, overlapped.[44]

He would now be expected to wear his uniform on almost all occasions while ashore, for working, on leave and on parade. He might abandon it at sea, especially small ships and submarines. He did not mind wearing it ashore and it was very popular with the public, especially with women. Tristan Jones was told by an army veteran of the last war, 'Well, matey, at least you'll be all right where crumpet's concerned. They go for the navy blokes a lot more than the army, see? Can't go wrong in your little old navy-blue suit, Can you?'[45]

Washing of clothes, or 'dhobying', was very important to the seaman. Even HO men posted to RAF bases for Fleet Air Arm training resented it when the RAF expected them to put their clothing in a communal laundry. In other cases, seamen were allowed to supplement their earnings by doing washing for others.

Messdeck Life

The messdeck was central to the seaman's life. In peacetime, a mess on a battleship was mixed but happy.

I was victualled in a mess, the members of which were mainly Irish or West Countrymen, since Queen Elizabeth *was a Devonport manned ship. We were a happy-go-lucky lot and many were the times we had a sing-song, with a couple of our Irish members playing piano accordians. The Cornish and Devon*

Naval uniforms 1939–45. Left: a captain's service dress. Centre: duffel coat and life vest as worn on active service. Right: a rating's uniform showing the separate collar.

types possessed a soft and pleasant accent which fascinated me, and one or two of them wore a single gold ring in one ear in the manner of gypsies. Some wore magnificent beards, black and smartly trimmed. As the only Portsmouth rating in the mess, I took a lot of ribbing from this gang of pirates, but I was glad to be of their number.[46]

The HOs and especially the CWs might intrude in this scene. Leading Seaman John Whelan was bemused when 12 CWs arrived on board. Their accents immediately attracted attention. 'Numbah twooo mess. Six of us hev to report to numbah twooo mess, the other six are going to numbah one mess'. But the atmosphere in mixed messes could be very jovial, especially in a happy ship, like the destroyer *Obstinate* when Tristan Jones served in her.

My mess was the after seaman's mess… I didn't know it at the time…that they were a crowd of the finest men I ever came across in my life, for all their personal peccadilloes. … I soon got to know all fifteen men in my mess very well, and sorted out the ones to cultivate and the ones to – not avoid – there was no such possibility on a crowded ship – slide by.

His messmates included leading seamen Pony Moore and Flossie Herbert, 'a handsome man of about thirty who'd once slept with the wife of a French cognac distiller'; recalled pensioners Tinger Ling and Rasher Williams, veterans of the last war; Rosy Lee a London Barrow boy and Jock McAllister a Hebridean 'with his angel face, his soft musical voice and his pink cheeks'. Brigham Young and Pincher Martin were HOs in their early twenties, the latter from a wealthy family. Roger the Lodger was an intellectual who read the *Daily Telegraph* and could confuse his superiors by switching from a Cockney to an Oxford accent. Jones also found two fellow Welshmen, Taff Williams and Organ Morgan, who 'treated me like a younger brother'.[47]

Homosexuality was not common, nor was it talked about much at the time, but the long absences of contact with the opposite sex made some kind of compromise necessary. According to George Melly, 'Sex on the *Dido* was comparatively low key but uncensorious. There were a few obvious homosexuals, the doe-eyed writer for one, many heterosexuals, and a fair number of those who would, on a casual basis, relieve sexual pressure with their own sex'.[48]

The Seaman and the Public

The public image of the seaman was one of the navy's greatest assets, in both recruitment and morale. This image was both reflected and reinforced by popular entertainment, particularly the cinema. The most famous example was *In Which We Serve*, made by Noel Coward and based very directly on the exploits of Lord Louis Mountbatten in HMS *Kelly*. It was much more subtle than the usual propaganda pieces, introducing issues such as boredom, fear and death, although its attitudes to class look ridiculously old-fashioned. Lower deck reaction to it was favourable, if slightly ambivalent. One insider felt that the film 'did NOT represent lower deck speech and manners', but he agreed that 'The average sailor loves to see patriotic stuff on the screen, although he might grumble like blazes when with his mates. Imagine the glow of pride, however, when sitting with his wife, girl

friend or 'tart wot I picked up' in the cinema. IWWS did have a real attempt at representing not only sailors at war, but families'.[49]

At the time, the British public saw the navy as the most reliable of the services. Before Dunkirk, the army suffered from the recollections of the Western Front; after Dunkirk, it was under the shadow of defeat for some years. The popular 1943 film *Went the Day Well?* provides a striking tribute to the reliability of the navy, though it was set entirely in an inland English village. The village is taken over by German paratroopers disguised as British soldiers, who quickly expose themselves through their cruelty and ruthlessness. The local Home Guard is alerted, but soon eliminated.

Seamen on a crowded mess deck of the destroyer escort *Garth* write letters home in 1944.

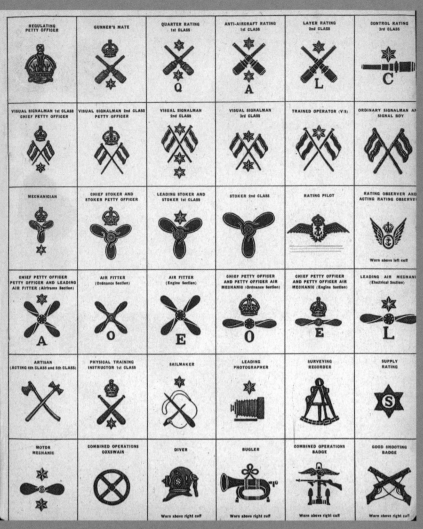

A selection of the many badges worn by ratings.

Resistance is led by an able seaman home on leave, who continues to wear his uniform throughout the affair. All classes (except for the odd traitor) unite in a common effort. Men in army uniform turn out to be spies, traitors or dupes, and acts of horrible cruelty are carried out or threatened by the disguised Germans; but the square collar and bell bottoms of the sailor remain the symbol of resourcefulness, leadership and success.

To the public who knew little of the seaman, he was held in great respect. As one correspondent told the social survey organisation Mass Observation in 1941, 'I know no sailors, but I think they are heroic'.[50] But people around the naval bases were less impressed, as young HOs copied the hard-drinking habits of the long-service men. According to one entertainer, sailors were a well-behaved audience on board ship, but ashore they were different.

Jack ashore…is still boisterous but inclined to be a little unkind, and changes the laughter for jeers, often spoiling a show with the intention of having a good time. In consequence many artists will not accept engagements at these Navy theatres at Portsmouth, Devonport, Sheerness and Chatham. The pity is that the 'birding' is never really meant, and perhaps just reaction of being away from the ship's company.[51]

Non-Substantive Rates

The seaman branch was the main home of the system of 'non-substantive' rates. Ratings as leading seaman and petty officer were 'substantive'. Non-substantive rates formed a parallel system which marked proficiency in a trade rather than leadership and management skill. A seaman did not have to specialise by acquiring a non-substantive rate, but he might find his role rather restricted and his promotion prospects poor. Skilled seamen were needed to steer the ship, to heave the lead and tend lines when mooring, to launch and

operate boats and to work anchor cables. But these tasks needed only a small number of men, like steering, or were used intermittently, like mooring. The seaman who did not acquire another skill was likely to find himself spending a great deal of time on menial tasks such as cleaning or looking after a petty officers' mess. In the gunnery branch, 'Although the Regulations permit advancement to Leading Seaman and Petty Officer without first qualifying for a "non-substantive" rating, such qualification is of great assistance and should in any case be undertaken as soon as possible after "substantive" advancement'.[52]

The exact relationship between substantive and non-substantive rates was a complex one. In the gunnery branch for example, according to the *Gunnery Pocket Book* of 1945, certain non-substantive ratings were only open to those with enough leadership skills to become leading seamen and petty officers. '*1st class ratings,* owing to the duties they have to perform, are reserved for C.P.O s, P.Os and leading seamen passed for P.O., holding a 2nd class rating. *2nd class ratings* are reserved for leading seamen, and able seamen passed for leading seaman, holding a 3rd class rating'.[53] In the torpedo branch, the non-substantive rating of Leading Torpedoman was not the same thing as leading seaman and could be held by a man in any rank from able seaman to chief petty officer.

In peacetime, men served some time at sea before being chosen for shore training in a non-substantive rate. In war, they were usually selected in the basic training schools, which were under increasing pressure to find men for the fleet. Others had some training afloat, for example as radar operators, before going on a formal course.

The Gunnery Branch

The gunnery branch regarded itself as the naval elite. Not only did it operate and direct the main weapons of the ship, it also ran the parade ground side of naval discipline. The senior gunnery rate in a ship, the

Chief Gunner's Mate, was expected to be a strict disciplinarian and the petty officers of the branch were trained in 'power to command' and barking orders in a military fashion. This tended to make it unpopular with other branches.

Just before the war the gunnery branch was reorganised into four sub-branches. First and second class ratings wore crossed guns, third class men had a single gun, with the appropriate letter underneath. Control ratings (C) operated range finders and other instruments. Quarters ratings (Q) operated the guns and took charge of the smaller ones. Layer ratings (L) aimed them and worked in the director towers. Anti-aircraft ratings (A) manned large and small guns. Large numbers of AA3s, or anti-aircraft gunners third class, were needed for the 55,000 Oerlikon guns that the navy used. One was in charge of each gun with a less skilled assistant, and he might become a kind of local hero if he was credited with shooting down a plane. Other sub-branches were added during the war, for specialists in merchant ship gunnery, boom defence and radar control, which would eventually replace visual range finding. Gunnery ratings were trained in the famous school, HMS *Excellent* on Whale Island in Portsmouth, where fitness and parade-ground discipline was as important as gunnery. There were other schools attached to the Plymouth and Chatham commands, and many smaller ones were opened during the war for in-service training between voyages.

Torpedomen and Submarine Detectors

The title of the torpedo branch was slightly misleading. It did indeed maintain and fire torpedoes and other underwater weapons such as mines and depth charges, but it also had responsibility for low power electrical systems, so torpedomen might find themselves posted to ships with no torpedoes. There were half-hearted attempts to split the branch into torpedomen proper and electricians, but most men continued to learn both aspects of the job and the navy failed to set up a properly integrated electrical branch during the war. Portsmouth-based torpedomen were trained at HMS *Vernon*, originally at Portsmouth but re-sited to Rodean School. Those who passed wore a single torpedo for a Seaman Torpedoman and crossed torpedoes for a Leading Torpedoman or a Torpedo Gunner's Mate. In wartime, the branch had more sub-divisions than any other, with skilled electricians known as wireman and specialists in controlled mining, landing craft, boom defence and minesweepers.

Asdic operators were rated as submarine detectors, with promotion prospects to the non-substantive rates of Higher Submarine Detector (HSD) and of Submarine Detector Instructor. The SD branch was forced to expand rapidly after peacetime neglect. It had only 1200 trained men in 1939, rising to 7600 in 1945. Originally it was based at Portland on the south coast of England but in 1940 it was moved to two training schools in the Firth of Clyde – HMS *Nimrod* at Campbeltown and *Osprey* at Dunoon further up the Firth. Often the HSD, who might only be an able seaman and rarely was higher than leading seaman in a corvette or frigate, was the senior operator in the ship and bore a great deal of responsibility. Sometimes an operator had to assert himself against his officers. Peter Gretton reports of the frigate *Tay*:

…the asdic operator reported 'echo right ahead'. We were rather sniffy about it, but he stuck to his guns, and the order to 'stand by' had just been passed to the depth charge party when the U-boat had the cheek to lift his stern out of the water, just underneath our port bow.[54]

Radar

Radar or RDF was an even newer branch than anti-submarine, and as yet it had no real hierarchy on the lower deck. Not all the ratings would be fully trained, due to the hug expansion of radar in 1941–2. The schools would provide three men for each set, and the others needed to keep up a continuous watch were to be acting RDF ratings, trained up on board. Captains were warned that there was no time in the schools to teach men fully. 'Commanding officers must therefore appreciate that Ordinary Seamen (R.D.F.) newly drafted to sea cannot be considered fully trained either in practical operating or in sea sense. This training must be continued afloat and every help and encouragement must be given to operators to learn'.

The main training school for radar operators was at HMS *Valkyrie* on the Isle of Man, where radar aerials were set up with a view over the Irish Sea. For security reasons ratings had no badge of their own until late in the war but their informal status was high. It was not unusual for a ship to be delayed in sailing because the key radar operator was absent.

Signallers

It was never quite clear how far signallers were considered part of the seaman branch, and how far they formed a branch of their own. They wore the square rig of the seaman and they were divided into two groups. Visual signallers used flags, semaphore and Morse code, wore a badge of crossed flags and operated mainly on the bridge. In peacetime, they were usually selected from the better-educated boys at the training schools and Nicholas Monsarrat liked working with them.

If you want an example of alert intelligence in the Navy, a young signalman, interested in his job and keen to get ahead, is probably the best specimen. From the very nature of his work, he knows more about the ship and her movements than any other rating; and he has the opportunity of learning much more besides. He sees almost every signal that comes in, on a very wide variety of subjects ranging from the First Lord's anniversary greetings to the provision of tropical underwear for Wrens. He spends long hours up on the bridge, in the centre of things, where he has the best opportunity of talking to his officers and of picking up fresh ideas.[55]

Radio operators were known as telegraphists and wore a badge of a lightning flash and wings. Originally they were responsible for maintenance as well as operating the sets, until a radio mechanic branch was formed later in the war. Telegraphists needed a good knowledge of Morse code and were often trained in civilian schools in wartime. Unlike the visual signallers and the members of the seaman branch they were not expected to assume military command of a compartment or a boat, so in that sense they were closer to the engineers and other specialists.

4 Engineers and Others

The Royal Navy was totally dependent on its engineers for all of its activities. No warship could operate for long without them, for even a static depot ship needed its electrical and other auxiliary services. Yet naval engineers had to work below decks in unpleasant conditions and at high temperatures, often knowing little about what was happening above. They were more at risk than other crew members when a ship sank: 'It is evident that casualties to men in sunk or damaged ships is affecting the number of higher Engine Room ratings available, as the proportion of casualties is usually highest in the Engine and Boiler Rooms'.[56]

But the lower deck did not have the same prejudice against engineering that was present among the officers. Ratings were aware that such technical skills could serve them well in civilian life, in a way that ability with guns or military discipline could never do. Engine room work tended to free men from the more menial and oppressive aspects of military life, such a cleaning decks or rifle drill. All sailors grumble, and in such a hazardous and uncomfortable war they had every right to; but the naval engineer was as happy as anyone else.

During the war there was a vast increase in smaller vessels such as coastal forces and landing craft, and each one had to have some kind of engineering staff. There was no great technological change in engine rooms during the war, but the engineering branch had to cope with a far wider range of power plants than ever before. Before the war nearly all warships (apart from submarines) had used the steam turbine engine. Hostilities brought the re-introduction of the steam reciprocating engine for escort vessels, the increased use of petrol engines for coastal forces and diesels for landing craft and other vessels. It was difficult to train experts who could operate and maintain all these engines, so some had to train in one type or another.

Selection

Apart from officers, the navy had two basic levels of skill for its engineers. Artificers were highly skilled, stokers were semi-skilled. In wartime there was not the time to train enough artificers to the highest standard, so some compromise was needed, not within the group itself but by creating 'dilutees' who could do some but not all of the skilled work. The navy found enough volunteers for its engine rooms despite the vast expansion. Including air personnel, between 14,000 and 15,000 were under training for engineering duties as the peak in 1943.[57]

Naturally it tried to find those with previous experience in civil life. Asked to investigate how trained engineering workers were deployed by the armed services, Sir William Beveridge had much praise for the navy.

The trade testing of the navy is centralized, standardized and objective. All the candidates for appointment as Engine Room Artificer or Ordnance Artificer are tested on uniform methods at one of the three home ports by performance against time of a set piece of work; all the candidates for appointment as Electrical Artificer are tested at one of two centres by a similar mechanical test; the test in each case normally lasts several days. Those who pass this test are guaranteed, as possessing a certain minimum of mechanical skill; those who fail it are given the opportunity of training up to it…

…there is an organised search for talent in the Navy. At each of the home ports officers of the engineering branch make a systematic investigation of all men at the general reception centre with a view to discovering men who can be trained for technical work. … This search for talent is conducted not on paper, by examination of forms, but by interviews making possible a real judgment of personal skill and capacity.[58]

As the war progressed the supply of skilled men tended to dry up and the navy had to identify those with educational qualifications to be trained as engine room, radio or air mechanics. A survey showed that men training for these trades had to come from the top 30 per cent of the intelligence range, equal to potential officers.[59]

Engine Room Artificers

The engine room artificer was one of the most skilled men on the lower deck. In peacetime most came from the dockyard towns or naval schools and had strong naval connections. They were recruited as apprentices at the age of about 16, and did a four-year course at Plymouth or Rosyth. They learned a skilled trade as a fitter, turner, boilermaker or smith and were able to make emergency repairs in out of the way places. They also learned how to take charge of an engine room. They had 'wide practical experience of reciprocating, turbine, internal combustion, compression ignition, refrigerating and hydraulic machinery; engine and boiler room refitting. Capable of fullest application of trade qualifications.'[60] The Admiralty was determined to maintain their standards even in wartime.

The training and education of Artificer Apprentices is intended not only to make them good Workmen, but to give them a real understanding of the tools, materials and machines they will have to handle, and also to make them self-reliant, ready and resourceful.

Opposite above: Stokers checking the temperature and pressure in the boiler room of a cruiser in November 1942.

Opposite below: The engine room of the turbine-driven escort aircraft carrier *Tracker*.

Below: The Chief ERA at work in the submarine *Tribune* in 1942.

Accordingly, their knowledge should not be gained simply from books or taken on trust from their teacher; they should be trained to approach subjects from the standpoint of observation, and to reason out their own conclusions.[61]

Nevertheless, much greater numbers were needed, and Hostilities Only men were also recruited, if they had at least two and a half years' experience in a relevant trade. They were given a short course in engine room work, but the Admiralty had to admit that their 'Efficiency as tradesmen varies widely'.

An engine room artificer wore the fore-and-aft rig for the entirety of his naval career. He started his working life afloat as an ERA fifth class, not yet fully trained and equivalent to a petty officer. After 12 to 18 months and gaining boiler room and engine room watch-keeping certificates, he would be rated fourth class and have the status of chief petty officer. He would then advance through the classes to become a chief ERA after at least six years' practical experience, though his badges did not change during that period. Indeed, he had no specific badge at all, only the three buttons of a CPO. A chief ERA might be the chief engineer of a small ship like a corvette, or in charge of the watch in a larger one. His promotion prospects were good by lower deck standards, and he could become a warrant or commissioned officer.

Mechanicians carried out the same duties as ERAs, though they entered by a different route. They began as stokers and were selected during the leading stokers' course, to begin two years' training at Plymouth. It was found that they responded well to this, although their experience made them a little rough for delicate work. Admiral Ford thought this was a much more economical way of training suitable men than the ERA apprenticeship, but if too many were recruited there might be a shortage of intelligent men to become stoker petty officers and chiefs. Mechanicians could also qualify for warrant rank, though even then the distinction for ERAs was maintained. They were known as warrant mechanicians rather than warrant engineers.

The supply of ERAs was not nearly enough to cope with wartime demands, and very few candidates could be recruited from civilian industry or the Merchant Navy, which had greatly increased needs of their own. Late in 1940 the navy set up a scheme to train a 'diluted' version of the ERA, to be known as the engine room mechanic. It was estimated that 2200 would be needed every year and they were to be selected from men 'either having some previous experience or a sufficient standard of intelligence and mechanical aptitude to enable them to be trained'. They were trained in Ministry of Labour facilities, a fact which rankled with naval officers.[62] Motor mechanics were trained in petrol and diesel engines, specifically for work on board coastal forces and landing craft.

Stokers

The title of 'stoker' came from the days before the First World War, when coal had to be shovelled into the furnaces of the boiler room. This was no longer necessary on oil-fired ships, and coal burners were rare outside the Patrol Service, which had different conditions of employment. The name lingered and suggestions to change the title to 'mechanic' fell on deaf ears for the moment. In the meantime, it was hoped that the stoker might lose his image of a muscular brute. 'He requires intelligence, mental alertness

and a reasonably high standard of education, if he is to watch-keep on machinery with understanding'.[63] Under the supervision of an ERA or engineering officer, the stoker 'tends coal or oil fired boilers, keeps watch on main and auxiliary machinery. Reads simple recording instruments, inspects self-lubricated bearings, oils open type engines, runs fire and bilge pumps'.[64] They made up the great mass of the engine room complement on nearly all ships, while a single one might operate the engines of a ship's boat or a small landing craft. Five hundred were entering the training schools every week at the height of the war.

The culture of the stoker was very different from that of the regular seaman. He had joined at the age of 18 or over and had never been broken by camps such as *Ganges*, so he tended to be more independent. As a seaman, Tristan Jones watched him at work.

I looked down through the iron gratings and saw Stokes calmly going about his business. … They appeared to be completely isolated from the world we knew topsides, and the most comfortable ratings in the ship, with no officers to oversee them directly. They certainly seemed the most content, even though they and we knew that only a quarter inch of steel plate stood between them and sudden, excruciating death.[65]

In peacetime the stoker was distinguished mainly by the age of his entry, but in wartime he was generally selected after the potential engine room mechanics and other intelligent men had been taken out, leading to a suspicion that the stoker was inferior in quality: '…the selection of these men has lowered the general standard of the stoker, and if the war lasts for many years will have a marked effect on the Engineroom Branch as a whole, since the skimming of the cream on entry removes the prospective

Cooks at work in the galley in 1942.

higher ratings of the future'. It was found that between 10 and 20 per cent of men under instruction were of 'low mentality' and 'semi-illiterates'.[66] Perhaps this group was represented by a Stoker Smith on the cruiser *Kent* in 1942. He resented being reprimanded by anyone, and any legitimate punishment was followed by requests to change his job or his ship. He had four unsuccessful attempts at the auxiliary watch-keeping course, 'a privilege which he ill deserves'. He was always clean, but of 'a surly nature'. The chief engineer had never seen him smile.[67]

Even so, the hierarchy of stokers had to be promoted from the 'rather thin cream' of the wartime navy, though, as in other branches, the majority of wartime petty officers and chiefs were regulars. A stoker second class was eligible for his first class rate after a year of service and on reaching the age of 18½, less if he was exceptional. After a further two years, and attaining an auxiliary watch-keeping certificate and passing an educational examination, he was eligible for leading stoker and was trained for three months in engineering skills at a Mechanical Training Establishment. At this stage he might be selected for further training as a mechanician, but otherwise he would qualify for promotion to stoker petty officer after two years, and for chief two years after that, provided he had a boiler room certificate.

Stokers had a higher proportion of senior rates than seamen. A River class frigate had one chief stoker, six stoker petty officers and six leading stokers as well as 12 stokers. A light fleet aircraft carrier had a total of 145, of whom 5 per cent were chiefs, 10 per cent were petty officers and 25 per cent were leading stokers. In the seaman branch the corresponding proportions were 1 per cent chiefs, 7 per cent petty officers and 9 per cent leading seaman.[68] On the other hand, stokers were not eligible for warrant and commissioned rank unless they had taken a different path as mechanicians. Despite this, Tristan Jones found that 'The Stoker POs were usually humane and friendly, with very little disciplinary bullshit about them. Often, if things were steady and quiet, the PO would be reading a cheap paperback under the forced draft fans, and his mate, the stoker, would be making cocoa or tea'.[69]

Engine Room Work

Engine rooms usually worked in three watches, even if the rest of the ship was in two watches. Capital ships and cruisers had enough men to maintain full power during three watches, destroyers and small vessels tended to use their speed in bursts and needed only to maintain three-fifths power at other times.[70]

There were three different areas of work: the engines proper, the boilers and the auxiliary machinery. A promising young stoker was expected to progress from the boiler room to the engine room, and then to begin work on the auxiliary machinery.[71]

Len Perry joined the destroyer *Beagle* late in 1943. His first job was cleaning the bilge pumps, 'plunging your arm into freezing, filthy bilge water'. After a while he was assigned to boiler control, which involved 'moving like a gazelle when the bridge called down for "Full Speed"'. He was promoted to keep watch on the distilling plant for fresh water, well aft in the ship where he had to lash himself against a pipe in rough weather. Then he went to the elite throttle party which controlled the speed of the engines on orders from the bridge. They were 'moved like finely honed and superbly trained athletes, moved as one team, instantly responding to every instruction from the bridge'.[72]

In the boiler room, the work began when the ship was ordered to sea and the boiler had to be lit or 'flashed up'. It took some time to get the water boiling and the ship ready to move. If the complement allowed, a petty officer or leading stoker would be in charge of the water level, as it was very dangerous to let it get too low.[73]

Engine room staff often knew little of what was happening above deck, as Perry found.

We never knew if the people on the bridge of Beagle *were having a bit of fun to relieve the boredom, or were about to drop depth charges, launch torpedoes, or take desperate avoiding action to dodge 'tin fish' or bombs. We were certainly under no illusions that nobody would tell us if a large hole was about to be ripped in the side of* Beagle.[74]

In port, boilers had to be cleaned at regular intervals and this was hard work for the crew. The boilers were shut down, cooled and emptied. The *Engineering Manual* gives only a vague idea of the hard and unpleasant labour involved.

All fittings inside the boiler are removed for cleaning, and the internal surfaces of a boiler are scrubbed clean with wire scrubbers, scrapers and light chipping hammers being used if necessary in cylindrical boilers. Special wire brushes are used for the tubes of water-tube boilers. Men working in water-tube boilers must not be allowed to take in with them anything which may fall into the tubes, and all articles used in the boiler should be mustered and accounted for before the boiler is closed.[75]

Electrical and Ordnance Artificers

The electrical artificer trained over the same period as an ERA and had the same conditions of service and promotion. He had a far wider range of skills than the torpedo ratings, who did simpler work.

Maintains and effects major repairs to ship's electrical equipment including gyro compasses and torpedoes. Undertakes armature winding etc., and repairs involving use of machine tools, together with maintenance work which torpedo ratings are not qualified to do. Has working knowledge of electronics and servicing valve amplifiers.[76]

Again the electrical artificers had to be diluted with less-skilled men. In this case they were the electrical mechanics who were selected from HO men 'of educational standard not less than 4th Form secondary school' but not necessarily with trade experience, and given six months' training.

The ordnance artificer trained in the same way, but specialised in the maintenance of guns and their mountings. He could refit the breech mechanism of a gun of any size, work on the hydraulics which operated the mounting, or line up the fire control instruments. He had an assistant, the able seaman qualified in ordnance, or QO. He was a gunnery rating and carried out some of the less-skilled tasks, but had to give up the rate on promotion to leading seaman.[77]

Artisans and Radio Mechanics

Artisans were distinguished from artificers in that their work could be done as easily on shore as at sea. They included shipwrights, blacksmiths, plumbers and painters. In general their status was equivalent to that of artificers, and they wore fore-and-aft uniform with a crossed hammer and axe badge on the collar. Most of them, however, had no path to warrant and commissioned rank, which enraged Churchill in 1939. Referring to Hitler's alleged early employment as a house painter, he wrote:

Will you kindly explain to me the reasons which debar individuals in certain branches from rising by merit to commissioned rank? … If a telegraphist may rise, why not a painter? Apparently there is no difficulty about painters rising in Germany![78]

Radio mechanic was a far newer branch, formed early in the war. It was intended to remove the need to train telegraphists in maintenance work and allow them to concentrate on signalling. Candidates were selected from young men with the school certificate in mathematics and given intensive training in civilian colleges. They were rated as leading hands on completion of the course and as petty officer a year later.

**Officers and a
writer at work in
the ship's office of
Rodney in 1940.
Even in a battleship
space is restricted.**

Chef had one of the hardest jobs, I would think, on a corvette. No doubt about it. He had a very small galley – if he's got three pans on top of the range then this was as much as he could do. A very small oven. And most of the times we had hot pot. We always had something on top there, a massive great big receptacle. We were limited to what we could carry, like meat. About four days and that was that, veg the same thing, about three or four days and that was gone. So then you went back to the old tinned stuff. And chef used to do miracles with some of these tins – his own concoctions.[81]

The officers' steward was trained in laying table and serving meals, in marketing (which in those days meant going to market to buy provisions), in serving wines, in cleaning cabins and in identifying and laying out all the various uniforms required by an officer for different occasions, from Number Ones worn on formal occasions to Number Fourteens, action dress – though in wartime there was rarely opportunity to wear anything but the most utilitarian clothing. Several writers identify the steward branch as the origin of myths about the sailor's homosexuality. According to Tristan Jones:

There were extremely few homosexuals among the seamen, stokers, torpedomen and such – I can remember only half a dozen in all the ships in which we served. They were most likely to be found among the stores and supply ratings, and officers' stewards. I don't believe that was because they were so much attracted to that kind of work, as that it gave them a niche on board where they could make themselves indispensable, and so be to some extent protected from the more pusser-faced officers and chiefs.[82]

Miscellaneous Ratings

The domestic and administrative sides of the navy were run by men who wore an inferior version of the fore-and-aft uniform, described as 'a cross between that of a taxi driver and a workhouse inmate'.[79] They were distinguished by star-shaped badges on the left arm, with a letter inside – W for writer or clerk, S for supply rating, C for ship's company cook, OC for officers' cook and OS for officers' steward. Medical standards were generally lower in these branches and men were allowed to wear glasses.

The writer was regarded as slightly superior to the other ratings in this uniform. In peacetime he was entered after an examination in English and arithmetic. He was divided into two main types. In a pay and cash office he would keep the ship's ledgers, carry out all pay accounting and income tax and send allotments to men's relatives. In a captain's or admiral's office he would do general clerical and secretarial work including 'personnel records, disciplinary matters and in general, naval administration'. Both types needed 'detailed knowledge of complex regulations'.[80] Ex-Post Office employees specialised in postal duties, and others were employed as interpreters. The supply rating was similar to the writer in status, and worked in store rooms on board ship and ashore. He might specialise in naval stores such as tools, hardware and cordage, or in provisions for messing purposes. A new breed of aviation stores rating emerged during the war.

With the class systems of the age, it is no surprise that the cooks were divided into two groups, for officers and for crews. Cooking was regarded as menial work rather than an art in Britain at the time, and ships' cooks were very much taken for granted, but it was hard work, especially on a small, unstable ship. Under the Standard Ration and Allowance Messing system, the cooks of the messes prepared the food for cooking, but the ship's cook still had to work hard in the conditions.

5 The Royal Marines

The Royal Marines date their foundation to 1664 when Charles II formed the Duke of York and Albany's Maritime Regiment of Foot. In 1755 they were taken firmly under Admiralty control, though they wore uniforms and had ranks similar to those of the army. Their duties varied over the years, but most of their men served on board ship as part of the crew, providing sentries or landing parties, helping to man guns and hopefully forming a buffer between mutinous seamen and their officers. In the 1930s the role was defined thus:

…in war and peace is to provide detachments which, whilst fully capable of manning their share of the gun armament, are specially trained to provide a striking force drawn either from the Royal Marine Divisions or from the Fleet, immediately available for use under the direction of the Naval Commander-in-Chief for amphibious operations, such as raids on enemy coast-line or bases, or the seizure and defence of temporary bases for the use of our own Fleet.[83]

The marines were self-effacing compared with their United States counterparts and the officers were 'rather smugly obsessed with their own obscurity', according to the novelist Evelyn Waugh, who served with them in wartime.[84] The corps was well aware of its many dichotomies. Every marine was 'a soldier and a sailor too' according to Kipling, and he had to be equally ready for land and sea service, or even

Field Officers

Other Officers
(white cap cover)

Other Ranks

General

Lieutenant
General

Major
General

Brigadier

Colonel

Lieutenant
Colonel

Major

Captain

Lieutenant

Second
Lieutenant

W.O.

Colour
Sergeant

Sergeant

Corporal

Lance Corporal

Provost Sergeant

Drum-Major

Band Corporal

Sergeant-Major

Company Sergeant-Major
and
Quartermaster Sergeant

Warrant Officer's
Badge

Bandmaster,
1st Class

Bandmaster,
2nd Class

Bugler

The rank badges of the Royal Marines.

flying duties in a small number of cases. The marines had highly aggressive roles as commandos, crews of landing craft or in landing parties. They had more defensive roles in protecting naval bases. They acted as domestic servants to both naval and marine officers, and some were artists in that they provided the band service for the navy as a whole. One of their duties was to provide bodyguards and messengers for the Prime Minister, and parties accompanied him on his overseas voyages. But their service as messengers was less successful. John Colville, one of Churchill's private secretaries, often found it easier to carry letters himself, as the marines 'move so slowly and with such dignity'.[85] In wartime the Royal Marines would find some of their traditional roles less important than before, but they would take on many new ones, for the corps always survived through its flexibility.

such as the Sten and the Lanchester, the Vickers heavy machine gun and the 2-inch mortar. Marine ranks were virtually identical to the army, with a few exceptions – warrant officers had naval rather than army status, so they were in effect junior officers, while sergeant majors were senior sergeants. The formal marine uniform consisted of a blue tunic and a peaked cap or white tropical helmet. It was still issued to ships' detachments and bands, but most marines wore battledress like the army.

The Royal Marines relied on both the army and the navy for much of their infrastructure. Administrative support at all levels was provided by the navy, and later by the WRNS. The navy also provided medical services, while much of marine training was based on the work and methods of the army. In return the marines provided some infrastructure for the navy, and ran much of its recruiting service.

The Organisation of the Marines

The corps was headed by the Adjutant-General, re-titled the General Officer Commanding and then the Commandant General in 1945. He came under the Second Sea Lord at the Admiralty, and the post was held by Sir Alan Bourne during the war. He was promoted to full general, unusually high for a Royal Marine. He had a staff of two general officers, two brigadiers and 18 other officers and warrant officers in his headquarters at Queen Anne's Mansions in St James's Park, within walking distance of the Admiralty building.[86]

Marines and officers were allocated to the three main divisions at Chatham, Portsmouth and Plymouth, which paralleled the manning divisions of the navy. Each was headed by a colonel-commandant and allocated men to ships or to other duties. There was also a depot at Deal in Kent, where recruits were trained. On shore they were organized in the same way as army infantry, with battalions each under a lieutenant-colonel, companies led by majors or captains, platoons headed by lieutenant with sergeants as seconds-in-command, and sections of about 10 men under corporals. Afloat, that organization was adapted to the needs of the ship but the marines were ultimately under naval command.

The marines used the standard army infantry weapons: the .303-inch Lee-Enfield rifle and the Bren light machine gun, sub-machine guns

Recruitment and Training

In recruitment, the marines were always in danger of falling between the two stools of the army and the navy. In practice, they always found enough men who wanted to combine the best of the two services. In peacetime, they recruited at a later age than the seaman branch of the navy, so they offered a career to men who wanted to see the world but were not attracted by the heat and confinement of the engine room. In wartime, they took on volunteers within the system of conscription, in the same way as the navy or air force. A surprising number found a family connection with the marines, while others were attracted by the prospect of service in big ships and the blue uniform which was still in use on certain occasions after the army had gone over entirely to battledress. That hope proved illusory – Raymond Mitchell volunteered in 1940 after seeing a poster of a marine in blue jacket and white helmet. But 'I spent my entire Service life in khaki and, save for a few transportational exceptions, entirely upon dry land'.[87]

Recruit training continued at Deal, but as with all services many more facilities were needed and annexes were opened. A new camp was set up for basic training on the River Exe in Devon and it had more than 4000 men in May 1944. Courses were shortened from 10 to 6 weeks in wartime, then increased again to eight. Men learned the traditional army skills of foot drill, field craft and the use of weapons. Potential NCOs were selected quite early and offered extra training in the evenings; they wore a diamond on each shoulder if successful.

The first wartime officers were chosen for the Royal Marine Brigade in 1939, by a mysterious selection process. The army now insisted that all potential officers go through the ranks, the navy at that stage preferred men with navigation experience, the RAF needed young and very fit men for flying, but this course was open to all. The results are vividly described by the novelist Evelyn Waugh in fiction, diaries and letters. But after that the marines went over to army style training. Potential officers were selected after a period in the ranks, and trained intensively in the Officer Cadet Training Unit in a converted hotel at Thurlestone in Devon. Critics said the system produced a superior private soldier rather than an officer able to make decisions.

The Royal Marines had nearly 11,000 men in 1939. By May 1941 this had more than trebled to 36,000. Expansion slowed down after that, but in December 1944 corps numbers had risen to 67,655.[88]

Shipboard Service

Shipboard service was traditionally the most important part of Royal Marine activity, but it was not a growth area in wartime, as new building of battleships, cruisers and aircraft carriers barely covered war losses. There were 7000 marines in shipboard detachments at the end of 1944, including bandsmen – a little over 10 per cent of the corps. In addition there were 570 serving in merchant ships as DEMS gunners.[89]

At one time marine gunners had been segregated in the Royal Marine Artillery, but that was merged with the Royal Marine Light Infantry to form a single corps in 1923. Now marines were entitled to train in gunnery on the same basis as Royal Navy ratings, and to qualify as quarter gunners, anti-aircraft gunners and so on. Marines traditionally manned one gun turret in battleships and cruisers, and a proportion of the anti-aircraft armament. Other marines served as sentries, as officers' servants (although gradually replaced by members of the steward branch) and took turns in other shipboard duties. Their training as soldiers continued as far as possible in the conditions, in case they had to form a landing party at short notice. A large battleship of the *King George V* class had 350 marines under a major. A light cruiser of the *Leander* class had 61 in the marine detachment under a captain, not including the band.[90] A flagship often carried a lieutenant-colonel as fleet marine officer.

It was rare for shipboard marines to land on active service during the war, as it reduced the effectiveness of the ship's armament. One exception was during the invasion of Madagascar in May 1942, when the detachment for the battleship *Ramillies* landed in the enemy's rear to create a diversion.

Marine Bands

Since 1903 the Royal Marines had provided all the band services for the navy. In peacetime, boys with a musical inclination were recruited and trained, in wartime, established musicians were taken on and trained on the Isle of Man and in Yorkshire. There were bands for each of the three divisions, which performed in ceremonial functions such as royal visits, and on the radio. Each large warship also had a band, ranging in size from 25 men in a battleship to 17 in a light cruiser. Their repertoire included popular as well as military and classical music, and they could perform for dances on board ship, or to keep the crew motivated during periods

The marines of *Queen Elizabeth* are inspected by the Free French General Catroux in 1942.

of hard work. In action they operated the transmitting station in the bowels of the ship, and their casualty rate was high when ships were lost.

Mobile Naval Bases

Defence of naval bases was a traditional marine role, and the marines founded the Mobile Naval Base Defence Organisation or MNBDO in 1923, after experiences with the unreadiness of Scapa Flow in the last war. Due to its lack of funds it remained a skeleton organization until after the outbreak of war in 1939, when MNBDO I was formed at Fort Cumberland in Portsmouth. It was intended to provide air and sea defence of forward bases, using 4- and 6-inch guns as coastal artillery, and long- and short-range anti-aircraft guns. It had an establishment of more than 4200 officers and men, but its equipment was slow in arriving. In 1941 it sailed for the Middle East and parties were landed on Crete during the German invasion, though too late to defend the base at Suda Bay. They served as infantry and formed part of the final rearguard with heavy casualties. Nine hundred of them were taken prisoner although Major R Garrett organized an escape in a landing barge, with over 100 people on board, the majority of whom were marines, which was propelled by sail for much of the way to North Africa.

MNBDO I continued in operation and later served in Ceylon. Meanwhile MNBDO II was formed near Portsmouth in 1941, with many officers transferred from army officer cadet training units (OCTUs), and a large proportion of inexperienced HO recruits. It formed part of the anti-aircraft defence of Malta in 1943 and then served in Sicily after the Allied invasion.[91]

The Royal Marine Engineers

A small force of Royal Marine engineers had served in the First World War but was soon disbanded. It was reformed early in 1940, with mostly civil engineers as officers, and skilled craftsmen as other ranks. Its main function was to provide new naval bases and air stations, and it was answerable both to the Civil Engineer in Chief of the Navy and RM headquarters. Originally it had two companies of seven officers and 500 other ranks each. These included divers and were equipped with heavy earth-moving machinery. By 1945 it had expanded to more than 10,000 officers and men, and it was planned to double that for the Pacific war, although that never happened. By that time it was organised in battalions of 1500 men, each under a lieutenant-colonel.

In Britain the RM engineers mostly carried out work on airfields and naval facilities in the remoter parts of Scotland where civilian labour was not available. In North Africa and Italy they put captured ports back into service. They helped with Mulberry Harbours and cleared ports during the invasion of Europe, and in the Far East they built a Coastal Forces base at Ceylon and began to restore the port of Singapore after its recapture at the end of the war. Commando engineers served mainly in demolition work.[92]

Other Activities

The marines were responsible for the famous 14-inch guns at Dover, designed to fire across the 21 miles of the English Channel to Calais.

They were set up in the autumn of 1940 and augmented by other guns from time to time, including some manned by the army. The marines provided many of the men for forts sunk in the Thames Estuary to deal with German minelaying aircraft and other raiders. One battalion helped with the repair of bomb damage in London, and another provided guards for vulnerable points along the coast.

In the field of special operations, the most famous activity was the raid by five two-man canoes under Major 'Blondie' Hasler in December 1942. They were launched from the submarine *Tuna* and two of them succeeded in attaching limpet mines to ships far up the River Gironde at Bordeaux; but only Hasler and his No. 2 survived the mission.

Marine officers could also serve with the Fleet Air Arm, and 31 pilots and two observers did so. Nine NCO pilots were also trained, but had to transfer to the navy as petty officers. Captain Oliver Patch took part in the raid on Taranto, and Major Alan Newson became a squadron commander.

The Royal Marine Division

The Royal Marine Brigade was formed early in the war, when Churchill was First Lord of the Admiralty. He planned to use it for offensive operations, perhaps in the Mediterranean if Italy entered the war. It comprised three battalions and was commanded by Brigadier St Clair Morford. It had three and later four battalions, but was split into 101 and 102 brigades in the summer of 1940, when 101 Brigade had 66 officers and 1350 men – about half the size of an army brigade. It took charge of coast defences west of Plymouth, then served in the abortive expedition to Dakar. A new brigade, 103, was formed late in 1940 to create the Royal Marine Division. It stood by for the capture of the Canary Islands in 1941, but it proved difficult to attach artillery and other specialist units from the army, so its personnel mostly became commandos or landing craft crew.

Marine NCOs under training at Deal in 1944.

Marines in Landing Craft

The question of using marines on board landing craft first arose during 1942. Landing Craft Gun and Landing Craft Flak were intended to engage mainly in the shore battle rather than with warships, and it made sense to man their guns with marines. Meanwhile the Royal Marine Division was being disbanded and it was suggested that ships with mainly RM crews might be under the command of marine officers. This ran counter to a good deal of naval tradition, but eventually it was agreed and marine officers were trained in the necessary navigation and watch skills before taking command.

The disbanded division also provided a pool for men to run smaller vessels, Landing Craft Assault and Landing Craft Mechanised. They were sent to camps on the Welsh coast to train as coxswains, stokers or deckhands. There were more than 9300 marines in landing craft by February 1944, and they operated two thirds of the assault craft which put British and Canadian force ashore in Normandy that year.

Commandos

Commando regiments were first formed after the Fall of France on the initiative of Churchill. They were intended to form an aggressive raiding force, without the drudgery and parade-ground discipline of normal military life. The Royal Marine Brigade might have been transformed into such a force, but it was held back for possible invasions overseas, and as one of the few intact military formations after Dunkirk it had an important role in home defence. Instead, the first commando regiments were formed from the army. But in 1942, when Mountbatten was head of Combined Operations, the first Royal Marine Commando was formed from volunteers within the corps, with a strength of 446 men after those less fit had been weeded out. It had no administrative tail, no heavy weapons and moved largely by sea, so it was an ideal role for the marines. It was eventually re-titled 40 Commando, and eight others were formed before the end of the war, either by converting existing battalions or by accepting volunteers.

Commandos trained in a notoriously tough course at Achancarry in western Scotland. Officers had to forgo privileges of rank and endure the same hardships as the men. There was physical training and high-speed marches.

All of this was interspersed with sessions of unarmed combat, bayonet practice, rope climbing and cat crawling along ropes stretched across the river while 'malignant' Army instructors did their best to shake men off, the 'Death Slide' where the river was crossed hanging onto a toggle rope looped over a steel hawser…and crossing the 'toggle bridge' as instructors hurled hand-grenades into the water below…[93]

Royal Marine Commandos saw action as part of the Dieppe raid in 1942, when an attack on the Channel port was foiled with heavy casualties. This was followed by Operation Torch, the landings in North Africa and invasions of Sicily, Italy and Normandy. They fought on Lake Commachio in Italy, on the island of Walcheren in the Netherlands, and in the Far East.

The Royal Marines were a transformed force by the end of the war. Out of 67,655 men at the end of 1944, more than 14,000 were engaged in active operation ashore in Italy, North West Europe and South East Asia. Nearly 18,000 were attached to Combined Operations, and 8000 more served in Royal Navy and Fleet Air Arm bases, mainly as drivers.[94] They had largely been replaced in menial duties such as servants. Their role on board ship was far less significant and only employed 8000 men, and their defensive work had never really borne fruit. Instead they served mainly as commandos or landing craft crews, in a highly aggressive spirit which is maintained by the modern marines.

6 The Wrens

Organisation

The Women's Royal Naval Service (WRNS) was first founded in 1917, as Britain mobilised its resources for total war, and the idea of women in the fighting services was gradually becoming accepted. It was disbanded at the end of that war, although its members kept in touch throughout the peace. In the inter-war period, women's position in society improved slightly. They gained the vote between 1918 and 1928, and professional work was gradually opened to them, but they were still regarded as inferior to men in almost every kind of work outside the home and family.

In 1939 it was decided to revive the service and a newspaper advertisement announced:

WOMEN'S SERVICE IN THE ROYAL NAVY
A number of women (initially about 1500) will be wanted to take the place
of Naval and Marine ranks and ratings in Naval Establishments upon
secretarial, clerical, accounting, shorthand and typewriting duties; and domestic
duties as cooks, stewardesses, waitresses and messengers.[95]

The idea was instantly popular and about 10 women applied for each place.

The wartime director of the WRNS, or Wrens as they were popularly know, was Vera Laughton Mathews, daughter of a well-known naval historian and once a suffragette who had campaigned for votes for women. She brought a great deal of administrative experience and dynamism to the role, and her frequent visits to naval bases earned her the nickname of 'Tugboat Annie'. Under her was Angela Goodenough, the daughter of an Indian Army officer, who was 'so calm and steadfast, so tireless' in the execution of her duties.[96] By late 1939 there were five Superintendents, one each for Chatham, Portsmouth, Devonport and Rosyth, and one for the officers' training course. There were nine chief officers, 26 first officers and 191 second officers. Nearly half of them, mostly in the more junior ranks, were the wives, widows or daughters of naval officers. Churchill welcomed this 'both as the evidence of the wish of these ladies to serve the State in the capacity which it seems natural for them to adopt, and because there is undoubted advantage to be gained to the Service from the especial ease with which they can assimilate its requirements'.[97] But the WRNS would have to broaden its base enormously in the course of the war.

Recruitment and Training

Women up to 30 were liable for conscription by 1942, but the WRNS was able to attract enough volunteers to fill its ranks – though of course some of them volunteered to avoid conscription. Many joined because of posters bearing the slogan 'Free a man for the fleet'. If accepted, they were given two weeks' intensive training. At first this was done in several centres around the country, which was suitable for the early phase of 'immobile' Wrens who continued to live at home. Later it was centralised at Hampstead and Mill Hill in London, and in a Victorian castle near Glasgow. During training the women wore an unattractive dress known as 'bluettes', apparently designed to 'make you pack in the whole daft idea and go home before your probationary fortnight was over'.[98]

The basic training in the central depots was extremely intensive, packed as it was into a puny two weeks, which was extended to three when pressure was less

acute. Drill and ceremonial figured largely and were taken by excellent Petty Officer Wrens under a qualified P.T. Officer. There were lectures on naval traditions, terms and customs, and on naval ranks, ratings and badges. … The syllabus included an excellent lecture on 'Security' with a film from the Naval Intelligence Department, and two very helpful lectures on sex hygiene from a woman doctor from the Central Council for Health Education. A further medical examination had to be got into the fortnight, as well as any necessary vaccination or inoculation and, after the 'Conscription Act', remedial dental work.[99]

Most women had already been selected for a particular trade, and they now went on to a specialist school. In 1943 there were 14 of these, mostly shared with male ratings, such as HMS *Cabala* at Warrington for coders, the Photographic School at Arundel and HMS *Vernon*, the Torpedo School.[100] Many went to the Supply and Secretariat School at Wetherby in Yorkshire.

Demetrius was pretty grim. The staff were nice and the course not too bad; but the whole set-up was so like a mild form of concentration camp that it got one down. It wasn't helped by the extreme cold 31 degrees fahrenheit of frost one morning … The course lasted six weeks – two weeks too long, in my opinion; we were all stale by the end of the month.[101]

After the initial burst of senior appointments, officers were selected from the ranks, except for women with specialist skills. Candidates went to a two- (and later three-) week course in the Royal Naval College at Greenwich, where even Vera Laughton Mathews, a regular visitor since childhood, was still impressed by the architecture. 'At the College

WOMEN'S ROYAL NAVAL SERVICE

JOIN THE **Wrens**

AND FREE A MAN FOR THE FLEET

APPLY TO DIRECTOR W.R.N.S., ADMIRALTY, S.W.1
OR THE NEAREST EMPLOYMENT EXCHANGE

A WRNS recruiting poster. The demure Wren is probably intended to appeal to parents rather than girls in search of adventure.

entrance the response "Director Wrens" would cause the great wrought-iron Anson gates to swing back, and in we would sweep past the chaste courts and classic columns'.[102] But things were far more squalid for the trainees, especially during the rocket attacks on London in 1944.

…we had to sleep on the ground floor of the Nurses Home on palliasses, which had to be taken up in the lift to the top floor, where we had our cabins, as this was the time of the Buzz bomb, life, to say the least, was somewhat disturbed. … We had to take our meals in relays in the Painted Hall so that there were never too many people in there at one time, and if there was an 'immediate alert', all the stewards departed to the shelter, and we just sat and ate on so that we could at least get something to eat.[103]

The course included 40 minutes of squad drill every morning, followed by lectures, often by very senior naval and civil service figures, on naval history and administration and on leadership, with a session of games or physical training at the end of most days.[104]

Uniform and Ranks

The First World War uniform with the sailor's collar was rejected for the new Wrens, who adopted a version of the 'fore and aft rig' with collar and tie and skirt instead of trousers. The first ratings hat was of floppy 'pudding basin' shape, but it was replaced by a version of the sailor's cap which proved more popular. The officer's and petty officer's cap was instantly successful. 'It suited nearly everyone I ever saw in it', wrote Angela Mack.[105]

There was some debate about the status of WRNS officers. They were given light blue stripes and ranks like first, second and third officer, which were closer to those of the Merchant than the Royal Navy, with a diamond rather than a curl above. As the ranks eventually evolved, the director had the broad and narrow stripes of a rear admiral, a superintendent had the four stripes of a captain, a chief officer had three, a first officer had the 'two and a half' of a lieutenant-commander, a second officer had two and a third officer had one. The ratings of chief wren, petty officer and leading wren were established quite early.

Wrens were divided into 'mobile' and 'immobile'. The former, like other members of the armed services, could be drafted anywhere, although not overseas in the early years. The immobiles were recruited locally in the vicinity of naval bases and stations and would continue to be employed there. They were often of high social class, like one driver of a utility vehicle.

The Tilly driver tooted impatiently. It was Lady Fiona McSavage, in a hurry to get back to ferry Naval Officers about. The Wrens who drove the Utilicons were all out of the Tatler. *They had long blonde hair well over their collars, and supercilious noses, and were never seen with their heads inside the bonnets of their vehicles.*[106]

Status

The acronym 'WRNS' was a fortunate choice in 1917, and it was soon translated into Wrens. In 1939 a civil servant first suggested that it might also be used as a rating title, producing 'Wren', 'Leading Wren' and eventually 'Chief Wren'.' It was a far stronger title than the army's ATS or Auxiliary Territorial Services, which was weak and meaningless; or the even RAF's Women's Auxiliary Air Force, or WAAFs. In fact the Wrens scored over the army in several ways. The khaki ATS uniform was unattractive and the service had a reputation for attracting undesirable women, while the army's prestige was low for most of the war in any case. In contrast, the Wrens had quite a high status and a good calibre of entry. The army and air force worried about women deserting and brought their own services under their respective discipline acts. The navy found that there was no real problem with the Wrens, and they remained outside the act. For disciplinary purposes they could be dismissed, fined or given extra duty, but they could only be imprisoned by the civil authorities for normal offences. To the rank and file of the navy, however, Wrens were not always welcomed. Some considered that the idea of women in uniform was a travesty. Others found that they adopted snobbish attitudes, however humble their backgrounds – they were 'officers' girls' who paid little attention to the ratings who were nominally their peers.

At first the Wrens came under the Civil Establishments Branch of the Admiralty, implying that they were civil servants in uniform rather than members of the services. This was rectified in 1941 when officers were transferred to the CW Branch and ratings to the Naval Branch. At first the authority of their officers and petty officers over naval personnel was questioned, but in 1942 it was established by an Admiralty Fleet Order. But disobedience to a Wren petty officer by a male rating would be considered only as 'an act prejudicial to good order and naval discipline' rather than a more serious offence.

Wrens were paid less than men, even if they replaced them in the same job, as was common in civil life at the time. Vera Laughton Mathews accepted this reluctantly on the grounds that women were not liable for the hardships of sea service. In general a woman earned about two thirds of a man's pay, though there were many anomalies in the naval service. On naval bases, the culture of the age and the

WRNS officers under training at Greenwich, being drilled by a Royal Marine instructor.

HAT INSIGNIA
Gold wreath for Medical Officers

SUPERINTENDENT
Ranks with Captain

CHIEF OFFICER
Ranks with Commander

FIRST OFFICER
Ranks with Lieutenant
Commander

SECOND OFFICER
Ranks with Lieutenant

THIRD OFFICER
Ranks with Sub-Lieutenant

Above: WRNS officers' rank stripes.

Opposite: A Wren visual signaller with the Fleet Air Arm in Scotland, using a signalling lamp.

explosive mixture of many young women away from home for the first time with sailors just returned from months at sea, demanded that Wrens' quarters be carefully segregated. There were some complaints about their living accommodation in the home commands, and of HMS *Collingwood* near Portsmouth it was claimed, 'This "ship" is the dread and horror of every Wren in every other "ship". Its name is legion as the "deep hole" of every WRNS inside and outside the service'.[107] But it was also found that Wrens' quarters overseas were superior to male accommodation.

Clerical and Administration

By the 1930s office work was already accepted as suitable for women, preferably unmarried, and it was one of the first roles of the Wrens on foundation. By the end of 1941 there were 1445 shorthand typists in the service, 1210 supply assistants, 1372 general writers and 1184 who specialised in pay.[108] There were women who worked all day in correcting charts or 'Kings Regulations', and in many other arcane naval matters. As officers, women also took on many more tasks. Audrey Deacon was secretary to the maintenance captain of the Plymouth Command.

At times we seemed to function almost as a Citizen's Advice Bureau – recipients of any type of problem. The subjects dealt with at different times included consultation with Departments of the City Council, discussions with YMCA and Toc H [a services welfare organisation], arranging for Dockyard Departments to deal with defects or difficulties in requisitioned premises, helping the newly-arrived Polish naval officers to sort out an enormous range of problems, exploring possible ways of camouflaging the china-clay spoil-heaps north of the city (which at onetime were thought to be helping German bombers to pinpoint the position of Plymouth)…[109]

Domestic Duties

By the end of 1941 there were 4517 stewards in the Wrens, and 2437 cooks. Wren cooks and stewards had to work in a great variety of kitchens ashore, from grand requisitioned hotels to the Nissen huts of training camps.

The Watch-Keeping system for cooks and stewards ensured their getting a good long spell off duty at least every other day. Even so, these girls were working under distinctly unfavourable conditions and I was amazed to find how lightly they took the trials and tribulations of their daily life. They groused, of course, but in the good-humoured way which is the prerogative of the lower deck, and they laughed far more than they grumbled. Remembering the peace-time view of domestic work as drudgery fitted only for those of low mentality, I marveled at the zest with which this group of Wrens attacked their various jobs. Some of them had been to famous schools, most had never seen a potato or a cabbage in the raw before they joined the service; now, under a system which made training interesting and ensured

that everyone took a turn at rough work, they were growing into excellent and careful naval housekeepers.[110]

As for medical work, much of that was already done by the women of the naval nursing services, but women also joined the sick berth branch as specialists such as X-ray operators.

Signalling and Communication

Women were accepted for signalling duties quite early on and a few were rated as chief petty officer with the Shore Wireless Service. It proved popular despite the obvious discomforts of visual signalling at all hours and in all weathers. One candidate describes her training by an aged RN chief petty officer.

We hoisted the International flags, we learnt what to look up in the Confidential Books, we were introduced to BR619, the Pendant List, which would be our bible, the FSB (Fleet Signals Book) and the AVSB (Auxiliary Vessels Signal Book), we learnt that in Morse you always flashed Ireland (R) and Iceland (C) in case someone read one dash too many and sent the convoy to the wrong place. We learnt about asdics and radiolocation, which were the newest thing. We learnt the Code Word Appendix, and the Alarm Signal Table, and the Sector System for Aircraft, and anchoring and harbour signals, and catapulting and alighting signals for aircraft carriers, and message prosigns, and the abbreviated plain language table.[111]

Wrens were also used as dispatch riders, which was not an easy job in the days of total blackout and before the building of the motorways. They took part, for example, in the planning for the Dieppe raid of 1942.

The orders had to be taken by dispatch Riders as far afield as Dover and Plymouth. The riders had to travel at night and along roads with no signposts, and even drivers well acquainted with the South Coast often lost their way in those days. This difficult duty was undertaken by Wren Dispatch Riders. Ten of these Wrens covered 10,000 miles in a fortnight and some were over twenty hours on the road.[112]

Recruiting and Training Duties

In 1941 the first Wren recruiting assistants were appointed. They were women with a teaching or social work background who were given the rate of petty officer and replaced the mature chief petty officers who interviewed naval candidates and assessed their suitability – after that, a young man's first contact with the navy was likely to be with a Wren. Sir Clements Markham of the Admiralty was at first sceptical about them, until he underwent a mock interview: 'My fears are completely at rest. I feel that I could tell my life story several times a day to Mrs O'Brian'.[113]

There was plenty of work for Wrens in the training bases of the navy. They operated cinema projectors and simulators such as the dome

teacher for training anti-aircraft gunners. Their role in the Tactical School at Liverpool became legendary. Training took place in a 'largish shed':

…around the walls of which were little curtained compartments not unlike bathing tents. In these sat the destroyer Captains with charts before them. On the floor, over which Wrens crawled at speed, was drawn another, immense chart and here the game was played according to instructions issued to the Wrens by the Naval Officer in charge.

The destroyer Captains in their little compartments plotted to outwit enemy attack. The Wrens on the floor counter-plotted, making chalk marks with rapidity, while others of their number flicked back the curtains in order to see how the Captains were getting on. It was an astonishing sight and, game or no game, it taught many valuable lessons.

The officer in charge nodded towards the Wrens. 'There's precious little they don't know about this business – and are they keen? Keen as mustard!'[114]

Opposite Top: The Wren coxswain of a motor launch at Plymouth in November 1944.

Below: Wren air mechanics arm a Sea Hurricane at RNAS Yeovilton.

Technical Trades

Originally Wrens were intended for the traditional 'women's work' of cooking, domestic service and office work. But the boundaries of what women could do expanded rapidly in all walks of life during the war, in the Wrens as much as anywhere else. The First Lord of the Admiralty was given a list of new trades open to Wrens for the Naval Estimates Debate of 1941 – aircraft checker and fitter, analyser, boats crew, cinema operator, courier, exercise corrector, fabric worker, machinist, marker, meteorologist, Morse transcriber, night porter, night vision tester, photographer, radio mechanic, range warden, recruiting assistant, radio operator, stores labourer, tailoress, workshop duties and X-ray assistant.[115]

Women were not trained for the gunnery branch of the navy, as that would have been very much against the culture of the time. However, the work of the torpedo branch was largely technical and in 1942 it was decided that women could be trained for that. There was some

objection to the term 'seaman torpedoman' as applied to women, but it was eventually accepted. Wrens (ST) worked as electricians in shore bases, and serviced torpedoes on ships and submarines in port, a role which attracted some attention from photographers.

Wren air mechanics were recruited from late 1941, and originally it was planned that they would do 'humdrum tasks' like battery charging, spark-plug cleaning and fabric repair. But they proved a great success and Rear-Admiral Ford of the engineering branch was impressed. They were keener than men and better at delicate work, though they lacked the skill with tools that most boys picked up from their fathers. He concluded: 'Their energy and intelligence put the men to shame'.[116] On qualification they were posted to naval air stations and unlike men they could not be posted to sea, so they were able to learn their jobs more thoroughly.

Wrens at Sea

In 1943 the question of sending Wrens to sea for long periods was considered, but the director pointed out that it would be impossible to employ mixed crews. Warships were already grossly overcrowded, and it would be impossible to find extra space to segregate women. Nor was it possible to man warships with entirely female crews, due to their lack of experience.[117] It was, however possible to employ women in harbour craft which did not require them to go into action, or to spend the night on board on a regular basis. The first ones were trained in October 1941 and it soon proved highly popular, despite the hazards of taking a party of ratings back to their ship after a run ashore.

Women also served as signallers in the great Atlantic liners which were now operating as troopships. Angela Mack joined the *Mauretania*.

Elizabeth had already worked out our rota of duty and she took me along to our 'office', a tiny narrow cabin fitted out with a working bench, two swing seats and a lockable cabinet for the code books, signal pads and so on. Here were the powerful transmitters and receivers with large dials to turn and pick up signals from far and near, indicators galore, and keys like small taps for sending Morse signals, and all the paraphernalia of a modern warship's communication equipment of those days crammed into a small area about the size of a small bedroom.[118]

Wrens were originally recruited for home service, and the first attempt to send them overseas ended in disaster in August 1941, when the troopship *Aguila* was torpedoed on the way to Gibraltar and a party of 22 was lost. By the end of the year numbers abroad were still quite small: 30 in the Far East, 25 at Gibraltar, 36 officers and 18 ratings in Washington and 101 of all ranks in the Middle East. However a further 400 or 500 were being sent to the last area. Only Wrens who volunteered could be sent abroad in the early stages, but that was altered by the indirect effect of conscription of women. Even so, the numbers remained quite small, with only 6000 in foreign parts at the end of the war.[119]

The Experience

The Women's Royal Naval Service was a highly successful organisation. As early as June 1941 the commanders-in-chief at the home bases were unanimous in praise of its members and sent 'eulogistic replies' when

questioned about their competence.[120] They constantly demanded more and more Wrens for the rest of the war.

Some women, such as upper-class immobile Wrens, were carrying out far more menial duties than they were used to, but they tended to do it with great style. Others may have exchanged one form of drudgery for another, perhaps moving from the kitchen of a house or hotel to one of a naval base. But for the most, naval service was an eye-opening experience with the chance to travel, to learn new trades, to share in the traditions of the Royal Navy and to see and take part in some of the greatest events of history.

Above: Wrens working on the plotting table of Western Approaches headquarters in Liverpool.

PART VII

The Battle Fleet

1 Ships of the Battle Fleet

HMS *Dreadnought,* the first modern battleship, was conceived by Admiral Sir John Fisher and launched in 1906. She had an all-big gun armament to fire effective salvoes at long range, a secondary armament for protection against torpedo boat attack, good armour protection and high speed provided by turbine engines. This remained the concept of the battleship over the next 40 years, though with many changes. There was a rapid increase in the size of the main guns, from the 12-inch of the *Dreadnought* to the 13.5-inch of the *Orion* class of the 1909 programme and the 15-inch for the superb *Queen Elizabeth* class ordered in 1912. After a gap, the British adopted the 16-inch gun for the *Nelson* and *Rodney* in the 1920s. With ever larger ships and reduced defence spending, there was an increasing tendency for emphasis on the individual ships rather than the battle fleet as a whole, and this was increased during the Second World War when the Germans had very few capital ships, each of great strategic value.

Important technical changes took place over the years. Director towers were fitted to control the main armament and the calibre of the secondary armament was increased. Oil replaced coal as the main fuel and more efficient engines were developed. Increased protection against torpedoes was needed. Existing ships were fitted with unattractive bulges outside the hull, new ones had this incorporated as part of the design. Bridges were greatly simplified in form to eliminate shot traps. Anti-aircraft armament was continually increased as the threat from the air grew. Aircraft catapults were fitted on the decks of capital ships, then removed towards the end of the Second World War as they proved to be ineffective.

The battlecruiser was another Fisher concept, faster than the battleship but with an almost equal heavy armament. The compromise was reduced armour protection. Fisher intended them as cruisers for commerce protection, but they became a fast division of the battle fleet, in which role their weak armour proved fatal – three of them blew up at Jutland.

As well as the heavy ships, the battle fleet needed fast cruisers for reconnaissance. They could also serve in multifarious duties, protecting commerce against surface raiders, and policing the British Empire in peacetime. The torpedo boat destroyer had been developed towards the end of the previous century, and was designed to fight off enemy torpedo boats, and launch attacks of its own. It grew in size like all warships, and became known as the destroyer. Once it became a fully seaworthy vessel, it proved even more versatile than the cruiser, though it was still designed mainly for its role with the battle fleet.

Throughout the inter-war period, the British navy continued to believe that the battleship was supreme, despite the doubts of younger officers and the air lobby. Lord Chatfield, First Sea Lord from 1933 to 1938, provided the ultimate defence of the great ships.

If we rebuild the battlefleet and spend many millions doing so, and then war comes and the airmen are right, and all our battleships are rapidly destroyed by air attack, our money will have been largely thrown away. But if we do not rebuild it and war comes, and the airman is wrong and our airmen cannot destroy the enemy's capital ships, and they are left to range with impunity on the world's oceans and destroy our convoys, then we shall lose the British Empire.[1]

Even in September 1941, the battleship was still seen as the leading element of naval power. When Churchill addressed the crew of the new carrier *Indomitable*, he 'spoke of the man of war and his wife, or sweetheart, the aircraft carrier, who goes out to find his dinner for him and sometimes cooks it and has it done to a turn so that the man of war may eat it'.[2] Such views did not survive the sinking of the *Prince of Wales* and *Repulse* by the Japanese three months later, followed by the great carrier battles between the Americans and the Japanese in the Pacific in the following year.

The Older Battleships

Apart from the aged and disarmed *Iron Duke* and *Centurion,* the oldest battleships in the fleet were the five ships of the *Queen Elizabeth* class, launched in 1913–14. The largest and most powerful battleships of the day, their building was supported by Churchill during his first period at the Admiralty: '… no doubt can be entertained of the decisive military advantages in the creation of a fast division of vessels of the maximum fighting power'.[3] They served well in the First World War, and had major refits between 1924 and 1934. They were given torpedo bulges and had two funnels trunked into one. All except *Barham* had even more extensive reconstructions in the 1930s. *Warspite,* for example, was fitted with new and far more efficient engines which increased her maximum horsepower from 75,000 to 80,000 but used a third less fuel. She had a new superstructure and a more powerful anti-aircraft armament. As they fought in the Second World War, the four modernised ships of the *Queen Elizabeth* class still had eight 15-inch guns, a speed of about 24 knots and armour plate up to 13 inches thick. The *Barham* – the only ship not to be modernised - was lost in 1941 but the others saw extensive service. The *Queen Elizabeth* served as Cunningham's flagship in the Mediterranean. The *Warspite* fought at Narvik and at Matapan and supported the landings at Salerno, Normandy and Walcheren.

The *Royal Sovereign* class of 1914–16 were essentially cut-price versions of the *Queen Elizabeths.* They retained the 15-inch guns but had much smaller engines and reduced speed. They were fitted with bulges in the 1920s but had less extensive alterations than the *Queen Elizabeths.* The were too slow for many operations in the Second World War, and the *Royal Oak* was in Scapa Flow in October 1939 when she

Opposite: The battleship *Warspite* at Gibraltar, in about 1938, with destroyers alongside.

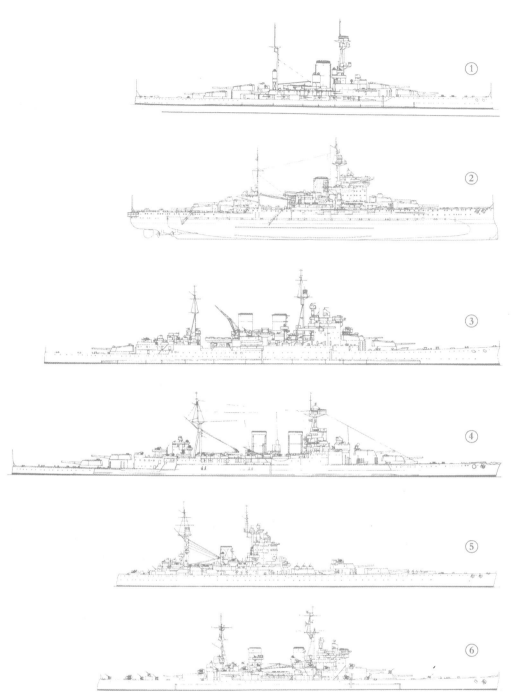

to the superstructure. The new ships had tall, angular bridge structures and single, straight funnels, with the secondary armament on either side. They had almost the speed of the *Queen Elizabeths*, with in-built torpedo protection, slightly heavier and better-designed armour, and a heavier broadside. They were known to the lower deck as 'the ugly sisters' or 'the pair of boots', while the officers called them 'the cherry trees' – cut down by Washington. The design was not repeated when battleship construction was resumed in 1936, but they proved effective ships with the Home Fleet, Force H and in the invasion of Normandy.

Battlecruisers

Only three battlecruisers remained with the Royal Navy in 1939. The *Repulse* and *Renown* had been begun early in the First World War, with the return of Fisher to the Admiralty and a wave of euphoria about the early success of the battlecruisers in eliminating a German commerce-raiding force at the Falklands in 1914. They were given 15-inch guns to match the *Queen Elizabeths*, but by the time they were ready in 1916 the concept had been discredited at Jutland. They had a good deal of reconstruction between the wars and it was hoped that a speed of 30 knots would allow them to be used as escorts for fast carriers. But *Repulse* was sunk by Japanese bombers in December 1941.

The *Hood* was designed just before Jutland but her construction was suspended while the lessons of the battle were considered. However, plans to increase her deck and magazine armour were never fully carried out. When she was commissioned in 1920 she was the largest warship in the world, with eight 15-inch guns to match any vessel afloat, and a speed of 31 knots. She was a handsome ship, the pride of the navy, and in 1923–4 she took the Prince of Wales on a world cruise during which the ship travelled 40,000 miles and was visited by 700,000 people. She was the flagship of the battlecruiser squadron of the Home Fleet in 1939–40, and subsequently became the flagship of Force H. In May 1941 she was sent in pursuit of the *Bismarck* but her inherent weakness caught up with her and she blew up on the fifth salvo from the German ship, to the shock of the British nation.

The *King George V* Class

In 1936 Britain resumed construction of battleships as the treaty limitations were about to expire, but the Admiralty jumped the wrong way. Since the 1935 treaty limited the size of big guns, they embarked on the design of ships to carry twelve 14-inch guns in quadruple turrets. The new ships had many positive features including good armour protection and the high speed (for a battleship) of 28 knots, but the US invoked an escape clause in the treaty and the Germans went for 15-inch guns, the Americans for 16-inch and the Japanese for 18-inch. Furthermore, two of the British ships' guns had to be left out because of stability problems, and the full broadside was weakened.

Churchill was well aware of the faults of the *King George Vs*. He was out of office in 1937 but he remembered how he had been instrumental in increasing the calibre to 15 inches a quarter of a century earlier and had a long correspondence with the First Lord of the Admiralty over it. His concern was revived in August 1941 when he crossed the Atlantic in the second ship of the class, the *Prince of Wales*. He deplored:

was sunk by *U-47*. The rest of the class served with the Home and Eastern Fleets, but were reduced to reserve or training ships near the end of the war, as the enemy threat reduced.

The *Rodney* and *Nelson,* launched in 1925, were the only British battleships built in the 1920s, and were odd ships by any standards. At the end of the First World War the Admiralty was planning giant battlecruisers of 48,000 tons. The Washington Treaty imposed a maximum of 35,000 tons, so the two new ships were cut down in size and designed to save weight as much as possible. They adopted the 16-inch gun for the first time, and put them in three triple turrets instead of four twin ones. This increased broadside weight from 15,360 pounds as in the *Queen Elizabeth* class, to 18,432 pounds. The three turrets were concentrated forward of the engines and superstructure, with the third one at a lower level than the second one so that it could not fire ahead. Nor could the guns be fired too far aft, without serious damage

The marring of the structure by the provision of the aerodrome amidships. Merely for the sake of having a couple of low quality aircraft, the whole principle of the citadel so well exemplified in the Nelson and Rodney has been cast aside.[4]

The screws overlapped and caused vibration, which made the after part of the ship uninhabitable at speed. Churchill commented: 'The vibration was almost worse than the noise. Small objects were given a life of their own. A penny, a bunch of keys, a book, a pencil, all dancing out of time, slowly jumped towards the precipice of the locker's edge, and one by one fell on the cabin floor.'[5] Matters were even worse when he crossed in the *Duke of York* in December, and was held up by bad weather. The ships had been designed with low bows to allow the guns to fire directly forward, and the sea broke over the decks. The passengers were confined below 'listening to the dull pounding of the great seas on the ship's ribs'.[6]

But the *King George V* class remained the best battleships available, as the larger ships of the *Lion* class were delayed and then cancelled because they would take too long to build. The *Vanguard*, with 15-inch guns and a much higher bow, did not enter service until after the war. The *Prince of Wales* had to retreat from the *Bismarck* after the *Hood* was sunk in 1941, and was herself sunk by the Japanese at the end of the year. The other ships served mainly with the Home Fleet, as three of them were kept in readiness to deal with any sortie by the *Tirpitz*. They escorted Russian convoys and the *Duke of York* led the sinking of the *Scharnhorst* in 1943. After the demise of the *Tirpitz* in 1944 they were free to move east and the *Duke of York* was present at the Japanese surrender in Tokyo Bay in 1945.

Cruisers

The cruiser had been important to the Royal Navy in the years of peace, and at the disarmament conferences it devoted much effort to getting what it regarded as an adequate number to act as a screen for the battle fleet and to patrol the seas in support of British commerce. It asked for 70 cruisers but never had more than 50.

Inter-war cruiser design oscillated between the desire to build the largest and heaviest armed ships possible to meet similar enemy cruisers, and the need for the largest numbers, which implied smaller ships. The heavy cruiser, with 8-inch guns, had been specifically created by the Washington Treaty in response to the British *Raleigh* class with 7.5-inch guns. The large ships were the three-funnelled *Kent*, *London* and *Norfolk* classes with four twin 8-inch gun turrets, followed by the slightly smaller *York* class with three turrets. After that the British began to favour smaller ships that could be dispersed round the oceans, and no more 8-inch ships were built after the *Exeter* of the *York* class was completed in 1931.

In theory the cruiser was the most flexible of warships. It had gun power inferior only to a battleship, long range and was almost as fast as a destroyer. It had a good anti-aircraft armament and often carried an aircraft or two of its own. It had a detachment of Royal Marines for shore operations, and torpedoes. The only gap was a lack of anti-submarine armament, for it was fast and mobile enough to evade any known submarines. Some cruisers were fitted with Asdic and depth charges for self-defence. This flexibility was attractive in peacetime, but was perhaps less valuable in war, when a cheap ship designed tightly round a particular task often proved the most useful.

The cruiser was suffering something of an identity crisis by 1939. It was redundant as a scout for a battle fleet, which no longer existed in its old form, and general reconnaissance was better done by aircraft (although the *Norfolk* and *Suffolk* did well in finding the *Bismarck* in 1941). The *Exeter, Achilles* and *Ajax* gained everlasting fame by hunting down the *Graf Spee* in 1939, but in general the threat to commerce came from the U-boat, and cruisers were too large, expensive and un-manoeuvrable to play a major role in hunting them. Cruisers no longer headed flotillas of destroyers, having been superseded by the purpose-built destroyer-leader. Destroyers themselves were larger than in the past, and took on some of the multifarious roles of the light cruiser. Inter-war cruisers were often built as a response to specific vessels of a potential enemy, and in wartime they were often most useful against vessels of a similar type, for example in the Mediterranean and in Arctic convoys. They took on a new role in anti-aircraft defence, and like battleships they proved useful in shore bombardment.

There were several projects for new designs of cruisers during the war, and construction started on some of them, but they were given low priority. Only two conventional cruisers, the *Bermuda* and *Newfoundland*, were begun and completed during the war, along with half a dozen of the *Dido* class. This contrasts with fleet destroyers which were cheaper, faster to build and almost as versatile – a dozen flotillas of eight ships each were begun and finished, and several more flotillas were under construction when the war ended. As a result, all the cruisers in the navy were of pre-war design and suffered from the faults of pre-war policy. More than any other type except carriers, they became overcrowded with people and equipment to an almost intolerable level.

The Older Cruisers

Several classes of cruiser survived from the time of the First World War. These included 13 of the C class of just over 4000 tons and a relatively light armament of five 6-inch guns, as well as eight ships of the slightly larger D class and two of the E class, much bigger at around 7500 tons and with seven guns. The four 'improved *Birminghams*' or *Raleigh* class, were of nearly 10,000 tons and had 7.5-inch guns. The old cruisers had mostly been built for service with the fleet in the North Sea rather than

1. The *Curacoa*, a C class cruiser of First World War vintage in 1941. A year later she was sunk in a collision with the *Queen Mary*.

2. The *Devonshire*, an 8-inch cruiser launched in 1927, as she was in 1944.

3. The *Exeter*, a smaller 8-inch cruiser launched in 1929.

4. The *Orion* of the *Leander* class in 1943. They were unusual for cruisers in having single funnels.

5. *Penelope*, one of the small cruisers of the *Arethusa* class, launched in 1935.

6. The *Sheffield* of the *Southampton* class, the first of the large 6-inch cruisers.

7. The *Edinburgh* (shown here as in 1942) and her sister *Belfast* could be distinguished by the large gap between the bridge and the funnels.

8. The *Fiji* or Crown Colony class was the standard type of cruiser, which continued to be built during the war. The *Bermuda* was completed in 1942.

9. The *Dido* class consisted of cruisers armed with dual-purpose 5.25-inch guns. The *Charybdis* was launched in 1940 and is shown as in 1942.

global war. Their lack of modern accommodation was often criticised by medical officers in 1939–45. The *Caradoc* of 1917 had poor ventilation, limited stowage space and behaved badly in rough seas. The medical officer of another ship commented that 'Nothing can get away from the fact that *Carlisle* is an old ship with inadequate and out of date ventilation, designed for work in the North (not the <u>Red</u>) Sea and that the ship's company lives under extremely unpleasant conditions below decks'.[7] Most of the old cruisers were converted to anti-aircraft ships while the *Vindictive* of the *Raleigh* class had a varied life as an aircraft carrier cruiser, training ship and finally as a repair ship. *Frobisher* and *Hawkins* also became training ships, as did *Dauntless* and *Diomede* of the D class.

Heavy Cruisers

Cruiser construction resumed quite quickly after the First World War, with the first of the *Kent* class being laid down in 1924. They were the first of the 8-inch ships allowed under the Washington Treaty, and they introduced the twin-gun turret to the British cruiser. They had eight main guns on a weight of 10,000 tons, as allowed by the treaty. To save weight they used the sides of the hull as an important part of the strength, which gave them flush decks and high freeboard. They had three raked funnels which gave an old-fashioned appearance. They were followed by the *London* class in the 1925–6 programme, similar but without torpedo bulges; and the *Devonshire* and *Norfolk* of the 1926 programme, with improved gun turrets.

The other ship of the 1926 programme was the *York*, with tonnage reduced to 8000. This meant she could carry only three twin turrets, though she needed the same engine power to maintain a top speed of 32 knots like her larger predecessors. She had two funnels. The following year the *Exeter* was ordered. She was similar, but with straight rather than raked funnels. The raked funnel helped carry smoke away from the bridge and was believed to improve appearance, but it was thought that it might make it easier for an enemy to judge the inclination of a ship. Ship designers would debate this issue over the next few decades.

The 8-inch cruisers were almost an embarrassment in the battle fleet. Analysis showed that smaller vessels had been much more effective in the last war, and the fleet orders of 1939 acknowledged that

their armament was not suitable for dealing with attack by light craft, while they formed 'large and unwieldy targets vulnerable to both gun and torpedo'.[8] The British were not sorry when the London Treaty of 1930 abandoned them in favour of smaller 6-inch ships.

Six-Inch Cruisers

Britain had already begun the design of a smaller class of cruiser, the *Leander* class of the 1929 and 1930 programmes, of just over 7000 tons, with eight 6-inch guns in twin turrets. They had single funnels which were unusual for cruisers and fooled the captain of the *Graf Spee* into believing he was being attacked by destroyers in 1939. Eight of these were built, followed by four more of the *Arethusa* class, similar but with rearranged machinery and two tall, thin funnels. In 1933 Britain was compelled to move to larger 6-inch gun ships to counter similar developments in the USA and Japan. The *Southampton* and *Newcastle* had the first triple 6-inch turrets to give a total of 12 main guns. They reverted to the raked funnels and had a displacement of nearly 9000 tons, not much less than a large 8-inch cruiser. They were considered a success and six more ships of the *Southampton* class were built, making them the standard modern cruiser at the beginning of the war.

Even larger 6-inch ships were planned. The *Belfast* and *Edinburgh* of nearly 10,000 tons were designed to have four quadruple 6-inch turrets, but these did not materialise so triple turrets were fitted. They had an unusually large gap between the bridge structure and the funnel, used to house the ship's aircraft. The *Belfast* was seriously damaged early in the war and rebuilt with a greater beam. By chance she is the only British cruiser of the period to be preserved.

The *Fiji* class was conceived in 1937 as a smaller version of the *Southamptons*, with the same 12-gun armament on a 8000-ton hull. The funnels were straight again and a large bridge structure dominated the appearance. A square or transom stern was used to save weight and length. All cruisers became overcrowded during the war, but this was particularly true of the *Fijis* and their variants. Some of them had X turret removed to save weight and increase the anti-aircraft armament. Eight *Fijis* were built, followed by three of the *Uganda* class, which had the reduced armament from the start. Most were under construction at the beginning of the war and they entered service from 1940–3. There were several projected cruiser designs during the war, but none materialised in time to take part.

The *Dido* Class

The *Dido* class was conceived in 1936 as a small, cheap cruiser on a hull derived from the *Arethusa* class, to serve as flagship of the rear-admiral in charge of the destroyers of a main fleet. Anti-aircraft armament was already a priority, and this was boosted by the adoption of the 5.25-inch gun, which could serve equally well in the anti-aircraft and anti-ship role. It was planned to fit five twin turrets, three of them superimposed forward of the bridge. The class proved successful in the anti-aircraft role and 16 of them were built, including five of the variant *Bellona* class. They were the only cruisers in production during the war, apart from a few *Fijis* which had been ordered before hostilities began. However, there were problems with the supply of the 5.25-inch gun, and the

secondary armaments of the *King George V* class battleships had priority. Some of the *Didos* had one turret omitted and replaced with a 4-inch gun, while the *Scylla* and *Charybdis* had 4.5-inch guns in all turrets.

The cruisers worked hard during the war and suffered heavy losses. Twenty-nine were sunk, including representatives of every class except the *Londons*. Two of the four *Arethusas* were lost and five of the *Didos* and *Bellonas*. Heavy cruisers accounted for 20,500 men early in 1944 and light cruisers had 11,600, compared with 17,000 men in battleships and 13,200 in fleet destroyers.[9]

Destroyers

The destroyer of 1939–45 was the most flexible of warships, and took part in almost every aspect of naval warfare. The American observer Joseph Wellings observed in 1941 that destroyers were 'always on the go'.[10] A battleship rarely sailed without three or four destroyers as escort. An aircraft carrier also needed a destroyer close behind, to rescue aircrew from planes that ditched in the water. At Narvik in 1940, destroyers and the battleship *Warspite* provided the only British success of the Norwegian campaign. At Dunkirk, 39 destroyers rescued almost a third of the Allied troops taken off. Four destroyers took part in a command raid on the Norwegian island of Vaagso in 1941. They could form part of a convoy escort, and their speed allowed them to come to the rescue of a beleaguered convoy. They carried Asdic and depth charges, and were fitted for minesweeping, though it was difficult to do that at destroyer speed. British destroyer design was usually very competent, but it was presumed that the war would be fought in home waters, the Mediterranean or the Pacific. Many ships were challenged by conditions in the Atlantic and Arctic.

The A to I Classes

With hundreds of ships left over from the First World War, the Admiralty did not look at destroyer design again until 1924. The leading destroyer builders were invited to submit designs for an improved W type, and those submitted by Thornycroft and Yarrow were successful. Both were launched early in 1926. The Thornycroft ship, the *Amazon*, was very fast and achieved nearly 38 knots on trials. The *Ambuscade* was of lighter construction and needed slightly less power. The following year the Admiralty held a conference and combined the best features of these ships to produce the A class. They were 323 feet long and of 1330 tons standard displacement, 30 per cent bigger than the wartime V and W classes. They had four 4.7-inch guns each, in single turrets, which were the first in British destroyers with full shields to protect the gun crews. The hull was rather angular with a raked bow and a high forecastle and a low

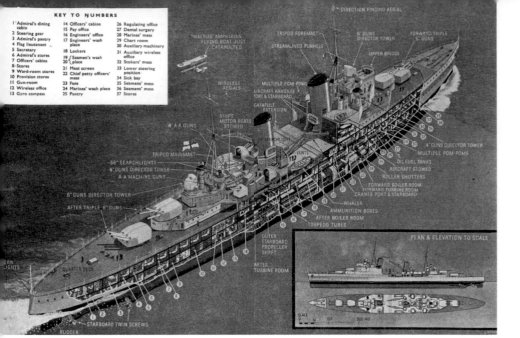

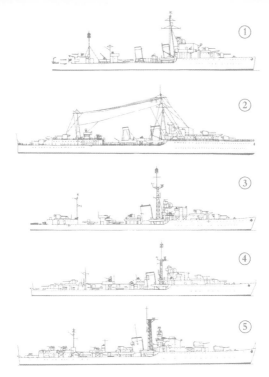

quarterdeck along half the length. Their 34,000 horsepower engines gave a speed of 35 knots. They had two raked funnels. Great emphasis was placed on torpedo armament, despite failures at Jutland, and they carried two sets of quadruple torpedo tubes amidships. Each ship had two 2-pounder guns as anti-aircraft armament. As well as eight ships to form a full flotilla, the Admiralty ordered a slightly larger leader, the *Codrington* of 1540 tons, carrying an extra gun amidships.

This process would be repeated annually for the next 10 years. Each year a flotilla was ordered with names beginning with successive letters of the alphabet, with a leader named after a famous admiral. Changes were introduced gradually. The C class of 1929 had a single 3-inch HA gun and had a more sophisticated director tower. The E class of 1931 had facilities for minelaying and two quadruple .5-inch machine guns as the anti-aircraft armament. The *Glowworm* of the 1933 order experimented with two quintuple torpedo tubes, and that became standard with the I class of 1935. Meanwhile, the H class of 1934 introduced a more streamlined bridge structure. The A to I classes were quite effective ships, but lacked anti-aircraft armament, as their 4.7-inch guns could only be elevated to 40 degrees. The design had changed very slowly since the VWs of 1918, and by the mid 1930s British destroyers were beginning to fall behind those built by other powers.

The Tribals

In 1934 the Admiralty began to consider building larger destroyers in response to those being built by foreign powers, especially the Japanese *Fubuki* class with six 5-inch guns in twin turrets. The new British class had a standard displacement of 1854 tons, 27 per cent more than the G, H and I classes, although they used a similar hull design. Their horsepower was increased to 44,000 giving a speed of 36 knots. Torpedo armament was less of a priority and only a single quadruple set of tubes was installed. Gun power was far more important and they had eight 4.7-inch guns in four twin turrets, hydraulically operated. Anti-aircraft armament was not much improved, although there was a quadruple 2-pounder pom-pom. The new ships were known as the Tribal class and 16 of them were built for the Royal Navy plus three for the Australians and eight for the Royal Canadian Navy. They were the most modern destroyers in service in 1939, and had the heaviest gun armament. They were often selected for special tasks, for example when the *Cossack* intercepted the *Graf Spee*'s supply ship *Altmark* in Norwegian waters early in 1940. On being posted in 1940, Ludovic Kennedy wrote:

Immediate inquiries revealed that the Tartar *was one of the famous Tribal class destroyers, completed a year before the war, the fastest, biggest and most modern destroyers in the fleet, formidably armed and superbly appointed and commanded by the cream of the Navy's destroyer captains. … I could not have asked for a better appointment.*[11]

The Tribals saw very hard service and 12 of the 16 British ships were lost.

The J, K, L and M classes

After the Tribals there was a move towards a smaller and simpler destroyer. The ships of the 1936 programme were fitted with two boilers instead of three with horsepower reduced to 40,000 and speed to 36 knots. The J class was the first in the twentieth century to have a single funnel, and the first with longitudinal framing, despite the protests of Clyde shipbuilders. They reintroduced the eight-torpedo armament, but had only three instead of four twin-gun mountings. The design was repeated in the K and N classes ordered in 1937 and 1939, with eight ships being built of each. Some were fitted as leaders but they were not significantly larger or better armed than the others. The Js and Ks were sent to the Mediterranean in 1940–1 and suffered heavy losses, including Mountbatten's famous *Kelly* of 1938. Overall the Js and Ks suffered almost as heavily as the Tribals – 12 out of 16 were lost.

The L and M classes of the 1937–9 programmes were based on the Js but with more beam, because they were to carry their main guns in fully enclosed mountings instead of being merely protected by shields.

This was far more efficient but increased the weight. The guns could elevate to 50 degrees, although this was still not enough for a satisfactory anti-aircraft role. The eight Ls served with Force H and the Mediterranean Fleet, the Ms with the Home Fleet until 1944.

The Emergency War Programmes

The First Emergency Flotilla of eight destroyers was ordered the day the war started. The O class combined the longitudinal framing and the two-boiler and single funnel arrangement of the J class with the four guns in single turrets as used by the A to I classes. There was a shortage of 4.7-inch guns, however, and some were completed with 4-inch. It produced a relatively cheap ship by destroyer standards, though they were still built by the usual warship yards and mass production methods were not used. The P class was similar, while the Q class, the Third Emergency Flotilla ordered in 1940, introduced the square or transom stern to use weight and space more efficiently. Successive emergency flotillas ran through the alphabet in the next three years, then started with four flotillas of Cs, grouped into Ca, Ch, Co and Cr classes. The *Cavalier* of the first group is the only survivor, now preserved at Chatham.

Changes were made with each successive flotilla. The S class of 1941 introduced a gun with 55 degrees elevation and the U class had lattice masts which gave much more support to the new radar equipment. The R class rectified a long-standing design fault. Until then officers' cabins were situated in the stern and it was sometimes impossible to relieve the officer of the watch due to heavy seas. The R class placed them under the bridge structure. Anti-aircraft armament was increased, partly by using the 20mm Oerlikon gun. The Qs had six of them, the Ts had 10 and the U class had a twin 40mm Bofors mount. Ninety-six ships were built to the same basic design.

Destroyers for the Pacific

Meanwhile the navy was aware that the war in the Pacific would demand larger ships with longer range and better anti-aircraft armament. The Battle class of the 1942 programme was a break from previous designs. Each ship was to carry twin 4.5-inch guns in two turrets forward, with an elevation of 80 degrees to make them effective for both anti-aircraft and anti-ship work. At more than 2300 tons they were considerably larger even than the Tribals. Three flotillas were ordered but only five ships were in service when the war with Japan ended.

Other designs included the Weapon class, smaller than the Battles and intended to use the shorter slipways in some yards; and the *Darings* of 1944, highly sophisticated vessels with all-welded construction, automatic loading of guns and the latest tachymetric system of anti-aircraft direction. They were too late for the war but formed an important part of the post-war navy.

Destroyers were the only type of ship from the traditional navy to remain in production throughout the war. They fought perhaps harder than any other type and 154 were lost, more than the total number in commission at the beginning of the war. Development was slow until the very end, and more effort was put into producing large numbers than building the perfect ship.

2 Life in the Battle Fleet

In the peacetime navy the big ships – battleships, battlecruisers, cruisers and aircraft carriers – were the focus of attention. Specialist seaman officers, trained in gunnery, torpedo or navigation, usually gravitated towards them. The big ship tended to use naval discipline and routine in its most rigid form. In peacetime a ship was probably attached to the Home or Mediterranean Fleet, where it was under the eye of the admiral. In wartime, discipline was more functional and relaxed even in great battleships, but peacetime standards survived, if they were not always implemented. This also had its effect in small ships, especially if commanded by regular RN officers or those who emulated them.

The Ship Hierarchy

Each large ship had a commanding officer, who actually held the rank as well as the position of captain, with a commander of the seaman branch as second-in-command. Battleships were allowed two gunnery officers, cruisers had one. A fully qualified torpedo officer was allocated to each ship of cruiser size and above, for electrical as well as torpedo duties, and each ship had a navigating officer. The rest of the seaman officer complement was made up of lieutenant-commanders, lieutenants and sub-lieutenants, according to the needs of the ship in action. There was one officer for each gun turret of 8-inches and above, one for each group of 6-inch guns in a light cruiser, two or three to take charge of the secondary armament, four more for various duties in fire control, and in peacetime another in charge of the anti-aircraft armament. The number of midshipmen was not fixed and depended on the needs of the operation. There were commissioned gunners and gunners in the director towers and control positions and in charge of ammunition supply: four in battleships of the *Nelson* class, two in a small cruiser. Battleships carried a boatswain and those equipped with torpedoes had a torpedo gunner.

The Role of the Commander

The commander or second-in-command of a large ship took on most of the responsibility for running it, leaving the captain to concentrate on strategy. It was a key job for an ambitious officer, for he had to do well to get further promotion. Nicknamed 'the Bloke', he was a familiar figure to the crew.

Rory O'Conor was a highly efficient and popular commander of *Hood* from 1933–6 before being promoted to become the youngest captain in the navy. He deplored voluminous standing orders and advocated a much simpler system. 'If Moses could control the people of Israel for forty years in the desert with Ten Commandments, it would be surprising if more were needed of the running of a ship'. O'Conor took laws on theft and murder for granted, and his commandments concentrated on the custom of the service, the good appearance of the ship, the conduct of the individual, courtesy to officers, the prompt execution of orders, punctuality (often timed by a stop watch), permission to leave work, reporting the completion of work, banning of gambling, and the right of a man to put his point of view to a senior officer. But the real Ten

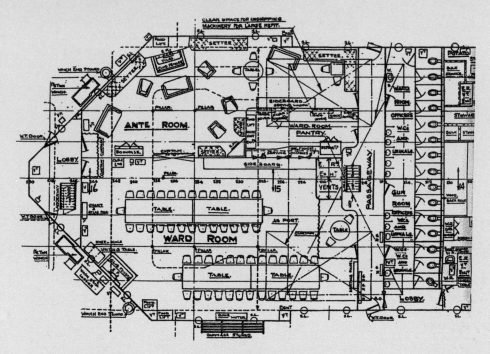

the *King George Vs*, where, unlike the other officers, they lived in hammocks rather than bunks.

Ratings were divided by trade as well as by rank. It was universal policy to separate seamen from stokers because of different standards of discipline and cleanliness – 'Oil and water don't mix' as the saying went. Officers' stewards and writers were separated for reasons of confidentiality; signallers regarded themselves as slightly superior to the seamen. Marines were always kept separate in their 'barracks', placed aft near the officers, because traditionally they had been regarded as a buffer against mutiny. There were separate messes for chief petty officers, engine room artificers, marine sergeants, the master-at-arms and the regulating petty officers, and various types of petty officer. Boys were kept apart, and the leading, able and ordinary seamen were divided among the many messes on board – a *King George V* class ship had 116 in total.[16]

Other ratings are accommodated in open mess spaces, i.e., spaces bounded by the ship's structure and not partitioned off in any way. Mess tables, stools, kit lockers for stowing clothes, mess racks, bread lockers, etc., are provided as necessary. The accommodation is based on a minimum requirement of 21 inches per man at table. Hammocks are slung from hooks secured to the beams.

Mess tables are usually supported by two hooks engaging in a small angle iron at the outboard end… When not in use the tables are stowed by hinging them about the outboard end and securing the inboard end by a hook suspended from the deck or beam… Hammocks are stowed in bins constructed of light perforated plating, with wood battens on the side and a wood grating at the bottom.[17]

In wartime the messdecks were even more crowded than this implies, with many men sleeping on lockers or in passageways. One rating describes conditions in a destroyer late in the war.

…it is about the size of a room in an average house. Most of the space is taken up by tables, lockers, cupboards, mess-traps, buckets, kitbags and hammocks, which leaves only a few square yards of space for the 30-odd ratings. Rabbits in hutches live better than this. … Overhead there are bars with grooves for the hammock ropes. These are only a foot apart; men sleep with their hammocks touching their neighbours on either side.[18]

Ship Organisation

Big ships tended to spend less continuous time at sea than small ones and mostly favoured the two-watch system in which the men had four hours on and four hours off, though even then engine room staff were on a three-watch system. The watches were known as port and starboard, and each divided into first or second parts, so that only a quarter of the men need be on duty in harbour. The watches and parts of watches needed equal numbers of men of equal skills from the various branches. A watch was also a period of time, usually four hours, except for the two two-hour 'dog watches' between four and eight in the afternoon, which meant that men did not have to stand the same watch day after day.

The seamen proper were also divided into 'parts of ship' for duty and welfare purposes. A major warship usually had four equal parts, known as forecastle, foretop, maintop and quarterdeck, from old sailing ship terms. Each group would keep that part of the ship clean and perhaps man the gun turret in the area, with the marines manning a turret and

Commandments are reinforced by codes of national law, which can only be understood after serious study, and O'Conor produced an influential book, *Running a Big Ship*, with much more detail.

Captain K C B Dewar suggested that the commander's job was quite easy if he knew how to delegate, but he was a maverick who had left the navy by 1939.[12] O'Conor was much more typical. Army officers, he wrote, were amazed to find that the commander got up at six in the morning to supervise the hands washing the decks, but the navy did things differently – '"Carry on, Sergeant Major" is not good enough'.[13]

The commander had a small staff to help him. The Lieutenant-Commander (Regulating) was his main assistant, who took much of his paperwork. The Chief Petty Officer (Regulating) kept the seaman's watch bill up to date, in consultation with his colleagues in the gunnery and torpedo branches. In addition, there was a writer or clerk, and a messenger. The Commander's Office issued daily orders to the crew, arranged training classes and published daily orders. In peacetime or during a quiet period it issued a weekly programme, but that was optimistic on active service.[14] The commander also supervised the master-at-arms (the 'Jaunty'), who was the senior petty officer on board, and the ship's police or regulating petty officers ('crushers').

Accommodation

The allocation of accommodation in a large ship was noticeably more complicated than in a small one, and it reflected the ship's hierarchy and its division into different trade groups. In a battleship serving as a flagship there was a mess for the admiral and his staff, and a separate one for the captain. The majority of the officers lived in cabins with recreation space in the wardroom, aft on the upper deck in the *King George V* class.

The ward-room of the Prince of Wales *was a large room some sixty feet in length …You stepped straight into it from the quarterdeck. It was divided into two parts: on the port side was the ante-room, furnished with easy chairs, a club lounge, a bookcase containing Chambers Encyclopaedia and a number of novels and other works…and on the starboard side was the dining room. In the dining-room were two long tables and a hatch where Royal Marines in white mess jackets served the food. Above the mantelpiece hung an irreverent Gillray caricature of the Prince Regent… At the end of the ante-room was a small bar, which was opened before lunch and dinner, where gin was sold at 3d and whiskey at 5d a glass.*[15]

The warrant officers had cabins and a mess. Midshipmen and the sub-lieutenant in charge of them had a separate mess, well below decks in

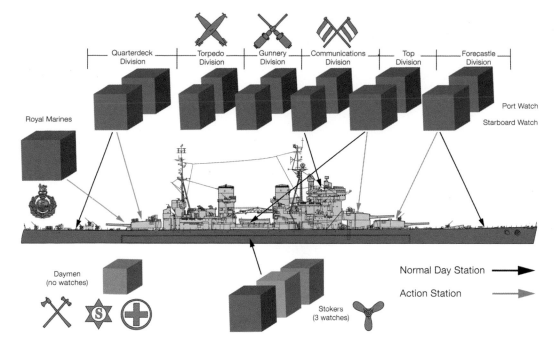

Quarterdeck Division
Torpedo Division
Gunnery Division
Communications Division
Top Division
Forecastle Division

Royal Marines

Port Watch
Starboard Watch

Daymen
(no watches)

Stokers
(3 watches)

Normal Day Station

Action Station

The organisation
of the crew of a
battleship.

secondary armament of their own. The specialists also had their own groups, and together these formed the divisional system. Each rating was attached to a particular division, for example of stokers, signallers or torpedomen. The division was under a hierarchy of officers, midshipmen and petty officers and allowed regular contact between officers and men for welfare, disciplinary and hygiene purposes.

The quarter bill allocated the men to their particular duties in action. Seamen were also allocated duties for the numerous tasks that had to be carried out, largely based on the watch and quarter bill. By 1932 there were lists for day action, night action, fire stations, collision stations, entering or leaving harbour, drill, abandon ship, landing parties, airing bedding, anchor watch, ammunitioning ship and many others, and more were added in war.[19]

Duties and Routine

At sea, the officer of the watch was in charge in normal times, though the captain was never far away in his sea cabin and probably remained alert if there was any possibility of action or danger. The captain of the destroyer *Eskimo* was

…on the bridge at all times during all manoeuvres, including large changes in course. At other times he remained in his emergency cabin, a deck below the bridge, reading light literature and sleeping. He…found out that he could not remain on the bridge all day and all night and be mentally and physically alert when an emergency arose.[20]

The officer of the watch had a quartermaster to supervise the steering, and boatswain's mates to transmit orders by means of whistle, and to keep an eye on what was happening on deck. Men normally did 'tricks' of an hour each as helmsman, lookout and so on. There were numerous other duties to be done – sweepers to clean up, the gunner's party to maintain the magazine, the 'captains of the heads' to clean the toilets, the sea boat's crew, who would be ready to launch in the case of 'man overboard' and many others. As the war progressed, the specialists such as radar and sonar operators had to develop their own organisation while lookout duties became ever more important for the ordinary seamen.

Men also had to be kept at readiness for long hours when in range of enemy aircraft. In 1941 in the light cruiser *Birmingham*:

The turret crews slept in their turrets. The 4" HA/LA [high angle/low angle] crews stood watch as follows; 1 mount crew actually on watch with starshells

ready to be fired on either side; 2 crews slept in the starboard hangar, about 40 yards form their mounts, 1 crew in the officers' galley compartment about 10 yards from the HA/LA mounts. LA control parties stood watch and watch – complete crews – additional men taken from the HA control which were not manned. Pom-poms and .5 machine guns not manned.[21]

In harbour it was usual to leave one part of a watch in charge of the ship, changing at noon every day. Side parties were posted to man the gangway and greet visitors with the appropriate ceremonies. At anchor or at a buoy, the ships' boats were lowered out and manned, and a capital ship usually had an attendant drifter to take men ashore on short leave or 'liberty'.

If they were very lucky the sailors might go ashore in one of the great naval ports such as Plymouth, where the civil population had long specialised in providing every service a sailor on leave might be prepared to pay for. But in wartime they were far more likely to find themselves among sparse houses, empty roads and waterlogged fields at Loch Ewe or Scapa Flow, where the football fields usually bore the sign 'All grounds unfit for play'.

The Effects of War

The big-ship navy was the last to feel the effects of wartime dilution by inexperienced and hastily trained new entrants, but by the third year of the war even it was showing signs of strain. Travelling across the Atlantic with Churchill in the *Duke of York* in December 1941, Captain Charles Lambe saw deficiencies in the crew of the ship:

…60% of the ship's company have never been to sea before. The proportion of RNR and RNVR officers is very high. They are a shapeless lot somehow and there is none of the active service sailor's swing about the ship. There seem to be no sailors who have swagger or are sex conscious. They are all worried little chaps doing a bigger job than they can cope with – civilians dressed up in fact. The lovely atmosphere of innocence combined with acute sophistication seems to be lacking entirely.

The Prime Minister agreed and remarked: 'They are not ready for fighting. Discipline and manners are lax. He'd never seen such a thing'.[22] But this was a little unfair as the *Duke of York* was not long in commission.

Captain Oram was more positive while in command of the cruiser *Hawkins* in 1942.

In effect the ship was steamed and defended by a cross-section of British provincial life with a handful of South Africans thrown in as leaven. The Jolly

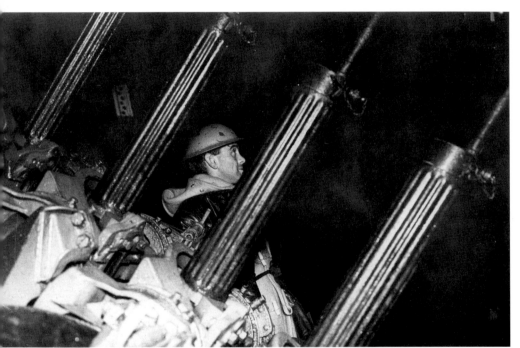

Jack of peacetime was a rare bird indeed, so rare that one was tempted to pipe a tear of affection for the breed, now a practically extinct prototype. The wartime sailor, faithfully modeling himself upon his glamorous predecessor, was conscious of the ready-made aura which attached to his own interpretation of the part. He was often dismayed to find that the dazzling mythology surrounding this sea business did not quite come up to expectation. There was much to be said for the 'new boys', though. The model set for them to follow was good and by his exacting standards we were able to run our complicated machines on a very weak mixture of RN spirit![23]

Life in Destroyers

Most destroyers were commanded by lieutenant-commanders and the second-in-command was known as the first lieutenant, or 'Jimmy the One' to the crew. It was an onerous job even in peacetime.

The First Lieutenant must be constantly supervising during working hours, which means that he must do nearly all his paper work – and make out his next day's programme – during the comparative calm of the Dog Watches; such problems as analyses must be deferred to even later in the day. After the first six months you will find the ship begins to 'run herself'.[24]

Destroyer discipline was traditionally far more relaxed than on big ships, even when they operated with the main fleets. Cunningham, a destroyer man himself, wrote:

Big ship time is said to be necessary to all. I have never found it so. What I do know is that any captain will tell you that the best officers to be found in big ships have come from submarines and destroyers. It is my experience here. I would rather be first lieutenant of a destroyer than about tenth down the list in a battleship.

I have always maintained there is more real discipline in destroyers than big ships, and of course we are always so much more in touch with our men. The skipper of a destroyer gets soaked to the skin on the bridge just the same as any sailor, but his opposite number [in a battleship] walks dry-skinned from his luxurious cabin where he has been sitting aloof from all goings on, to an equally luxurious bridge.[25]

Destroyers were usually organised in flotillas of eight ships, plus a leader which was slightly larger. The flotilla was headed by a Captain (Destroyers) in the leader, with a commander in one of the other ships as 'half-leader' or second-in-command. The flotilla leader had specialist gunnery, navigation and torpedo officers with warrant officers to support them and in port they would assist the other ships in these tasks. The system was based on the idea of a unified organisation like the Grand Fleet of the last war, in which the flotillas would stay together and return to the same port at regular intervals. In practice destroyers were used very differently in 1939–45, carrying out miscellaneous tasks in ones or twos. Sub-Lieutenant Roderick Macdonald of the *Fortune* rarely saw his flotilla officers as the ships were detached all round the world. The system was 'too inflexible to allow for deployment and losses in a World War'.[26] Ships were left to their own devices without specialist help.

3 The Fleet in Battle

Quarters

Battle was the supreme test of every warship and the numbers in her crew were assessed with that in mind. Every ship had a quarter bill, a list that gave every man's station in action. In ships which carried them, Royal Marines usually manned one of the main gun turrets plus a proportion of the secondary and anti-aircraft armament. Marine bandsmen were sent down to the bowels of the ship to work the equipment in the transmitting station. Not all the three watches of stokers were needed in the engine room at one time, so about 25 per cent of them helped with the manning of the guns and others formed damage control parties about the ship.

Gunnery ratings came into their own in action. The quarters, layer and control ratings naturally had to work very closely together on individual guns and turrets, often directing less qualified men. The largest turrets in the navy, the 16-inch of the *Nelson* class, needed a gunner's mate, 15 seaman gunners and two other seamen in the gun house; seven gunnery ratings and nine other seamen in the cordite handling room; four gunnery ratings and 21 others in the magazine; a gunner's mate, and eight gunnery ratings in the shell handling room and eight gunnery ratings and 17 others in the shell room, a total of 93 men.[27] A destroyer's 4.7-inch gun had a quarters rating 2nd class in command, probably a leading seaman or petty officer. The gunlayer and the trainer, who pointed the gun in the vertical and horizontal directions, were both layer ratings 3rd class. The other four members, with no gunnery qualifications, were the trayworker who loaded the gun, the projectile supply number who handled the shells, the cartridge supply number who handled the propellants, and the sightsetter who

was responsible for passing on messages and checking that gunsights and fuses were accurately set. The 1945 *Gunnery Pocket Book* stressed the importance of teamwork; 'the crew does not consist of seven men doing seven jobs but is a team doing one job'.[28]

In a modern war, when air attack might have come at any moment in the Mediterranean or Arctic theatres, it was necessary to find a compromise between constant readiness and giving the crew some rest. Four different states of readiness had evolved by the end of the war, for both anti-ship or low angle (LA) operations and for anti-aircraft or AA. The first degree was used when the enemy might be encountered at any moment and full crews were closed up ready for action. In the second degree, groups of men might be fallen out in turn, and some could rest at their quarters. In a fleet or squadron, one or more ships might be detailed as guard ships to give the others a rest. The third degree was often known as defence stations. One watch out of two manned half the guns in the ship when action was possible but not imminent. This degree of LA readiness was normally used at night in operational areas, while AA defence stations were in operation when the threat of air attack existed over a long period. This was hard on AA gunners and some men from the LA armament were trained to assist them. In the fourth degree, one of the LA guns was manned, or a quarter of the AA armament.[29]

Fire Control

Long-range gunnery systems had evolved within the navy over the previous 35 years or so, and were highly efficient by 1939. The task was a complex one – to hit a small target up to 20 miles away which might move unpredictably, from a platform which was itself moving forward, and might well be rolling and pitching in the sea. Only a direct hit

Opposite top: Lookouts in the *Devonshire* in the Indian Ocean.

Opposite middle: Seamen man the anti-aircraft guns of a destroyer during the night watches.

Opposite bottom: A destroyer flotilla at sea in wartime.

Below left: The distribution of men in gun turrets and magazines in the mid-1930s.

Below right: A low-angle fire control team, for action against surface ships.

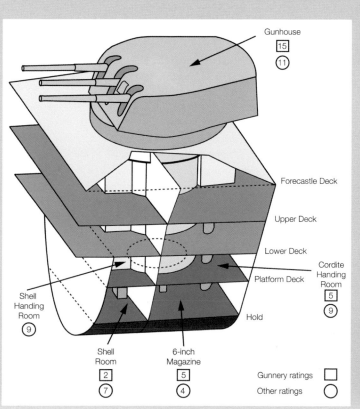

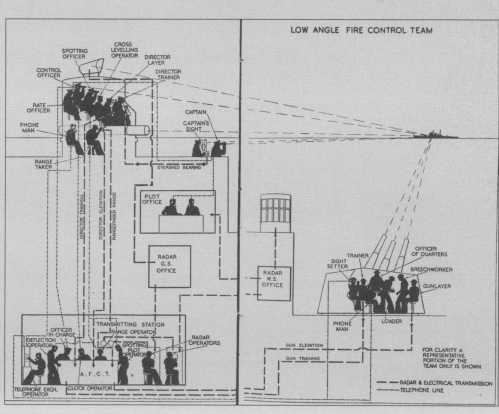

counted in naval gunnery, and a target ship might have moved more than a quarter of a mile during the time of flight of the shot alone; other factors included wear on the gun barrels and wind. To give the greatest accuracy, guns were normally centrally aimed and fired.

In gun action, the captain of the ship identified the target to be engaged. He pointed his sight at it and its bearing was automatically transmitted to the director control tower high in the ship. Inside the director, three officers sat towards the rear of the cylindrical compartment, looking forward through small windows. The control officer in the centre was in charge of the operation of the guns. To his right was the spotting officer who reported on the fall of shot, as 'short' or 'over; or 'straddle' if the aim was accurate and shots were falling on both sides of the target. On the other side was the rate officer, whose job was to observe and if possible measure any changes of course or speed by the target. He used an instrument called an inclinometer, which measured the distance between the masts or other features of the enemy, and any sudden change could be noted.

Further forward and lower down in the director were the ratings of the control team. The director layer was a senior gunnery rate with considerable responsibility. 'On the Director Layer, more than any other individual in the ship, except perhaps the Control Officer, depends the success of the gunnery action'. He sat on the left-hand side of a gyro-compass, looking through stablilised binoculars or a telescope at the enemy. He operated a handle which elevated or depressed the guns to control the range, and also observed the spread of each salvo and its accuracy of aim. On the other side of the gyro-compass was the director trainer, also a senior rating. Using similar binoculars or telescope, he kept the director pointing at the target. The cross level operator applied corrections for the roll and other movements of the ship. The range might be taken by a man inside the director, though the range finders attached to battleship turrets were wider and therefore more accurate, while radar provided an even better alternative by the end of the war. The last member of the director team was a telephone operator.

Information from the director and other sources was sent automatically to the transmitting station low down in the ship. A battleship or cruiser was equipped with an Admiralty Fire Control Table, a destroyer with the slightly simpler Fire Control Clock. In either case it was a manually operated mechanical computer. Data was fed in by turning a handle the right amount, and this gave corrections

to the aim. The processed data was transmitted to the gun turrets, and the guns were laid and trained according to it. Firing was done by the touch of a button inside the director, once the operator knew that all guns in the salvo were loaded, and he 'hunted the roll' to find the right moment in the ship's movement to aim accurately.

In the early stages of an action the 'ladder' system was used to find the range of the target. Two salvoes were fired to establish the line of the target, spread slightly over a third of the length of the target. Two more were fired with some spread to find the range, and corrected in 400-yard steps until the target was straddled.

A normal salvo in a ship with twin turrets was to fire one gun in each turret, while the other reloaded. The nine-gun *Rodney* normally fired her nine main guns in salvoes of five and four, but when she took part in the sinking of the *Bismarck* in 1941 she also fired one eight-gun salvo and there were seven-gun ones. According to an American observer on board:

Damage sustained from contusion of broadsides very considerable, causing undue discomfort to personnel and much work to make compartments habitable.

Tile decking in washrooms, water closets and heads were ruptured throughout the ship. Urinals were blown off bulkheads, water pipes broken, and heads flooded. Longitudinal beams were broken and cracked in many parts of the ship having to be shored. … The overhead decking ruptured and many bad leaks were caused by bolts and rivets coming loose. All compartments on the main deck had water flooding the decks.[30]

Anti-Aircraft Gunnery

Anti-aircraft gunnery had very different problems from anti-ship action. Aircraft were far more vulnerable and a near miss with an exploding shell could destroy one. They could be seen much further away, and picked out by radar. On the other hand they flew about 10 times faster and were far more manoeuvrable. In addition, the Royal Navy lagged behind in anti-aircraft gunnery, partly because rivalry with the RAF made realistic exercises more difficult, partly because of a certain amount of complacency. Between the wars it failed to develop tactics against dive bombers, and rejected plans for a tachymetric system which would have made it far easier to track the movement of aircraft.

There were several methods of aiming anti-aircraft guns. The most primitive, known as hosepipe shooting, consisted of merely following the line of tracer and moving it towards the target. This was mainly used by hastily-trained merchant ships crews. Slightly more sophisticated was 'eyeshooting'. Gunners used sights with two or three rings, each representing 100 knots of an aircraft's speed.

The method of using the sight is very simple. Look at the aircraft, note its direction of flight and estimate its aim-off speed. Point the gun so that the aircraft is flying towards the centre of the sight, with its nose the distance from the centre corresponding to your estimate of its aim-off speed. As the attack develops and the aim-off speed increases, bring the nose of the aircraft further and further out from the centre, always adjusting direction of aim-off to keep the aircraft flying towards the centre of the sight.[31]

It was not particularly effective with the slower firing pom-pom gun, and Joseph Wellings of the US Navy observed: 'The close range weapons

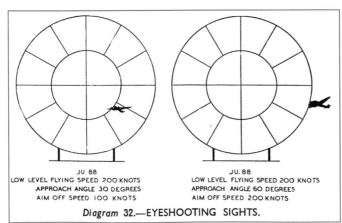

JU 88
LOW LEVEL FLYING SPEED 200 KNOTS
APPROACH ANGLE 30 DEGREES
AIM OFF SPEED 100 KNOTS

JU 88
LOW LEVEL FLYING SPEED 200 KNOTS
APPROACH ANGLE 60 DEGREES
AIM OFF SPEED 200 KNOTS

Diagram 32.—EYESHOOTING SIGHTS.

The basic principle of eyeshooting.

have no remote control nor director to date. I have met two skippers who claim to have shot down planes with pom-poms. I am convinced that any hits were only due to the volume of fire'.[32] It was more effective with the 20mm Oerlikon, though there was a tendency for gunners to open fire too soon and expend their magazine before the enemy was within range.

High-level bombing proved ineffective against ships, because they could move out of the way in time. Roderick MacDonald describes his experience as a midshipman in the battleship *Valiant* off Norway.

…we were both posted at the back of the bridge with binoculars to alert the captain. 'Bomb doors open, sir.' Then 'Bombs away!' He then put down the wheel hard one way or the other. It always worked, as the explosions and columns of water erupted where we would otherwise have been.[33]

Low level bombing was effective in the early stages against merchant ships, but could be driven off by gunfire. The Germans did not develop the torpedo bomber very far, although the Japanese did and used it against the *Prince of Wales* and *Repulse*. But the most effective air weapon against ships was the dive bomber, and the Germans had a suitable aircraft in the Junkers 87 Stuka. The range changed rapidly during a dive, which made range finders and fuse setters ineffective. The standard method in the early stages was barrage fire. The shells could be set to explode at a fixed range from the ship, forcing the aircraft to pass through a barrage. But dive bombers proved one of the most serious threats against British warships, and sank many ships in the battle for

Crete alone. Good anti-aircraft gunnery had to await the arrival of the stabilised tachymetric anti-aircraft gun towards the end of the war, and the proximity fuse just after it.

Gunnery Practice

There were several types of gunnery practice, each with its own advantages and disadvantages. 'Towed Target Battle Practice' had the disadvantage that 'it is very slow and spotting the fall of shot is very inaccurate. It is impossible to simulate a quick alteration of course'. A target towed by a motorboat was faster, but not very manoeuvrable. A radio-controlled target ship had 'the great advantage that both ships have complete mobility but is restricted by the fact that only shells below a certain calibre may be used'. In 'throw-off firing', one ship fired her guns at another, but they were offset by 6 degrees from the true aim so that they should hit the water a fixed distance away. Both ships were fully mobile, but it was very difficult to measure the fall of shot accurately. Another variation of this was 'throw-short firing', in which the fire control system was adjusted so that all shots would fall well short of the target.[34]

Besides firing with their main armament, cruisers and battleships were equipped for 'sub-calibre' firing. Guns of a smaller calibre could be fixed in line with the big guns in the main turrets and fired in exercises. Practice of this kind conserved the barrels of the main guns, saved on ammunition, and gave good practice for the control system and the trainers and layers over a relatively short range. It gave little realistic practice to the loading numbers.

The crew of a four-barrelled pom-pom take aim at the target.

Top: The crew of a 20mm Oerlikon wearing anti-flash gear and helmets during the Dieppe raide of 1942.

Above: A practice target in use off Trincomalee in 1944, to calibrate the guns of the cruiser Newcastle.

Fleet Tactics

For nearly three centuries the fleet had relied on the line of battle as its main tactic. All the battleships were arranged in a single line ahead so that one did not mask the fire of another. It was seldom used during the Second World War, because there were rarely enough battleships together to form a line. Furthermore, it would be easily disrupted by air attack as ships had to manoeuvre to avoid bombs. One exception was the Battle of Java Sea in February 1942, when a mixed group of British, Dutch, American and Australian cruisers and destroyers formed up against the Japanese. There was immediate confusion as one ship dropped out of the line, followed by disaster in which there were heavy losses.

Between the wars the Tactical School at Portsmouth had evolved new methods of fighting, and Cunningham paid tribute to them, finding that his action off Calabria in July 1940 followed almost exactly 'the lines of the battles we used to fight out on the table'.

First we had the contact of long-range reconnaissance aircraft; then the exact positioning of the enemy relative to our own fleet by the Fleet Air Arm aircraft from the carrier, and the informative and accurate reports of their trained

observers. Next, the carrier's striking force of torpedo bombers went on to attack, though on this occasion, through no fault of theirs, they were not successful. Meanwhile the cruisers, spread on a line of bearing, pushed in to locate the enemy's battle fleet, and finally the heavy ships themselves came into action.[35]

In battle, commanders preferred to split their forces and attack from many different directions. The action against the *Graf Spee* in December 1939 was perhaps the last to be fought under old conditions, with minimum effect from aircraft and radar. Commodore Harwood used his three ships to divert the fire of the enemy's two turrets, though in practice the Germans do not seem to have been affected by this. At the second Battle of Sirte early in 1942, Phillip Vian used several forces of cruisers and destroyers emerging from smoke screens in different directions to drive off a larger Italian force.

Destroyer Tactics

As well as the numerous and miscellaneous duties that were found for them in wartime, destroyers still had the basic role of screening fleets of battleships, cruisers and aircraft carriers against aircraft, surface ship and particularly submarine attack. Their organisation was still based on the flotilla of about eight ships under a Captain (D), though this was rarely used in battle. Lieutenant-Commander Wellings of the US Navy was told by a destroyer captain that 'the most important difference between peacetime training and operating in war was that he now had to think for himself. Usually there is no division commander to follow and operations orders with their elaborate annexes are never seen. It was a 'captain's war'.[36]

For screening a force, the destroyers might adopt a formation such as the one used to protect the carrier *Furious* and two cruisers in October 1940. The heavy ships formed a single line with four destroyers ahead. A and D were 3600 yards out on either side, just ahead of the bows of the leading cruiser. B and C were 2800 yards diagonally ahead of the same point, and 2500 yards apart. This meant that there was no anti-submarine protection on either side of the big ships, so it was considered suitable at speeds of 15 to 18 knots which a U-boat could not keep up with, and when Asdic conditions were fairly good. Another type of screen, used by the *Hood* and *Repulse* in November 1940, consisted of six destroyers. The capital ships were in line ahead with three cruisers astern of them. There was a destroyer on each side of the *Repulse* about 1000 yards out, with the same for the *Hood*. Two more destroyers patrolled 1000 yards ahead, 1500 yards apart.[37] But destroyer screens were not always impenetrable. *U-331* managed to pass through the one escorting the battleship *Barham* in November 1941 and sank her with torpedoes.

In the early stages of the war there was a belief that torpedo attack by destroyers was becoming obsolete. There were relatively few large targets for them, and the fear of air attack resulted in the removal of some torpedo tubes. Destroyers were at their best under cover of night or smoke screens, but big ships were fitted with radar first and could counter such attacks. However, failures such as the attempt to stop the *Scharnhorst* and *Gneisenau* passing through the Channel in 1942 highlighted the need for a stronger torpedo armament. By this time most destroyers were fitted with radar themselves and they regained some of the initiative.[38]

British destroyers had their torpedo tubes mounted amidships, and they could only fire about 60 degrees forward of the beam. In the early

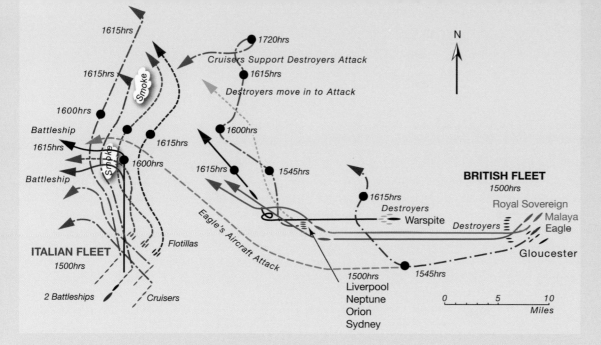

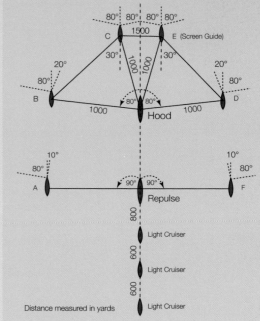

Above left: The
action off Calabria
in July 1940, when
Cunningham's fleet
compelled an
Italian force to
retreat, although
two of his three
battleships were too
slow to keep up
with the fleet.

Above right: The
destroyer screen
protecting the *Hood*
and *Repulse* in
November 1940.

stages of the war this meant that they had to turn almost broadside on to the enemy before firing, giving him good warning. Later they were fitted with gyro-angled torpedoes, which could be set to turn after firing, so that a destroyer could launch an attack directly ahead, directly astern, or in several other directions.

Vian was perhaps the most successful British destroyer officer of the war and, like many of his contemporaries, he reacted against old methods. Roderick Macdonald of the destroyer *Fortune* contrasted the official battle orders with Vian's less formal document.

I opened the charthouse safe and took out two large Confidential Books, the Fighting Instructions and the Destroyer Fighting Instructions. ... The former, a glossy, scarlet, expensively bound volume, appeared to be devoted to a re-run of the Battle of Jutland. The blue, less ormolu, loose leaf Destroyer publication also had absolutely no relevance to the impending engagements.

In contrast Vian's orders 'had the supreme virtue of clarity and simplicity. Destroyers on the side threatened by enemy ships would form up for a torpedo attack in as near as possible to a concave half circle, described as the shape of an open umbrella, with the handle aimed at the enemy'.[39] Destroyer attack patterns in the Mediterranean also included the star pattern, with ships converging from different directions. In the Home Fleet, the problem was of attacking a single heavy unit such as the *Bismarck* or *Scharnhorst* rather than a fleet. Units of three or four destroyers were used to surround the enemy, using whatever radar they had at the time.

A destroyer attack was an exciting affair as Tristan Jones relates about the assault on the *Scharnhorst* in 1943.

Our stern went down, the bow shot forward, then we went...like staghounds at last, at long bloody last, off the leash. ... Faster and faster, plunging and swaying, pulsing with strain until her whole hull screamed in protest. ... All we could see of the nine other destroyers were their pale wakes, until Captain (D) in Onslow opened up with his four-inchers. Crash after crash shook our hull...and how the Torps got the tinfish away in any semblance of an aim I'll never know. Out slid the tinfish, long and sinister, and splashed into the darkness.[40]

Even the threat posed by a torpedo attack could be effective against a nervous opponent and Vian used it to force a powerful Italian squadron to retreat at the Second Battle of Sirte in March 1942.

Smoke screens were an important part of destroyer operations, especially in the early stages of the war before radar became universal. They could be created by aircraft, or by floats dropped in the water. All steam-powered warships had means of injecting oil fuel to produce a thick cloud of black smoke in a very short time. In addition destroyers and MTBs (which of course were not steam-powered) had chlorosulphuric acid equipment and could discharge smoke by three nozzles over the stern. When using smoke, captains had to take account of humidity, which might affect the rate at which it dispersed, and wind direction and strength.[41]

Shore Bombardment

In the past shore bombardment had been regarded as very much a secondary task for warships, except for a special group known as monitors, with the maximum gun power on the smallest hull. Battleships, cruisers and even destroyers were considered too valuable to risk against forts and batteries on shore. This began to change in the second half of the war, as the German and Italian fleets were reduced and amphibious operations became ever more prominent.

Shore bombardment became important during the Mediterranean campaign. The navy had its first unhappy experience of attacking static targets when it destroyed the French fleet at Mers el-Kebir in 1940. It destroyed shipping and oil tanks at Tripoli in April 1941, but Admiral Cunningham considered that this was not to be repeated. 'We have got away with it once but only because the German Air Force was engaged elsewhere'.[42] Techniques were developed during the successive invasions from late 1942 onwards. It demanded a good deal of sea superiority so that the bombarding ships could be spared from other duties. A certain amount of air superiority was also necessary, but ships suffered many air attacks during the Italian campaign of 1943–4, while on D-day they suffered most from 'friendly fire' by aircraft and guns. During the Italian campaign the cruiser *Mauritius* carried out 134 day and 25 night bombardments at ranges up to 22,500 yards at Salerno. She fired more than 6000 shells on coastal and inland batteries, defended areas, towns, roads, groups of vehicles, one ammunition dump and one factory.[43]

It was best if the bombarding ship was stationary during the attack. After the bombardment of Walcheren in late 1944, the captain of *Warspite* considered that it was too dangerous to anchor even if the water was shallow enough, for it would take too long to get under way if there was a counter attack. He preferred to have a marker buoy dropped with the ship using her engines to keep a fixed distance from it. If this was not desirable, then the ship should steer on a fixed line. Nevertheless, the *Rodney* did anchor while bombarding a battery on the island of Alderney shortly afterwards.

Shore bombardment was a truly inter-service operation, requiring close liaison between land, sea and air. Slower reconnaissance aircraft were shot down too easily, so fast single-seat fighters were used to spot the fall of shot. It was important that the pilot was briefed adequately and had a chance to make contact with the bombarding forces. Mike Crossley describes his experiences in a Seafire.

Today, D-Day, we worked very hard indeed. Don and I flew three times over France, spotting for 'Spunyarn' (Warspite) flying a total of six hours fifty. Cloud was rather low and this meant we had to go well below light flak height to do our spotting. … My first flight took off at 0735, with Don Keen as my number 2. We spent 45 minutes over France spotting on a heavy gun position near the coast at Trouville. The shoot was fairly accurate, by the clock method, but the broadsides had no effect as the guns could be seen still firing at the same time through the clouds of white concrete dust flung up by Warspite's shells.[44]

Meanwhile, joint naval and army parties selected targets on shore. Tactics varied according to whether they had landed themselves or not. In Normandy and at Walcheren there were complaints that naval forces did not know enough about the movements of their own troops and opportunities were missed. For example, a group of tanks appeared but the bombarding forces had no way of confirming that they were enemy. Naval guns could reach some miles inland, and during the Normandy invasion a Panzer regiment parked south east of Caen had a shock when *Rodney*'s 16-inch shells, fired at a range of 32,000 yards, began to explode among them.

As a result of the experience of the invasion of Sicily in 1943, it was concluded that the best aiming technique was to make a few one or two-gun salvoes to get the range, and establish the line of the target. Once the line was found within a 200-yard bracket, deliberate fire was opened, followed by rapid fire. The captain of the *Warspite* believed that:

Deliberate shooting achieves little and is wasteful of time. I have no doubt in my mind that this ship has secured the best results by getting within say 100 yards of the target after crossing and then quickly 'plastering' with that range for three or four salvos or until the fall of shot wanders.[45]

The navy was proud of its role in shore bombardment and felt that it justified the continued role of the gun in naval warfare. Certainly it had an effect on enemy morale and they took cover as soon as the spotting aircraft appeared. But naval guns were not designed for this kind of pin-point accuracy, or for sustained firing. Mike Crossley claims that some shots were 2 miles from the target, and only about 1 per cent hit the target at long range.[46]

4 Naval Bases

The battle fleet required two kinds of base, the functions of which sometimes overlapped. It needed operational bases such as Scapa Flow, where the fleet could anchor between sorties, relatively safe from surface, submarine or air attack but well positioned to intervene if the enemy moved. And it needed repair bases with the specialised facilities to deal with large warships.

The navy always found it more difficult to get money for infrastructure than for ships and men, and the period between the wars was worse than most as limited funds were concentrated on keeping up the numbers of the battle fleet. Vote 10 of the Navy Estimates, for 'Works, Buildings and Repairs at Home and Abroad', never exceeded £2½ million in the early 1930s out of a total budget of more than £50 million. This was less than a third of the cost of a modern battleship. The only major building project was the ill-fated base at Singapore. Even in 1936, as Vote 10 crept up to £2,537,500, the list of projects was not ambitious.

The principal new works for which provision is made comprise new quarters at Bermuda for single workmen transferred from the Home Dockyards, underpinning and underwater repairs to wharf walls at Malta, reconstruction of a jetty at Plymouth, and a new boathouse at Portsmouth.[47]

Below left: The destroyer *Westcott* of 1918 creates a smokescreen.

Below right: A cruiser's guns fire in support of a landing.

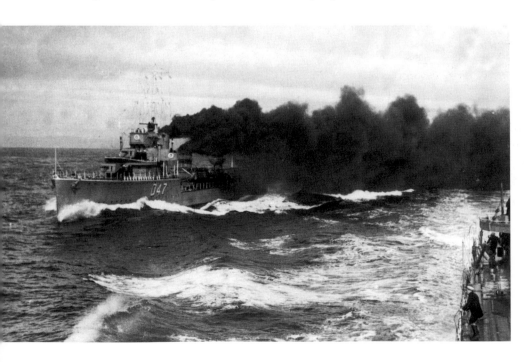

In wartime this neglect would be reflected in two main areas. Fleet anchorages such as Scapa Flow were dangerously unprepared, and docking facilities for large ships were inadequate. The Royal Navy had only nine docks worldwide which were capable of taking the largest battleships and aircraft carriers. Three were at Rosyth, two each at Portsmouth and Devonport, and one each at Gibraltar and Singapore.[48]

The battle fleet was more dependent than other parts of the navy on the traditional naval bases. The aforementioned bases had dry docks large enough for the biggest battleships and aircraft carriers, cranes and other equipment to deal with heavy engines and guns, and a specialised labour force for the requirements of armour plate and the naval style of ship construction. Other types of ship, such as escorts, were generally smaller and built to mercantile standards, so they could be repaired anywhere with a shipbuilding industry, such as the Tyne, Mersey or Clyde. Coastal forces were even smaller and could be repaired, as they were built, by yacht-builders or woodworkers.

The Dockyards Under Attack

In past ages, naval strategists had believed that a fleet could decline action and stay in port as a 'fleet in being' which still had decisive effect on the war. But by 1939 no port was completely safe from bombing, long-range gunnery and submarines, not to mention the threat of invasion. All nations suffered from this, and one need only mention the attacks at Taranto and Pearl Harbor, the destruction of the French at Mers el-Kebir and the sinking of the *Royal Oak* and *Tirpitz*. Ships were little safer in port than at sea in 1939–45.

The older home naval bases, at Chatham, Sheerness, Portsmouth and Plymouth, had been founded in the days of sail and expanded in the early steam age for war against France. They were all in the south of England and were highly vulnerable to air attack after the Fall of France provided the enemy with ideal bases. Chatham was slightly more difficult to find than the others, and was close to the more tempting target of London, so it suffered less damage. Portsmouth endured several heavy raids, for example on the night of 10/11 January 1941, when 153 aircraft dropped 140 tonnes of bombs. Churchill visited the town and his private secretary saw 'a dismal sight…where one whole street we went along had just ceased to exist'. Plymouth was not even protected by an island like Wight, and was an ideal distance from France on short nights. It became one of the most heavily bombed towns in Britain. After a series of five raids in nine days in April 1941, 600 civilians were left dead and 40,000 were homeless. Large parts of the dockyard were destroyed, including most of the historic Officers' Terrace. German bomber crews began to doubt the wisdom of further attacks and one wrote: 'The target is again Plymouth. Does it really make sense to drop so much on the south coast, just because it lies nearest to us?'[49] Visiting Plymouth in his ship, Commander Donald Macintyre was horrified to find 'what a backwater the great port of Plymouth and Devonport had become, with the shifting of the nerve centre of the Atlantic war to Liverpool and its satellite ports'.[50]

Rosyth, in the Firth of Forth on the east coast of Scotland, was slightly better positioned against the German threat but it had been neglected between the wars and was smaller than the other bases. It attracted some attention from the *Luftwaffe* in the early stages of the war when warships in the Forth were bombed, but an air attack involved a long flight over the North Sea in which the aircraft could easily be picked up by radar, and Rosyth was left alone during the main blitz. But Scapa Flow was famously penetrated by *U-47* early in the war and the battleship *Royal Oak* was sunk.

The overseas yards were even more vulnerable. Gibraltar and Alexandria were both infiltrated by Italian midget submarines and the battleships *Queen Elizabeth* and *Valiant* were seriously damaged in the latter port. Malta was paralysed by bombing for much of the war.

Dockyard Facilities

The main feature of any dockyard, from where the name comes, was the dry dock, which could be drained of water for access to the underwater hull of a ship. Such docks were scarce in 1939–45, partly because of the lack of pre-war investment. There was no time or resources to build any new docks in wartime. A typical dry dock was lined in stone, with huge steps on each side, to provide bases for the props that would support a ship under repair. Each had a floating gate known as a caisson. Some dry docks, such as those in the older part of Chatham Dockyard, opened directly onto the river front, but that made movement difficult due to tidal conditions. Most modern dry docks were accessible through wet docks – large rectangular areas of water where ships could be protected from the rise and fall of the tide. Large electric cranes were fitted around the dry and wet docks, for lifting heavy machinery and parts.

Floating docks could be used instead of fixed dry docks. They were relatively inexpensive and could be towed from one base to another, but this might take a long time and they could be sunk by torpedo or bombing – AFD (Admiralty Floating Dock) 8 was sunk at Malta in 1940 and AFD 23 collapsed at Trincomalee while lifting the battleship *Valiant* in 1944. Eight docks of 2750 tons each were built for the use of destroyers and smaller ships. Each was fitted with two 5-ton electric cranes.[51]

A dockyard needed space for ships which were awaiting repair, were laid up in peacetime or whose crews were resting. Some were accommodated in wet docks, where the rise and fall of the tide was controlled and they were safe from torpedo attack, if not aerial bombardment. Others were moored alongside wharves and jetties and yet more were tied up to buoys inside the harbour, or had to anchor offshore. A suitable anchorage was an important feature of any dockyard or naval base. Ashore, a dockyard was equipped with workshops of various kinds, for ironworking, boatbuilding, woodworking and storage.

The Dockyard Workforce

The royal dockyards were managed by the Director of Dockyards, a senior flag officer who reported to the Third Sea Lord. Many of the senior management were members of the Royal Corps of Naval Constructors. Each major dockyard had its own Admiral Superintendent, assisted by a Captain of the Dockyard. There was a manager for the Constructive Department assisted by various naval constructors, and a large staff of civil engineers to maintain the yard itself. Traditional titles such as Master Rigger and Boatswain of the Yard were maintained alongside newer ones such as Admiralty Chemist and Senior Electrical Officer. The Engineering Department was headed by a naval captain or rear-admiral.

The largest part of the labour force consisted of shipwrights, for in the dockyards they remained the principal workers on the hull of a ship, in contrast to private industry. They formed the largest group in the Naval Construction Department, but were supplemented by smiths, joiners, pattern makers, plumbers, coppersmiths and painters. The Marine Engineering Department included engine fitters and bricklayers (for boilers) as well as many kinds of metalworker. The electrical engineering division had electrical fitters and electricians at various levels of skill. More traditional trades were represented by the sailmakers and riggers. The dockyard workers were generally union members, and the management usually tried to adopt a conciliatory approach during negotiations with them. This went against the grain with many admirals, for sailors tended to regard the dockyard 'mateys' as lazy and inefficient, with no respect for naval tradition.

Traditionally, skilled dockyard workers were trained by apprenticeship in the dockyard schools, though in wartime the yards accepted skilled men who had been trained elsewhere, and partly-trained 'dilutees' who could do selected parts of the job. There were nearly 100,000 workers in the home and overseas yards at the beginning of the war, rising to 128,000 at home at the end of 1941, and nearly 45,000 abroad.[52] At Chatham the number of male workers hardly increased at all during the war, from 9750 to 9755, while more than 1500 were released to the armed forces and 2000 went on to other services such as yards abroad. Their numbers were augmented by 579 male dilutees and the female workforce grew from 130 to nearly 2000. Chatham had long employed 'ladies' for sewing in the flag loft, and 'women' for heavier work in the ropery, but now they took on many new tasks and the class distinctions were obscured.

Rosyth Dockyard had only just been re-activated after more than a decade of closure, and there was no pool of skilled labour to draw on within the area. In 1939 it employed 10 naval officers, 32 senior and 133 junior civil servants and 1670 industrial workers, with a total wage bill of £10,390 per week. Naturally there was a need for vast expansion and 1695 men were transferred from the southern yards and paid an extra allowance of 21/- (£1.05) per week each. There was just one woman among the industrial employees in 1939. By the end of the war there were 2204 women workers in the yard along with 7096 men. There were 21 naval officers, 101 senior civil servants and 409 junior.

Other Naval Facilities

As well as the facilities of the dockyard itself, which were devoted to servicing the ships, a full naval base needed to handle the people, the weapons and the other supplies. Portsmouth and Plymouth were the most complete in this respect. Portsmouth had many different facilities, mostly on the peninsulas and islands round the natural harbour. East of the entrance was the Gunwharf or HMS *Vernon*, the torpedo depot for the base. On the western side of the entrance were Haslar naval hospital and Fort Blockhouse, the peacetime headquarters of the submarine service. Further in was the town of Gosport and the Royal Clarence Victualling Yard. Priddy's Hard was on a peninsula just to the north, and included the main armament depot. Opposite was the dockyard itself, and north of that was Whale Island, the home of the gunnery school HMS *Excellent*. At this point the channel into the harbour divided into two streams. To the west was Fountain Lake, with the great training camp HMS *Collingwood* and the armament depot at Bedenham on shore. The

Bomb damage in Portsmouth, painted by Richard Eurich. 'Good old Bubbles!' is written on one of the walls, a reference to Admiral Sir William James, the Commander-in-Chief, who was the model for a painting by Millais in his childhood.

eastern channel, known as Portchester Lake, led past Whale Island and the firing range at Tipner, to the ancient castle of Portchester. Portsdown Hill, behind the town, had tunnels for underground fuel storage. The town of Portsmouth included the main naval barracks, heavily bombed in 1940–1, and several temporary camps where seamen between ships could be accommodated. The Royal Marine Barracks was at Eastney, east of the town. On the Gosport side was HMS *St Vincent*, the initial training base for the Fleet Air Arm; HMS *Sultan* for the training of engineers and HMS *Daedalus*, the airfield at Lee-on-Solent. Even in peacetime the whole area was dominated by the navy, and far more so in wartime.

Harbour Craft

The navy maintained a large fleet of civilian-manned tugs, ammunition vessels and supply boats for use in harbour. They were manned by several different departments, such as the King's Harbourmaster which controlled the tugs, the Victualling Department and the Civil Engineer which controlled the dredgers. Portsmouth had more than 40 craft in 1939, including 16 tugs, some of which were paddle boats with greater manoeuvrability. Tugs were usually needed for going alongside a jetty, as warships had no sideways power. They were even more important when

manoeuvring a ship into a dock. Portsmouth had two sailing barges, able to carry ammunition in safety and several towed lighters. The navy adapted the design of the Clyde puffer for victualling vessels or VICs. At Scapa Flow, requisitioned fishing drifters were allocated on the basis of one per ship and two per aircraft carrier, but were kept in a common pool, known as the 'marine menagerie' because of the great variety of craft. They were used to ferry crew and stores to and from ships. In August 1942 there were more than 150 vessels including trawlers, ferries and yachts, as well as wood and steel drifters powered by steam or diesel.

The Home Bases

The naval base at Chatham had been in relative decline since the seventeenth century. More recently, it had been hit by the Dreadnought revolution, for its narrow, winding channels and smaller docks could not cope with the larger ships. The older 80-acre site – which today is the Historic Dockyard – was by this time mainly being used for storage, administration and lighter industrial activity, although the older building slips were used for submarines, a Chatham speciality. The newer dockyard was to the north of the old one and was three times the size. It had been created in the nineteenth century by cutting

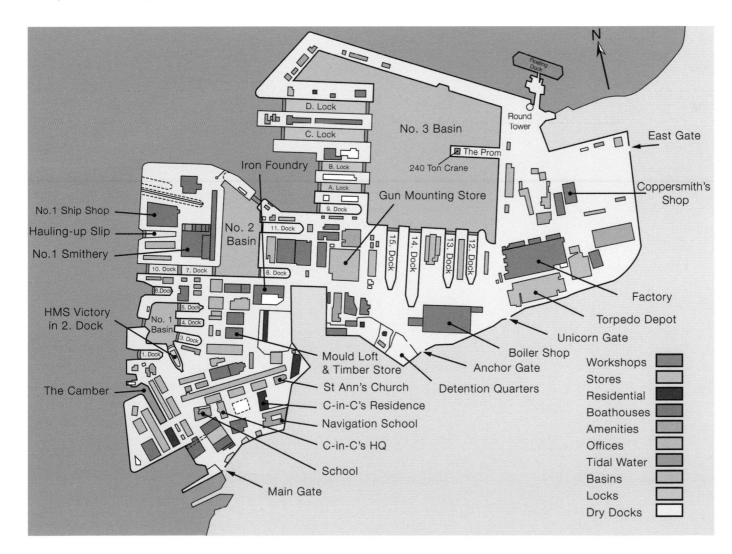

Portsmouth Dockyard in wartime.

three huge wet docks between the mainland and St Mary's Island. Chatham was 11 miles up the River Medway, which restricted its use. Early in the war the yard concentrated on the repair of destroyers and smaller ships due to the fear of bombing, but a few cruisers including *London* were later refitted there. During the war the yard carried out 804 dry-dockings of ships of cruiser size and below, and repaired or refitted 1360 ships.[53]

At the mouth of the Medway where it joined the Thames Estuary was the smaller dockyard of Sheerness. Its first role in wartime was as a base for the ships which evacuated Dunkirk. For the rest of the war it serviced the ships which protected the entrance to the Thames Estuary.

Portsmouth was protected by the Isle of Wight, which created the great naval anchorage of Spithead off the port. Like Chatham, the yard consisted of an older area and a large steam yard, dominated by huge wet docks, to the north. The dockyard only built a cruiser, two submarines and two floating docks during the war but it repaired the battleship *Nelson* after mine damage and refitted many cruisers. It came into its own in the preparations for D-Day, when more than a thousand landing vessels of various types were fitted out, and Spithead served as one of the main assembly points. Portsmouth Dockyard staff also constructed and fitted the headquarters at Fort Southwick, from where the invasion was planned, and built the first two midget submarines.

The base at Portland was protected by the eponymous island on one side and large breakwaters on the other. In peacetime it was useful for anchoring ships exercising in the Channel and it was the centre for anti-submarine warfare. In wartime it was more vulnerable to bombing that any other base, and was used much less.

Devonport Dockyard at Plymouth was the most westerly of the home yards. It was situated up the River Tamar, which led into Plymouth Sound. That area was protected by a large breakwater which created a fine naval anchorage. The yard carried out some well-known repairs, including those to the cruiser *Exeter* after the Battle of the River Plate and the rebuilding of the *Belfast* after serious mine damage. It carried out some special tasks, such as converting the old battleship *Centurion* to look like one of the *King George V* class as a decoy, and the preparation of the ex-American destroyer *Campbeltown* for the raid on St Nazaire. It had facilities for the largest ships and recovered quite quickly from the effects of bombing – 90 per cent of its facilities were back in use after the last and heaviest raid in 1941.

Rosyth Dockyard had opened in 1916 after many delays. Situated on the Firth of Forth in the shadow of the famous bridge, it consisted of a large square wet dock built out into the Firth, with three large dry docks on its landward side. Neglected between the wars, it became very useful due to its relative safety. All five of the *King George V* class battleships were taken there for fitting out, as were some of the fleet aircraft carriers. The famous battleship *Warspite* was repaired after mine damage, and her 15-inch guns were replaced.

Choosing the Northern Base

The navy was well aware that it needed a northern anchorage as the main operational base for the Home Fleet, from which it could attempt to seal off German access to the oceans. Loch Ewe on the north-west coast of Scotland was considered as a base for the main fleet

early in 1940, when the new defences of Scapa were being repaired. Also known as Aultbea from the name of the largest village in the area, or more cryptically as 'Port A', it was relatively easy to keep clear of mines, though at that time the sweepers were not available. Unlike Rosyth and the Clyde it was not protected by the RAF's fighter cover. Enemy aircraft could approach the Loch over the sea and arrive without any warning, so the main fleet would be highly vulnerable in the area.[54] This was apparently confirmed on 4 December 1939 when the battleship *Nelson* was damaged by a magnetic mine on entering the Loch. It had been laid by a U-boat and defences were soon improved.

The strategic advantages of the different bases were considered by the Admiralty. The Clyde, Loch Ewe and Rosyth were 'equally acceptable', though Loch Ewe was slightly nearer the probable area of operations. But Scapa was the best sited and it was agreed that it 'should have absolute priority in the Naval quota of A/A defence' and become the main base of the Home Fleet. Rosyth should be the base for light forces operating locally in the North Sea, and the Clyde for armed merchant cruisers. Loch Ewe should be 'developed as an alternative anchorage when material becomes available after the other three bases have been fully protected'.[55]

The Development of Scapa

Scapa Flow in the Orkneys had many advantages as a naval anchorage. It was a large area of water about 7 miles square, of suitable depth for anchoring. It was well sited to close the entrance to the North Sea, and, as it turned out, to support campaigns in Norway and protect convoys to Russia. With a little work it could be made safe from aerial and submarine attack, though that was tragically behind at the start of the war. A small naval base was set up at Lyness on the island of Hoy to service the warships anchored in Scapa Flow, and many other facilities were deployed in depot ships afloat. At the height of the war the boom defence of Scapa Flow employed 1100 naval personnel and 130 civilians. In addition to the laying, opening and maintenance of boom defences, groups of trawlers and drifters were used as minesweepers and anti-submarine vessels around Scapa.

After the sinking of the *Royal Oak* it was decided to close Kirk Sound, Skerry Sound, East Weddel Sound and Water Sound within the anchorage permanently, though the enormous tides of the area made the project very difficult. Up to 1200 Italian prisoners of war were employed at the peak, with an average of 920 Italians and 350 British workmen during most of the work. This created some difficulties, because technically it was a breach of the Geneva Convention to employ prisoners on direct war work. It is commonly believed that the 'barriers' they constructed eventually became known as 'causeways', linking the islands, because the latter term implied more peaceful uses.

In the early stages Scapa remained was as unpopular with the seamen as it had been in the last war. Ludovic Kennedy, then a junior officer on a destroyer, wrote:

The islands were treeless, just heather and grass, seabirds and sheep, and across the bare face of the Flow tempests blew, often for days on end. There were no women, shops, restaurants, just a couple of canteens that dispensed warm beer, a hall for film shows and the occasional concert party'.[56]

Opposite top:
Rosyth Dockyard
in 1943.

Opposite middle:
Workers entering
the gates of
Plymouth
Dockyard in
October 1940.

Opposite bottom:
Naval tugs tow a
battleship into a
lock in 1940.

Left: The home
dockyard and naval
bases, 1939–45.

The facilties were gradually improved over the years. D A Rayner of the destroyer *Shikari* visited in August 1943 after a three-year gap and found:

There had been fantastic changes. Where there had been miles of muddy roads and open fields there were now hard roads and serried ranks of good huts. There were canteens for the men and there was also a giant mess for the officers. A busy town had sprung up in the salty wilderness, and there were even Wrens about on roads where before only the male of the species had ever been seen.[57]

The Overseas Bases

The great overseas naval bases, at Gibraltar, Malta, Alexandria, Singapore, Bermuda, Hong King and Simonstown at the Cape of Good Hope, were products of British imperialism and the need to protect trade worldwide. Some of them, notably Bermuda, were on the fringes of this particular war but were useful for training and other purposes. Simonstown, while far from the scene of action, was an essential staging post on the route to the East while the Mediterranean was closed to shipping. Others were almost too close to the scene of action. Gibraltar would have become extremely precarious if Fascist Spain had been persuaded to join the Nazis. Alexandria was evacuated at one stage as Rommel's armies advanced across North Africa. Malta was bombed into impotence for much of the war, and Singapore and Hong Kong were taken by the Japanese before they had any real effect.

Gibraltar had been a British possession since it was taken from the Spanish in 1704. It had a poor harbour, until a programme of works at the turn of the twentieth century allowed the building of long breakwaters to create an enclosed space of water. Three dry docks were built, including the Prince of Wales Dock, which could cope with the largest ships. Gibraltar was always short of supplies, but the slopes of the rock were concreted over to allow rainwater to be collected. The Spanish never gave up their claim on the island and it took a great deal of diplomacy (and the threat to invade the Canary Islands) to prevent an alliance with Germany, which would have been fatal to British Gibraltar. The civil population of 14,000 was evacuated in 1940, although 4000 remained behind for dockyard work and local defence. The Admiralty was able to build an airstrip across the land linking the rock to the mainland, though that was a sensitive issue with the Spanish. The port was easily visible from Spain, so there was no security, and Italian submarines operating from a secret Spanish base did some damage to merchant shipping. But Gibraltar was a vital base for guarding the strait that bore its name, for Force H, which operated in the Western Mediterranean and the Atlantic, as a staging post for convoys into the Mediterranean and towards Malta, and for the invasion of North Africa in 1942.

Malta had been in British hands since 1800. It had a very central position in the Mediterranean, several excellent harbours, first-class dockyard facilities and strong defences against seaward attack, though not against aerial bombing. In peacetime, it was highly popular with sailors of all ranks who made short visits, but less so with the army who had to stay there for longer periods. The young Stoker Sydney Greenwood was entranced during a visit to Valetta in 1935.

Opposite: British naval bases throughout the world.

Below: Scapa Flow showing the defences.

Each of the closely joined buildings was either a place of entertainment or some other facility for our benefit. Barbers' shops, bed-and-breakfast, fortune telling; all doing a roaring trade. Music filled the air. A dozen public house pianos mingled with the small bands from the bigger saloons with names such as Egyptian Queen and Silver Horse. Smells of lovely fatty fried food invaded the nostrils of sailors unused to rich living. ... Men got drunk and there were brawls; but it was all kept in hand by naval patrols provided by the ships.[58]

This changed completely in wartime. Malta, only 50 miles from the coast of Sicily, was bombed incessantly by the Germans and Italians. The people craved independence but supported the Allied cause: the island won the George Cross and a place in British hearts.

The main harbours of Malta were on either side of the city of Valetta on the north coast, founded and fortified by the Knights of St John who had ruled the island until 1798. To the east of the city was Grand Harbour, used for battleships, cruisers and aircraft carriers. To the east of that were the 'three cities' of Cospicua., Vittioroso and Senglea where most of the dockyard workers lived. French Creek opened off Grand Harbour and included four dry docks and other facilities forming the main dockyard area. Dockyard Creek on the other side of Senglea had another dry dock and sheltered mooring facilities for cruisers. There was a naval hospital at Bighi on another peninsula and the entrance to the harbour was protected by Fort St Angelo to the east, and a breakwater to the west. At the other end of Grand Harbour were basins for barges and small craft and the Corradino Heights had two of the common features of twentieth-century naval bases, fuel tanks and football pitches. The whole harbour was overlooked by the magnificent fortifications of the Knights.

Marsamxett Harbour on the other side of Valetta was only slightly inferior. The side away from Valetta was divided by Manoel Island with its fort. The two creeks thus created, Lazaretto and Sliema, were used for destroyers and submarines. The Commander-in-Chief of the Mediterranean Fleet had a house in Valetta itself, though for the early part of the war he had to operate from Alexandria. The bombing of Malta was much reduced after 1942. Its dry docks and repair facilities were restored to use and it operated as a major base for the invasions of Sicily and mainland Italy.

In the Eastern Mediterranean, the Royal Navy became highly reliant on its improvised base at Alexandria. Egypt had been theoretically independent of British rule since 1922 and was neutral in the war, but under an agreement of 1936 the British were allowed to base large forces there, including the use of the harbour at Alexandria. In fact, much land fighting took place on Egyptian soil, including the Battle of El Alamein in 1942, though the British political position in Egypt remained slightly precarious.

The ancient city of Alexandria was sited on a T-shaped peninsula with a natural harbour on each side. The western harbour was the most developed, with an outer harbour of nearly 1400 acres and an inner one of 464. The whole was protected by a breakwater but the entrance was shallow, with 35 feet of water through the Great Pass as the only viable route for big ships. This left only a foot or two of clearance for a battleship. The Royal Navy had the use of the Gabbari dry dock, which could take small cruisers, and AFD 5 was towed there from Portsmouth. It was large enough to handle a battleship but Cunningham worried constantly that it might be sunk, perhaps with a ship inside. The submarine depot ship *Woolwich* was sent there in 1940 to act as a tender for destroyers. Workshops used by the Khedival shipping line and the Alexandria tramways were taken over and shore facilities were gradually built up. It was difficult to attract enough workmen from Malta and the Egyptians were not considered satisfactory – after an air raid they insisted on taking that day off and the following one. The Mediterranean Fleet suffered badly from the lack of maintenance facilities. The battleship *Malaya*, for example, had

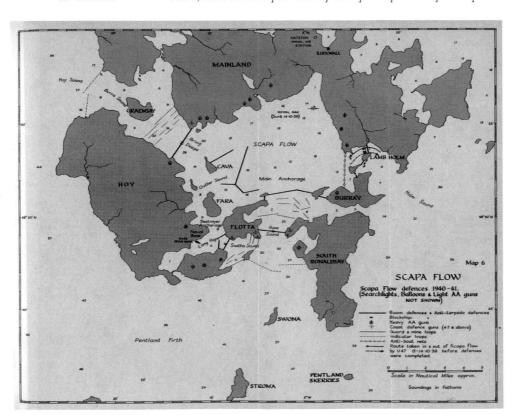

Map 6

SCAPA FLOW

Scapa Flow defences 1940-41.
(Searchlights, Balloons & Light AA guns
NOT SHOWN)

'condenseritis' – trouble with the condensers in her boiler system – and could not keep up with the fleet, and the boilers of the *Ramillies* and *Royal Sovereign* were in bad shape.[59]

Before the war the navy had developed the concept of a mobile naval base. This was partly tested at Suda Bay on Crete, which was taken over as an advanced refuelling base during the campaign in Greece in 1940–1. A convoy left Alexandria on 29 October 1940, including two RFA tankers, a netlayer, a minesweeper and escorted by two cruisers and two destroyers. The monitor *Terror*, with her 15-inch guns, was brought from Malta as a defence and an effective anti-submarine boom was fitted, but an improvised torpedo net was 'nothing more than a dummy'[60] – the cruiser *Glasgow* was hit by airborne torpedoes and later the *York* was sunk by Italian MTBs. The Royal Marines' Mobile Naval Base Defence Organisation arrived on the island but was soon caught up in the fight against the German airborne invasion, and lost 1200 men as part of the rearguard while the island was evacuated.

The idea for a great naval base at Singapore was adopted in 1921 and became increasingly important the following year when Britain's alliance with Japan was ended on the insistence of the Americans. It was an imperial rather than British: the Malay States and the governments of Australia and New Zealand naturally had a stake in it, and the costs were to be shared. A site was chosen on the Sembawang River in the Old Sound between Singapore Island and the mainland, 12 miles north of the city of Singapore. A town for 12,000 workers was planned. Progress was slow in an era of government cuts, and the scheme was suspended in 1924. The initial scheme was for a large wet dock and four great dry docks. This was soon cut down to a single large dry dock supported by a floating dock, with an open Stores Dock where destroyers could lie alongside, and two wharf walls. There was a long and debilitating controversy over whether the base should be defended by guns or bombers. It was 1928 before the main engineering contract was placed. Work was suspended again the following year after just over £2½ million of a £8.7 million project had been spent, and an imperial conference agreed to a five-year postponement. The first milestone was reached in 1938, when a 1000-foot dry dock was opened with great ceremony. But two sides of the Stores Dock remained uncompleted, along with part of the north wall, which was left as a pitched slope, unsuitable for mooring. The whole concept was useless without strong land, sea and air forces to defend it. When the Japanese attacked in 1941–2, the *Prince of Wales* and *Repulse* were lost, army and air forces were inadequate and the defences mostly faced to seaward. The Japanese advanced down the Malayan peninsula and the garrison surrendered into miserable and mostly fatal captivity, in what Churchill called 'the worst disaster and largest capitulation in British history'.

Bases in India, such as Bombay and Calcutta, were maintained during the war. On the return to the East in 1944, the British used the base at Trincomalee in Ceylon (Sri Lanka). Sydney in Australia had a great natural harbour, which was planned as the main base for the British Pacific Fleet, while the mobile naval base concept was being revived to deal with the great distances in the Pacific.

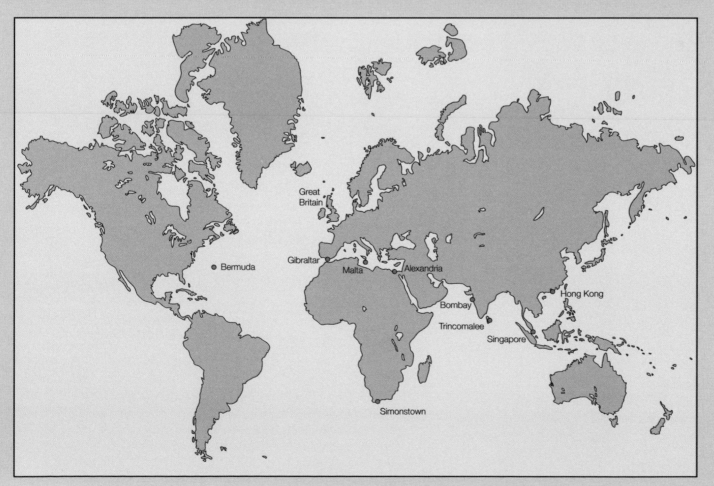

PART VIII
Naval Aviation

1 Aircraft Carriers

The Royal Navy had pioneered naval aviation in the First World War, and eventually reached the conclusion that only a 'flat-top' aircraft carrier could be fully effective. Development slowed down after that, and as result the navy's carriers at the beginning of the war were a mixed bag, mostly conversions of merchant ships or warships, with only one modern purpose-built ship.

Prototypes

The *Argus* of 1918 was the world's first true aircraft carrier, with a completely flat deck for landing on and taking off. Numerous experiments in the First World War had shown that it was relatively easy to launch an aircraft from a ship, but much harder to land it on the stern in the airflow created by the superstructure. The *Argus*, converted from a liner, was on trials when the war ended. She continued in service until the next war, but her 470-foot flight deck was too short for modern operations. She served in trade protection and as a training carrier in the Clyde, and delivered aircraft to Malta.

The *Eagle* of 1924 was built on the hull of a battleship ordered by Chile, with a longer flight deck of 652 feet. She introduced the 'island superstructure' set off to the starboard side to leave the flight deck uninterrupted, and established that this was a practical proposition. She served in the Mediterranean and South Atlantic until she was sunk in Operation Pedestal, the Malta convoy of August 1942.

The *Hermes*, also of 1924, was the first carrier to be built as such from the bottom up, and the only one for some years. At 10,850 tons she was smaller than the *Argus* and she was little changed between the wars. She served in the Far East at the beginning of the war and was sunk by Japanese dive bombers in April 1942.

Conversions

The *Furious, Glorious* and *Courageous* were light battlecruisers, ordered by Fisher early in the First World War for an expedition into the Baltic that never took place. As planned, the *Furious* was to have two 18-inch guns and the others four 15-inch each. The three were eccentric ships by any standards and were known to the lower deck as the *Useless, Helpless* and *Hopeless*. *Furious* was quickly fitted with a take-off deck forward, then a landing deck aft but air currents over her central superstructure made this arrangement impractical. In 1925 she emerged from dock as a fully converted carrier, without the island superstructure introduced by *Eagle* and *Hermes*. She had a small retractable conning tower on the foredeck and even smaller ones, for navigation and aircraft control, on either side. *Glorious* and *Courageous* followed in 1928 and 1930, this time with a small island. All three ships had a flight deck which stopped well short of the bows and stern, and it was planned that the hangars could be opened forward to allow aircraft to take off from that level, an idea which was later abandoned. With more than 22,000 tons displacement and speeds of 30 knots, the three ships provided the navy with valuable experience during many exercises in the 1930s. The *Furious* carried 33 aircraft, the others 48 each and they increased the potential air power of the inter-war fleet dramatically. *Glorious* and *Courageous* were both squandered in the early stages of the Second World War. *Courageous* was torpedoed on a futile anti-submarine patrol in 1939, and *Glorious* was sunk by the guns of the *Scharnhorst* and *Gneisenau* after Captain D'Oyly-Hughes misunderstood her role during the Norwegian campaign. *Furious* served with the Home Fleet for most of the war.

The *Ark Royal*

In 1933 the navy began the design of a new carrier and the *Ark Royal*, laid down at Cammell Laird's shipyard in Birkenhead in 1935, incorporated all the experience so far. She was similar in size and speed to the three conversions, but she was built from the bottom up, which allowed a far more efficient design. She had hangars on two decks to carry 72 aircraft. Her flight deck of 720 feet was far longer than any used before. Unlike previous carriers, her aircraft were fully enclosed in the hangars, although they were not protected by

Opposite: An aircraft lands on an escort carrier in a convoy, as seen by the pilot, with the batsman in view on the port side of the flight deck, in a wartime poster by Roy Nockold.

Below: A take-off from the decks of the *Courageous*, in about 1935, with a destroyer following in case of accident.

armour. With a complement of 151 officers and 1630 ratings, she entered service late in 1938.

The *Ark Royal* was the only modern carrier in service at the beginning of the war and soon became one of the most famous ships in the world. When building, her hull towered above the houses of Birkenhead and her height gave her a distinctive appearance. In September 1939 Adolf Francke of the *Luftwaffe* was decorated and promoted for sinking her in the North Sea, though in fact she was barely damaged and he made no such claim himself, and was eventually driven to suicide by the strain. German propaganda asked, 'Where is the *Ark Royal*?' and the ship became a symbol of British defiance as well as German duplicity. She had a highly active career. She chased the *Graf Spee* then took part in the Norwegian campaign. She became part of Force H, and attacked Mers el-Kebir, bombed Genoa in Italy and Cagliari in Sardinia, hunted the *Bismarck* and escorted Malta convoys. She was hit by a single torpedo launched by *U-81* off Gibraltar in November 1941. Nearly all the crew were saved, but she sank due to poor damage control. But by that time, several more modern carriers had joined the fleet.

Armoured Carriers

By 1935 the British were becoming concerned about the increasing power and value of aircraft, and their ability to inflict damage. British

Below: The Ark Royal *sinking in 1941, with the crew being taken off by destroyer.*

Bottom: A Swordfish landing on the Illustrious, *the first of the armoured carriers.*

carriers were already well protected against accidental fires, and it was now decided to armour the flight decks so that the aircraft in the hangars would be safe from bombing. Two new ships, the *Illustrious* and *Victorious*, were designed on the general lines of the *Ark Royal* but with their hangars protected by 3-inch armour on the decks above and below, and 4½ inches on the sides. In effect, the hangars were large boxes which contributed to the strength of the ship and kept the aircraft secure. But the price was high. A single hangar was adopted to save weight, and the new ships carried only 36 aircraft in the first instance, half of those on the *Ark Royal* and far fewer than equivalent American and Japanese carriers.

A third ship of the class, the *Formidable*, was ordered in 1937 as the Admiralty began to seek ways to increase the aircraft complement. The *Indomitable* was given less armour but a smaller hangar under the main one, allowing her to carry 45 aircraft. She was followed by the *Implacable* and *Indefatigable* which could carry 60. The armoured carriers were of around 23,000 tons with a speed of about 30 knots, except for the last two which could make 32 knots.

The armoured carriers, especially the first four which were completed in 1940–41, were the core of the British carrier force for most of the war. *Illustrious* launched the aircraft which damaged the Italian fleet at Taranto and survived a heavy air attack in the Mediterranean in January 1941, and heavier still when she was being repaired in Malta. The *Indomitable* withstood bombs and torpedoes and there are indications that the Americans envied the armoured deck, especially when kamikaze attacks began in the Pacific. Five of the ships were damaged by Japanese suicide bombers and a report in May 1945 commented that 'without armoured decks, TF 57 [the British Pacific Fleet] would have been out of action (with 4 carriers) for at least 2 months'.[1]

By 1940 the British were planning larger carriers which eventually grew to nearly 37,000 tons, but the new *Eagle* and *Ark Royal* were not launched until well after the war. Even larger ships, of 45,000 tons, were cancelled at the end of the war.

CAM and MAC Ships

Meanwhile design policy was moving towards smaller ships which could be built quickly and cheaply and spread over the oceans. The question of convoy protection was extremely urgent in the spring of 1941, and 35 merchant vessels were fitted with catapults to launch a single, expandable Hurricane fighter against German Focke-Wulf reconnaissance aircraft. Known as catapult aircraft merchant or CAM ships, they had some success but it was a desperate measure.

In 1942 another idea was adopted, by fitting merchant ships with flight decks so that they could fly off and land a small number of low-performance aircraft for anti-U-boat patrol in the air gap in the middle of the Atlantic. Suitable ships were selected, with a speed of at least 11 knots and room for a flight deck of at least 390 feet by 62 feet. The first, the *Empire MacAlpine*, was ready in April 1943, just as the tide in the Battle of the Atlantic was on the turn. She carried a flight of four Swordfish, as well as a full cargo of grain and was operated by a Merchant Navy crew and Fleet Air Arm aircrew and mechanics. Six grain ships were converted in this way, with a lift and a small hangar aft. Thirteen oil tankers were also built or converted and had no hangars so aircraft had to stay on deck when not flying. Two of these were operated by Dutch crews. Known as MAC

ships or merchant aircraft carriers, they made 216 Atlantic crossings in 1944 alone and flew more than 2600 sorties. Although they mounted only about a dozen attacks on U-boats, their deterrent effect was important.

Escort Carriers

Since at least 1926 the Royal Navy had been planning for small aircraft carriers to escort individual convoys, but the projects were always pushed aside in favour of larger carriers. In 1941 the captured German merchant ship *Hanover* was converted and re-named *Audacity*. Carrying six or eight Martlet fighters, she escorted several convoys, shot down five enemy aircraft and damaged several others before being torpedoed at the end of the year. The *Activity* was also converted from a merchant ship in 1942, and was to escort many convoys for the rest of the war, followed by the *Pretoria Castle*, *Nairana* and *Vindex* in 1943. But merchant ships were in short supply, and the Royal Navy was to find a much larger source of escort carriers in the United States.

The US Navy was already developing its own ideas on escort carriers and the first one, based on a standard merchant ship hull, was completed as a carrier and turned over to the Royal Navy as HMS *Archer*. She entered service in at the end of 1941, although she had many teething troubles due to her fast building and the inexperience of her crew. Four more of that class followed, each with a wooden flight deck 442 feet long, a tonnage of 8200 and a speed of 16 knots. They carried an air group of 15. They were followed by the eight ships of the *Attacker* class, which entered service in 1942–3. They were larger at 11,420 tons, and were followed by 23 ships of the *Smiter* or *Ruler* class, mass-produced in Henry Kaiser's yard at Seattle in 1943–4, and taken to Vancouver for fitting out. They were of 15,610 tons and, like all the American ships, they had very small, rectangular islands. They could carry up to 24 aircraft, and were approaching the British concept of a light fleet carrier in size, although they were built much more quickly.

The American-built carriers retained the American title of CVE, the code letters for escort carriers. Most were modified to British standards in accommodation and safety, though HMS *Dasher* was not and blew up with great loss of life in the Clyde in March 1943. The adoption of the American crash barrier made it feasible to operate high-performance aircraft from quite short fight decks, albeit in small numbers. As a result the CVEs were often diverted from their original task of convoy escort. When they first entered service late in 1942 the first four were used to support the invasion of North Africa and they did not begin convoy escort until 1943, when they began to fill the air gap. Even so, they were used for many other operations. Four of them took part on the attack on the *Tirpitz* in April 1944, while others supported the Allied invasion of southern France or were sent to the Pacific.

The Light Fleets

By late 1942 the Royal Navy had already begun to plan for a cheaper carrier, which could nevertheless keep up with the fleet and operate high-performance aircraft. The loss of the *Prince of Wales* and *Repulse* confirmed the need for carriers to accompany battleships, and four classes of 'light fleet carriers', totalling 24 ships, were ordered in 1942–3. They had adequate flight decks, were almost 700 feet long, and could make 25

knots. They were lightly built according to merchant ship standards, with none of the armour which protected the *Illustrious* and her near sisters.

Only four of the light fleets were in commission by the end of the war with Japan and they played no part in the conflict. They were, however, a triumph of design and some lasted many years in service. Many were transferred to Allied nations and they were used by France, the Netherlands, Brazil, Argentina, India, Australia and Canada. The *Hermes* was not launched until 1953, but went on to lead the British fleet in the Falklands War nearly three decades later.

The Design of a Carrier

According to one of Britain's leading aircraft carrier designers of the period, J H C Chapman of the Royal Corps of Naval Constructors:

The aircraft carrier presents the naval constructor with some of the most difficult problems encountered in warship design. On a hull possessing most normal warship features, provision must be made for the operation and maintenance of several squadrons of aircraft. If operated ashore, a carrier's aircraft would require an airfield extending over several square miles with air control, hangar, maintenance shops, petrol stowage, bomb dumps, barrack blocks and messes, transport and runways thousands of feet in length. In the carrier this has to be compacted into a ship about 800 feet long with a flight deck of less than two acres.[2]

Fleet carriers needed powerful engines. Not only did they have to keep up with the fleet, they might have to turn away to launch aircraft and

Top: The *Empire MacAlpine*, the first of the merchant aircraft carriers.

Above: The escort carrier *Rajah*, completed at Seattle in 1944.

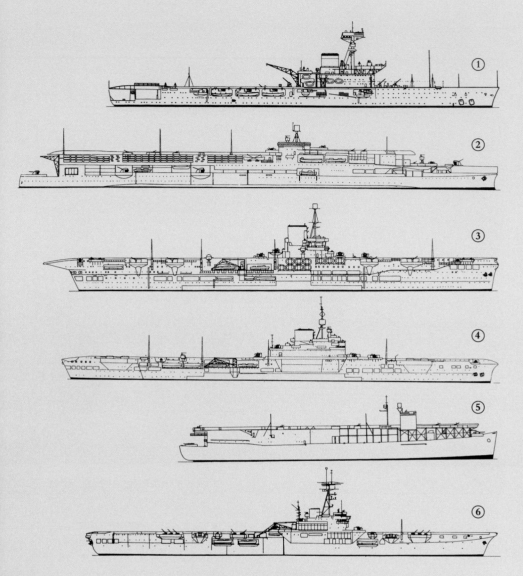

Above: British aircraft carriers.

1. The *Hermes*, the first carrier built as such from the keel up. She was too small for the job, and was sunk by Japanese air attack in 1942.

2. The *Furious*, converted from a light battlecruiser, as she was in 1942.

3. The *Ark Royal*, with her double hangar deck, was significantly higher than later carriers.

4. The *Illustrious* in 1940.

5. The *Emperor*, an escort carrier completed in 1943.

6. The *Colossus*, the first of the light fleet carriers to enter service, at the end of 1944.

then catch up with it again. The four-shaft geared turbines of the *Implacable* and *Indefatigable* generated 148,000 shaft horsepower, more than any other ships in the wartime fleet, and gave a speed of 32 knots. Escort carriers needed less speed. None of the American-built ones had more than 10,000 horsepower, with speeds of around 17 knots. Engines were kept low in the ship to avoid interrupting the hangars, and this was not too difficult with turbines which took up little vertical space.

The 'normal warship features' mentioned by Chapman included anchors in the bows. Mooring lines had to be used as in any other ship and rectangular holes were left in the hull near the bows and stern for handling them. There were more apertures midships on each side for the ship's boats. Pumps were needed in the lower hull, though these proved inadequate in the case of the *Ark Royal*.

Accommodation on aircraft carriers was in principle the same as on other warships, with messes for all the different ranks and trade groups as on a battleship. It was even more crowded, however, partly because of the higher proportion of officers. As originally planned, the *King George V* class battleships had 109 officers and 1536 men, while the *Illustrious* class carriers had 121 officers and 1208 men in a hull a third smaller. The situation became far worse as extra aircraft were added and even more officers' accommodation was needed. The complement of the *Victorious* rose by 67 per cent in wartime, that of the *King George V* by 23 per cent.[3] The only compensation for the crews was that when there was no flying, the flight deck was available for games and recreation.

A carrier needed a defensive armament. *Furious* carried 5.5-inch guns but exercises in the 1930s tended to establish that carriers should not be expected to fight large surface ships, and after that mainly anti-aircraft armaments were fitted. The *Illustrious* class carried sixteen 4.5-inch guns in sponsons along the side of the flight deck, in countersunk twin mountings designed not to protrude above the flight deck and interfere with flying. Pom-poms were common in the early years but soon the Oerlikon and then the Bofors proliferated. The *Attacker* class, for example, had eight Bofors and up to 35 Oerlikon mounted on sponsons at two levels along each side. The kamikaze threat in the Pacific meant that even more guns had to be added.

The Flight Deck

Early British flight decks were not completely flat, for 'round-down' was used both forward and aft in an attempt to streamline the airflow. However, it tended to reduce the space available for stowing aircraft on deck and was eliminated during refits from about 1943. A standard layout for the flight deck had evolved by the later stages of the war, and it was not much affected by the size of the carrier. Aft were the arrester wires which would stop an aircraft on landing. Early in the war the numbers were limited due to production difficulties, but by 1944 a fleet carrier had nine of them, designed to stop an aircraft of up to 20,000 pounds in weight at a speed of up to 60 knots. An American-built CVE also had nine wires; a merchant aircraft carrier had four. A platform for the deck landing control officers or batsman was placed to port opposite the wires.

Forward of them was an open space used for short-term stowage on a larger carrier, then several safety barriers, copied from the Americans early in the war. These were net-like structures which could be raised during a landing to stop any aircraft which missed the wires, and lowered to allow planes to move forward to clear the area. Most carriers had an 'accelerator', later known as a catapult. It could launch an aircraft at between 50 and 75 knots according to type. It was useful for take-off in light or contrary winds, and could cope with up to 25 knots of side wind.

Carriers needed lifts to take the aircraft between the hangars and the flight deck. The *Furious, Glorious* and *Courageous* had cross-shaped lifts to suit the shape of the aircraft of the day with their wings unfolded, but it was found that rectangular lifts offered more flexibility. Most carriers had two lifts on the centreline, one forward and one aft, and this was essential if landing and taking off were going on at the same

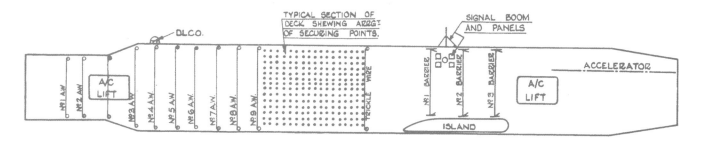

time. The *Ark Royal* had three, two to starboard and one to port, to service her two hangars. Grain ships converted to MACs had one lift, while converted oil tankers had none.

Fleet carriers had mobile cranes so that crashed aircraft could be removed quickly, and CVEs had aircraft handling booms on either side. Night flying lights were fitted, carefully designed so that they would not give the ship away to surface craft. Outriggers were fitted in later years, so that an aircraft could be hung partially over the side out of the way of landing operations. Fleet and light fleet carriers had rows of large gantries along each side with the main radio aerials slung between them. They were raised vertically when in use, and lowered then flying was in progress.

The Superstructure

The island superstructure of a fleet carrier was its nerve centre. It was given a streamlined form in the *Ark Royal* and some later ships, to reduce interference over the flight deck. A certain amount of space was taken up by the need to trunk funnel gases through it, but the superstructure contained a number of key areas.

The most obvious was the compass platform from which the ship was steered, four decks above the flight deck on most fleet carriers. Close to it was the Commander's (Flying) control position, fitted with many instruments and with good communication to allow the head of the air group to control operations on the flight deck. The air operations room was on the deck below the compass platform, and was used by aircrew to get the latest information before flying, especially when a separate briefing room was not provided. The captain usually had his office inside the island, and the air department office was close to it, with a communicating door or hatch. A lecture room was placed inside the superstructure in the *Indomitable* class and later, equipped with bookcase, blackboard and easel. By the end of the war there were plans to add an air intelligence office where officers could peruse secret matters in seclusion. The aircraft direction room was still in the superstructure at the end of the war, though there were plans to move it down below to be protected by armour. It contained the main aircraft plot, fed with information by the ship's radar and other sources. The fighter direction officer worked there, controlling the defence of the carrier against attack. At flight deck level was the flight deck control room, from where the aircraft on deck were directed. It had direct contact with the Commander (Flying). Ready rooms for the aircrew were placed as close to the flight deck as possible, equipped with notice boards, drawers for personal equipment, settee bunks for resting between operations and lockers for flying gear.

Below Decks

Below decks, the space tended to be dominated by the huge hangars. British designers were very concerned with safety and the hangars of the

Illustrious class were divided into three sections, 166 feet, 124 feet and 166 feet long, with fire curtains between them. Each was 62 feet wide and 16 feet high. The *Indomitable, Implacable* and *Indefatigable* also had lower hangars, with sections 83 feet and 125 feet long. Light fleet carriers had single hangars, while American-built CVEs had no fire curtains in the first instance. British carriers also had spraying and flooding arrangements for use in case of fire and were lighted with three rows of 500-watt bulbs, corresponding with the rows of stowed aircraft. Their decks had arrangements for securing aircraft in bad weather. Aircraft were usually pushed manually into place when stowing them but some carriers had transporters or rail systems to move them sideways, as it was difficult to get the last two or three aircraft into the corners. All this was supervised by the hangar control officer, and by the end of the war there were plans to give him a position 8 feet or 10 feet above the deck

Workshops were situated around the hangars, including shops for engine stripping, cleaning and assembly, aircraft metal working, sparking plug servicing, electrical and instrument repair, and radio and radar repair. Parachutes had to be hung and repacked regularly and a 40-foot table was provided, with a hanging compartment. This was not available on escort carriers, which had to make their own arrangements.

Aviation fuel was stored in compartments low in the ship, forward and aft of the engine room. Ready-use ammunition was kept in small quantities just below the flight deck. Bomb lifts were fitted on larger carriers, and special trolleys were used to transport and load them. Torpedoes were mostly stowed at the ends of hangars.

Aircraft spares were stowed ingeniously to save as much space as possible. The favourite site was suspended from the deck above, between the beams. Engines, wings and even fuselages could be hung there and CVEs could carry the equivalent of six Seafires between the beams. Spare propellers were hung from sides or bulkheads or kept

disassembled. Smaller spare parts were kept on racks aft of the after lift on fleet carriers. In addition, each squadron had a supply of ready-use stores and specific spaces to keep them in.

Offices were needed for the air department of the ship. Apart from the air office near the captain's cabin, the Commander (Flying) was expected to use his cabin as a personal office. The air engineer officer had an office fitted for work on plans, and shared it with the air electrical officer. Each squadron on board also had some space for administrative work, equipped with 'cupboards, racks, notice board, radiator, telephones, desks and chairs for at least three people'.[4]

2 The Personnel of the Fleet Air Arm

Apart from Combined Operations, and Coastal Forces, which had no permanent post-war existence, the Fleet Air Arm was the navy's greatest single growth area during the war. In 1939 it had a few trained pilots and observers but virtually no servicing crews of its own. By September 1944 it had more than 63,000 men and it was the only branch which was still expanding at the end of the war, in preparation for the conflict with Japan.

The Fleet Air Arm Hierarchy

Naval aviation was normally administered by the Fifth Sea Lord, a member of the Board of Admiralty. However, Admiral Sir Frederick Dreyer was appointed Chief of the Naval Air Service in July 1942, because Churchill believed that he would 'bring a fresh mind to bear on these problems'. His seniority meant that he would outrank other members, and he was not able to sit on the Board of Admiralty. This made it difficult for him to get his policies adopted, and he left after six months and the old system resumed.[5]

Under the Fifth Sea Lord were several admirals including those in charge of carrier training and naval air stations. The naval staff also had

divisions dealing with naval warfare, and airfield and carrier requirements. The Fleet Air Arm was established as a separate manning division soon after the naval takeover in 1939, on a par with Chatham, Portsmouth and Plymouth. It would not have been possible to split the highly-specialist personnel between the three existing divisions, and in any case there were no suitable airfields near to Chatham and Plymouth. Instead, the headquarters was established at Lee-on-Solent near Gosport.

At sea, aircraft carriers were nearly always commanded by officers who were not airmen, for there was no supply of senior officers who had flown themselves. This was a problem early in the war when Captain D'Oyly-Hughes of the *Glorious* had very bad relations with his senior aircrew before the ship was lost in 1940. It was not necessarily a disadvantage later, for distinguished captains such as Dennis Boyd of the *Illustrious* and admirals such as Lumley Lister of Operation Pedestal worked with great efficiency and won the respect of their aircrews.

Under the captain was the ship's air staff, who tended to stay on board when the squadrons disembarked in port. It was headed by the Commander (Flying), an experienced pilot, with another commander who had served as an observer. The ship had three or four other officers for technical and staff duties, and warrant officers responsible for stores and to supervise the air mechanics.[6]

Recruitment

It was important for the Fleet Air Arm to establish a strong identity with the public, to prevent all the suitable aircrew candidates being attracted to the RAF. It did this by combining the long-standing prestige of the Royal Navy with the glamour and excitement of

Below left: The shoulder straps of a lieutenant-commander in the RNVR air branch, and his observer's badge.

Below right: Rear-Admiral McGrigor, the Captain and the Commander (Flying) watch fighters landing from the control position of the carrier *Indefatigable* in 1944.

flying. But this did not remove all the problems. An RAF flier knew that he was the centre of attention, part of the elite of the force and instantly recognisable to the public by the winged badge on his breast. In the navy, the ship always came first, and aircrew wore less prominent wings on their sleeves. The navy refused to subvert the normal promotion structure for the sake of its aircrew, and promotion was far slower than in the RAF.

Old boys of public schools, returning to their schools on visits as Midshipmen and Sub-Lieutenants, saw their contemporaries, who had joined the R.A.F., returning as Squadron Leaders and Wing Commanders, a fact which not unnaturally had an adverse effect on recruitment for the Naval Air Arm.[7]

In the RAF, promotion depended almost entirely on leadership in the air, whereas in the navy it depended on vacancies and on the performance of other duties. Up to the rank of wing commander (equivalent to a naval commander) an RAF pilot had very few administrative duties, whereas every naval air officer was expected to take a full part in the running of the squadron.

The Fleet Air Arm's advantage was that it could almost guarantee a commission to pilots and observers, whereas the RAF used an increasing proportion of sergeant aircrew during the war. Public schoolboys tended to expect a commission whatever service they joined, but middle-class boys from the grammar schools were less secure and might be lured to the Fleet Air Arm. But this did not mean that the force was entirely middle class. John Godley, an old Etonian who later inherited the title of Lord Kilbracken, found that four or five of his 16 contemporaries in training were also public school boys, though shy to admit it.[8]

Officers and Rating Aircrew

Originally the Admiralty had envisaged that a large proportion of aircrew would be ratings, just as many RAF aircrew were sergeants during the war. One of the motives for the split with the RAF in 1937 was the desire to train rating pilots and observers, because of the shortage of officers. As late as March 1941, the establishments for Fleet Air Arm squadrons allowed for about a third of pilots in fighter squadrons to be petty officers.[9] But in practice the Admiralty had already found a way of distinguishing air officers from others, by using

the air branch of the RNVR. Its officers wore the well-known wavy stripes with the letter A inside the curl. According to Charles Lamb:

The badge was designed to warn all beholders that the wearer knew nothing about the Navy, or about seamanship or navigation, and could not be expected to answer any question which was not about aviation. In other words, it was the only badge ever worn by a naval officer to indicate that the wearer was not *qualified to do something.*[10]

This allowed the navy to recruit large numbers of pilots and observers direct from civilian life without having to give them a full training as naval officers. It was convenient, because the Admiralty now believed that they needed 'officer-like qualities'. An RAF pilot usually knew the aim of his mission before he left – to intercept a raid, or bomb a city, for example. The situation was naturally more fluid at sea, and the Fleet Air Arm pilot might find an enemy naval force and have to decide whether to engage it, with what weapons and tactics he had, or to wait for help. He might have to direct the battle fleet or its guns onto a target, clearly a job for an officer. As a result, the great majority of pilots and observers were commissioned officers during the war. A few pilots remained as petty officers, either because they had blotted their copybooks during training, or were regarded as unsuitable to become officers. They were mostly confined to second-line duties.

Selection and Early Training

Air crew recruitment was one of the most important tasks of the war. All aircrew were volunteers for a hazardous but glamorous role, and they needed good eyesight and very high medical standards. Their selection took priority over everything else, and a young man could even get out of a reserved civilian occupation if he volunteered successfully for aircrew. The RAF founded the Air Training Corps (ATC) in 1941 to catch candidates young, from the age of 14. It was far more successful than the Sea Cadets sponsored by the Admiralty, but its charter included the recruitment of boys to the Fleet Air Arm as well. Raymond Lygo was in the ATC when he first came across the Fleet Air Arm. 'They were more than just pilots, they were in the Navy, they were part of our great tradition of the sea'.[11]

Above left: Recruits are issued with their flying kit at HMS *St Vincent.*

Above right: British and American trainees walk to their aircraft to begin training at Bunker Hill, Indiana. The aircraft are Boeing Stearman Kaydets.

This painting by Stephen Bone shows the flight deck of an aircraft carrier, probably the escort carrier *Pursuer*. Grumman aircraft are ranged towards the stern, and the flight deck crews are colour coded according to function.

Candidates were selected by interview and stiff medical examination. They were sent to HMS *St Vincent* at Gosport for initial naval training, under the watchful eyes of Chief Petty Officer Wilmott, 'of the yellow fangs and the bloodshot and unremitting eye and a voice like a rusty winch, and Petty Officer Trim who had been twenty years a postman and was not relishing his recall to the colours'.[12] They learned naval discipline in the same way as all new entrants, by foot drill. They were trained in a certain amount of seamanship, for they had to co-operate with ships and report on enemy activities. They also learned about the navigation and the theory of flight before being sent on to flying training. They were also selected, finally, for further training as a pilot or observer.

Pilots

Pre-war Fleet Air Arm pilots were taught to fly at RAF Leuchars in Scotland. Early in the war the RAF trained them in airfields in central England, but an air raid on Luton in 1940 revealed the problems with that. Some training continued further north, but in the meantime a school was set up at Kingston in Ontario, Canada. Even before America entered the war in December 1941 many pilots were trained by the US Navy under the Towers Scheme. In British schools they did their initial training in aircraft such as the De Havilland Tiger Moth and the Miles Magister, during which the first solo, after about 10 hours flying, was a major event.

One taxied out (but with what excruciating care!), took off into wind (but with what concentration!), climbed to 600 feet, made a circuit, and (but with what checkings and re-checkings of trim and flaps, of speed and height!), landed; a series of actions one had performed many times before, and which was not, when all was said and done, very difficult. But oh the terror of it, the unassailable achievement!
First solo- underlined in red![13]

After initial training, pilots went on to more advanced schools, flying trainers such as the North American Harvard, or obsolete aircraft such as the Fairey Battle. According to Hugh Popham, 'We had learnt how to fly an aeroplane; now we had to learn to use it; and so the routine of turns, navigation exercises, precautionary landings, gave way to formation flying, dive bombing and firing practice at a towed target'.[14]

On qualification, pilots were awarded their wings to be worn on the sleeve, though it was done with far less ceremony than in the RAF. They were selected for specific types of aircraft such as fighter, torpedo bomber or reconnaissance. They usually returned to the United Kingdom for further training, as operational flying involved much closer co-operation with the fleet, and learning British rather than American methods. They went to operational training bases such as Crail in Scotland for torpedo bombers, Yeovilton in Somerset for fighters, and Dundee for the amphibians used in ships' flights. Simulators were much used at this stage, including the Torpedo Attack Trainer, which allowed a pilot to practice aiming a torpedo quite realistically. They also had to learn deck landing, practicing on a short runway at RNAS Arbroath then doing their first landings on *Argus*, the world's oldest carrier, in the Firth of Clyde.

Observers

The navy used the term observer to describe the 'back-seaters' in its aircraft. They were equivalent to navigators in the RAF, but in the navy that term was already taken by ship navigators. Furthermore, the observer had many other duties, such as spotting for gunfire, ship recognition and operating the radio and rear guns when a telegraphist air gunner was not carried. In many ways the navy regarded the observer as more important than the pilot. The most intelligent men were often selected for the duty, and they remained eligible to take command of aircraft and squadrons, unlike non-pilot aircrew in the RAF.

Observers, unlike pilots and servicing crews, were almost entirely trained within the navy. After initial training at *St Vincent*, half were sent to Arbroath in Scotland and the others to the more exotic location of Piarco in Trinidad. They were given a good deal of ground training in navigation and meteorology, still in the rating of leading airman and wearing square rig. In the air, their instructors were usually officers who were unhappy at the menial work they had been assigned to.

'And where would we be going today?' 'If you don't mind, Sir, could we please depart over the Seaforth Hotel swimming pool on a course of 095 degrees.' It was always the swimming pool: an imaginary aircraft carrier would 'sail' from that point at a speed of 25 knots on a course of 030 degrees, thus bringing it close to the little port of Stonehaven after an hour, by which time we would have completed a dog leg course over the sea and would attempt to arrive over, or 'intercept' the carrier at the appropriate time and place on the coast. These attempts brooked much sarcastic comment from our pilots. 'Lost again are we? And where would you suggest we go now if we're not to miss lunch?'[15]

Air fitters at work on the engine of a Swordfish on board the *Ark Royal*. RAF men were employed throughout the war.

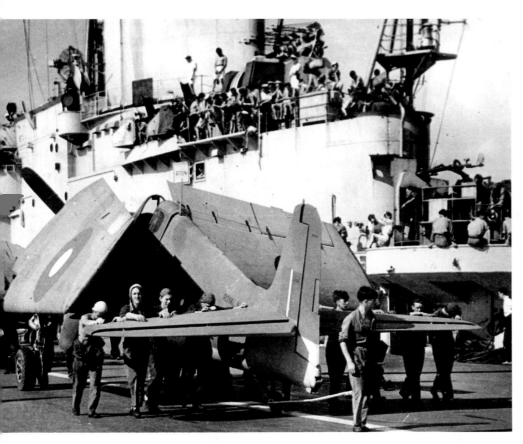

Aircraft handlers moving a Hellcat on the deck of the *Indefatigable* early in 1945.

There was no escape from it all. Your Corsair was in the hangar, one deck up. The flight deck, that torrid arena in the grim game of life and death was two short ladders beyond that. Life was lived, utterly and completely, within a space of about 10,000 yards. Within that area we ate, slept, drank, chatted with our friends, attended church, watched films, took our exercise – and flew, landed or crashed our aircraft.[16]

Clear successes such as Taranto and the *Bismarck* operation were quite rare and most of the Fleet Air Arm's flying was to deter aircraft or submarines.

Crews had to be constantly reminded that 'no contact' did not mean 'no success'. We had absolutely no means of knowing how many times an enemy was forced to dive and therefore rendered less of a threat. Crews had to think positively that 'no contact' very probably could still mean 'attack prevented'.

To compound the problem, the navy had no system of rotating its aircrew and saw leave as 'a cure for everything'. It is not surprising that many naval pilots cracked up under the stress. John Godley, for example, lost his self-confidence after more than a thousand hours on active service. Even in command of a training squadron, he tended to avoid flying, and this fear continued for many years after the war.[17]

Servicing Crews

It is characteristic of aviation that it employs far more people on the surface to maintain the aircraft than in the air. Just after the war it was pointed out that a battleship's 15-inch gun turret needed one officer and 75 men for its fighting crew and four more for maintenance. A 16-plane fighter squadron, whose pilots were all officers in wartime, needed 160 highly specialised men to maintain the aircraft.[18] This was apart from the men who operated the aircraft carrier on which they might be based.

In the case of technical officers, the navy was slightly ahead of the RAF. It was only recently that aircraft had become sophisticated enough to need the constant attention of engineering officers. In the past, servicing was left to mechanics and aircrew had a vested interest in seeing that they did the job properly. The navy founded its air engineer branch on the eve of war, taking in men from the engineering branch for retraining, and some trainee pilots. Officers came from civilian colleges, from civilian industry and from the lower decks of the navy. There were 800 air engineering officers in the Fleet Air Arm by the autumn of 1943, and a need for 2000 was forecast for 1946.

The Fleet Air Arm had no reserve to find skilled men on the outbreak of war. It was able to borrow a few from the RAF, which had serviced the inter-war aircraft. Some remained attached to the Fleet Air Arm for most of the war and served in carriers and other ships, but it proved difficult to persuade them to transfer to naval uniform. Civilians with suitable skills were urgently needed in the expanding aircraft industry. It planned to use personnel on four different levels. At the top were the artificers, equivalent to those employed in the engine room and elsewhere and with chief petty officer status once they were fully trained. It did not intend to skimp

The observer's badge was designed in 1942, in time for a great expansion of numbers. It had two wings, unlike that of the RAF navigator who only had one, but they were clipped short. Like the pilot's badge, it was worn above the braid on the left sleeve.

Telegraphist Air Gunners

The one branch of Fleet Air Arm aircrew which was dominated by ratings was the telegraphist air gunners. They had the basic rank of leading seaman, whereas all RAF aircrew were at least sergeants, one rank higher. They were recruited from men who were physically fit enough to become aircrew, but did not have the education required of pilots and observers. After basic naval training at *Royal Arthur* and *St Vincent*, they went on to RAF Worthy Down to learn the two parts of their trade. Gunnery was mostly with single machine guns on flexible mounts in the rear cockpit, and was taught by firing at a drogue towed by another aircraft, and on simulators. For the telegraphist part, they had to learn Morse code, as radio telephony was not reliable at long ranges.

Flying Stress

The Fleet Air Arm did not suffer the high casualty rate of parts of the RAF such as Bomber Command, but it endured other kinds of stress. Long-range navigation over the sea was very wearing on observers, while all aircrew knew the risks of deck landing from accidents they had witnessed. Aircraft were often poorly adapted to the naval role, and the high accident rate of the Seafire during deck landings was well known. In addition, aircrew had to suffer all the discomforts of shipboard life, including overcrowding, noise and disturbance, heat in the Pacific and movement of the ship in the Atlantic. Unlike RAF aircrew they could not leave the base to forget their problems.

on their training, and selected young men were sent on a three-year course from 1938. The navy disagreed with the RAF about the length of training needed and for once it set up its own course, which moved to Newcastle-under-Lyme after bombing in the south east. Air artificers would specialise in either airframe and engine or ordnance and electrical. They were trained to become highly skilled and responsible men.

As senior electrical and ordnance maintenance rating in Fleet Air Arm, takes charge of workshop and junior maintenance ratings on repair, overhaul, modification and inspection of electrical and ordnance equipment of aircraft. Services, repairs and overhauls electrical gear controlling the firing of guns and cannons, operation of gun turrets, torpedo, bomb, depth charge settings and torpedo dropping gear. Services and installs magentos and ignition harnesses, electric generators, starters, batteries, cameras, oxygen equipment, sights and all aircraft instruments, gauges and dials…[19]

But the first three-year course only started just before the war, and only 300 were trained per year, so it was not the answer to the Fleet Air Arm's short-term needs.

Air fitters were selected from 'men with two and a half years' civilian experience who passed trade test, or from superior types not necessarily possessing any previous trade experience'[20] and trained in a shortened version of the artificers' syllabus. They wore fore-and-aft uniform from the beginning and were rated as leading seamen soon after qualification, with fast promotion to petty officer and chief, or the opportunity to qualify as fully-fledged artificers. They were also more specialised, in either airframe who wore the letter 'A' under their badge, engine (E), electrical (L) or ordnance (O). In addition, radio mechanics were regarded as equivalent though they were not necessarily specialised in air work. Air fitters were trained by the RAF in huge bases, such as Hednesford near Birmingham, where more than 5000 naval personnel were stationed in Autumn 1943. A torpedo bomber squadron was allocated a chief air artificer and eight air artificers in March 1941, along with an electrical and an ordnance artificer; but it was recognised that these rates were in short supply and 'Air Fitters of any rate and appropriate trade may be employed in lieu until the necessary Artificer ratings become available'.[21] Like artificers, air fitters were qualified to sign Form 700 indicating a plane's airworthiness.

Below them were the air mechanics, who wore the square rig of the seaman until promotion to petty officer. An air mechanic was a 'Semi-skilled maintenance rating employed on minor inspection and repair by replacement.'[22] Few had any previous trade experience but they were sent on 18 weeks' technical training under the auspices of the RAF. Like the fitters, they were divided into airframe, engine, electrical and ordnance and wore a two-bladed propeller badge instead of the four blades of the fitter. Air mechanics were needed in large numbers, for by 1944 a squadron was allocated one air mechanic (A) and one (E) for each aircraft with an air mechanic (O) between two and an (L) between three.[23]

For most of the war the navy used general service seamen to manhandle aircraft, in what it regarded as 'unskilled work on the flight deck and in the hangar'. Each squadron had about a dozen

men for its own needs, while for more general purposes a large carrier of the *Illustrious* class was allocated 30 men under a petty officer and four leading seamen. In wartime it was also allowed 30 more reserve and HO men of low status.[24] By 1943 the importance of handling parties was more clearly recognised – if nothing else, they could relieve skilled men from heavy duties. Ninety men were allocated to the handling parties of fleet and light fleet carriers.[25]

3 Aircraft

The Role of Naval Aircraft

The naval aircraft as used in the Second World War was invariably a fixed wing machine, which could land either on the deck of an aircraft carrier or on the sea alongside another warship. In 1942 the Admiralty gave serious consideration to equipping merchant ships with the newly invented helicopter, or its forerunner the autogyro which could land vertically but needed a short take-off run. Detailed plans were produced for flying platforms, but the first Sikorsky Hoverflies only entered service in February 1945.[26]

The Admiralty, unlike the inter-war RAF, was deeply and rightly concerned about the problems of navigating an aircraft over a featureless sea to find its target and then back to a mobile platform. It had moved on from the early 1920s when it insisted on room for a full-sized chart table as used on board ship. This had necessitated a very wide fuselage, and produced some of the ugliest and slowest aircraft ever built. But naval aircraft design, apart from single-seat fighters, still demanded room

Swordfish wings being constructed in an aircraft factory in Yorkshire.

late in the war. It was possible to adopt the 'pusher' layout, perhaps with the engine mounted high above the fuselage and the propeller behind it as in the Walrus, but this was associated with low performance. Other aircraft had the engine in front of the cockpit, tending to restrict the pilot's view forwards and downwards. Purpose-built naval aircraft, such as the Swordfish and the Martlet, often had the cockpit slightly raised to give a better view for deck landing, and perhaps the cockpit level with the leading edge of the wing, as with the Barracuda. Adapted landplanes, such as the Seafire, did not enjoy these advantages.

One problem of the Fleet Air Arm was that its aircraft tended to serve in small numbers aboard ship, which meant that multi-purpose designs were needed. This tended to cause delays in production, so that they were often obsolete before they entered service. In July 1940 the Commander-in-Chief of the Home Fleet complained:

There is no getting away from the fact that the Walrus, the Swordfish and the Skua, which after 10½ months of war are still the main aircraft with which the Fleet Air Arm are equipped, are the slowest aircraft of their respective types in the world.[27]

Out of about a dozen large firms in the British aircraft industry, there were two which specialised in naval aircraft (as distinct from large flying boats operated by the RAF). Blackburn Aircraft of East Yorkshire had produced a whole line of torpedo bombers in the inter-war years, but only two of their aircraft, the unsuccessful Skua and Roc, were in use during the war. The Fairey Aviation Company of Hayes near London, on the other hand, produced many wartime types, including the torpedo bombers Swordfish, Albacore and Barracuda, and the two-seat fighters Fulmar and Firefly. The company's chief designer before the war, Marcel Lobelle, was something of a genius, though unlike R J Mitchell of Spitfire fame he mostly worked with difficult naval specifications and never produced a successful high-performance aircraft. Like all British aircraft firms in wartime, Fairey set up 'shadow factories' in co-operation with other companies and most Swordfish, for example, were built by Blackburn at Leeds.

The jet engine did not reach the Fleet Air Arm until just after the war, and only the Germans used diesels on aircraft, so aero engines were petrol-driven and fell into two main types according to the arrangement of the cylinders and the cooling system. In the radial, the cylinders were arranged in a circle round the crankshaft, so they could be cooled by the airflow. This type was slightly lighter because it did not need a complex cooling system. It was favoured by the Americans and used on their Pratt and Whitney Double Wasp, which had 18 cylinders in two rows, and was used in the Corsair, Martlet and Hellcat, while the Wight Cyclone was used in the Avenger. The radial engine created more drag and restricted the pilot's forward view. The British tended to associate it with low-performance aircraft, and various types of Bristol engine were used in the Swordfish, Gladiator, Albacore and Walrus. For the British had the classic Rolls Royce Merlin, an in-line engine with 12 cylinders arranged in two rows, angled at 60 degrees above the crankshaft. It needed a liquid cooling system using ethylene glycol which transferred the heat to a radiator, but it took up less space in the nose of the aircraft. The Merlin was used in the Fulmar, Sea Hurricane, Seafire and Barracuda, while its successor, the Griffon, was fitted to the later Seafires and the Firefly.

for the observer and his charts and equipment. This was a serious constraint on design. Two- or three-seater aircraft had to be built within the limits of aircraft carrier stowage, and often using the same engines as single-seaters because these were the only ones available.

The Problems of Design

The military aircraft had developed fast in the late 1930s. It had already acquired an aluminium alloy internal structure instead of a wooden one and it now began to use a metal skin as well (though progress in this was not complete by 1939 and the high-performance Hurricane still had partly fabric-covered wings and fuselage in its earlier versions). It now had a retractable undercarriage to reduce drag and an enclosed cockpit. Aero engines had improved in power-weight ratio, fuel consumption and reliability. Most obvious of all, the monoplane was rapidly succeeding the biplane. The older type had relied on two wings for its main strength, with one braced against the other by a system of drag-creating wires. The modern monoplane had its wing braced internally by cantilever construction as in a bridge, giving the potential to fly much faster. The Fleet Air Arm was left behind by these developments at the beginning of the war, for several reasons. Partly it was due to the long-standing rivalry with the RAF, which had often left the naval arm at the end of the queue for the latest technology. Partly it was the changeover to naval control, which could not have come at a worse time in this respect. And partly it was because the navy itself was doubtful if the latest high-performance aircraft could be operated from ships, and to a certain extent questioned the need to do so when anti-aircraft gunnery was believed to be adequate to protect the fleet.

Virtually all naval aircraft were small and therefore single-engined, despite some promising experiments with the De Havilland Mosquito

Because of the very limited space on aircraft carriers, naval aircraft needed folding wings, which placed another constraint on design. If they were biplanes the pivot point on the lower wing had to be directly below that on the upper, which meant that the designer could not stagger the wings as he often did on landplanes. There was more flexibility with monoplanes. They could simply fold upwards, but there might be problems with the height in of the hangar. The Seafire's wing needed a double fold, with the wingtips going in the opposite direction. A successful but complex method, used on many American aircraft, was for the wing to twist and then fold backwards. The high wing of the Barracuda posed other problems, and it needed special handles for the crew to reach it. The folding wing also limited the position of the undercarriage. It had to be wide enough to make the aircraft stable on landing, and the Seafire was a failure in this respect, but if it was situated too far out on the wing, like the Hurricane, it would make it difficult to fold. In the most successful arrangements, the undercarriage either folded directly backwards, or into the fuselage.

Sources of Naval Aircraft

British naval aircraft came from four main sources. First, there were the obsolescent biplanes, the Gladiator, Walrus and Swordfish, which were outclassed by landplanes but performed heroically in service. They filled a gap at the beginning of the war, and were useful against the lower performance aircraft used by the Italians. In areas where there was no real air opposition, such as the middle of the Atlantic, the Swordfish remained useful throughout the war.

Secondly, there were newly-developed monoplanes. They suffered from two problems: they had low priority in development, which often made them obsolete by the time they entered service, and they were often expected to do too many things at once. Thus the Skua fighter dive-bomber and the Barracuda torpedo dive-bomber were disappointing performers.

Thirdly, there were the adapted landplanes. The Fulmar fighter was already obsolete on entering service; the Sea Hurricane and Seafire filled important gaps but they were not easy to adapt to the specialised conditions of carrier warfare.

Fourthly, there were supplies from America. The US Navy had never had to work very closely with the Army Air Force, so it was less tempted to adapt landplanes for naval purposes. It had much greater control over the supply of aircraft than the Fleet Air Arm, so it was able to produce several highly successful designs that were well conceived for carrier operation, some of which were made available to the British. All the Fleet Air Arm's most successful fighters – the Martlet, Hellcat and Corsair – came from America.

Single-Seat Fighters

Of all the advances in aviation in the years before 1939, none was more stunning than the improvement in single-seat fighters. In 1936 the RAF's standard interceptor was the Bristol Bulldog with a top speed of 174 mph per hour and an armament of two machine guns. By 1938 it was beginning to re-equip with the Spitfire, with twice the speed and four times the gun power.

In June 1940 the navy perceived several main roles for its fighters: to destroy enemy aircraft shadowing a fleet or a convoy, to intercept enemy striking forces, to destroy enemy spotter planes in battle and to protect one's own spotters, and escort their own striking forces for an attack. The last aim was recognised as the most difficult, as it needed two-seater aircraft able to navigate across the sea over long ranges.

The Gloster Gladiator was the last biplane fighter used by the RAF, from a line which stretched back to the Grebe of 1923. The Gladiator had a metal frame and metal skin from the cockpit forward, keeping up with the progress in metal construction, but apart from that its only concession to modernity was an armament of four machine guns instead of two, and an enclosed cockpit for the pilot. With a top speed of 245 mph it was 100 mph slower than its monoplane contemporaries. However, it was available in 1939 and the navy had to defend its base at Scapa Flow, which was outside the RAF fighter umbrella. Thirty-eight RAF machines were converted for carrier work by adding an arrester hook, catapult points and an inflatable dinghy stowed under the fuselage. Sixty more were built specially for naval use.

Despite its obsolescence and the small numbers in service, the Sea Gladiator made a surprisingly important contribution to history. It fought in the Norwegian campaign and in the Mediterranean, where it formed the sole fighter defence of the fleet when war with Italy began in 1940. In the same year Sea Gladiators loaned to the RAF gained legendary status as Faith, Hope and Charity in the defence of Malta.

Top: A Swordfish cockpit.

Above: A Fairey Barracuda in flight.

There was a feeling that their machine gun armament was not sufficient against such robust planes as the Focke-Wulf Condor.

The Supermarine Spitfire, designed by R J Mitchell, was one of the most successful, famous and beautiful aircraft of all time, and it was adapted for naval use. This occurred quite late in the development of the Spitfire, which had reached Mark V, with two 20mm cannon, by 1942. About a hundred aircraft were fitted with arrester hooks and went to sea as 'Spitfires (hooked)'. A naval version, with a more effective arrester hook and lashing points, was known as the Seafire IB and entered service with 807 Squadron in June 1942. The first version built from the beginning for naval use was the Mark II, which also had catapult spools. The Mark III added folding wings and it became the most common version, more than 1200 of the 2000 Seafires produced.

The Hurricane dropped from the production lines mid-war, but the development of the Spitfire continued, with the Seafire not far behind. The Seafire Mark XV was the first with the new and more powerful Griffon engine giving a top speed of 384 mph; but it only entered service in May 1945.

Despite being produced by a company called Supermarine, and its descent from a line of seaplanes that won the Schneider Trophy for Britain, it was not easy to adapt the Spitfire to a carrier-based fighter. It was too delicate, its range was too short and its undercarriage was too narrow. It

…was never an aeroplane designed for deck landing and, unless one put it down very carefully, it would either leap back off the deck and go into the barrier, or worse still over the top of the barrier… Or, if it got too slow, it would stall on the approach…or it would drift slightly and break an undercarriage, or it would burst tyres and then have to be towed forward with some difficulty. All this caused the recovery of the Seafire to be a more lengthy process than was the case with Avengers and Hellcats.[29]

The Grumman F4F-3 or Wildcat entered service with the US Navy and Marines in 1937. They were also ordered by Britain, France and Greece and 91 aircraft of the French order, with non-folding wings, were diverted to the Fleet Air Arm on the Fall of France, replacing Sea Gladiators in the defence of Scapa Flow in September 1940. They were known as Martlet Is to the British; the Martlet II, with folding wings and a more powerful engine, went to sea with 802 Squadron in August 1941. With a speed of 300 mph, good manoeuvrability and a reliable Pratt and Whitney Twin Wasp engine, the Martlet II carried a powerful armament of six 0.5-inch guns and was an important addition to the fighting power of the fleet. Later versions, known as the Wildcat to the British as well as the Americans, were 20 mph faster. More than 1100 of them were supplied to the Royal Navy. They were succeeded by the Grumman Hellcat, which reached a speed of 380 mph, and were first used by 800 Squadron in July 1943. More than 1100 of these were supplied and they were mostly used in the Pacific.

The Chance-Vought Corsair was another classic design, one of the fastest carrier-borne aircraft with a speed of up to 415 mph in its later versions. It had an inverted gull wing to allow a shorter undercarriage, but its cockpit was too far aft and the pilot's view was poor on landing. It was initially rejected as a carrier aircraft by the US Navy, but the Fleet Air Arm was able to use them in this role, partly by raising the

The Hawker Hurricane was the RAF's first monoplane fighter, recognisably descended from a line of biplanes produced by the company since the First World War, and still retaining a certain amount of fabric covering in its construction. Though it was more conventional than the Spitfire and had a slightly inferior performance, it was the principal defence of Britain against air attack in 1940. Its introduction to naval service was almost accidental, when some had to be evacuated from Norway by the carrier *Glorious*. This was the first time high-performance modern aircraft had landed on a British carrier, and it opened many eyes in the navy, including the Commander-in-Chief of the Home Fleet.

…we have made a 'false God' of the business of flying on and off a carrier but now that it has been done by four RAF pilots in Gladiators at their first attempt and ten Hurricanes have been flown onto a carrier the matter should be reconsidered.[28]

It was October before serious investigations began into using the Hurricane at sea, and January 1941 before the first 20 modification kits with arrester hooks and catapult spools were ordered. In the meantime, another version, the Sea Hurricane 1A, was fitted with catapult spools only, for it was intended as a single-mission fighter to be catapulted from merchant ships and land in the sea afterwards. The first aircraft carrier version, the Sea Hurricane 1B, was in service by the spring of 1941, filling a major gap in the fleet's defence. All Sea Hurricanes were conversions from landplanes and they never had folding wings, which limited the numbers that could be carried. Around 800 aircraft were converted, but the type was superseded by the Seafire and American fighters from 1942 onwards. As a catapult fighter, Sea Hurricanes were launched only eight times and they shot down seven enemy aircraft for the loss of one pilot.

cockpit to improve the view. The Corsair formed part of the escort for the raid on the *Tirpitz* in 1944 and served in large numbers in the Pacific. Nearly 2000 were delivered to the Fleet Air Arm.

Two-Seat Fighters

The single-seat fighter was adequate to defend the fleet, but the Admiralty felt the need for a two-seater carrying an observer, in order to protect bombers on long-range offensive operations. Fighters could use the bombers' navigation on the way out, but might well become separated in air combat over the target and have to find their own way home. This problem tended to diminish during the war as increasingly effective radio navigation aids were fitted, but a new problem began to emerge. Enemy aircraft could now attack the fleet at night using their radar, and night-fighter defence was essential. RAF experience showed that a second crew member was needed to operate the air interception (AI) radar and the two-seat fighter had a new lease of life.

The Fairey Fulmar was adapted from a light bomber which had already suffered heavy losses in France before it joined the Fleet Air Arm in mid-1940. It had the same Merlin engine as the Spitfire, but in the Fulmar it had to power an aircraft of 11,000 pounds, nearly twice the weight of a Spitfire, so its top speed was only 246 mph. Five hundred and sixty-three entered service, forming a large proportion of the fighter defence of the fleet in the crucial years of 1940–2.

The Americans did not develop the two-seat fighter and several projected British aircraft failed to materialise. The only other two-seat naval fighter was the Fairey Firefly, first used by 1770 Squadron in July 1943. Its performance was rather better with a Rolls Royce Griffon engine and a top speed of 319 mph. By the end of the war 658 of them had been built.

Torpedo Bombers

The torpedo bomber was the most effective offensive weapon of the Fleet Air Arm, and perhaps of the navy as a whole. British naval aircraft launched 609 torpedoes in anger during the war and had a hit rate of 33.5 per cent, compared with 22 per cent for submarines and 16 per cent for destroyers. But torpedo carrying was only one task of a multi-role aircraft, which had to be equipped to spot a ship's gunfire, carry out reconnaissance over wide areas of sea, and later to carry out anti-submarine attack.

The Fairey Swordfish, the Fleet Air Arm's standard aircraft at the beginning of the war, was first flown in 1934 as a multi-purpose aircraft. According to Fleet Air Arm legend: 'when trying it out with all those different loads some wag remarked that, "No housewife on a shopping spree could cram a wider variety of articles into her stringbag." The name stuck and from that moment the pilots always called it the 'Stringbag'.[30]

It was the only biplane to serve in combat throughout the war. It took part in the attack on the Italian fleet at Taranto in 1940 and launched the torpedo that fatally damaged the *Bismarck* in the following year. However, it failed to stop the *Scharnhorst* and *Gneisenau* in their Channel dash in 1942, with heavy losses. Its top speed of only 139 mph did not inhibit it; it found an afterlife in the new MAC ships and escort carriers, as a low-performance anti-submarine aircraft

operating in areas of ocean where enemy air power was weak or non-existent. It also operated from shore bases in this role late in the war.

The Swordfish was a hard act to follow, and its successors were disappointing. The Fairey Albacore introduced an enclosed cockpit and a slightly improved performance but it retained the biplane layout and never supplanted the Swordfish on the production lines. It entered service in March 1940 but did not join aircraft carriers until later in the year. It was phased out by the end of 1943.

Its successor was the Fairey Barracuda, the first British monoplane in the role. It, too, suffered from lack of priority and delays in production and it was built to a very demanding Admiralty Specification issued in 1937. Reconnaissance and navigation were regarded as important, necessitating a high wing and large windows under it for the observer. For the same reason the torpedo was carried externally rather than in a bay like the American Avenger. Very long undercarriage legs were needed, and wing folding was awkward. Huge flaps were used to assist take-off and control the aircraft in its dive-bombing role. The engine planned for it failed and it was underpowered with the Merlin. The tailplane tended to flutter during the trials and was raised to near the top of the fin, adding to the strange appearance. Nevertheless, the Barracuda was quite successful after entering service in January 1943, though it did little actual torpedo bombing. Its most famous success was a dive-bombing attack on the *Tirpitz* in a Norwegian fjord in 1944. Its career in the Pacific war was cut short when it was phased out in favour of American aircraft, to ease supply problems. More than 2000 were built.

The Grumman Avenger was the main American aircraft in the torpedo-bombing role from its introduction in 1942. The first of nearly a thousand Avengers (originally known as the Tarpon to the British) entered service with the Fleet Air Arm at the beginning of 1943. Like the Barracuda, it rarely dropped torpedoes in action, but was used in a bombing role, often from escort carriers. It was a monoplane with a long enclosed cockpit with room for the pilot, observer and a telegraphist air gunner operating a rear turret.

A cutaway view of the Supermarine Walrus.

Dive Bombers

Though the RAF was scornful of dive-bombing, the navy saw quite early on that it provided a very effective way of hitting a moving target such as a ship. When its specification was issued in 1934, the Blackburn Skua was seen as a very advanced monoplane design, but it fell into a common trap of British naval aircraft design. By August 1939 it was complained that:

Due to the 3½ years which have elapsed since the inception of the design, these aircraft are already obsolescent, although not yet in production. As fighters – for which purpose they are primarily required, they are in My Lords' opinion too slow; being monoplanes their lack of speed is not offset by their manoeuvrability [or rate of?] climb which would be attained by a biplane of comparable speed.[31]

One hundred and ninety Skuas were ordered and they entered service with the *Ark Royal* in 1939. As a fighter it shot down the first German aircraft by the Fleet Air Arm on 25 September 1939. As a dive bomber it sank the cruiser *Königsberg* during the Norwegian campaign, but it was too slow at 225 mph and was phased out of operational service by early 1941.

The American Curtiss Helldiver was highly successful in the Pacific, with the result that the British were only allowed 26 of them, built in Canada, and they saw no operational service. The Albacore and Barracuda had some provision for dive-bombing and the latter aircraft distinguished itself in the role, but the lack of a successful specialised dive bomber remained a gap in the navy's range of weapons.

Floatplanes and Flying Boats

Large ships, cruisers and battleships could carry a small number of aircraft for reconnaissance and spotting for gunfire. They could be catapulted into the air and then land on the sea. Wheeled aircraft such as the Swordfish could be converted for this by adding floats, at some cost in performance, while specially-designed flying boats had a hull for landing on water.

The Fairey Seafox floatplane was a typical pre-war biplane, one of a series produced by the company. Small numbers served with the fleet and the Seafox had its greatest moment when one was launched from *Ajax* to spot for the fire of three cruisers in the Battle of the River Plate in 1939. It remained in service until July 1943.

The Supermarine Walrus was a flying boat, one of the classic aircraft of the war. It was produced by the same company as the Spitfire and Seafire, by the same designer. It, too, had its origin in machines designed to win the Schneider Trophy, but it is difficult to imagine two more different aircraft. The Walrus was a biplane with a hull for landing in the water, an engine mounted well above the fuselage to keep it clear of the sea, and a 'pusher' layout in which the engine was ahead of the propeller. It also had retractable wheels to land conventionally. It had a crew of three, with a pilot in a rather angular enclosed cockpit, an observer buried deep in the fuselage but with access to a position ahead of the pilot for a forward-firing gun; and a telegraphist just behind the observer with his own rear-firing gun aft in the fuselage. The Walrus had a top speed of 135 mph and a cruising speed of 40 mph less. Its good flying qualities made it popular.

Turns are made with slow dignity, as one might imagine a 60-seater bus on a smooth road. Pipes and tobacco come out, the transparent panel is slid over our heads, but the side window is left open for fresh air. The engine makes a steady roar

but sufficiently above and behind us to make conversation possible. On a rough day the Walrus behaves more like a cow than a bus – a very friendly cow however.[32]

About 500 served with the Fleet Air Arm before catapult flights were disbanded from 1944. The Walrus continued in use with the RAF for air-sea rescue.

The Supermarine Sea Otter was intended as a replacement for the Walrus. It had a tractor rather than a pusher layout for the propeller and was generally more streamlined, but by the time it came into service in 1944, the original concept was obsolete.

Training and Second-Line Aircraft

Since the Fleet Air Arm was essentially an operator of shipboard aircraft, it was rather restricted in its use of support aircraft. Most of its pilot training was carried out by the RAF or the Canadian authorities, and for its operational training it tended to use the actual aircraft that crews would fly in service. For training observers and air gunners it used a variety of aircraft, including the multi-seat Airspeed Oxford and De Havilland Dominie, and the smaller American Stimson Reliant. Another training role was the target tug for anti-aircraft fire. The Boulton-Paul Defiant, a failed RAF fighter, was used by many fleet requirement units. Another approach was to use a radio-controlled drone. The Queen Bee was a version of the De Havilland Tiger Moth trainer, used on both landplane and floatplane versions. The latter could be catapulted from ships of the fleet and landed after exercise.

The Fleet Air Arm had a variety of small transport aircraft for communication work. These included the British biplane the De Havilland Dominie and monoplane Airspeed Envoy, as well as the American monoplane the Beech Expediter. The Fleet Air Arm used small numbers of twin-engined RAF types such as the Bristol Beaufighter, Vickers Wellington and De Havilland Mosquito for training and shore-based photo reconnaissance.

Weapons

Operational naval aircraft carried guns, mostly for self-defence. Guns on flexible mountings were operated by the telegraphist air gunners and usually consisted of a single light machine gun firing aft, except for the Walrus which could also mount one firing forward. The short-lived Blackburn Roc, a variant of the Skua, carried a four-gun turret as used on RAF bombers. The Grumman Avenger was more successful with its turret mounting a single .5 calibre gun, with a .3 calibre weapon below.

Apart from that, naval aircraft had forward-firing guns aimed by pointing the aircraft. Early British-built aircraft had .303 machine guns, from the single one carried by the Swordfish to the eight-gun mountings of the Fulmar and Sea Hurricane. American aircraft such as the Martlet introduced the more powerful .5-inch gun, and the Seafire and later versions of the Sea Hurricane brought in 20mm cannon with its exploding shell.

The standard air-launched torpedo was 18 inches in diameter, compared with 21 inches for a normal ship-launched one. The Mark XII in service at the beginning of the war weighed 1548 pounds – less than half a shipboard torpedo – and had a range of 1500 yards at 40 knots. A later version, the Mark XV, had a range of 2500 yards at the same speed.

Depth charges and mines were generally too heavy to be used by shipborne aircraft, though depth charges were used by Coastal Command, and mines were laid by Bomber Command. Naval aircraft could carry a variety of bombs, although of course not the huge ones developed by the RAF in the war. Probably the most successful ones were those of 500 and 1000 pounds carried by Barracudas in the attack on the *Tirpitz* in 1943. Unguided rockets proved a very effective way of attacking surfaced U-boats after their introduction in 1943 and many Swordfish operating from escort carriers or shore bases were fitted to carry them in two racks of four. The standard rocket was just over 6 feet long and had a warhead of 60 pounds.

4 Aircraft Techniques and Tactics

Much of Fleet Air Arm flying was similar to that of the RAF and other aerial services, but there were many techniques that had to be specially learned: flying off and landing from aircraft carriers and ships, navigating over a featureless sea and in torpedo and dive bomber attack on ships, for example. The differences began when aircraft were made ready for flight on the crowded decks and hangars of a carrier.

Deck Take-off

During operations, aircraft were kept in several states of readiness on the deck and in the hangars of a carrier. On Stand-By, they were ranged in a position for take-off. This meant that the aircraft required were set out on the after part of the deck, leaving the forward part clear for the first take-off run. The engines warmed up and the aircrew were briefed but not necessarily in the aircraft. At Readiness, they were at 10 minutes notice for launching, with the engines warmed and the flight leaders ready for a final briefing. If Available, they were in the hangar ready to be ranged. If on Stand-Off, they were at 30 minutes notice to be ranged, and if Released, at two hours notice.

Although aircraft could be launched from carrier decks by catapult, it was a slow process and it was far more common to turn the carrier into the wind for both take-off and landing – in the Home Fleet in 1943, this was regarded as having the relative wind 10 degrees on the port bow. By the *Air Fighting Instructions*, flying might begin while the carrier was still turning and was still 20 degrees off the wind.[33] A carrier would hoist the appropriate flag five minutes before turning. The admiral could decide whether to turn the whole fleet into the wind, or just the carrier in question, which would then have to catch up at the end of flying operations.[34] When launching a large formation, the *Fighting Instructions* of 1942 suggested an interval of 15 seconds between planes, although the *Illustrious* claimed 10 to 13 seconds in December 1940.[35]

The take-off usually began towards the stern of the flight deck.

The flight deck officer waves his little flag around his head to tell me to wind the engine up to full revolutions. Hold it for a moment. Then down with the

flag, off brakes and away. Don't seem to be going very fast when the deck runs out, but with a 30 knot wind the take off speed relative to the ship was only 60 knots. Over the bows. Hand ready on the undercarriage retraction lever. Better to have the wheels up if you don't make it. Gentle turn to starboard, no point in being run over by the ship if you do go in.[36]

Aircraft were usually launched in sub-flights of three, with the leader of each formation taking off first. Those in the air would fly back and forwards at 1000 feet over the intended course of the flight until all were in the air and the formation was assembled.

Deck Landing

Desk landing was the defining skill of the aircraft carrier pilot. The pilot was guided down by the deck landing control officer, generally known as the batsman because of his main tools. His signals were mandatory.

I picked up Lieutenant McQueen quite early, a little doll-like figure with his arms comfortingly held horizontal. Intense concentration and instant response to his every movement. Initially it all seemed in slow motion, then things happened in a rush. Suddenly the ship materialised all around me, the batsman gave the cut, the plane thumped on to the deck, the hook caught a wire and held. I was on. … Crewmen were jumping out of the cat walks on both sides of the flight deck, giving signals. Brakes on, to stop the plane rolling back with the wind over the deck. Brakes off, to let it go again to disengage the hook from the wire. Retract arrester hook. Flaps up, brakes off, so that the flight deck party can push the plane back to the after end of the flight deck.

Aircraft parked on the flight deck of the *Indomitable* in 1943.

superstructure and turned into the wind, while its ends were extended to give a suitable take-off run. The Type D was mounted in a fixed position across the upper deck in capital ships and large cruisers. Both types were powered by a cordite charge through a system of gearing. The aircraft was mounted on a trolley and run back along rails to the downwind position. A launch often gathered a large crowd. The acceleration was intense and the crew had to be well strapped in, but a Walrus, for example, reached its flying speed before the end of the run and was automatically released from the trolley at the end.

Where possible landings were planned in smooth water, either in the shelter of a harbour or fjord, or in smooth water at sea. When this was not possible, the 'slick' technique was used. The ship began with the wind about 60 degrees over its stern and began to turn slowly through about 20 degrees, so that a patch of smooth water known as the slick was created, in which the aircraft would land. Whatever the type of landing, the aircraft would motor up to the ship, preferably on the leeward side. The telegraphist air gunner climbed precariously to the upper wing and prepared the slings. On reaching the ship, the aircraft was hoisted on board.

Navigation

The Fleet Air Arm navigator/observer had special difficulties. He often had to find his way over a featureless sea, and return to a platform which might have moved many miles since he left it. Of course the Royal Navy had vast experience in sea navigation, and unlike the RAF it never underestimated the difficulties, but there were two main differences in the air. Movement was much faster and course was very much affected by the wind, which was far harder to predict than tides and currents in the sea. But navigation was especially important. If an enemy force was seen, its position had to be reported accurately.

The observer was trained in astral navigation and carried a sextant for taking sun and star sights, but this was only useful on longer flights and when visibility was clear. Mostly he worked by dead reckoning.

I check the time of departure, fix the position of the ship at that time and from there start my plot marking with my estimated position at six minute intervals (At 95 knots ground speed we travel 9.5 miles in six minutes – it is easy to make one minute sub-divisions by eye).

I check the air speed, then the course on one of my compasses. I glance behind and there is no sign of the ship we have just left. Too late to take a back bearing to check our track. It is time to find a wind.[38]

Meteorology was part of an observer's training and its importance soon became clear.

The early weeks were spent more in the class-room than in the air. It had never occurred to me to wonder how one set off from an aircraft carrier, flew in all directions, blown by unforeseen winds, and arrived back to whatever spot in the ocean the carrier might have sailed to in the meantime.[39]

Weather forecasts were rarely accurate enough and the observer had to use the Four Point Windfinding Procedure. A smoke float was dropped into the sea from one of the bomb racks and the pilot steered away from it, then on a compass course towards it, allowing the observer to measure

---

Above: A Wildcat taking off from the *Formidable* during operations off North Africa in November 1942.

Opposite: Batsman's signals, as established by Admiralty Fleet Order in 1941.

1. Correct approach.
2. Go higher.
3. Go lower.
4. Go round again.
5. Throttle back and land.
6. Go to starboard.
7. Go to port.
8. Too fast.

If the pilot should miss all the arrester wires, he would hit the safety barrier, which was a great asset. It was kept up as each aircraft landed, then lowered to allow the plane to pass forward as the next one came down. Landing could take place much more quickly without taking the aircraft down to the hangar one by one. Aircraft could be 'parked' forward on the deck until there was time to take them below.

Crashes on landing were quite common, and the captain of the *Illustrious* lamented 'the number of excrescences upon which an aircraft can become attached – viz. 4.5" directors, pom-pom mountings, aircraft cranes, etc'.[37] A crane was supplied to remove the wreckage as quickly as possible and allow landing to continue, but it was not strong enough to lift a Fulmar. *Illustrious's* captain recommended tractors and derricks. Aircraft often fell over the side on attempting to land, and a destroyer was detailed to stand by to rescue the pilot.

After landing the pilot was expected to fill in the appropriate form, as described in the Fleet Air Arm's most famous song.

In the Royal Air Force, a landing's OK
If the pilot gets out and can still walk away.
But in the Fleet Air Arm the prospect is grim,
It's bloody hard luck if the pilot can't swim.
[Chorus] Cracking show, I'm alive,
But I've still got to render an A25.

Operating from Battleships and Cruisers

The techniques used by battleships and cruisers for launching and recovering their amphibian aircraft were very different from those of carriers. Ships with narrow beam had the Type E catapult of girder construction, which was fitted on a turntable high in the

how far the aircraft was blown off course. It was time-consuming, but leaders of formations were urged to carry it out as the group assembled. They were to pass the information to other crews, so that in the event of separation they would be able to find their way to the target, or home.

If navigation was unsuccessful in finding the way back, an aircraft carrier could use its radio and radar to direct them in, though in an operational area it would be very reluctant to break radio silence to do this. A better alternative was the large radio beacon fitted on major carriers. When hoisted up the mast for operations, it rotated through 360 degrees sending out a narrow-beam signal. The radio in each aircraft was tuned to this and could home in on it.

Reconnaissance and Spotting

A reconnaissance might be ordered over a specified geographical area, or an area in relation to the fleet such as a sector of 70 degrees in front of it. It demanded good navigation and the observer was expected to plot the aircraft's position every 20 minutes, as there might not be time to do it once the enemy was sighted. For night searches, parachute flares might be used for illumination. On finding a submarine, a reconnaissance aircraft would normally attack it immediately if at all possible, as it was likely to dive. If it was a surface ship he would have to be very careful about his identification, especially of merchant vessels whose characteristics were less easy to classify. If the target was definitely an enemy he might shadow it. The reconnaissance aircraft would provide the commanders with information on enemy movements, and perhaps direct a striking force on him. By 1944, with the increased use of radar, even night shadowing was possible, although it imposed a strain and if possible the aircraft was relieved every two hours.[40]

The pre-war navy placed great importance in spotting the fall of shot for the guns of a battleship or cruiser. A Fairey Seafox was indeed launched with great difficulty during the *Graf Spee* action. There were problems with its communication and it had no effect on the fighting, though it did report the enemy's movements as *Graf Spee* left harbour to be scuttled. After that, aerial spotting had almost no effect in battle.

Defence of the Fleet

By September 1941 carrier officers were aware that a 'standing patrol' was necessary above the fleet in areas where enemy action was at all possible – 'The rate of climb of the fighters in use (Fulmars) is insufficient to enable them to take off from the deck and climb to the required height in the time taken by enemy aircraft from the point of first detection by Type 279 [radar]'. The patrol had to be at least sufficient to deal with an enemy reconnaissance aircraft, and was at a height of 12,000 feet or more.[41] In the British Pacific Fleet, Raymond Lygo found that the Combat Air Patrol was not the most exciting form of flying.

To be perfectly honest, it was fairly boring in 887 to be patrolling at 30,000 feet for an hour at a time (our total endurance being one hour forty minutes from take off to landing), and seeing nothing but your wingman or your flight companions as we solemnly patrolled and countered at the end of each patrol line back and forth over the fleet.[42]

Fighter tactics were generally adapted from RAF practice, with modifications to suit naval conditions. The *Naval Air Fighting Instructions* of 1942–3 allowed for flexibility.

Fighter tactics are constantly changing and it is not intended to cramp individual squadron commanders in any way, as it is highly desirable that they should use their own initiative to devise formations and tactics to meet local needs and conditions.[43]

A fighter attack was divided into three stages: the tactical approach, which began the moment the enemy was sighted; close combat which began when he was within range, even if fire had not necessarily been opened; and the break away after the combat ceased. Surprise was considered a great advantage in air fighting, but this conflicted with the overriding need in naval air warfare to engage the enemy quickly before he reached the fleet. Therefore, it was rarely possible to use the sun, clouds or enemy blind spots to attack unexpectedly. In the attack, three main groups of manoeuvre were recommended. Sugar was used by a flight or a single aircraft to attack a single enemy aircraft from astern. The Queenie or Double Queenie was used to attack the outer aircraft of an enemy formation from the quarter. In Harry, one flight or section made a head-on attack on any aircraft of a formation.

Fighter pilots avoided an attack on the bomber from dead astern, as that gave an easy shot to the tail gunner. The quarter attack was more popular but also difficult.

…some pilots took to it almost immediately. They were those who could judge speeds of approach, angles off and 'curves of pursuit', by using eyesight and the equally marvellous computer in their brains to arrive at 250 yards from the target, with an overtaking speed of about 50 miles an hour and an angle off of about 30 degrees. They would then have about three seconds of firing time as they closed the range from 250 to 100 yards. During this time, their front guns would fire off about 500 bullets, 10 per cent of which should, if correctly aimed, hit something vital.[44]

In order to get maximum protection from air attacks that might come at any time and from several directions, the navy's fighter direction system was developed over the years. By the end of the war each carrier had an aircraft direction room in its island superstructure. Specialist fighter direction officers were being trained – they required

…high personal qualities since the safety of the Fleet at sea depends on an accurate interpretation of enemy aircraft and will on occasions rest entirely in the hand of the F.D.O. Officers recommended should, therefore, possess a quick, clear-thinking brain, be able to react to new situations, be able to do mental arithmetic accurately and have a clear voice for microphones.[45]

On duty, the flight direction officer (FDO) sat in an elevated position near the centre of the room. In a flagship he would have the fleet FDO sitting next to him. The main display plot was in a circular table surrounded by several plotters, with interceptor plots on either side, supervised by deputy FDOs who directed individual formations. Information came in from many sources, including the ship's own radar and that of other ships, and reports of pilots in the air. They were in constant control of the carrier's fighters, and any other fighters that might be placed under their command.[46]

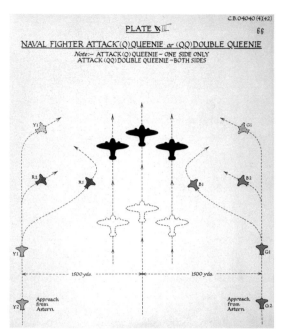

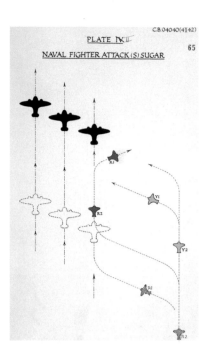

Right: Types of attack by naval fighters.

Opposite above: Fairey Albacores flying in Vic formations.

Opposite below: A Swordfish dropping a torpedo in an exercise before the war.

Attack

The torpedo turned out to be the most effective weapon of the Fleet Air Arm, especially early in the war. It flourished in the early stages of the Mediterranean campaign.

Operations were carried out against ships in harbour at Taranto and Tobruk and against an Italian convoy South of Malta and during the battle of Matapan, all of which met with considerable success. This phase ended when the arrival of German aircraft in the Mediterranean with the loss of Crete prohibited the use of carriers in the Eastern Mediterranean.[47]

According to John Kilbracken who piloted a Swordfish for most of the war, 'Dropping a torpedo is an extremely tricky business'. Aircraft approached at a suitable height then dived to sea level when in close range of the target, hoping to spend not more than 10 seconds at that level. Dropping height was between 50 and 70 feet and an ideal range was around 1000 yards. The pilot had to allow for the movement of the target and usually aimed slightly ahead: '…over a minute will elapse, if you drop from 1000 yards, before the tin-fish reaches its target, which will meantime have travelled 800 yards if steaming at 20 knots. So you must judge her speed, aim the right distance ahead and guess what avoiding action she may take'.[48] By 1942, night attacks were possible when led by an aircraft carrying ASV radar. The leader ordered the striking force to break formation and dive to the attack, then dropped flares in a pre-determined position to guide them in.[49]

Fleet Air Arm pilots learned dive-bombing from the Americans. The pilot flew the plane over the target until it disappeared between the leading edge of the wing and the fuselage. He then cut the throttle, opened the dive brakes and went into an almost vertical attitude, though the aircraft was actually moving about 70 degrees to the vertical. He was in the dive for about 10 seconds, during which the speed did not greatly increase due to the brakes. He used the gunsight to aim the bomb and had to take care to pull out at the right moment, as he could not see the altimeter directly.[50] Dive-bombing was accurate against the static target of the *Tirpitz* in 1943, though the relatively light bombs did not penetrate the armoured target.

Attacking formations had to expect enemy opposition, and they were not always optimistic about overcoming it. Their guns were not expected to be much use against enemy aircraft, so they had to rely on a suitable

formation, fighter defence and evasive action. The formation was based on the 'Vic' or sub-flight of three aircraft in a V formation, or multiples of such a group. Fighters might escort fast aircraft such as the Avenger, though they no longer used a weaving motion as the pilots had to observe their leader instead of looking out for the enemy. Biplanes such as the Swordfish and Albacore were too slow to be escorted closely and the fighters could only provide a general cover in the area. Torpedo planes, though slow, were mostly highly manoeuvrable. This could be used to put off an enemy fighter pilot, who had to aim off for deflection. The standard plan was for the leader of each sub-flight to go into an undulating motion, while the other two went into corkscrews. The senior observer of the group controlled the motion.

Carrier Groups

British aircraft carrier doctrine developed slowly and fragmentarily, with very different experiences in the Atlantic, Mediterranean and Arctic before they reached the Pacific. It was rare to operate carriers in groups in the early stages, because they were in short supply due to the loss of the *Glorious* and *Courageous* and the slow building of others. Even when several could be assembled, they were often of different generations and capabilities, as when the *Argus, Eagle* and *Indomitable* escorted a Malta convoy in August 1942.

The invasion of Salerno in September 1943 was the first to be heavily opposed, and it was at the limit of land-based fighter range. Two fleet carriers and four escort carriers were employed in the British force, enough to give some lessons for the future. They operated 20 to 30 miles offshore. The maximum size of a group was considered to be six carriers, though four was more common. In larger forces, groups of four would operate 10 miles apart. A circular screen round the force was provided by 10 destroyers 3000 yards apart, though it was considered that 14 would have been a more suitable number. After some consideration, Admiral Vian decided to control the battle from a cruiser rather than a carrier, and another cruiser operated close inshore to give fighter direction with its radar. In cruising formation, the large ships, including the carriers, would form a line, with a large force of destroyers ahead and smaller numbers on the flanks. When operating aircraft, a square formation was considered suitable for a fleet of four carriers, 10 cables or 2000 yards apart, so that they did not interfere with one another's flying operations. Unless they were short of fuel, the destroyers would turn into the wind with the carriers during flying off.[51]

Servicing

Maintenance of naval aircraft poses many difficulties which are not present on land. It is done in very confined spaces on a moving platform, often when the weather is too rough to allow flying. Each carrier has to be self-contained, and it is not possible to bring in expertise or spare parts at short notice. Naval aircraft have to endure harsh conditions at sea and in deck landing, and often have to switch rapidly from one role to another.

Nevertheless, the Fleet Air Arm tended to follow RAF procedures in its servicing. There were four main types of aircraft inspection, undertaken before a flight; daily; a 'minor' inspection after every 40 hours flying or quarterly, whichever was the shorter; and a major inspection after every eight minor ones. Work was recorded on RAF Form 700, which was signed by the pilot before a flight. In the early stages of the war the record was eventually transferred to a logbook and the forms destroyed. However, this was dropped to save paper and the forms were retained as the only record. 'The Form 700 became extremely dirty and almost unreadable, and there were never enough "boxes" on the log cards to carry the necessary information'.[52]

Each aircraft type had a handbook which outlined maintenance procedures. The Supermarine Walrus could land on water and it was necessary to drain the hull and clean weeds off it occasionally. There was a detailed schedule for oiling, with some parts lubricated by anti-freezing oil, some by anti-freezing grease and some by grease gun. The Barracuda was a monoplane with cantilever wings, so it was not necessary to adjust the bracing wires as on a biplane. When unfolding the wings for flight, the training edge was set hydraulically but there was a complex four-part procedure for setting the rest. The flying controls had to be checked regularly and there were detailed instructions on how to fill and drain the fuel tanks in the wings.[53]

In the early stages of the war servicing was carried out on a squadron basis. This had the advantage of keeping a strong link between the air and servicing crews, but it tended to be wasteful of specialist manpower. Only a few of the most specialised ratings belonged to the crew of each carrier, and the rest were attached to the squadrons and landed, with stores and equipment, when the carrier entered harbour and the aircraft transferred to a shore base. There was a gradual movement from 'the pre-war sub-division on a rigid and parochial squadron system' to a 'wholly centralised sausage-machine of the closing stages of the war in the Pacific'. Shore bases evolved in different ways, but Henstridge and Yeovilton developed centralised systems, which, it was claimed, saved 20 per cent in manpower.[54]

Naval aircraft were precious at the beginning of the war and crews worked hard to maintain and repair them. Later it became increasingly common to ditch damaged sub-assemblies or even complete aircraft over the side, for space was very limited on a carrier and there was neither time nor room for a long-term repair. This was perhaps encouraged by the practice of keeping disassembled aircraft suspended

under the deckheads of hangars. In other cases, aircraft were sent to shore bases for major repair or maintenance. This was reasonably practicable in home waters, but in the longer distances of the Pacific it was necessary to employ specialist maintenance carriers, such as the *Unicorn*, for longer and heavier jobs.

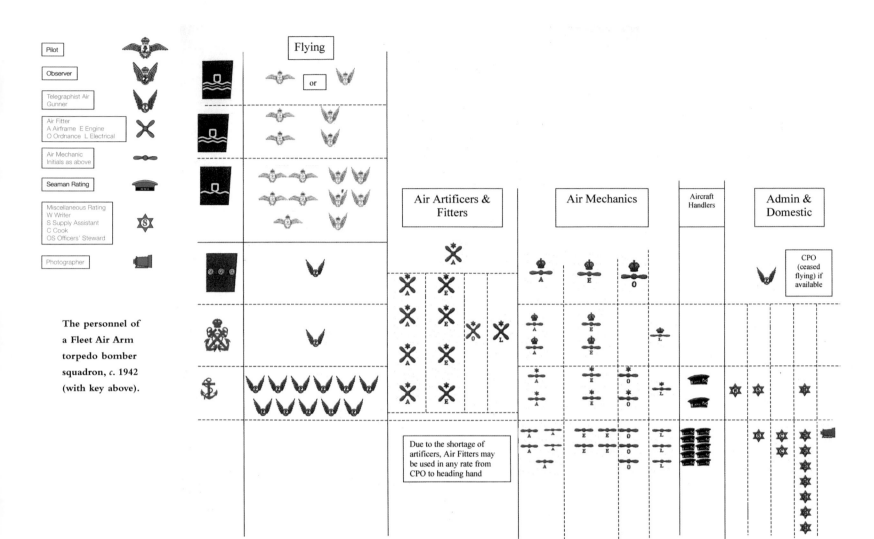

The personnel of a Fleet Air Arm torpedo bomber squadron, *c.* 1942 (with key above).

5 Squadrons and Bases

The Squadron

Until 1933 the basic Fleet Air Arm unit was the flight of about six aircraft. After that it was the squadron, which was based on the equivalent formation in the RAF. To avoid confusion with the RAF, Fleet Air Arm squadrons were numbered from 700 upwards, with numbers up to 749 for catapult squadrons, 750 to 799 for training units, 800 to 809 and 870 to 899 to single-seat fighters with groups in between for torpedo bombers, spotter reconnaissance squadrons and so on. A typical squadron had a dozen aircraft of the same type, divided into two flights, as in the RAF, but in practice there were many variations on this. At one extreme was a squadron such as no. 700, which supplied cruisers and battleships with catapult aircraft like the Walrus. It had 65 aircraft when it was formed in 1940, and it never came together as a unit. Another variation was a squadron formed to serve in a small aircraft carrier with more than one type of aircraft; for example 824 Squadron had nine Swordfish and six Sea Hurricanes on *Striker* in late 1943.[55] Later it was decided that all the aircraft of the same type on a larger carrier should be in the same squadron. Thus in 1944, 887 Squadron had 24 Seafires on *Implacable*.[56]

Normally a squadron was led by a lieutenant-commander, the equivalent of the RAF rank of squadron leader. Since the navy was always reluctant to use temporary rank, some were commanded by senior lieutenants. In theory, the flight commanders were to be lieutenants, but sometimes there was a shortage of senior men and a squadron commander might find himself with only sub-lieutenants under him. Squadron officers usually had subsidiary duties besides flying, for example in adminstration, engineering or in organising sport or entertainment. The telegraphist air gunners usually had a petty officer or chief as their leader.

The squadron also had about up to 90 ratings and marines for non-flying duties. By the establishment of March 1941, a 12-aircraft torpedo-bomber squadron had a chief petty officer airman who had ceased flying and was employed in administrative duties, although it was recognised that these were in very short supply and for the moment general service ratings would be used instead. It had seven air artificers, one ordnance and one electrical artificer, with six CPO and PO air mechanics (A) and (E). They led a group of 14 air mechanics, and alongside them were six air mechanics (O) and the same number of electrical mechanics, each led by a CPO. In all there were 43 technical ratings, making up exactly half the ratings of the squadron. There were three writers and supply assistants for administration, plus a few more men for parachute packing and 'regulating' or disciplinary work, and a photographer. The Royal Marines provided a dozen men to act as wardroom attendants and batsmen for the officers, though these were gradually replaced by members of the steward branch.[57] Many of the technical staff were seconded from the RAF, especially early in the war before the Fleet Air Arm had time to train its own technicians.

A Fleet Air Arm squadron led a nomadic life, even by naval or air force standards. In 1943 alone, for example, 824 Squadron had 15 changes of base, serving in three different carriers and seven different shore bases, including five spells in Machrihanish in Scotland.[58]

Royal Naval Air Stations

The aim of the Fleet Air Arm was to operate ship-based aircraft, so in theory it had no need for operational land aerodromes, although this was modified in practice. The force took over the air defence of Scapa Flow for a time, and contributed to the defence of Malta. In addition, the Fleet Air Arm needed airfields for several other purposes. Initial and intermediate flying training was largely conducted by the RAF and overseas, but operational training in specialised tasks such as torpedo bombing and deck landing needed bases. The Fleet Air Arm had second-line bases for aircraft maintenance and storage. And aircraft carriers usually disembarked their planes when in port, so that they could continue with training and take part in operations. Airfields were needed near all the main fleet bases.

In May 1939, the Fleet Air Arm took over five airfields from the RAF. Four were too close to the threat of bombing and too far from the operational fleet bases to be of much use in the war that was to follow. Lee-on-Solent was near the dockyard at Portsmouth and would form the headquarters of the Fleet Air Arm. Ford in Sussex was used for training observers and later air photographers, and for reserve aircraft storage. Worth Down in Hampshire was the air gunners school and school of aircraft maintenance. Eastleigh in Kent was used only for ground training. Donibristle in Fife was close to the dockyard at Rosyth but it had only two runways at a narrow angle to each other and on a very restricted site, so it was useful only as a second-line base.

Other stations were taken over from the RAF during the war, including Stretton in Cheshire and Eglinton in Northern Ireland. The navy also launched a building programme, its largest civil engineering project during the war. By mid-1944 there were 24 Royal Naval Air Stations in commission at home, plus seven not yet commissioned and 15 that were satellites to other stations and were quaintly known in naval parlance as 'tenders'.[59]

Each station was named as a ship in conventional naval fashion, and the authorities had to dig deep into the ornithology textbooks to find names such as HMS *Sanderling* for Abbotsinch (now Glasgow Airport), HMS *Shrike* at Maydown and *Godwit* at Hinstock. The title of HMS *Fledgling*, the Wrens training centre at Millmeece, showed some imagination. A Royal Naval Air Station was usually commanded by a captain, not necessarily a flier himself. In February 1944 HMS *Landrail* at Machrihanish had 80 officers on its staff, not including those of visiting squadrons, and 38 WRNS officers. Besides the usual accountants, chaplains, dentists, doctors and storekeepers, their duties included training in fighter direction, air gunnery, dive-bombing and operating link trainers, flying control and air engineering.

The Sites

Since the skies of southern England were soon filled with aircraft both friendly and hostile, most Fleet Air Arm bases were located elsewhere. Some were situated near the main wartime fleet bases. Machrihanish on the Kintyre peninsula served the many warships in the Firth of Clyde, while Hatston and Twatt on Orkney were close to Scapa Flow. Many more were in Scotland, including those at Crail and Arbroath on the east coast. Some were in north-west England, such as Inskip in Lancashire, and Maydown and Eglinton were in Northern Ireland.

Hugh Popham called Machrihanish the 'Crewe Junction of the Fleet Air Arm', which was not a compliment, as he considered it

…the uniquely desolate station you arrive at in the early hours of the morning, wait about at, and finally depart from, none the wiser. …supremely it is the place of departure, from which one flies to deck-land within the shadow of Ailsa Craig; an uneasy, queasy staging-point, a bowl in the hills full of the filthiest weather in the British Isles.[60]

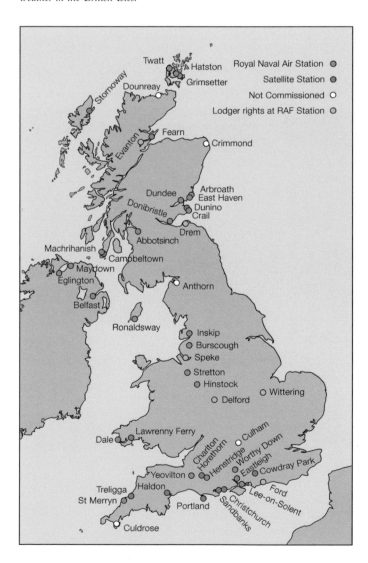

Naval air stations in the United Kingdom, mid-1944.

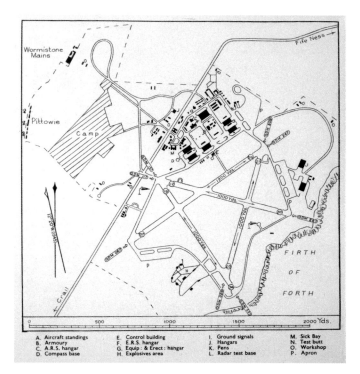

Right: The naval air station at Crail in Fife.

Below: RNAS Twatt in Orkney in the winter of 1945.

A. Aircraft standings
B. Armoury
C. A.R.S. hangar
D. Compass base
E. Control building
F. E.R.S. hangar
G. Equip: & Erect: hangar
H. Explosives area
I. Ground signals
J. Hangars
K. Pens
L. Radar test base
M. Sick Bay
N. Test butt
O. Workshop
P. Apron

The Layout of an Air Station

Air stations taken over from the RAF had the conventional layout of the service, with three runways each 50 yards wide. New naval air stations mostly had four runways. One suggested explanation was that naval pilots, trained to land on carriers which were steaming into the wind, were not used to dealing with cross winds. Another was that winds were strong and highly variable on many of the sites allocated to the navy.

The runways were arranged in various forms, always crossing one another but not all at the same point, to avoid the possibility of a single bomb putting the station out of action. Henstridge in Somerset was the only airfield in Britain with five runways, apart from Arbroath which had a very short one for deck landing training.

Since the navy did not operate heavy aircraft or have to scramble fighters several at a time, runways at the new naval air stations were only 30 feet wide. They were made of tarmac rather than concrete which was cheaper but less durable. HMS *Nightjar* in Lancashire had four runways 30 yards wide, between 1000 and 1200 yards long. They were angled at roughly 45 degrees to one another to give the maximum range of landing possibilities. A perimeter track ran round the airfield for the movement of aircraft, and most had 'frying pan' shaped areas, each to hold a single aircraft when dispersed against enemy air attack. A few airfields were far simpler than that. Dunino, a satellite of Crail in Fife, was simply a grass field a few miles from the main aerodrome.

The Buildings

The pre-war RAF tried to maintain certain architectural standards in its buildings, even during its expansion period of the late 1930s. This was not possible for either the navy or the RAF in wartime, so most Royal Naval Air Stations relied heavily on temporary accommodation. The most common was the Nissen hut, invented by a colonel in the Canadian army in 1915. Sleeping accommodation at HMS *Blackcap* at Stretton in Cheshire was divided into three sites. No. 1 as used for 196 officers and men of the ship's company while the others held 70 and 162 officers and men of visiting squadrons. Sixteen ratings were accommodated in each Nissen hut, or eight petty officers. Four officers lived in a hut, with two in a cabin at each end, while lieutenant-commanders and above might have a single cabin. They were heated by slow combustion stoves, but the medical officer considered that they might become rather stuffy at night when blackout boards were in place. Drainage was into the station's own sewage farm, but only No. 1 site had proper WCs – the others had latrine buckets that were emptied each night.[61]

Various types of hangars were used in Royal Naval Air Stations. Some were large in order to put maintenance facilities under the smallest number of roofs. The navy preferred to concentrate certain maintenance activities in large hangars and each station had an Electrical Repair Shop and an Aircraft Repair Shop, each with a large, specially fitted hangar. Others were very small to disperse the aircraft and protect against attack. The navy had a slight advantage here, in that its aircraft could fold their wings to take up less space. Lee-on-Solent,

an ex-RAF station, had six different types of hangar including two large Type Cs from the inter-war period. Three of them were of the very common Bellman type, which had been designed by an engineer of the Directorate of Works to be erected in a hurry by unskilled labour. The 12 Mains hangars were relatively small sheds where dispersed aircraft could be serviced. The station also had several old seaplane sheds, although these were no longer used. Arbroath had six Bellmans, two smaller versions known as half Bellmans, six sheds for aircraft with folded wings and 76 more sheds along the roads up to 5 miles away for dispersing aircraft.

One distinctive naval feature was the control tower. It was usually larger than a RAF tower, three stories high with an air watch office on the roof. It included garages for a crash tender and an ambulance on the ground floor, with offices for the meteorological staff, the air intelligence officer and RAF liaison on the first floor, and wireless telegraphy and the air traffic controller on the second floor.

Eventually the RAF followed with larger control towers.

Airfields needed many other facilities. Arbroath had storage for 72,000 gallons of aviation fuel, 77 tons of bombs and more than a million rounds of machine gun ammunition. It had building for fuel tenders, bomber and gun turret training and all the trappings of a military post, for example the guard room at the entrance and the officers' mess. The operations block was partly underground and there were more domestic buildings such as latrines and laundries, a church which served several denominations, a squash court and a gymnasium which could be converted into a concert hall.[62]

Crete was lost in May 1941, largely due to the Germans capturing the aerodrome at Maleme. After that there was increasing concern about airfield defence against both bombers and paratroopers, which fell on the Royal Marines. In May 1944 they had static units at several Royal Naval Air Stations on the east and south coasts, each consisting of three officers and 110 other ranks.[63]

A Seafire at RNAS Yeovilton in September 1943.

PART IX

The Submarine Service

1 The Organisation of the Submarine Service

Submarines were not as central to British strategy in this period as they were to Germany, or indeed to the post-war British navy. As Admiral Binney noted in 1943: 'Formerly submarines were considered to be the weapon of the weaker power at sea. Their use by the British Empire was visualised chiefly for scouting and lookout, during and after a fleet action, and for anti-submarine purposes'.[1] The Submarine Service was quite small, with only 9090 ratings in September 1944,[2] though it was growing with the launching of new boats – 3226 men were allocated to 50 new submarines planned for 1943. One of the difficulties of the service, as Admiral Binney noted, was that when a submarine was lost the crew was almost certainly lost with it.[3] Despite its small size the service was highly publicised, and it was one of the few to take the war direct to the enemy in the middle years of the war, so its prestige was high. In *Send Down a Dove*, a novel based on Charles MacHardy's own experience, a young ordinary seaman spent his leave in Glasgow. 'He'd roamed the centre of the city, going from bar to bar and getting a kick out of it as he noticed people's eyes lighting up with respect as they caught sight of his H.M. Submarines cap tally. He wished he could also have worn his white roll-neck submarine jersey, but they were forbidden ashore.'[4]

Flag Officer (Submarines)

The Submarine Service was a relatively compact organisation even in wartime, with its own drafting arrangements and traditions, and a very high morale engendered by success in action, public esteem and good relations between officers and men. Men were drafted from the peacetime headquarters at Fort Blockhouse at Gosport in the entrance to Portsmouth harbour. The headquarters of the Flag Officer Submarines was also at Gosport in peacetime, but in 1939 it was moved north. As well as administering the Submarine Service the admiral was expected to take operational command of boats in home waters, and it was intended to give good liaison with Commander-in-Chief Home Fleet at Rosyth and with a nearby Coastal Command headquarters. Sir Max Horton, who took command in January 1940, was unhappy with the distance from London and wrote:

…the Flag Officer Submarines, at the time being in command of all S/Ms in home waters under C-in-C Home Fleet, sought an HQ in the Firth of Forth with his operational staff, while the material side remained at Portsmouth – thus the majority of papers had to make a nice little trip of 450 miles each way to be minuted, and the personal touch between the two divisions of the staff was almost completely lost. Further, the Flag Officer Submarines, as personal adviser

to the Admiralty on S/Ms, was quite out of touch, and his own operational supervision was not so good.

I couldn't bear such an organisation, despite the golf course just outside the front door, and decided to move nearer the Admiralty where one would be at least in close personal touch with at least one of my masters.[5]

Horton had his way and moved to a block of flats in London.

The Flotillas

British submarines were organised in flotillas, usually based on a depot ship, except at Dundee where local buildings and a dock were converted. Submarines were not expected to provide full technical and administrative support from their own resources, and the depot ship was supposed to give better living and recreational facilities for crews between patrols. Depot ship crews were not counted as part of the Submarine Service, which was restricted to those who actually went to sea in the boats. Each flotilla was headed by a Captain (Submarines) who directed operations. In June 1939 the *Forth*, headquarters of the Second Flotilla,

Opposite: The wardroom of an S class submarine, with a view towards the crew's quarters, painted by Stephen Bone.

Below: Submarines alongside their depot ship in the Holy Loch in April 1942.

Lieutenant-Commander Wanklyn (with beard) and the officers of the *Upholder*.

had a commander as second-in-command, a paymaster lieutenant as secretary, with engineer and paymaster commanders in charge of their various departments, and specialist gunnery, torpedo, anti-submarine and navigating lieutenants, with a warrant shipwright, telegraphist electrician, schoolmaster, writer and supply officer. In all there were 28 officers and warrant officers and a crew of more than 1100 men.

When the war began all the operational British submarines in home waters were sent to flotillas at Blyth and Harwich on the east coast of England, and at Rosyth and Dundee. After the Fall of France there was a move to the west and several depot ships moved to the Holy Loch and Rothesay Bay in the Firth of Clyde. The *Cyclops* in the Holy Loch was the headquarters of the Seventh Flotilla, providing submarines for anti-submarine and Combined Operations training. Later the *Forth* was ordered to go to the Holy Loch, while the *Cyclops* would move to Rothesay. By August 1940 the submarine force in Scotland consisted of the *Forth* and *White Bear* in the Holy Loch with the Second Flotilla, consisting of eight boats, mostly of the modern T class; the Seventh Flotilla at Rothesay with *Cyclops* and 15 older boats, mostly used for training; and the Third Flotilla at Rosyth with the *Titania* and five modern boats, mostly of the S class. The submarine base at Harwich was closed on 5 November and only the Ninth Flotilla remained on the North Sea coast, operating from Dundee.

Submarines from the Clyde ranged widely over the seas, from Norway to the Mediterranean. Their main task was to patrol the waters of the Bay of Biscay and attack enemy ships and submarines using the bases there.

The ward-room of HMS Forth *had been nicknamed the Globetrotters' Club. Submariners sprawled in the deep chairs and swapped yarns with officers from other boats with whom they had shared depth charges in the Mediterranean. Men back from the Bay of Biscay discussed tactics and experiences with friends down from the Arctic Circle or across from Norway. There was great talk about Norway.*[6]

In the Mediterranean, the First Flotilla operated from Alexandria and the famous Tenth Flotilla was formed at Malta in September 1940, mainly with U class boats, and operated with great success against Axis supply lines to North Africa.

Submarine Captains

A submarine captain was in a unique position during an attack. Captains of other ships relied heavily on gunnery or torpedo officers

to direct the armament, but the submarine captain was the only one with a clear view of the target through his periscope, and he aimed largely by directing the boat onto it. He had a truly independent command, for submarines usually operated singly or occasionally in pairs, and had little radio contact with higher authority.

Submarine captains had invariably served some time as junior officers in submarines, but one of the lures of the service was that command might come very early. Submarines were usually commanded by lieutenant-commanders, some by lieutenants. In 1940 the average seniority of lieutenants qualifying for command was 5½ to 6½ years. This had dropped to 1¼ to two years by the first half of 1943.[7]

Potential submarine commanders set out from *Cyclops* on practical courses, which soon became known as 'Perishers'. One theory suggests that this was simply a corruption of the 'Periscope' Course, another that they were so-called because failure would bar the candidate from any further appointments in the Submarine Service. Edward Young describes his experiences in 1943. After two weeks shore training at Gosport near Portsmouth he was billeted in a local hotel but had to catch a boat to the *Cyclops* every morning before breakfast. He describes his first mock attack.

I swept [the periscope] rapidly across the green shores of Bute…swung past the entrances to Loch Fyne and Kilbrannan Sound, and continued along the steep shores of Arran, which rose nearly three thousand feet to the imposing summit of Goat Fell. The only ship in sight apart from the target was an outward-bound merchantman steaming down the main channel of the Firth of Clyde. Completing the circle I came back once more to the target, still going away to the eastward. … Waiting for the White Bear *to turn, I felt horribly uncertain of myself. … In as calm a voice as I could muster, I gave the order, 'attack team close up.'*

After three hard weeks Young was sent to Scapa to practice with modern warships and conducted a mock attack on the battleship *King George V*. He passed, as did all but one of his course, and was appointed to command an old submarine operating as a 'clockwork mouse' from Rothesay.[8]

Officers

A typical submarine had three junior seaman officers. The first lieutenant was responsible for administration, as in all small ships, and also for the trim of the boat when going into action. The second lieutenant was in charge of navigation, with a junior lieutenant in charge of gunnery and the torpedoes. All could stand a watch on the surface or underwater. In peacetime, submarine officers formed a separate group within the seaman branch, bearing the letters 'SM' against their names in the *Navy List*. At the beginning of the war the officers were nearly all regulars, though one RNR officer was now included in each course of 16 men. Edward Young was one of the first three RNVR officers to volunteer for submarines from *King Alfred* in 1940, and after that increasing numbers entered the service. By 1941 half of submarine officers were reservists, and a proportion of 60 per cent was accepted for the peak year of 1943. Most, but not all officers were volunteers – in September 1942, all RNR officers were shown as having entered willingly, compared with 69 per cent RN and 63 per cent RNVR.[9] Most RNVR officers were new to the Submarine Service after they were commissioned, for very few CW candidates served in submarines, in which there was no room for any kind of spare man.

The engineer officer was the only type of specialist to be found in large numbers in the wardrooms of the Submarine Service and one was allocated to each seagoing boat, except the smaller U class. He might be a lieutenant or a commissioned or warrant engineer and was responsible mainly for the diesel engines and all the pumping machinery which was vital in a submarine. He could also stand a watch when necessary, for the concept of 'one man one job' did not apply in submarines. Submarine engineer officers had to be able to operate on their own, to be adaptable and to use their initiative in an emergency. Many newly appointed warrant officers were drafted in against their will, because in 1940 it was necessary 'to obtain Engineer Officers at any price and regardless of previous submarine experience'.[10] Most non-volunteers, it was said, soon became reconciled to the 'smell of diesel fuel'. A hundred and nineteen engineer officers were trained for submarines during the war, of which 37 were regular RN lieutenants, 15 were temporary lieutenants and 56 were in the commissioned and warrant grades.

The Drafting of Ratings

The wartime growth of the Submarine Service was quite slow compared with some branches of the navy. It expanded from 2909 regular rating and 474 mobilised reservists at the beginning of the war, to a peak of just over 9000 officers and men at the peak in September 1944 – rather less than threefold. However, casualties were high and 306 officers and 2567 men were lost, while many others had to be drafted out because of medical problems. More than 10,000 ratings were trained for the service during the course of the war, with a peak of 3221 in 1943.[11] The service had high prestige and offered certain advantages such as comradeship and extra pay at the rate of 9d to 3s 9d (3.75p to 18.75p) per day, but it was not to everyone's taste, and it demanded high medical standards.

There were many difficulties in recruiting adequate numbers of ratings. It was established that the service was to have absolute priority from the manning depots, but that was not enough. From 1940 HO men were accepted, and it was no longer necessary to have a non-substantive rating to join the service. It became increasingly common to draft men in against their will, and in 1941 some men at HMS *Dolphin* refused duty because they had not volunteered. It was established that 'service in the Royal Navy involved a liability for any kind of naval service, and this included service in submarines'.[12] It was discovered that some men were committing offences to have themselves debarred from submarines, until the rules were changed to prevent this. More positively, lectures were held and Admiralty Fleet Orders publicised the advantages of the service.

Submarine Training

Submarine training started with six weeks' theoretical instruction in the Portsmouth depot, HMS *Dolphin*, during which, according to Arthur P Dickison, 'We never set foot in a submarine'. Instead they spent two weeks being drilled in escape procedure, and the use of the Davis Submerged Escape Apparatus in a mock submarine compartment at the bottom of a tank.

The experience of that water slowly rising up my body made the hairs stand up on the back of my neck and when it touched my chin I was not far off

The crew of the *Storm* celebrate their return from the Far East in April 1945.

panicking. One of my fellow trainees did. When the water was at chin height the pressure was equalised and the instructor opened the hatch at the top of the chamber. In turn, we ducked under a canvas tube and floated up to the surface, 100 feet above. On subsequent runs most of us achieved more confidence but sadly there were two of the class who could not get it right'.[13]

On average about 12 per cent failed the course, often at this stage.[14]

The class then went on to the submarine base at Blyth in Northumberland for two months' practical training in an old seagoing submarine. Then they went to the Seventh Flotilla based in HMS *Cyclops* off Rothesay in the Firth of Clyde, where they trained in old boats left over from the First World War. It was noted that men from the Chatham port division had a far higher failure rate than those from Portsmouth and Plymouth – 39 per cent compared with 12.5 and 10 per cent. The authorities rejected any suggestion that 'town-bred' men from the London area were inferior, as men were spread evenly through the home ports during the war.[15]

The final stage was the working up of a boat with its operational crew in the Firth of Clyde. In 1942 Arthur P Dickison of HM Submarine *Safari* found that: 'The two months based at HMS FORTH were hectic. We were in and out of the Holy Loch and into the Clyde Estuary on trials and exercise to bring the boat and her crew up to operational standard'.[16] In 1944 Arthur Hezlet took the *Trenchant* through her working up and trials. Guns were fired at sleeve targets – long pieces of fabric towed by aircraft – and sub-calibre firing was carried out against surface targets. One of the biggest tasks was torpedo attack.

Practice in making attacks was done in three stages. In every submarine base and depot ship there was a Submarine Attack Teacher in which, with model ships and a rotating 'submarine' with a short periscope, attacks could be simulated. The second stage was to make dummy attacks at sea in the submarine, using ships as targets. The third stage was the same as the second but practice torpedoes were fitted with dummy heads set to run under the target. The complexity of these exercises could be varied from an attack when the target steered a straight course at moderate speed to others when the target zig-zagged or used high speed. Finally exercises could be carried out with escorts round the target. In Trenchant we carried out some of all of these exercises during a period of some three weeks.[17]

The Ratings

Each submarine had a Chief ERA under the engineer officer, with an average of 15 to 18 years' service in submarines in 1941. A T class boat had four more ERAs with service ranging from 11 years to three patrols. The senior one was the 'outside ERA' who took responsibility for the equipment outside the engine room, such as pumps, compressors, periscopes and steering gear. The others stood watch in the engine room. ERAs were in particularly short supply and were drafted in from many sources including general service, newly trained men and civilian industry. A T class boat had a chief stoker, several stoker petty officers, four or five leading stokers and about a dozen stokers.

The coxswain, usually a chief petty officer, was the senior rating on any boat. As well as his disciplinary and administrative functions he was expected to have knowledge of first aid, as there was no medical specialist on board. Most men had a non-substantive rate as torpedomen, gunners, submarine detectors and signallers.

New ratings were added to the complements over the years, after careful consideration of the effect they would have on space on board – cooks and anti-aircraft gunners in 1942, Asdic and radar ratings in 1943, and then telegraphist and sick berth ratings for ships serving on the very long patrols in eastern waters.[18] The standard crew of a T class boat was five officers and 55 men, but that tended to increase over the years.

Life at Sea

Able Seaman Sydney Hart describes his first patrol from HMS *Forth* in the early months of the war.

A narrow gang plank ran down to Triad's *slippery deck; we scrambled down it in single file, passed our kits through a small hatch, and so squeezed ourselves into our ship's interior. The atmosphere was warm and stuffy. The lights seemed dull and listless by contrast with the late autumn sunset outside. So we went through the engine-room into the small mess, cramped as it normally was, and now, with our steaming bags all over the place, looking like any London Tube at the rush hour. For us this state of affairs would be normal for three weeks duration or thereabouts.*

The submariner had to endure many discomforts as well as overcrowding. The smell of diesel oil permeated the boat and everyone's clothes and person. It was only possible to use the toilet at certain times and with permission, as the waste was discharged directly into the sea rather than into a holding tank. Hot meals were not available when the boat was submerged in the daytime, as the galley used too much battery power.

The Submarine Service was essentially nocturnal. There were three watches, but only bunks for two thirds of the men, so they had to 'hot-bunk'. Men off duty were encouraged to rest while the boat was submerged, to save air. The submarine surfaced at night to charge its batteries and make more progress to its destination with the much higher speed of its diesel engines. These were fully manned under the Chief ERA, the wireless operators worked hard receiving messages, the radar and Asdic operators took up their stations, the cook prepared hot meals and the rest of the crew acted as lookouts in rotation, in case of sudden air attack.

The boat submerged at dawn and the employment pattern changed. Some of the seamen worked as helmsmen and on the hydroplanes and an ERA operated the blowing and flooding panels. An Asdic operator provided the main contact with the outside world and the electrician operated the motors. According to Arthur Hezlet, 'Conditions when submerged on patrol were really quite good. It was silent and there was no motion caused by the sea. Normally the air-conditioning system was operating and it felt cool and pleasant'.[19]

2 Submarines

In the 1920s and early 30s the British had experimented with submarines in various roles: with high surface speed to operate in conjunction with the main fleet, as monitors with heavy guns for shore bombardment, as a submersible cruiser which could engage any ship up to a destroyer, and even as aircraft carriers. All these had proved failures, and had led to several well-publicised disasters. By 1939 the Royal Navy saw the submarine as a vessel mainly for attack by torpedo, with light guns for self-defence. It could launch mines through its torpedo tubes, though that was quite rare, and most offensive minelaying was now done by aircraft. Submarines were also to prove useful for clandestine operations – landing agents or commandos on an enemy held coast. But the main role was torpedo attack. Since the British had long tried to ban submarine attacks on merchant shipping, they planned to use their own submarines for attacks on relatively fast warships, so they could fire a salvo of up to 10 torpedoes at once. But in fact this never happened. Their most important victories against large warships were to damage the cruiser *Karlsruhe* in 1940 and force her sinking, and to sink the Japanese cruiser *Ashigara* in 1945. The great majority of attacks were against enemy transports. In the course of the war RN submarines fired 5121 torpedoes in action during 1671 attacks, making an average of three torpedoes per salvo. Of their attacks 776, or 46 per cent, were successful, which was greater than any other type or torpedo attack.[20]

During the First World War British submarines were given numbers such as *H-28*, *L-26* and so on. From 1926 new boats were given names, but this policy was stopped in 1940, probably for security reasons. This infuriated Churchill, and late in 1942, after a string of successes in the Mediterranean, he complained that numbering of boats was insulting to 'the officers and men who risk their lives in these vessels. Not even to give them names is derogatory to their devotion and sacrifice'.[21] He ordered them to be re-instated. Crews were given a certain amount of choice of names, even though the best ones had already been taken up by destroyers and other vessels. Ben Bryant held a discussion in the wardroom of *P-211*.

We fancied ourselves as a hunter and felt that Shikari *would be splendid, but there was still an old destroyer claiming that lovely name. From that we passed to* Safari, *and one and all in the wardroom decided that was the name we should like to have.*[22]

Design and Building

The Submarine Service benefited from its compactness in many ways, and this applied to ship design as much as anything else. There was very close liaison between builders and operators. G W Pamplin was in charge of submarine design up to 1944. Alfred Sims served as a Constructor-Commander on the staff of Sir Max Horton for most of the war and became very close to the submariners and their operations. At the end of the war he took charge of submarine design.[23]

There were relatively few builders of submarines, compared with surface ships. Portsmouth and Devonport built a small number, but Chatham was the only royal dockyard that did much submarine construction. For commercial yards, the Admiralty relied on three firms – Vickers-Armstrong at Barrow-in-Furness and Tyneside, Cammell Laird on the Mersey and Scotts on the Clyde. Submarine production was never a priority in Britain. For the first two years of the war there was a net loss, for the 31 boats built did not compensate for 34 sunk. Production got into its stride later on and peaked between September 1943 and March 1944 when 22 were completed. By this time Cammell Laird alone was launching an S class boat every six weeks, and two were handed over in December 1943 alone. In all 164 submarines were built during the war, compared with 76 lost.

The increased use of welding was one of the great changes introduced in submarine construction during the war. The techniques were still very new in Britain at the war's outset and obviously submarines were very vulnerable in the case of any failure. Early war-built submarines had welded frames and riveted plating. In 1941 new submarines of the S and T classes were ordered to be all-welded. Great care was taken with the process. It was carefully supervised, and tested by X-ray and by pumping high-pressure air inside the hull. The weight saved was used to give thicker hull plating – riveted S class boats could dive to 300 feet, welded ones to 350 feet. The A class went a stage further and introduced pre-fabrication.

The Submarine Hull

The core of any submarine was the pressure hull, which contained all the accommodation and most of the engines and machinery. It was usually cylindrical in section, with constant diameter throughout most of its length. It tapered towards the bow and stern. On a typical British boat it narrowed at the bows but maintained the same height to allow room for torpedo tubes. At the stern it retained a circular section but it gradually reduced in diameter, with the lower part sloped upwards to give space for the propellers to operate.

A submarine needed large tanks which could be filled with water to allow it to submerge. The British tended to favour saddle tanks, huge blisters along either side of the pressure hull. The U class, however, used single tanks which formed part of the pressure hull. Submarines of the period spent a good deal of time on the surface and had a casing over the pressure hull to produce a reasonably flat deck. This could also fill with water when the boat was submerged. The T class and the early U class had a raised bow which contained an extra torpedo tube and could help sea-keeping on the surface in rough weather, but it sometimes made life difficult when submerged. It was not easy to keep level at periscope depth, and the bow was re-designed in later boats. The hull was fitted with hydroplanes fore and aft to control the depth. These could be turned up when the boat was coming alongside in harbour.

Inside the Pressure Hull

The pressure hull of a typical submarine of the T class was divided into six roughly equal compartments along its length, each separated by a watertight bulkhead. Forward in the narrow part of the bow were the six internal torpedo tubes. Next came the torpedo storage compartment, with six reload torpedoes on racks on either side, and a hatch above through which the torpedoes were loaded. The space was also used for crew bunks and mess tables, and there was an escape hatch for emergency use. The third compartment was used for most of the accommodation, with messes for seamen, petty officers and ERAs. Most of the batteries for the electric motors were under this compartment and the control room aft. This area contained the wardroom for the officers, although the captain's cabin was situated just aft in the next compartment, from which the ship was controlled. The two periscopes were in the centre of the control room, and on the port side sat the operators of the hydroplanes and the ERA who controlled the ballast tanks. The steering wheel was just forward of the periscopes. There was a hatch and ladder for access to the conning tower above when on the surface, and a separate one forward to reach the main gun. Aft on the port side were small cabins for wireless and later radar operation and equipment. On the other side was the galley, situated centrally to aid food distribution.

Aft of the fourth watertight bulkhead was the engine room, with a diesel and an electric motor on each side. The last compartment, where the pressure hull began to narrow, contained a cramped stokers mess and the steering machinery of the ship. The after escape hatch was situated there.

The submarine *Seadog* manoeuvres in the Holy Loch in 1942, with *Thunderbolt* in the background.

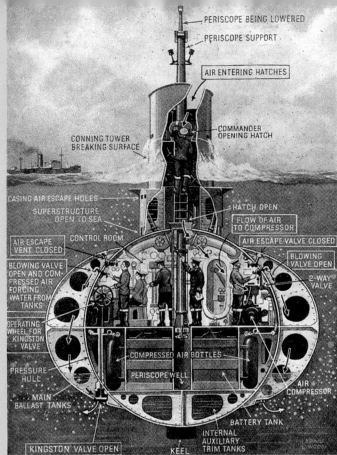

The cross section of a submarine coming to the surface.

Submarines had two propellers, held away from the hull by brackets as in surface ships. The U class boats had a problem with 'singing' propellers, which made a whistling noise that might give the submarine's position away. Tests were carried out in the Admiralty Experimental Works at Haslar and the propellers were given finer edges and higher quality machining.

Submarines used a system of hydraulic telemotors to power the rudder and hydroplanes. Boats could originally be steered directly from the bridge, but this gear was removed from the T class when radar was fitted after 1943, and orders had to be sent down to the control room. To surface, it was necessary to use air to blow the ballast tanks. This was compressed by a machine in the stern, and stored in cylinders in the engine room and wardroom areas.

External Fittings

The conning tower of a submarine gave an elevated position from which the vessel could be directed or 'conned'. At the top of the tower was the bridge where the captain, officer of the watch and lookouts operated on the surface. In 1939 there were experiments with an enclosed bridge or 'cab'. This reduced resistance underwater, but an open bridge was needed to keep a good lookout and the cabs were removed. There was much concern about airflow over bridges but the position of the gun made it difficult to improve it.

A submarine carried two periscopes, usually a high power one with a magnification of 1.5 to six, and a small or attack periscope, which was less easily detectable by enemy lookouts. When not in use both were retracted within fixed tubes protruding above the conning tower. The jumping wire ran forward and aft from these periscope standards, and was used to deflect any anti-submarine nets or mine cables the boat might encounter.

Asdic was fitted to all submarines and was a primary means of detecting targets. The usual model was Type 129, first fitted to *Seawolf* in 1937. It was the first to be designed for fitting to the keel of a submarine, and was placed under the foremost torpedo tubes. It could operate for 'hydrophone effect' when the operator listened

The layout of other classes was not very different. In the smaller U class, the first two compartments had to maintain the same length as the size of the torpedoes was constant, but the accommodation and engine compartments were rather shorter, and the after compartment was not used for accommodation.

A submarine usually had two diesel engines side by side in the after part of the boat. The three ships of the River class of the early 1930s had 10-cylinder engines of 5000 horsepower, but most were much less than that. The prolific S class of 1940 had two eight-cylinder engines of 950 horsepower each. Those of the coastal U class had 400 horsepower, while those of the A class, designed for the Pacific war, had 2150 horsepower. Under the surface a submarine needed electric motors, which were charged up by the diesels while on the surface. The motors themselves were quite small, but large numbers of batteries were needed and these took up much of the space under the decks. Oil fuel was mostly carried under these, in the lowest part of the hull, with larger tanks under the engine room where there were no batteries.

The longitudinal section of a T class submarine.

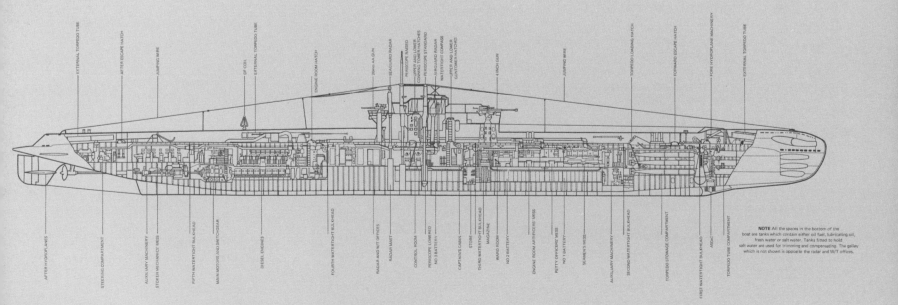

rather than sent out pings. Radar was first fitted to the *Proteus* in 1941 but the service was lukewarm about its value. Type 267W was not ready until late in the war and boats for the Far East were fitted with the American Type SJ.

Armament

Torpedoes were carried inside the pressure hull in the bows of all operational submarines, four in the case of the small U class, six in the S and T classes. British submarines also carried external torpedo tubes, outside the pressure hull. This allowed an increase of armament and the huge 10-torpedo salvo of the T class, but they could not be reloaded at sea, nor could the torpedoes be serviced, so they were always less reliable than those fired from internal tubes. The large salvo of the T class soon proved impracticable, and there was a need for torpedoes which could fire aft as a boat withdrew. From late 1939 the midships external tubes were arranged to fire aft, and an aft-firing external stern tube was fitted.

The British always regarded the gun as the secondary armament of the submarine. According to the original scheme for the T class, 'A gun is the least important of all other Staff Requirements'.[24] The *Submarine Gunnery Manual* of 1943 stated that the gun armament was a 'useful junior partner' to the torpedo, for use against lightly armed enemy ships or for defence against aircraft. But the gun's importance tended to increase as attacks on merchant ships became more common and the problems of air defence increased. Submarine guns made 150 successful attacks on enemy ships up to July 1943, and 30 partially successful.[25] Main guns were upgraded. The 4-inch gun of the T class was gradually improved, while the 4-inch replaced the 3-inch on the S class, and the 3-inch replaced the 12-pounder on the U class. Oerlikon anti-aircraft guns were added to the rear of the conning towers of the S and T classes.

British submarines usually carried their guns high above the surfaced waterline. This did not help stability, but it allowed the gun to be brought into action as the boat was surfacing, and it made it easier to use in rough weather.

Older Submarines

After its foundation in 1901, the Royal Navy's Submarine Service evolved its boat design quite rapidly and by the end of the First World War it had the highly satisfactory 'improved H' class of 423 tons on the surface. The larger boats of the L class were developed from the E class which had been the most successful type during the war. Nine of the H class survived into the Second World War, along with three of the Ls, mostly used for training purposes. These two classes also provided the basis for most subsequent British designs, which were evolutionary rather than revolutionary until after the Second World War.

The first inter-war submarine was the experimental *X-1*, carrying 5.2-inch guns. It was a failure and had the distinction of being the only British warship built after the First World War to be scrapped before the Second. The overseas patrol submarines of the O class, the prototype of which was laid down in 1924, were designed with the long distances of the Pacific in mind. They were adopted by the British

and an enlarged version of 1926 displaced more than 2000 tons submerged. The P and R classes, built in 1929–30, were similar. Their size made them rather unmanoeuvrable and future patrol submarines were smaller.

The River class was designed in 1929, as an attempt to produce a submarine which could keep up with the battle fleet and launch torpedo attacks on an enemy. This had been tried with the steam-powered K class of the First World War, with disastrous results. The Rivers had huge diesel engines of 10,000 horsepower and the impressive speed of nearly 22 knots. Unfortunately it became clear that future battleships would be much faster than that, and the attempt was abandoned. Only three out of a projected 20 Rivers were built.

The New Classes

During the war, British submarine design was to concentrate on three main classes – the large T class, medium S class and the small U class. The only new type to be developed, the A class, was too late to have any effect on the war. The S class had first been conceived in 1930 as replacement

A seaman climbs up the conning tower of an S class submarine, in a painting by Stephen Bone.

218

Top: Checking the
torpedo tubes.

Right: An X-craft
or midget
submarine, with her
commander and
one of the crew
on deck.

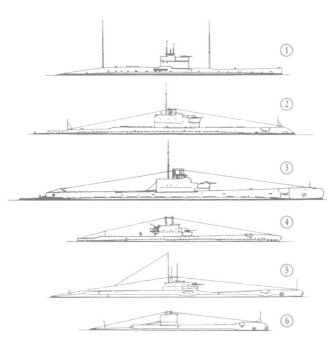

Above: Classes of submarine.
1. L class *L-9* in 1920.
2. O class *Osiris* as completed in 1928.
3. The *Thames* as completed in 1932. She was sunk in 1940.
4. S class *Saga* as completed in 1945.
5. The *Triumph* of the T class in 1939.
6. U class *Undine* in 1937, sunk in 1940.

for the ageing H class, for offensive patrols in home waters and the Mediterranean. They were small compared with the O class and its successors, displacing 730 tons at full load on the surface and 927 submerged. The four original boats were succeeded by a lengthened version with improved internal layout. Eight of these were launched in 1933–5, and in 1939 five more boats of a third version were ordered. At the beginning of the war it was planned to concentrate production on the larger T class and the smaller U class, but the S class was found to be a suitable size for operations in the North Sea and was reintroduced. Fifty of them were built from 1942 onwards, to add to the 12 pre-war boats.

The T class was conceived during the early 1930s, when overall submarine tonnage was limited by the Treaty of London. At 1573 tons submerged, it was smaller than the O and P classes but was expected to undertake a Far East role if necessary. Fifteen had been ordered by the end of 1938. The class suffered a setback when the *Thetis* was lost on trials in Liverpool Bay in 1939, but changes were made and it proved a very successful design, just big enough to undertake most of the navy's tasks in the west. It remained in steady production throughout the war and 51 more were built.

The U Class was originally designed mainly to replace the old H class for training both submarine crews and anti-submarine operators – coastal patrol was seen as a secondary function. The first three were completed in 1938 and were found suitable for operations, so the training role faded into the distance. They soon got priority because of the simplicity of their construction and fitting and 68 were built during the war. They proved very useful in the confined waters of the Mediterranean.

X-Craft

Early in 1942, following the Italian success in Alexandria Harbour, Churchill enquired into British progress with regard to penetrating enemy

ports. Sir Max Horton's idea for a midget submarine was making slow progress, so a 'chariot' or human torpedo was designed as a stopgap, using ideas from captured Italian machines. They were 22 feet 3 inches long and the crew of two sat astride them on the outside, wearing a specially designed diving suit. They could move for five or six hours a speed of 2.5 to 3 knots, and leave a detachable warhead attached to the hull of a target ship. They failed to penetrate the fjord where the *Tirpitz* was moored in 1942, but had some success against Italian warships in the Mediterranean in 1943.

The first X-craft or midget submarine was ready during 1942. It was conceived by Commander Cromwell Varley, who had left the navy between the wars to set up a marine engineering business, and built by Vickers-Armstrong at Barrow. It was 51 feet 4 inches long in its developed version and carried a crew of four in very cramped conditions. Powered by diesel on the surface and electricity underwater, it could make a speed of just over 6 knots surfaced and slightly less underwater. Only after hydroplanes were fitted, and these were operated by hand, as was the rudder. Side charges were dropped under an enemy ship, set to explode up to 16 hours later. Twelve of these X-craft were built. Six took part in an operation against the *Tirpitz* in September 1942, towed to the area behind larger submarines of the S class. Two reached the target and the enemy battleship was damaged but not sunk. A larger version, the XE-craft, was designed for operation in the Pacific, with an air-conditioning plant and better fresh water supply. Twelve of these were built, and in July 1945 two of them attacked ships in Singapore Harbour.

Depot Ships

British submarines rarely used shore bases, and were supplied by depot ships moored in the major ports. This allowed a certain amount of tactical flexibility, as when the main bases shifted to the Firth of Clyde after the Fall of France. The ships came from several sources. The *Bonaventure*,

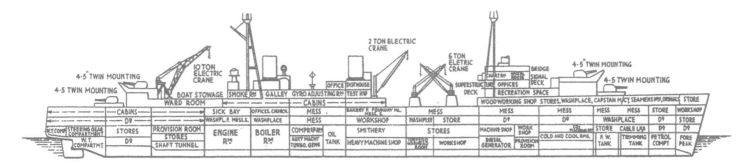

Montclare and *Wolfe* were converted merchant ships; the *Vulcan* had been built as a torpedo boat depot ship well before the First World War; while the *Adamant, Maidstone* and *Forth* were built for the service in 1937–40.

A typical depot ship, such as the purpose-built *Forth* of 1939, was equipped with extensive workshops and machine rooms, a foundry, a periscope repair room, a bakery and cold store for food. Externally it had 6- and 10-ton cranes. Its engines were quite small and its top speed was only 17 knots. It was defended by eight 4.5-inch guns and had a crew of 1167. Submarines would usually moor alongside it when in port. It had reasonably comfortable accommodation for the officers, but the crews' quarters were Spartan to say the least, and depot ships were never popular with the submarine crews.

They are the biggest disgrace in the Navy. I could tell you scores of tales from my own experience. Of submarine crews preferring to go on patrol rather than stay in the depot ships on food fit only for the gash bucket. Of ratings carrying their dinner on the deck and ditching it over the side in front of the Commander (who was probably waiting for his six-course lunch). Of crews sleeping in their boats when off patrol, although that was against the rules, because there was no room to sleep in the depot ship. Submarine crews are far worse off than the depot-ship ratings.[26]

3 Submarine Techniques

Patrol

British submarines began the war by patrolling off Norway to supplement the short range of maritime aircraft, but lost *Oxley* to another British submarine, *Triton*. Patrols in the Heligoland Bight close to Germany were ended early in 1940 due to heavy losses, but those off Norway continued after the German occupation, often in support of Arctic convoys. During the passage of PQ 18, four boats were stationed off the Lofoten Islands and three off northern Norway to give warning of enemy activity. *Storm* was one of three boats allocated areas off North Cape in November 1943, as her captain describes.

When approaching a new patrol billet he must adjust the submarine's speed so as to be able to dive at dawn in the right position, and not so far out to seaward as to waste a day in getting close in. He must choose the best approach when keeping clear of shoal water and for early precise identification of the landfall. ... I was more worried about possibilities [of going aground or drifting out into the Atlantic] than I was of encountering the enemy...[27]

After the Fall of France submarines patrolled the narrow seas against invasion but suffered heavy losses from enemy patrols. They were sent to the Bay of Biscay to patrol against U-boats leaving and returning from missions, but that was only marginally successful as losses balanced

victories. They had further difficulties when the RAF carried out an offensive in the area, and probably sank HM Submarine *Unbeaten* in error. They operated unsuccessfully off Brest against the *Scharnhorst* and *Gneisenau,* and Ben Bryant found that it was 'a boring business, waiting about for the battle-cruisers that did not come out'.[28]

Submarines were far more successful in the Mediterranean, attacking enemy coastal shipping and severely disrupting the supply lines with North Africa. There was little 'remote control' from base. They

...normally did patrols of two or three weeks, or less if they ran out of torpedoes, of which we carried twelve. They would be given an area of sea, but no-one knew their whereabouts in that area unless SOS calls from the enemy were intercepted. Nothing was more infuriating for a C.O. than to be moved just when he had gathered the information to make a strike.[29]

Altogether they sank 286 ships totalling more than a million tons, including 16 submarines. In return, they lost 45 boats.[30]

British submarines also operated in the Far East. Because they were smaller than American boats, they were allocated areas such as the Strait of Malacca. Alistair Mars was not happy about working under American control and found the orders far too prescriptive.

...it was infuriating to a man brought up on the intelligent elasticity of the Royal Navy... A chap was given an area and told to get on with it. He usually had complete freedom of action. He just toured around, fed with the latest information from Intelligence, and sank whatever initiative, prowess, skill and good fortune brought his way.[31]

Diving

Submarines of the age were basically submersibles, far faster on the surface than underwater, forced to spend much of their time on the surface using diesel engines for propulsion and to charge the batteries which supplied the electric motors. Most submarines on patrol stayed on the surface all night and dived when the sun rose. The official manual described the procedure for diving, using a combination of hydrophones and flooded tanks to increase displacement.

Assuming the submarine to be shut off for diving and proceeding ahead on her main motors, the main tanks are flooded, the foremost hydroplanes are put to 'dive helm,' i.e., leading edge down and the after planes also to 'dive helm,' i.e., leading edge up. Both sets of planes are now forcing the submarine to take an angle down by the bow, and as she loses her buoyancy the angle will gradually come on and the vessel start to dive.

When the angle has reached the desired amount, about 4 to 5 degrees, the helm is taken off the hydroplanes and reversed as the submarine nears the depth ordered. This forces the stern down and the bow up and the vessel will return to the horizontal. Large pressure gauges, graduated to show the depth in feet and pressure in lbs. per sq. in., together with large clinometers to indicate the angle of the ship are fitted over the hydroplane controls.

As soon as it is known that the main tanks are full, the main vents are shut, so that the tanks are ready for instant blowing.[32]

Normally this was done with the full crew, but an experienced one could do without disturbing the watch off duty, as Edward Young, for example, was able to do in the *Storm* after months of training.[33]

Crash diving was necessary if any unidentified ship or aircraft was sighted. The captain or officer of the watch on the bridge sounded the alarm Klaxon, and in case it did not work he also shouted 'dive' down the voice pipe. He might order an alteration of course to avoid presenting a broadside to the enemy, or to make it easier to dive in rough seas. It was now very important that every officer and rating did the right thing, or the submarine would be exposed on the surface, or in a very dangerous condition below it. In the control room, the rating on watch vented the tanks and put the hydroplanes to dive until relieved by the duty ERA. The engine room staff disengaged the diesels which could quickly suck the boat dry of air, and put the electric motors to full speed. At the fore end of the boat the planes had to be turned out to operate. The submarine went to 60 feet as the lower hatch and the bridge voice pipe were closed, and the torpedo tubes and Asdic were manned ready for action.[34] A minute was the normal time for a crash dive, measured from the first order to the boat being out of sight, but if the ballast tanks were kept partly filled and the fore hydroplanes turned out, it could be reduced to 30 or 40 seconds.[35]

Underwater

Once underwater, it was the first lieutenant's job to keep the boat in trim, or level in the water. He had to work out in advance how much water was needed in each of the ballast tanks, taking into account the ever-changing state of the boat's fuel, stores and crew. Failure to do this might result in a boat which could not dive at all, or one which would hurtle towards the bottom unless the main tanks were blown. Edward Young was delighted on *Umpire*'s first dive, because 'within two minutes Bannister had caught the trim'.[36] However, some helm was nearly always needed on the hydroplanes to maintain the boat level. The foremost planes were used to keep the depth, the aftermost ones to alter the angle. This was naturally more difficult at slow speed, and depended on co-operation between the hydroplane operators. It was even more difficult in rough weather, and at periscope depth where the effects of a disrupted surface were felt more clearly. To avoid detection it might be necessary to hold a boat stopped, in which case the trim had to be perfect when the motors were turned off. Even then, the bow would probably tend to drop slightly and the crew had to be moved about the ship to compensate. In shallow water a boat might lie on the bottom. Again the trim had to be perfect, and the boat was brought in very slowly in a direction to stem any current.[37]

A submarine would use its hydroplanes to go deeper. The water pressure would reduce its volume and more water was needed in the tanks to compensate for this. It had its risks during a pursuit, for the tanks could be noisy. Submariners were increasingly aware of different density layers underwater, especially in areas such as the entrance to the Baltic where different streams of water met. These could affect the trim but could also be used to confuse pursuers.

Using the Periscope

Submarines were equipped with Asdic, which they mostly used for hydrophone effect rather than give their position away by constant pinging. Apart from that, the periscope was the only contact with the

Track charts of patrols by the submarine *Tuna*. Left: An abortive operation off Norway in November 1941. Right: The Bay of Biscay, December 1940.

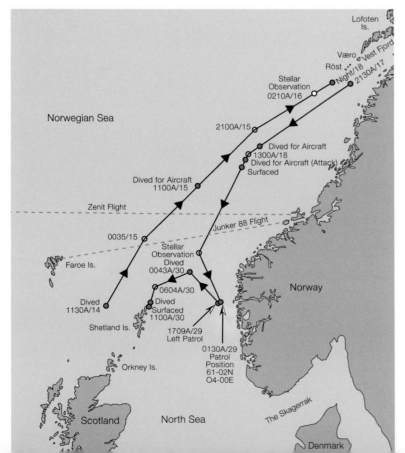

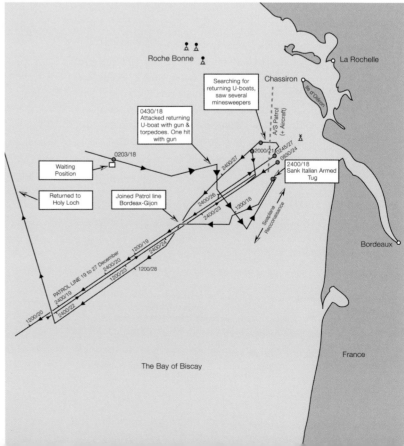

outside world when submerged, but it had to be used sparingly. It could only be employed when the boat was at a relatively shallow depth, which made the submarine vulnerable in itself. A periscope made a wash which could be seen, especially by aircraft, and the instrument itself could be spotted by a sharp lookout even when the boat was stopped. A commander had to develop 'periscope eye', the ability to assess and memorise a situation, to 'keep a running plot of all vessels in the vicinity in your head, memorising ranges, speeds, rates of change of bearing and courses of both yourself and the enemy'[38] in short glances above the surface. He would use the high power periscope for searching and could magnify up to six times to look closer at a suspicious object. The periscope also had a skyscape, which allowed him to search for enemy aircraft, essential before surfacing. He had to be careful about using such a large instrument close to the enemy and in an attack he would switch to a smaller one with much less magnification.

Operation of the periscope required some athleticism and skill, especially during an attack.

At such times the C.O. would be alternating between grovelling on the floorboards and stretching out to his full height. If you add to this gymnastic procedure the effort of training the periscope – you could only see in one direction at a time and so you had to walk round it, sometimes on your knees, pulling the eye-piece with you so as to be able to sweep the horizon – it all mounted up to quite a strenuous operation physically.[39]

Surfacing

Submarines usually surfaced at nightfall unless they were in the presence of the enemy, to charge their batteries and make much faster progress to their destination. A T class boat, for example, could make less than 9 knots underwater and only for a limited period of time. On the surface it could travel at 15 knots for up to 15,000 miles. Edward Young describes the action of surfacing.

'Blow all main ballast!' Valves on the control panel were opened one after the other, and there came a roar of air under high pressure expanding into the ballast tanks. The hydroplane operators turned their wheels to put the planes to 'rise.' The ship took a slight bow-up angle as we began moving towards the surface. Number One stood at the foot of the ladder calling the changing depths to the Captain, who was now releasing the clips on the upper hatch; 'Twenty-five feet, sir… Twenty feet, sir… Fifteen feet, sir…' and then the Captain thrust his arm up and swung the hatch open. A few drops of water came down the tower, the signalman and the look-outs clambered up and as the Channel swell took charge of us I had to hang on to one of the periscope wires to steady myself. 'Stop blowing,' shouted Number One above the din of the roaring air. Orders came down the voice-pipe from the Captain, and soon the diesels were thundering and the ship began to gather speed.[40]

Torpedo Attack

At night, a submarine would usually attack on the surface. Before an attack, the commander had to decide how many, if any, torpedoes to use. Merchant ships below 1500 tons were considered too small for a torpedo, while a larger ship might merit two, and a major warship

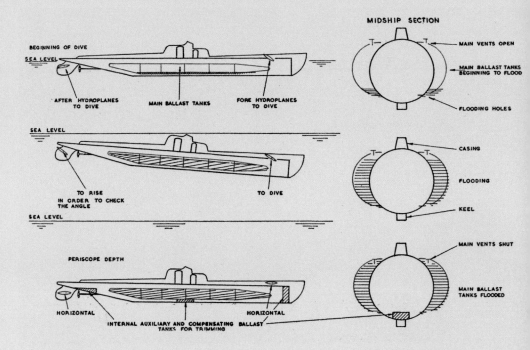

would justify a full salvo of perhaps six. The commander might be under orders to reserve a salvo of torpedoes for large warships, as Edward Young was in the Malacca Strait in 1944, until they were cancelled to allow him to attack merchant ships.[41] The commander would also have to decide the spread of a salvo, to give the maximum chance of one or more hitting.

In the daytime, the attack was made submerged. Since the target was almost certainly faster, the submarine had to get into a position ahead of it. Torpedoes had a range of up to 10,000 yards, but a hit at a range of more than 2000 yards was largely a matter of chance. The ideal range was about 600 yards, but anything from 500 to 1500 yards was possible. The submarine had to get into a firing position well in advance, as the target was moving faster than the submarine could turn. He had to keep his speed low to avoid detection, to find his way round any escorts which might be screening a valuable target, and to avoid sudden movements which might cause the first lieutenant to lose the trim and perhaps cause the boat to break surface. The commander would estimate the enemy's speed by observation of its bow wave; its inclination by the distance between its masts, and its distance by means of a range finder on the periscope, though that involved raising it high out of the water. In directing the attack, the commander could use the Submarine Torpedo Director or 'fruit machine'. This was a kind of mechanical computer invented by Commander Wadham in 1929.[42] Captain Ben Bryant, however, dismissed it as 'the most rudimentary of attack instruments', and preferred not to use it but do the sums in his head. The commanding officer set the attack angle on the periscope, and fired when the target was in place. Then he had to wait.

The seconds ticked away; at 45 knots the torpedo would take over two minutes to get there. The torpedo officer was counting the seconds. Two minutes and still the ship sailed on.

The method of diving a submarine.

Above left: Petty Officer Woodley, the second coxswain of the *Tribune*, at the forward hydroplane controls.

Above right: A submarine captain training on the attack teacher, with the 'fruit machine' behind him.

An awful feeling of despair came over me; at last, after all those months of waiting, we had got a chance to attack and I had missed.

Suddenly a great column of water rose high above the masts. Almost immediately she started to settle by her stern. Her fore foot slowly reared out of the water, to fall back as the whole ship sank upright to the bottom…[43]

Submarine Gunnery

Submarine guns had some success in the right circumstances. They were little used in North European waters and only 10 successful attacks on ships were recorded, sinking an average of less than 250 tons per ship They were far more commonly used in the Mediterranean, where they sank more than 70,000 tons of shipping in 268 attacks, though the ships were still very small, averaging about 264 tons. Ben Bryant suggested that the 12-pounder gun as fitted to the U class was 'as near useless a weapon as could have been thought of'.[44] This was perhaps true in northern waters, but in the Mediterranean against small caiques and schooners, U class boats sank nearly 16,000 tons in 88 attacks, not far behind the T class with the much more effective 4-inch. Bryant himself, in the *Safari*, was confident that guns were useful in the Mediterranean despite strong air patrols, because few aircraft had radar for use at night. In the Far East 452 vessels of 64,000 tons were destroyed by gunfire.[45]

Submarine commanders were warned to make sure that the gun was functioning properly before surfacing for an attack, as it might deteriorate underwater. They could allow the gunlayer to look at the target through the periscope in advance. They would try to choose a range at which the enemy could not reply: more than 2000 yards if he carried machine guns, 4000 yards if he had a 40mm gun. It was important that the gun crew got into action quickly, even if they were

drenched as the submarine surfaced, and it should come up on an even keel to improve their aim. Submarines were warned never to engage aircraft if there was any possibility of diving.[46]

British submarines mostly worked alone, but the 'wolf pack' was developed later in the war. This was very different from the much larger German group, and normally consisted of two boats which had trained together. In the Mediterranean it was used by *Shalimar* and *Seadog*. One surfaced to attack an enemy landing ship which fled, only to encounter the other. Another tactic was for one boat to attack on each quarter, so that whichever way the target tried to turn it would present a full broadside.[47] Arthur Hezlet used the tactics well in the Malacca Strait and his *Trenchant* co-operated with *Terrapin*, using Asdic to communicate underwater. They sank a submarine chaser and a coaster, and drove three other coasters ashore. Separately, they also sank two coasters, four junks, two lighters and a tug.[48]

Evasion

Once its presence was known to the enemy the submarine usually had to dive to escape, and there it was at a disadvantage as long as its position was known. The crew braced themselves for an attack by depth charge. The enemy normally used hydrophones to detect submarines, rather than active sonar, which might give the target more warning of the approach. It was a tense time for commanders and crew.

This was what I disliked most of all, this silent waiting, wondering when the next explosion would come, and whether it would be nearer than the last one, and when it came taking it without a chance to retaliate, unable to do anything but creep quietly away, not knowing what the enemy was doing, the barometer of hope rising and falling with the asdic reports.[49]

But there were evasive techniques that could be used when there was some depth or sea room.

Once detected you would have to speed up, make a wake – which you hoped he would mistake for the submarine itself – and alter course and depth. It was no good doing this till he was committed to the attack, particularly as you usually had more than one hunter and the noise you made would be followed. You wanted to get him to drop his charges. You waited until he seemed to be committed to steaming over you to drop them; then, and then only, you would speed up and alter course to get out of the light. This manoeuvre called for a nicety of timing, but even if you did not judge it very cleverly, he still had to set his charge to the right depth, so you had an extra chance, except in shallow water. … For the C.O. it was an absorbing business, and you had far too much to think about to have time to be frightened.[50]

Rescue

Submarine crews were trained in the use of the Davis Submerged Escape Apparatus or DSEA. This consisted of a breathing bag, a metal canister holding soda lime, a rubber mouthpiece, oxygen flasks and a valve connection. It was self-contained and delivered pure oxygen to the wearer's mouth. It could also be used in smoke or as a gas mask. If an escape was contemplated, the men gathered under one of the three hatches, forward, aft or under the gun. The DSEA was put to the ready position and the compartment was flooded. Men escaped one by one, the senior officer or rating working the valves and supervising the process before escaping last.[51] When the *Umpire* was sunk in a collision in 1941 Edward Young escaped without the apparatus because he thought it would be too restrictive in a tight environment, though most of the crew used it. He saw men 'coming up at fairly regular intervals, strange Martian creatures with their DSEA goggles and oxygen bags, and rendered almost unrecognisable by black oil which had flooded up from the bilges'.[52] Such measures may have given some confidence to crews but were rarely useful in action. Surveying submarine manpower, Admiral Binney was coldly realistic: '…whenever a submarine is lost, the crew is unfortunately lost with it'.[53]

Clandestine Operations

Submarines were the main means of landing small parties of commandos on enemy coastlines, and carrying out many other clandestine operations. This required good navigation, and patience as when Ben Bryant's *Safari* landed a Combined Operations pilotage party off Algiers.

Trimmed right down, to show a minimum of silhouette, the submarine would creep right close to the enemy beach. The final run in would be made at slow speed on the electric motors so as to avoid noise and wash. She would then stop, about half a mile off shore. The fore hatch would be opened, taking care that there was no sound – sound travels well over water… Silently, everyone wearing plimsolls to make no noise on the steel casing, the canoes would come up through the torpedo hatch, the final assembly being made on deck. Then the canoes would be put carefully over the side, the torpedo hatch shut and maybe the bow trimmed down a bit to make it easier for the intrepid surveyors to get into their canoes.[54]

Patience was also needed when a group was being recovered. *Safari* landed a party of commandos on the North African coast and their recovery is described by her signaller.

At 0220 a folboat was sighted out from the harbour and I was ordered to call it on the [radio?] telephone as it was heading away and would have passed us. … It altered course towards us. …one of the Army officers reported to the bridge and spoke to the Captain. There was no sign of the others anywhere. It seemed that on arrival on shore someone had dropped their machine-gun and the home guard had opened up with rifle fire and sent up some flares, but according to the Army officer everyone had got away from the shore. Ten minutes late a dinghy was sighted with some figures on board and they were soon alongside. Another 10 minutes the other dinghy containing ten men was sighted. … The missing man was a sergeant and even though we were very near to the shore we cruised around for yet another hour… Nothing was heard of him…[55]

Submarines also participated in some famous operations. Six of the S and T class towed the X-craft to the attack on the *Tirpitz* in the north of Norway in 1943. The *Tuna* launched Major Hasler and his six canoes for a raid on Bordeaux in 1941, a task which required considerable navigational accuracy as the men had to find their way to the river mouth several miles away. The *Seraph* under Lieutenant Bill Jewell dropped a body carrying false papers off the coast of Spain to fool the Germans into believing that the next invasion would not in fact be on Sicily. Jewell became something of a specialist in clandestine work – he also transported General Mark Clark of the US Army to Algiers for secret talks with the French authorities there, and brought back General Giraud.

Submariners using the Davis escape apparatus in the tank at Gosport.

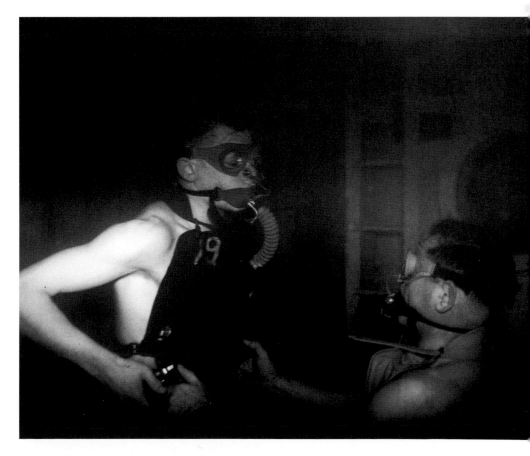

PART X

Escorts

1 Escort Vessels

The specialised escort vessel, designed to protect convoys of merchant ships against submarine and to a lesser extent aircraft attack, became one of the most important types in the war. At the beginning, escort design was bedevilled by the two problems of exaggerated faith in Asdic, and the unexpected switch of the war from British waters to the North Atlantic after the Fall of France. As a result it took some time to produce suitable vessels, and they were taken from many sources: destroyers and modified destroyers, fishing and whaling craft, anti-submarine ships of the inter-war years and specialised designs for the Atlantic. Both British and American ships were used, so many different types and classes performed overlapping functions.

At the very minimum, an escort vessel needed the means to find and destroy a submarine – Asdic to detect it, depth charges to attack it underwater and a gun to destroy it on the surface. There were plenty of hulls that could be converted to do this, including civilian trawlers at one end of the scale, and medium-sized warships at the other, though neither of these were ideal vessels for the work in other respects. Later in the war, escort vessels carried ahead-throwing weapons such as Hedgehog and Squid, and radar to detect submarines on the surface. These, too, came to be regarded as minimum requirements.

There were also minimum speed requirements for an escort. Obviously it had to be able to keep up with the convoy being escorted, and a little faster to allow for zigzags and other manoeuvres. Ideally it had to be faster than an enemy submarine on the surface, which could do about 17–18 knots. Speed was also useful in catching up with the convoy again after the long hunt of a U-boat, or in a support group which had to move quickly to the aid of a convoy. Range was just as important as the war moved further and further out into the Atlantic. Very few of the ships available at the beginning of the war carried enough fuel to cope with this, and techniques for refuelling at sea were still primitive.

Because of the initial assumption of a coastal U-boat campaign, and because nothing else was available, the Royal Navy used more than 200 trawlers manned by the Patrol Service as escort vessels in the early stages of the war. They were withdrawn to other duties such as coastal patrol as soon as larger escorts became available.

An escort vessel had to have good sea-keeping qualities, but again these were not always available. Some of the early destroyers were too delicate for Atlantic work until they were converted, and early corvettes, though perfectly safe, were based on a design used by hardened seafarers and were far too lively for the civilian seamen who manned them in practice. Crews would quickly become seasick and exhausted and this was detrimental to their efficiency. Ships designed with the Atlantic in mind, such as the River and Loch class frigates, were far more efficient in this respect, although the North Atlantic could never be made comfortable.

A certain minimum length was needed for this, close to the 300 feet of the Rivers and the Lochs, but that tended to counteract another factor, manoeuvrability. A short ship like a corvette had small turning circle, which was very useful in pursuit of a submarine taking evasive action.

In the Battle of the Atlantic itself, it was possible to concentrate on pure anti-submarine performance as surface ship and air attack were less likely than in the Mediterranean or the Arctic convoys. But a good all-round escort vessel would need to defend itself against air attack at least. If surface ship attack was likely, as when the *Bismarck* entered the Atlantic in 1941, or off Norway during the Arctic convoys, then battleships, cruisers and destroyers would operate in support. For air attack, many escort vessels were ill-equipped for self-defence even by the rather low British standards early in the war. This did not matter in mid-Atlantic where enemy aircraft could not reach, but it did in other areas.

Finally, escort vessels were needed in large numbers, so cheapness and ease of production was as important as anything else. This meant accepting less than perfect standards of finishing, simplified hull design, merchant ship rather than warship methods as there were far more merchant shipbuilding yards, and ultimately prefabrication. By these methods, several hundred escort vessels were built or acquired during the war.

Destroyers

The latest types of destroyer were reserved for work with the fleet and for special tasks requiring fast and well-armed ships, so the duty of convoy escort fell mainly to the older ones. The destroyer's speed of up top 36 knots (more than twice a corvette) could be useful in coming to the relief of a beleaguered convoy, as *Larne* and *Lance* did with the Gibraltar convoy OG71 in August 1941. But in general they were faster than was needed for close escort with merchant ships that rarely exceeded 10 knots, and against U-boats that did not exceed 18 knots on the surface.

The destroyers of the V and W classes were the latest type at the end of the First World War, and incorporated much of the experience. They were designed for a war in the North Sea rather than the Atlantic, so they had limited range and poor sea-keeping qualities. The officers' quarters in the stern were often cut off from the bridge by rough seas. Their powerful engines, developing 27,000 shaft horsepower, gave a speed of 34 knots, but this was largely wasted escorting convoys that rarely did more than 10.

Many ships were rearmed; their six torpedo tubes were of little use in the U-boat war and were generally removed. Nevertheless, the ships were often used by the senior officers in command of escort groups, partly because they were faster than corvettes or frigates. Large numbers served in the Battle of the Atlantic, because nothing else was available.

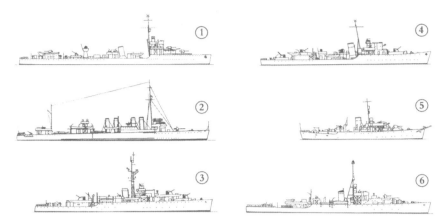

Above: Types of escort vessel.

1. The *Vansittart* of the V class as converted to a long-range escort, shown in 1943.

2. One of the *Clemson* class of American destroyers built in 1918–19, some of which were transferred to the Royal Navy in 1940.

3. The *Hind* of the modified *Black Swan* class of sloops, built in 1943.

4. The *Bicester* of 1942, one of the second type of Hunt class of destroyer escorts.

5. The *Bryony*, a corvette of the Flower class in 1942.

6. The *Fal*, a River class frigate, in 1942.

Other old destroyers were sometimes used, such as the S class of 1918–20. D A Rayner was ambivalent on taking command of the *Shikari*.

Before going on board I walked around her admiring the cunning of the draughtsman who had put her lines on paper. It was only a pity that she had not been built on a bigger scale, for then she would have been the perfect escort vessel. It appeared to the seaman's eye that she was carrying far too much gear on the upper deck – as indeed she was…and certainly her designer had never meant her to carry 110 depth charges on the upper deck, with all their heavy throwing gear.[1]

One type of relatively modern destroyer often used on escort duty was the H class, particularly six ships under construction for Brazil at the beginning of the war and taken over by the Royal Navy. Captain Donald Macintyre complained about the poor torpedoes and fire control equipment in *Hesperus* when first completed, but Rayner was far more satisfied with *Highlander*. 'What ships they were! … She was really the most beautifully fitted warship I had ever seen. … At sea, too, she would be far more comfortable than any previous ship'.[2]

The Town class destroyers were far less popular. In September 1940 Churchill was delighted to receive 50 old destroyers from the United States in exchange for the use of certain naval bases – the first concrete support from that source. However, the ships themselves, built in 1917–20, were poorly designed and were no more suitable for the Atlantic than the corvettes. In his book *Destroyer from America* John Fernald tried to be as kind as possible about their qualities, but his characters claimed that they had 'long narrow lines', which were 'more like a college eight than a ship'.[3] The most famous of the class, the *Campbeltown* (ex USS *Buchanan*), was used to smash the lock gates at St Nazaire during a famous raid of 1942. According to her medical officer she originally had good

officers' accommodation, with comfortable bunks, running water in each cabin and steam radiators for heating. The wardroom was smaller than would be expected on a British ship, but the Americans had provided good showers and lavatories. The ratings were accommodated in fixed bunks instead of hammocks, which took up a great deal of space and restricted other activities. The blackout of the galley was so poor that meals could not be cooked after dark and the sick bay was 'totally inadequate'.[4]

Destroyers usually had numerous guns, though some of them were too small to be effective. The VWs had four 4-inch guns, the Towns had three in single mountings. More modern destroyers like the Hs had the much more effective 4.7-inch gun, with director control towers to allow very accurate aiming. All destroyers carried depth charges, although generally in small numbers compared with purpose-built escorts.

Sloops and Destroyer Escorts

The sloops *Sandwich* and *Bridgewater* of 1928 were the first attempts at medium-sized warships after the First World War and were based on wartime experience. They were intended for minesweeping, anti-submarine operations and for showing the flag in the Empire. The type evolved in several designs over the next few years. It had a long forecastle for good sea-keeping, because unlike a destroyer it did need torpedo tubes amidships. It had a low quarterdeck for either dropping depth charges or operating minesweeping gear. By the early 1930s it had evolved into a mainly anti-submarine vessel, with good anti-aircraft capability in its guns.

The *Black Swan* class was the culmination of inter-war design. Once the designers had given up the subsidiary roles of peacetime flag-showing and minesweeping, they evolved a very successful class of escort vessels, with a heavy gun armament for the role. The most famous ship of the class was the *Starling*, group leader of F J Walker's Second Support Group, which sank six U-boats in a single voyage early in 1944. More than 30 of the type were built.

The ships of the Hunt class were conceived as small destroyers, without the features that were not needed on escort work – torpedoes and high speed. They were known as escort destroyers and had a speed of just over 30 knots, compared with 36 for a modern destroyer. There was a serious mistake during the design of the ships and their stability was much less than intended, so armament had to be reduced to four 4-inch guns. Later versions had broader hulls to carry heavier gun armament. For all their problems they were successful ships. In all, 86 ships were built, although they were expensive and not suitable for mass production.

Corvettes

According to Sir Stanley Goodall, the Director of Naval Construction, the Flower class of corvettes originated in a conversation between him and Admiral Sir Roger Backhouse, the First Sea Lord (1938–9), when

…war clouds were gathering thick and fast and it was evident that the storm would break. He sent for me and said he was concerned about ships for anti-submarine duties. We must have great numbers. Of the types then in service

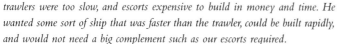

trawlers were too slow, and escorts expensive to build in money and time. He wanted some sort of ship that was faster than the trawler, could be built rapidly, and would not need a big complement such as our escorts required.

About this time Mr William Reed of Smith's dock came to see me. He enlarged upon the properties of the whale-catchers of the Southern Pride class built to the British Corporation's classification. It seemed to me that ships with the characteristics of Southern Pride *would meet the requirements outlined by Sir Roger Backhouse.*[5]

The resulting ships had a simple triple-expansion engine of 2750 horsepower, giving a top speed of 16 knots, which was not enough to catch a surfaced U-boat. They carried 40 depth charges at first, and a single 4-inch gun in the bows to deal with submarines on the surface. They proved very uncomfortable in service when transferred from the English Channel and North Sea to the Atlantic.

Steps were taken to improve the Flowers. They were given longer forecastles to make them drier and bilge keels to prevent rolling. The design was fundamentally sound and safe despite initial appearances, and the Flowers were the most common type of escort vessels for practically all of the war. A hundred and forty-five were built in Britain for the Royal Navy and 95 more in Canada. They were able to take most of the latest devices in time, including radar, Hedgehog and, later, Squid. The number of crew quickly rose from 85 to 108.

Work began on the design of another type of corvette in 1941. Though the River class frigates were now in production, it was recognised that many shipyards were too small to build them and the Castle class emerged. They were 252 feet long, 47 feet more than the Flowers, and had the same engine, but improved design gave them a speed of 16.5 knots. Many of them were fitted with early Squid mortars, which made them quite effective and good value for money.

Frigates

In the autumn of 1940, as soon as it became apparent that the Flower class corvettes would have difficulty in Atlantic operations, the Admiralty began the design of a new class, known at first as twin-screw corvettes. They were 40 per cent larger than the Flowers, with flared bows to meet the waves and twice the engine power. The Admiralty originally wanted a speed of 22 knots to chase U-boats, but 20 knots was the most that could be achieved without much larger ships or engines. Nearly all the River class ships were fitted with Hedgehog as the main anti-submarine armament, but this was an afterthought in the design and the position on the forecastle was unsuitable. The title of the class was changed to frigate in March 1943. The first ships entered service in the spring of 1942, and eventually 59 River class frigates were built for the Royal Navy and 70 more were built in Canada for the Royal Canadian Navy.

They were quickly succeeded by the Loch class, with the hull redesigned for welding and prefabrication. Since they carried Squid instead of Hedgehog, they were very successful on operations. Another version, the Bay class, had a mainly anti-aircraft armament for use in the Pacific. Twenty-five Lochs and 19 Bays were completed for the Royal Navy during the war, along with others for Canada and Australia .

The Captain class frigates were built in the USA in 1942–3 and loaned to the Royal Navy under lend-lease. Originally a programme of 520 ships was planned for Britain, but 78 were built for the Royal Navy and 565 for the US Navy as DEs (destroyer escorts). Some were powered by diesel-electric engines. The design was a combination of British and American practices and proved quite seaworthy in action, although with some problems in bad weather. Their main guns were 3-inch, which was too light for anti-submarine work, but they also carried a heavy anti-aircraft armament which made them useful on routes where air attack was likely. They were faster than the River

Far left: The decks of the *Wallace* **of the VW class escorting an east coast convoy in 1941.**

Top: The sloop *Scarborough,* **launched in 1930, in peacetime.**

Above: The Hunt class destroyer escort *Talybont* **as completed in 1943.**

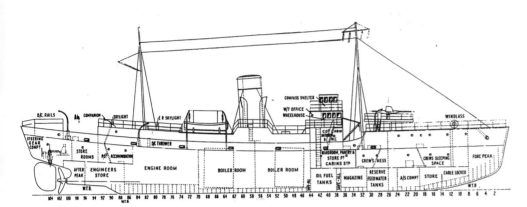

2 Life in the Escorts

Apart from submarines, aircraft carriers and the big ships of the battle fleet, escort vessels in the Battle of the Atlantic were the only ships which habitually went to sea for weeks at a time. A battleship can still serve as a deterrent, part of a 'fleet in being', even if it stays in harbour. An escort vessel is only earning its keep if it is at sea, protecting the supply lines. Much of this was done in the worst weather of the North Atlantic, and convoy escort posed special challenges for the hardiest sailors, not to mention the inexperienced temporary RNVRs and HOs who actually manned the ships. It is described graphically in Nicholas Monsarrat's novel *The Cruel Sea,* as well as his works of non-fiction, such as *Three Corvettes.* It also features in many less well-known memoirs of the period.

The Theatres of Action

For most people the North Atlantic is an undistinguished mass of rough weather, grey seas, huge waves and perhaps icebergs. For the sailors of the escort forces it was all that, but it also had its notable milestones. In the early stages of the conflict there was the line of 17° or later 19° West, the furthest out that escorts operated. After 1941 there were CHOP or change of operational command lines, where direction was handed over from Britain or Canada to America, or vice versa. More sinister was the air gap in the middle of the ocean, where aircraft rarely operated before 1943 and the U-boats were at their most effective. For all the disadvantages, Atlantic escort at least allowed a predictable routine. A slow convoy from Halifax to Britain took about 17 days; a fast one took about 13 days. Commander Peter Gretton was able to plan his wedding several months in advance, knowing that the system would allow him to be there on the day.

There was a different kind of war on the east coast of Britain. Convoys were protected from submarine attack by minefields, but air attack was common and the E-boats remained a threat. According to Peter Gretton, then first lieutenant of a destroyer:

Coastal convoys were a very different affair from ocean convoys. They were smaller for one thing and were never more than two columns so that the ships could keep in the narrow swept channel. Their shape was long and thin, therefore, and station-keeping was even more difficult than in the open sea because of the tides and the bends in the narrow channels which twisted their way through the sand-banks of the east-coast route. We used to pick up a north-bound convoy off Southend and drop it off Methyl [sic] opposite Leith in the Firth of Forth, reversing the process shortly after arrival, and returning with a south-bound convoy.[6]

The Arctic convoys to Russia introduced other factors. They were vulnerable to air, submarine and surface ship attack, as well as bad weather and extreme cold.

It was miserable watch-keeping in winter; our main occupation, day and night, was knocking ice from the gun breeches, the masts and the rigging. In a destroyer plunging around in high winds, that is not a passive duty. It snowed most of that trip, even more when the wind was down. The snowflakes fell like confetti at some hellish wedding. Doom cracked wide open in smoke and noise.[7]

Top: A section of a Flower class corvette in an early state, with a short forecastle.

Above: The *Hibiscus,* a Flower class corvette.

class, with a speed of 23.5 knots. They were mainly used in support groups and took part in the sinking of 35 U-boats from October 1943 onwards.

The Ideal Escort

The Royal Navy ended up using a great variety of craft on escort duties: two classes of corvette, a variety of destroyers, several types of destroyer escort, frigates of both British and American design and sloops of pre-war types. All had different good and bad points, and were useful in slightly different roles.

The ideal escort vessel was never developed during the war, but the Loch class was probably closest. It was the first British class specially designed for true mass production. It had reasonable speed, the best sea-keeping of any class, good radar and sonar and the best anti-submarine weapon in the Squid. Another approach was to look at a three-tier system of escorts with slightly different functions. Some could be rather slow, to fill the gaps in the escort screen. The Castle class corvettes, slightly faster and better designed than the Flower class, would fill this role. Then there was a need for a larger, faster ship to lead the group and carry out anti-submarine hunts. The Lochs were best for this, followed by the Rivers and Captains. Finally there was a role for fast ships to form support groups to go to the aid of beleaguered convoys. The Hunts, once their early faults had been corrected, were suitable for this role, though in practice the *Black Swans* proved even better.

Officers and Crews

The escort force was mostly stratified by type of engagement in the navy. Escort group commanders, such as F J Walker, Peter Gretton and Donald Macintyre, were usually regular RN, though D A Rayner reached the position as a permanent RNVR officer. Commanding officers of ships, apart from destroyers, were mostly RNR, though a few temporary RNVRs such as Nicholas Monsarrat took command. First lieutenants were often RNR, some were RNVR. The junior officers were nearly always temporary RNVR, except the engineers who were often commissioned from warrant rank. On the lower decks, the petty officers were regular RN, while those below them were overwhelmingly HOs.

In the early stages all ships suffered from a shortage of experienced officers.

Our officers consisted of a Lieutenant-Commander and three raw R.N.V.R subs, and, apart from a few stalwart Active Service ratings, the men were as new to the job as we were. … It shocks me now to think of the behaviour in the early days of we three subs to our C.O., and I can only defend out actions by pleading that the results justified the means. The C.O was in no way to blame, he was no more qualified to command a warship than we to act as officers of the watch…even if we

were completely lacking in technical knowledge of how to run and work a ship, both at sea and in port, we were so single-minded in our purpose and ruthless in our methods that nothing would have stopped us. We had to get the ship into reasonable sea and fighting trim, without the slightest knowledge or training of how to do it.[8]

Later in the war Rayner noticed a different breed. 'Of the officers I could make neither top nor tail. Although they were the legatees of the robust tradition of the Western Approaches, they were totally different from their forebears in background, outlook and training. This does not mean that they were inefficient. They were merely products of the Radar Age. … Responsibility sat rather heavily on shoulders not yet broad enough to bear the weight'.[9]

All ships carried more officers and men than they had been designed for. The complement of the Flower class corvette increased from 85 to 109. Frigates were designed for 100 men but usually had about 140 on service. They had eight to 10 officers including a surgeon-lieutenant and an engineer, who was a sub-lieutenant or warrant officer. The ratings included a CPO as coxswain, three more seamen petty officers and four leading seamen. The seaman branch also included six Asdic operators as well as radar operators and gunners. There were five or six signalmen and coders under a yeoman, plus a radio mechanic. There was

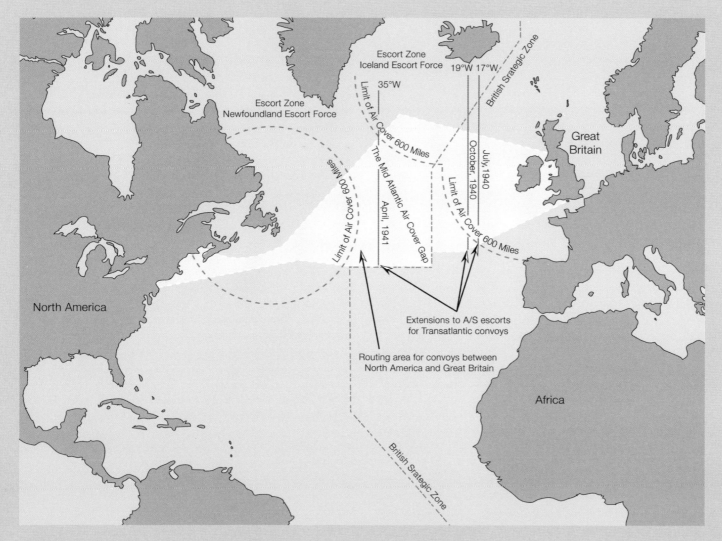

The areas in which the Battle of the Atlantic was fought.

such equipment, does not entitle the Commanding Officer of that ship to believe that his ship is ready for all contingencies. Much more is needed before it can be claimed to constitute an efficient fighting force. The Commanding Officer has to be satisfied that every officer knows not only his own duty but that of every other officer and the whole ship's company has to be moulded into one team. This cannot be accomplished if the cook in the galley is inefficient or if there are leaks in the seamen's messdeck, if the men are undisciplined while onshore or untidy in their dress. Neither can efficiency be expected if smooth working is hampered by minor defects. Not until every man in the ship is happy in the knowledge that he knows his job and shows a carefree disposition in his mess, can a ship be considered efficient.[13]

a chief ERA and three ERAs. There was one chief stoker, six stoker petty officers and six leading stokers as well as 12 stokers. Miscellaneous ratings included a sick berth attendant, a supply assistant, a leading cook and his assistant and three stewards and a cook for the officers.

In the destroyer *Winchelsea,* the medical officer complained that the living spaces only had 81.5 cubic feet of air per man, compared with the recommended 200 cubic feet. Accommodation was '…further decreased by the absence of stowage for gear such as duffel coats, oilskins etc. During wet weather, the amount of wet clothing which accumulates seriously affects the dryness of living spaces'.[10] His opposite number in the *Keppel* complained that 'There are many in every mess unable to sling a hammock and some are necessarily poorly accommodated. Sweating of the ship is considerable, and when the sea is over the forecastle, water rises quickly to two inches in the mess decks'.[11]

Tobermory

Each newly commissioned escort vessel was sent to work up under HMS *Western Isles* at Tobermory, under the command of Commodore Sir Gilbert Stephenson. He had retired as a vice-admiral in 1928 but came back as a commodore of convoys before taking command of *Western Isles* in 1940. He had a fierce and energetic personality, and delighted in surprising the crews of ships sent to him. He was equally delighted when they responded in kind.

There was a corvette which kept a fire hose rigged in readiness, and when someone tried to scramble on board unannounced, let him have it full blast. When the officer of the deck looked over the side he saw the Commodore himself, drenched to the skin and dancing up and down in his launch, laughing and saying 'Well done – oh, well done'.[12]

Though the personality of the commander might appear to dominate, there was in fact a syllabus. For a Castle class corvette the training lasted 18 gruelling days, including 35 hours of sea time doing anti-submarine and anti-aircraft exercises, 37 hours of gunnery and anti-aircraft drills and 160 hours of classroom instruction. The aims of the school were as much to do with teamwork as technical instruction.

To equip a major war vessel with up-to-date armament – depth charges, oerlikons, hedgehog, squid, asdics, radar and D/F – and be satisfied that part of the ship's company is sufficiently conversant with the method of operation of

After Tobermory, ships went straight to the Battle of the Atlantic in the early stages of the war. From late 1942 they went to Larne in Northern Ireland for more technical training as part of an escort group.

Bad Weather

Life in a small ship in wartime could be utterly exhausting, even without an attack by the enemy. The early Flower class corvettes were by far the worst. There was a saying in the navy: 'Corvettes are all right. The bloke who invented corvettes is a genius. The only trouble is he didn't invent the men to go with them'.[14]

John Palmer describes his introduction to life as a junior officer in the *Clematis*.

We left at 0700, wind freshening from the North-West. It didn't look healthy – visibility was poor and low cloud was making the west coast look as sinister as it can look beautiful. It wasn't healthy. By 0930 I had been sick – so had nearly everyone else – and by 103 there were six inches of fuel oil and water in the wardroom and in my cabin. It got worse steadily. By lunchtime no one was really capable. Life seemed hardly worth living, I remember. That night, or rather the next morning, when I was keeping the morning watch, was the worst I can remember. I could hardly stand. Waves broke green over the open bridge and she was rolling so far that the boats touched the water on either side.[15]

Things could get even worse, as described by Nicholas Monsarrat:

One measure of rough weather is domestic, but reliable. Moderate sea, the lavatory-seat falls down when it is tipped up; rough sea, the radio-set tumbles off its bracket in the wardroom.

Apart from the noise it produces, rolling has a maddening rhythm that is one of the minor tortures of rough weather. It never stops or misses a beat, it cannot be escaped anywhere. If you go through a doorway, it hits you hard; if you sit down, you fall over; you get hurt, knocked about, continuously, and it makes for extreme and childish anger. When you drink, the liquid rises towards you and slops over; at meals, the food spills off your plate, the cutlery will not stay in place. Things roll about, and bang, and slide away crazily; and then come back and hurt you again.

Exhaustion began to set in, especially when the ship was operated in two watches.

Strain and tiredness induce a sort of hypnosis: you seem to be moving in a bad dream, pursued not by terrors but by an intolerable routine. You come off watch at midnight, soaked, twitching, your eyes raw with the wind and staring at shadows; you brew up a cup of tea in the wardroom pantry and strip off the top layer of sodden clothes; you do, say, an hour's intricate ciphering, and thereafter snatch a few hours' sleep between wet blankets, with the inflated life-belt in your ribs reminding you all the time that things happen quickly.; and then, every night for seventeen nights on end, you're woken at ten to four by the bosun's mate, and you stare at the deckhead and think: My God, I can't go up there again in the dark and filthy rain, and stand another four hours of it. But you can, of course: it becomes automatic in the end.[16]

Conditions might improve slowly, as Monsarrat records.

There's respite now, anyway: hot meals instead of tea and corned beef sandwiches; sleep without being tipped out of your bunk, a whole watch without getting wet. The upper-deck petty officer gets to work squaring up, the seaman gunner of the watch cleans the Lewis and Hotchkiss guns, the leading signalman checks over his rockets and flares…[17]

The sailors' dress owed little to the traditional naval uniform.

If it was wet, you know raining, you'd be dressed in a pair of sea boots, a pair of heavy sea boot stockings, coat, a mackintosh coat o top of that, a sou-wester, a towel tied round your neck, a pair of gloves and a pair of binoculars and you'd clamber up this crow's nest and get inside it.[18]

The Dangers

Most of the U-boat attack was against merchant ships rather than their escorts, so their losses were not excessive. But they did happen, and could often be horrific. Captain Charles Cuthbertson describes his experiences in the sinking of the corvette *Zinnia* in 1941.

I was stepping out of the bridge asdic house and facing the funnel and about 25 feet from the explosion. The asdic house collapsed and parts of the ship were thrown in the air. She immediately heeled over on to her starboard beam ends, and in five seconds had capsized through 120 degrees. The blast did not hurt me and the capsizing hurled me into the water on the starboard side abreast the bridge. Looking upwards I saw the deck of the ship coming over on top of me, when she broke in two about the funnel, and a swirl of water took me down. When I came to the surface again my lungs and stomach were filled with oil fuel, and I was partially blinded. The time was now about twelve seconds after the explosion. I could see the bows rising vertically out of the water, they disappeared within a few seconds. HMS Zinnia had sunk in 15 or 20 seconds. There was no wreckage.

I heard many cries for help in the water, and estimated there were about 40 men floating. I could do nothing to help them. The water was thick with oil fuel, and it was all I could do to keep my balance in the swell, and with my nose and mouth above the oil. I remained afloat for 40 minutes before finding the trunk of a body which had been blasted and was buoyant, this kept me afloat for the remaining 30 minutes. One corvette passed close without sighting me, eventually at 0530 I was picked up by a boat from another corvette, HMS Campion. I had to be hoisted inboard, could only crawl along the deck, and was completely blinded. I was still fully clothed.[19]

Almost as traumatic was the picking up of men from torpedoed merchant ships.

Survivors in the mess decks, filling every available space: asleep on the deck, on benches, against bulkheads: sitting at tables with their heads between their hands, talking, shivering, wolfing food, staring at nothing. Some of them half naked, wrapped in blankets and makeshift shoes: some with pathetic little cardboard suitcases, hugged close: puzzled black faces, pinched yellow ones, tired bleary white masks that still muster a grin. Men half-dead, men cocky as bedamned: men suffering from exposure, frost-bite, oil fuel poisoning, cuts, gashes, broken limbs: men hanging to life by a wet thread.[20]

Officers' Accommodation

Even in such small vessels officers had some privileges, especially in the allocation of space. A Canadian report of November 1943 found that in a River class frigate 15 per cent of the accommodation space was for the use of a dozen or so officers, 58 per cent was for about 130 men, and the remaining 27 per cent was for neutral spaces such as passages and the sick bay. Taken in these terms, the average officer took up nearly three times as much space as a seaman.[21] The captain had a cabin as in virtually all ships, including the frigate *Ettrick* when commanded by Monsarrat. 'My own cabin, with bathroom attached, was a big one, and adequately comfortable: though here again the wartime finish was apparent'.[22] His junior officers lived in the wardroom.

The wardroom…was in much the same state of overcrowding as the messdecks: two subs had to eat at a separate table, and the competition for the sofa at the end of a meal recalled the after-dinner rush at a residential hotel… Wartime austerity was much in evidence as regards the furnishing – bleak iron radiators instead of a stove, and chairs of that modern tubular design which makes 'the shape of things to come' so morbid a prospect.[23]

Captains usually dined with the other officers in the wardroom, but were warned against spending too much time there.

'Monkey' Stephenson enforces his will on a group of seamen.

The corvette *Clematis* pitching in the sea.

Another way of 'reverting to type' is to become too much of a wardroom officer. In the smallest ships the Captain is inevitably a member of the mess and its president, but in ships like a destroyer he is an honorary member, and has a comfortable day cabin of his own in which to sit. He should normally have lunch and dinner in the wardroom as this will help him to know his officers, but his continued presence is bound to have a somewhat restricting influence, as is exemplified by the tradition that officers should stand when the Captain comes into the mess. A Captain should therefore not outstay his welcome.[24]

Daily Routine

Transferring from the Tribal class destroyer *Tartar* to an old V and W on convoy escort, Ludovic Kennedy found that life was very different.

…in the Wanderer [actually Watchman] it was the desperate crawling about the ocean at eight or nine knots, the remaining with the convoy in all weathers and conditions (having the ability but not the sanction to go elsewhere), that in the long run made the service so demanding.[25]

He describes the routine beginning of a watch.

The first hour or two of the watch passed quietly. Orders as to what we were to do in any situation had already been passed to us from the escort leader and Commodore, and there was nothing to do now but watch and wait. We zigzagged slowly across the face of the convoy. Occasionally the Captain came up from his cabin for a chat and a smoke: otherwise I was alone on the bridge.[26]

Officers in the wardroom of a destroyer on escort duty.

In such small vessels one would expect the men to know each other, but according to Monsarrat, 'Strange people come to surface when "Action Stations" is sounded – stokers I had no idea were on board, rare faces that never see the light of day'. The division system was used to keep contact between officers and men.

…it is, to my mind, the Navy's most admirable organisation, and if the other services have no parallel to it, that is probably what is wrong with them. … Briefly, a ship's company is divided into 'divisions', according to the various branches – seamen, stokers, communications, etc: each group of men has an officer to look after it, an officer specially charged with its welfare and regulation. It is to him that they look in all their difficulties, whether concerned with promotion, training for a higher rate, doubts about their pay, internal quarrels and problems, domestic complications, compassionate leave, complaints of unfairness or favouritism. This division into small groups, if conscientiously applied, makes for a high degree of confidence between officers and men.[27]

Occasionally captains ordered 'divisions', a parade on deck, when conditions permitted. The captain of HMS *Clematis* did a rare inspection in July 1941. 'This morning the Captain inspected the mess decks after the great drive to get bunks and lockers clean. They looked quite surprisingly clean, far better than I have ever seen them before, with all the bunks properly made'.[28]

In good weather the crew settled down to routine tasks. Each mess had its cooks who prepared food. Younger men tried to avoid the task of 'captain of the heads' who cleaned the toilets, but three-badgers saw it as 'a quiet number'. As for the rest of the crew:

…when the hands fell in in the morning and detailed off to working parties, it was nearly always a chipping hammer or a paint brush, that was at sea, or in harbour, you were chipping old paint and putting on fresh paint. … And there were difficult moments when you were covered in paint when you tried to climb up from the stage over the fo'c's'le and try to get back on board and your hands are slipping.[29]

When attack seemed likely, the whole crew was ready for action.

In the Tay the ship's company was at defence stations, with only half the officers and men closed up, but every man off watch was lying fully dressed ready to rush to his action station whenever the alarm bells rang. No less aware of the situation were the men in the boiler and engine rooms, well below the water-line, whose chances of survival if a torpedo struck were remote. There were indeed men who, unable to stand the thought of being trapped below when off duty, were trying to get some rest in corners of the wet, cold upper decks. …

For those on watch above decks, exposure to the weather was unending. On the bridge, at the guns, and on the quarter-deck aft, where the depth charge crews waited for action, the men were faceless ghouls, wrapped in duffel coats, the hoods drawn over their heads… As the spray came sweeping, rattling over them, each man ducked, then waited calmly until the arrival of the next wave's onslaught.[30]

Shore Time

The arrival in port was a time of great relief, as Monsarrat describes.

It was the prelude to a whole range of delights about to be showered on us; sliding through the dock gates towards our berth, getting the first heaving-line ashore, then the head-rope, then the stern-wire; ringing off the engines – their first respite for perhaps four hundred hours: the curious warm silence which fell on the ship as the mail came on board and was doled out: the first guaranteed night in port, first drink, first undressing for a fortnight, first bath, first good sleep.[31]

It was even more joyous for a captain, such as Donald Macintyre of the destroyer *Hesperus*.

The first night in harbour after these voyages will always be highlighted in my memory. After the long, anxious days at sea in all weathers it was an unforgettable joy to be able to come aft to one's harbour cabin, to slough off one's clothes for the first time in many days and lie wallowing in a hot bath. …

The enemy we knew we could cope with, but the vindictive savagery of the Atlantic gales and the mountainous waves they raised, which came snoring down the wind at us, towering high above our heads, many a time put the fear of God into me. It was almost a tangible joy, therefore, to be snug in harbour in a secure berth, with a westerly gale moaning through the rigging, and knowing that an undisturbed night in one's bunk and between sheets lay ahead.[32]

The members of the crew had 'a love of home grafted deep inside them, to a degree which a cynic might not credit'[33] and the prospect of leave was very welcome. Boiler cleaning allowed some leave to the ship's company, with only a skeleton crew left behind.

With the boilers blown down, the whole ship is very cold: she is lit by unreliable shore-lighting which has a habit of packing up when you need it most; she has a general air of disuse not lessened by most of her innards being spread out over the engine-room casing. All officers except yourself are on leave. You sit and sit (and drink and drink) and nibble at the enormous amount of paper-work before you; other corvette officers in the same position come over to grouse in company.[34]

Normally half the crew went on leave at once, including all but one anti-submarine rating. They returned and the rest went off, leaving most of the anti-submarine team to practice together on the numerous simulators in the port. As the crew reassembled after leave, their work began right away. Training between convoys was a vital part of the Western Approaches regime, as described by Commander Peter Gretton:

Before leaving on each escort duty, two or three days and nights were spent exercising off the entrance to the River Foyle, working with submarines, firing

A convoy enters Falmouth harbour in 1942, as seen from above the signal station on St Anthony's lighthouse, painted by John Platt.

at targets and carrying out the multitude of jobs which might fall to a convoy escort. In fact, the men sometimes complained that they felt more tired after the pre-convoy exercises than after the convoy itself!

He thought this was one of the main reasons for the British victory in the Atlantic and contrasted it with the U-boat crews' lack of practice between operations.[35] The ship was now ready to take out its next convoy and the cycle began again.

3 Escort Techniques

The war against the U-boat attracted the attention of the very highest in the land. In March 1941 Churchill announced that 'In view of various German statements, we must assume that the Battle of the Atlantic has begun'. He later admitted that 'The only thing that ever really frightened me during the war was the U-boat peril',[36] and for several years in the middle of the war he chaired the Anti-U-Boat Committee in Downing Street every second week, bringing together all those involved in the Battle of the Atlantic. The navy was, of course, represented, along with the RAF and those who managed the docks, transport, shipbuilding and the shipping industry.

Below: The Operations Room in Derby House, Liverpool. The main Atlantic plot is to the left, with the home waters plot in the background.

Bottom: A convoy conference in progress.

The operations in the anti-U-boat war were conducted by the area commands. Nore and Rosyth shared responsibility for the east coast convoys, while Western Approaches command, with its headquarters in Liverpool, ran the Battle of the Atlantic from the British side of the ocean. There, Sir Percy Noble and later Sir Max Horton conducted the battle with great skill from Derby House in Liverpool.

The Convoy System

The sinking of the *Athenia* on the first day of the war led the Admiralty to introduce convoy straight away, for all merchant ships except very fast ones (over 15 knots) which could evade U-boats. Merchant ships were on charter to the Ministry of War Transport, which arranged their cargoes and their destinations. The navy, in the person of the Naval Control of Shipping officer at the port of departure, allocated the ship to a convoy. This might depend on the speed of the ship. Ships in slow convoys needed a minimum of 7 knots; those in fast ones needed 10 or 11. Each convoy route had two or three code letters, sometimes given for slightly frivolous reasons – troop convoys to the Middle East were WS, or Winston's Specials. Sometimes the name of the port was incorporated, so those coming from Halifax were HX, or HXF for fast convoys. SC from North America did not mean 'slow convoy', but referred to Sydney Cove in Nova Scotia where they assembled. The PQ series to Russia ended soon after the disaster to PQ17, and they were later resumed under the new code JW for security reasons. In all, there were more than 500 convoy codes, ranging from AB to ZT.[37]

Each convoy route had its own cycle. The east coast system started straight away, running almost daily between London and the Tyne or Forth. In the early stages in the Atlantic, convoys were only escorted out to 17°W, then 19°W from October 1940, and by that time they were routed round the north of Ireland to or from the Clyde or Liverpool. Use of bases in Iceland allowed escort to be extended to 35°W, about halfway across the Atlantic, from April 1941, and from then on there was a gradual introduction of 'end to end' escort to the Canadian bases, although the whole journey was not usually done by the same group. The HX convoys ran on a four-day cycle and from mid-1942 New York replaced Halifax as the western end. A convoy leaving New York was met at the Halifax Ocean Meeting Point or Homp off Newfoundland and then escorted by British, Canadian or American warships to Eastomp where a British escort took over for the last part of the journey. From July 1942 there was a change of operational control for an eastbound convoy from American to British at the 'Chop' line at 26°W, though this was moved westwards late in the war. By the middle of the 1942 there was an interlocking convoy system covering the whole American coast and down into the Caribbean.[38]

Convoy Organisation

Convoy commodores were often very senior retired RN officers, with the rank of Commodore RNR. Each was in charge of the merchant ships of the convoy, and was stationed in the ship at the head of the central column. Even in his reduced rank, the commodore was two grades senior to the escort group commander, but regulations made it clear that the 'The Commodore of the Convoy is to take charge of the convoy as a whole, subject to the orders of the senior Officer of the Escort'.[39] Donald Macintyre was able to use this 'obscure passage of the convoy instructions which did place the ultimate safety on the shoulders of the escort commander' on the one occasion when he differed from the commodore.[40]

Each convoy started with a conference attended by naval officers, the commodore and the masters of all the merchant ships involved. Joseph Wellings attended one in Halifax in September 1940.

The Halifax Naval Control Service Officer was in charge of the conference. The captain of all the ships in the convoy, plus the captain of the ocean escort, and the convoy commodore attended the conference. Each captain was given a copy

of the sailing order, a copy of the convoy formation, and a copy of the pamphlet entitled 'Pamphlet Instructions for the Conduct of Convoys'... The Commodore of the convoy, Rear-Admiral Plowden, made a few brief remarks that information had been received that the Germans were using magnetic pistols in their torpedoes which would explode the torpedo as it passed under the ship. All ships were urged to use their degaussing device, which neutralises the magnetism of the ship, all the way across the Atlantic. When one of the captains asked about the use of fog signals, the convoy commodore stated that the odd-numbered column leaders would sound the Morse equivalent of their column number every half hour. ... At the end of the conference each captain received his sealed envelopes containing the secret routing instructions. The conference lasted about 45 minutes and the convoy sailed 1½ hours later.[41]

Convoys outward bound from the United Kingdom often started from several different ports so the captains were briefed separately. Such convoys assembled at Oversay between the Mull of Kintyre and Northern Ireland, and the process might take several hours. Convoys were arranged in several columns forming a rectangle much broader than it was long, with the columns perhaps 600 yards apart and each ship 400 yards behind the one ahead. There was some attempt to keep ships going to different destinations together, but that often had to be modified if circumstances changed. The size of ocean convoys increased over the years. In the early stages it was considered impossible to control more than 35 ships, but it was eventually proved that larger convoys used escorts more efficiently. The record was held by HX300 of July–August 1944, which had 166 ships.

Escort and Support Groups

Escort vessels were organised into groups, under the overall command of the Captain (D) of the port where they were based. Each was normally led by a commander, except that those promoted captain in the normal course of things, such as F J Walker, often stayed with their groups to give continuity. There were several experiments with giving the group commander the equivalent of a flagship with a captain under him, but this was not easy in such small ships and the system worked best when the group commander was also captain of the ship he sailed

in, with a strong first lieutenant under him. Groups tended to include several different types of ship, reflecting what was available in the early stages, but it soon became clear that each class had a different role – trawlers were often all that was available to start with, corvettes eventually provided the numbers, destroyers had the speed to fill gaps or catch up after the hunt of a U-boat, and the new frigates of 1942 had the sea-keeping and range for longer operations.

The ocean escort system was not fully developed in July 1940, when there was only one escort vessel for every two convoys. In October, as the Atlantic battle became more serious, there were nine destroyers, 10 sloops, 10 corvettes and 18 trawlers escorting 20 convoys, an average of two per convoy. A year later the corvettes had begun to enter service in larger numbers and there were 45 of them, with 30 destroyers including the ex-US Town class, with sloops and trawlers to make the total up to 94, an average of six per convoy. This was the number of ships in the 5th Escort Group in April 1941 when it escorted convoy HX122 and sank *U-99* under the ace Otto Kretschmer. Numbers tended to dip during the winter months and in March 1943 the ill-fated convoy HX229 was escorted by three destroyers and two corvettes when it encountered a

Wrens marking up the plot in the Western Approaches Tactical Unit in Liverpool. The trainees sit in the curtained areas behind them.

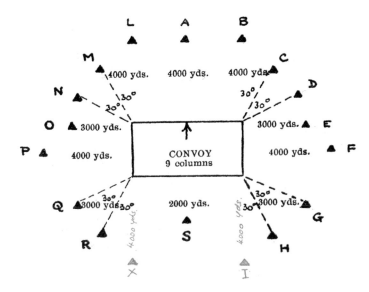

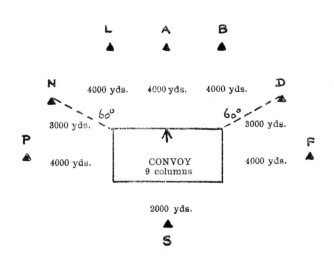

Convoy formations. The one on the right is for eight escorts, the one on the left is a generic diagram for all purposes.

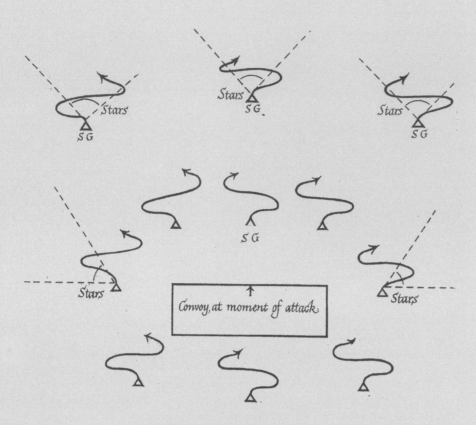

Convoy, at moment of attack

Operation Pineapple.

large concentration of U-boats. The acting group commander made the disastrous if understandable mistake of detaching escorts to rescue survivors, leaving the screen even weaker. But by July there were 82 escorts at sea, including some of the new frigates, for 11 convoys, giving an average of 7.5 per group, and the U-boats were on the run.[42]

At first each group developed its tactics independently, which caused problems when a ship operated with a strange group.

'Krakatoa Sir.'

'Krakatoa Yeoman? What on earth's that?' You would say raising yourself from your couch.

'Seems to be a code word Sir. Starshell on the other side of the convoy now, Sir – and rockets too. Funny group this, Sir. Wish we could get back to our own group – do at least speak English there, Sir.'[43]

Likewise, when two groups operated together in August 1941, 'many of them missed their old leader's voice, and may on occasion have waited for an executive order which never came'.[44] But tactics tended to be similar between the groups, even if the signals were different.

Captain Gilbert Roberts worked out the ideal system in his Tactical School at Liverpool. The whole thing was promulgated by means of the Atlantic Convoy Instructions, and reinforced by group training courses. A school was set up in Northern Ireland based on the yacht *Philante* and escort groups were sent there for training between convoys. It was perhaps less memorable than the course at Tobermory but no less gruelling and it concentrated on tactics rather than teamwork and character-building.

By the *King's Regulations,* the protection of the convoy was the first duty of the escort, and destroying U-boats or other attackers was secondary. It was not easy for an escort to spend a great deal of time attacking a U-boat which had been forced to submerge, for a slow ship like a corvette was little faster than some convoys and might take days to catch up again. The idea of forming special support groups, which would be ready to go to the help of a beleaguered convoy in

mid-ocean, was considered early on but it was March 1943 before enough ships were available to implement it, and five support groups were formed. They tended to be more uniform than escort groups, because they needed faster ships to rush to the aid of a beleaguered convoy or break up a concentration of U-boats. The First Support Group, for example, was mainly River class frigates, and F J Walker's famous Second Support Group, which held the record for the number of U-boats destroyed, used *Black Swan* class sloops.

Convoy Escort

The ocean escort was grouped round its convoy. In November 1940, they were placed 3000 yards apart, though it was recognised that this was not infallible with the limited number of ships available.

…a U-boat attempting an attack may well be sighted or heard by hydrophone effect before she reaches a firing position. If she gets through the escort unobserved and undetected, the first intimation that an attack has taken place, is generally the flash or noise of a torpedo explosion.[45]

Standard formations evolved for daytime, when there was sufficient light for a periscope attack, and night when a surfaced attack might escape detection. With a typical seven-ship escort in the daytime, one would be stationed 4000 yards forward of each side of the convoy, with others 3000 yards out at 60 degrees. Two more were 4000 yards out on the beam. Attack from astern was unlikely as the convoy was faster than a submerged U-boat, but it was recommended that whenever possible one ship should be stationed astern as a 'whipper in' to deal with stragglers and emergencies. By night, there would only be one ship ahead of the convoy, with two astern. By 1943 it was assumed that all ships had radar; if any were absent or their sets were out of action, the screen should be rearranged to close the gap. With extra ships, the commander might order an extended escort with ships 12,000 yards ahead in good conditions In rough weather ships might be stationed some distance upwind.

Asdic's main limitation was that its range was no more than 2500 yards, which meant that it was difficult to give all-round cover to a convoy when escorts were in short supply. Even with the stronger escort groups of 1943, it was recognised that 'the convoy torpedo zone is too large for the number of escorts normally available to provide complete asdic cover'. If he was reasonably sure that attack from astern was unlikely, a commander might use a day-screening pattern with all ships in line abreast ahead of the convoy to detect any U-boats that might be lying in wait hoping to be overrun by the convoy and then attack from inside.

In a danger area, a convoy might zigzag to spoil the aim of the U-boat commanders. There were 43 standard patterns of zigzags available in 1940, 14 of which were suitable for convoys of various types. Pattern 15 was for a convoy of any speed, in low visibility or heavy seas, when large alterations of course were considered dangerous. The convoy ran on its normal course for precisely five minutes, then turned 30 degrees to port. After another 10 minutes it turned 30 degrees to starboard, and 30 degrees to starboard again after five minutes. There were five more alterations of course until after an hour the convoy was back on its normal course, having covered about 91 per cent of the distance run towards its destination. Convoy zigzag No. 16 was more complex. It involved 16 alterations of 15, 25, 30 and 35 degrees over two hours and was in general use in clear weather in submarine infested areas.[46] Convoy zigzagging became unfashionable later in the war, but escorts continued to do it to increase the area of their Asdic cover. By day they followed the motions of the senior officer, at night they steered independently within prescribed limits.[47]

Reactions to Attack

By November 1940 it was established that in the event of a night attack,

All escorts on the engaged side, or on both sides if the side of the attack is in doubt, turn 90 degrees outwards together and proceed at full speed for a distance of ten miles from the convoy, firing starshell over the whole arc away from the convoy to illuminate the area.[48]

This later became known as a 'raspberry', or 'half raspberry' in its abbreviated form. The use of fruit code names became common, as did the principle of 'turning night into day' to the disadvantage of a surfaced U-boat. By 1943 there were several different operations that might be ordered in the event of a threat. If there was an Asdic contact close ahead of the convoy, the ship would counter attack at once and hoist a warning signal. If it was further away, she would attempt to identify the contact more carefully before warning and attacking. A hydrophone effect contact at night probably meant a surfaced boat. The escort would alter course towards it and try to get a radar echo. With a radar contact, she would again alter course towards it at maximum speed and report it by radio. On sighting a U-boat at close range an escort would either open fire or ram, then drop shallow depth charges over the site. If she saw a torpedo track she would take avoiding action, hoist a warning signal and then run along the track of the torpedo hoping to find the submarine that had fired it.

If a ship in the convoy was torpedoed by day, the senior officer would make the code word 'Artichoke' over the radio. The ship in the 'whipper in' position would steer towards the casualty, while those on the forward positions would go on the reciprocal course and those on the flanks would continue forward until they reached the suspected position of the U-boat. It was hoped to 'cover as far as possible the area in which the U-boat is likely to be'. If the attack took place by night and it was believed to be from a single U-boat, 'banana', the successor to raspberry, was used. By 1943 the value of turning night into day by use of illuminants was being questioned, with the increased use of radar and the risk of spoiling the vision of lookouts. A suspected pack attack was met by 'pineapple' in which the all the escorts would go to full speed, transmit on their Asdic and zigzag wildly to increase the cover. If a U-boat was believed to be submerged in a particular area at night, Operation Observant was carried out. The first escort to arrive searched round a square with 2-mile sides after marking out the central point with a flare. The second went to the edge of the square opposite the first. If escorts could be spared from the convoy long enough, they might hunt the U-boat to exhaustion so that it was forced to surface after its air was used up.[49]

Air Support

Convoys could be supported from the air by two main sources. Carrier-borne aircraft began to appear with the introduction of the MAC ship and later the escort carrier. They generally operated low-performance aircraft such as the Fairey Swordfish. They communicated with the carrier on the convoy radio telephone wavelength, which was linked with the escort commander. Their crews were trained by the navy and they could be briefed and debriefed on board the carrier, so good liaison was maintained. The only difficulty was of command, because the carrier captain was often senior to the escort group commander.

John Kilbracken flew 'Vipers' from *Empire MacAlpine,* consisting of two or three hours clockwise round the convoy, keeping it in sight at about 15 miles range. He was more nervous when sent out to chase a reported U-boat, his first time out of sight of land and ships.

On such flights, the monotony and vastness of that unending expanse beneath us becomes so intense that any break is always welcome – a slick of oil, a flight of sea-birds, a large patch of seaweed, a whale or an iceberg – and we would swoop down to examine it. All eyes skinned but nothing to be seen. And we start our square search, which will take another hour, of the area surrounding it.[50]

It was recognised that the majority of such patrols would only have a deterrent effect. Nevertheless, escort carrier borne aircraft had their first major engagement in May 1943, when *Biter's* planes attacked six U-boats, and sank one. Later in the month *Bogue's* aircraft made six attacks in a few hours, sinking one submarine and helping a convoy to get through without loss.

Communication with shore-based aircraft, operated and trained by the RAF, was generally more difficult. Captain Macintyre railed against the futility of many early patrols due to poor training and communication. 'A code of very brief signals was devised to cut down signalling to a minimum. A typical one was the signal IGO [by flashing light] which meant, "My time with the convoy is up, I am returning to base."'[51] Things began to improve with better liaison. From the air, Sunderland pilot Alan W Deller reported:

As soon as the senior officer was satisfied as to our identity he flashed us instructions for the type of patrol he wanted us to carry out, we having told him how long we could stay with the convoy … The naval operators, evidently feeling that we were a long way up there in the sky, turned up the volume on their powerful sets to the point where their speech was so overmodulated as to be almost unintelligible, largely just a meaningless roaring noise. So communication tended to be mainly by lamp and here the difficulty often was that senior officers of escorts did not fully appreciate how relatively short our time with them had to be: they were apt to indulge in lengthy exchanges in Morse by signal lamp when we wanted to get off on our patrol.[52]

Depth Charges

The depth charge was simply a container filled with explosives set to explode when the water pressure indicated a certain depth. They could be dropped from rails, providing the ship was going fast enough to avoid blowing her own stern off with the explosion, or fired 40 yards out from

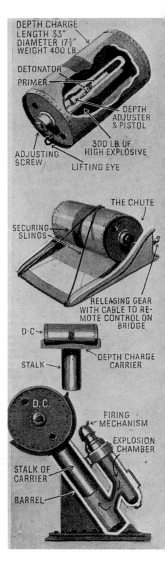

Depth charges and the means of dropping and throwing them.

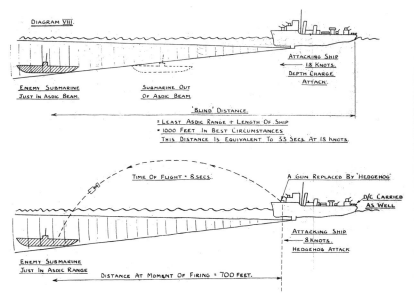

Above left: The advantages of attacking by Hedgehog, avoiding the blind area under the escort.

Above right: The Squid triple-barrelled anti-submarine mortar.

throwers on either side of the ship to increase the spread of a pattern. They came in normal types with a 150-pound weight to sink it, and heavy with a 300-pound weight to make it sink more quickly in deep attacks.

Early estimates about how much damage a depth charge could do at a distance were too optimistic, and the Battle of the Atlantic was fought in deep waters, so new tactics were necessary. The 14-charge pattern was developed, with settings at 150, 300 and 385 feet. It was found that one charge tended to interfere with another, and the 10-charge pattern then became standard 'when carrying out a deliberate attack on a contact which is very likely to be a U-boat, in waters of 40 fathoms or more'. For a shallow attack, the charges were set at 100 and 225 feet, for a medium attack at 150 and 300 feet, and for a deep pattern at 150 and 385 feet. On the buzzer signal to fire, two charges, one normal and one heavy, were fired from the throwers on each side, and a normal and a heavy charge were released from the rails. Four seconds later when travelling at a speed of 18 knots, or after travelling 40 yards, another normal and a heavy charge were released from the rails, and this was repeated after a further 4 seconds or 40 yards.[53] Eight, seven and five-charge patterns could also be used, mostly from ships which were not fitted for the full complement.

If there was enough time, ships and depth charges to mount an extensive attack, the U-boat's fate was probably sealed. The plaster attack was developed by Walker's celebrated Second Escort Group and consisted of three ships dropping as many charges as possible at five-second intervals, as they did in June 1943.

…the three ships steamed over the 'pinged' position of the U-boat dropping a continuous stream of depth charges…the sea heaved and boiled under the non-stop impact of the explosions. Twisting and turning always leaving a trail of charges, the ships 'plastered' the area of U-202. In three minutes a total of seventy-six depth charges had rocked and shaken the attacking ships almost as much as it had the U-boat.[54]

The creeping attack was also developed by Walker's group but used by others.

The creeping attack made use of the fact that the U-boat's hydrophones were masked by its own propeller noises from hearing a ship coming up slowly from right astern. So one ship would hold contact at about 1,000 yards astern of the U-boat and would direct a consort up to the U-boat's wake at the slowest possible speed to overtake. Then, as the consort crept into position over the unsuspecting U-boat, at an order from the directing ship, a stream of twenty-six depth-charges set to their maximum depth would go down to explode accurately around the target.[55]

New Weapons

The greatest single problem with depth charge attack was that the target would disappear from the Asdic some distance from the ship, especially if it was deep. The attacking ship had to make intelligent guesses about its movements and drop the depth charges almost blind – U-boat captains knew this well and manoeuvred unpredictably during this interval. Ahead-throwing weapons were developed to attack the U-boat while it was still in Asdic range. The Hedgehog consisted of 24 spigot mortars firing a charge of up to 35 pounds of explosive ahead of the ship, to land in a circle 100 feet in diameter in which it was hoped would include the U-boat. Fitted to River class frigates and to many corvettes and other ships, it was rushed into service in 1942 to beat its rival, Squid, and crews were inadequately trained. Aiming and firing were much more complex than with depth charges, and the early success rate was low. The charges only exploded if they actually hit the submarine, so they did not have the psychological impact, on both sides, of the depth charge. Nevertheless, orders were given to use the Hedgehog when possible, to avoid the dangers posed by the German acoustic torpedo. This tended to make its reputation worse, as it was fired without proper preparation. Success rates dropped to less than 7 per cent between April and July 1943. A series of trials off Londonderry established faults in maintenance and procedure. Once these were corrected, Hedgehog had a success rate of 37 per cent. By that time its main rival was in service and was proving even more successful.

Squid was a three-barrelled mortar fired from the forward part of the ship. Unlike Hedgehog it used depth rather than contact charges, and it was aimed using direct links to the ship's Asdic, including automatic depth settings for the charges. Fitted on Castle class corvettes and the new Loch class frigates, it soon proved highly successful, especially in twin mounts, which had a success rate of 40 per cent early in 1945.

In September the frigate *Lagan* was the first ship to be sunk by the new German acoustic torpedo, known to the Allies as GNAT. It was only effective against ships doing between 10 and 18 knots, so unlike other weapons it was aimed at escorts rather than merchantmen. It was countered by reducing speed in an attack, which made Hedgehog rather than depth charges necessary, and by towing a noise-making machine known as Foxer behind the ship. That worked, but it made much more noise than the ship itself and could give her position away. Another technique was 'step aside' in which an attacking ship would alter course suddenly.

Attack on the Surface

The convoy escort had two main means of attacking a U-boat on the surface – gun and ramming. The 4-inch gun fitted on many escorts was 'the light "Woolworth" type, developed for merchant ships, with a comparatively short range'. It had no great superiority over the U-boat gun, but the submarine was not likely to stand and fight.[56] Destroyers had bigger and better guns, and also had more sophisticated aiming systems using directors, but corvettes and frigates had to rely on the marksmanship of the gunners to achieve hits. Even then, the 4-inch was barely enough to penetrate a stout U-boat hull, and many escaped.

Ramming was considered a suitable tactic at first. By its nature a submarine has very little reserve buoyancy, so a small penetration of the hull is likely to be fatal. Twenty-seven U-boats were rammed with some degree of success in 1940–3, and in about half of these cases ramming was the major cause of sinking. But ramming was not certain to sink the boat, and it could often harm the rammer – the destroyer *Oribi* rammed *U-531* at 22 knots in May 1943 and her bow was considerably damaged. After that captains were ordered to ram only if there was no other way of preventing imminent danger.[57]

Air Defence

In ocean convoys the main air threat was from the long-range Focke-Wulf Kondor. These four-engined aircraft were the longest range machines the Germans had at the time, but their primary role was reconnaissance. The appearance of one in the vicinity of a convoy tended to signal an imminent attack. Before MAC ships and escort carriers became general, the single-use Hurricane fighters were deployed against them.

Russian convoys generally had the resources of the Home Fleet, including aircraft carriers, for their defence. East coast convoys could be protected by RAF fighters but had to carry out a good deal of their own defence as well. The convoys were long and narrow to fit into the space between the shore and the east coast minefield. They generally sailed from the well-defended Thames Estuary in daylight, then rounded East Anglia by night, where they were closest to the Dutch coast. Next day they were between the Wash and the Tyne, where the risk of air attack was much less.

4 Escort Bases

Most Second World War escort bases were in one sense or another improvised, because the Fall of France closed the ports in the south and east, and the U-boat war extended far wider than anyone had predicted. There was no time for extensive civil engineering work, so escort bases were either natural harbours such as Loch Ewe, or established commercial ports such as Liverpool. In some bases, such as the Clyde and Liverpool, warships and merchant ships shared the facilities. Others, such as Londonderry and Harwich, were mainly used by warships. Escort vessels had administrative, technical and personnel support in the bases where they found themselves. Each British group in the Battle of the Atlantic was attached to a port such as Liverpool, Londonderry or the Clyde, but it might also find support while waiting at St John's in Newfoundland or Freetown in Sierra Leone, for example. It was a system that worked quite well, with shore officers who were close to the needs of the ships and gave them priority. Donald Macintyre felt that this contrasted with more established bases such as Plymouth: 'We were intruders there and made to feel ourselves nuisances'.[58]

Apart from a large harbour, a good escort base needed a headquarters, often with an operations room, and an accounting base for the ships. It had to be defended against attack from the air, surface vessels, submarines, torpedoes and mines. In view of the excessively short range of many escort vessels, fuel supply was critical. It needed recreation facilities for crews between missions, and good transport to send them on leave – Liverpool's location, with a good rail network, was the best provided for this. It had various training establishments, including a school, for merchant ship gunners, and simulators for continuity training. Londonderry, for example, had a Night Escort Attack Teacher, an Anti-

A *Luftwaffe* **reconnaissance photograph of Liverpool. Gladstone Dock, the main escort base, is on the top left.**

Submarine and Tactical School, two Anti-Submarine Attack Teachers, depth charge, Hedgehog and Squid drillers, a mock up of a U-boat for boarding parties, and gunnery, signals, direction finding and radar schools.[59] A base also needed repair facilities for merchant ships and warships suffering from the effects of enemy action or rough weather.

Naval Control of Shipping

All the branches of the inshore navy were to be found in the typical base: the Patrol Service, Controlled Minefields, Coastal Forces, Boom Defence and the Examination Service. One important element was the Naval Control of Shipping Office (NCSO). This was manned by former officers, later assisted by Wren officers. They controlled the routing of convoys which, they were urged, 'should never be allowed to become a routine matter'. They decided which ships should sail independently, or in fast or slow convoys. They conducted the convoy briefing and made up the information packs that were issued to each captain.[60]

One of the most important bases was at Southend, from where ships entering the Thames Estuary were controlled. At the beginning of the war it had a strength of one captain and 11 other officers of the RN and RNR, with four signallers, a writer and two civilian clerks. By 1944 HMS *Leigh* was under the command of a commodore who doubled as NCSO Thames, with a staff of 78 officers and 25 Wren officers by early 1944. The latter were advised that a female boarding officer should have already been in a boat's crew to learn seamanship; to have 'a complete lack of sense of modesty' as she was likely to find sailors in all states of undress on boarding; to be able to resist continuous offers of drinks; and to be 'elastic and acrobatic' enough to climb ladders and planks.[61]

The core of the command was formed by two dozen commanders, RNR, who had experience of both the Royal and Merchant navies. Fifteen of them had been recalled from retirement to serve. There was little difficulty with routing as there was only one path inside the east coast minefields, but timing was very important so that convoys were not exposed during daylight in the most dangerous sectors. Unlike other commands *Leigh* was closely involved in the headline events of the war: the evacuation from Dunkirk, the London blitz and the Normandy landings. It handled a total of 3367 convoys, of which two thirds were along the east coast.[62]

Liverpool

Liverpool was one of the world's great ports, vying with London for the leading position within Britain. It was largely an artificial creation, with many miles of enclosed docks on the east bank of the River Mersey and more on the other side at Birkenhead. It had very little naval presence in peacetime, but with the virtual closure of the Port of London and the English Channel to ocean shipping, it became the main entry point to the United Kingdom for most of the war. It also became the base for many escort vessels, which were moored in Gladstone Dock in the northern end of the port. Nicholas Monsarrat was a native and it was his favourite base, despite regular bombing in 1940–1.

Liverpool, the hub of the Western Approaches command, was a target well worth hitting. There were never less than a hundred ships in harbour, loading and unloading: plus their tugs, and the oil storage tanks, and eleven miles of docks with their cranes and ammunition barges and ship-repair yards and warehouses and dock-gates and the whole network of rail-linkage which bound it to the rest of England. Worth hitting, it was now hit, with relentless energy, for eight nights on end.[63]

The Clyde

Together the main Clyde ports of Glasgow and Greenock were much smaller than Liverpool or London, accounting for about 4 per cent of British trade before the war. Their rail links with other parts of the country were not extensive, and they had small dock labour forces. However, the Firth of Clyde was further from bombing than any other industrial part of Britain (despite devastating raids on Clydebank on 13 and 14 March 1941) and offered a large area of anchorage in the Tail of the Bank off Greenock, and in several sea lochs. To supplement the port facilities, dockers were brought up from London. A scheme of 'overside discharge' was started, in which the cargoes of arriving ocean merchant ships were unloaded into coasters to go to smaller ports round the country. A new port was created at Faslane on the Gareloch, intended for the export of military personnel and goods, such as the heavy equipment for the Torch landings in North Africa.

The Clyde also served as a main base for escort forces. It was less popular than Liverpool, partly because the ships had to moor in a rather exposed position at the Tail of the Bank rather than come alongside.

The great anchorage at the mouth of the Clyde was always choc-a-bloc with hundreds of ships, ranging from coasters to the huge passenger liners running as troopships. To the uninitiated they were berthed in the most complete confusion and with barely room to swing with the tide. The oiler to which one was invariably ordered on arrival was berthed in a remote and awkward spot.

Somehow one always arrived after dark and it was always raining cats and dogs and usually blowing a gale as well… Cursing miserably, peering desperately through the downpour and the dark, one would creep tortuously through the seemingly solid mass of darkened ships…. Arrived at our anchorage finally at the Tail of the Bank, the odds were that there would be no peace, for the poor holding ground meant anchor watch and steam on the engines at the slightest blow.[64]

Londonderry

The idea of using Londonderry originated in September 1940. It had declined as a port since 1922 when the independence of Eire cut it off from most of its hinterland. It was on the fringes of the United Kingdom, and the western shore of the River Foyle leading up to it was Irish territory. It was 4 miles upstream, in a narrow river with rather run-down facilities including jetties and a graving dock. It was of little use for merchant ships, because it had no direct link with the British rail system, but its greatest advantage was its situation. Apart from Campbeltown near the end of the Kintyre peninsula, it was the closest British port to the area in which the Battle of the Atlantic was fought, which made it ideal in view of the short range of many escort vessels. Furthermore, Campbeltown was isolated and in a very sparsely populated area. Londonderry was close to industrial Belfast and had a large civilian labour force, for Northern Ireland was not subject to conscription.

Captain P Ruck-Keene built up the base and in February 1942 it was

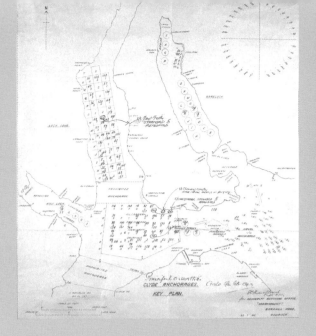

given priority 'to relieve the Clyde and give greater endurance to the escort forces'.[65] The river was deepened, a repair workshop was built, and berths were constructed on the east side of the river for escorts to moor several deep. Maintenance was only carried out in urgent cases.

The aim of the maintenance and repair base is to service the vessels so that they continue running efficiently. Approved alterations and additions are only progressed or carried out when such action is possible within the turn round periods.

By February 1941 thirty-six ships were based at Londonderry. The base had a staff of 1455 by the beginning of 1944, headed by a Commodore (D). Commander D A Rayner describes the approach to Londonderry.

Leaving the dispassionate sea behind you as you go up the River Foyle, the friendly, green land enfolds you. Further and further your ship noses her way up the tortuous channel, until an S bend at Lishally entirely shuts out all sign of the sea. Your ship steams on between the walls of woodland, so that her salt-encrusted sides are almost brushed by the overhanging branches; and your bow wave and wash, which for weeks have been lost among the immensity of the ocean, now slip-slop amongst the tree roots, and stir the long tendrils of seaweed on half-tide ledges. Another S-turn, and there before you lies the enchanted city, silhouetted against the light of the noon-day sun. In the shadow of the wharf would be lying a long single line of escorts. … In later years the line became four or five deep, and ninety per cent of them were ready for sea.[66]

Londonderry became the main eastern Atlantic base for British, Canadian and American escorts, and 15 groups were stationed there by July 1943.[67]

East Coast Bases

Harwich Harbour is one of the best in eastern England north of the Thames, a natural anchorage formed by the confluence of the rivers Stour and Orwell. It had been well known to the navy since the time of Samuel Pepys two and a half centuries earlier. The training base HMS *Ganges* was on the peninsula between the two rivers, and there were Coastal Forces and RAF bases at Felixstowe to the north. Harwich served many purposes in wartime, including the base for the sloops and corvettes which escorted the coal convoys to London and the south. Most of the naval facilities were at Parkeston Quay, the continental ferry port 3 miles up the Stour – the town quays at Harwich were used for local defence craft and salvage and rescue tugs. A large temperance club for ratings was set up at Parkeston, while their superiors had the use of the Michaelston Naval Officers' Club, established by the maintenance captain of the port and situated in beautiful grounds 2½ miles from Parkeston. Various hotels

and houses were taken over, but the LNER Hotel remained an anomaly. It was in civilian hands but could only be reached by those with a naval pass. The base appears, thinly disguised, in Monsarrat's *East Coast Corvette.*

The Naval Base from which we operated was small and self contained, a sort of feudal village, graded in rank and consequence, where everyone knew everyone else; and like other villages it had its odd characters, its oldest inhabitants, its scandal-mongers, and its essential unity and comradeship. … But it led, sometimes, to an outlook which might with justice be described as restricted. … But these were odd backwaters and eccentricities, by no means the general rule. The place was justly renowned as being one of the best Naval Bases in Great Britain; it had about it, both ashore and afloat, an air of unruffled solidity and comradeship which is the only sure foundation for success in sea warfare.[68]

The 1st Corvette Flotilla was based at Harwich for the whole of the war. It used several sloops, initially for anti-submarine patrol and escort duties. By 1940 it was clear that aircraft were the greater threat in the area and they were converted to AA ships, with Oerlikons and 2-pounder pom-poms.

Loch Ewe

Loch Ewe in north-west Scotland had been used as a fleet anchorage in the First World War, and it was revived in 1939 when Scapa became untenable for a while. It was empty for most of 1940, until December when it was decided to develop it for convoys heading round the north of the country to avoid the English Channel. Soon it was being used to assemble parts of convoys going to Halifax, Sierra Leone, Iceland, Gibraltar and North Africa. Its mouth was defended by trawlers and 6-inch gun batteries. It soon had a total staff of 1535, including 175 Wrens. Of these, the most difficult were the crews of the merchant oilers and auxiliaries who were 'continually going ashore without leave, getting drunk, breaking leave etc'. A large oil tank was built, a cinema was erected, but shore accommodation remained a problem, with only a small hotel for officers' quarters and headquarters. Loch Ewe was one of the remotest of bases, with no rail facilities, and even the shore staff had restricted leave. There were no shore amusements except those provided by the navy, such as football pitches. In 1941 the base was handling an average of 80 merchant ships and 20 escorts per week.[69]

The Western Atlantic

Halifax in Nova Scotia is a great natural harbour, in an inlet 4 miles long and nearly a mile wide at its entrance, with an area of 13 square miles

Above left: The Clyde anchorages, with the naval anchorages on the right, and the others reserved for merchant ships. The red marks show ships that went aground in a storm of 1943.

Above right: Londonderry, with the escort base on the right.

A convoy enters Murmansk through a channel cleared by an icebreaker, with the aurora borealis in the winter sky. A painting by Charles Pears.

inside. It was far from the main agricultural and industrial centres of Canada so it was under-employed in peacetime, which left a good deal of space in war. It was already a Canadian navy base and it became the main assembly point for fast convoys across the Atlantic. Some escort forces were also based there, with 47 Canadian and 14 British warships in June 1942.

Convoys also assembled at Sydney, a commodious but little used natural harbour 250 miles east of Halifax, until the middle of 1942 after which they pressed on to New York. Sydney was defended by a local force of corvettes and minesweepers, a few of which were manned by the Royal Navy.

St John's in Newfoundland was a smaller natural harbour, no more than 700 yards wide and 2100 yards long. Much of the space was taken up with small and dilapidated old wharves. It had no confined approach channel, which made it easy to enter but difficult to defend. There were some who protested in May 1941 when it was decided to develop St John's as a major escort force base, but it had one great advantage – it was the closest point of North America to Britain, and formed a counterpart to Londonderry. Even so, as the naval song put it, 'From Newfy to Derry's a bloody long way'. Although Newfoundland was not part of Canada at the time, the Canadian government agreed to fund the base to the sum of $16 million. A new base was designed to accommodate 5000 men in an area almost the size of Toronto, but like many such works it was not completed on

time. At its peak at the beginning of 1944 nearly 90 British, Canadian and Free French ships were based there, but that was only part of its work, for during 1942 it repaired 834 naval ships in more than 9000 man days. It was a port of refuge for vessels who got into trouble in the North Atlantic, an assembly point for convoys to Greenland and other places in the region, and a port for merchant ships waiting for convoy after repairs.[70]

Iceland

Iceland was occupied by British forces in May 1940 to forestall a possible German invasion. The government and population maintained an 'attitude of undemonstrative aloofness' to the occupiers but were more friendly to the Americans who formally took over the occupation in July the following year. British forces remained on the island, to the concern of the Icelandic Government. The British used Iceland as an advanced base for the Home Fleet in the first instance. The harbour in the capital Reykjavik, was too small and difficult to protect, so they developed Hvalfjord. It was developed as a base during the Battle of the Atlantic, for destroyers and escorts carrying out the middle phase of a transatlantic escort. From 1941 it was also used for the assembly of Arctic convoys to Russia.

Hvalfjord was a useful if stormy harbour. 'The holding ground…is good, but squalls come down the valleys between the mountains with

Philoctetes were still in use. The Freetown escort force protected ships on their way south towards South Africa and the Far East.

Russian Bases

In summer, Artic convoys headed for Archangel, the Soviet Union's main northern port. It had a population of 281,000 in 1939 and good rail links to Leningrad, Moscow and the Urals. Convoys passed through the White Sea, sailing from one lighthouse to another by a 2-mile-wide channel maintained by Russian minesweepers. They hoisted international flag signals to identify themselves to the Russians and went down the Dvina Channel. Ships of up to 22-feet draft were able to cross the bar into the port. Larger ones anchored outside, but still needed anti-submarine protection, which was largely provided by their own escorts. Meanwhile, the skies above were patrolled by aircraft, including Hurricanes and American Tomahawk fighters supplied by these very convoys.

Corvettes and trawlers berthed at a timber yard; destroyers at Voskresennski Quay, or they had to anchor offshore, as did cruisers. The wharves were of rough wood, there were no bollards and shore berthing parties could not be guaranteed. While in port ships were kept at four hours' notice for steam and were recommended to have at least one boiler in operation to heat the ship and run auxiliary machinery. They were warned to watch out for large pieces of timber floating down the river and to withdraw their Asdic domes. A certain amount of oil fuel was available from lighters, but Russian coal was considered inferior and was to be avoided.

If crews were allowed ashore, their welcome and facilities were very limited. They could only be landed at Voskresennski Quay, there was a strict curfew, Russian sentries had a tendency to shoot on sight, and a strong presence by the secrete police, the NKVD, was taken for granted. Sailors were warned strictly not to sell any of their tobacco or other goods ashore. There were, however, tennis, football and hockey grounds and a 'large commodious club provided by the Russian seamen's trade union. But even there, vodka and spirits were not to be consumed'.[72]

Archangel was closed in winter unless icebreakers were used, and ships went to Murmansk where the Atlantic drift kept the port ice-free. Again the crews were not particularly welcome in the town at the head of the Kola Inlet.

Polyarnoe, deep in snow and in almost perpetual darkness, was a cluster of dreary-looking wooden buildings about half a mile inland. There was a sort of track leading to it which we had permission to use for exercise, but every hundred yards there were sentries in fur hat and with fixed bayonets, ready to prod us if we dared strike out on our own. ... There was little to do in Polyarnoe except walk to the village and back, read and drink.[73]

great violence during bad weather'. Nissen huts were built on both sides of the fjord. Net and anti-aircraft defences were prepared. At first ships refuelled from naval oilers, but a farm at Hvitanes near the end of the inlet was rented and used as a fuel depot. Eventually there were 52 tanks holding 54,000 tons of furnace oil, 7650 of diesel and 32,000 of petrol. This was much more than naval needs in the area, and it was used for transhipment of fuel for other purposes. The staff of the base reached 818 under a rear-admiral in 1941. The depot ship *Hecla* was used for the repair of destroyers and escorts, while Royal Marine engineers began the construction of a base on shore. The Admiralty considered that Hvalfjord was an anchorage 'of considerable strategic importance', but it was politically insecure and diplomatically difficult, and plans were made to evacuate it as soon as the war was over.[71]

Freetown

Freetown in the British colony of Sierra Leone was the only large natural harbour in West Africa, and was strategically situated on the 'Atlantic narrows' only about 1500 miles from the coast of Brazil. There were ambitious plans to develop it as large naval base, but the money was never forthcoming to complete a deep-water quay and associated works. However, by 1944 a corvette jetty and naval barracks were well advanced in the Kissy area, though the base and repair ships *Edinburgh Castle* and

PART XI
The Coastal Navies

1 Coastal Forces

Coastal Forces was one of the great growth areas of the wartime navy, expanding from almost nothing to more than 20,000 men, using a varied force of very small warships outside the general line of development, and attracting a great deal of publicity during the war. Yet their success was highly ambiguous. They were not as obviously necessary as major warships, escort vessels and landing craft for example, no matter how ingenious their designers or how brave their crews.

Early Development

There were two essential problems with British coastal forces – the lack of any development for more than 15 years in a highly technical field, and the lack of a suitable engine.[1] The British had used fast power boats known as coastal motor boats in the First World War, but there was no post-war naval interest until 1935 when Hubert Scott Paine of the British Power Boat Company persuaded the Admiralty to invest in one of his designs. Scott Paine was something of an enthusiast and his claims for fast craft were exaggerated. He also upset his commercial rivals such as Vosper and Thornycroft by his exclusive deal with the Admiralty. In the meantime the Germans and Italians made good progress in the field, and Scott Paine's 60-foot boat proved unsatisfactory, though it led to a re-birth of interest. In 1936 Vospers produced a larger, 68-foot boat, MTB 102, which could reach a speed of 43.7 knots. In 1938 the British Power Boat Company responded with a 70-foot boat, and the Admiralty decided to go ahead with orders for boats of that length from Vospers and Thornycroft.

The fast ships of Coastal Forces were motor torpedo boats or MTBs and motor gunboats or MGBs. Many of these were of the 'hard chine' hull form, with very distinctive edges between the upper and lower part of the hull. They were designed for 'planing', using 'dynamic lift' to raise most of the hull out of the water at high speeds of 40 knots or so. The bottom was V-shaped, because a flat bottom would slam too much in the waves and when it re-entered the water as the boat slowed down. This form tended to create a short, wide boat, and a typical MTB was about two and a half times as wide as a destroyer in proportion to its length. This made it inefficient at lower speeds. Because of the lack of continuous development there were many problems with matters such as propeller design. The amount and distribution of weight was crucial, especially when planing, but coastal forces suffered from the usual wartime additions of guns and other equipment, often fitted at flotilla level without the consent of the naval constructors.

MTBs

The motor torpedo boat was intended to carry two or more torpedoes on a minimum size of hull at a maximum speed, to attack enemy merchant ships and warships in coastal waters. It had a certain attraction as a cheap, fast craft manned by non-naval personnel which could potentially destroy a ship of many times its own value. But it was these very factors which made it unpopular with the Admiralty in the inter-war period, and enhanced its appeal to weaker navies such as Germany and Italy.

After the competition between the builders in the late 1930s, most construction of MTBs was based on the Vosper design, with a hull form that did not change much. Typical boats, built between 1942 and 1944, were of 37 tons on a length of 72½ feet. They had a speed of 38–40 knots if fitted with their intended engines, two torpedo tubes, a 20mm gun and two machine guns and were operated by a crew of 13.

The British Power Boat Company (BPB) continued to build boats to its own design, as did other firms such as White of Cowes and Camper and Nicholson. The BPB type had a distinctive hull with its maximum breadth well forward and a deck which rounded down towards the bows to improve the view forward. Other boats were supplied under lend-lease by the Electric Boat Company (Elco) of New Jersey.

MGBs

There was no need for a motor gunboat until 1940, when the fall of Norway, the Netherlands and France created the possibility of short-range warfare in the 'narrow seas' around Britain. The British MTB was not big enough to carry a defensive armament of its own, and it was not suitable for fighting off E-boat attacks on convoys. A group of about a dozen motor anti-submarine boats or MA/SBs were already under construction, mostly by BPB, and were unemployed because the enemy did not launch an inshore campaign. Most of them were converted into motor gunboats by fitting 2-pounder and 20mm guns, but they were slow at 23 knots. Various other vessels were taken over from defeated

allies, from commercial orders for other countries, or transferred from the United States. The first British boats designed as MGBs were again produced by BPB and had the characteristic hull shape. They were 71 feet long, had a speed of up to 40 knots and were fitted with a 2-pounder, two Oerlikons and four machine guns. Others were designed by the yacht-builders Camper and Nicholson and the American firm of Higgins, so the force remained small and miscellaneous until the larger boats of the Fairmile type came into being.

Steam gunboats were built mainly because the petrol engines of MGBs were too noisy for a surprise attack. They had a certain amount of success, but their numerous steam pipes and boilers were vulnerable to a single hit, and armouring them added greatly to the weight. In any case, fast craft were likely to be given away by the huge white bow wave as much as by the noise. Only seven steam gunboats were built, but they were given names rather than numbers.

MLs

Early in the war the Fairmile Company of Cobham approached the Admiralty with an idea for a 110-foot motor launch for anti-submarine purposes. Twelve of this boat, known as the A type, were ordered but proved too slow for an MTB and too weak for general purposes. The B type was even slower at 20 knots, but more robust and eventually 568 of them were built at home and abroad. Initially they carried a 3-pounder gun and two machine guns, with a complement of 16.

In 1943 Admiral Binney found that MLs were mainly involved in coastal convoy escort but performed different functions in each of the home commands. Such versatility often meant that they were not ideal for any of the tasks. Out of six flotillas in the Nore, three were used as close escorts where E-boat attack was likely. The others normally operated to the east of convoys to give early warning of attack, though they were too slow to intercept E-boats. Their main value with the convoys was as lifeboats for torpedoed or bombed ships. In Orkney and Shetland it was felt that MLs were unsuitable for nine months of the year due to bad weather, except one flotilla for the defence of Scapa. In the Western Approaches, coastal convoy escort was regarded as 'soul-destroying work', which was undermining the spirit of 'keen and efficient officers and ratings'. MLs were slightly more useful in the Plymouth and Portsmouth commands, where convoys were more compact than on the east coast and the boats formed a large part of the

fitted to the engine to increase the speed to 32.5 knots. Later craft were fitted as combined MTBs and MGBs, with four 18-inch torpedo tubes, two 6-pounders, Oerlikons and machine guns. In all 228 were completed, 19 of them for the RAF as air-sea rescue launches.

HDMLs

Harbour defence motor launches were used for anti-submarine patrols along booms and at harbour entrances, for the destruction of submarines detected by hydrophones and other devices, for patrol against surface attack and as lookouts for enemy minelaying. The first design was produced late in 1939, after the *Royal Oak* was sunk at Scapa. They were wooden round-bilge craft with a length of 72 feet and a speed of 11 or 12 knots. They were fitted with Asdic and armed with a 3-pounder gun, an Oerlikon and two Lewis machine guns. They were manned by two officers, two petty officers and eight ratings.[3] Four hundred and fifty of them were built. W J Holt considered them one of his best designs: 'In a seaway they seemed to possess an unusual harmony of weight, buoyancy and shape forward, in relation to pitching and speed, which enabled them to move in rhythm with the seas to make the best of prevailing conditions'.[4] Admiral Binney was sceptical about their value in 1943, as there had been no U-boat attacks on British ports since the *Royal Oak* three years earlier. He considered that the fishing drifter, manned by the Patrol Service, was superior in every respect.[5]

Building

The great majority of coastal forces craft were built in wood. One major advantage was that they did not compete with merchant shipping and larger warships for either materials or skilled labour, because their frames were often cut out by woodworking firms such as furniture makers, and assembled by yacht-builders. These included well-known yacht-builders such as Camper and Nicholson at Gosport and Alex Robertson at Sandbank in Scotland; and builders of inland pleasure craft such as Herbert Woods at Potter Heigham on the Norfolk Broads.

The Fairmile boats used the most developed system of mass production. The hull was based on plywood frames, cut out very economically by a woodworking company in Brentford near London. A bell-casting company made the propellers, a wire-netting manufacturer the rudders, and a radiator company made fuel and water tanks. The whole kit could be sent to a boat-builder's for erection and launch.[6]

Despite the best efforts, there were many problems with the wooden hulls. According to Holt:

As a result of heavy driving, it was found that the boats were prone to break their plywood frames in the forward part of the boat; also the keel scarphs were liable to pull and work, and the scarphs of the gunwales and deck stringers in the way of the engine room were liable to crepitation. It was found necessary to double the number of plywood frames forward and to fit steel angle bars along inboard edges of the plywood frames to act as a tension strip to prevent fracture.[7]

All this tended to undermine the original idea of a fast, light craft.

escort due to the shortage of destroyers. But on the whole Binney found 'no real enthusiasm' for MLs. None had ever sunk a U-boat and they were too slow to engage E-boats. They were only used because nothing else was available, and their presence would 'make a U-boat think'.[2]

The Fairmile D

The Fairmile Company continued to develop its 110-foot hull, and the C type of 1941 was a motor gunboat. Twenty-four were built, but it was still too slow at 26 knots. Meanwhile W J Holt, the chief coastal forces designer in the Naval Construction Department, had stepped in. A destroyer type of bow was joined to a motor boat stern, to give less pounding of the hull at high speed. After tank testing it was decided to use the hard chine hull form and a new boat of 110 feet was developed, far longer than previous British coastal units. It had four Packard engines giving a total of 5000 horsepower and a speed of just under 30 knots. The Fairmile D or 'Dog boat' proved a great success in several roles. Of the first 96 built, half were completed as MTBs, initially with two torpedo tubes, and half as MGBs, with the 2-pounder gun as the main armament. Development continued and reduction gearing was

Armament and Equipment

The standard armament of the early MTB was a pair of 21-inch torpedoes, one on each side. The Mark 8✱✱ torpedo was largely reserved for submarines and MTBs had to make do with older Mark 4 and 5 models until 1942. The following year the supply of 18-inch torpedoes increased and they had new warheads with 545 pounds of Torpex. It was now possible to fit four 18-inch tubes in larger MTBs, and two in smaller ones. However, its range was limited to 2500 yards and it was difficult to get that close to a well-escorted enemy convoy. Early ideas for rail discharge of torpedoes by Scott Paine and ram gear by Thornycroft were discarded and MTB torpedoes were carried in and fired from tubes on each side of the boat. A very simple sight was fitted to early boats for aiming, but it was too easy to confuse the settings for enemy angle with the bow angle in the dark, and a Mark 2 version, introduced in 1944, remedied these defects and allowed for steering by the coxswain, and radar control.[8]

Coastal forces carried a great variety of gun armament, and 18 different types are listed for the Fairmiles alone. Early motor torpedo boats carried only .303-inch machine guns in addition to the main armament. This was gradually increased as encounters with E-boats grew, and power-mounted .5-inch guns were added. Motor gunboats usually had the 2-pounder pom-pom as their main gun, and larger guns were fitted later on. Boats were increasingly fitted with radar, though the first type, 268PU, was very unsatisfactory and only had a range of 2 miles against an E-boat.

Officers and Men

Coastal Forces formed a separate manning division within the navy, equivalent to the three home ports or the Fleet Air Arm, but much smaller. It included 1294 officers and 7721 ratings in November 1942, and a total of 20,855 officers and ratings in September 1944.[9] Nearly all, about 98 per cent, were temporary RNVR officers and Hostilities Only ratings. In December 1940 they were placed under the Rear-Admiral, Coastal Forces, but that appointment later lapsed and they were integrated with the home commands. Each area had a Captain, Coastal Forces, and boats were organised in flotillas, normally eight boats under a lieutenant-commander. However, up to half the boats in any flotilla might be unserviceable at any given moment.

Coastal Forces was one of the most highly publicised parts of the navy, and attracted some very high-profile officers. One of the most famous was Peter Scott, son of Scott of the Antarctic, and destined to become the first great nature presenter on television. The 15th MGB Flotilla at Dartmouth included Guy Hamilton, a future film director, David Birkin, the husband and father of two famous singers, and Mike Marshall, an Oxford and England rugby player.[10] The Admiralty found the publicity useful in attracting ambitious young men who otherwise might have been drawn towards the air force. It quoted the career of the great Coastal Forces hero Robert Hichens:

…he thought how kind the sea had been to the small leggy boy of seven who had an important job to do twenty-five years later; for here he was in command of a flotilla of small but immensely powerful warships, each with the proud White Ensign blowing out straight in the wind of her own speed, each with her mighty roaring engines possessing the power of thousands of horses, each with

her deadly armament which had just blown to bits a strongly escorted enemy convoy, each with her crew of skilled sailors for whose lives he was responsible. … Not only Hitch but a lot of other men who were boys not so long ago have found that kind of astonishment…[11]

The fact that Hichens had been killed a year earlier did not seem to diminish the impact. Coastal Forces continued to attract large numbers of applications from newly-commissioned officers in HMS *King Alfred*. A typical boat was commanded by a lieutenant, with one or two sub-lieutenants under him according to size.

The complement of Coastal Forces varied quite considerably, from two officers and eight men in the earliest ones, to more than 30 in larger ones. Some of the crew were trained gunners, although this was not always helpful in action. In MGB 658, Lieutenant Cornelius Burke took his men to a rifle range and selected his gunners for good marksmanship, ignoring any gunnery badges they might have. Asdic operators were needed in boats with an anti-submarine function, and radar operators were added when sets became available.

Coastal forces crews were trained in HMS *St Christopher* at Fort William, before going on to HMS *Bee* at Weymouth on the south coast to work up.

A very complicated timetable was arranged so that lectures (for both officers and men) occupied the days, and frequent tactical exercises occupied the nights. The programme for each boat gradually worked up to a crescendo, so that by the time she was due to leave, she had an efficient crew, accustomed to snatching odd hours of sleep and hasty meals between fuelling and sea-time, and therefore prepared for operations immediately she arrived at her operational base.[12]

Later the course moved to Holyhead in Anglesey to make way for the D-Day invasion forces.

MTBs and MGBs could have a very unpleasant motion even in quite moderate seas. Their chief designer, W J Holt, spent much time at sea in different craft and admitted that 'the motion of a corvette in a seaway is positively stately in comparison with the motion of a coastal force craft in the same seaway'.[13] It was the engine room crews who got the worst of this, stuck down below with the smell of petrol and obliged to open and close the throttles of engines whose propellers were racing while they were out of the water. A large boat needed a skilled motor mechanic and two semi-skilled stokers. Their training was haphazard in the early stages of the war, and was largely conducted by the makers of the boats or engines, until special schools were set up such as HMS *Attack* at Portland. But it was only in the last two weeks of a 10-week course that trainees went afloat. 'During this period they begin to get their sea legs, are seasick and learn how to handle their engine'.[14] This did not always work and some men had to be relieved because of chronic seasickness.

Bases

By late 1942 there were Coastal Forces bases all round the British coast, serving different functions. *Wasp* at Dover and *Fervent* at Ramsgate were part of the Dover Command and heavily engaged with light enemy forces in the Channel. Between them they had 20 MGBs, seven MTBs and 17 MLs in November. Nore Command had bases at Brightlingsea,

Felixstowe, Lowestoft, Great Yarmouth and Immingham and was perhaps the most active command of all, involved in the protection of coastal convoys and attacks on enemy coastal shipping. It had 45 MGBs, exactly half the total in home waters, 24 MTBs and 35 MLs. Rosyth Comand only had a small base at Invergordon, but Orkney and Shetland had one on each archipelago, defending Scapa Flow and attacking shipping in Norwegian coastal waters when the weather and light were suitable. It had eight MTBs and 24 MLs in November 1942, but extra flotillas could be drafted in when needed. Western Approaches was far from the coastal war, but it included the main training bases at Fort William and Ardrishaig. It also ran coastal convoys escorted by the command's 25 MLs, though they acted only as a deterrent as there was no German activity in the area at the time. On the south coast of England, Plymouth Command was also active in the English Channel, though there were difficulties about its boundary with Portsmouth. In June 1943 the enemy was able to lay a minefield off the Eddystone Lighthouse because of poor communication between the two commands.[15] There were bases in the natural harbours of Falmouth, Fowey and Dartmouth and one in Devonport Dockyard, with a total of eight MTBs and 19 MLs. Weymouth had the working-up base, HMS *Bee,* while Portsmouth Command had bases along the coast at Portland, Gosport and Newhaven equipped with the six steam gunboats, 15 MGBs, 16 MTBs and 28 MLs.[16]

Sometimes MTBs and MGBs were compared with bomber aircraft, because they undertook short missions and needed a large amount of maintenance. They were highly dependent on bases for supplies, recreation and other facilities. They also needed a large shore staff. In August 1943 HMS *Beehive* at Felixstowe, one of the most active of the bases, had 350 men in the crews of its boats, plus 60 base staff, 153 maintenance staff and 70 men in the pool for drafting to boats as needed.[17] In home waters, the bases were usually situated ashore in requisitioned accommodation. HMS *Fervent* at Ramsgate on the coast of Kent used a holiday camp, 'Merrie England', to house up to 450 men, and even the ballroom was fitted out as a messdeck. The yacht club had accommodation for up to 60 officers in double cabins, and also housed the operations room and intelligence library.[18] HMS *St Christopher,* the training base at Fort William in Scotland, used a collection of hotels as quarters for officers and Wrens, with the seamen in Nissen huts. It was preferable for the men to sleep ashore if not on operations, as the boats had thin skins which made them uncomfortable in northern waters, and were subject to a good deal of unhealthy condensation of 'sweating'.[19] But most of the crews of larger boats such as the Fairmiles slept on board, especially in the Mediterranean.

Operations

Coastal Forces were slow to get into action. There were only about 30 encounters with the enemy up to the end of 1941, including some rather desultory ones. There were none at all in the first quarter of 1941, and two in the spring, both 'indecisive actions' with E-boats 'who did not stay to fight'. Coastal Forces took part in two atypical actions early in 1942. MTBs from Dover and Ramsgate were among the weapons which the British threw in the direction of *Scharnhorst* and *Gneisenau* during their Channel dash in February, to no effect. They were more successful in the

raid on St Nazaire, which destroyed the huge dry dock there. Meanwhile, more conventional actions were beginning to increase with 78 encounters in the first quarter of 1943, rising to 109 in home waters in the first half of 1944. By that time Coastal Forces were very much involved in the invasion of Normandy. They protected the routes taken by the landing ships, and a picture of the Fairmile Ds of the 55th Flotilla at Gosport became one of the classic images of the period. Coastal Forces continued to support the army's advance and battled for control of the shallow waters off the Netherlands. They had 50 encounters with the enemy during 1945, until the surrender of Germany.[20]

On the east coast of England, the main task was defending coastal convoys carrying coal into London from E-boat attack. MGBs were used, because the torpedoes of MTBs were not suitable against such small, fast and shallow targets. MGBs were also not suitable for close escort, as their planning hulls were not efficient at low speeds. A convoy usually had an escort of destroyers, trawlers and corvettes, so coastal forces were used to intercept the E-boats. They were inhibited by their small size and poor sea-keeping, for it is recorded that on 16 nights when E-boats were out in the autumn and winter of 1943–4, Coastal Forces were not able to operate on four of them. Nor were they able to defend the convoy directly, because they were slower than E-boats. Most raids were first detected by the escorts or shore radar and the MGBs were directed onto them, but they tended to reach them on the way home after the raid. The main advantage of coastal forces in this role was that that their shallow draught allowed them to pursue the enemy across minefields.[21]

The main role of MTBs in the North Sea was to attack enemy shipping, particularly convoys off the Dutch coast. They were not particularly successful in this, despite exaggerated wartime claims. In fact they sank only 40 merchant ships in northern Europe, a total of just under 60,000 tons. The peak year was 1943, when 13 ships of more than 26,000 tons were sunk.[22] MTBs also sank 70 enemy warships, mostly small ones escorting convoys.

In the Mediterranean, coastal forces saw action along the coast of North Africa, and they supported the invasion of Sicily and Italy. After that they operated on both sides of Italy, helping with the capture of islands in the Adriatic and moving up the west coast to attack enemy coastal shipping.

In action, motor gunboats relied on good marksmanship rather than scientific gunnery. In describing the lessons of action, L C Reynolds of MGB 658 unconsciously echoed Nelson's dictum that 'No captain can go far wrong if he places his ship alongside one of the enemy'.

...once any action had begun, the results achieved depended on the crews, not the officers. What the S.O. and each C.O. did was to place the ship as close as possible to the enemy; from that point on the aim and the continuous shooting of the gunners was all that really mattered, and finally accomplished the results.[23]

A gun action happened very fast. Commander McCowen of the 53rd MTB Flotilla reported on an attack on a convoy in March 1944: 'We held the stage for perhaps 15 seconds, and then the enemy opened a heavy and sometimes accurate, but mostly wild, fire on the unit from all directions, with the exception of one coaster, which was heavily hit by our initial burst.[24]

Details of a common type of magnetic mine.

2 Mine Warfare

The Threat

Statistically the mine could be seen as the greatest single threat to British shipping in the Second World War. It sank 281 British warships, compared with 271 by aircraft, 172 by submarine and 109 by surface craft. However, the ships sunk by mines were usually small – only one cruiser and nothing bigger, compared with 23 destroyers, 23 submarines and more than a hundred trawlers and drifters.[25] The effect on the enemy was just as serious. More than 1500 enemy vessels were sunk or damaged by mines laid by surface vessels and submarines, including three capital ships damaged and. 414 merchant vessels sunk.[26] In addition, whole areas were denied or made unsafe to one side or the other through mining, with a profound effect on strategy, and large numbers of personnel were employed in dealing with mines. Fifty-seven thousand British sailors were serving in nearly 1500 minesweepers in mid-1944.[27]

Yet minesweeping was quite low in the pecking order of naval prestige. It was not formally recognised as a specialisation for officers. It was not a separate manning division like Submarines or Coastal Forces, it had no non-substantive badges and minesweepers generally were unglamorous ships. The crews of minelayers never had the satisfaction of seeing hits on the enemy and those of

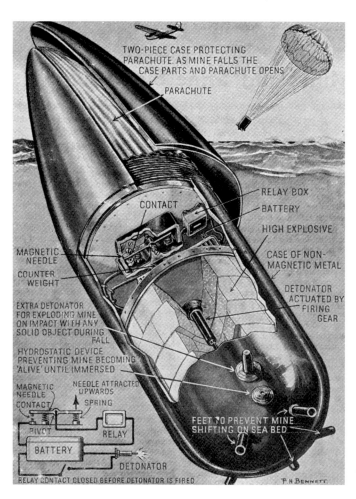

sweepers needed some imagination to see the end product of their work. John Miller, an ex-yachtsman officer, volunteered for minesweeping because 'I felt for humanitarian reasons that I didn't want to shoot at the enemy'. But minesweeping officers did sometimes become heroes. Commander Norman Morley was awarded the Distinguished Service Cross and three bars for clearing the way to landings at Sicily, Salerno and Anzio.[28]

Types of Mine

The moored contact mine had been in use since the Crimean War nearly 90 years earlier. In the developed version, as used since the beginning of the twentieth century, it was attached to a sinker which went to the bottom of the sea. The mine itself was fastened by a wire and floated to the correct depth just under the water. If a ship hit one of the 'horns' on the side of the mine, it would detonate. British contact mines could be used in depths of up to a mile.

Influence mines did not need direct contact. The best known was the magnetic mine, introduced by Germany early in the war. It was dropped in relatively shallow water, and was detonated by the magnetic field of a ship passing over. At first it was regarded as Hitler's secret weapon, and indeed it damaged the battleship *Nelson* and the cruiser *Belfast* as well as many merchant ships. But Britain was not far behind in such mines, and an intact German example was recovered off Shoeburyness in Essex in November 1939. Countermeasures were soon devised, at some cost. As well as minesweeping, these included degaussing, or reducing the magnetic field of ships by passing electrical cables round them.

Other types of influence weapon included the acoustic mine, which was set off by the sound of a ship. It was first used in August 1940, but as with magnetic mines the Germans started to use them before they had adequate stocks, allowing time to develop countermeasures. The most difficult type of all was the pressure mine, set off by the waves of a passing ship. This was first used by the Germans immediately after D-Day, and the only way of dealing with it was to have a well-protected or expendable ship pass over it. Minefields were even more deadly if several types of mine were combined, or if delayed action fuses were set so that it would only become active after several ships had passed.

Controlled minefields were used near harbour entrances. They were electrically linked to the shore and could be de-activated when friendly vessels were passing. The navy had a controlled mining service that numbered 1368 men in November 1944, mostly working ashore and unfit for sea service.[29]

Minelaying

Offensive minelaying was usually done close to enemy shorelines and was intended to sink his ships in home waters, or to restrict the areas in which they could operate. The British laid mines off the coast of Germany and all the occupied countries using surface ships, submarines and aircraft. In the Bay of Biscay, a large minefield was used to help stop U-boats getting to and from their bases. Defensive minelaying was intended to protect one's own coast and shipping. Mines were laid across the English Channel and entrances to the North Sea at the beginning of the war, but these were soon outflanked

by the German advance. Far more useful was the East Coast Barrage, running a few miles offshore from the Thames Estuary to the north of Scotland. It was very valuable in protecting shipping from U-boats and surface attack, except by E-boats which could often pass over it. Other fields were laid at the entrances to the Irish Sea, and to prevent a counterattack on the invasion forces in 1944. In all, about 185,000 mines were laid for defensive purposes in 340 different operations.

Surface ships were the oldest form of minelayers. They were most useful for defensive purposes, and merchant ships could be converted easily. Train ferries, such as the *Shepperton* and *Princess Victoria*, were obviously useful with their flat open decks and stern ramps, but the most prolific minelayer was the *Port Quebec*, converted from a Port Line cargo ship of 5396 tons. She laid more than 33,000 mines as part of the 1st Minelaying Squadron.

Offensive minelaying was far more difficult for surface ships, but six very fast ships – the *Abdiel* class – were built for this. With an overall length of 420 feet they resembled small cruisers, but had a much greater speed of nearly 40 knots and could carry up to 156 mines. However, they were also found useful for other tasks such as keeping the beleaguered garrison of Malta supplied, and spent comparatively little time in their designed duties. Only the *Apollo* laid more than 8000 mines. Three of them were sunk – the *Latona* by bombing in 1941 before she had laid any mines. Eight destroyers also laid mines, but again three were sunk.

Submarines had been used as offensive minelayers in the First World War, and mines could now be launched from torpedo tubes so that a specially-designed boat was not necessary. But in practice only six boats of the *Porpoise* and *Narwhal* classes were used in the role, plus the Free French *Rubis*. Five of them were lost, the *Seal* and *Grampus* after laying only about 50 mines each, and only the *Rorqual* laid more than a thousand mines in her career. The aircraft turned out to be the most successful means of offensive minelaying. Usually the work was carried out by Bomber Command of the RAF, often as part of a diversion from a raid on a city. More than 54,000 mines were laid by aircraft but again the cost was heavy and it is estimated that 500 aircraft were lost on these duties.[30]

The minelayer *Welshman* carrying supplies into Valetta.

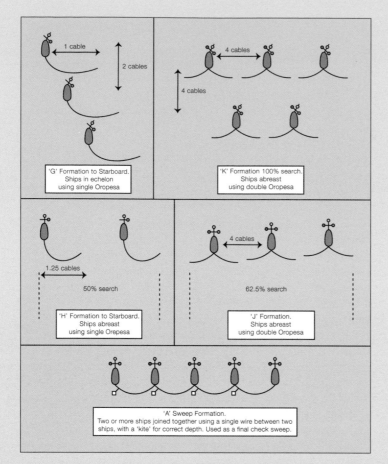

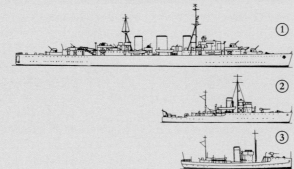

Sweeping Techniques

The main method of sweeping moored contact mines was with the oropesa sweep, developed just after the First World War and tested in a trawler of that name. A wire sweep was streamed at a distance from the ship by the torpedo-shaped oropesa float, and its central part was held at the right depth by angled blades known as kites and otters. The sweep was fitted with wire cutters along its length, and the cable of a moored mine would be drawn towards one of these and severed. The mine would float to the surface where it would be destroyed by gunfire. All this needed a high standard of old-fashioned seamanship with ropes and wires.

Contact minesweepers needed a safe area to begin operations. The edge of a particular minefield might be known, in which case the sweepers could start to work from the outside. Otherwise the sweep might begin through the centre of the field at high tide, when the shallow-draught minesweepers could hope to pass over in safety. Light markers known as danbuoys marked the cleared area, and measuring gear was used to establish its position accurately so that the edge of the next sweep could be done in safety.

Sweepers usually worked in formation, with the leading ship in a safe area. Using the G formation, the ships sailed in echelon and each following ship of the flotilla was protected behind the sweep of the one ahead, so a large area could be cleared. Each ship covered an area of one cable or 220 yards. The A sweep formation had all the ships side by side in a line, linked by a single wire. This was used as a final check after an area had been cleared. In the K formation, the ships streamed oropesas on both sides and operated in two lines, at a certain risk to the leading ships, but providing 100 per cent coverage.

The LL sweep was used against the magnetic mine. It consisted of two electric cables towed astern of the ship, one 575 yards long the other 225 yards, to spread the area affected by the electric current between them. The minesweepers were degaussed by passing a current round them to neutralise their magnetic field. Two ships sailed together and a current was passed between the sweeps at short intervals, hopefully detonating any mines inside it. But some mines would only detonate after a fixed number of ships had passed, so the same area often had to be swept many times to be declared safe.

The SA sweep was used against acoustic mines. It attempted to simulate the noise of a propeller, mostly using a spring hammer which was worked electrically. It could be towed astern or mounted in a flooded area in the ship's bows.

Types of Minesweeper

An ideal minesweeper needed a powerful engine to tow the sweep through the water. It needed a clear deck aft where the gear could be handled, and good manoeuvrability. It should have good internal subdivision to limit damage if a mine was hit, and preferably a shallow draft which would allow it to operate inshore and pass over contact mines in certain tidal conditions. If intended for operations far from its base it needed fuel storage, crew accommodation and guns for defence.

Many different types of vessels could be adapted for minesweeping. Destroyers could operate sweeps for moored mines at either high or low speed, but the high-speed sweep covered only a very small area and destroyers were too expensive and deep draughted to be useful in the role. Thirty-two passenger paddle steamers were requisitioned early in the war because of their shallow draught, but they were difficult to control in rough seas and their lack of internal subdivision made them very vulnerable. Early sloops, and the frigates of the River class were originally intended to double as fleet minesweepers and some had a full range of equipment, but in the event the Rivers were not needed and were perhaps too deep draughted. Many fishing vessels were converted and used by the Patrol Service. In September 1940, 261 trawler-minesweepers were in service, rising to more than 400 a year later. The numbers tended to decline as other types of sweeper were developed.

Large vessels were known as fleet minesweepers, which was a misleading title. Some, with speeds of at least 20 knots, were indeed intended to accompany the fleet and prepare the way in front of it in shallow waters. But others were given the title merely because they could operate the largest kind of sweep, the Mark I, at 11.5 knots and had a free speed of 15 to 17 knots. Older sweepers included the coal-burning *Aberdare* ('Smokey Joes') of 1918 vintage and the *Halcyon* class of 1933–9.

The *Bangor* and *Bathurst* classes were built in the early years of the war with various types of engine, but the classic design was the *Algerine* class, which was designed in 1940 and first entered service in the March 1942. They were largely built in Canada and 29 were in service in home waters by September 1944, with 22 more serving abroad. The *Algerine* class was designed for turbine engines but most were built with triple expansion due to shortages of turbine blades. They were of up to 1325 tons at full load and had a top speed of 16.5 knots with a crew of up to 138. Larger than previous vessels of the type, they proved very satisfactory in service.

Training

Apart from a small number of regular officers who had specialised in minesweeping, at the beginning of the war the service was dominated by fishing skippers recruited through the RNR and appointed warrant officers. But they were not successful in modern conditions. 'The trawler skippers could be a problem. They were nearly all professional fishermen and great seamen, but they were not easily amenable to naval discipline, nor did they take kindly to too much flag signalling'.[31]

Port Edgar on the Firth of Forth was commissioned as HMS *Lochinvar* in November 1939 as the main minesweeping training base. Officers were sent for a course combining practical sea experience with lectures in minesweeping, gunnery and seamanship. Twenty arrived every three weeks. They spent the first two days at sea in trawlers or paddle steamers watching crews working up, then a week of lectures on minesweeping, one on gunnery practice, another on general drill, and a fourth week on seamanship. After that they had three weeks of practical training on trawlers specially fitted with gunrooms to accommodate 10 officers. Each took a turn as first lieutenant, and there were practical exercises, as described by the government pamphlet *His Majesty's Minesweepers*:

On 'Action Stations' they will range the guns on an imaginary submarine or hostile aircraft. Masked figures will race along the decks when the gas alarm is given, on fire duty or putting out collision mats. The commands 'Man Overboard' and 'Away Seaboats' demand the appropriate drill. Sweeps are veered out in various formations. Dan-buoys are laid and recovered, the fog-buoy streamed, the anchor weighed by hand.[32]

Brendan Maher and his colleagues had seen the pamphlet when he joined the course in 1943, and laughed at the claim that all the men were 'picked volunteers'. In the trawlers:

We streamed sweeps, set depths, changed depths, swept occasional dummy mines set there for a purpose, gave steering orders, and navigated (not difficult to do when one is in constant sight of the Forth Bridge). We also spent a few hours in the engine room and watched the stokers as they endlessly shovelled coal into the nearly blinding glare and flare of the firebox. ... We rotated duties on these trawlers and gained a little experience doing each of the things that had to be done – except stoking.[33]

Charles McAra, who really had stated a preference of minesweepers, found the seagoing course was 'a strenuous, cheerful time, but very dirty as the trawlers were coal-burning and the washing facilities minimal'.[34]

3 The Patrol Service and Harbour Defence

The Royal Naval Patrol Service was founded in 1907, and in peacetime it consisted of fishermen who did some part-time training with the navy. In the First World War it manned much of the Auxiliary Patrol, which carried out a large part of the anti-submarine work. Its main roles were minesweeping and anti-submarine patrol, largely in defence of harbours, and it overlapped to some extent with coastal forces and general service.

In 1939 the Admiralty planned to take up 100 trawlers for anti-submarine work and 200 for minesweeping, manned by more than 3000 seamen and engineers.[35] As with most things in wartime, it expanded far beyond that with more than 60,000 men in about 3000 small vessels. Largely by chance, the Patrol Service was the only one of the 'navies within the navy' to have its own badge. As First Lord of the Admiralty in 1940, Churchill authorised a unique, small metal badge for those who had served six months on minesweepers. It was soon extended to coastal anti-submarine work, and became associated with the Patrol Service.

Officers

In wartime the Patrol Service was headed by a senior Royal Naval officer, Captain Piercy in 1939 and Commodore de Pass from 1941.

A minesweeping training ship operating from HMS *Lochinvar* in the Firth of Forth. A danbuoy is being lowered to mark the swept area.

Right: The crew
of the trawler
Cornelian after
shooting down a
German Heinkel
111 bomber
in 1942.

Opposite bottom:
The trawler
Cherwell at sea.

He had a considerable staff in his headquarters at Lowestoft, from where ratings were trained and drafted to the boats and ports where they were needed. It was a fully fledged manning division on a par with the three home ports, and its men had the prefix LT (for Lowestoft) before their service number.

The key figures in the Patrol Service were the skippers, warrant officers appointed from among experienced fishermen. They wore the intertwined braid of the RNR and could be promoted to Chief Skipper, the equivalent of a commissioned warrant officer, and eventually to Skipper Lieutenant. There were 400 of them in the navy in 1939 and 525 more were quickly taken on from the fishing fleet, plus 300 more promoted from the rating of second hand.[36]

The Skipper RNR was a very different figure to the traditional naval officer. Skipper Lang of the *Loch Tulla* was 'a first rate seaman and knew things about the way of a ship at sea which no one not trained in sail could have understood'. His navigation was by eye rather than chart and sextant and he had a fund of weather lore.

'Wind'll freshen from the south'ard before midnight, Sir.'
  'How so Skipper?'
  'See those gulls Sir, throwing water over their backs – sure sign of a southerly wind that Sir.'
  'Thick weather or clear Skipper?' I'd ask.
  'Oh thick Sir, with a mizzel of rain. Did you notice how red was the rust on that buoy we passed a while back – blood red it was. 'Twill be as thick as the Earl o' Hell's riding boots tonight.'[37]

The new German magnetic mines needed a different approach and the old-fashioned Skipper RNR became redundant.

There was little increase during the war in the number of minesweeping officers of the RNR Skipper class … The reason lay partly in the reluctance to deprive the food producing fishing industry of all the most knowledgeable trawler and drifter-men, and partly in the realisation, born of war experience, that the average Skipper could not contend with the intricacies of influence sweeping. The necessity for meticulous station keeping, navigational accuracy and constant vigilance ran counter to his ingrained habits. The temporary reserve officer of the other classes, usually better educated, more amenable to training and bringing to the task a fresh, enthusiastic and unbiased mind, proved far more efficient and reliable.'

RNR skippers had made up 43 per cent of minesweeping officers at the beginning of the war. By the end they were only 6 per cent while RNVR officers formed 63 per cent.[38]

Ratings

The mate of a small Patrol Service vessel held the rating of second hand, equivalent to a petty officer. Originally they were fishermen who held a Board of Trade certificate, but they were soon augmented by men with experience of other kinds of small boats rated as Second Hands (Small Craft Only). There was a suspicion that both groups were under-qualified for the role.

The Patrol Service began to take on HO seamen from general service quite soon after the start of the war, to allow for its great expansion. It was given permission to train signallers and in 1942 it began to train its own gunners in a school 11 miles south of Lowestoft. They wore non-substantive gunnery badges with the letter P underneath.

At first the engines of Patrol Service vessels were all steam reciprocating, and they were manned by skilled enginemen who were equivalent to ERAs, and by stokers. Petty officer stokers were drafted in from general service to make up the numbers. In 1940 the Patrol Service began to take responsibility for motor minesweepers, but its members had no experience of this type of power. About 600 ratings were enrolled soon after Dunkirk, all with some experience of diesel engines, and they were given training by the manufacturers. By the end of the war the Patrol Service included 17,000 engine room ratings, more than a quarter of the total. These included nearly 7000 enginemen and chief enginemen.[39]

The authorities were ambivalent about the quality of men in the Patrol Service. Concerned about the numbers that failed officer training, Combined Operations headquarters suggested that candidates who were above average in the Patrol Service 'do not compare favourably with candidates from other sources'. But at the same time it was found that Patrol Service submarine detector trainees could learn the operation of sets much more quickly and this was put down to their higher standard. 'Almost certainly the P/S gets a better quality of rating, since someone at Lowestoft looks after their interests'.[40]

The Ships

Fishing trawlers were designed to tow equipment through the water and could be adapted for minesweeping. The Admiralty began planning the Patrol Service ships in 1933 with the design of the *Basset,* a trawler of 775 tons, and the slightly smaller *Mastiff* of 1938. But it was always recognised that the main expansion of the Patrol Service would come through requisitioned fishing vessels which would find it difficult to pursue their normal business in war conditions. Whalers were the largest and fastest and were suitable for anti-submarine duties, though not for inshore work.

Trawlers were the most common. The largest ones, designed to operate in rough seas off Iceland, were about 900 tons with a crew of up to 50 and were often used as ocean escorts in the early stages of the war. Smaller ones were used inshore for coastal patrol and escort and harbour defence. Drifters were a different type of fishing boat, used to catch herring in the North Sea. They had small endurance, poor accommodation and inadequate sea-keeping, but were highly manoeuvrable and could be used to tow a small LL sweep in certain conditions, or for harbour defence. Yachts came in many shapes and sizes, from the *Cutty Sark* of 884 tons used as a submarine tender, to small craft with a crew of five or six. In all, about 1700 civilian vessels were taken over in the course of the war. Their conversion posed some problems, particularly when guns and equipment had to be mounted high up, affecting their stability. In general, the fish hold was converted into crew accommodation. An anti-submarine coastal escort trawler usually had a 4-inch gun to deal with a surfaced submarine, Oerlikons and machine guns for self-defence, and about 25 depth charges.

But even after conversion, commercial trawlers often retained their characteristics, well known to the fishermen who sailed them in peacetime. According to D A Rayner:

Loch Tulla was unique amongst trawlers. … Regal, Istria and Brontes were as much alike as three pins. It was not until they developed little idiosyncrasies of their own under their new commanding officers that you could tell them apart at a distance of a mile. The Davy again was different. … Looking at her, one had the impression that her designer had tried to do something special, but the arrow of his thought seemed to have missed the target. To a seaman it did not appear that the bow matched the stern.[41]

Large commercial trawlers of the period had too deep a draught for coastal work, but specially designed Admiralty trawlers of the *Tree,*

Below: A stoker in the engine room of the trawler *Stella Pegasi*.

Dance, Shakespeare and *Isles* classes proved more useful inshore. They were of 770 tons deep load with a crew of 35 to 40 and a speed of 12.5 knots. Motor minesweepers were designed for short-range operations in clearing local harbours and estuaries, so they did not need much fuel storage, accommodation or speed. They used diesel engines, and had wooden hulls to reduce their magnetic signature. Those built between 1940 and 1944 were of 295 tons deep load with a speed of 10 to 11 knots and a crew of 20. Slightly larger ones were built from 1943–5 and 220 were in service in September 1944. Another type, known as the British Yard Minesweeper or BYMS, was built in America under lend-lease.

Bases

Lowestoft was chosen as the headquarters of the Patrol Service as early as the Munich Crisis in 1938. It was a major centre of the fishing industry with a good harbour for small craft. It faced the German enemy across the North Sea, but was closer to London than other fishing ports of similar size. It was not needed for any other naval purposes, and the town's secondary function in peacetime as a holiday resort meant that it had plenty of spare hotel accommodation, which could be requisitioned, and good rail connections. It served as a depot, for training, and for men awaiting draft.

Patrol Service vessels were soon spread around the ports of the United Kingdom and abroad. At Plymouth, the naval base was protected by four anti-submarine groups, a total of 16 trawlers, in the spring of 1941. All of these were manned by the Patrol Service except two ex-French ships manned by Dutchmen. There was also a small anti-submarine group of two yachts, of 500 tons each. In addition, the Patrol Service provided eight minesweeping groups with 16 vessels, and two small trawlers and two drifters.

The nearby port of Fowey had a narrow entrance but had two trawlers, one large one small, two drifters, two motor fishing vessels and two motor boats in service, all manned by the Patrol Service except the small trawler, which was run by the Free French. Falmouth, further to the west, was a major port and had a total of 21 Patrol Service vessels, including three river steamers. Grimsby, the original home of many of the trawlers, was defended by 55 craft including 11 harbour defence patrol vessels, four examination service vessels and six motor fishing vessels for patrols on the Humber Estuary.[42]

Whereas Coastal Forces took some years to build up to a high level of activity, the Patrol Service was in the thick of the action from the beginning. Its ships were involved in the Norwegian campaign, and saw far more overseas service than originally planned. In September 1944 it had nearly 5000 men in the Mediterranean, more than 1800 with the Eastern Fleet and others on both sides of the Atlantic, in South Africa and in Iceland.[43] It also suffered its share of casualties, losing 3218 killed, more than half of who were 'missing, presumed killed on war service'.[44]

Boom Defence

Boom defence was something of a misnomer, for nets rather than booms were now used to defend the entrances to harbours and estuaries. The nets were made of links rather like chain mail and consisted of three main types. Anti-boat booms were shallow and were for protection against torpedo boats. Anti-torpedo booms were to guard against torpedoes that might be launched outside the anchorage; and anti-submarine booms were much deeper and stronger than the others. They were prepared on shore with the buoys that held them up and the anchors and chains which in turn fixed these in place. They were loaded onto netlayers, mostly converted from paddle steamers or small ferries with a wide, open deck aft to stow the net. Meanwhile, boats laid out buoys to mark the position, and netlaying began.

By the beginning of the war booms had already been laid at Scapa, the Firth of Forth, Dover, Portsmouth and Portland, and were under construction at Harwich, Plymouth and the Firth of Clyde, with one at Milford Haven due to start being laid in mid-September 1939. Overseas, they were laid or being laid at all the main bases.[45]

Boom defence vessels were also constructed or converted to maintain and service the boom. The Admiralty had begun to design these by 1935, and planned to use purpose-built craft in the first instance. In contrast to the last war they used larger vessels, so only 29 were to be used at Scapa instead of 96.[46] The ships of the Bar class were of 959 tons with a crew of up to 44 officers and men. They usually served as boom gate vessels, with gear to open and shut the boom to allow access. The *Bayonet* class ships were smaller at 780 tons and were used in shallower

BOOM BARRAGE WITH THE GATE OPENED FOR THE PASSAGE OF A FRIENDLY VESSEL

BUOYS

GATE BEING OPENED

BOOM DEFENCE VESSELS

TOWING GEAR

AFTER WINCH FOR TOWING CABLE

3 INCH GUN

LIFEBOAT

SEARCHLIGHT

NAVIGATING BRIDGE

HEAVY DERRICK FOR LIFTING FLOATS & BUOYS

LIFEBOAT

HATCH

GALLOWS FOR SUPPORTING BOOM

FORWARD WINCH

STARBOARD GALLOW

BOOM GALLOWS FOR PAYING OUT AND RETRIEVING NET BOOM

MANNER IN WHICH THE LINKS OF WIRE ARE ARRANGED

Details of a boom defence vessel. The inset shows the method of operating the gate in the boom.

water. These ships were easily distinguished by their gallows in the bows, for lowering and lifting buoys. As usual, far more were needed in practice and about 90 trawlers were converted for the work.

The Boom Defence Service was civilian manned in peacetime, but on the outbreak of war they were taken into the navy at the appropriate rate, with their pay made up to civilian standards. By late 1940 it was necessary to recruit more men, either experienced deckhands from the Merchant Navy or new entrants from the training schools. The Boom Defence Service was considered a separate manning division with nearly 9000 ratings in September 1944. As well as the crews of the vessels, it included recalled naval artisans such as blacksmiths and shipwrights, who were essential for repairing buoys and equipment. It also employed civilian staffs on shore, particularly in the early stages when new booms were being set up. The skilled riggers of the Boom Defence Service, who worked at splicing wire rigging, setting up and repairing moorings and so on, were given a specialist badge in 1941, consisting of a shackle crossed with a marlinspike. They were rated as leading seaman and above. They also had their own mechanism for training gunners and wiremen, with the letters BD under the usual badges.

Controlled Mining

As well as the permanently active minefields in enemy waters and offshore from friendly coasts, the navy used controlled minefields that could be turned off to allow the safe passage of friendly vessels. Practice varied from place to place. In commercial ports the minefields were normally left at 'safe' to allow traffic to pass. At a naval anchorage such as Scapa they were kept permanently 'active' except when necessary.[47] Again the Admiralty planned this quite early of this and in 1936–7 it launched three vessels of the *Linnet* class of 585 tons to lay the mines and their equipment with considerable accuracy. As always, needs expanded in wartime as overseas ports were taken over and the threat from the midget submarine increased. Trawlers and cable ships were converted for the work, and a class of eight self-propelled minelaying lighters proved successful.

Again, the controlled minelaying branch was a separate manning division of the navy with 1368 ratings in 1944. It needed a high proportion of wiremen and skilled electricians who maintained the electric connections. It worked with the harbour defence operators branch, which was even smaller with 1320 men, who served ashore and provided the lookouts and operators who turned the minefields on and off.

The Examination Service

The function of the Examination Service was 'to identify and ascertain the character and intentions of vessels (excepting war vessels) seeking entrance in order that the defences may have warning of the attempted entry of suspicious or unfriendly ships'. Known British-owned vessels would be examined cursorily, and those joining convoys would be looked over at the assembly point. It operated in most of the ports of Britain, with a variety of vessels manned in different ways. On the Clyde for example, there were six

vessels ranging from 25 to 229 tons, owned by a government department, a railway company, the MacBrayne shipping line and private owners. Some were manned by the Patrol Service, some by merchant seamen on T124 Agreements, and the *Wee Cumbrae* of 37 tons had four men paid by the London, Midland and Scottish Railway Company. The staff was headed by a commander and a lieutenant-commander, and the examination was to be done by six officers from the Scottish Fishery Board, and four Merchant Navy masters, all commissioned in the RNR. On the River Humber, on the other hand, four out of five Examination Service vessels were manned by the Patrol Service. Meanwhile, in the Isle of Wight area, the Examination Service dealt with 3456 inward bound ships in the first six months of war, and 1020 outward bound.[48]

The enemy made no attempt to infiltrate harbours in this way and by 1943 it was found that very few searches of cargo were being carried out. Examination Service craft usually approached incoming vessels and gave them the necessary signals for entering port. In effect, they were becoming a part of the pilotage service, and the Examination Service was greatly reduced after that.[49]

British-controlled harbours were penetrated several times during the war, but apart from *U-47* at Scapa Flow there were no serious losses in home waters. This was largely due to a German policy of carrying the U-boat war out to sea for most of the conflict, so it is difficult to know how far the harbour defence forces acted as a deterrent. In the Mediterranean it was rather different, with Italian manned torpedo attacks on Alexandria and Gibraltar, and torpedo boat assaults on Suda Bay and Malta.

Below: The mine and other defences of Hoxa Sound, the main entrance to Scapa Flow.

KEY

— Indicator Loop

— Mine Loop or Guard Loop

— Boom Defence

⬤ Barrage Balloon

⊕ Harbour Defence Asdic

● Harbour Defence Searchlight

● AA Searchlight

◍ AA Gun

◑ Coast Defence Gun

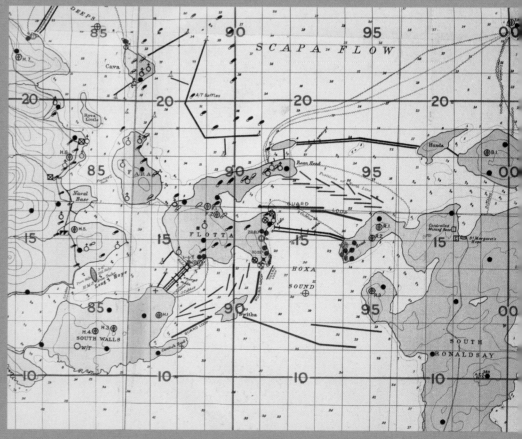

PART XII
Amphibious Warfare

1 Combined Operations Personnel

Co-operation between the three armed services was much neglected before the war. Experiences of amphibious operations in the First World War such as the Dardanelles had been very unhappy, and the war was largely fought in separate compartments. In the 1920s and 30s the service chiefs were often barely on speaking terms as they competed for funds and influence. At the beginning of the Second World War each service had its own idea of how it would be won. The navy would blockade Germany and starve it out as they had done in 1918, the army would build up its strength and invade in co-operation with the French by about 1942, and the RAF, if let off the leash, would bomb them into submission. All this collapsed with the Fall of France in 1940. It was clear that all three services would have to co-operate closely to return the army to Europe.

Combined Operations Organisation

Within days of the Fall of France Churchill was considering ways to get back to the continent. The Chiefs of Staff appointed General Bourne of the Royal Marines as Commander of Raiding Operations but this was too limited for Churchill's vision. He appointed Admiral of the Fleet Lord Keyes as Director of Combined Operations. He was over 70 by this time, but in the previous war he had led a famous raid on Zeebrugge, and had only just failed to become First Sea Lord in the 1930s. Keyes made a good deal of progress in setting up bases, developing craft and mounting commando raids, but he was forceful and opinionated and ultimately annoyed Churchill with his constant criticism of the Prime Minister and others.

Lord Louis Mountbatten was as well-known as Keyes but better connected, for he was a cousin of the King and his father had once been First Sea Lord. He had served as a signal officer then in command of the destroyer *Kelly*, whose sinking was used by Noel Coward as the basis for the film *In Which We Serve*. In 1941 he was a captain and preparing to take over the carrier *Illustrious* when he was given Keyes' job. When he protested Churchill replied, 'You fool! The best thing you can hope for is to repeat your last achievement and get yourself sunk'. He was immediately promoted Commodore and later to Acting Vice-Admiral, and parity with the Chiefs of Staff.[1] He had much greater influence than Keyes and got almost everything he wanted until he left after two years to become Supreme Allied Commander in Burma.

His successor, Sir Robert Laycock, was much less flamboyant. He was well connected as the son-in-law of a Privy Councillor and member of the Royal Horse Guards, but this was trivial in comparison with Mountbatten. He was glad to get into Combined Operations to escape a posting in chemical warfare and he took part in several operations including the evacuation from Crete – he became the model for Evelyn Waugh's admirable Colonel Tommy Blackhouse in *Sword of Honour*.

Combined Operations had its headquarters in Richmond Terrace in Whitehall, built in 1822 as eight very grand dwelling houses and situated opposite the entrance to Downing Street. Naturally it was a joint service organisation, though according to Arthur Marshall of the army it was 'a largely navy-orientated place' where 'briskness was the thing' and 'there was a refreshing breeziness and a feeling that at last the war was getting somewhere'. Senior naval officers continued to refer to offices as cabins and messages as signals, and to pick on both army officers and the RNVR, although the RAF 'seemed to pass muster'.[2]

Combined Operations was given its own badge in 1942. It consisted of a gun, anchor and eagle and was worn by all three services in addition to other rank, trade and good-conduct badges. For most of the Mountbatten era the force was almost independent, but it was reintegrated with the army, navy and air force as D-Day approached. Its biggest single duty was to man landing ships and craft, so the majority of its personnel were naval. In April 1943, just before the great expansion for D-Day, there were nearly 44,000 of them, including nearly 30,000 in landing craft, more than a thousand in beach commandos and reconnaissance units and more than 6000 in landing ships.[3] By mid-1944 there were more than 50,000 men in landing craft alone.[4]

Opposite: Vice-Admiral Lord Mountbatten, Chief of Combined Operations, inspects the anti-aircraft gunners of the combined operations ship *Empire Pride* in 1943.

Below: Richmond Terrace in Whitehall.

Above left: Landing Craft Vehicle and Assault on a beach near Inveraray, with many others moored in the Loch.

Above right: The Combined Operations base at Tignabruaich in the Forth of Clyde, *James Cook*, was used to train landing craft navigators.

Training

The Combined Training Centre was set up at Inveraray on Loch Fyne in July 1940. It was away from other activities but had good access to the water and was safe from air raids. Seamen ratings, nearly all HO men straight from the training camps, were sent there for a four-week course in the new craft and practised landing on the shores of the loch. Engineers included motor mechanics with petty officer rate for the larger craft and they were trained at Northney near Portsmouth. Stokers were used as assistants in the larger craft, and took charge of the engine rooms in the smaller ones. Though it was hoped that all personnel would know how to start, stop and run an engine in an emergency, even the smallest craft had a stoker-driver in charge of it.

Inshore navigation was an important issue. In the case of landing ships, they had to find the 'lowering position', usually 7 miles offshore, where they would lower the landing craft, full of assault troops or tanks, from their davits for the final run to the shore. From that point the major and minor landing craft would have to work with considerable accuracy. According to the Director of Combined Training:

The chief problem with which they will have to contend is the pilotage one, of finding the right beach within 100 yards at the right time. To train an officer or a coxswain to do this with any success requires considerably more than three weeks, in view of the instruction in Beach Pilotage, and Navigational Aids, as well as ordinary Pilotage that is involved.[5]

A Combined Operations pilotage school, HMS *James Cook*, was set up at Tighnabruaich in the Firth of Clyde in November 1942. Many other bases were also set up in this region to cover the various aspects of amphibious warfare. There was a headquarters at Largs and a signal school at Troon on the Ayrshire coast, a training school for amphibious tank warfare at Toward on the other side of the Firth of Clyde, and a base at Rosneath on the mouth of the Gareloch for engineering personnel. On the other side of Scotland, Tank Landing Craft crews were trained at Bo'ness on the Firth of Forth. As D-Day approached, there was a gradual move south, although that brought ships closer to enemy action and danger. Bases were also set up in the Middle East and Far East for local needs.[6] A separate organisation, mostly in north Wales, trained Royal Marines who now manned a large proportion of minor landing craft. Roy Nelson describes his training in the months before D-Day.

I was in U 20 Squad – we were allocated to either U (coxswain and deck hands) or V (stokers) squads. Our instructors were mainly RN personnel, and from 3 weeks we had basic seamanship training. Then it was on to Burma Camp for gunnery training in light ack-ack, Oerlikon, pom-pom and Vickers guns. … Our accommodation in a row of large Victorian houses was adjacent to a jetty on the

foreshore of the river. It was here that we finally got to see a landing craft, old LCPs [Landing Craft Personnel] being used for our handling instruction. We would be taken out by our instructor into Barmouth Bay and there practice [sic] our newly acquired seamanship and take turns at the wheel.[7]

Many landing craft officers were trained by normal wartime methods at *King Alfred*, but by 1942 it was recognised that a much higher proportion of officers was needed for landing craft – two officers and 10 men in a Landing Craft Tank, for example. A special shortened course was set up at Lochailort in Scotland, served by two trains a day on the West Highland Railway from Glasgow. It was a tough course of six weeks involving much trekking over mountains, and some questioned whether it was really suitable for the kind of officers needed.

Crews

Landing ships were usually manned by Merchant Navy seamen on T124X agreements, with a naval party to man the landing craft that they would launch. There were 974 officers and 4554 men of the Merchant Navy on this duty in April 1943. A typical ship of the Glen class was manned by 28 Merchant Navy officers and 263 men, with 12 naval officers and 220 men to crew 14 landing craft. She also carried 87 army officers and 1000 soldiers.[8] Captain David Bone found that there could be conflict between his Merchant Navy seamen and the Royal Navy men of the landing craft, for example when shore leave was given.

Our merchantmen, being solidly independent, resented any questioning about a warrant for a run ashore. When mixed groups of merchant and navy men gathered at our one regulating gangway, the naval P.O.….held up the dispatch of the liberty boat. This provoked resentment on the part of the navy men entitled, and vulgar torrents of abuse from hotheads of our merchant crew.[9]

A Tank Landing Craft was naval-manned and had a captain and first lieutenant, six seamen including a coxswain who should be at least a leading seaman, a wireman, a motor mechanic, leading stoker and stoker for the engine room. Gavin Douglas describes the crew of his in 1944.

The crew of my own craft were all little more than boys: the eldest was twenty-five, and only three out of the ten hands carried were entitled to draw a rum issue, which means that only three were more than twenty. My Motor Mechanic, in charge of the craft's machinery with two assistants, was a fair-haired, boyishly smooth-faced expert of nineteen, and the First Lieutenant was a happy-go-lucky New Zealander of twenty-one. At the age of forty-five, I felt the complete horny-handed old sea-dog in such company.

Only one or two of the hands had been at sea before. The coxswain had seen most of the Mediterranean landings in minor landing craft and was a fair seaman, but none of the others was much advanced from the landsman he had been not many months before.[10]

The crew of a Landing Craft Infantry (Large) was not very different, but with three more seamen and two more in the engine room. Alec Guinness became very fond of his crew in LCI(L)124.

There are about three of them who bore me or whom I can't take much notice of — but the others I find enchanting. I believe I must have quite the best crew over here. They are inclined to be a bit grubby and I bawl at them until they look smart, but they are all so cheerful and gay.[11]

Minor landing craft had much smaller crews. The largest ones, the Landing Craft Mechanised, had five seamen and one stoker, the Landing Craft Assault had three seamen and a stoker, and the Landing Craft Vehicle and Personnel and Landing Craft Vehicle had three men apiece including the stoker. It was hoped that the coxswain in command of each would be a leading seaman and it was necessary to bend the usual rules of seniority to create men with acting temporary ratings. It was normal to select possible candidates at Inveraray and send them on for operational experience, replacing them with others who had already seen some service as coxswains of the craft.[12] There was an officer in charge of each group of three craft.

Group Training

After learning skills as officers, coxswains, seamen, engineers, gunners and signallers, landing craft crews were then brought together. Three areas of training needed particular attention: the handling and

navigation of the craft at sea, operating in company with other craft, and the special handling during beaching. To some officers though this was the most difficult:

The special problems connected with beaching the Landing Craft and with the management of the troops embarked, are popularly regarded as the main item in the training of Landing Craft crews. Actually however, they constitute the least difficult part of Naval Training. The average seaman can quickly be taught how to beach a Landing Craft and any officer of average power of command and common sense, can learn how to handle troops without difficulty. On the other hand the training needed to operate in company at sea is far and away the most difficult to provide. It calls for real experience in realistic conditions, which can only be provided by exercising in company in waters similar to those in which the force will have to operate.

Gavin Douglas describes the integration of his LCT(4) into larger formations.

Assumed to be a trained ship's company, we joined a flotilla of twelve craft. We practiced [sic] certain manoeuvres, mostly in moving as a flotilla and in working by signal flags or radio-telephony. We formed, wheeled and turned, and drove on to the beaches together. … D-Day was coming nearer, and after a few weeks' training as a flotilla we moved south. At a West Coast port we joined three more flotillas and were part of 'Q' Squadron under a Lieutenant-Commander of the Royal Navy. Four days after we joined the Squadron, hardly knowing our new mates, and not having worked with them at all, we continued on to Plymouth. That was two weeks before D-Day.[13]

A squadron of Landing Craft Tank or Infantry had a commanding officer with two assistants, a boatswain, gunner's mate, leading telegraphist, yeoman of signals, shipwright, electrical artificer and

The crew of
Landing Craft Tank
2130 at the time
of D-Day.

wireman, a medical officer, sick berth attendant and writer. It comprised three flotillas of 12 craft each, headed by a flotilla officer, petty officer, signalman, writer and supply assistant. Each flotilla had a maintenance staff of 15, headed by an engineer officer and a chief ERA.

Pilotage Parties and Beach Commandos

A landing on the island of Rhodes was planned while the British were in Greece in 1941, and Nigel Clogstoun-Willmott trained by swimming 25 lengths in the baths at Cairo every day, before landing by folbot canoe and exploring the beach on the island. He found that the charts were wildly inaccurate, and some features were shown a mile from their true position, but the landing never took place. Clogstoun-Wilmott went on to set up reconnaissance parties for Operation Torch, though at first they were treated by suspicion by senior officers at Gibraltar. Their value was established when several groups landed miles from their target.[14] Combined Operations Pilotage Parties were set up after that experience. By November 1942 the standard party consisted of three naval and one military officers, two seamen ratings as coxswains and paddlers for the canoes, an artificer or mechanic, a commando corporal and a draughtsman from the Royal Engineers. The size of the unit was restricted by the carrying capacity of a submarine.[15]

Beach parties were planned to co-ordinate the movement of vessels, troops and vehicles during and after a landing. They emerged informally during the voyage to Madagascar in 1942. It was Mountbatten who suggested the title 'commando' rather than 'party', because to the seamen the latter term implied an unpleasant work detail. But commando implied a more combative role, and when two petty officers helped clear pill boxes and snipers in Normandy, a senior officer suggested that they were doing the job of the army. 'The word

"Commando" is regrettable, I consider, as it implies a completely false role for this party'.[16] Eventually two dozen of them were formed and most of them were trained at HMS *Armadillo* among the Clyde sea lochs. Originally a full beach group consisted of three officers and 112 other ranks from the army, an officer and three men from the RAF, and two naval officers and 16 ratings.[17] The petty officers in the party were trained in seamanship, elementary pilotage, beach drill, gunnery, first aid and many other matters.[18] They had to have above average 'power of command' in order to control bewildered parties of troops on the beach. All ranks had to be able to 'endure hard work for long hours with little food, and having to live in the open for up to a week'.[19]

2 Landing Vessels

The problems of landing an army had greatly increased since the First World War, for it was now necessary to land tanks and artillery and their fuel, ammunition and stores with the first wave of troops. Planners had largely discounted the need for amphibious warfare in the 1920s and 30s, and progress in landing craft design was slow, so a great deal had to be improvised hastily. It is surprising how often the designers were right, and how much of the landing craft of the early 1940s is reflected in present-day design. Battleships have disappeared, submarines are now very different, destroyers and frigates have changed their functions, but the basic landing craft has survived.

The British attempted long-range landings at Dakar in 1940, and more successfully on Madagascar and North Africa in 1942, but in general they operated over much shorter ranges than the Americans, crossing the Mediterranean or the English Channel. Influences came from a wide variety of sources on both sides of the Atlantic – converted merchant ships and Thames barges, shallow-draught oil tankers, powered pleasure craft and even a traditional local craft, the Northumberland coble. The techniques and materials of the motor industry were often used in production. The navy had one basic design of battleship during the war and three or four submarine designs, but according to one authority there were 38 different types of landing craft and eight types of barges and even that does not exhaust the full range of possibilities.[20] Broadly, landing craft were used for three different roles: to carry and land personnel, to carry and land vehicles, and in support functions such as control, navigation, bombardment and supply of food. Landing vessels could also be classified according to function. The nomenclature was not always applied precisely, for example in the case of landing tanks, but in general a landing ship took troops and vehicles within a few miles of the beach and then loaded them into landing craft for the actual assault. Major landing craft made the whole journey from loading port to beach, while minor landing craft did the trip from the landing ship to the beach.

An opening bow ramp or doors is often seen as the main characteristic of a landing craft. This was not universally true, as men could jump from a conventional bow or vehicles could disembark aft, but it would not be easy to design a landing craft which could beach stern-first without damaging its propeller. Certainly the opening bow offered many

A beach commando headquarters during the Normandy invasion.

advantages, landing troops and vehicles in the shallowest possible water and getting them straight into action. Conventional naval architects were doubtful about it and feared leaks. Rowland Baker of the Royal Corps of Naval Constructors insisted on a sump to collect water in the design of the Tank Landing Craft Mark 1 in 1940.[21] Leaks were less of a problem than anticipated, but the bow ramp of small landing craft did tend to restrict speed. The most essential characteristics of any craft intended to land on a beach were shallow draught and a flat bottom, and these, too, could restrict performance and sea-keeping.

British landing craft did much of the work alongside the Americans in the D-Day invasion of 1944, an achievement that must rank with the winning of the Battle of the Atlantic in the scale of historical achievement. From a fleet of about two dozen vessels before the war, it built up to a force of 44 landing ships, 115 tank landing ships, 1265 major landing craft, 3777 minor landing craft and 276 barges in May 1945, despite losses of more than 1300 vessels.[22]

Landing Ships

Even before the Fall of France, the Admiralty planned landing operations in German territory and began to convert three passenger ships of the Glen Line, the *Glenroy*, *Glenearn* and *Glengyle*. They were of nearly 10,000 tons and were converted to carry 14 landing craft and more than a thousand troops, with a crew of 291 plus 232 for landing craft crews. Rated as Landing Ships Infantry (Large), they proved very successful and saw much service in the Mediterranean, Normandy and the Far East. All were updated several times during the war to carry more troops and landing craft, at some cost in stability. Other LSI(L)s included the *Keren* and *Karanja* of the British India Steam Navigation Company, which were converted in 1942 and could carry 1500 troops. They had Merchant Navy crews during the early part of their service. In the *Karanja*, according to Evelyn Waugh, the sergeants lived in relative luxury in second-class cabins, while the quarters for the rank and file were extremely cold.[23] In the same ship, Rowland Draper found that 'the food, which was cooked by Merchant Navy cooks, was appalling', because the Goanese stewards had no experience of preparing potatoes.[24] A Dozen American-built merchant ships were converted to LSI(L)s in 1943, and many more ships served for particular operations.

Cross-channel ferries obviously became redundant after the Fall of France and in October 1940 the Admiralty took over several Belgian ships. They were reasonably fast but had limited capacity and therefore short range. They had a certain amount of cabin space, but also wide promenade decks which could be used to stow landing craft. They were classed as Landing Ships Infantry (Small). The *Prince Charles*, built in 1930, was of nearly 3000 tons with a speed of 24 knots. Her decks had a combination of the original passenger and crew bunks and hammocks for crew and troops. She could carry 377 troops with eight landing craft.

Ferries designed for slightly longer voyages, such as the *Ulster Monarch* and the *Isle of Guernsey*, had more cabin space but no promenade decks where landing craft could be stowed. The davits projected from the side, an improvised and ungainly arrangement.

All British infantry landing ships were converted from merchantmen. Army officers found that their fittings were not ideal, and Major Plowden of the Royal Engineers commented:

The soldier in battle order takes up an extraordinary amount of space…the minimum width of any companionway or alleyway should be about 12 feet! It has been found extremely difficult to marshal troops at their action stations as it is nearly always necessary for troops to pass through troop spaces other than their own…

More adequate drainage should be provided in troop spaces and latrine accommodation; few people who have not seen them can have any idea of the indescribable mess which these places become in rough weather. …

Then a most important point is sea kindliness. …one of my main worries was not that the gale would interfere with the physical act of landing, but that the troops would be in no condition to work when they got to the beaches on account of seasickness.[25]

The British also tried to develop a ship which could launch landing craft to take ashore large numbers of tanks, or to carry extra landing craft to ferry them from ship to shore. Two Landing Ships Stern Chute were converted from train ferries and carried landing craft on deck and launched them over the stern, but this was a dangerous procedure. Three Landing Ships Gantry used travelling cranes to hoist heavily loaded landing craft into the sea, but the concept was not fully developed. The best long-term solution was probably the Landing Ship Dock in which a large compartment at the stern was flooded to allow landing craft to reload with heavy vehicles; but it never saw service during the war.

Tank Landing Ships

The problem of landing tanks was solved by a fine example of Anglo-American co-operation. Urged on by Churchill to find a ship which could land them anywhere in the world, British constructors turned to shallow-draft oil tankers used on Lake Maracaibo in Venezuela. They went on to design the *Boxer* class or Landing Ship Tank Mark 1, which could carry 13 tanks and move at up to 13 knots. But they beached in 5 feet 6 inches of water forward and a long ramp was needed to get the vehicles and men ashore. The Americans were asked to help in building and design and in the winter of 1941–2 they produced the LST(2), which could carry up to 18 tanks over an ocean at a maximum speed of 10 knots, and could beach in 3 feet of water forward. Its bow doors would open, a short, steep ramp would be lowered and the tanks and vehicles would disgorge straight onto the beach. The LST(2) was 327 feet long with a light displacement of 1468 tons, with a crew of 13 officers and 73 men. It turned out to be a classic design; able to load in port, transport its cargo across a sea or

A Landing Ship Tank unloading a lorry during the Normandy invasion.

ocean and then land it on the beach. Thousands were mass-produced in America and many were sent to Britain under lend-lease. They took part in all the major landings and their design had much influence on the ro-ro ferries of post-war years.

Tank Landing Craft

In June 1940, again under pressure from Churchill, the Admiralty began to look at a craft to land three of the largest tanks of the time, 40 tons each, in 2 feet 6 inches of water. A prototype, the Landing Craft Tank Mark I, was built on Tyneside with many novel features, including a ramp with a hinge just above the waterline and a double floating dock-type of hull, but it created alarm as it swung from side to side going down the river. A few were built and shipped out to the Eastern Mediterranean.

The next version, the LCT(2), had 2 feet more beam but was not a success.

The Mark 2 must have been designed by a madman. It had three Scott-Paine Sealion engines, using high-octane petrol, with a home-made reverse gear which required a man on each gear lever, each pulling back with all his strength to operate a friction band which had a life of 50 hours. … Although we had three engines there were only the usual double telegraphs, so we had to use our ingenuity to rig up a telegraph for the centre engine. This was the vital one, for the craft would only steer with the slipstream from this engine on to the single rudder in the centre.[26]

The LCT(3) came next in 1941–2, with more satisfactory engines and a 32-foot section inserted bringing the length to 192 feet. Two hundred and thirty-five were built, mostly by structural engineers. It could carry up to 11 tanks. This was followed by the LCT(4), which was designed entirely by structural engineers to standards that shipbuilders found alarming. It was shorter and broader than the LCT(3) and was slower at 10 knots. Some regarded it as expendable,

to be abandoned on a beach, if necessary, after landing its cargo, but this was denied by the authorities. '…an attempt was always made to recover the more seriously damaged craft, either in one piece or two, and at least one returned to the U.K. under its own power, towing its fore-end!'[27]

One RNVR officer describes his LCT(4) as loaded for D-Day.

My craft carried six Sherman tanks, two half-track supply trucks, and a Red Cross jeep. With this load, we carried four officers and fifty-four GIs. To accommodate these soldiers we had, officially, two small cabins and a troop space about fifteen feet by five feet. My crew were a hospitable crowd, and the Yanks were all as willing to take what came. I, the First Lieutenant, one Army Officer and the Flotilla Officer slept in the wardroom. The other officers had the cabins. The non-commissioned officers had the troop space, and the rest of the troops were given bedding on the mess-deck and engine room decks.[28]

Landing Craft Infantry

The Landing Craft Infantry (Large) was an American design intended originally to meet British needs. It was able to cross the oceans and could carry more than 200 troops at up to 14 knots. It had no bow doors and troops disembarked by means of gangways on either side of the bows. This meant that it was unsuitable for the first wave of an invasion, but it brought in follow-up troops at all the major landings in Europe. It was built in America for both the British and American navies.

British sailors were amazed to find their craft fitted out to American standards.

I was overcome to find that I had my own cabin, with fitted wardrobe, filing cabinet, desk, safe, and interior spring bunk complete with reading light. There were showers for both officers and ratings, and the ratings had a very spacious messdeck, quite apart from their sleeping quarters, where every man had his own bunk. The galley was beautifully equipped, with an enormous cold storage room and refrigerator adjoining.[29]

Alan Villiers, the well-known sailor and writer, describes it from another angle.

They steered like tramcars with electric power and a gadget like a carman's switch; they looked like welded steel orange boxes, and their plates were so thin that in places they yielded at the tread of their sailor's feet, like sheets of thin plywood. They were mass-produced like automobiles, and women welded them together at assembly points on the east coast of the United States. They were powered with eight bus engines each, in two banks of four called quads, each quad being geared to a variable pitch propeller which was adjusted electrically. To go astern, both propellers had to be adjusted to negative pitch.

But despite his unrivalled experience in square-rigged ships, Villiers found them to be 'splendid sea boats', able to cross oceans and withstand much damage.[30]

Small Personnel Landing Craft

The only type to be developed in Britain between the wars was the Motor Landing Craft built by J S White of Cowes in 1926 to carry 100 troops. Proposals for improvement came to nothing until 1928 when the Inter-Service Training and Development Centre began to take an interest. Alternative designs were produced commercially but were not very satisfactory. The Admiralty produced the Assault Landing Craft 2, later the LCA. It was 38 feet 9 inches long and had a bow ramp, bulletproof side decks and an armoured steering position forward in the developed version. Nearly 2000 were produced during the war, at a rate of 60 per month in 1944.

Meanwhile the Americans adopted another approach. Andrew Jackson Higgins, a colourful boat-builder of New Orleans, used his experience with speedboats to design a light craft which could carry 30 men at 18 knots. It had a conventional bow rather than a ramp. Instead of the armour of the LCA, the Eureka or Landing Craft Personnel (Large) as the British called it, relied on speed for protection and it could drive some way up a beach, or over the top of a shallow sandbank. Some were bought for the Royal Navy. At the same time, the LCP (Small) was being developed in Britain. It was short, and light enough to be slung from ordinary merchant ship davits.

The smallest type of landing vessel was the folbot, a folding canoe that would be dismantled for stowage inside a submarine and used for commando operations. The standard model was 18 feet long and was paddled by two men.

Landing Craft Mechanised

In the inter-wars years the British had continued to study the problem of designing a craft which could land a single tank or large vehicle. By 1938 they had evolved the Landing Craft Mechanised Mark I, which could carry 16 tons at 7½ knots. It was simply a floating pontoon with the sides built up, and the tank deck was above the waterline. At the time of Dunkirk the prototype was the only

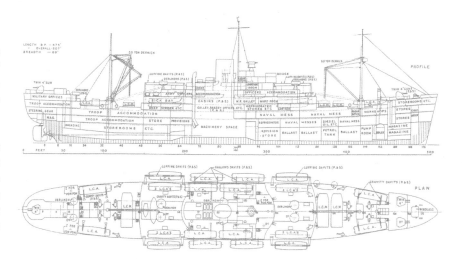

Landing Ship Infantry (L) of the Glen class, which served all through the war.

vessel capable of beaching with a tank. Many more were ordered, often built by railway companies.

The US Marine Corps looked at the LCM(1) in 1941, but it could not carry a large enough load for their purposes. They consulted with Higgins, who lowered the deck to below the waterline to increase stability, and produced the LCM(3) which could carry a 30-ton tank. The British ordered 150 while the Americans were still sceptical, and eventually thousands were built for Allied use. The LCM(1), however, continued in use, because it was light enough to be hoisted with its load on board. Higgins also produced the Landing Craft Vehicles and Personnel, or LCV (P), based on his LCP. It adopted the bow ramp and could carry a 3-ton lorry or 36 troops.

Landing Barges

The classic Thames sailing barge was designed for the shallow waters of London's estuary, with a flat bottom and shallow draft so that it could pass over sandbanks and unload on beaches. Twenty-five of them took part in the evacuation of Dunkirk and their use for the reverse operation was obvious. Stripped of their sails and fitted with engines, more than 400 of them were converted for various functions. New crew members, dreaming of appointments to destroyers or MTBs, were disappointed.

The following day we were taken down to Fishbourne, Wootton Creek . We arrived at the water's edge and there in the river, moored head to stern, were a number of shapes the like of which I had seen so often on the London River: barges with their backsides shorn off and some planks of timber held together to form a ramp and a wheel box; not even a resemblance of a bridge. There was some sort of contraption up forward resembling a machine gun, which turned out to be a twin Hotchkiss made obsolete in the 1914 war.[31]

Some were able to carry up to three tanks, others took oil supplies into the beach area and bore large signs indicating the type of fuel carried, for example 'Diesel'. Some carried anti-aircraft guns, some were fitted for emergency repair of other boats, some carried water, and others were fitted with kitchens to feed the crews of minor landing craft during the operation. 'The kitchen craft closely resembled an overgrown caboose set on a barge, and its many smoking stove-pipes made this unseaworthy Noah's Ark look most out of place battling it out in the mean sea towards Normandy, where it was badly needed'.[32]

Guns and Flak

Naval ships could provide gunfire support during a landing, and land artillery could sometimes be used from a landing craft, but as often happened it was found that specially designed equipment was the best. The Landing Craft Gun, in various sizes, could go close inshore and engaged directly in the land battle. Captain J A Good of the Royal Marines served in a Landing Craft Gun (Medium) in 1944–5 and became committed to the concept.

The LCG(M) armed with 25 pdr had a dual role and purpose. First, being mounted in a naval turret, and having naval sighting arrangements, they were capable of firing on the move at sea, either at targets afloat or, as intended, at targets ashore. Second, being field artillery pieces, and having Royal Artillery control arrangements as well, they could act, when firmly beached, as a section of field artillery. Very versatile we were! …

We in LCG(M)s were a proud lot, justly so, for our craft were purpose built and had been well conceived and designed. It was the fact that they had a pointed bow that made them look like a ship…[33]

The Landing Craft Rocket was an amazing vessel, armed with 792 rocket projectiles – for a second or two it had the firepower of 80 cruisers or 200 destroyers – but it was very difficult to aim, and took several hours to reload.

Ships also needed protection from the air during a landing, in addition to what was provided by the naval escorts. Landing Craft Flak came in several forms. Some had 4-inch high-angle guns, some 2-pounder pom-poms.

Headquarters Ships

One lesson of the Dakar affair was that a seaborne invasion needed dedicated headquarters ships, as conventional warships such as cruisers were in danger of being called away to perform their usual duties. This was reinforced during the North Africa landings late in 1942, when the American cruiser *Augusta* had to leave her station with the staff on board. By that time the British had already converted the ex-passenger ship *Bulolo* as the first headquarters ship, followed by the *Largs*. Smaller ships, such as frigates, which proved unsuitable for ocean service for one reason or another, were converted to LSH (Small), capable of directing the landing of one brigade 'brick' during an invasion. Fighter Direction Ships or LSFs were also fitted out with sophisticated radar, plotting equipment and radio to control the air battle above the landing.

Below: Landing Craft Assault at sea in June 1943, led by a motor launch.

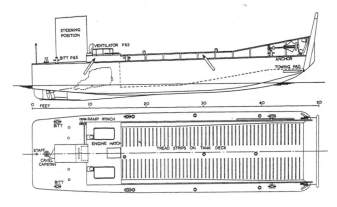

3 Combined Operations Techniques

The Experience

The Combined Operations organisation had a chance to build up a cumulative experience of landing troops on hostile shores, and to learn from some quite serious mistakes. Withdrawals such as Dunkirk, Greece and Crete provided some experience of the dangers of operating ships close inshore. The abortive attack on Dakar in 1940 showed the need for ships to land tanks and to carry the headquarters. The landing of marines on Madagascar established the need of a beach organisation. The disastrous raid on Dieppe in 1942 provided many lessons, including the effectiveness of German coastal batteries, the dangers of choosing the most obvious landing place, and the problems of communication if too may radio sets are in use at once. The North African landings later in the year were unopposed, but they emphasised the need for good training of landing craft crews and for navigation aids, the importance of reconnaissance to ascertain certain facts, such as the exact gradient of beaches, and that army commanders should not go ashore until their signals headquarters are established. The landing on Sicily the following year was relatively easy, but the operation at Salerno on mainland Italy met the heaviest opposition so far. The value of gunfire from large warships was established, and the use of carriers to establish air superiority was generally successful. Army commanders learned that it was dangerous to press on too far without securing the flanks. At Anzio later in the year, they learned the opposite lesson, that a force should not remain static on the beaches and allow the enemy time to regroup.

British experience was different from that of the Americans in the Pacific. The Americans had no policy of commando raids, and they generally landed on small islands where navigation and the identification of the correct beach were not great problems. On the other hand they were dealing with a fanatical foe. The Germans were skilled and dedicated soldiers, but not as suicidal as the Japanese, and they usually had a line of retreat so did not have to fight to the finish, unless the Führer ordered it in one of his disastrous tactical interventions. Nevertheless, the British kept in touch with American developments in tactics.

Planning

The original idea of Combined Operations was perhaps to build up from small commando raids to bigger operations. This did not work, as there proved to be a large gap between raids and full invasions. The Dieppe raid was between the two, but it was an appalling failure.

It was important to chose the site of a landing carefully. The most far-reaching decision was to invade Normandy rather than any other part of northern Europe. The Germans had always assumed that it would be done over the shortest sea route in the Strait of Dover, but the length of time at sea was irrelevant, as ships and craft would have to be assembled in many ports from south Wales to East Anglia. The Calais area had few suitable beaches, and any preparations directly opposite would be obvious to the enemy (alhough ships in Dover harbour were used for deceptive purposes). Mountbatten staged a well-managed conference at Largs in Scotland in 1943, a kind of 'psychological motor show' and persuaded the senior officers present that Normandy was the place.

The army generally would have preferred to land in darkness, but the navy favoured dawn, so that it could approach under cover of darkness and make the final approach in the light. It usually had its way. A suitable beach needed to have a reasonably steep slope, or the landing craft would have to beach a long way from the shore – this made much of the Dutch coast, for example, unsuitable for landing. Tides and currents were powerful in northern Europe, though not in the Mediterranean. Strong currents might push craft sideways and had to be allowed for. Landing at high tide would give a shorter distance for the troops to cross between the landing point and the enemy defences, but in fact the Normandy landings took place at low tide to expose enemy beach obstacles. This placed a vital constraint on the time of the landing, making it necessary to choose days when low tide was close to dawn.

Detailed operation orders were produced and issued to commanders of landing craft. Under American command for the Normandy landings, Gavin Douglas commented:

That paper work deserves a book to itself. Each craft carried sacks of the stuff and as I had the Flotilla Officer onboard I carried his lot as well. We stacked it in drawers, on top of shelves, under tables and in our bunks. There were thirty books of photographs of the beaches: dozens of magnificently printed and coloured charts; Intelligence reports of some fifty types foolscap sheets… We sat down and worked through the lot, picking out the few pages from each book that would concern out own part in 'Operation Overlord' and made them into a slim, understandable book.[34]

Reconnaissance

Detailed photo reconnaissance was vital in planning a landing, to show the latest state of the defences. It was not complete, for it did not necessarily show the height of a feature, the state of the beach or the water and tidal conditions, so it had to be supplemented by information gained on the spot.

The Admiralty Hydrographic Department had a vast fund of knowledge of the world's coastlines, but it was not always detailed enough to plan a landing. In some places, the charts were out of date and inaccurate, which is where the Combined Operations Pilotage Parties (COPP) came in. They used a version of the folbot canoe, improved to fit their own needs. They landed at night after being launched by

Canadian survivors of the disastrous raid on Dieppe return to Britain in August 1942.

mainland of Italy. It found that beach No. 11 was 5000 yards long and had an excellent gradient of 1:20 except for an 800-yard bank to the north. The beach was not easy to pick out, however, and pilotage instructions were offered;

When within about ½ mile you will see through your glasses the white sand beach, terminating at the northern end in the cliffs and high ground in the vicinity of NICOMERA. …
The under-water surface is sand and there are no obstacles, natural or otherwise, apart from the bank mentioned above, over the entire length…[37]

Even after the first wave of the landing, decisions could be changed by further reconnaissance. Patrick Bayley was beachmaster during the Sicily landings and he found that the allocated beach was not suitable for heavy landing craft. He found a rocky shore a few miles away, where pillboxes could be pulled down to create a smooth surface and the heavy equipment was landed there in record time.[38]

The Voyage

Landing craft were 'combat loaded', with the equipment that would be needed first ready to be landed quickly. Control of troops in a cross-channel invasion required some skill among the officers of major landing craft. They needed 'Ability to maintain discipline and an aggressive spirit both among the crews themselves and among the troops embarked, under conditions of exceptional stress through enemy action'.[39]

The planning of an operation depended very much on the distance to be covered on the approach. In a commando raid such as the attack on Lofoten Island off northern Norway in March 1941, the troops would travel both ways in Landing Ships Infantry or smaller vessels. In one involving a long sea voyage, such as Madagascar, the force would travel in a big-ship convoy with naval escort and carriers to provide air cover. The number of troops carried was also determined by the length of the voyage. A Landing Ship Tank, for example, could carry 400 men on a short voyage but only 170 on a long one.[40]

A short sea crossing, such as the landings in Italy and Normandy, would carry the troops out mainly in landing ships and put them ashore in Landing Craft Assault. They might travel in three types of convoy, according to speed. The slow assault convoys would leave first, consisting of the slower Landing Ship Tank Mark III and some stores ships, with speeds of 6 to 10 knots. The 'craft convoy' of Tank Landing Ships and Craft and Landing Craft Infantry travelled at 10 knots. The fast assault convoy had a speed of 12 knots and included Landing Ships Infantry (L) and Landings Ships Personnel. During the voyage of the craft convoy the Landing Craft Tank would form lines astern along the centre, with LCI(L)s on the outside, with the whole force protected by a naval escort of cruisers and destroyers.[41] Though the Germans managed to invade Norway without it, the British and their allies insisted on a large margin of sea superiority for large-scale operations, especially if they were opposed. Invasion forces en route were protected by major warships, anti-submarine vessels, coastal forces and fighter aircraft. Minesweepers went ahead to clear paths towards the beaches.

The route towards a landing involved several stages. The craft would set out from various ports, for example, in the case of the Normandy

submarine. As well as checking the navigational features shown on charts, they could test the strength of a beach for heavy equipment, and carry out many detailed surveys.[35] They were tasked with finding pilotage directions for the assault convoy as well as the landing ships on the beaches, to establish the nature of the beach with its gradients, obstacles and exits to the shore. The submarine carrying them might take photographs in daylight through its periscope, but pilotage parties preferred to work in moonless nights, and they claimed that with training in night stalking they could operate within 20 yards of an enemy sentry. They would draw silhouettes of the coast, both from the lowering position 7 miles offshore, and about 3 miles off to check the route. They would make recommendations about any leading marks that might be there already, or any navigational aids that could be put in place for the landing. They would check the surface of the beach to see if it would bear heavy vehicles. They used underwater writing pads to make notes, and wrote them up as soon as they were back on board the submarine or other vessel carrying them.[36]

COPP No. 5 was landed by the submarine *Shakespeare* in the Gulf of Gioia in July and August 1943, in preparation for the first landing on the

invasion. They would reach a rendezvous point, just south of the Isle of Wight and known informally as 'Piccadilly'. Normally this was to be in daylight on D minus one, to allow the craft to assemble, 'in a position carefully chosen so that it does not disclose the exact assault area to the enemy'.[42] Then they sailed in protective formation towards the landing beaches. In the Normandy invasion this was down the 'spout', a channel cleared of mines which gradually widened towards the destination.

After experience in North Africa, the difficulty of finding the right spot on the right beach began to be appreciated. Landing Craft Navigation were equipped with chart tables and fully qualified navigators to direct the forces in. For the Normandy landings the midget submarines *X-20* and *X-23* sailed from Portsmouth on 2 June and were on station a day and a half later, but did not know that the invasion would be postponed for a day, making life very difficult in such cramped craft. They took accurate bearings from points on shore and when the main force arrived they directed it in by flashing lights on telescopic masts.[43]

Assault Formations

The assault began in earnest when the landing and headquarters ships arrived at the lowering point, 7 miles offshore in the case of the British forces on D-Day. Captain David Bone of the landing ship *Circassia* watched a well-trained crew in exercise. The ships anchored and then lowering began.

Other than the first shrilling of the bos'n's pipe there were no high words of command although I could mark the crews scrambling into the craft and the swift but unhurried embarkation of the Marines from the 'sally ports' on the ship's high deck levels. … Suddenly, at some sign I could not see, or word I could not hear, all the lower craft on the side nearest to us were lowered swiftly and steadily into the water, cast off and formed line ahead…the upper bank was as quickly lowered and then joined the snake-like line of sea-hornets. …there were twelve craft. About 400 armed men sent off, outboard the ship on a mission, well within five minutes.[44]

Slower craft went into the water first to begin their journey towards the beach. In the bad weather that day, this was hazardous in itself. According to Major Porteus of No. 4 Commando:

As my landing craft hit the water, we took a large wave over the side. A foot of water swilling round our feet. Get pumping – Damn! The bilge pumps not working, so get bailing with tin hats. Difficult in the cramped conditions on board, especially as some men being sick.[45]

The assault craft would approach the beach in carefully timed waves. Each was in line abreast, so that large numbers would arrive at the same time and present the greatest problem to the enemy defences. For the invasion of Normandy, a line of swimming or DD tanks, manned by the army, was expected to land first on each beach. In the bad weather this proved very difficult. Forty were launched from landing craft 500 yards offshore on Sword Beach and 32 of them made it ashore, but on Juno and Gold most of them were taken ashore in the Landing Craft Tanks, often arriving later than other forces. The next wave consisted of

Landing Craft Gun, which would not land until later but would engage the enemy defences at close range. Then came a line of LCTs carrying AVREs (Assault Vehicles, Royal Engineers), which would use flail tanks and low-velocity guns to clear mines and obstacles on the beach. They were closely followed by Landing Craft Assault carrying the first wave of infantry, who would touch down precisely at H-hour. Behind them were Landing Craft Flak and Rocket, and LCTs carrying self-propelled

Above: A selection of charts and orders used in Operation Neptune, the naval side of the invasion of Normandy.

Left: Typical formations for an assault landing.

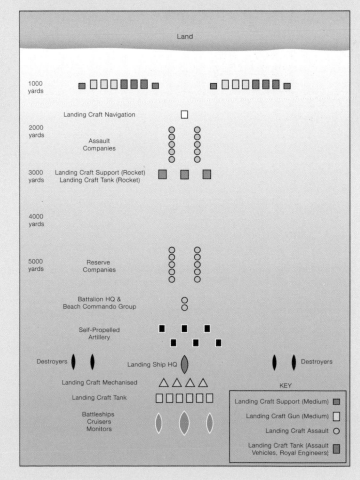

army guns, which would also stay slightly offshore for the moment and use their weaponry. Then came several waves of LCAs with infantry and commandos at intervals of 10 or 15 minutes. The headquarters ship for this force of one army brigade group or 'brick' was stationed not far offshore and the flanks were protected by Hunt class destroyer escorts 4000 yards offshore, and fleet destroyers with longer range guns further out.

The Landing

The commander of each craft had to find his way ashore in the final stages. According to Lieutenant-Commander Rupert Curtis of LCI(S) 519:

My mind concentrated on finding a path through the underwater obstructions. Fortunately at that state of the tide, the tops of many of them were still visible sprouting above the surface of the sea, many with lethal attachments.

Right: Landing Craft Rocket in action.

Below: A Landing Barge Kitchen (easily identifiable by its high superstructure and chimneys) supplies a variety of landing craft moored alongside.

Working completely by instinct…I felt I could discern a clear path through the menacing stakes. It looked a bit of a zig-zag but I backed my instinct and took 519 through with rapid helm orders. We emerged unscathed and I called for more power from the engine room to thrust our bows hard on to the beach to ensure as dry a landing as possible. Then we kept both engines running at half speed to hold the bows in position.[46]

In theory the authority of the naval commander over the troops ended when the craft touched shore. The assault landing craft carrying Lieutenant L E Anderson hit an obstacle which stuck through the bottom of the boat 'which made it spin like a roulette wheel in the rough sea'. After an argument with the coxswain it was agreed that they went ashore and the troops waded out, up to their necks in water.

In his waterlogged craft, Major Porteus was not sorry to reach the beach. 'Approaching the beach all hell going on but anything preferable to this horrible boat. As the front ramps went down, she finally sank in three feet of water'.[47]

It was important to let go of the kedge or stern anchor so that the craft could be hauled off after the load was discharged, as Able Seaman John Holden found in training.

We were constantly wet through with rain and sea spray, doing endless landings on the beach from early morning to late evening. The worst part was if we lost our kedge anchor wire by dropping the stern anchor too soon. Apart from the skipper losing face in front of the other LSTs, it was a cold, wet job for a boat to fish for the cable with grappling hooks. The practice paid off, however, as we never lost our kedge anchor during operations in the face of the enemy.[48]

Landing on Sicily, Alec Guinness's cable was cut by a passing ship and the LCI(L)'s kedge anchor was lost. The ship drifted diagonally to the beach and the troops had to climb over the side. It was 10 days before a passing destroyer towed her off.[49]

Air and Sea Support

Bombing and bombardment from the sea might begin some time before the landing, although the strategists had to be careful not to give the site away. In the case of Normandy, the air attack concentrated on transport facilities, which helped conceal Allied intentions. Parachute and glider troops were landed on the flanks of the invasion to secure bridgeheads and prevent counterattack.

Artillery support of a landing came in three phases. During the approach the heavy artillery from ships' guns could saturate the beach batteries and defences without risk to their own troops. Landing Craft Rocket were deployed just before the troops landed, providing an impressive display of pyrotechnics for a few seconds. The first six were used at Sicily in 1943 and opened up 500 yards from the beach, heartening the troops of the Highland Division who were about to land.[50]

At H-hour, as the first landings took place, the situation was more difficult as ships' guns were not accurate enough, and the army's own artillery had not yet landed. This was where the Landing Craft Gun came into its own.

A Mulberry Harbour. The success of the breakwaters in providing a calm area is clearly seen.

The LCG(M) armed with 25 pdr had a dual role and purpose. First, being mounted in a naval turret, and having naval siting [sic] arrangements, they were capable of firing on the move at sea, either at targets afloat or, as intended, at targets ashore. Second, being field artillery pieces, and having Royal Artillery control arrangements as well, they could act, when firmly beached, as a section of field artillery. Very versatile we were![51]

The third phase was the advance inland, when long-range ships' guns became useful again in firing at enemy batteries and strong points and targets of opportunity as pointed out by reconnaissance aircraft of forward observation officers.

As well as reconnaissance, aircraft were necessary to give fire and bombing support at sea and ashore, and to provide a fighter screen over the operation. There was one headquarters ship for each beach in the Normandy invasion. They anchored offshore at first light on D-Day, and the army command remained on board for about six hours until their signals units were set up ashore. By this time fighter direction ships manned by the RAF were used as well, so the headquarters ships had little to do in that matter. The ships remained on station for more than a week after that, mostly doing naval duties such as directing landing craft.[52]

On the Beach

In the book and the film *The Longest Day* the public was given a very one-dimensional view of the beachmaster with an image of Captain Colin Maud standing alone with his dog on Juno Beach, waving a stick and shouting 'Get a move on'.[53] In fact the beachmaster was leader of a skilled and varied team controlling movement by sea and land in an impromptu but very busy port, often under enemy fire. Between the first phase of the landing and the capture or building of the first port, the beachmaster and the beach commandos had to control the build-up of forces. Some lessons had been learned from the Italian landings. It was suggested that the most difficult task was controlling the landings of the Landing Craft Mechanised, whose visual signalling was often poor with such a small crew, and whose engines tended to drown out a loud hailer. Wheeled vehicles should be landed near a roadway, tracked vehicles should never be on a wire roadway as they would destroy it. Heavy armoured vehicles should not be landed on a beach, and squadrons or batteries should not be split between different parts of the beach. Two boats were necessary to intercept arriving craft and give them instructions. Special parties

were now able to repair damaged craft on the beaches, so a large kit of tools was no longer needed.[54]

There were further lessons from Normandy. Beach parties worked continually for two or three days and went into two watches, and some parties appointed cooks to keep them supplied with food. Jeeps and motorbikes were needed to maintain contact on long beaches, especially when the signal unit became separated, necessitating the use of flashing light signals. Casualties were highest among officers and petty officers, which perhaps justified the complement of three officers, two petty officers, two leading seamen and 20 able or ordinary seamen in a unit.[55]

Supplying the Armies

After the frustration of the Dieppe raid the Allies realised that it would be very difficult to capture a major port intact, but armies would still have to be supplied on a scale beyond what could be landed on open beaches. After the Quebec Conference in July 1943 they began Operation Mulberry, to build artificial harbours and tow the elements across the Channel to Normandy. 'Phoenixes' were floating concrete caissons up to 200 feet long that were sunk to form breakwaters. These were supplemented by old merchant ships which were scuttled, and by rafts known as bombardons which formed an outer floating breakwater. Inside the space thus created were floating jetties held in place by piles in water deep enough for ships to unload, connected to the beach by causeways held up by small floating units known as beetles. Other quays were used for unloading stores from Tank Landing Ships.

The blockships and caissons were the first to set sail for the invasion, from faraway ports such as Oban. Construction of the two Mulberries began soon after D-Day, but was severely hampered by storms on 19–22 June. The American Mulberry never recovered, but the British one at Arromanches eventually enclosed an area of 3 square miles and landed thousands of tons of stores before it was closed in mid-November. Five much simpler ports known as Gooseberries were also set up off landing beaches, consisting of breakwaters formed by old ships. These proved very effective, as did landing goods by DUKW, the American-designed amphibious truck.

PLUTO, or Pipe Line Under The Ocean, was a scheme to supply the Allied forces in northern Europe with fuel. From a base on the Isle of Wight, *Latimer* and other vessels laid a 3-inch pipe to Cherbourg beginning on 8 August 1944, and later a triple pipeline to Boulogne. But there difficulties with the shore connections and Pluto delivered only 8 per cent of the supplies needed.[56]

Conclusion

When the war finally ended with the surrender of Japan after the dropping of the atom bombs in 1945, the Royal Navy was showing signs of exhaustion. It had lost 1500 ships and vessels ranging from the battlecruiser *Hood* and the aircraft carrier *Ark Royal* to 21 dumb barges. Its men had spent long years at sea and were ready for a rest. Of the million men and women who served, more than 50,000 would not come back. The wartime navy was quickly demobilised, and the system was fair enough to prevent any serious discontent, although very few wartime ratings wanted to volunteer for the post-war navy – the Admiralty was rather shaken by an essay on 'Why I Prefer Civvy Street' by a rating in the cruiser *Black Prince*. By 1949 it had been reduced to 144,000 men, a sixth of its wartime strength. The infant technologies of the later stages of the war – nuclear weapons, guided missiles, jet aircraft – would combine with recently established ones such as radar and amphibious warfare to produce a new kind of navy. Socially, the navy was slow to respond to changes in the outside world but by about 1960 it had got rid of the worst of its class distinctions and became a very effective modern force, though always constrained by budgets which were much less than what it wanted.

The Royal Navy came out of the Second World War with almost unsullied credit. It had no disasters on the scale of the army's defeats in France, Greece and Crete. It did not have any morally and strategically dubious campaigns on the scale of the RAF's bombing of Germany – its most controversial episode, the destruction of the recently-allied French fleet at Mers el-Kebir, was imposed from above and was directed against ships and servicemen, not civilians. It made a substantial contribution to almost every campaign in every theatre of the Second World War, despite a national base which was under threat of invasion, was bombed and had grossly over-stretched personnel and industrial resources. It maintained and developed forces for every kind of warfare, on, under and over the sea and on the interface with the land – the only navy to do so fully, apart from the United States with much greater resources. It ended the war with restored prestige and vastly increased experience, but without its old position as the world's greatest sea power.

Certainly the navy had serious faults. It maintained a system of class distinction which was already being challenged during the war. It had placed exaggerated faith in the battle fleet before the war, to the neglect of anti-submarine warfare, amphibious operations and coastal warfare. It was able to catch up in time in the first two of these fields, but not in the third, which was arguably far less important in any case. It failed to develop an adequate method of anti-aircraft gunnery, and in the early stages it did not even appreciate the importance of this failure. It tended to place too little faith in the self-discipline of its sailors, and maintained draconian punishments for minor misdemeanours. Conversely, it expected too much of them in action or in service, believing that they would endure and even relish harsh conditions for long periods. As a result, men were worn out from flying or combat stress when a period of rest could have restored them. It refused to think defensively and neglected to develop life jackets and efficient lifeboats, and was late with damage-control techniques. None of these faults lost a major battle or campaign, although individual ships such as the *Hood*, *Ark Royal*, *Prince of Wales* and *Repulse* suffered from them. But more generally, the faults caused unnecessary waste of talent and loss of life.

The navy's strong points shone through this. Having finally freed itself from the malaise of the late nineteenth and early twentieth centuries, it allowed initiative to its middle-ranking officers. It proved very adaptable and developed an amphibious warfare organisation out of almost nothing. Its training methods were far from perfect, but it absorbed hundreds of thousands of men and women into the esoteric naval culture, motivated them and gave the vast majority of them a lasting affection for the navy, with all its faults. That was one use for its tradition. The other one was the hatred of failure, the refusal to break off an operation when it was going badly. Sir Dudley Pound was no Nelson, but one phrase of his echoes the great admiral. 'So long as a ship remains afloat and has even one gun in action she may cause damage to the enemy'. This was in contrast with the captain of the *Graf Spee* who scuttled his ship, and with the U-boat captains who failed to press their attacks home in the summer of 1943 and had to be rebuked by Dönitz.

Without the Second World War, the Royal Navy would seem very different from a historian's perspective, looking back to the faraway days of Nelson for its last great triumphs. Before the previous world war in 1914–18, it got practically everything it wanted from taxpayer and government, but failed to shine in action. Before the Second World War it complained constantly about neglect, but performed very well. After the war, it carried out various thankless tasks in connection with winding down the British Empire, or the Cold War. It maintained the submarine nuclear deterrent, but that role was unpopular with large elements of the public and boring for those who carried it out. It had three unpopular 'cod wars' with Iceland over fishing rights, and it played second fiddle to the army in two Gulf wars. Only in the relatively small Falklands Conflict of 1982 did it show anything of its former fame and skill, but even that did not prevent a long-term decline in numbers, finance and public interest. But its conduct in the Second World War allows it to be remembered as one of the decisive forces of the twentieth century, which prevented the invasion of Britain in 1940, struggled for control of the Mediterranean, fought the longest campaign of all in the Battle of the Atlantic, and put much of the Allied armies ashore in Normandy in 1944.

A U-boat captain surrenders to British officers in May 1945.

Appendices
1 Ship Classes

Notes to tables;
Some figures, such as standard displacement and complement, are highly variable within a class and over a period of time. As far as possible, the figure at the beginning of the war or when the ship entered service is used. Anti-aircraft is omitted, as it was variable throughout the war

Capital Ships

Name of class	Dates of building	Standard displacement in tons	Length overall in feet	Maximum speed in knots	Crew	Main armament	Secondary armament	Armour, maximum thickness
Queen Elizabeth★	1912-16	Approx. 31,000	645ft 9in	24	1124	Eight 15in guns	Twelve 6in guns	13in
Royal Sovereign	1913-17	29,150	624ft 3in	21½	1146	Eight 15in guns	Twelve 6in guns	13in
Renown	1914-16	32,000	794	30	1181	Six 15in guns	Twenty 4.5in guns	11in
Hood	1916-20	42,670	860	31	1341	Eight 15in guns	Twelve 5.5in guns	15in
Nelson	1922-7	33,313	710	23	1314	Nine 16in guns	Twelve 6in guns	14in
King George V	1937-42	36,727	745	28	1422	Ten 14in guns	Sixteen 5.25in guns	15in

★ as modernised

Cruisers

Name of class	Dates of building	Standard displacement in tons	Length overall in feet	Maximum speed in knots	Crew	Main armament	Secondary armament	Armour, maximum thickness
C	1914-18	Approx. 4200	451	29	400	Five 6in guns	–	3in
D	1916-19	4850	471	28	450	Six 6in guns	–	3in
E	1917-20	7550	570	33	572	Seven 6in guns	–	2½in
Raleigh	1915-21	Approx 9770	605	30½	712	Seven 7.5in guns	–	2½in
Kent	1923-8	9750	630-33	31.5	685	Eight 8in guns	Eight 4in guns	5in
London	1925-9	9850	630-33	32.3	700	Eight 8in guns	Eight 4in guns	5in
Norfolk	1926-30	9975	633-35	32.3	710	Eight 8in guns	Eight 4in guns	4in
York	1926-31	8250	575	32	623	Six 8in guns	Four 4in guns	3in
Leander	1929-35	6895-5720	554	32.5	570	Eight 6in guns	Eight 4in guns	4in
Arethusa	1930-7	5720	500	32.3	500	Six 6in guns	Eight 4in guns	2in
Southampton	1933-8	9100	591ft 6in	32	748	Twelve 6in guns	Eight 4in guns	4in
Belfast	1936-9	10,550	613ft 6in	32	850	Twelve 6in guns	Twelve 4in guns	4½in
Dido	1936-42	5600	480-530	33	530	Ten 5.25in guns	–	3in
Fiji	1937-43	8530	555ft 6in	33	920	Twelve 6in guns	Eight 4in guns	4in
Swiftsure	1941-5	8800	555ft 6in	31.5	960	Nine 6in guns	Ten 4in guns	4in

Fleet Destroyers

Name of class	Dates of building	Standard displacement in tons	Length overall in feet	Maximum speed in knots	Crew	Gun armament	Torpedo armament
A & B	1927-30	1337-60	323	35.25	138	Four 4.7in	Eight 21in
A & B Leader	1928-30	1540	343	35	185	Five 4.7in	Eight 21in
C, D, E & F	1929-32	1400	329	36	145	Four 4.7in	Eight 21in
E & F Leaders	1931-5	1495	343	36.75	175	Five 4.7in	Eight 21in
G & H	1933-6	1370	323	36	145	Four 4.7in	Eight 21in
G & H Leaders	1933-7	1456	337	36.5	178	Four 4.7in	Eight 21in
I	1936-7	1370	323	36	145	Four 4.7in	Ten 21in
Tribal	1935-9	1959	377	36.5	250	Eight 4.7in	Four 21in
J, K & N	1936-41	1773	356ft 6in	36	218	Six 4.7in	Ten 21in
L & M	1937-42	1935	362ft 6in	36	226	Six 4.7in	Eight 21in
O & P	1940-2	1550	345	37	212	Four 4in	Eight 21in
Q & R	1940-3	1725	358ft 3in	36.75	225	Four 4.7in	Eight 21in
S, T, U, V&W	1941-4	1730	362ft 9in	36.75	225	Four 4.7in	Eight 21in
Z & C	1942-5	1730	362ft 9in	36.75	222	Four 4.5in	Eight 21in
Battle	1942-8	2325	379	35.75	308	Four 4.5in	Eight 21in

Aircraft Carriers

Name of class	Dates of building	Designation	Standard displacement in tons	Length overall in feet	Maximum speed in knots	Crew	No. of aircraft	Armament	Armour
Argus	1914-18	–	14,550	566	20	401	20	Six 4in guns	–
Eagle	1913-20	–	21,630	667ft 6in	22½	950	21	Twelve 6in guns, four 4in guns	4½in belt
Hermes	1918-24	–	10,850	598	25	664	20	Ten 6in guns, four 4in guns	3in belt
Furious	1922-5★	Fleet	22,450	786ft 5in	30	1218	36	Ten 5.5in guns, two 4in guns	3in belt
Courageous	1924-30★	Fleet	22,500	786ft 7in	30	1216	48	Sixteen 4.7in guns	3in belt
Ark Royal	1935-8	Fleet	22,000	800	31	1580	60	Sixteen 4.5in guns	4½in belt
Illustrious	1937-41	Fleet	23,000	753ft 3in	30.5	1229	33	Sixteen 4.5in guns	4½in belt, 3in deck
Indomitable	1937-41	Fleet	23,000	753ft 11in	30.5	1392	45	Sixteen 4.5in guns	4½in belt, 3in deck
Implacable	1939-44	Fleet	23,450	766ft 4in	32	1585	33	Sixteen 4.5in guns	4½in belt, 3in deck
Colossus	1942-46	Light Fleet	13,190	693-695	25	1300	37	–	–
Audacity	1939-41★	Escort	11,000	467ft 3in	15	?	6	One 4in, one 6pdr guns	–
Attacker	1941-6	Escort	10,200	496ft 1in	18.5	646	18-24	Two 4in guns	–
Ameer	1942-4	Escort	11,400	496ft 8in	18	646	18-24	Two 5in guns	–

★Date when converted

Submarines

Name of class	Dates of building	Surface displacement in tons	Submerged displacement in tons	Length overall in feet	Maximum speed surface in knots	Maximum speed submerged in knots	Crew	Torpedo armament	Gun armament
H	1917–20	423	510	171ft 9in	11.5	10.5	22	Four 21in	–
Odin	1924–9	1475	2038	283ft 6in	17.5	8	53	Eight 21in	One 4in
Parthian	1928–30	1475	2040	289ft 2in	17.5	8.6	53	Eight 21in	One 4in
Thames	1931–5	1850	2680	345	22	10	61	Six 21in	One 4in
S (War Emergency)	1931–45	715	990	217	14.75	9	48	Seven 21in	One 3in
T (War Emergency)	1936–45	1090	1573	273ft 3in	15.25	9	61	Eleven 21in	One 4in
U (short hull)	1937–44	540	630	196ft 10in	11.25	10	31–33	Four 21in	One 12pdr
A	1943–7	1120	1620	279ft 3in	18.5	8	61	Ten 21in	One 4in
X	1942–5	26.9	29.7	51ft 7½in	6.6	6	4	–	–

Escort Vessels

Name of class	Designation	Dates of building	Standard displacement in tons	Length overall in feet	Maximum speed in knots	Crew	Gun armament	Anti-submarine armament
V–W	Destroyer	1917–19	1100	312	34	134	Four 4in	Depth charges
Town	Destroyer	1917–19	1190	310	35	114	Four 4in	Depth charges
Modified *Black Swan*	Sloop	1941–5	1490	299ft 6in	19.75	192	Six 4in	Depth charges
Hunt Type 1	Escort Destroyer	1938–40	1000	280	28	147	Four 4in	Depth charges
Hunt Type 3	Escort Destroyer	1940–3	1050	280	27	168	Four 4in	Depth charges
Flower	Corvette	1939–44	1070	205	16	85–109	One 4in	Depth charges
River	Frigate	1941–4	1460	301ft 4in	21	140	Two 4in	Hedgehog, depth charges
Castle	Corvette	1941–4	1060	252	16.5	120	One 4in	Squid, depth charges
Captain	Frigate	1943–4	1192	289ft 5in	19.5	156	Three 3in	Hedgehog, depth charges
Loch	Frigate	1943–5	1435	307	20	114	One 4in	Two Squid, depth charges
Bay	AA Frigate	1944–6	1600	307	19.5	157	Four 4in	Hedgehog, depth charges

Coastal Forces

Name of class	Designation	Dates of building	Standard displacement in tons	Length overall in feet	Maximum speed in knots	Crew	Gun armament	Torpedo armament	Other armament
BPB Type	Motor Torpedo Boat	1936–9	22	60ft 3in	33	9	Eight .303in	Two 18in	–
MTB 102	Motor Torpedo Boat	1937	32	68	35.5	10	One 20mm	Two 21in	–
Vosper type	Motor Torpedo Boat	1942–4	37	72ft 6in	39.5	13	One 20mm, two .5in	Two 21in	–
BPB type	Motor Torpedo Boat	1942–5	37	71ft 9in	39	17	One 2pdr or 6pdr, four .303in	Two 18in	–
BPB type	Motor Anti-Submarine Boat	1939–40	23	70	23	9	Eight .303in	–	Depth charges
BPB type	Motor Gun Boat	1942	47	71ft 9in	40	12	One 2pdr, two 20mm, four .303in	–	–
Steam gunboat	Steam Gun Boat	1941–2	165	145ft 3in	35	27	Two 2pdr, four .5in	Two 21in	–
Fairmile B	Motor Launch	1940–4	65	112	20	16	One 3pdr, two .303in	–	–
Fairmile D	Motor Torpedo Boat	1942–4	90	115	31	14	One 2pdr, two 20mm, four .5in, four .303in	Two 21in	–
HDML	Harbour Defence Motor Launch	1940–4	54	72	11.5	10	One 1pdr, one 20mm, four .303in	–	–

Minesweepers and Patrol Service Vessels

Name of class	Dates of building	Standard displacement in tons	Length overall in feet	Maximum speed in knots	Crew	Gun armament
Aberdare	1917–19	800	231	16	74	One 4in, one 12pdr
Bangor	1940–2	605	174	16.5	60–87	One 3in
Algerine	1941–4	940–980	225	16.5	85–138	One 4in, four 40mm
MM	1940–4	165	119	11	20	Two .5in
BYMS	1942–4	207	135ft 6in	14	30	One 3in, two 20mm
Tree, Dance, Shakespearean and Isles	1939–44	545	164	12.25	35–40	One 4in or one 12pdr, depth charges

Landing Ships

Name of class	Designation	Dates of building	Standard displacement in tons	Length overall in feet	Maximum speed in knots	Crew	Landing craft carried	Troops carried	Vehicles carried
Glen	LSI(Large)	1938–9	9800	507	18	523	24 LCA, 3 LCM	800	–
Keren	LSI(Large)	1930	9890	471ft 6in	17	297	9 LCA, 1 LCS(M), 2 LCP(L), 2 LCM	1296	–
Prince Charles	LSI(Small)	1929–30	2950	359ft 6in	24	207	8 LCA	384	–
Boxer	LST	1942	3616	400	17	169	1 LCM	193	13 x 40-ton tanks
Bulolo	LS Headquarters (Large)	1938	9111	412ft 6in	15	264	–	–	–
Landing Ship Tank (2)	LST (2)	1942–5	1625	327ft 9in	10	86	–	–	20 x 25-ton tanks

Landing Craft

Name of class	Dates of building	Standard displacement in tons	Length overall in feet	Maximum speed in knots	Crew	Troops carried	Vehicles carried	Armament
Landing Craft Tank (2)	1941–3	296–453	135	10	12	–	Three 40-ton tanks	–
Landing Craft Tank (3)	1941–4	350 to 640	190ft 9in	11.5	12	–	Five 40-ton tanks	–
Landing Craft Tank (4)	1942–5	200 to 586	187ft 3in	10	12	–	Six 40-ton tanks	–
Landing Craft Infantry (Large)	1942–3	234 to 384	158ft 6in	14	24	188	–	–
Landing Craft Assault	1940–4	9 to 13.5	41ft 6in	10	4	35	–	–
Landing Craft Personnel (Large)	1940–2	6.5 to 10.75	36ft 9in	10	3	25	–	–
Landing Craft Mechanised (1)	1940–4	21 to 36	44ft 9in	7.5	6	100	One 16-ton tank or six jeeps	–
Landing Craft Mechanised (3)	1942–4	22 to 52	50	11	3	60	One 30-ton tank	–
Landing Craft Vehicles and Personnel	1943	11.5	36	9	3	36	One 3-ton lorry	–
Landing Craft Gun (Large) (3)	c.1943	491	190ft 9in	10	47	–	–	Two 4.7in guns, fourteen 20mm guns
Landing Craft Flak (4)	c.1943	415	187ft 3in	11	66	–	–	Four 2pdr guns, eight 20mm guns
Landing Craft Rocket (ex-LCT) (2)	c.1944	296–453	135	10	17–18	–	–	792in x 5in rockets

2 Main Aircraft Types

Manufacturer	Name	Dates in service	Number used	Function	Crew	Speed mph	Guns	Other Armament	Range miles
Supermarine	Walrus	1935–45	+/- 500	Spotter-reconnaissance amphibian	3	135	Two flexible .303in MGs	–	444
Fairey	Swordfish	1936–45	2391	Torpedo, spotting, reconnaissance	3	139	One fixed, one flexible .303in MG	18in torpedo	546
Gloster	Sea Gladiator	1938–41	98	Fighter	1	245	Four fixed .303in MGs	–	320
Blackburn	Skua	1938–41	190?	Fighter, dive bomber	2	225	Four fixed .303in MGs	One 500lb bomb	720
Grumman	Martlet (Wildcat)	1940–5	1123	Fighter	1	320	Four fixed .50in MGs	–	838
Fairey	Albacore	1940–3	800	Torpedo bomber	3	159	One fixed, one flexible .303in MG	One 18in torpedo	930
Fairey	Fulmar	1940–5	563	Day and night fighter	2	246	Eight fixed .303in MGs	–	830
Hawker	Sea Hurricane	1941–4	800+	Fighter	1	315	Eight fixed .303in MGs	–	500
Supermarine	Seafire (Merlin engine)	1942–5	1700	Fighter	1	332	Two 20mm cannon, four .303in MGs	–	280
Chance Vought	Corsair	1943–5	1977	Fighter	1	374–415	Four fixed .50in MGs	–	1562
Fairey	Barracuda	1943–5	2150	Torpedo and dive bomber	3	235	Two flexible .303in MGs	One 18in torpedo or four 500lb bombs	853
Grumman	Avenger (Tarpon)	1943–5	958	Torpedo bomber	3	259	Two fixed .50in MGs, one flexible .30in MG, one flexible .50in MG	One 18in torpedo or four 500lb bombs	1910
Fairey	Firefly	1943–5	658	Fighter and reconnaissance	2	319	Four 20mm cannons	–	1088
Grumman	Hellcat	1943–5	1182	Fighter	1	380	Six fixed .50in MGs	–	945

3 The Board of Admiralty, 1939-45

First Lord of the Admiralty
3 September 1939 — Winston Churchill
12 May 1940 — Albert V Alexander
29 May 1945 — Brendan Bracken
4 August 1945 — Albert V Alexander

First Sea Lord
12 June 1939 — Admiral of the Fleet Sir Dudley Pound
15 October 1943 — Admiral of the Fleet Sir Andrew Cunningham

Deputy First Sea Lord
29 July 1942 — Admiral Sir Charles Kennedy-Purvis

Second Sea Lord and Chief of Naval Personnel
30 September 1938 — Admiral Sir Charles Little
1 June 1941 — Vice-Admiral Sir William Whitworth
8 March 1944 — Vice-Admiral Sir Algernon Willis

Third Sea Lord and Controller
1 March 1939 — Vice-Admiral Sir Bruce Fraser
22 May 1942 — Vice-Admiral Sir Frederick Wake-Walker

Fourth Sea Lord and Chief of Supplies and Transport
1 October 1937 — Rear Admiral G S Arbuthnot
1 April 1941 — Vice-Admiral Sir John Cunningham
8 May 1943 — Vice-Admiral F H Pegram
10 March 1944 — Vice-Admiral A F E Palliser

Fifth Sea Lord and Chief of Naval Air Services
19 July 1938 — Vice-Admiral Sir Alexander A M Ramsay
21 November 1939 — Vice-Admiral C G G Royle
14 May 1941 — Rear-Admiral Lumley Lyster
(in abeyance, July 1942 to January 1943, Admiral Sir Frederick Dreyer, Chief of Naval Air Services, was not a member of the board)

Fifth Sea Lord and Chief of Naval Air Equipment
14 January 1943 — Vice-Admiral Sir Dennis Boyd
(Became Fifth Sea Lord (Air) on 1 May 1945)

Deputy Chief of Naval Staff (Vice Chief from 22 April 1940)
1 January 1939 — Rear-Admiral Tom Phillips
21 October 1941 — Vice-Admiral Sir Henry Moore
7 June 1943 — Vice-Admiral Sir Neville Syfret

Assistant Chief of Naval Staff (Trade)
10 January 1939 — Rear-Admiral H M Burrough

25 July 1940 — Rear-Admiral H R Moore
21 October 1941 — Vice-Admiral E L S King
7 December 1942 — Rear-Admiral J H Edelsten
Membership of the board ended, 30 October 1944

Assistant Chief of Naval Staff (Weapons)
9 September 1941 — Rear-Admiral R H McGrigor
8 March 1943 — Rear-Admiral W R Patterson

Assistant Chief of Naval Staff (Foreign)
8 April 1940 — Vice-Admiral Sir Geoffrey Blake
1 December 1940 — Rear-Admiral Sir Henry Harwood
Post ended, 4 April 1942

Assistant Chief of Naval Staff (Home)
27 May 1940 — Rear-Admiral A J Power
Post ended, 28 May 1942

Parliamentary and Financial Secretary
28 May 1937 — Geoffrey Shakespeare
4 April 1940 — Sir Victor Warrender
Post ended, 9 February 1942

Parliamentary Secretary
9 February 1942 — Lord Bruntsfield

Financial Secretary
9 February 1942 — G H Hall
28 September 1942 — J P L Thomas

Parliamentary and Financial Secretary
8 August 1945 — J Dugdale

Civil Lord
15 July 1938 — Captain U A M Hudson
5 March 1942 — Captain R A Pilkington

Controller of Merchant Shipbuilding and Repairs
1 February 1940 — Sir James Lithgow

Permanent Secretary
23 July 1936 — Sir Archibald Carter
5 December 1940 — Sir Henry Markham

4 Commanders-in-Chief, 1939-45

Home Commands

	Date appointed
Nore	
Based at Chatham	
Admiral Sir Studholme Brownrigg	9 January 1939
Admiral Sir Reginald Plunkett-Ernle-Erle-Drax	1 December 1930
Vice-Admiral Sir George Lyon	2 April 1941
Admiral of the Fleet Sir John Tovey	7 July 1943
Portsmouth	
Admiral Sir William James	30 June 1939
Admiral Sir Charles Little	1 October 1942
Admiral Sir Geoffrey Layton	1 May 1945

	Date appointed
Naval Air Stations	
Based at Lee-on-Solent	
Rear-Admiral R B Davies	24 May 1939
Rear-Admiral R A C Moody	30 September 1941
Rear-Admiral C V Robinson	12 May 1943
Vice-Admiral Sir Dennis Boyd	1 June 1945
Plymouth	
Admiral Sir Martin Dunbar-Nasmith	24 October 1938
Admiral of the Fleet Sir Charles Forbes	1 May 1941
Lapsed by February 1942, then reappointed	
Admiral Sir Ralph Leatham	12 May 1943

Western Approaches	Date appointed
Based at Liverpool	
Admiral Sir Percy Noble	17 February 1941
Admiral Sir Max Horton	19 November 1942

Rosyth
Vice-Admiral Sir Charles Ramsey	25 August 1939
Vice-Admiral Sir Wilbraham Ford	15 February 1942
Admiral Sir William Whitworth	1 June 1944

Dover
Vice-Admiral Sir Bertram Ramsay	24 August 1939
Vice-Admiral Sir Henry Pridham-Whippel	1 August 1942

Home Fleet
Afloat
Admiral Sir Charles Forbes	12 April 1938
Admiral Sir John Tovey	2 December 1940
Admiral Sir Henry Moore	1 August 1942

Admiral (Submarines)
Based at Aberdour then Northways
Admiral Sir Max Horton	9 January 1940
Rear-Admiral C B Barry	9 November 1942
Rear-Admiral G E Creasy	

Northern Patrol
Based at Ardrossan
Rear-Admiral E J Spooner	16 July 1940
Lapsed by August 1942	

Reserve Fleet
Vice-Admiral Sir Max Horton	26 July 1937
Lapsed January 1940 then reappointed	
Rear-Admiral C F Harris	15 January 1944

Orkney and Shetland
Based at Lyness
Vice-Admiral Sir Hugh Binney	22 December 1939
Vice-Admiral Sir Henry Harwood	15 April 1944
Rear-Admiral P Macnamara	1 March 1945

Overseas Commands

America and the West Indies (Later Western Atlantic)	Date appointed
Based at Bermuda	
Vice-Admiral Sir Charles Kennedy-Purvis	10 March 1940
Vice-Admiral Sir A T B Curteis	5 August 1942
Vice-Admiral Sir Irvine Glennie	11 October 1944

South Atlantic
Afloat, then based at Freetown, then Simonstown
Vice-Admiral Sir Sidney Meyrick	15 April 1937
Vice-Admiral Sir Robert Raikes	1 August 1940
Vice-Admiral Sir Campbell Tait	26 February 1942
Vice-Admiral Sir Robert Burnett	1 May 1944

Naval Expeditionary Force
Based in France then Germany
Admiral Sir Harold Burrough	19 January 1945

Iceland
Vice-Admiral B C Watson	26 October 1943

West Africa
Vice-Admiral A M Peters	27 November 1943

Mediterranean Fleet
Afloat, then based at Algiers and Taranto
Admiral Sir Andrew Cunningham	1 June 1939
Sir Henry Harwood	April 1942
Admiral Sir Andrew Cunningham	January 1943
Admiral Sir John Cunningham	15 October 1942

Levant
Admiral Sir Henry Harwood	20 February 1943
Vice-Admiral W G Tennant	30 October 1944

Eastern Mediterranean
Based at Alexandria
Vice-Admiral Sir Bernard Rawlings	28 December 1942

Western Mediterranean
Based at Algiers then Taranto

	Date appointed
Vice-Admiral J G A Miles	15 July 1944

North Atlantic
Based at Gibraltar
Admiral Sir Dudley North	November 1939
Vice-Admiral Sir Frederick Edward-Collins	31 December 1940
Vice-Admiral Sir Harold M Burroughs	10 September1943

Force H
Sir James Somerville	June 1940
Rear-Admiral E N Syfret	10 January 1942
Vice-Admiral H U A Willis	24 February 1943

China
Based at Singapore
Admiral Sir Percy Noble	9 December 1937
Vice-Admiral Sir Geoffrey Layton	10 July 1940
Became the Eastern Fleet	

East Indies
Based at Colombo
Vice-Admiral R Leatham	2 April 1939
Vice-Admiral G S Arbuthnot	22 April 1941
Admiral Sir Arthur Power	22 November 1944

Australian Squadron
Based in Hobart
Rear-Admiral J G Grace	16 September 1939
Rear-Admiral V A C Crutchley	30 March 1942
Commodore J A Collins	13 June 1944
Commodore H B Farncock	January 1945

Naval Headquarters, India
Vice-Admiral John Godfrey	22 May 1943

Eastern Fleet
Admiral Sir James F Somerville	12 February 1942
Lapsed by January 1945	

British Pacific Fleet
Admiral Sir Bruce Fraser	December 1944

5 Daily Pay for Selected Substantive Rates, 1941

Minimum pay for the rate given in each case.

Equivalent rate	Seamen	Signallers	Telegraphists	Artificers	Stokers	Artisans	Writers	Cooks (ships)	Marines
Boy	Boy 2nd Class 9d	Signal Boy 1s 3d	Boy Telegraphist 1s 3d	-	-	-	Entry suspended	-	Boy Musician 1s 3d
Ordinary	Ordinary Seaman 1s 6d	Ordinary Signalman 2/0	Ordinary Telegraphist 2/0	-	Stoker 2nd Class 2/0	-	-	Assistant Cook 2/0	Marine 2/0
Able	Able Seaman 2s 6d	Signalman 3s 3d	Telegraphist 3s 3d	-	Stoker 1st Class 3/0	-	Writer 3s 6d	Cook 3s 3d	-
Leading Rate	Leading Seaman 3s 10d	Leading Signalman 4s 10d	Leading Telegraphist 4s 10d	Artificer 5th Class 5s 7d	Leading Stoker 4s 10d	Artisan 5th Class 4s 4d	Leading Writer 5s 1d	Leading Cook 4s 10d	Corporal 4s 7d
Petty Officer	Petty Officer 5s 6d	Yeoman of Signals 6s 6d	Petty Officer Telegraphist 6s 6d	Artificer 4th Class 8/0	Stoker Petty Officer 6s 6d	Artisan 3rd Class 6s 9d	Petty Officer Writer 6s 9d	Petty Officer Cook 6s 6d	Sergeant 6/0
Chief Petty Officer	Chief Petty Officer 7/0	Chief Yeoman of Signals 8/0	Chief Petty Officer Telegraphist 8/0	Artificer 3rd Class 9/0	Chief Stoker 8/0	Chief Artisan 8s 9d	Chief Petty Officer Writer 8s 3d	Chief Petty Officer Cook 8/0	Colour Sergeant 8/0

Source, *Appendix to the Navy List*, December 1941

Selected Non-Substantive Rates

Gunnery rates open to marines and seamen, the others open to members of the Seaman Branch.

		Gunnery		Torpedo	Submarine Detector
Quarters Rating 3rd Class 3d	Layer Rating 3rd Class 3d	Control Rating 3rd Class 3d	Anti-aircraft Rating 3rd Class 3d	Seaman Torpedoman 3d	Submarine Detector 6d
Quarters Rating 2nd Class 6d	Layer Rating 2nd Class 6d	Control Rating 2nd Class 6d	Anti-aircraft Rating 2nd Class 6d	Leading Torpedoman 6d	Higher Submarine Detector 9d
Quarters Rating 1st Class 1s 6d	Layer Rating 1st Class 1s 6d	Control Rating 1st Class 1s 6d	Anti-aircraft Rating 1st Class 1s 6d	Torpedo Gunner's Mate 1s 6d	Submarine Detector Instructor 1s 9d

Abbreviations

AA Anti-Aircraft	
AB Able Seaman	
AFD Admiralty Floating Dock	
AFO Admiralty Fleet Orders	
AIO Action Information Organisation	
ASV Air to Surface Vessel	
ATC Air Training Corps	
ATS Auxiliary Territorial Services	
BL Breech Loading	
BYMS British Yard Minesweeper	
CAM Catapult Aircraft Merchant	
COPP Combined Operations Pilotage Party	
COS Chiefs of Staff	
CPO Chief Petty Officer	
CW Commission and Warrant	
DEMS Defensively Equipped Merchant Ships	
DF Direction Finding	
DNC Director of Naval Construction	
DSO Distinguished Service Order	

ERA Engine Room Artificers
FDO Flight Direction Officer
FONA Flag Officer North Atlantic
GRU Gyro Rate Unit
HA High Angle
HF/DF High Frequency Direction Finding
HO Hostilities Only
HP High Frequency
HSD Higher Submarine Detector
IFF Identification Friend of Foe
LA Low Angle
LCA Landing Craft Assault
LCG Landing Craft Gun
LCI Landing Craft Infantry
LCM Landing Craft Mechanised
LCP Landing Craft Personnel
LCT Landing Craft Tank
LF Low Frequency

LSI Landing Ship Infantry
LST Landing Ship Tank
MAC Merchant Aircraft Carrier
MASR Monthy Anti-Submarine Report
MF Medium Frequency
MGB Motor Gun Boat
ML Motor Launch
MNBDO Mobile Naval Base Defence Organisation
MTB Motor Torpedo Boat
NAAFI Navy, Army and Air Forces Institute
NCO Non Commissioned Officer
NCSO Naval Control of Shipping
NID Naval Intelligence Department
OCTU Officer Cadet Training Units
PO Petty Officer

PPI Plan Position Indicator
QARNC Queen Alexandria's Royal Naval Nursing Service
QF Quick Firing
R/T Radio Telegraphy
RAAF Royal Australian Air Force
RAF Royal Air Force
RCNC Royal Corps of Naval Constructors
RDF Radio Direction Finding
REME Royal Electrical and Mechanical Engineers
RFA Royal Fleet Auxiliary
RFR Royal Fleet Reserve
RM Royal Marines
RN Royal Navy
RNAS Royal Naval Air Station
RNR Royal Naval Reserve
RNVR Royal Naval Volunteer Reserve

SBA Sick Berth Attendant
SD Submarine Detectors
SOE Special Operations Executive
STAAG Stabilised Tachymetric Anti-Aircraft Gun
TA Traffic Analysis
TAG Telegraphist Air Gunner
TBS Talk Between Ships
TLC Tank Landing Craft
VAD Voluntary Aid Detachments
VICS Victualling vessel
VLF Very Low Frequency
W/T Wireless Telegraphy
WAAF Women's Auxiliary Air Force
WO Warrant Officer
WRNS Women's Royal Naval Service

Notes

PART I: THE ROYAL NAVY IN PEACE AND WAR

1 Rear-Admiral W S Chambers, *Max Horton and the Western Approaches*, London, 1954, p.51
2 National Archives, ADM 116/5771
3 Ibid.
4 Walter Schellenberg, *Invasion 1940 – The Nazi Invasion Plan for Britain*, London, 2000, p.27
5 Ibid., pp.9, 95
6 *Instructions for American Servicemen in Britain*, 1942, Oxford, 2005, no page number

PART II: THE STRUCTURE OF NAVAL POWER

1 National Archives, T161/1083, 161/1042
2 Lord Alanbrooke, *War Diaries*, eds Danchev and Todman, London, 2001, p.273
3 Lord Ismay, *Memoirs*, London, 1960, p.159
4 John Colville, *The Fringes of Power, Downing Street Diaries, 1939-1955*, London, 1985, p.159
5 *Mariner's Mirror*, 1937, p.19
6 John Gilbert (ed.), *The Churchill War Papers 1939-40*, London, 1993, p.75
7 National Archives, ADM 116/4331
8 John Colville, op. cit., p.285
9 Viscount Cunningham of Hyndhope, *A Sailor's Odyssey*, London, 1951, p.577
10 Ibid., p.597
11 Lord Ismay, op. cit., p.51
12 Lord Alanbrooke, op. cit., pp.244-6
13 National Archives, ADM 1/10288
14 John Gilbert (ed.), *The Churchill War Papers*, Vol. III, London, 2000, pp.47-8
15 H K Oram, *The Rogue's Yarn*, London, 1993, p.228
16 Oliver Warner, *Admiral of the Fleet, the Life of Sir Charles Lambe*, London, 1969, p.98
17 *The Times*, 16 December 1946
18 Celia L Jones, *Navy Mixture*, Edinburgh, 1995, pp.8, 11
19 E N Gladden, *The Civil Service, its Problems and Future*, London, 1948, p.169
20 *Shorter Oxford English Dictionary*, 1973 edition, vol. I, p.398; *Mariner's Mirror*, 1937, pp.16-17
21 National Archives, ADM 1/13557
22 Celia L Jones, op. cit., p.12
23 Robin Brodhurst, *Churchill's Anchor*, Barnsley, 2000, pp.134-35

24 Sir Phillip Vian, *Action This Day*, London, 1960, p.63
25 Oliver Warner, *Cunningham of Hyndhope*, London, 1967, p.93
26 S W Roskill, *The War at Sea*, vol. III, part II, London, 1961, p.421
27 National Archives, ADM 199/1456
28 W S Chalmers, *Max Horton and the Western Approaches*, London, 1954, pp.150-51
29 CAFO 2682/44
30 Sir Angus Cunninghame-Graham, *Random Naval Recollections*, Gartocharn, 1979, p.259
31 Sir Phillip Vian, op. cit., pp.81, 85
32 Sir William James, *The Sky was Always Blue*, London, 1951, p.199
33 W S Chalmers, op. cit., p.153
34 National Archives, ADM 1/16003
35 Viscount Cunningham of Hydnhope, op. cit., p.465
36 National Archives, ADM 239/241
37 National Archives, ADM 1/28902
38 Donald Macintyre, *U-Boat Killer*, reprinted London, 2002, p.25
39 National Archives, ADM 239/241
40 Ibid.
41 David Reynolds, *In Command of History*, London, 2004, pp.248-49
42 K C B Dewar, *The Navy From Within*, London, 1939, pp.297-98
43 Corelli Barnett, *Engage the Enemy More Closely*, London, 1991, p.105
44 Navy Lists
45 F H Hinsley, *British Intelligence in the Second World War*, vol. 2, London 1981, pp.17-38, *passim*
46 David Syrett, *The Battle of the Atlantic and Signals Intelligence: U-Boat Tracking Papers, 1941-47*, Navy Records Society, 2002, pp.372-4
47 Ibid., p.139
48 Ibid., pp.386-400
49 D K Brown, *Nelson to Vanguard*, London, 2000, p.212
50 Nixie Taverner, *A Torch Among Tapers*, Bramber, 2000, pp.282-3
51 Joseph Wellings, ed. Hattendorf, *On His Majesty's Service*, Newport, Rhode Island, 1983 p.85
52 Sir Phillip Vian, op. cit., pp.16, 19
53 J A G Troup, *On the Bridge*, 3rd edition, London, 1950, p.45
54 Ibid., p.75

55 Admiralty, *Manual of Seamanship*, BR 68, Vol. II, 1932, reprinted 1939, p.174
56 John Fernald, *Destroyer From America*, London, 1942, p.10
57 S Gorley Putt, *Men Dressed as Seamen*, London, 1943, p.85
58 Admiralty, *Manual of Navigation*, vol. 1, 1938, p.128
59 National Archives, ADM 1/19170
60 S Gorley Putt, op. cit., p.78
61 Noel Wright and A C G Sweet, *How to Prepare Food: Tips and Wrinkles for Cooks of Messes in Standard Ration Ships*, Ipswich, 1941
62 Admiralty, BR 93, *Manual of Victualling*, 1939, vol. 2, p.85
63 Ibid., p. 94
64 National Archives, ADM 101/574
65 National Archives, ADM 1/12114
66 S Gorley Putt, op. cit., p.80
67 Anon, *HMS Mauritius*, Ayr, 1945, pp.49-50
68 H Miller, *Service to the Services*, London, 1971, *passim*
69 National Archives, ADM 1/27143
70 *Manual of Seamanship*, vol. II, pp.76-8
71 J P W Mallalieu, *Very Ordinary Seaman*, London, 1946, p.105
72 *Manual of Seamanship*, vol. II, pp.60-63

PART III: ENEMIES AND ALLIES

1 *Fuehrer Conferences on Naval Affairs*, London, 2005, p.360
2 Bernard Kroener et al., *Germany and the Second World War*, Oxford, 2003, vol. 5, part 2, p.1037
3 *Fuehrer Conferences on Naval Affairs*, p.336
4 Ibid., p.179
5 Heinz Schaeffer, *U-Boat 977*, London, 1952, p.31
6 Jak P Mallman Showell, *German Navy Handbook*, Stroud, 2002, p.23
7 Gilbert Norman Tucker, *The Naval Service of Canada*, Ottawa, 1952, vol. II, pp.275-83
8 Donald Macintyre, *U-Boat Killer*, London, 1956, p.78
9 Marc Milner, *North Atlantic Run*, London and Toronto, 1995, p.159
10 NMM, MS 93/008
11 Frances Margaret McGuire, *The Royal Australian Navy*, Melbourne, 1948, pp.85, 91, 92, 339

12 S D Waters, *The Royal New Zealand Navy*, Wellington, 1956
13 H J Martin and Neil Orpen, *South Africa at War*, Cape Town and London, 1979, *passim*
14 Studs Terkel, *The Good War*, London, 1985, p.392 ff.
15 *Brassey's Naval Annual*, 1939, pp.63-73
16 A C Hardy, *Merchant Ship Types*, London, 1924, p.137
17 C B A Behrens, *Merchant Shipping and the Demands of War*, London, 1955, p.22
18 W H Mitchell and L A Sawyer, *Empire Ships of World War II*, Liverpool, 1965, *passim*
19 C B A Behrens, op. cit., p.174n
20 National Archives, ADM 1/15854
21 National Archives, WO 32/10913, AFO 4048/41
22 CAFO 2313/43
23 National Archives, ADM 1/15685
24 F C Dreyer, *The Sea Heritage*, London, 1955, p.253
25 AFO 3606/40
26 R Baker (ed.), *British Warship Design*, London, 1983, p.55
27 Lord Kilbracken, *Bring Back My Stringbag*, London, 1996, pp.113-29
28 C B A Behrens, op. cit., p.112
29 John Colville, *The Fringes of Power*, London, 1985, p.452
30 Kenneth Edwards, *Operation Neptune*, London, 1946, p.85
31 Ministry of Information, *Coastal Command*, London, 1942, p.90
32 Alan W Deller, *The Kid Glove Pilot*, Newtownards, 2004, pp.118-19
33 MASR, April 1943
34 Sir Phillip Joubert, *Birds and Fishes, the Story of Coastal Command*, London, 1960, pp.125-6
35 Ibid., p.211
36 Bill Gunston, *Classic World War II Aircraft Cutaways*, London, 1995, p.34
37 Sir Phillip Joubert, op. cit., p.127

PART IV: THE SHIPS

1 National Archives, ADM 116/4331
2 Quoted in D K Brown, *Nelson to Vanguard*, London, 2000, p.193
3 D K Brown, *A Century of Naval Construction*, London, 1983, p.157
4 Ibid., p.337
5 Ibid., pp.210-11

6 R Baker (ed.), *British Warship Design*, London, 1983, p.114

7 D K Brown (ed.), *The Design and Construction of British Warships*, vol. 1, London, 1995, p.114

8 Buxton and Aldcroft, *British Industry Between the Wars*, London, 1979, pp.81-2

9 Sir Wescott Abell, *The Shipwright's Trade*, reprinted London, 1948, p.204

10 Quoted in J F Clarke, *Building Ships on the North-East Coast, Part 2*, Whitley Bay, 1997, p.330

11 *A Shipbuilding History 1750-1932*, London and Cheltenham, c. 1932

12 Ministry of Information, *Build the Ship*, London, 19—, p.27

13 Ian Macdonald and Len Tabner, *Smith's Dock Shipbuilders*, Seaworks, 1986, no page numbers

14 J F Clarke, op. cit., pp.334-5

15 Ian Buxton, 'British Warship Building and Repair', in Stephen Howarth and Derek Law (eds), *The Battle of the Atlantic, 50th Anniversary International Naval Conference*, London, 1994, p.95

16 *The Design and Construction of British Warships*, vol 1, p.129n

17 *A Century of Naval Construction*, p.200

18 W F Knight, *His Majesty's Bristol Built Escort Ships*, Bristol, 1995, *passim*

19 Ian Buxton, op. cit., p.92

20 National Archives, ADM 116/4331

21 P M Rippon, *The Evolution of Engineering in the Royal Navy*, vol. 2, Tunbridge Wells, 1994, p.112

22 *Nelson to Vanguard*, p.210

23 Admiralty, *Machinery Handbook*, BR 77, 1941, p.5

24 R Baker (ed.), op. cit., p.209

25 P M Rippon, op. cit., p.27

26 P G A King, *Not All Plain Sailing*, np, 1970, pp.112-14, 119

27 National Archives, ADM 116/4331

28 National Archives, ADM 234/59

29 John Wingate, *HMS Belfast*, Windsor, 1971, pp.12-16, 66-71.

30 Admiralty, *The Gunnery Pocket Book*, BR 224/45, 1945, pp.31-3

31 Ibid., p.56

32 Ibid., pp.62-7

33 *Nelson to Vanguard*, pp.207-9

34 National Archives, ADM 239/239

35 John Coote, *Submariner*, London, 1991, p.17

36 National Archives, ADM 239/239

37 MASR, December 1942, p.40

38 National Archives, ADM 234/151

39 *The Gunnery Pocket Book*, pp.177-8

40 MASR, Sept 1942, p.40

41 National Archives, ADM 259/38 p.2

42 Willem Hackman, *Seek and Strike*, London, 1984, p.281

43 National Archives, ADM 220/109

44 National Archives, ADM 239/307

45 National Archives, ADM 220/109

46 National Archives, ADM 239/307

47 National Archives, ADM 239/307

48 National Archives, ADM 234/539

49 Derek Howse, *Radar at Sea, the Royal Navy in World War 2*, Basingstoke, 1993, p.250

50 Ibid., p.89

51 Derek Howse, op. cit., p.78

52 Ships Covers, National Maritime Museum

53 National Archives, ADM 101/623

54 A J Sims, *The Habitability of Naval Ships Under Wartime Conditions*, Transactions of the Institution of Naval Architects, 1945, p.64

55 Ibid., p.52

56 Betty Nelson Cuttyer, *Anchors*, London, 1999, pp.129-30

57 Admiralty, *Manual of Seamanship*, vol. 1, pp.295-9

58 Rory O'Conor, *Running a Big Ship on Ten Commandments*, Portsmouth, 1937, p.191

59 Ludovic Kennedy, *On My Way to the Club*, Glasgow, 1990, p.48

60 Rory O'Conor, op. cit., p.27

61 Anon, *HMS Mauritius*, Ayr, 1945, p.83

62 National Archives, ADM 199/466

63 Rory O'Conor, op. cit., p.120

64 Alec Guinness, *Blessings in Disguise*, London, 1985, p.119

65 Peter Hodges, *Royal Navy Warship Camouflage*, London, 1973, *passim*

66 National Archives, ADM 298/5

67 National Archives, ADM 1/19235

68 National Archives, ADM 101/615

69 National Archives, ADM 298/5, 319/1

PART V: NAVAL SOCIETY AND CULTURE

1 B Warlow, *Shore Establishments of the Royal Navy*, Liskeard, 1992, p.132

2 Sir Roderick Macdonald, *The Figurehead*, Bishop Auckland, 1993, p.76

3 John Gilbert (ed.), *The Churchill War Papers*, Vol. III, London, 2000, p.378

4 B Lavery, *Hostilities Only*, Greenwich, 2004, pp.26, 27

5 Godfrey Winn, *Home From the Sea*, London, 1944, pp.60-1

6 National Archives, ADM 1/17685

7 Nicholas Monsarrat, *HM Frigate*, London, 1946, p.7

8 R Ransone-Wallis, *Two Red Stripes*, London, 1973, p.10

9 National Archives, ADM 101/574

10 Admiralty, *Notes for Medical Officers on Entry into the Royal Navy*, BR 767, 1943

11 Ibid., p.8

12 Admiralty, *The Treatment of Battle Casualties Afloat*, BR 1443 (42), 1942, p.4

13 National Archives, ADM 101/563

14 *The Treatment of Battle Casualties Afloat*, p.5

15 National Archives, ADM 101/598

16 National Archives, ADM 101/592

17 National Archives, ADM 101/624

18 J L S Coulter, *The Royal Naval Medical Service*, vol. I, London, 1954, pp.97-108

19 Ibid., pp 48-9

20 National Archives, ADM 101/631

21 J L S Coulter, *The Royal Naval Medical Service*, vol, II, London, 1954, p.76

22 National Archives, ADM 101/660

23 *The Treatment of Battle Casualties Afloat*, p.5

24 Admiralty, *First Aid in the Royal Navy*, BR 25, 1943, p.3

25 Admiralty, *The Gunnery Pocket Book*, BR 224/45, 1945, p.143

26 *First Aid in the Royal Navy*, pp.51, 57

27 J L S Coulter, op. cit., vol. II, p.339

28 Navy Records Society, *The Beatty Papers*, vol. 1, 1989, p.141

29 J L S Coulter, op. cit., vol. II p.48; vol. I, pp.48 ff.

30 National Archives, ADM 101/609

31 Hannan Swaffer, *What Would Nelson Do?*, London, 1946, pp.60-1

32 National Archives, ADM 116/6066

33 National Archives, ADM 156/209

34 National Archives, ADM 1/18941

35 National Archives, ADM 1/15801

36 *King's Regulations and Admiralty Instructions*, 1943, p.1509

37 National Archives, ADM 231/235, p.10

38 J N Pelly, *An Officer's Aide Memoire*, HMS *King Alfred*, 1943, pp.20-1

39 National Archives, ADM 231/235, p.13

40 J N Pelly, op. cit., p.19

41 Ibid., p.17

42 John Fernald, *Destroyer From America*, London, 1942, pp.61-3

43 Nicholas Monsarrat, *Three Corvettes*, reprinted London, 2000, p.22

44 *King's Regulations*, p.1509

45 National Archives, ADM 1/16827

46 Sir Angus Cunninghame-Graham, *Random Naval Recollections*, Gartocharn, 1979, p.273

47 David Twiston Davies(ed.), *The Daily Telegraph Book of Naval Obituaries*, London, 2004, pp.37-8, 249

48 Sir Roderick Macdonald, op. cit., pp.142-3

49 Geoffrey Willans, *One Eye on the Clock*, London, 1943, pp.13-14

50 H V Morton, *Atlantic Meeting*, London, 1942, p.86

51 Admiralty, *Manual of Seamanship*, vol. II, 1932, p.11

52 Ibid., p.13

53 Anon, *HMS Mauritius*, Ayr, 1945, p.26

54 Nicholas Monsarrat, *Life is a Four Letter Word*, London, 1970, p.26

55 Admiralty, *Manual of Seamanship*, vol. 1, p.7

56 *Globe and Laurel*, February 1945

57 *HMS Mauritius*, op. cit., pp.91-2

58 A B Campbell, *Customs and Traditions of the Royal Navy*, Aldershot, 1956, pp.27-9

59 S Gorley Putt, *Men Dressed as Seamen*, London, 1943, pp.34-5

60 George Melly, *Rum, Bum and Concertina*, London, 1977, p.57

61 Robert Burgess and Roland Blackburn, *We Joined the Navy*, London, 1943, p.7

62 J P W Mallalieu, *Very Ordinary Seaman*, London, 1946, p.5

63 Piers Paul Read, *Alec Guinness*, London, 2003, p.122

PART VI: OFFICERS AND RATINGS

1 W S Churchill, *The Second World War*, Vol. 1, *The Gathering Storm*, London, 1965, p.692

2 Charles Owen, *No More Heroes*, London, 1975, p.131

3 National Archives, ADM 116/3926

4 Rory O'Conor, *Running a Big Ship on Ten Commandments*, Portsmouth, 1937, p.27

5 K C B Dewar, *The Navy from Within*, London, 1939, p.62

6 D A Rayner, *Escort, the Battle of the Atlantic*, London, 1955, p.27

7 Ibid., p.23

8 Ludovic Kennedy, *On My Way to the Club*, London, 1990, p.93

9 Ewen Montagu, *Beyond Top Secret U*, London, 1977, pp.17, 19

10 *Hansard*, vol. 378, cols 1088-89

11 F S Holt, *A Banker All at Sea*, Newtown, Australia, 1983, p.103

12 Ibid., p.103

13 Alec Guinness, *Blessings in Disguise*, London, 1985, p.108

14 *Hansard*, vol. 387, col. 598

15 *Navy List*, June 1939, pp.312-13, 278

16 George Melly, *Rum, Bum and Concertina*, London, 1976, p.8

17 National Archives, ADM 1/17944

18 National Archives, ADM 231/235, p.20

19 John W Davies, *Jack, the Sailor With the Navy Blue Eyes*, Bishop Auckland, 1995, p.264

20 John Whelan, *Home is the Sailor*, London, 1957, p.178

21 *A First Lieutenant's Handbook*, c. 1932, NMM pamphlet collection, p.8

22 Ibid., p.21

23 Admiralty, *Manual of Seamanship*, BR 68, 1932, p.31

24 Tristan Jones, *Heart of Oak*, 1984, reprinted Shrewsbury, 1997, p.88

25 George Melly, op. cit., p.7

26 Joseph Wellings, ed. Hattendorf, *On His Majesty's Service*, Newport, Rhode Island, 1983, p.67

27 John Palmer, *Luck On My Side*, Barnsley, 2002, p.26

28 Chris Howard Bailey, *The Battle of the Atlantic*, Stroud, 1994, p.23

29 National Archives, ADM 186/77

30 D A Rayner, op. cit., p.66

31 Nicholas Monsarrat, *Three Corvettes*, reprint London, 2002, pp.187-8

32 National Archives, ADM 231/235

33 D A Rayner, op. cit., p.213

34 National Archives, ADM 1/12133

35 John Davies, *The Stone Frigate*, London, 1947, p.162

36 Hannen Swaffer, *What Would Nelson Do?*, London, 1946, p.89

37 Tristan Jones, op. cit., pp.29, 44-5

38 Nicholas Monsarrat, op. cit., p.188

39 Piers Paul Read, *Alec Guinness*, London, 2003, p.122

40 *The Royal Navy as a Career*, 1937 edition, p.4

41 J Lennox Kerr and David James, *Wavy Navy, by Some Who Served*, London, 1950, p.194

42 H K Oram, ed. Wendy Harris, *The Rogue's Yarn*, London, 1993, p.229

43 James Callaghan, *Time and Chance*, London, 1987, p.58

44 John Davies, op. cit., p.39

45 Tristan Jones, op. cit., p.19

46 Leonard Charles Williams, *Gone on a Long Journey*, Havant, 2002, p.72

47 Tristan Jones, op. cit., pp.216-19

48 George Melly, op. cit., p.164

49 Quoted in Anthony Aldgate and Jeffrey Richards, *Britain Can Take it*, Oxford, 1984, p.216

50 Mass Observation archive, Brighton University, no. 886-7

51 Anon, *HMS Mauritius*, Ayr, 1945, pp.62-3

52 Admiralty, *Gunnery Pocket Book*, BR 224/45, 1945

53 Ibid., pp.1, 3

54 MASR, June 1944, p.30

55 Nicholas Monsarrat, op. cit., p.189

56 National Archives, ADM 1/12133

57 National Archives, ADM, 1/17685

58 National Archives, PRO PREM 4/55/3

59 National Archives, PRO ADM 1/16774

60 National Archives, LAB 29/249-

61 Admiralty, *Training of Artificer Apprentices*, BR 91, 1936, p.17

62 National Archives, ADM 1/17685

63 Ibid.

64 National Archives, LAB 29/249

65 *Heart of Oak*, p.195

66 National Archives, ADM 1/17685

67 National Archives, ADM 101/609

68 National Archives, ADM 1/20375, 186/77

69 Tristan Jones, op. cit., p.195

70 Admiralty, *Engineering Manual for His Majesty's Fleet*, BR 16, 1939, p.25

71 Admiralty, *Machinery Handbook*, BR 77, 1941, p.iv

72 Ian Hawkins (ed.), *Destroyer*, London 2003, pp.233-4

73 *Engineering Manual*, p.141

74 Ian Hawkins (ed.), op. cit., p.234

75 *Engineering Manual*, pp.23-4

76 National Archives, LAB 29/249, p.8

77 Ibid., p.19

78 W S Churchill, op. cit., Vol. 1, *The Gathering Storm*, p.688

79 John L Brown, *Diary of a Matelot, 1942-45*, Lowesmoor, Worcester, 1991, p.8

80 National Archives, LAB 29/429

81 Chris Howard Bailey, op. cit., p.101

82 Tristan Jones, op. cit., p.187

83 National Archives, ADM 193/19

84 Mark Amory (ed.), *The Letters of Evelyn Waugh*, London, 1980, p.453

85 John Colville, *The Fringes of Power*, London, 1985, p.300

86 James D Ladd, *By Sea by Land, the Royal Marines, 1919-1997*, London, 1998, p.137

87 Raymond Mitchell, *They Did What Was Asked of Them*, Poole, 1996, p.16

88 National Archives, ADM 181/131, 116/5346; James D Ladd, op. cit., p.128

89 National Archives, ADM 116/5346

90 James D Ladd, op. cit., pp.523, 527

91 Ibid., pp.70-91, 501-3

92 Ibid., pp.538-9

93 Raymond Mitchell, op. cit., p.23

94 National Archives, ADM 116/5346

95 Vera Laughton Mathews, *Blue Tapestry*, London, 1949, p.51

96 Ibid., p.267

97 *Hansard*, vol. 357, col. 1222, 1939

98 Stephanie Batstone, *Wren's Eye View*, London, 1994, pp.14-5

99 Vera Laughton Mathews, op. cit., p.179-80

100 AFO 1728/43

101 Audrey Deacon, *Diary of a Wren, 1940-1945*, Spennymoor, 2001, p.135

102 Vera Laughton Mathews, op. cit., p.184

103 Audrey Deacon, op. cit., p.128

104 National Archives, ADM 1/13981

105 Angela Mack, *Dancing on the Waves*, Little Hatherden, 2000, p.55

106 Stephanie Batstone, op. cit., p.139

107 National Archives, ADM 1/17100

108 National Archives, ADM 1/12114

109 Audrey Deacon, op. cit., p.xi

110 Eileen Bigland, *The Story of the WRNS*, London, 1946, p.62

111 Stephanie Batstone, op. cit., pp.38-9

112 Eileen Bigland, op. cit., p.viii

113 B Lavery, *Hostilities Only*, Greenwich, 2004, p.35

114 Eileen Bigland, op. cit., p.95

115 National Archives, ADM 1/12114

116 National Archives, ADM 1/17685

117 National Archives, ADM 1/12133

118 Angela Mack, op. cit., p.69

119 Vera Laughton Mathews, op. cit., p.266

120 National Archives, ADM 1/11114

PART VII: THE BATTLE FLEET

1 Lord Chatfield, *It Might Happen Again*, London, 1947, p.99

2 John Colville, *The Fringes of Power*, London, 1985, p.442

3 John Gilbert (ed.), *The Churchill War Papers*, Vol. II, London, 1994, p.1922

4 Ibid., Vol III, 2000, p.1075

5 H V Morton, *Atlantic Meeting*, London, 1943, p.39

6 Lord Moran, *Winston Churchill, the Struggle for Survival*, London, 1966, p.7

7 National Archives, ADM 101/561

8 National Archives, ADM 239/261, p.14

9 National Archives, ADM 116/5345

10 Joseph Wellings, ed. Hattendorf, *On His Majesty's Service*, Newport, Rhode Island, 1983, p.75

11 Ludovic Kennedy, *On My Way to the Club*, Glasgow, 1989, p.104

12 K C B Dewar, *The Navy From Within*, London, 1939, p.159

13 Rory O'Conor, *Running a Big Ship on Ten Commandments*, Portsmouth, 1937, p.47

14 Ibid., pp.39-41

15 H V Morton, op. cit., pp.43-4

16 National Archives, ADM 101/598

17 R H Newton, *Practical Construction of Warships*, London, 1941, p.275

18 Hannen Swaffer, *What Would Nelson Do?*, London, 1946, p.29

19 Admiralty, *Manual of Seamanship*, BR 68, 1932, vol. II, p.15

20 Joseph Wellings, ed. Hattendorf, op. cit., p.66

21 Ibid., p.167

22 Oliver Warner, *Admiral of the Fleet, the Life of Sir Charles Lambe*, London, 1969, pp.102-3

23 H K Oram, ed. Wendy Harris, *The Rogue's Yarn*, London, 1993, p.229

24 *A First Lieutenant's Handbook*, c. 1932, NMM pamphlet collection, p.8

25 Quoted in Oliver Warner, *Cunningham of Hyndhope*, London, 1967, p.62

26 Sir Roderick Macdonald, *The Figurehead*, Bishop Auckland, 1993, p.195

27 National Archives, ADM 186/77

28 Admiralty, *The Gunnery Pocket Book*, BR 224/45, 1945, pp.143-4

29 Ibid., pp.179-80

30 Joseph Wellings, ed. Hattendorf, op. cit., pp.234

31 *Gunnery Pocket Book*, p.162

32 Joseph Wellings, ed. Hattendorf, op. cit., p.76

33 Sir Roderick Macdonald, op. cit., p.6

34 *Gunnery Pocket Book*, p.189-90

35 Viscount Cunningham of Hyndhope, *A Sailor's Oddysey*, London, 1951, p.260

36 Joseph Wellings, ed. Hattendorf, op. cit., p.62

37 Joseph Wellings, ed. Hattendorf, op. cit., pp.53-4

38 National Archives, ADM 239/239

39 Sir Roderick Macdonald, op. cit., pp.106, 105

40 Tristan Jones, *Heart of Oak*, 1984, reprinted Shrewsbury, 1997, p.251

41 National Archives, ADM 234/275

42 S W Roskill, *The War at Sea*, vol. 1, London, 1954, p.433

43 Anon, *HMS Mauritius*, Ayr, 1945, p.23

44 R 'Mike' Crossley, *They Gave me a Seafire*, Shrewsbury, 1986, p.118

45 National Archives, ADM 199/2505, 1/18009, 1/16160

46 D K Brown, *Nelson to Vanguard*, London, 2000, pp.199-200

47 First Lord's Statement, *Brassey's Naval Annual*, 1936, p.358

48 D K Brown, op. cit., p.199

49 Winston G Ramsey (ed.), *The Blitz Then and Now*, vol. 2, London, 1988, pp.390, 424, 575, 574

50 Donald Macintyre, *U-Boat Killer*, reprinted London, 1999, p.154

51 Ian Buxton, 'Admiralty Floating Docks', Part 2, in *Warship Supplement 78*, 1984, pp.9-17

52 National Archives, ADM 1/12114

53 National Archives, ADM 199/1456

54 National Archives, ADM 1/11922

55 Ibid.

56 Ludovic Kennedy, op. cit., pp.111-12

57 D A Rayner, *Escort, the Battle of the Atlantic*, London, 1955, p.148

58 Sydney Greenwood, *Stoker Greenwood's Navy*, Tunbridge Wells, 1983, p.34

59 Viscount Cunningham of Hydnhope, op. cit., p.270

60 Ibid., p.289

PART VIII: NAVAL AVIATION

1 D K Brown, *Nelson to Vanguard*, London 2000, p.205

2 Quoted in ibid., p.40

3 National Archives, ADM 205/52

4 National Archives, ADM 329/361; *Aircraft Carrier Handbook*

5 Sir Frederick Dreyer, *The Sea Heritage*, London, 1955, p.393

6 AFO 1021/41

7 Admiralty, *The Navy and the Y-Scheme*, 1944, p.14

8 Lord Kilbracken, *Bring Back My Stringbag*, reprinted London 1996, pp.3-4

9 AFO 1021/41

10 Charles Lamb, *War in a Stringbag*, London, 1977, p.43

11 Sir Raymond Lygo, *Collision Course*, Lewes, 2002, p.62

12 Hugh Popham, *Sea Flight*, London, 1954, p.12

13 Ibid., p.22

14 Ibid., pp.33-4

15 Gordon Wallace, *Carrier Observer*, Shrewsbury, 1993, p.23

16 Norman Hanson, *Carrier Pilot*, Cambridge, 1979, p.146

17 Quoted in A G H Goddard, 'Operational Fatigue' in *Mariners Mirror*, vol. 91, no. 1, February 2005, pp.54-55, Lord Kilbracken, op. cit., pp.216-31

18 National Archives, ADM 1/19264

19 National Archives, LAB 29/249

20 National Archives, LAB 29/249

21 AFO 1021/41

22 National Archives, LAB 29/249

23 AFO 1759/44

24 AFO 1021/41

25 National Archives, ADM 1/20375

26 National Archives, ADM 1/12189

27 National Archives, ADM 1/1120

28 National Archives, ADM 1/11207

29 Sir Raymond Lygo, op. cit., p.112

30 Charles Lamb, op. cit., p.56

31 National Archives, ADM 1/9725

32 Quoted in Owen Thetford, *British Naval Aircraft*, London, 1991, pp.324-5

33 National Archives, ADM 239/419

34 National Archives, ADM 1/16345

35 National Archives, ADM 199/847

36 H J C Spencer, *Ordinary Naval Airman*, Tunbridge Wells, 1992, pp.106-7

37 National Archives, ADM 199/847

38 Gordon Wallace, op. cit., p.38

39 Ibid., p.22

40 National Archives, ADM 239/419

41 National Archives, ADM 199/847

42 Sir Raymond Lygo, op. cit., p.111

43 National Archives, ADM 239/419

44 R 'Mike' Crossley, *They Gave Me a Seafire*, Shrewsbury, 2001, p.48

45 CAFO 1162/43

46 National Archives, ADM 239/361

47 National Archives, ADM 199/847

48 Lord Kilbracken, op. cit., p.34

49 National Archives, ADM 199/847

50 H J C Spencer, op. cit., pp.69-79

51 National Archives, ADM 1/16345

52 National Archives, ADM 1/19264

53 National Archives, AIR 10/2081, 10/2799

54 National Archives, ADM 1/19264

55 Ray Sturtivant and Theo Balance, *The Squadrons of the Fleet Air Arm*, Tonbridge, 1994, p.211

56 Sir Raymond Lygo, op. cit., pp.104-5

57 AFO 1021/41

58 Ray Sturtivant and Theo Balance, op. cit., p.214

59 National Archives, ADM 239/362

60 Hugh Popham, op. cit., p.4

61 National Archives, ADM 101/602

62 Graham Buchan Innes, *British Airfield Buildings of the Second World War*, Earl Shilton, 1995, *passim*

63 National Archives, DEFE 2/984

PART IX: THE SUBMARINE SERVICE

1 National Archives, ADM 205/28

2 National Archives, ADM 116/5346

3 National Archives, ADM 205/28

4 Charles MacHardy, *Send Down a Dove*, London, 1968, p.159

5 W S Chalmers, *Max Horton and the Western Approaches*, London, 1954, p.72

6 John D Drummond, *HM U-Boat*, London, 1958, p.149

7 National Archives, ADM 239/414, p.5

8 Edward Young, *One of Our Submarines*, reprinted London 1982, pp.130-5

9 National Archives, ADM 239/414

10 Ibid.

11 Ibid.

12 National Archives, ADM 116/5771

13 Arthur P Dickison, *Crash Dive*, Stroud, 1999, pp.ix-x

14 National Archives, ADM 205/28

15 National Archives, ADM 116/5771

16 Arthur P Dickison, op. cit., p.xii

17 Sir Arthur Hezlet, *HMS Trenchant at War*, Barnsley, 2001, p.32

18 National Archives, ADM 116/5771

19 Sir Arthur Hezlet, op. cit., p.55

20 National Archives, ADM 239/239

21 W S Churchill, *The Second World War*, Vol. IV, *The Hinge of Fate*, London, 1951, p.815

22 Ben Bryant, *Submarine Command*, London, 1958, p.214

23 D K Brown, *A Century of Naval Construction*, London, 1983, p.227-8

24 Ships Covers, T class, National Maritime Museum

25 National Archives, ADM 239/215

26 Hannen Swaffer, *What Would Nelson Do?* London, 1946, p.35

27 Edward Young, op. cit., p.176

28 Ben Bryant, op. cit., p.125

29 Ibid., p.144

30 S W Roskill, *The War at Sea*, vol. 3, part 2, London, 1960, p.107

31 Alistair Mars, *Court Martial*, London, 1954, pp.30-1

32 National Archives, ADM 239/45

33 Edward Young, op. cit., p.222

34 National Archives, ADM 239/45

35 Sir Arthur Hezlet, op. cit., p.30

36 Edward Young, op. cit., p.53

37 National Archives, ADM 239/45

38 Ben Bryant, op. cit., p.158

39 Ibid., pp.157–8

40 Edward Young, op. cit., p.29

41 Ibid., p.224

42 National Archives, ADM 1/24278

43 Ben Bryant, op. cit., p.88

44 Ibid., p.146

45 National Archives, ADM 234/235

46 Ibid.

47 Ibid.

48 Sir Arthur Hezlet, op. cit., p.126

49 Edward Young, op. cit., p.229

50 Ben Bryant, op. cit., pp.50–1

51 National Archives, ADM 1/10239

52 Edward Young, op. cit., pp.60, 63

53 National Archives, ADM 205/28

54 Ben Bryant, op. cit., p.218

55 Arthur P Dickison, op, cit., pp.118–19

PART X: ESCORTS

1 D A Rayner, *Escort, the Battle of the Atlantic*, London, 1955, p.131

2 Captain Donald Macintyre, *U-Boat Killer*, reprinted London 2002, pp.10–11; D A Rayner, op. cit., pp.188–9

3 John Fernald, *Destroyer From America*, London, 1942, p.25

4 National Archives, ADM 101/561

5 R Baker (ed.), *British Warship Design*, London, 1983, p.112

6 Sir Peter Gretton, *Convoy Escort Commander*, London, 1964, p.6

7 Tristan Jones, *Heart of Oak*, 1984, reprinted Shrewsbury 1997, p.237

8 J Lennox Kerr (ed.), *Wavy Navy*, London, 1950, p.168

9 D A Rayner, op. cit., p.218

10 National Archives, ADM 101/615

11 National Archives, ADM 101/609

12 J Lennox Kerr (ed.), op. cit., p.80

13 MASR, October 1944, p.14

14 J Lennox Kerr (ed.), op. cit., p.37

15 John Palmer, *Luck On My Side*, Barnsley, 2002, p.23–5

16 Nicholas Monsarrat, *Three Corvettes*, reprinted London 2000, p.31

17 Ibid., p.29

18 CHB 111

19 National Archives, ADM 237/558

20 Nicholas Monsarrat, op. cit., p.60

21 Ships Covers, 645, Canadian ships, National Maritime Museum

22 Nicholas Monsarrat, *HM Frigate*, London, 1946, p.16

23 Ibid.

24 National Archives, ADM 231/235

25 J Lennox Kerr (ed.), op. cit., p.123

26 Ibid., p.126

27 Nicholas Monsarrat, *Three Corvettes*, op. cit., p.57, *HM Frigate*, op. cit., p.14

28 John Palmer, op. cit., pp.83–4

29 Chris Howard Bailey, *The Battle of the Atlantic*, Stroud, 1994, p.27

30 Sir Peter Gretton, *Crisis Convoy*, London, 1974, pp.7–8

31 Nicholas Monsarrat, *Life is a Four Letter Word*, London, 1970, p.15

32 Captain Donald Macintyre, op. cit., p.113

33 Nicholas Monsarrat, *Three Corvettes*, op. cit., p.123

34 Ibid., p.47

35 Sir Peter Gretton, op. cit., pp. 37, 170–1

36 W S Churchill, *The Second World War*, vol. II, *Their Finest Hour*, London, 1967, p.529

37 Arnold Hague, *The Allied Convoy System*, London, 2000, pp.109–14

38 D W Waters and F Barley, *The Defeat of the Enemy Attack on Shipping*, Navy Records Society, 1997, pp.29–35

39 National Archives, ADM 199/2372

40 Captain Donald Macintyre, op. cit., p.22

41 Joseph Wellings, ed. Hattendorf, *On His Majesty's Service*, Newport, Rhode Island, 1983, p.3

42 D W Waters and F Barley, op. cit., Table 11

43 D A Rayner, op. cit., p.79

44 MASR, Aug 1941, p.28

45 MASR, November 1940, p.14

46 National Archives, ADM 1/13415

47 National Archives, ADM 239/344

48 MASR, November 1940, p.14

49 National Archives, ADM 239/344

50 Lord Kilbracken, *Bring Back My Stringbag*, reprinted London 1996, p.125

51 Captain Donald Macintyre, op. cit., p.95

52 Alan W Deller, *The Kid Glove Pilot*, Newtownards, 2004, p.77

53 CAFO 40/2176

54 Terence Robertson, *Walker RN*, London, 1956, p.103

55 Captain Donald Macintyre, op. cit., p.146

56 Ships Covers, National Maritime Museum

57 D K Brown and Phillip Pugh, 'Ramming' in *Warship* 1990, pp.18–34

58 Captain Donald Macintyre, op. cit., p.154

59 National Archives, ADM 239/248

60 National Archives, ADM 199/2369

61 Eileen Bigland, *The Story of the WRNS*, London, 1946, p.174–5

62 National Archives, ADM 199/1456

63 Nicholas Monsarrat, *Life is a Four Letter Word*, op. cit., p.85

64 Captain Donald Macintyre, op. cit., pp.120–1

65 National Archives, ADM 1/17805

66 D A Rayner, op. cit., p.78

67 National Archives, ADM 187/27

68 Nicholas Monsarrat, *Three Corvettes*, op. cit., pp.77–8

69 National Archives, ADM 1/31049

70 National Archives, ADM 116/4540

71 National Archives, ADM 116/5262, 199/674

72 National Archives, ADM 1/13155

73 Ludovic Kennedy, *On My Way to the Club*, Glasgow, 1990, p.142

PART XI: THE COASTAL NAVIES

1 See Engines chapter for more detail

2 National Archives, ADM 1/1308

3 R Baker (ed.), *British Warship Design*, London, 1983, pp.133–5

4 Quoted in D K Brown, *Nelson to Vanguard*, London, 2000, p.140

5 National Archives, ADM 1/13108

6 John Lambert, *The Fairmile D Motor Torpedo Boat*, London, 1985, p.7

7 R Baker (ed.), op. cit., p.142

8 National Archives, ADM 239/239

9 S W Roskill, *The War at Sea*, vol. II, London, 1956, p.252; National Archives, ADM 116/5346

10 David Twiston Davies, *The Daily Telegraph Book of Naval Obituaries*, London, 2004, p.411

11 Admiralty, *The Navy and the Y-Scheme*, London, 1944, pp.4–5

12 L C Reynolds, *Motor Gunboat 658*, reprinted London, 2002, p.19

13 R Baker (ed.), op. cit., p.124

14 National Archives, ADM 1/17685

15 National Archives, ADM 1/15006

16 National Archives, ADM 1/15685; S W Roskill, op. cit., vol. II, p.252

17 National Archives, ADM 1/15685

18 National Archives, ADM 1/15904

19 R Baker (ed.), op. cit., p.165

20 National Archives, ADM 1/18997

21 National Archives, ADM 219/195

22 S W Roskill, op. cit., vol. III, part II, 1960, p.473

23 L C Reynolds, op. cit., p.116

24 David Twiston Davies, op. cit., p.177

25 HMSO, *Ships of the Royal Navy: Statement of Losses During the Second World War*, 1947, pp.40–1

26 J S Cowie, 'The British Sea Mining Campaign, 1939–1945', in *Royal United Services Institution Journal*, 1948, p.35

27 National Archives, ADM 239/245

28 David Twiston Davies, op. cit., pp.132, 56

29 National Archives, ADM 116/5346

30 J S Cowie, op. cit., p.34

31 Paul Lund and Harry Ludlam, *Out Sweeps*, London, 1978, p.125

32 Ministry of Information, *His Majesty's Minesweepers*, London, 1943, pp.30–3

33 Brendan A Maher, *A Passage to Sword Beach*, Shrewsbury, 1996, pp.35, 45

34 Charles McAra, *Mainly in Minesweepers*, London, 1991, p.57

35 National Archives, ADM 1/9936

36 National Archives, ADM 1/19713

37 D A Rayner, *Escort, the Battle of the Atlantic*, London, 1955, p.30–1

38 D W Waters and F Barley, *The Defeat of the Enemy Attack on Shipping*, Navy Records Society, 1997, p.186

39 National Archives, ADM 1/17685

40 National Archives, ADM 1/11361

41 D A Rayner, op. cit., pp.38–9

42 National Archives, ADM 208/6

43 National Archives, ADM 116/5346

44 National Archives, ADM 1/19713

45 National Archives, ADM 1/9843

46 National Archives, ADM 1/16994

47 National Archives, ADM 1/10413

48 National Archives, ADM 199/334

49 National Archives, ADM 1/15289

PART XII: AMPHIBIOUS WARFARE

1 Phillip Zeigler, *Mountbatten*, London, 1985, p.156

2 Arthur Marshall, *Life's Rich Pageant*, London, 1984, p.155

3 Amphibious Warfare Headquarters, *History of the Combined Operations Organisation 1940–1945*, London, 1956, p.59

4 National Archives, ADM 1/15685

5 National Archives, DEFE 2/898

6 *History of the Combined Operations Organisation*, pp.92 ff.

7 Anthony J Perrett, *Royal Marines in Wales*, Portsmouth, 1992, pp.116–17

8 R Baker (ed.), *British Warship Design*, London, 1983, p.5

9 David W Bone, *Merchantmen Rearmed*, London, 1949, p.190

10 J Lennox Kerr (ed.), *Wavy Navy*, London, 1950, p.223

11 Piers Paul Read, *Alec Guinness*, London, 2003, p.158

12 National Archives, ADM 1/14725, DEFE 2/1430

13 J Lennox Kerr (ed.), op. cit., p.224

14 David Twiston Davies, *The Daily Telegraph Book of Naval Obituaries*, London, 2004, p.89

15 National Archives, DEFE 2/987

16 National Archives, DEFE 2/961

17 *History of the Combined Operations Organisation*, p.142

18 National Archives, ADM 1/14725

19 National Archives, DEFE 2/929

20 D K Brown, *Nelson to Vanguard*, London, 2000, p.142

21 Ibid.

22 S W Roskill, *The War at Sea*, vol. III, part II, 1961, pp.438, 450

23 Michael Davis (ed.), *The Diaries of Evelyn Waugh*, London, 1976, p.493

24 Paul Lund and Harry Ludlam, *The War of the Landing Craft*, London, 1976, pp.16–17

25 R Baker (ed.), op. cit., p.35

26 Paul Lund and Harry Ludlam, op. cit., p.40

27 R Baker (ed.), op. cit., p.210

28 J Lennox Kerr (ed.), op. cit., pp.224–5

29 Paul Lund and Harry Ludlam, op. cit., p.63

30 Alan Villiers, *The Set of the Sails*, London, 1950, pp.273–5

31 W D 'Jim' Jarman, *Those Wallowing Beauties*, Lewes, 1997, p.29

32 Ibid., p.115

33 J A Good, typescript in the Royal Marines Museum, Eastney

34 J Lennox Kerr (ed.), *Wavy Navy*, op. cit., p.226

35 National Archives, DEFE 2/987

36 National Archives, DEFE 2/1116

37 Ibid.

38 David Twiston Davies, op. cit., p.248

39 National Archives, DEFE 2/898

40 National Archives, DEFE 2/1319

41 Ibid.

42 Ibid.

43 C E T Warren and James Benson, *Above Us the Waves*, London, 1953, p.200

44 David W Bone, op. cit., pp.189–90

45 Toni and Valmai Holt, *The Visitor's Guide to the Normandy Beaches*, Ashbourne, 1994, p.183

46 Ibid., p.177

47 Ibid., pp.136, 183

48 Brian Macdermott, *Ships Without Names*, London, 1992, p.28

49 Piers Paul Read, op. cit., p.164

50 David Twiston Davies, op. cit., p.70

51 J A Good, typescript in the Royal Marines Museum, Eastney

52 National Archives, DEFE 2/241

53 Cornelius Ryan, 'The Longest Day', reprinted in *War* 1999, p.247

54 National Archives, DEFE 2/961

55 National Archives, DEFE 2/961

56 Adrian Searle, *PLUTO*, Shanklin, 2004, pp.60, 78, *passim*

Bibliography

Printed Books

General Histories

Calder, Angus, *The People's War, Britain, 1939-1945*, St Albans, 1982

Kennedy, Paul, *The Rise and Fall of the Great Powers*, London, 1988

Mowat, Charles Loch, *Britain Between the Wars, 1918-1940*, reprinted Cambridge, 1987

Taylor, A J P, *English History, 1939-45*, reprinted Oxford, 1975

Naval Histories

Barnett, Corelli, *Engage the Enemy More Closely*, London, 1991

Kennedy, Paul, *The Rise and Fall of British Naval Mastery*, reprinted London, 1991

Pemsel, Helmut, *Atlas of Naval Warfare*, London, 1977

Potter, E B, *The Great Sea War*, London, 1960

Roskill, S W, *The War at Sea*, 4 vols, London, 1954-61

Wells, John, *The Royal Navy, An Illustrated Social History*, Stroud, 1994

Biographies, etc., of Leading Figures

Brodhurst, Robin, *Churchill's Anchor*, Barnsley, 2000 (for Sir Dudley Pound)

Chambers, Rear-Admiral W S, *Max Horton and the Western Approaches*, London, 1954

Chatfield, Lord, *It Might Happen Again*, London, 1947

Chatfield, Lord, *The Navy and Defence*, London, 1942

Churchill, W S, *The Second World War*, 6 vols, London, 1948-54

Cunningham of Hyndhope, Viscount, *A Sailor's Odyssey*, London, 1951

Gilbert, *Churchill, A Life*, London, 1991

Gilbert, *The Churchill War Papers*, London, Vol. I, 1993, Vol. II, 1994, Vol. III, 2000

Jenkins, Roy, *Churchill*, London, 2001

Reynolds, David, *In Command of History*, London, 2004 (for the writing of Churchill's war history)

Vian, Sir Phillip, *Action This Day*, London, 1960

Warner, Oliver, *Cunningham of Hyndhope*, London, 1967

Zeigler, Phillip, *Mountbatten*, London, 1985

Personal Memoirs

Amory, Mark (ed.), *The Letters of Evelyn Waugh*, London, 1980

Batstone, Stephanie, *Wren's Eye View*, London, 1994

Brown, John L, *Dairy of a Matelot, 1942-45*, Lowesmoor, Worcester, 1991

Bryant, Ben, *Submarine Command*, London, 1958

Cherry, A H, *Yankee RN*, London, 1951

Coote, John, *Submariner*, London, 1991

Crossley, R 'Mike', *They Gave me a Seafire*, Shrewsbury, 1986

Cunninghame-Graham, Sir Angus, *Random Naval Recollections*, Gartocharn, 1979

Davies, John W, *Jack, the Sailor with the Navy Blue Eyes*, Bishop Auckland, 1995

Davis, John, *Lower Deck*, London, 1945

Davis, John, *The Stone Frigate*, London, 1947

Deacon, Audrey, *Diary of a Wren, 1940-1945*, Spennymoor, 2001

Deller, Alan W, *The Kid Glove Pilot*, Newtownards, 2004

Denton, Eric, *My Six Wartime Years in the Royal Navy*, London, 1999

Dewar, K C B, *The Navy from Within*, London, 1939

Dickison, Arthur P, *Crash Dive*, Stroud, 1999

Dreyer, F C, *The Sea Heritage*, London, 1955

Fernald, John, *Destroyer From America*, London, 1942

Greenwood, Sydney, *Stoker Greenwood's Navy*, Tunbridge Wells, 1983

Gretton, Sir Peter, *Convoy Escort Commander*, London, 1964

Gretton, Sir Peter, *Crisis Convoy*, London, 1974

Guinness, Alec, *Blessings in Disguise*, London, 1985

Hanson, Norman, *Carrier Pilot*, Cambridge, 1979

Hezlet, Sir Arthur, *HMS Trenchant at War*, Barnsley, 2001

Hill, Richard, *Lewin of Greenwich*, London, 2000

Holt, F S, *A Banker All at Sea*, Newtown, Australia, 1983

James, Sir William, *The Sky was Always Blue*, London, 1951

Jones, Tristan, *Heart of Oak*, reprinted Shrewsbury, 1997

Kennedy, Ludovic, *On My Way to the Club*, Glasgow, 1990

Kilbracken, Lord, *Bring Back my Stringbag*, London, 1996

King, P G A, *Not All Plain Sailing*, np, 1970

Lamb, Charles, *War in a Stringbag*, London, 1977

Lygo, Raymond, *Collision Course*, Lewes, 2002

Macdonald, Sir Roderick, *The Figurehead*, Bishop Auckland, 1993

Macintyre, Donald, *U-Boat Killer*, reprinted London, 2002

Mack, Angela, *Dancing on the Waves*, Little Hatherden, 2000

Maher, Brendan A, *A Passage to Sword Beach*, Shrewsbury, 1996

Mallalieu, J P W, *Very Ordinary Seaman*, London, 1946

Mars, Alistair, *Court Martial*, London, 1954, pp.30-1

McAra, Charles, *Mainly in Minesweepers*, London, 1991

Melly, George, *Rum, Bum and Concertina*, London, 1977

Monsarrat, Nicholas, *HM Frigate*, London, 1946

Monsarrat, Nicholas, *Life is a Four Letter Word*, London, 1970

Monsarrat, Nicholas, *Three Corvettes*, reprinted London, 2000

Montagu, Ewen, *Beyond Top Secret U*, London, 1977

Oram, H K, *The Rogue's Yarn*, London, 1993

Owen, Charles, *No More Heroes*, London, 1975

Palmer, John, *Luck on My Side*, Barnsley, 2002

Popham, Hugh, *Sea Flight*, London, 1954

Putt, S Gorley, *Men Dressed as Seamen*, London, 1943

Ransome-Wallis, R, *Two Red Stripes*, London, 1973

Rayner, D A, *Escort, the Battle of the Atlantic*, London, 1955

Read, Piers Paul, *Alec Guinness*, London, 2003 (includes many diary extracts)

Reynolds, L C, *Motor Gunboat 658*, reprinted London, 2002

Spencer, H J C, *Ordinary Naval Airman*, Tunbridge Wells, 1992

Taverner, Nixie, *A Torch Among Tapers*, Bramber, 2000 (with regard to Rory O'Conor)

Wallace, Gordon, *Carrier Observer*, Shrewsbury, 1993

Wellings, Joseph, ed. Hattendorf, *On His Majesty's Service*, Newport, Rhode Island, 1983

Whelan, John, *Home is the Sailor*, London, 1957

Willans, Geoffrey, *One Eye on the Clock*, London, 1943

Williams, Leonard Charles, *Gone in a Long Journey*, Havant, 2002

Winn, Godfrey, *Home from the Sea*, London, 1944

Young, Edward, *One of our Submarines*, Reprinted London 1982

Collected Accounts and Oral History

Bailey, Chris Howard, *The Battle of the Atlantic*, Stroud, 1994

Connell, G G, *Jack's War*, London, 1985

Davies, David Twiston (ed.), *The Daily Telegraph Book of Naval Obituaries*, London, 2004

Kerr, J Lennox and James, David, *Wavy Navy, by Some Who Served*, London, 1950

Official Documents

Technical manuals

Admiralty, *A Seaman's Pocket Book*, BR 827, 1943

Admiralty, *Engineering Manual for His Majesty's Fleet*, BR 16, 1939

Admiralty, *First Aid in the Royal Navy*, BR 25, 1943

Admiralty, *Machinery Handbook*, BR 77, 1941

Admiralty, *Manual for Officers' Stewards*, BR 97, 1932

Admiralty, *Manual of Navigation*, Vol. I, Vol. III, 1938

Admiralty, *Manual of Seamanship*, Vol. I, 19—, Vol. II, 1932

Admiralty, *Notes for Medical Officers on Entry into the Royal Navy*, BR 767, 1943

Admiralty, *The Gunnery Pocket Book*, BR 224/45, 1945

Admiralty, *The Treatment of Battle Casualties Afloat*, BR 1443 (42), 1942

Admiralty, *Training of Artificer Apprentices*, BR 91, 1936

Staff histories

Admiralty, *Monthly Anti-Submarine Report*, 1939-45

Admiralty, *The Navy and the Y-Scheme*, 1944

Amphibious Warfare Headquarters, *History of the Combined Operations Organisation 1940-1945*, London, 1956

Waters, D W and Barley, F, *The Defeat of the Enemy Attack on Shipping*, Navy Records Society, 1997

Official histories

Coulter, J L S, *The Royal Naval Medical Service*, 2 vols, London, 1954

Ellis, L F et al., *Victory in the West*, Vol. I, *The Battle of Normandy*, London, 1962

Hinsley, F H, *British Intelligence in the Second World War*, Vol. 2, London 1981

Other Official Publications

Appendix to the Navy List, December 1941, June 1944

King's Regulations and Admiralty Instructions, 1943

Navy Lists – copies available in the National Archives and the National Maritime Museum

The Royal Navy as a Career, 1937 edition

Naval Architecture and Engineering

Baker, R (ed.), *British Warship Design*, London, 1983

Brown, D K (ed.), *The Design and Construction of British Warships*, Vol. 1, London, 1995

Brown, D K, *A Century of Naval Construction*, London, 1983

Brown, D K, *Nelson to Vanguard*, London, 2000

Buxton and Aldcroft, *British Industry Between the Wars*, London, 1979

Buxton, Ian, 'British Warship Building and Repair', in Stephen Howarth and Derek Law (eds), *The Battle of the Atlantic, 50th Anniversary International Naval Conference*, London, 1994

Newton, R H, *Practical Construction of Warships*, London, 1941

Rippon, P M, *The Evolution of Engineering in the Royal Navy*, Vol. 2, Tunbridge Wells, 1994

Roberts, John, *British Warships of the Second World War*, London, 2000

Ship Lists and Reference

Campbell, N J M, *Naval Weapons of World War II*, London, 1985

Enton, H T L and Colledge, J J, *Warships of World War II*, 8 parts, London, 1962-3

Gardiner, R (ed.), *Conway's All the World's Fighting Ships, 1905-2*, London, 1985

Gardiner, R (ed.), *Conway's All the World's Fighting Ships, 1922-46*, London, 1980

Histories of Individual Branches and Aspects

Submarines

Akerman, Paul, *Encyclopaedia of British Submarines, 1901-1955*, Penzance, 1989

Lipscomb, F W, *The British Submarine*, Greenwich, 1975

Warren, C E T and Benson, James, *Above us the Waves*, London, 1953

Convoy Escort and Anti-Submarine Warfare

Baker, Richard, *The Terror of Tobermory*, Edinburgh, 1999

Hackman, Willem, *Seek and Strike*, London, 1984

Hague, Arnold, *The Allied Convoy System*, London, 2000

Middlebrook, Martin, *Convoy*, reprinted London, 2003

Robertson, Terence, *Walker RN*, London, 1956

Williams, Mark, *Gilbert Roberts and the Anti-U-Boat School*, London, 1979

Minesweeping

Lund, Paul and Ludlam, Harry, *Out Sweeps*, London 1978

Ministry of Information, *His Majesty's Minesweepers*, London, 1943

Royal Marines

Ladd, James D, *By Sea by Land, the Royal Marines, 1919-1997*, London, 1998

Mitchell, Raymond, *They Did What Was Asked of Them*, Poole, 1996

Perrett, Anthony J, *Royal Marines in Wales*, Portsmouth, 1992

Wall, Major P H B and Ritson, Lt G A M, *The Royal Marine Pocket Book*, 4 parts, Aldershot, 1945

Amphibious Warfare

Edwards, Kenneth, *Operation Neptune*, London, 1946

Fergusson, Bernard, *The Watery Maze*, London, 1961

Lund, Paul and Ludlam, Harry, *The War of the Landing Craft*, London, 1976

Macdermott, Brian, *Ships without Names*, London, 1992

Intelligence

Syrett, David, *The Battle of the Atlantic and Signals Intelligence: U-Boat Situations and Trends, 1941-45*, Navy Records Society, 1998

Syrett, David, *The Battle of the Atlantic and Signals Intelligence: U-Boat Tracking Papers, 1941-47*, Navy Records Society, 2002

Wrens

Bigland, Eileen, *The Story of the Wrens*, London, 1946

Mason, Ursula Stuart, *The Wrens, 1917-77*, Reading, 1977

Mathews, Vera Laughton, *Blue Tapestry*, London, 1949

Shore Bases

Hewison, W S, *This Great Harbour – Scapa Flow*, Stromness, 1985

Warlow, B, *Shore Establishments of the Royal Navy*, Liskeard, 1992

Wells, John, *Whaley, the Story of HMS Excellent*, Portsmouth, 1980

Reserves, etc.

Featherbe, F C, *Churchill's Pirates*, Rochester, 1994 (the Royal Naval Patrol Service)

Howarth, Stephen, *The Royal Navy's Reserves in Peace and War*, Barnsley, 2003

Kerr, J Lennox and Granville, Wilfred, *The RNVR*, London, 1957

Operations

Grove, Eric, *Sea Battles in Close Up, World War 2*, Vol. 2, Shepperton, 1993

Grove, Eric, *The Price of Disobedience*, Stroud, 2000

Holt, Tonie and Valmai, *Visitor's Guide, Normandy Landing Beaches*, Ashbourne, 1994

McKee, Alexander, *Black Saturday*, London, 1960

Phillips, C E Lucas, *Cockleshell Heroes*, London, 1977

Stephen, Martin, *Sea Battles in Close Up, World War 2*, Shepperton, 1991

Winser, John de S, *The D-Day Ships*, Kendal, 1994

Other Navies

Fuehrer Conferences on Naval Affairs, London, 2005

Henry, Mark, *The US Navy in World War II*, Oxford, 2002

Jenkins, H J, *A History of the French Navy*, London, 1973

Kroener, Bernard, et al., *Germany and the Second World War*, Oxford, 2003

Martin, H J and Orpen, Neil, *South Africa at War*, Cape Town and London, 1979

McGuire, Frances Margaret, *The Royal Australian Navy*, Melbourne, 1948

Milner, Marc, *North Atlantic Run*, London and Toronto, 1995

Schaeffer, Heinz, *U-Boat 977*, London, 1952

Showell, Jak P Mallman, *German Navy Handbook*, Stroud, 2002

Tucker, Gilbert Norman, *The Naval Service of Canada*, Ottawa, 1952, Vol. II

US Navy, *Naval Orientation*, 1945

Waters, S D, *The Royal New Zealand Navy*, Wellington, 1956

Merchant Shipping

Behrens, C B A, *Merchant Shipping and the Demands of War*, London, 1955

Bone, David W, *Merchantmen Rearmed*, London, 1949

Chell, R A, *Troopship*, Aldershot, 1948

Hardy, A C, *Merchant Ship Types*, London, 1924

Jordan, Roger, *The World's Merchant Fleets, 1939*, London, 1999

Mitchell, W H and Sawyer, L A, *Empire Ships of World War II*, Liverpool, 1965

Woodman, Richard, *The Real Cruel Sea*, London, 2004

Uniforms, Personnel, etc.

Anon, *The Royal Navy Today*, London, c. 1942

Lavery, B, *Hostilities Only*, Greenwich, 2004

Mollo, Andres (ed.), *Uniforms & Insignia of the Navies of World War II*, London, 1991

Swaffer, Hannan, *What Would Nelson Do?* London, 1946

Sumner, Ian and Baker, Alix, *The Royal Navy, 1939-45*, Wellingborough, 2001

Ship and Ship Type Histories

Anon, *HMS Mauritius*, Ayr, 1945

Hawkins, Ian (ed.), *Destroyer*, London, 2003

HMSO, *Ships of the Royal Navy: Statement of Losses During the Second World War*, 1947

Hobbs, David, *Royal Navy Escort Carriers*, Liskeard, 2003

Lambert, John and Ross, Al, *Allied Coastal Forces of World War II*, 2 vols, London, 1993

March, Edgar J, *British Destroyers, A History of Development, 1892-1953*, London, 1966

Moore, George, *Building for Victory*, World Ship Society, 2003

Poolman, Kenneth, *Escort Carrier, HMS Vindex at War*, London, 1983

Taverner, Nixie, *Neptune's Legacy*, Fleet Hargate, 2003

Wingate, John, *HMS Belfast*, Windsor, 1971

Winton, John, *Carrier Glorious*, reprinted London, 1999

Anatomy of the Ship series

Lambert, John, *The Fairmile D Motor Torpedo Boat*, London, 1985

Lambert, John, *The Submarine Alliance*, 1986

MacKay, John, *Corvette Agassiz*, 2004

Ross, Al, *Destroyer Campbeltown*, London, 1990

Roberts, John, *Battlecruiser Hood*, London, 1982

Watton, Ross, *Aircraft Carrier Victorious*, 2004

Watton, Ross, *Battleship Warspite*, London, 2002

Watton, Ross, *Cruiser Belfast*, London, 1985

Aviaton

Francis, Paul, *British Military Airfield Architecture*, Sparkford nr Yeovil, 1996

Freidman, Norman, *British Carrier Aviation*, London, 1988

Goddard, A G H, 'Operational Fatigue' in *Mariners' Mirror*, Vol. 91 no. 1, February 2005

Gunston, Bill, *Classic World War II Aircraft Cutaways*, London, 1995

Harrison, W A, *Fairey Swordfish and Albacore*, Marlborough, 2002

Innes, Graham Buchan, *British Airfield Buildings of the Second World War*, Earl Shilton, 1995

Jefford, C G, *Observers and Navigators*, Shrewsbury, 2001

Joubert, Sir Phillip, *Birds and Fishes, the Story of Coastal Command*, London, 1960

Ministry of Information, *Coastal Command*, London, 1942

Nicholl, G W R, *The Supermarine Walrus*, London, 1966

Ray and Theo Balance, *The Squadrons of the Fleet Air Arm*, Tonbridge, 1994

Sturtivant, Owen Thetford, *British Naval Aircraft*, London, 1991

Other Technical and Specialised Topics

Anon, *A First Lieutenant's Handbook*, c. 1932

Burgess, Robert and Blackburn, Roland, *We Joined the Navy*, London, 1943

Campbell, A B, *Customs and Traditions of the Royal Navy*, Aldershot, 1956

Cowie, J S, 'The British Sea Mining Campaign, 1939-1945', in *Royal United Services Institution Journal*, 1948

Hodges, Peter, *Royal Navy Warship Camouflage*, London, 1973

Howse, Derek, *Radar at Sea, the Royal Navy in World War 2*, Basingstoke, 1993

Nelson-Curryer, Betty, *Anchors*, London, 1999

O'Conor, Rory, *Running a Big Ship on Ten Commandments*, Portsmouth, 1937

Pelly, J N, *An Officer's Aide Memoire*, HMS King Alfred, 1943

Sims, A J, *The Habitability of Naval Ships under Wartime Conditions*, Transactions of the Institution of Naval Architects, 1945

Troup, J A G, *On the Bridge*, 3rd edition, London, 1950

Wright, Noel and Sweet, A C G, *How to Prepare Food; Tips and Wrinkles for Cooks of Messes in Standard Ration Ships*, Ipswich, 1941

Manuscripts
National Archives

It is not particularly useful to give a detailed list of references, apart from those cited in the text. It is better to do a keyword search on the catalogue on a particular subject. Some lateral thinking is often necessary. For example, the best description of the duties of individual classes of naval ratings is to be found, not in the Admiralty papers, but in Ministry of Labour LAB 29/249. Some of the most useful series are:

ADM 1 and 116: miscellaneous papers, best searched by keyword

ADM 101: medical journals of selected ships

ADM 182: Admiralty Fleet Orders, miscellaneous mine of information. The set in the Library of the Royal Naval Museum, Portsmouth, is much easier to browse.

ADM 187: Pink Lists, 208, Red Lists, 209, Blue Lists, 210, Green Lists, give the stations of various different types of ship at approximately three-day intervals throughout the war.

ADM 199: war history cases and papers

ADM 205: First Sea Lord's papers

ADM 217: convoy reports, Western Approaches

ADM 234: non-confidential reference books, BR series

ADM 237: convoy records

ADM 239: confidential works of reference, CB series

ADM 264: Naval Air Publications

National Maritime Museum
Draughts and Ships covers

Plans of virtually all naval ships are held in the National Maritime Museum, but an appointment and a good deal of time is needed to look at them properly. These are accompanied by the Ships Covers – large files

on the development of each design. They are an invaluable source but as D K Brown puts it, they contain, 'The Truth, Nothing but the Truth but often very far from the Whole Truth.'

Pamphlets

This collection is one of the undiscovered treasures of the museum, with many rare and unique copies of obscure but very useful works, such as Captain Pelly's *An Officer's Aide Memoir*.

Films

Collections of training and propaganda films issued on video and DVD by the Imperial War Museum are very useful for explaining difficult points. These include:

Protect the Convoy, 2005

The Royal Navy at War, 2002

The Royal Navy at War – Fleet Air Arm, 2005

The Royal Navy at War – Know Your own Navy, 2005

The Royal Navy at War – Naval Instructional Films, 2005

The Royal Marines at War, 2003

Shipyards and Docks at War, 2004

Find, Fix and Strike about the Fleet Air Arm is issued by Canal + Images International, 1999

Picture Credits

Anova Books Ltd is committed to respecting the intellectual property rights of others. We have therefore taken all reasonable efforts to ensure that the reproduction of all content on these pages is done with the full consent of copyright owners. If you are aware of any unintentional omissions please contact the company directly so that any necessary corrections may be made for future editions.

Index